HANDBOOK

of CLINICAL

HEALTH

PSYCHOLOGY

Volume 3.
Models and Perspectives in Health Psychology

HANDBOOK
of CLINICAL
HEALTH
PSYCHOLOGY

Volume 3.
Models and Perspectives in Health Psychology

Editor-in-Chief
Thomas J. Boll

Volume Editors
Robert G. Frank, Andrew Baum,
and Jan L. Wallander

AMERICAN PSYCHOLOGICAL ASSOCIATION
WASHINGTON, DC

Published by
American Psychological Association
750 First Street, NE
Washington, DC 20002
www.apa.org

To order
APA Order Department
P.O. Box 92984
Washington, DC 20090-2984
Tel: (800) 374-2721
Direct: (202) 336-5510
Fax: (202) 336-5502
TDD/TTY: (202) 336-6123
Online: www.apa.org/books/
E-mail: order@apa.org

In the U.K., Europe, Africa, and the Middle
East, copies may be ordered from
American Psychological Association
3 Henrietta Street
Covent Garden, London
WC2E 8LU England

Typeset in Goudy by World Composition Services, Inc., Sterling, VA

Printer: Sheridan Books, Ann Arbor, MI
Cover Designer: Nini Sarmiento, Baltimore, MD
Project Manager: Debbie Hardin, Carlsbad, CA

The opinions and statements published are the responsibility of the authors, and such
opinions and statements do not necessarily represent the policies of the American
Psychological Association.

Library of Congress Cataloging-in-Publication Data

Handbook of clinical health psychology / edited by Suzanne Bennett Johnson, Nathan
Perry, and Ronald H. Rozensky.—1st ed.
    p. cm.
    Includes bibliographical references and index.
    Contents: v. 1. Medical disorders and behavioral applications—
    ISBN 1-55798-909-5 (alk. paper)
    1. Clinical health psychology—Handbooks, manuals, etc. 2. Health behavior—
Handbooks, manuals, etc. I. Johnson, Suzanne Bennett. II. Perry, Nathan W.
III. Rozensky, Ronald H.

R726.7.H354   2002
616.89—dc21   2002018260

ISBN: 1591471060

British Library Cataloguing-in-Publication Data
A CIP record is available from the British Library.

Printed in the United States of America
First Edition

CONTENTS

CONTRIBUTORS

Michael H. Antoni, Department of Psychology, College of Arts and Sciences, University of Miami, Coral Gables, FL

Andrew Baum, Behavioral Medicine and Oncology, University of Pittsburgh Cancer Institute, Pittsburgh, PA

Cynthia D. Belar, Office of the Education Directorate, American Psychological Association, Washington, DC

Laura M. Bogart, RAND Corporation, Santa Monica, CA

Dean G. Cruess, Department of Psychology, University of Pennsylvania, Philadelphia

Douglas L. Delahanty, Department of Psychology, Kent State University, Kent, OH

Patrick H. DeLeon, past president, American Psychological Association, Washington, DC

Jason N. Doctor, Department of Rehabilitation Medicine, University of Washington School of Medicine, Seattle

Craig K. Ewart, Center for Health and Behavior, Department of Psychology, Syracuse University, Syracuse, NY

Michael J. Forlenza, Behavioral Medicine and Oncology, University of Pittsburgh Cancer Institute, Pittsburgh, PA

Robert G. Frank, Department of Clinical and Health Psychology, College of Public Health and Health Professions, University of Florida, Gainesville

Margaret A. Gardea, Department of Psychiatry, University of Texas Southwestern Medical Center, Dallas

Robert J. Gatchel, Department of Psychiatry, University of Texas Southwestern Medical Center, Dallas

Karen Glanz, Department of Behavioral Sciences and Health Education, Rollins School of Public Health, Emory University, Atlanta, GA

Robert L. Glueckauf, Department of Medical Humanities and Social Sciences, Florida State University, Tallahassee

Jessie C. Gruman, Center for the Advancement of Health, Washington, DC

Robert M. Kaplan, Department of Family and Preventive Medicine, University of California, San Diego

Joshua C. Klapow, Department of Psychology, Department of Healthcare Organization and Policy, Center for Outcomes Effectiveness Research and Education, University of Alabama at Birmingham

Laura C. Leviton, Robert Wood Johnson Foundation, Princeton, NJ

Jeffrey S. Loomis, Center for Research on Telehealth and Healthcare Communications, College of Public Health and Health Professions, University of Florida, Gainesville

Niccie McKay, Department of Health Services Administration, College of Public Health and Health Professions, University of Florida, Gainesville

James G. Murphy, Center for Alcohol Studies, Brown University, Providence, RI

David W. Nickelson, Office of the Practice Directorate, American Psychological Association, Washington, DC

C. Tracy Orleans, Robert Wood Johnson Foundation, Princeton, NJ

Ruth Ullmann Paige, private practice; former member of the Board of Directors, American Psychological Association, Washington, DC

Rebecca K. Papas, Department of Clinical and Health Psychology, College of Public Health and Health Professions, University of Florida, Gainesville

Frank Penedo, Department of Psychology, College of Arts and Sciences, University of Miami, Coral Gables, FL

Nathan W. Perry Jr., Department of Clinical and Health Psychology, College of Public Health and Health Professions, University of Florida, Gainesville

Martha M. Phillips, Department of Psychiatry, Center for Mental Healthcare Research, University of Arkansas for Medical Sciences, Little Rock

James M. Raczynski, College of Public Health, University of Arkansas for Medical Sciences, Little Rock

Richard C. Robinson, Department of Psychiatry, University of Texas Southwestern Medical Center, Dallas

Ronald H. Rozensky, Department of Clinical and Health Psychology, College of Public Health and Health Professions, University of Florida, Gainesville

John M. Ruiz, Department of Psychology, University of Utah, Salt Lake City

Morgan T. Sammons, U.S. Navy Bureau of Medicine and Surgery, Washington, DC

Neil Schneiderman, Division of Health Psychology, Department of Psychology, University of Miami, Coral Gables, FL

Brian D. Smedley, Institute of Medicine; former American Psychological Association Congressional Science Fellow, Washington, DC

Timothy W. Smith, Department of Psychology, University of Utah, Salt Lake City

Sally Tarbell, Department of Psychology, Northwestern University, Chicago, IL

Jalie A. Tucker, Department of Health Behavior, School of Public Health, University of Alabama at Birmingham

Cheryl C. Ulmer, consultant, McLean, VA

Jan L. Wallander, Sociometrics Corporation, Los Altos, CA; University of Alabama at Birmingham

Lari Wenzel, Health Policy and Research, College of Medicine, University of California, Irvine

Jeffrey D. Whitton, Center for Research on Telehealth and Healthcare Communications, College of Public Health and Health Professions, University of Florida, Gainesville

INTRODUCTION TO THE SERIES

THOMAS J. BOLL

The history of psychology in medicine predates the formal development of psychology. For the many millennia in which medicine has made a contribution to humankind, most of its contribution was in fact psychological. Until sometime in the middle part of the 20th century, medicine had very little of either science or technology to offer. For example, no general anesthetic existed until the end of the 19th century, and no antibiotics were available until the 20th century. Most of the miracles of surgical intervention and restoration occurred sometime after that. Before this time, common sense, diet, rest, and bedside manner was the doctor's stock-in-trade.

With the advent of "miracle medicine," a great deal has been gained and much has been lost. What has been gained is obvious. Medicine has allowed us to "fix" many disorders and conditions and make many once-fatal illnesses curable. It has also, however, placed the emphasis on the role of the physician as the sole person responsible for healing. This thinking, in turn, has to a considerable extent removed not only the patient's role but also the role of the interaction between doctor and patient. In many instances, patients are essentially passive recipients of pharmacological, surgical, and other biomechanical interventions. It was not until the end of the 20th century and the beginning of the 21st century that what is now amusingly referred to as "alternative medicine" was rediscovered. Western allopathic procedures have become the mainstream, and all of the procedures that were for millennia the entire armamentarium of medicine are now only "alternative." Many of these procedures have roots in specific cultures and have continuously been in practice, whereas others are being re-recognized.

A positive effect of the biomedical revolution has been the prolonged life of many people with chronic illnesses. It is now common for individuals with diabetes, hypertension, hyperlipidemia, cerebral disorders, and coronary artery diseases to live not only long but also active and productive lives. At the same time, many early killers and limiters of life such as smallpox, whooping cough, and polio have been eliminated or largely controlled. However, this resulting longevity has led to the presence of increasing numbers of individuals with other illnesses of previously relatively small import (e.g., arthritis, dementing disorders), which has focused attention on the need for care of chronic illness and the elderly population.

Chronic care is an overbroad term that involves a return to nonbiomechanical interventions for individuals who simply cannot be "fixed." These individuals must, through their own participation as well as through the cooperation and active participation of significant others and a broad range of individuals in the "health care system," work to ameliorate symptoms, minimize dysfunction, increase capacity, and enhance quality in their lives. Much of this change was predicted by Nicholas Cummings and others in their seminal work at the Kaiser Foundation in the 1960s (Cummings & Follette, 1968; Follette & Cummings, 1962, 1967). Unfortunately, this knowledge is only recently gaining general acceptance with the health care community and general public. The remarkable work of Dean Ornish with end-stage cardiovascular disease demonstrates that behavioral interventions for "real" medical conditions work because they are "real" interventions (Ornish et al., 1990). Time in the hospital, time for recovery after surgery, and amount of medication required for seizure management and pain management can all be reduced with behavioral and biobehavioral techniques. This reality seems, all too slowly, to be seeping into the awareness of physicians, the general patient population, and—even more slowly—third-party payers.

The purpose of the books in this series is to detail the contributions of health psychology to scientific knowledge and effective evaluation and intervention. The books covered by the *Handbook of Clinical Health Psychology* discuss the diagnoses contained in the *International Classification of Diseases, Ninth Revision* (World Health Organization, 1996) and the contributions of psychological and behavioral evaluation and intervention to each of these areas of medical disorder and dysfunction. Major systems of the body and the disorders attendant thereto are considered, as are lifestyle factors that affect health, in which health psychology has contributed to the development and implementation of effective methods for health promotion and for primary, secondary, and tertiary illness prevention. These books also discuss a wide variety of specific disorders and crosscutting medical conditions (e.g., sleep problems, obesity) and delineate techniques, results, and interventions that have been found to be effective and continue to be developed. Finally, the theoretical underpinnings for each of these scientific advances and clinical applications are discussed.

All of this information makes these handbooks the first comprehensive effort to characterize the field of health psychology. The three volumes seek to describe the scientific basis of the endeavor; to delineate the specific techniques, technologies, and procedures for evaluation and intervention in the field; and to demonstrate the applications of health psychology to the full range of diagnostic entities recognized in medicine today.

REFERENCES

Cummings, N. A., & Follette, W. T. (1968). Psychiatric services and medical utilization in a prepaid health plan setting: Part II. *Medical Care, 6,* 31–41.

Follette, W. T., & Cummings, N. A. (1962). [Psychiatry and medical utilization]. An unpublished pilot project.

Follette, W. T., & Cummings, N. A. (1967). Psychiatric services and medical utilization in a prepaid health plan setting. *Medical Care, 5,* 25–35.

Ornish, D., Brown, S. E., Scherwitz, L. W., Billings, J. H., Armstrong, W. T., Ports, T. A., et al. (1990). Can lifestyle changes reverse coronary heart disease? *Lancet, 336,* 129–133.

World Health Organization. (1996). *International classification of diseases, ninth revision, clinical modification.* Geneva: Author.

Volume 3.
Models and Perspectives in Health Psychology

INTRODUCTION TO VOLUME 3: MODELS AND PERSPECTIVES IN HEALTH PSYCHOLOGY

ROBERT G. FRANK, JAN L. WALLANDER, AND ANDREW BAUM

Volume 3 is the third and final volume in the *Handbook of Clinical Health Psychology*. Each of the volumes in the series addresses the contributions of psychology to our understanding and management of health conditions. Volume 3 examines models and perspectives psychologists use to provide heuristic paradigms. The text is divided into four parts: overview, research perspectives, clinical issues, and public health and policy perspectives.

Chapter 1, by Baum, Perry, and Tarbell, constitutes the overview. The authors trace the evolution of psychology from a behavioral social science into a health science. They note the intertwined relationship between psychology and health services. As chronic conditions have increasingly accounted for premature mortality, the importance of health psychology has increased. Using the concept of behavior-borne illness, they note the importance in behavior change to improving health outcomes. Baum and colleagues recognize the increased importance of studying behavior change and decreased emphasis on psychopathology.

Part II contains six chapters. These chapters cover a broad array of topics ranging from biobehavioral issues to personality factors in chronic health conditions. Common to the chapters in this section is an emphasis on basic psychological science contributions to health. These chapters provide a broad understanding of the implications of integrating psychological research into the delivery and understanding of health care. In chapter 2, Cruess, Schneiderman, Antoni, and Penedo provide a broad-based description of biobehavioral contributions to disease. Cruess and colleagues show that although there is much more to learn, it is now clear that psychological and social processes clearly influence disease outcomes in several significant medical conditions, including coronary heart disease, infection, HIV/AIDS, and some cancers. One important pathway underlying susceptibility is the immune system, and Forlenza and Baum explore current research and theory underpinning psychoneuroimmunology in chapter 3. This chapter provides a broad overview of research linking thoughts, behaviors, and mood with the status and functional ability of the immune system, including basic concepts, hypotheses, and findings. The authors of this chapter provide an understanding of relationships among neuroanatomical, neurochemical, and neuroendocrine systems and behavior. They show how perturbations in one system, including psychologically mediated changes, can affect other systems. The dynamic balance between immune system "enhancement" and "suppression" is considered and suggestions for ideal disease states for psychoneuroimmunology are provided. Recognizing the historic and scientific significance of recent efforts to sequence the human genome, Wenzel and Glanz (chapter 4) provide a timely review of behavioral aspects of genetic contribution to disease. Using cancer genetics as a prototype, the authors describe the interplay between psychological and biological issues in the area of genetics, ultimately suggesting important translational aspects of this work as well. In chapter 5, Smith and Ruiz address personality and health, one of the most studied issues in psychology. The authors provide a comprehensive discussion of current research, considering cardiovascular outcomes as an exemplar and describe the relationship between disease, premature mortality, and personality. Social and physical environment also plays an important role in these relationships, and the relationship between psychological and environmental factors is considered in Bogart and Delahanty's chapter 6 on psychosocial models. This chapter provides a comprehensive review of current theoretical models and the explanatory value of each approach. In chapter 7, Ewart addresses how integrated behavioral theory can directly affect health promotion and disease prevention. He provides a comprehensive review of current models, assessing the value of each, recognizing the limitations of any single theory to account for the myriad of health behaviors.

Part III addresses specific clinical issues in four chapters. In the first of these, chapter 8, Papas, Belar, and Rozensky address professional issues underlying clinical health psychology practice. The chapter provides an important discussion of the interaction between psychological health care practitioners and complex regulatory issues. Chapter 9 by McKay and Frank turns to a different aspect of professional environment, payment and economic issues controlling reimbursement for health care services. The chapter provides a review of fundamental drivers controlling health care reimbursement as well as examining future trends. Complementary health care—in other words, interventions outside the realm of traditional Western medicine—has become one of the most rapidly growing areas of health care. In chapter 10, Gardea, Gatchel, and Robinson provide a primer on the topic and interactions with psychology. In chapter 11, Glueckauf, Nickelson, Whitton, and Loomis define telehealth, providing a review of commonly used telehealth equipment and regulatory issues and research affecting psychological practice within this arena.

Part IV considers the possibility of modifying health services through governmental and systems interventions. Although the previous parts examined basic research within clinical health psychology and the delivery of individual services, this part considers population-based interventions and the role of policy in affecting such interventions. The five chapters in this section provide an opportunity for clinical health psychologists to work with large populations and policies governing their care. In chapter 12, DeLeon, Paige, Smedley, and Sammons examine the nature of public policy and opportunities for psychologists to engage in policy work. Recently, psychologists have found increasing opportunities in the field of public health. In chapter 13, Tucker, Phillips, Murphy, and Raczynski define the field of behavioral epidemiology. They review basic epidemiological concepts and discuss the applications of psychological principles to epidemiology. Orleans, Ulmer, and Gruman provide a comprehensive overview of the role of behavior in U.S. national health goals in chapter 14. This important chapter demonstrates the importance of clinical health psychology to achieving the types of health outcomes that public policy visionaries believe possible. In chapter 15, Leviton and Raczynski challenge the normal perspective of clinical health psychologists. The authors review and describe interventions with large communities that contrast to the typical single-subject intervention common to clinical health psychology. In the final chapter, chapter 16, Klapow, Kaplan, and Doctor describe the emerging field of health outcomes and progress toward meeting the importance of health outcomes in assessing national health priorities. The authors argue that clinical health psychology can play an important role in designing and measuring these health outcomes.

Taken together, the 16 chapters in this book provide a timely and exciting view of the future of clinical health psychology. The reader, whether a graduate student deciding on which opportunities beckon him or her or an established researcher, will understand the changes the field is experiencing. The remarkable body of research and theory described in these pages suggests clinical health psychology has much to offer for those seeking to understand health and morbidity.

I

OVERVIEW

1

THE DEVELOPMENT OF PSYCHOLOGY AS A HEALTH SCIENCE

ANDREW BAUM, NATHAN W. PERRY JR., AND SALLY TARBELL

Psychology has evolved since its inception as a "brass instrument" science in the 19th century. Buffeted and shaped by events outside its science as well as within, psychology gradually developed a systematic applied focus and developed interventions for problems ranging from mental health and psychopathology to social influence and persuasion. Since World War II, psychology has entered and reshaped the workplace, schools, community activism, the legal arena, and other real-world settings. In none of the settings have these changes been more evident or important than in the health care environment, verifying for many that psychology is, among other things, a behavioral life science inextricably tied to biology and chemistry, with an important role for safeguarding health and well-being. The impact of psychology in health care has moved well beyond simply caring for medical patients who become distressed by their disease, treatment, or prognosis. As chronic illnesses have become more commonplace and account for the majority of disability and premature mortality, psychology has become more prominent in the management of illness, maintenance of health, prevention and detection of disease, and the operation of the systems delivering care. At the same time behavioral and biobehavioral factors and processes have become important in models of the etiology and progression of diseases such as heart disease and cancer. This chapter describes prominent aspects of this behavioral revolution in health care and the growing recognition that what we think, how we feel, or how we behave inexorably influences our health and well-being. It is also about how this revolution has changed how psychology operates in these settings.

Specifically, we consider the changes in psychological perspectives that have accompanied changes in health care. As suggested earlier, applied psychology has been involved in health for many years, caring for patients and their families who experience difficulty managing distress associated with medical problems and helping them cope with often unwanted developments. However, this has historically been done from a traditional mental health perspective, with an emphasis on psychopathology. The changes we consider have not eliminated this traditional focus but rather have greatly broadened it to include the majority of patients and family members who do not experience psychopathology or overwhelming distress. These changes also suggest incorporation of psychological variables in models of disease etiology and treatment and important adjuncts to patient care, prevention, and palliation. Although clearly rooted in more traditional areas of psychology, this new health psychology is based on some fundamentally different concepts and assumptions.

PSYCHOLOGY AS A HEALTH SCIENCE

The implications of changes in psychology and in health care are as profound as are recent changes in public health, health care financing, and other relevant arenas. They are also intertwined with these evolving areas. Since the advent of systematic–universal vaccination programs, enhancement of sanitation, and widespread use of antibiotics, the nature of the major causes of illness, disability, and death have changed. As threats associated with influenza, tuberculosis, and polio receded in the 20th century, chronic diseases emerged anew (see Figure 1.1). Heart disease, stroke, cancer, diabetes, arthritis, and other diseases have taken their place as a primary focus for intervention, with implications for a range of health care issues. Chronic diseases often require substantial lifestyle changes and behavioral change as a strategy for risk management, and disease management has become more important. These diseases also pose new psychologically relevant challenges for patients, families, and health care providers seeking to manage diseases rather than cure them, to prevent their recurrence or progression, and to provide care for conditions that persist for long, open-ended periods of time. Chronic lifestyle illnesses are generally more costly to treat than acute illnesses, and the changing nature of major threats to health have dictated new ways of structuring health care as these costs have

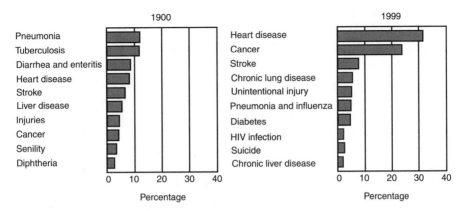

Figure 1.1. Changes in cause of death (1900–1999). From "Control of Infectious Diseases, 1900–1999," by Centers for Disease Control and Prevention, 1999, *Morbidity and Mortality Weekly Report, 48.* In the public domain.

increased (see Figure 1.2). Health care costs will continue to increase as our population ages, and although the import of increasing dominance of health maintenance organizations (HMOs) and promised emphasis on prevention and health promotion on these costs is not yet clear, the confluence of these and other changes have helped deliver a new and exciting paradigm for psychology and for patient care.

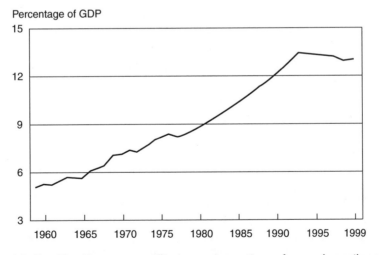

Figure 1.2. Total health care expenditures as a percentage of gross domestic product (GDP). From Health Care Financing Administration. In the public domain.

HEALTH PSYCHOLOGY

As we have noted, health psychology reflects a relatively new product of the evolution of research and theory in our field. It challenges traditional dichotomous views of the mind and body and argues for a more unified perspective based on their interaction. Health psychology is inherently holistic; its theories are based on close interaction of biological and psychological processes, and its targets and concerns have become increasingly of joint biological and behavioral determination of thoughts, moods, and behavior. It has imported advances in technology, molecular biology, and patient care and achieved an unprecedented degree of integration between brain–behavior domains and more traditional physiology, biochemistry, and other areas of medical science. It has also become more pervasive in traditional public health and medical arenas. As costs have increased and diseases have become more chronic and disabling, there has been a renewed focus on prevention, early detection, and behavior management. Science has long recognized these aspects of health promotion as essential and largely behavioral, but greater emphasis on behavior seems now to characterize our efforts to control serious disease. Stress, tobacco use, alcohol and drug abuse, diet, exercise, and other behavioral or lifestyle variables are a major focus of most attempts to promote good health and prevent illness.

The impetus for the development of this field was in part the changing social and cultural climate as well as technological advances, health care economics, and rapidly changing population trends. Most of all it grew as a result of the apparent inadequacy of traditional medical models to explain, prevent, or manage chronic illness. But where did the new field come from? Several sources can be traced, some widely recognized (such as the seminal work on autonomic regulation by Neal Miller [e.g., Miller, 1969]) and others less often discussed (e.g., Cannon, 1927; Wolff, 1953). It is safe to say that health psychology did not spring full-blown into the professional arena. Rather, it reflects the products of many developments, theoretical currents, and methodological and treatment innovations.

Psychology has strong biological roots, having grown from medicine and physiology as well as philosophy and social science. However, these roots have long been subject to tensions related to psychology's multiple identities as a social science, a natural science, and a life science. Philosophical origins of psychology have been well-described, and in its closeness to these roots, psychology is a social science, related to areas such as sociology, anthropology, and the decision-making sciences. In other ways, it resembles a physical science with its emphases on quantitative measurement, prediction, and overarching laws of behavior deriving from views of physics and "mental chemistry." However, some of the most important contributions to the development of psychology in the 19th century were from biology and the undeniable importance of the brain, nervous system, and the endocrine and immune systems in regulating thoughts, emotions, and bodily function and have been evident for years. These biological roots typically do not receive as much attention within psychology as have more traditional areas such as learning and cognition, and psychology's growth has been marked by only a modest emphasis on the biological determinism context of behavior or the close interaction of mood and behavior with biological systems.

This is not to suggest that health psychology is all biology (or that it should be) or that more traditional emphases of psychology are not central to health psychology. The 20th century has seen a number of developments that contributed to the growth of this field, some of which were essentially biobehavioral in nature or suggested more holistic perspectives. The applied demands of two world wars and in Korea, Vietnam, and the Middle East, changes in health and illness that we have already been noted, and the advent of modern psychopharmacology are all of this past century. The 20th century also saw the discovery and refinement of sophisticated models of conditioning and learning, some of which implicitly or explicitly view behavior as a joint function of mind and body (e.g., Pavlov, 1927; Skinner, 1998). Miller's work provided new perspectives on the brain and nervous system, challenging traditional views about which bodily functions are involuntary or under volitional control and how much control one has over them (e.g., Miller, 1969). Other work suggested that there are general processes (such as stress) or personality variables (such as Type A behavior) that can predict or predispose serious disease (e.g., Ader, 1981; Glass, 1977; Lazarus, 1966; Selye, 1976). To some extent these changes arose out of parallel developments in biological sciences and in psychosomatic medicine, a pioneering discipline focused on illnesses with biological causes that are produced, in part, by psychological processes. Psychosomatically oriented physicians were wrestling with the limitations of an exclusively biological model of disease that were becoming apparent as the 19th century ended. Although the theories and methods used by these investigators were often different than those used in psychology, the fields were clearly linked, and psychosomatic medicine became an important foundation for health psychology. Today, the fields overlap considerably and have continued to grow toward each other.

Many of these ingredients developed more or less independently of one another. They remained to be stirred into something new, just as many areas of psychology were catalyzed by World War II or by the IQ debate (Jensen, 1987; Kamin, 1974). For health psychology, catalyzing elements included new health care challenges—the increasing, uneasy realization that diseases such as heart disease had substantial behavioral components and the unprecedented problems posed by behavioral pathogens such as tobacco use (e.g., Matarazzo, 1980). Perhaps the most critical of these catalysts was the HIV/AIDS epidemic, which presented society with a progressive, often fatal illness for which there was no cure and that was transmitted almost exclusively through behavior. This epidemic presented unprecedented opportunities and responsibilities for psychologists (e.g., Baum & Nesselhof, 1988). In addition to the technological and medical revolutions that were spawned, behavioral scientists found themselves face to face with a killer disease that most of the time could be prevented by behavior change. For the first 10 to 20 years of our experience with HIV and AIDS, behavior change was the only approach to disease control; abstinence or monogamous sexual activity, safer sexual practices, and modification of IV drug use offered the best hope of curbing the spread of HIV and preventing infection. In addition, the progression of HIV disease appeared to be variable, and it became increasingly likely that behaviors and biobehavioral processes could also affect disease course and treatment outcomes. Drawing in models of health beliefs, persuasion, psychoneuroimmunology, stress, and other behavioral phenomena, this epidemic was a crucible for the development of health psychology.

Of course, if one considers tobacco use in the same light, then diseases such as lung cancer or head and neck cancer are also dangerous diseases that can be prevented by behavior change. The 10 leading causes of death in the United States in 1990 were tobacco use, poor diet, lack of exercise, alcohol, infectious agents, toxics, firearms, compromising sexual behavior, motor vehicle accidents, and illicit drug use (McGinnis & Foege, 1993). Investigation of these public health problems, most of which have substantial behavioral components, was linked to many early contributions to the development of health psychology, from within behavioral sciences and from other disciplines and arenas. The development of research on coronary-prone behavior (e.g., Glass, 1977), of psychoneuroimmunology (Ader, 1981), on health beliefs and expectations (e.g., Wallston & Wallston, 1984), of work on surgery and reduction of fear and distress (e.g., Johnson, 1973; Johnson & Leventhal, 1974), and of research on tobacco use, obesity, and neuroscience all led directly to new approaches in health psychology. The rise of cognitive–behavioral approaches, new techniques for helping to control pain, and the increasing ascendance of prevention in mental health also contributed. A detailed history of the field is beyond the scope of this chapter. It is sufficient to note the great variety of divergent trends and developments that have contributed to this field and the absolute emphasis it places on the constant interplay of behavioral and biological variables in the maintenance of health and etiology of illness. In the rest of this chapter we argue that changing currents in the field and in society are consistent with this new perspective and new ways of thinking about our science and about health care delivery. The successful blending of several areas of psychology with public health and more traditional biomedical sciences has helped change the way we view health and disease. Behavioral and biobehavioral factors affecting our health have been identified, and we live in an era of unprecedented awareness of the importance of people's choices and actions in determining their health. We know that a variety of behaviors and social variables can contribute to development of disease and have reason to believe that psychosocial interventions can help prevent illness, affect how well treatments work, and influence how long people survive. Quality of life, adherence, and stress have become common to the lexicon of medicine, and the pervasive roles of behaviors such as smoking, diet, and exercise have been recognized in the pathophysiology of disease. Nowhere is this revolution more apparent than in the evolution of this new approach in patient care and psychological health service delivery, preemptive efforts of maintaining good mental and physical health, and active intervention to prevent problems and to facilitate adjustment and coping with disease.

Applied to patient care, the behavioral medicine or health psychology model is not a replacement for more traditional clinical psychology. It addresses fundamentally different concerns than do these approaches and should be considered complementary to them. It is concerned primarily with preventing adjustment problems and helping mentally healthy people cope with extraordinary circumstances associated with health and illness rather than with psychopathology or treatment of mental illness. It is also concerned with disease prevention and risk management through applications of behavioral principles and with disease management. Its scope includes psychopathology, seeking first to prevent it or minimize its impact, seeking more fundamental change in behavior that will mitigate negative aspects of illness and assist people in managing and surviving it. It is an interdisciplinary model, often more closely aligned with medicine, surgery, pediatrics, or other medical specialties than with psychiatry. It is equally applicable across all phases of the medical system, from routine screening and outpatient care to extraordinary interventions and palliative care. And it seeks to provide support, skills, and information that make it easier for people to manage health and illness.

In these respects, health psychology is more than clinical psychology applied to medical settings and more than traditional psychiatric approaches to mental health. For patients with serious acute or chronic disease or for those undergoing aversive or stressful medical procedures, it seeks to identify existing resources, build on these resources, and develop support and resiliency factors that will minimize distress later on. Its outcomes include mood and well-being but go well beyond them, looking at adherence to preventive or treatment regimens, preparation for surgery and management of distress associated with medical tests or procedures, modification of pathophysiological processes and symptom reduction, and the development of well-informed patients who become actively involved in their care.

PSYCHOLOGY IN MEDICAL SETTINGS

Although there is not one simple way to describe how psychology has fit into the medical world, psychology has historically found itself a junior partner of psychiatry, charged with treating episodes of psychopathology that developed in medical settings and with identifying risk factors contributing to adjustment problems or poor disease management. This remains a critically important role, as research suggests that one third of medical inpatients and substantial numbers of people with other serious or chronic diseases develop diagnosable psychopathology during the course of identification, treatment, and living with these diseases (Katon & Sullivan, 1990). Management of these crises is essential to appropriate care for these patients and, untreated, mental health problems can negatively affect medical outcomes. Depression, for example, is associated with shorter survival and higher incidence of coronary events following an initial heart attack (Carney, Freeland, Rich, & Jaffee, 1995) and has been linked to suppression of indexes of immune system function and adherence to prescribed regimens (Herbert & Cohen, 1993; Weisse, 1992). Application of traditional psychological and psychiatric care to mood disorders and other mental health syndromes manifest in medical settings has worked well and is an essential part of health care today.

As these considerations suggest, the role of psychology in medical settings has moved far beyond dealing with patients at risk or with psychopathology. As noted earlier, the early appearing field of psychosomatic medicine struggled against the mind–body dichotomy then (and still) dominant in medical settings. The struggle was shared by pioneer psychologists and psychiatrists who today make up a core of what has come to be labeled behavioral medicine. These psychologists led a major development in both basic and applied psychology into health and clinical health psychology, respectively. The impact has been so great that applied psychologists have defined themselves as health service providers, and the American Psychological Association (APA) changed its mission statement to include the word "health" in the past few years. Psychosomatically oriented psychiatrists had far less of an impact in the field of psychiatry and have, in fact, lost ground as psychiatry moved back toward biology during the last two decades of the 20th century. Health psychology is the beneficiary of these earlier struggles against dualism. Modern academic health science centers in the United States contain a vast array of medical specialists to diagnose and treat every medical illness. A psychologist in such a setting can expect patient referrals, consultations, or research opportunities from every one of these medical specialties. This demand can be so great that psychology has responded as medicine—with increased specialization by individual psychologists.

Health psychology also assumes a proactive stance through prevention and early intervention in primary, secondary, and tertiary care. Traditional approaches have been more reactive, treating problems after they have become serious, but health psychology anticipates them and works to prevent them from occurring. An example of a reactive approach would be starting pain treatment after an invasive procedure has been completed and pain is experienced. Newer approaches to pain management are based on the idea that it is easier to prevent pain from ever being felt than it is to reduce it once it has appeared (Turk, 2002). Experience tells us that the preemptive approach is usually more effective than treatment that "chases the pain" (Turk, 1996). We believe the same is true for most health problems. Health psychologists eschew the notion that you cannot treat pain if you do not yet have it, seeking to head it off before it becomes a problem.

This preoccupation with inoculation and preventive intervention, which sets health psychology apart from many more traditional psychological forays into the medical arena, is by no means its only distinguishing characteristic. As we will see in the next section, health psychology is a specialty that is important in many medical contexts. Treatments are ordinarily based on knowledge of psychological *and* biological disorders and their interactions. The clinical health psychologist applies treatments that are empirically based and seeks to evaluate interventions through clinical trials. Health psychology also emphasizes active participation by the patient in his or her treatment, using a variety of techniques to educate patients, involve them in monitoring symptoms, and empower them to understand and influence the course of care. Interventions are usually short-term and goal-oriented. We will consider these characteristics in greater detail before turning to some of the implications of this evolving model of patient care.

HEALTH PSYCHOLOGISTS AS PART OF THE HEALTH CARE TEAM

Health psychology providers may have their primary appointment in any of many medical departments, a division or section of psychology or behavioral medicine in a medical department, or in some cases in a department of psychology. This range of venues highlights the diverse array of services offered by psychologists in medical settings as well as the broad applicability of behavioral health services to health care. The health psychologist becomes an integral part of multidisciplinary treatment teams that can include not only medical colleagues but also allied health disciplines such as pharmacy, physical, and occupational therapy, nursing, nutrition, and in the pediatric setting, child life. The psychologist ideally will participate in daily medical rounds, in interdisciplinary rounds, and in treatment planning or care conferences. This participation not only involves active consultation to staff on optimal methods to manage patient behavioral and psychological health issues, especially as they affect the patient's health status, but also on how patient–staff interactions can influence patient symptoms. For example, in the pediatric setting nursing staff may inadvertently reinforce pain behaviors by refusing to give analgesics unless the child is markedly expressive (e.g., screaming, crying). Patients quickly learn that if they ask for pain medicines without producing these behaviors they will be less likely to get them, thereby reinforcing maladaptive pain behaviors rather than active coping with pain. The health psychologist may consult with the medical staff to change the medication schedule from an "as needed" to a set schedule to reduce the likelihood of problematic staff–patient interactions. Alternative ways to promote patient coping rather than "sick" behaviors may be suggested, and health psychologists also provide consultation on the use of valid methods of assessment to help guide staff in making judgments about medication administration.

Because health psychologists work with several medical subspecialties and across hospital settings, they are often thrust into a unique position, helping to coordinate care among multiple practitioners. By doing so they can provide a coherence to care that can be lost when a patient is simultaneously receiving services from multiple practitioners. One striking example of this occurred when a health psychologist was consulted to help a patient with chronic pain management. In an effort to understand the patient's complex medical history, the psychologist uncovered many inconsistencies in her symptoms and their response to treatment as described by the several physicians involved in her care. Efforts to clarify these inconsistencies led to the discovery of several factitious medical problems, and ultimately, to a major reduction of the intensity of this patient's medical care and referral for psychiatric care.

To function effectively as part of a multidisciplinary health care team, the health psychologist needs to be knowledgeable about psychological treatments and disorders, as well as medical disorders and their treatments. It is critically important to recognize the impact of various medical procedures and disorders on mood and behavior. For example, steroids may depress mood or produce euphoria, whereas stroke, brain metastases, low cardiac ejection fraction, and high ammonia levels found in end-stage liver disease will all influence patients' mental status, fatigue, and mood. Knowledge of the patient's medical regimen, prognosis, and impact of medical treatments and recommendations about patients' lifestyles also are essential to accurately understand the patient's adjustment to illness and motivation to effect behavioral change. Without this understanding the health psychologist is not credible to the health care staff and cannot communicate effectively with either the patient or the health care team. For example, psychologists are commonly members of formal organ transplant teams where the patient and social support resources must be part of the complex evaluations of several questions or issues, including whether the procedure be done or how to increase chances of success. Most medical settings develop consultation patterns between practitioners that over time could loosely be called "teams," and psychologists are often part of these networks.

Before health psychology intervention is initiated the clinician also needs to be familiar with standards of care for the management of medical symptoms. For example, helping a patient manage postsurgical symptoms with behavioral medicine techniques first requires an assessment of the adequacy of the patient's pharmacological management (e.g., analgesics or anxiolytics scheduled at regular intervals versus prn (*pro re nata* or "as needed")). The health psychologist will be less effective if he or she does not address pharmacological issues with the health care team as well as provide consultation to the patient and staff on behavioral methods of control. Thus, the health psychologist truly becomes a partner in the medical team in managing the patient's symptoms.

To the fullest extent possible health psychology interventions are based on empirically validated treatments. What often distinguishes the clinical work of the health psychologist from that of some other specialties or subspecialties is the ability to cite treatment efficacy studies when explaining care to a referring physician or to a patient and to give a clear description of what will be involved in the treatment as well as the time commitment required. Although treatment protocols or guidelines for each clinical problem encountered do not yet exist, behavioral medicine and health psychology clinicians work to advance the science of intervention through studies of treatment effectiveness and individual difference variables that may affect treatment outcome.

As has been implicit throughout this discussion, health psychology is also characterized by an emphasis on active patient participation. The patient is given an overview of treatment and detailed information about disease characteristics. Treatment is not done to or for the patient. Rather, the patient is an active learner, even when it comes to palliative care. Often patients will need to be socialized to this active role. A psychoeducational approach is taken whereby patients are taught about the nature of the intervention as well as their role in its implementation. The analogy of a coach or teacher is often used to describe the clinician's role, with the patient taking on the role of a competent student. Most patients are viewed as mentally healthy people experiencing aversive or extraordinary circumstances, and they are offered the opportunity to learn additional skills for managing psychological and physical symptoms. The patient's active participation in treatment may include symptom recording/behavior logs; practicing skills such as relaxation, imagery, and cognitive coping and problem solving methods; and becoming more involved in decision making about his or her health care. Treatment is typically short-term and goal-oriented, with treatment contracts renegotiated as needed to accommodate new symptoms or changes in medical care. Booster sessions are provided as indicated to prevent relapse after the initial treatment regimen is completed. Because the presenting problem may range from acute trauma to chronic illness, the different sequences in this model may range from days to years or even decades. This model of care fits well with increased demands for efficient outcomes-based care necessitated by managed care and reductions in health care funding, but it is based on optimal effect on health status rather than the economics of health care.

A PREEMPTIVE FOCUS

Important defining characteristics of health psychology interventions are that they focus when possible on preventing or preempting distress or health problems rather than crisis intervention and are focused on adjustment and coping. Because this is a relatively new approach in medical settings (physicians and nurses often think of behavioral interventions only when patients are very distressed), a major component in establishing health psychology services is teaching physicians and allied health professionals what it is that health psychologists can do to improve health status. Our experience suggests that many of the things health psychologists do are readily embraced and used once physicians, nurses, and other medical staff learn what *can* be done. At the same time, health psychologists can help determine when in the course of a patient's treatment behavioral medicine intervention can be most effective. Optimal involvement of health psychologists requires that they meet patients at initial entry into the health care system to screen for psychosocial or biobehavioral risk and resiliency factors and offer patients opportunities to augment current positive health behaviors and coping skills and to reduce behavioral risk factors. How these appraisals are communicated to the patient is an area where the psychologist has much to contribute as well. For example, how much information is necessary to secure his or her active and effective participation versus providing so much that disruptive anxiety is created? This prevention focus contrasts with the traditional psychiatric consultation–liaison model where intervention typically occurs only after psychiatric symptomatology is evident.

Prevention activities are not limited to managing symptoms and preventing extreme or debilitating emotional disturbances. Health psychology approaches can be used for primary prevention of disease, as in programs designed to encourage healthy eating and for modification of known risk factors such as a sedentary lifestyle and smoking. Behavioral medicine intervention also can be a primary effective treatment, rather than an adjunct to biological treatments, as is the use of stress management and biofeedback-assisted relaxation training for migraine headaches (Hatch, 1993). Health psychology interventions are also used for symptom reduction, as in the treatment of conditioned vomiting related to chemotherapy (Redd et al., 2001). As noted earlier, nonadherence to medical regimens has a pervasive negative influence on health outcomes and is another important target for health psychology.

The work that health psychologists do with their patients is intentionally transparent, with goals and techniques clearly explained to the patient and other health care providers. The psychologist provides frequent, brief, data-based communication to referring physicians that keeps the physician apprised of the patient's progress without compromising patient confidentiality. Furthermore, it is likely that some of the intervention will be conducted in collaboration with the referring practitioners and simultaneously involved in the delivery of care.

Health psychology intervention is often directed both to patients and their family members, because changes in lifestyle risk factors and coping skills often involve modifications that affect the entire family. For example, when one family member is diagnosed with diabetes and needs regularly scheduled meals that are low in concentrated sugar the needs or preferences of other family members may not be met, and adjustment by each is necessary. When a family member is stricken with breast cancer or another life-threatening disease, the changes in roles, distress, and general disruption are shared by all. In pediatric behavioral medicine, particularly for children in the preschool years, the child's parents often become active partners in the delivery of interventions, such as when they prompt their child to use relaxation and imagery techniques for procedure-related pain and distress.

The behavioral medicine toolbox includes a variety of techniques for managing physical and psychological symptoms. The diversity of these approaches can be illustrated by considering a few brief examples. An adult patient with chronic obstructive pulmonary disease who panics at episodes of dyspnea would be educated about the role of anxiety in exacerbating feelings of shortness of breath and taught specific breathing techniques to reduce hyperventilation. He or she would be asked to keep a log of symptoms to chart treatment response and to promote feelings of effectiveness in coping with the symptoms, and would be taught energy conservation techniques to help reduce the frequency of the dyspnea episodes. Family members would be included in treatment to the fullest extent possible to help support and coach the patient in these newly developing skills and to provide support for treatment adherence and the maintenance of positive health behavior changes, such as smoking cessation.

Another example is a pediatric patient who displays distress related to frightening or painful medical procedures. This patient would be presented with a developmentally appropriate explanation of the procedures causing him or her pain and taught a series of behavioral pain management skills such as breathing, relaxation, and mental imagery to reduce pain and attendant distress. Again, family involvement would be central, and parents would be coached on how to reinforce their child's active coping efforts and to reduce their own distress, enabling them to provide optimal support for their child. At the same time, medical and nursing staff would be informed about the behavioral pain management intervention and how they can support its successful implementation.

TRAINING AND PROFESSIONAL ISSUES FACING HEALTH PSYCHOLOGY

In spite of the progress cited in the integration of health psychologist into the health care of patients and their families, there are too few formal clinical health psychology training programs. Current clinical health psychologists often have a background in clinical or counseling psychology, and then use clinical practica, internships, and postdoctoral positions to develop specific clinical skills in health psychology. Rarely are such skills taught formally to the psychology graduate student, and most behavioral health practitioners in the field have had to substantially supplement their formal didactic training with courses from medical schools and graduate schools of pharmacy, public health, and the biological sciences. Although the clinical health psychologist can acquire a basic level of specialty skills through continuing education courses offered at national conferences, most often the depth of skills required to function as a competent clinical health psychologist is acquired on the job. The medical environment bears little resemblance to the mental health clinic, the psychiatric hospital, or the college counseling service where many psychologists have received a majority of their clinical training. Considering the complexity of the skills required of the clinical health psychologist, including collaborating with several different disciplines on the care of patients with a multitude of medical and psychological concerns, we believe it would be optimal to provide more systematic teaching for the psychologist considering a clinical career in health psychology.

The evolution from individual experiential training in clinical health psychology to formal program training is accelerating. Although exact numbers are not available, it is estimated that there are between 30 and 40 predoctoral programs that are self-described as clinical health with a formal sequence of didactic and practicum courses. Many of these appear as tracks or areas within accredited clinical psychology programs. There are a similar number of internship or postdoctoral programs in medical settings. In addition, the APA has recognized clinical health psychology as a practice specialty. The specialty recognizes two paths to those students aspiring to be clinical health psychologists. One is to graduate from a recognized traditional specialty program and complete a two-year postdoctoral program in clinical health psychology. This path recognizes the evolving nature of the specialty. The second path also requires completion of a traditional specialty but includes a predoctoral program in clinical health psychology. Graduates of the latter could, of course, participate in postdoctoral training if they wished but it would not be required. The APA Committee on Accreditation has been asked to accredit both kinds of programs, and the recommended guidelines and types are explicitly given in the petition to recognize the specialties that were in turn based on an earlier conference (Arden House, 1983).

Training for a clinical health psychology specialty should look substantially different than traditional training in clinical psychology, although the latter is seen as a necessary base. A primary addition to the clinical training would be courses in the mechanisms of disease, where the student would be exposed to the basics of pathophysiology. Education about pharmacology and medications would extend beyond the mechanisms of action of psychotropic medications and cover basic classes of other therapeutics, such as analgesics, antiinflammatory agents, and medications for particular illnesses such as chemotherapeutic agents for cancer and antihypertensive and cholesterol-lowering agents for heart disease.

The implications of these needs and requirements include a broadening of traditional psychology training and expansion of practica in medical settings and with medical patients. Traditional psychology course work needs to be preserved, and trainees still need formal courses in statistics and experimental design, assessment, psychopathology, and clinical intervention (including interviewing, clinical techniques, and so on). Basic work in cognition, learning, sociocultural factors, motivation, and on models of behavior change are also still needed. In addition, greater emphasis on developmental/life-span issues, with a good deal of attention to aging family systems, and diversity are needed, as is basic course work in physiology, pharmacology, neuropsychology, and mechanisms of disease. Emphasis on more biological foundations of behavior must be renewed and coupled with more innovative instruction on how the human body works, how it metabolizes and responds to drugs, and on pathophysiology if health psychologists are to be as effective as possible.

Equally important is the development of new practical opportunities for students at the pre- and postdoctoral levels. Rotations in medical settings and with medical patients are important for several reasons. Medical settings, like most environments, are marked by unique cultural characteristics and by a set of expectations, informal rules, and traditions that are different from academic or mental health settings. In addition, working as part of a multidisciplinary team, working with families or caregivers, and dealing with aged or infirmed patients all require special knowledge, relevant experience, and the kind of understanding of the forces that buffet health and well-being that is best gained in real-world practice. Finally, effective care of these patients is best facilitated by experience with and guided interventions for patients in real-world settings. For these and other reasons, assessment experiences directed toward screening for psychotic patients and personality disorders as well as treatment practica that provide opportunities to apply basic techniques of health psychology intervention (e.g., relaxation, cognitive–behavioral stress management, imagery, progressive muscle relaxation, biofeedback, hypnosis) are important. It is also critical that these rotations include consultation with physicians and health care teams and include a range of clinical targets, including pain, risk factor reduction and management (e.g., smoking cessation, exercise, diet, stress), weight management and assessment/treatment of eating disorders, addictive behaviors, pediatrics, geriatrics, and specialized services (e.g., transplantation, cardiology, oncology, metabolic diseases). These practica inevitably suggest some restriction of more traditional rotations unless new, longer training models are adopted. Regardless, they seem necessary if we are to achieve the success that our society needs and our science and clinical approaches are capable of achieving.

These suggestions have focused on training of the clinical health psychologist and assume that the research training under the scientist–practitioner model will remain unchanged. This research training is a second unique strength that the clinical health psychologist brings to the multidisciplinary team and greatly enhances the value of the psychologist to the team. The term *clinical health psychologist* refers to someone who may do either research or clinical work, or often both, whereas *health psychologist* usually refers to someone who is primarily or solely concerned with research. This awkward distinction is of course not always completely accurate but helpful for those trained in basic areas of psychology who do not wish to be involved in diagnosis and treatment. Psychology as a profession and as a discipline can contribute so much through direct service to individuals and through research on health and health policy.

Perhaps the greatest issue or problems in psychology related to health are not in education within psychology but with the public and the medical professions. We discussed earlier how we needed to educate other health care providers about what psychology could do to contribute to patients' health, and we certainly do need to increase those educational efforts. We also need to increase those efforts with every group that helps in developing health policy. It is reassuring that the role of behavior (and concomitantly, psychology) is increasingly appreciated. However, the dichotomy between health and mental health is still so prevalent that a psychologist ordinarily cannot be reimbursed for seeing a patient who is referred for medical care unless the patient has a psychiatric diagnosis. At the same time, behavioral research can expect to receive less than 10% of the total National Institute of Health budget, regardless of the role behavior is known to play in disease and mortality (Kabor, Sharpe, Silver, & Wurtz, 2002). As conditions improve and more attention and awareness of the importance of behavioral approaches to health and health care becomes evident, the research and clinical discoveries that have driven the field will expand. For the time being, however, there is still much to be done.

CONCLUSION

We have argued that the development of psychology as a health science reflects the confluence of many forces and developments. The face of disease and causes of premature mortality have changed over the past century, and this has been marked by increasing prominence of diseases with strong lifestyle components or origins. These behavior-borne illnesses and syndromes are a result in part to unhealthy behaviors such as tobacco use, overeating, and lack of exercise and appear to be influenced by stress, coping, personality, one's social relationships, and other psychosocial factors that interact closely with inherited and somatic gene mutations and environmental forces. People are living longer, and this has also contributed to changes in the prevalence of some diseases and syndromes. These general changes have increased the salience of behavioral and biobehavioral factors in models of disease etiology, also increasing their importance in prevention efforts. More holistic approaches to health and disease and increasing calls for unification of persistent elements of Cartesian dualism have evolved and become more common. Funding agencies and professional societies have designated various epochs as reflecting dramatic change in emphasis and focus; hence we had the "Decade of the Brain" and now the "Decade of Behavior." Perhaps our next such designation should reflect the need to better integrate mind and body and to learn to really think of them as simultaneous extensions of each other.

The changes noted have been particularly important in the emergence of psychology as a health science. Research on disease and health have been irrevocably altered, and emphasis on these new linkages will undoubtedly increase further. At the same time, these developments spell significant changes for the practice of psychology and for health care in general. Now, in addition to "responsibility" for care, prevention, and rehabilitation of mental disorders and psychopathology, we must consider the unusual, unique, or interactive demands of chronic disease management (many major health threats require long-term management instead of or in addition to acute care) and treatment of normal or everyday behaviors or habits that may contribute to future disease or ill health. The primary focus in the health care settings is more often not psychopathology but rather the context in which habitual or risky behavior develops and the distress that results when psychologically healthy people confront the often extraordinary threat and demands associated with major illnesses such as heart disease or cancer. These additional concerns raise new issues and suggest new training venues and emphases. How well we can incorporate these new issues and adapt to changes in what we do as trainers and educators may ultimately determine how successful we will be.

There are other pressures and causes of change in the health care environment that have been mentioned. Similarly, there are other important aspects of health psychology and behavioral science contributions to health and to illness prevention, most notably community and population-level approaches and health care policy. These other perspectives are part of the overall changes that led to or accompanied the development of health psychology and should increasingly become a target for psychological training, research, and application. We have chosen not to emphasize them because they reflect other issues and forces that are beyond the scope of this chapter. Dramatic advances in technology and scientific knowledge, from imaging to the genome, have revolutionized the ways we think about behavior and about health and disease. Changes in how health care is managed and paid for, how prevention and early detection are considered, and how health care is accessed are also critically important and offer new challenges and opportunities for health psychologists. The changing nature of our population, changing cultural mores and social pressures, and the introduction of new health hazards are also important. Our task, as we enter the Century of Unification of mind and body medicine and science, will be to adapt to and shape these disparate forces and to generate new and equally challenging opportunities and problems.

REFERENCES

Ader, R. (1981). Behavioral influences on immune responses. In S. M. Weiss, J. A. Herd, & B. H. Fox (Eds.), *Perspectives on behavioral medicine* (pp. 163–182). New York: Academic Press.

Arden House. (1983, May 23–27). National working conference on education and training in health psychology. *Health Psychology*, 2(Suppl.).

Baum, A., & Nesselhof, S. E. (1988). Psychological research and the prevention, etiology, and treatment of AIDS. *American Psychologist*, 43(11), 900–906.

Cannon, W. B. (1927). The James–Lange theory of emotions: A critical examination and an alternative. *American Journal of Psychology*, 39, 356–372.

Carney, R. M., Freedland, K. E., Rich, M. W., & Jaffe, A. S. (1995). Depression as a risk factor for cardiac events in established coronary heart disease: A review of possible mechanisms. *Annals of Behavioral Medicine, 17*(2), 142–149.

Centers for Disease Control. (1999). Control of infectious diseases, 1900–1999. *Morbidity and Mortality Weekly Report, 48,* 621–629.

Glass, D. C. (1977). *Behavior patterns, stress, and coronary disease.* Hillsdale, NJ: Erlbaum.

Hatch, J. P. (1993). Headache. In R. J. Gatchel & E. B. Blanchard (Eds.), *Psychophysiological disorders, research and clinical applications* (pp. 111–150). Washington, DC: American Psychological Association.

Herbert, T. B., & Cohen, S. (1993). Depression and immunity: A meta-analytic review. *Psychology Bulletin, 113,* 472–486.

Jensen, A. R. (1987). Individual differences in mental ability. In J. A. Glove & R. R. Ronning (Eds.), *Historical foundations of educational psychology. Perspectives on individual differences* (pp. 61–88). New York: Plenum Press.

Johnson, J. E. (1973). Effects of accurate expectations about sensations on the sensory and distress components of pain. *Journal of Personality and Social Psychology, 27*(2), 261–275.

Johnson, J. E., & Leventhal, H. (1974). Effects of accurate expectations and behavioral instructions on reactions during a noxious medical examination. *Journal of Personality and Social Psychology, 29,* 710–718.

Kabor, P. Sharpe, A., Silver, H., & Wurtz, S. (2002). Behavioral and social science research in the FY 2003 budget. In *AAAS Report XXVII: Research and development TY 2003* (chap. 20). Retrieved January 21, 2004, from http:/www.aaas.org/spp/rd/03pch20.pdf

Kamin, L. J. (1974). *The science and politics of IQ.* Potomac, MD: Erlbaum.

Katon, W., & Sullivan, M. D., (1990). Depression and chronic medical illness. *Journal of Clinical Psychiatry, 51,* 3–11.

Lazarus, R. S. (1966). Story telling and the measurement of motivation: The direct versus substitutive controversy. *Journal of Consulting Psychology, 30,* 483–487.

Matarazzo, J. D. (1980). Behavioral health and behavioral medicine: Frontiers for a new health psychology. *American Psychologist, 35,* 807–817.

McGinnis, J. M., & Foege, W. H. (1993). Actual causes of death in the United States. *Journal of the American Medical Association, 270*(19), 2207–2212.

Miller, N. E. (1969). Learning of visceral and glandular responses. *Science, 163,* 434–445.

Pavlov, I. P. (1927). *Conditioned reflexes.* New York: Dover.

Redd, W. H., DuHamel, K. N., Vickberg, S. M. J., Ostroff, J. L., Smith, M. Y., Jacobson, P. B., et al. (2001). Long-term adjustment in cancer survivors integration of classical conditioning and cognitive processing models. In A. Baum & B. Andersen (Eds.), *Psychosocial interventions for cancer* (pp. 77–97). Washington, DC: American Psychological Association.

Selye, H. (1976). *The stress of life* (Rev. ed.). New York: McGraw-Hill

Skinner, B. F. (1998). The experimental analysis of operant behavior: A history. In R. W. Rieber & K. Salzinger (Eds.), *Psychology: Theoretical–historical perspectives* (2nd ed., pp. 289–299). Washington, DC: American Psychological Association.

Turk, D. C. (1996). Biopsychosocial perspective on chronic pain. In R. J. Gatchel & D. C. Turk (Eds.), *Psychological approaches to pain management* (pp. 3–32). New York: Guilford Press.

Turk, D. C. (2002). Clinical effectiveness and cost effectiveness of treatments for chronic pain. *Clinical Journal of Pain, 18,* 355–365.

Wallston, B. S., & Wallston, K. A. (1984). Social psychological models of health behavior: An examination and integration. In A. Baum, J. E. Singer, & S. Taylor (Eds.), *Handbook of psychology and health* (pp. 23–53). Hillsdale, NJ: Erlbaum.

Weisse, C. S. (1992). Depression and immunocompetence: A review of the literature. *Psychological Bulletin, 111*(3), 475–489.

Wolff, H. G. (1953). *Stress and disease.* Springfield, IL: Charles G. Thomas.

II
RESEARCH PERSPECTIVES

2

BIOBEHAVIORAL BASES OF DISEASE PROCESSES

DEAN G. CRUESS, NEIL SCHNEIDERMAN, MICHAEL H. ANTONI,
AND FRANK PENEDO

There is considerable evidence that within the context of our genetic endowment, constitutional factors, sociocultural variables, and the physical environment, important psychosocial and biological processes interact to influence health outcomes. Adverse health effects can be exacerbated by such harmful behaviors as smoking, poor diet, excessive alcohol consumption, and a sedentary lifestyle. In addition, psychosocial stressors may affect disease processes through their impact on the autonomic nervous system (ANS) and the hypothalamic pituitary adrenal (HPA) axis. During recent years there has been increasing awareness that common pathways appear to link genetic predispositions, adverse environments, and psychosocial variables with various disease outcomes. Although the mediating variables and their interactions have not all been identified, an outline of the pathways is becoming clearer. Figure 2.1 provides a schematic diagram depicting some of these pathways.

Genetic predisposition and adverse environmental factors affecting the nervous system can influence perceptions. These can lead to emotional experiences and changes in behavior or neural regulation, which in turn may exacerbate disease processes. This may influence a host of physical

31

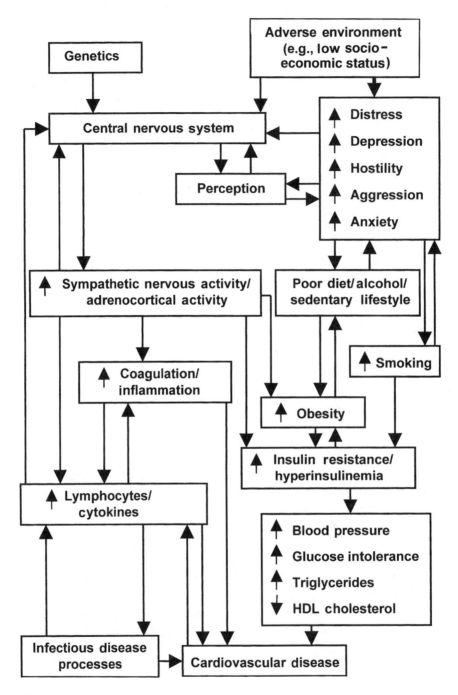

Figure 2.1. Schematic diagram depicting proposed pathways linking biobehavioral variables and cardiovascular and infectious diseases.

disorders as disparate as cardiovascular and infectious diseases. It should be noted that the regulatory systems involve extensive feedback loops. Thus, even information from damaged end organs may be transmitted back to the brain by means of chemical messengers of the immune system called cytokines, which may then evoke feelings of malaise and sickness (Appels, Bär, Bär, Bruggeman, & de Baets, 2000; Danzer, 2001).

In this chapter we focus on some of the biobehavioral pathways that may link certain psychosocial variables to coronary heart disease (CHD), several infectious diseases, and some cancers. A large body of research has examined the biobehavioral factors associated with an increased risk for CHD. Therefore, we begin by summarizing the role of specific health behaviors and psychological factors in CHD and examine some of the possible biological pathways that may be involved in the disease process. Then we proceed to examine biobehavioral pathways in the manifestation or progression of infectious diseases, including human immunodeficiency virus (HIV). Finally, we review the effects of psychosocial stressors on cancer, particularly breast cancer and malignant melanoma.

STRESS AND CORONARY HEART DISEASE

Cardiovascular disease including CHD and stroke is currently the leading cause of death in the United States. Several biobehavioral risk factors such as obesity, physical inactivity, smoking, hypertension, and diabetes mellitus are associated with the development of CHD and may operate through specific biological pathways to undermine health. It is also known that psychosocial stress has major effects on the ANS and HPA axis, which can further contribute to an increased risk of CHD. Thus, psychosocial stress may exacerbate risk by influencing health behaviors as well as by direct pathobiological mechanisms.

Biobehavioral Risk Factors and Coronary Heart Disease

Most deaths in the United States are linked to behavioral risk factors (McGinnis & Foege, 1993). The major preventable cause of death and illness is cigarette smoking. A combination of unhealthy dietary patterns and lack of physical activity is the second-leading factor contributing to mortality. Thus, it is important to understand the relationship between behavioral risk factors and disease.

Diet

Diet has a profound influence on numerous facets of health including risk for developing CHD. Total serum cholesterol and its major components, low-density lipoprotein (LDL) and high-density lipoprotein (HDL) choles-terol, are strongly related to an increased risk of CHD. Although circulating levels of lipids and lipoproteins are mainly influenced by genetic and homeo-static mechanisms (Breslow, 1991), dietary behavioral factors such as the consumption of saturated fats may also lead to fluctuations in the levels of lipids and lipoproteins (Arntzenius et al., 1985). A diet composed of excess saturated fats may further lead to obesity, which can result in an increased risk for developing atherosclerosis (Armstrong, Dublin, & Wheatley, 1951) and hypertension (Sims, 1982).

One of the mechanisms by which diet may affect health is through its influence on adrenergic activity. Activation of the sympathetic nervous system (SNS) is suppressed by caloric restriction (Young & Landsberg, 1977b) and stimulated by overeating (Young & Landsberg, 1977a). Elevated body mass index (BMI) and increased caloric intake are also associated with higher urinary norepinephrine output, a major stress hormone in humans (Troisi et al., 1991). Furthermore, a diet high in fats and carbohydrates also stimulates SNS activity (Landsberg & Young, 1985), which may have profound effects on health. The effects of overeating on the SNS appear to be mediated by insulin (Landsberg, 1992). Increased norepinephrine output has been associated with hyperinsulinemia (Triosi et al., 1991). This is consistent with the observation that exogenous insulin infusions lead to an increase in plasma norepinephrine levels (Rowe et al., 1981) and an increase in sympathetic nerve discharge to muscle (E. Anderson, Balon, Hoffman, & Sinkey, 1992).

There is a large body of research showing that dietary sugars can also contribute to both increased plasma insulin and SNS activity. Dietary sugar induces an increase in catecholamine excretion and blood pressure in both spontaneously hypertensive and control rats (Fournier, Chiueh, & Kopin, 1986). Replacement of complex carbohydrates with fructose in rats causes increases in blood pressure, impairments in insulin-stimulated glucose use, and elevations in serum triglyceride levels (Hwang, Ho, Hoffman, & Reaven, 1987).

There is evidence that dietary sugar also contributes to hyperinsuli-nemia, and through its effect on insulin as a mediator of SNS activity appears to have an additional impact on both blood pressure and lipid metabolism. When plasma insulin concentration has been assessed in rela-tionship to serum lipids, significantly higher insulin levels have been found in individuals with elevated LDL and very low-density lipoprotein (VLDL) levels (Burke, Webber, & Srinivasan, 1986). Relationships have been shown relating dietary patterns, insulin resistance, hyperinsulinemia, and SNS ac-tivity, which have also been related to changes in blood pressure and lipid profiles. Recent evidence points to the possibility that there may be some additional dietary substances that affect an individual's risk for developing

CHD. The role of nutrients in the atherosclerotic process and of precipitating or preventive factors, such as antioxidant vitamins, phytosterols, and arginine, have been examined and may operate independently of LDL cholesterol levels (Menotti, 1999).

Stress may also affect CHD risk through modification of diet (Brindley, McCann, Niaura, Stoney, & Suarez, 1993). Life stress is known to influence eating behavior in both humans (Greeno & Wing, 1994; Robbins & Fray, 1980) and animals (Robbins, Everitt, & Sahakian, 1981). For example, persons experiencing occupational stress are more likely to consume alcoholic beverages and coffee (Conway, Vickers, & Ward, 1981) and consume increased calories, fat, and a greater proportion of calories from fat (McCann, Warnick, & Knopp, 1990). Job loss has also been linked to weight gain (Morris, Cook, & Shaper, 1992). A prospective study found that an imbalance between effort and reward and loss of control account for a large proportion of job stress (Bosma, Peter, Siegrist, & Marmot, 1998). Therefore, the relationship between psychological and emotional stress, alterations in diet, and an increase in obesity may contribute to a greater risk for CHD.

SNS activation has further been implicated as an underlying mechanism through which psychosocial factors affect CHD risk. Catecholamines are released during psychological, emotional, or physical stress and can subsequently mobilize lipid stores from adipose tissues (Heindel, Orci, & Jeanrenaud, 1975). These lipids are then hydrolyzed to free fatty acids for energy production during muscular activity (Zieler, Maseri, Klassen, Rabinowitz, & Burgess, 1968). Therefore, activation of the SNS elicited by physical exertion, including the fight–flight response, can lead to the effective use and rapid clearance of free fatty acids from within the circulation. However, when lipid mobilization induced by strong emotions is not accompanied by vigorous physical activity, free fatty acids are not cleared as quickly and may be converted to triglycerides by the liver. They are subsequently circulated within the bloodstream as a component of VLDL cholesterol (Schonfeld & Pfleger, 1971). Some of the VLDL remnants are also converted to LDL cholesterol and are released again into the circulation; LDL cholesterol is the source of most lipids in atheroma (Miller, 1980).

The interaction of psychological stress and diet in the promotion of CHD has been studied extensively in nonhuman primates (Kaplan, Manuck, Clarkson, Lusso, & Taub, 1982; Kaplan, Manuck, Clarkson, Lusso, Taub, & Miller, 1982; Shively, Kaplan, & Adams, 1986). Because cynomolgus monkeys tend to form dominance hierarchies based on the outcome of aggressive encounters among group members, periodic redistribution of these living groups leads to an increase in aggression. When male cynomolgus monkeys were maintained on a low-fat diet, dominant animals living in a socially unstable environment developed significantly more coronary atherosclerosis than dominant animals in the stable condition or subordinate animals in either condition (Kaplan et al., 1982). Thus, atherosclerosis was significantly enhanced both by psychosocial (e.g., unstable living environment) and constitutional factors (e.g., dominance) in this paradigm.

Exercise

Maintaining adequate physical activity can also have a vital impact on cardiac health. There is considerable evidence that aerobic fitness is inversely related to blood pressure in both normotensive and hypertensive individuals (Erikssen, Forfang, & Jervell, 1981; Hickey, Mulcahy, Bourke, Graham, & Wilson-Davis, 1975; Paffenbarger, Wing, Hyde, & Jung, 1983). Decreases in SNS activity (e.g., norepinephrine levels) are also associated with enhanced fitness (Kiyonaga, Arakawa, Tanaka, & Shindo, 1985; Nelson, Jennings, Esler, & Korner, 1986). Both weight loss and aerobic exercise decrease blood pressure (Reisen, Frohlich, & Messerli, 1983) and insulin resistance (Golay, Felber, & Dusmet, 1985; Jennings, Deakin, Dewar, Lanfer, & Nelson, 1989) among obese individuals. It has also been shown that following a prolonged program of exercise training reduction in blood pressure is related to a decrease in insulin resistance as opposed to overall weight loss (Krotkiewski et al., 1979). Therefore, it appears that increasing aerobic fitness may lower blood pressure by decreasing insulin resistance.

Increased physical activity is also associated with elevations in HDL cholesterol and decreases in triglycerides and LDL cholesterol independent of body weight, diet, and smoking (Thompson, Cullinane, & Sady, 1988). Both cross-sectional (Hollenbeck, Haskell, & Rosenthal, 1985) and longitudinal (DeFronzo, Sherwin, & Kraemer, 1987) studies have shown an inverse relationship between aerobic fitness and insulin resistance. It appears that regular exercise is necessary to maintain insulin sensitivity, because reducing activity results in an elevation of insulin response to an oral glucose tolerance test (Heath, Gavin, & Hinderliter, 1983) and an increase in insulin resistance (King, Dalsky, & Clutter, 1988) within just 10 days after reducing activity. Exercise has long been used to deal with psychosocial stress (Rostad & Long, 1996). Beyond the physical benefits that exercise offers, research shows that regular aerobic exercise can also have psychological and emotional benefits as well (Leith & Taylor, 1990). Therefore, maintaining a regular exercise regimen has important benefits for both psychosocial and physical health.

Smoking

Cigarette smoking leads to adverse physiological changes in the lungs and heart and thus represents a major risk factor for developing a number of chronic diseases, including CHD. Smoking acutely increases heart rate, blood pressure, and stress hormone (e.g., cortisol) levels (Benowitz, Kuyt,

& Jacob, 1984; Kerschbaum, Pappajohn, & Bellet, 1968; Robertson, Tseng, & Appalsamy, 1988). Frequency of smoking often increases during stressful events (Epstein & Perkins, 1988; Twisk, Snel, Kemper, & van Mechelen, 1999), and the intensity of smoking has been related to adverse personality characteristics such as hostility (Scherwitz, Perkins, & Chesney, 1992).

Compared to nonsmokers, smokers have significantly higher concentrations of serum total cholesterol, VLDL cholesterol and triglycerides, and significantly lower concentrations of HDL cholesterol (Craig, Palomaki, & Haddow, 1989; Cullen, Schulte, & Assmann, 1998). The detrimental effects of cigarette smoking on HDL cholesterol may result from the acute effects of smoking on increases in triglycerides, VLDL cholesterol, and free fatty acids (Brischetto, Connor, Connor, & Matarazzo, 1983). It may also be a result of the differences in diet and distribution of body fat observed between smokers and nonsmokers (Barrett-Connor & Khaw, 1989). Smoking also increases platelet reactivity in hypercholesterolemic patients with low HDL levels or high levels of triglycerides (de Padua Mansur, Caramelli, Vianna, Chamone, & Ramires, 1997). Thus, there are a number of pathways through which cigarette smoking may affect cardiac health.

Alcohol

Excessive alcohol use can also have detrimental effects on cardiac health. Regular consumption of excessive amounts of alcohol may account for the variability in lipids and lipoproteins seen in CHD (Castelli et al., 1977). The prevalence of hypertension is 50% higher in people who consume three to five alcoholic beverages daily, and 100% higher among those who consume more than six alcoholic beverages daily as compared to those who consume little or no alcohol (Klatsky, Friedman, Siegelaub, & Gerard, 1977). Furthermore, consumption of large amounts of alcohol can also lead to acute blood pressure elevations (Maheswaran, Gill, Davies, & Beevers, 1991), increased catecholamine levels (Kaysen & Noth, 1984) and hypertension (Klatsky et al., 1977). The increased prevalence of hypertension has also been linked to higher levels of plasma catecholamines (Kaysen & Noth, 1984) independent of weight gain (Friedman, Klatsky, & Siegelaub, 1982). Excessive alcohol use acutely raises both systolic and diastolic blood pressure by about 7 mm Hg (Maheswaran et al., 1991).

Mild to moderate alcohol consumption, however, may benefit cardiac health. Some researchers have found a protective relationship between alcohol consumption and CHD, especially among smokers (Manttari, Tenkanen, Alikoski, & Manninen, 1997). Rimm, Williams, Fosher, Criqui, and Stampfer (1999) conducted a meta-analysis of all experimental studies that assessed the effects of moderate alcohol intake and found that alcohol use is related to lower risk of CHD. Among the mechanisms accounting

for the benefit of moderate alcohol consumption are increased HDL cholesterol and inhibition of blood coagulation (Goldberg, Soleas, & Levesque,
1999) and decreased platelet activity, especially with red wine consumption
(Ruf, 1999). However, some studies have not found either a protective or
deleterious effect of mild to moderate alcohol consumption on CHD risk
(C. Hart, Smith, Hole, & Hawthorne, 1999; Shaper & Wannamethee,
2000). Thus, future work is needed to clarify these discrepancies.

Insulin Metabolic Syndrome and Coronary Heart Disease

Insulin metabolic syndrome is a distinct pattern of risk factors implicated in the development of both diabetes and CHD. The syndrome's
hallmarks include glucose intolerance, hyperinsulinemia, dyslipidemia (e.g.,
high triglycerides, low HDL cholesterol, and high LDL cholesterol, particularly involving small, dense particles), obesity, hypertension, and increased
prothrombic and antifibrinolytic factors (Garvey & Hermayer, 1998). The
relationships among some of these variables are depicted in the lower right-
hand quadrant of Figure 2.1. It is important to point out that chronic stress
has been shown to moderate certain aspects of metabolic syndrome. For
example, Alzheimer's caregivers with CHD have a greater preponderance of
metabolic syndrome risk factors than noncaregivers with CHD (Vitaliano,
Scanlan, Siegler, McCormick, & Knopp, 1998). Thus, psychosocial and behavioral factors may play a vital role in the exacerbation of insulin metabolic
syndrome. We will now examine some of these factors individually.

Obesity

Obesity is an independent risk factor for CHD. Obese adults are almost
twice as likely to be hypertensive than those who are not obese (Sims,
1982). Central or upper body obesity is an even more powerful determinant
of elevated blood pressure than global measures of obesity, such as body
mass index (Blair, Habicht, Sims, Sylvester, & Abraham, 1984). It has also
been shown that CHD among obese patients is often more severe than that
of normal-weight individuals (Morricone et al., 1999).

Non–Insulin-Dependent Diabetes Mellitus (NIDDM)

Insulin resistance occurs in 25% of nonobese individuals with normal
glucose tolerance and in most people with impaired glucose tolerance or
with NIDDM (Reaven, 1988). The magnitude of the deterioration of glucose
tolerance in these groups appears to be related to the ability of pancreatic
beta cells to compensate for the defect in insulin action. Therefore, people
who are insulin-resistant but able to maintain normal glucose tolerance are
able to compensate for the insulin resistance by hypersecreting insulin.

However, patients with NIDDM are unable to increase their insulin secretion sufficiently to prevent hyperglycemia.

Hypertension

Numerous population studies have reported positive associations between fasting plasma insulin levels and blood pressure (e.g., Fournier, Gadia, Kubrusly, Skyler, & Sosenko, 1986; Modan et al., 1985). This relationship has typically persisted even after adjusting for obesity and diabetes. There are several mechanisms through which hyperinsulinemia secondary to insulin resistance may contribute to the development of hypertension. These processes include renal sodium retention, SNS hyperactivity, smooth-muscle hypertrophy, and altered transport and composition of cellular electrolytes. It is well-known that the prevalence of hypertension is higher in societies that consume large amounts of sodium (Tobian, 1983). It is also known that hypertension in persons with NIDDM or obesity is associated with elevated sodium content and volume expansion (Feldt-Rasmussen et al., 1987).

Another mechanism by which insulin can lead to hypertension involves SNS activation. Overeating of carbohydrates or fats in rats has resulted in increased SNS activation and blood pressure (Landsberg & Young, 1985). Thus, it appears that the pathways relating insulin resistance, hyperinsulinemia, SNS activation, and increases in blood pressure may be operating concurrently in the development of hypertension.

Another way in which hyperinsulinemia may be involved in the pathogenesis of hypertension is through stimulation of vascular smooth-muscle hypertrophy. Regulation of systemic circulation can be influenced from a narrowing of the lumen of resistance vessels (Folkow, 1978; Mulvany, 1984). Insulin may contribute to this process either directly or indirectly through the stimulation of growth factors, including insulin-like growth factor (Kleinman & Fine, 1988). Therefore, it appears that multiple biobehavioral mechanisms may account for the effects of hypertension on CHD risk.

Inflammation, Depression, and Coronary Heart Disease

During the past few years increasing evidence has shown that inflammation is critical for the development and progression of atherosclerosis, and that the former view that coronary risk is related to the passive accumulation of fat in the arterial wall is incorrect (Libby, Ridker, & Maseri, 2002). In fact, half of all patients who have had a myocardial infarction do not have above average LDL levels. Most heart attacks stem from ruptured plaques that then trigger the emergence of thrombi that block blood flow. The development of atherosclerosis and a cause of rupture is inflammation.

Several of the traditional risk factors for CHD may operate in part via inflammation. Thus, for example, LDL retained in the vascular cell wall undergoes oxidative modification (Berliner, Leitenger, & Watson, 1997). The resultant modified lipids can induce the expression of adhesion molecules and proinflammatory cytokines as mediators of inflammation in macrophages and vascular cell walls. Smoking also causes oxidants to form that could hasten the oxidation of LDL constituents. The hyperglycemia associated with diabetes enhances glycation that in turn can stimulate inflammatory pathways in vascular endothelial cells. Other aspects of the metabolic syndrome (e.g., obesity) can also promote oxidative stress leading to inflammation.

Chronic extravascular infections (e.g., gingivitis) can lead to the production of inflammatory cytokines that may accelerate the development of remote atherosclerotic lesions (Danesh, Collins, & Peto, 1997). Intravascular infection might also provide a local stimulus. Human plaques often are infected by microbial agents such as *Chlamydia pneumoniae*. Chlamydia can release endotoxin and heat shock proteins that can stimulate the production of proinflammatory mediators by vascular endothelial cells (Kol, Bourcier, & Lichtman, 1999).

Depressive symptoms, especially fatigue and feelings of general malaise, often precede or are associated with acute coronary syndrome (Carney et al., 1988). In patients with CHD, the prevalence of major depression is nearly 20% and the prevalence of minor depression is about 27%, whereas in the general population the point prevalence for major depression is about 3% (Schleifer et al., 1989). The feelings of depression or fatigue are only modestly associated with low left ventricular ejection fraction or amount of vessel disease but are predictive of increased recurrent myocardial infarction and cardiac death (Frasure-Smith et al., 1995). Appels et al. (2000) compared blood and biopsy samples obtained from coronary lesions of depressed versus nondepressed patients treated with directional angioplasty because of severe angina. The depressed patients had higher antibody titers against cytomegalovirus and higher levels of proinflammatory cytokines.

The possibility that proinflammatory cytokines mediate the relationship between depression and acute coronary syndrome is of particular interest because acute myocardial infarction patients have a four-fold risk of dying within six months if they are depressed (Frasure-Smith et al., 1995). Previous research has shown that proinflammatory cytokines that bind to receptors on vagal afferent neurons ultimately projecting to the hypothalamus and other limbic structures, lead to "sickness" behavior closely resembling depression (Danzer, 2001). Thus, although depression may contribute to increased risk of myocardial infarction via behavioral (e.g., poor lifestyle habits) and physiological (e.g., HPA activation) pathways, it may also be the result of ongoing, subclinical heart disease. The alternative pathways linking depressed affect and CHD are shown in Figure 2.1.

Potential Stress Mechanisms in Coronary Heart Disease

The exact causal pathways linking behavioral and psychosocial variables to chronic disease outcomes are not completely known, but plausible biological links have been identified. As previously discussed, one set of pathways links lifestyle factors and CHD. Another set of pathways link psychological variables (e.g., hostility, depression) and psychological stressors (e.g., social isolation, job strain, racism) to CHD. Thus, for example, depressed affect (Anda et al., 1993) and anger proneness (Williams et al., 2000) have been prospectively associated with an increase in CHD mortality. As indicated in Figure 2.1, there appear to be overlapping and interactive segments along the pathways linking behavioral and psychosocial factors to disease outcomes.

Serotonin

It is known that a number of adverse personality and behavioral characteristics, including hostility and depression, as well as greater levels of eating, smoking, and alcohol consumption, often occur together. These characteristics are associated with CHD risk, and are also linked to increases in SNS activity, specifically decreases in the neurotransmitter serotonin. There is evidence of reduced brain serotonin levels in relation to elevated levels of depression (Risch & Nemeroff, 1992), hostility (Coccaro et al., 1989), increased aggression, decreased affiliation in cynomolgus monkeys (Kyes, Botchin, Kaplan, Manuck, & Mann, 1995), and also alcoholism (Ballenger, Goodwin, Major, & Brown, 1979). Increasing serotonin levels has also been shown to lower blood pressure in spontaneously hypertensive rats (Fuller, Holland, Yen, Bemis, & Stamm, 1979); reduce aggression in monkeys (Tompkins, Clementa, & Taylor, 1980); and decrease smoking (Gawin, Compton, & Dych, 1989), eating (Levine et al., 1989), and alcohol use (Naranjo & Sellers, 1986) among humans. Thus, the serotonergic system may represent one underlying pathway through which psychological factors—particularly depressive symptoms—affect CHD risk.

Sympathetic Nervous System

Stress is a common part of life, and everyday we all cope with a range of stressful experiences. Acute stress leads to increases in blood pressure, heart rate, and SNS activation (Krantz & Manuck, 1984). Activation of the SNS in response to stress is an adaptive response and results in an increased secretion of catecholamines (e.g., epinephrine and norepinephrine) as the body prepares the fight-or-flight response. Higher levels of catecholamines lead to increases in blood pressure and heart rate. More oxygenated blood and glucose are required to respond to stressful events, and this often occurs at the expense of the digestion of food and other bodily functions. Also, one's cognitive attention becomes focused on coping with a stressful situation, which further depletes vital resources if the stress becomes chronic. These types of SNS reactions may have important implications for CHD risk.

Because insulin metabolism seems to play a major role in the relationship between behavioral variables and CHD, the contribution of the SNS in both etiology and pathogenesis of CHD is vital. SNS activity is involved in the production of free fatty acids, increases in blood pressure, vascular and left ventricular hypertrophy, platelet activation, and the induction of ventricular fibrillation. Although the SNS interacts with insulin metabolism, SNS activation may also be considered an etiologic agent. Thus, in some instances increased sympathetic activity may be a primary mechanism underlying the increase of both insulin levels and blood pressure (Brindley et al., 1993).

Increased SNS activity may also provide a primary mechanism for atherogenesis. SNS activity increases plasma triglycerides through lipoprotein lipase (Pykallsto, Smith, & Brunzell, 1975). The SNS may induce insulin resistance and thus stimulate the production of VLDL cholesterol and decrease HDL cholesterol synthesis. By stimulating alpha-adrenergic receptors, the SNS may also influence LDL cholesterol catabolism (Sacks & Dzau, 1986). Because increased SNS activity may contribute to the initiation of hypertension (Julius, 1993), specific features of hypertension are more likely to contribute to increased CHD risk. An increase in SNS activity can promote coronary thrombosis by increasing platelet aggregation (Ardlie, Glew, & Schwartz, 1966) and hematocrit levels (Julius, 1993).

SNS activation may also lead to left ventricular hypertrophy. For example, norepinephrine-stimulated hypertrophy of myocardial cells is produced by an alpha-1 adrenergic response (Simpson, 1983). An increase in SNS activity also acts as a trophic factor in vascular hypertrophy (M. Hart, Heistad, & Brody, 1980). There is also considerable evidence that increased SNS activation is particularly pronounced during the early phases of hypertension. An increase in both cardiac beta-adrenergic (Julius, Pascual, & London, 1971) and vascular alpha-adrenergic (Esler et al., 1977) drive is observed during use of selective autonomic blockades. Overall, SNS activation may play a key mechanistic role underlying psychosocial and behavioral effects on CHD risk.

How an individual responds to stressful circumstances can have a profound influence on his or her risk for CHD. Specific negative emotional states such as depression (Carney et al., 1988; Frasure-Smith, Lesperance, & Talajic, 1995), anxiety (Carney et al., 1998), hostility (Barefoot,

Dahlstrom, & Williams, 1983; Siegman, Townsend, Civelek, & Blumenthal, 2000), and anger (Verrier & Mittelman, 1996) have been associated with greater cardiac events and mortality. For example, Kawachi, Sparrow, Spiro, Vokonas, & Weiss (1996) prospectively examined 1,305 men from the Normative Aging Study and found that high levels of expressed anger were associated with greater risk of coronary events. A type-D personality (e.g., a tendency to suppress emotional distress) has also been found to predict cardiac events and long-term mortality in patients with CHD. Because these types of emotional states and personality styles have also been associated with increased SNS arousal, they may operate at least partially through SNS pathways in influencing cardiac health.

Another possible stress mechanism is through overactivation of the HPA axis. When the hypothalamus is stimulated it secretes corticotropin-releasing hormone (CRH). CRH stimulates the pituitary to synthesize adrenocorticotropin hormone (ACTH) into the bloodstream. ACTH then causes the adrenal glands to release cortisol, the major steroid of the HPA axis. The HPA axis is regulated by a negative feedback loop, in which elevations of ACTH and cortisol both signal a decrease of CRH production. Although the effects of catecholamines are almost immediate and transient, cortisol is slower acting and more likely to influence blood flow and glucose production during prolonged stress responses.

In summary, neuroendocrine mechanisms appear to play a significant role in how stress affects health and risk for CHD. Acute stress-induced increases in catecholamines and glucocorticoids are a normal part of the body's adaptive response to stress. However, chronic stress leads to sustained levels of stress hormones, which in the long term may compromise numerous bodily systems, including the immune system, influencing the ability to protect against specific foreign pathogens. A proinflammatory cytokine, interleukin-6 (IL-6), elevated during distress states, has been implicated in the pathogenesis of CHD, because it not only stimulates SNS and HPA activation but is also associated with central obesity, hypertension, and insulin resistance (Yudkin, Kumari, Humphries, & Mohamed-Ali, 1999). Future research examining the effects of stress on the immune system among patients with CHD will help clarify these types of mechanisms. We now examine the effects of stress on the immune system in the development of infectious illness.

STRESS AND INFECTIOUS DISEASE

The effects of psychosocial and behavioral stessors on the immune system have been studied in initially healthy people. These studies have shown that stress-immune relationships are importantly influenced by neuroendocrine activity. An increasing body of evidence supports the view that relationships between psychosocial variables and disease are influenced by endocrine-immune relationships such as are depicted in Figure 2.1. It should be kept in mind, however, that the relationship between psychosocial variables and disease also depends on pathogen exposure and host vulnerability, because not everyone exposed to a psychosocial stressor develops an infectious disease.

Psychosocial Factors Related to Immune Function in Medically Healthy Persons

Psychological factors, such as distress and negative affect, seem to have an adverse affect on immune function. A commonly used immune system indicator of depressed affect is lymphocyte proliferative response to mitogens (i.e., in-vitro test that measures the ability of lymphocytes to undergo DNA synthesis and clonally expand when stimulated with plant lectins). A meta-analytic review of studies relating depression and immunity found a consistent relationship between depression and decrements in a variety of immune measures, including lymphocyte proliferative response and related lymphocyte populations, especially in older individuals and those with greater severity of depression (Herbert & Cohen, 1993). Even among those not meeting full criteria for a diagnosis of depression, a linear relationship was found between depressed mood and impairments in cell-mediated immunity.

Other reviews have documented a lower percentage and number of total lymphocytes and lower natural killer cell cytotoxicity (NKCC) and neutrophil activity among patients diagnosed with depression (Weisse, 1992). In this report, the largest immune decrements were found among patients with unipolar depression, older age, and more severe clinical symptoms of depression requiring hospitalization. Fewer studies have shown parallel remission of depression symptoms and enhancement of immune function among patients undergoing treatment. One study found that treatment with a serotonin reuptake inhibitor decreased depressive symptoms and restored neutrophil activity to control levels across a 6-week period (O'Neill & Leonard, 1986).

A substantial number of stressful experiences have been found to relate to impairments in immune system functioning, including medical school and law school bar examinations (Glaser et al., 1987), sleep deprivation (Palmblad et al., 1976), caregiving for sick or demented relatives (Glaser & Kiecolt-Glaser, 1997), death of a spouse (Irwin et al., 1997), marital separation and divorce (Kiecolt-Glaser et al., 1988), nuclear reactor accidents (McKinnon, Weisse, Reynolds, Bowles, & Baum, 1989), and natural disasters (Ironson et al., 1997). The most consistent immune impairments tend to be functional measures associated with cellular immunity such as decrements in lymphocyte proliferative response to mitogens (Kemeny et al., 1995), NKCC (Kiecolt-Glaser et al., 1987), increased antibody titers to Epstein Barr virus (EBV; Kiecolt-Glaser, Dura, Speicher, Trask, & Glaser, 1991), and herpes simplex virus (HSV; Glaser, Rice, Speicher, Stout, & Kiecolt-Glaser, 1986). These types of stressors have also been related to disturbances in cytokine regulation, including interferon-γ (IFN-γ) production (Glaser et al., 1986) and changes in interleukin-2 (IL-2) production and receptor gene expression (Glaser et al., 1990). Thus, certain negative psychosocial factors are associated with immune impairments and may play a role in the body's ability to fend off pathogens.

In their comprehensive meta-analytical review of the literature, Herbert and Cohen (1993) found that in 38 studies, stressors were associated with a wide array of immune system measures, the most consistent of which were lymphocyte proliferative response to mitogens, NKCC, immunoglobulin levels, herpes virus antibody titers, and circulating white blood cells. Among these immune parameters, the effect sizes ranged from low to moderate for lymphocyte proliferative response and NKCC, to quite large effect sizes for antibody titers to HSV and EBV. Among the more quantitative measures, total white blood cells, suppressor/cytotoxic T-cells, and natural killer (NK) cells showed the largest effects. Although acute stressors are related to increases in cytotoxic/suppressor T-cells, NK cells, and NKCC, longer term stressors are related to decreases in these same measures. This difference may be a result of the differential emotional reactions likely to accompany short- versus long-term stressors and potential differences in short-term versus chronic activation of neuroendocrine response systems known to affect communications between cells of the immune system (McEwen, 1998).

The immune measure that is most often associated with a variety of stressful experiences as well as depression is NKCC. This in vitro indicator measures the ability of an NK cell to spontaneously kill targeted tumor cells when placed in culture, and represents an important part of the innate immune system repertoire in mounting a response against intracellular viral infections and tumors (Herberman, 1991). Impairments in NKCC have been associated with bereavement (Irwin, Daniels, Smith, Bloom, & Weiner, 1987), depression and depressed affect (Irwin & Gillin, 1987), anxious symptoms following a natural disaster (Ironson et al., 1997), the chronic stress of being a caregiver for a dependent relative (Esterling, Kiecolt-Glaser, & Glaser, 1996), decrements in social support (Baron, Cutrona, Hicklin, Russel, & Lubaroff, 1990), and marital discord (Kiecolt-Glaser et al., 1988). Thus, stressful events may impair a person's ability to fight off infections.

An in vivo functional measure that is also consistently related to stressors is immunoglobulin-G (IgG) antibody titers to latent herpes virus infections such as EBV and HSV. Elevations in these antibody titers may reflect either reinfection with or reactivation of the virus, and chronically elevated titers may result from inadequate cellular immune surveillance of these reactivated viruses (Glaser & Gotlieb-Stematsky, 1982). Elevated HSV antibody titers have been related to such disparate events as marital separation and divorce (Kiecolt-Glaser et al., 1988), caring for a demented relative (Glaser & Kiecolt-Glaser, 1997), and being a resident near Three Mile Island during the period following the nuclear reactor accident (McKinnon et al., 1989). These associations represent some of the strongest stress-immune relationships to date. More recently, lymphocyte proliferative responses to HSV antigen has been found to be suppressed among caregivers of ill relatives (Glaser & Kiecolt-Glaser, 1997), and virus-specific T-cell response to EBV is decreased during medical school examinations (Glaser et al., 1993). These findings suggest some potential cell-mediated immune pathways through which stressors relate to increases in antibody titers to herpes viruses.

Potential Moderators of the Stress–Immune Relationship

Underlying stress–immune research is the basic assumption that psychosocial factors relate to the immune system through alterations in neuroendocrine functioning (Maier, Watkins, & Fleshner, 1994). Some neuroendocrine responses can be altered by an individual's cognitive appraisals (e.g., controllable versus uncontrollable) and coping responses (e.g., active versus passive) to stressful circumstances. For example, when faced with a major stressor deemed unpredictable or uncontrollable, an individual may engage in more passive coping strategies that may further exacerbate stress and impact on health. Immune impairments and increases in stress hormones have been observed in people reporting perceived loss of control and social losses in situations such as divorce and bereavement (Calabrese, Kling, & Gold, 1987). The stress–immune relationships might be influenced, in part, by neurohormonal changes linked to cognitive appraisals, coping responses, and resources available for dealing with stressful stimuli (Schneiderman et al., 1994). Among individuals undergoing stressful circumstances, perceived loss of control, helplessness/hopelessness, and low self-efficacy have also been associated with impairments in immune functioning (Wiedenfeld et al., 1990). More passive coping strategies (Antoni et al., 1995) and insufficient emotional expression about traumatic or stressful events (Lutgendorf, Antoni, Kumar, & Schneiderman, 1994) have also been associated with decreased lymphocyte proliferative response to mitogens and elevated antibody titers to EBV. Social support (Esterling et al., 1996), marital distress (Kiecolt-Glaser et al., 1988), and hostile interactions between marital partners (Kiecolt-Glaser, Malarkey, Cacioppo, & Glaser, 1994) have also been related to decrements in several cellular immune functions. Therefore, how an individual confronts and copes with a stressful situation can have a substantial effect on immune function and perhaps influence the development of infections.

Stress and Upper Respiratory Infections

Stressful circumstances and perceived stress have been related to the development of upper respiratory infections (P. Evans & Edgerton, 1991; Roghman & Haggerty, 1973). Some studies have explored this same stress–infection relationship experimentally among individuals deliberately exposed to viral pathogens, such as rhinoviruses (common cold viruses). These studies have shown that persons experiencing more stressful life events and higher perceived stress are more likely to develop cold symptoms and actual infections after viral exposure (Cohen, Tyrrell, & Smith, 1991). In this well-controlled study, experimenters exposed healthy research participants to nasal drops containing either rhinovirus or saline. Rates of respiratory infection and colds increased in a dose–response manner with increases in psychological stress. The effects remained even after controlling for relevant covariates (e.g., age, type of respiratory virus). A corollary study in which the same participants completed questionnaires assessing stressful life events, perceived stress, and negative affect found that higher scores on each of the three stress measures was associated with greater risk of developing a cold (Cohen, Tyrrell, & Smith, 1993). Thus, stress may enhance susceptibility to infections such as the common cold.

STRESS AND HIV/AIDS

The effects of psychosocial and behavioral stressors on health have also been examined among individuals with HIV disease. HIV systematically attacks multiple components of the immune system, resulting in susceptibility to infections and cancers typical of Acquired Immunodeficiency Syndrome (AIDS), as well as other common pathogens usually kept in check by a healthy immune system. HIV infection is now viewed as a chronic disease influenced by a wide variety of psychosocial and behavioral factors (Schneiderman, Antoni, & Ironson, 1997), which can affect the ability to maintain optimal cell-mediated immunological control over existing and novel pathogens.

Important Immune Parameters in HIV Infection

HIV binds with a specific receptor on a type of T-lymphocyte called a T-helper-inducer (CD4) cell. As HIV progresses, there are decrements in

CD4 cells and impairments in the ability of T-lymphocytes to respond to antigenic challenge (DeMartini, Brodie, de la Concha-Bermejillo, Ellis, & Larimore, 1993). Reductions in CD4 cell counts are predictive of the onset of physical symptoms and overall clinical decline in HIV disease (Pantaleo, Graziosi, & Fauci, 1993). Next we review some immune system components relevant to HIV infection and disease progression.

Natural Killer Cell Cytotoxicity

Cytotoxicity is a type of vital type of immune function that offers protection against replicating HIV, as well as surveillance over other pathogens. Psychosocial stressors such as bereavement are associated with decreases in NKCC (Irwin et al., 1987). Because CD4 cells are depleted both quantitatively and qualitatively, NK cells may compensate to some extent for HIV-induced CD4 cell deficiencies (Ironson et al., 2001). Although NKCC also seems to decrease over time during HIV and AIDS, Solomon, Benton, Harker, Bonavida, and Fletcher (1993) found that HIV positive people who were asymptomatic despite very low CD4 counts (< 50 cells/mm3) had NKCC in the normal range, suggesting a compensatory mechanism of NKCC. Conversely, impairments in NKCC facilitated herpes virus reactivation in HIV-infected individuals (Glaser & Kiecolt-Glaser, 1987), a possible cofactor of HIV progression (Rosenberg & Fauci, 1991).

Herpes Viruses

As noted above, psychosocial stressors are related to reactivation of some herpes viruses. Immunological control over the reactivation of latent viruses such as herpes viruses may influence the course of HIV infection (Rosenberg & Fauci, 1991). Glaser and Kiecolt-Glaser (1987) have argued that if stressors affect the immune system's ability to control latent herpes viruses in other populations, then these same stressors may also influence herpes virus-mediated progression among HIV-infected individuals. Immune indexes that reflect the potential contribution of reputed cofactors of HIV disease progression include rising antibody titers to herpes viruses such as EBV, which are quite prevalent among HIV-infected individuals. Furthermore, herpes virus reactivation may also "transactivate" HIV-infected cells, contributing to increases in viral load. HIV-infected individuals who experience increased life stressors, distress, depression, and an inability to manage effectively or cope with these stressors or encounter social isolation may be at greater risk for reactivation of herpes viruses. Both NKCC and T-cell-mediated cytotoxicity are generally responsible for keeping these types of viruses in check. In addition, stress-associated impairments in cytotoxicity may facilitate herpes virus reactivation in HIV-infected individuals with subsequent HIV replication and progression to AIDS (Antoni et al., 1995).

It is important to point out that herpes viruses are known to suppress a wide number of immunological functions, including cytokine production and lymphocyte proliferation to mitogens (Rinaldo, 1990). This suggests that HIV and various herpes viruses may interact to disrupt immunological control of viral infections and possibly contribute to the severity and chronicity of disease.

Because several herpes viruses prevalent in HIV-infected individuals are known to have immunosuppressive effects, reactivation of these viruses could have implications for progression to AIDS (Griffith & Grundy, 1987). These surveillance effects may be observed as rising antibody (IgG) titers to EBV, HSV-2, as well as human herpesvirus type-6 (HHV-6), and cytomegalovirus (CMV). It is conceivable that the inability to survey these latent viruses could manifest in more advanced symptoms, such as EBV-associated Burkitt's lymphoma (Doll & List, 1982) and oral hairy leukoplakia (Eversole, Stone, & Beckman, 1988); CMV-associated retinitis, encephalitis, hepatitis, adrenalitis, and gastrointestinal pathologies (Schooley, 1990); and HSV-associated proctitis (Goodell et al., 1983), esophagitis (Levine, Woldenberg, Herlinger, & Laufer, 1987), and aseptic meningitis (Dahan, Haettich, Le Parc, & Paolaggi, 1988). EBV reactivation has been associated with factors promoting HIV replication and progression to AIDS (Rosenberg & Fauci, 1991). CMV antibody titers are also important because they are an opportunistic pathogen in HIV infection and have been shown to enhance susceptibility to other secondary opportunistic pathogens among immunosuppressed patient groups. For example, among HIV-infected individuals, the age-adjusted relative risk of developing AIDS was 2.5 times higher in those who were seropositive for CMV compared to those who were CMV seronegative (Webster, 1991).

In summary, several specific immune parameters may have an impact on HIV disease progression. Innate immune functions such as NKCC may compensate in conferring protection against extant viral infections. Through direct immunosuppression or transactivation of HIV, latent herpes viruses may also be considered as potential cofactors in progression to AIDS. HIV-associated effects on cells of the immune system may perpetuate a downward spiral in the ability of the immune system to survey and control latent viruses that, when left unchecked, may increase the replication of the primary virus.

Potential Stress–Immune Interactions in HIV

There are an increasing number of studies examining the effects of psychosocial stressors among people with HIV, as well as research exploring the biobehavioral processes of HIV infection and subsequent disease course. Some potential mechanisms have been offered to explain these associations, including stress activation of latent HIV to a more vigorous replicating state and stress-related alterations in the immune system (Glaser & Kiecolt-Glaser, 1987). Several of these psychosocial factors, such as stressors (Glaser et al., 1987), maladaptive coping (Esterling, Antoni, Kumar, & Schneiderman, 1990), and social isolation (Glaser, Kiecolt-Glaser, Speicher, & Holliday, 1985) have been related to impaired immunity in a wide variety of healthy populations. Some studies have also examined a possible link between these psychosocial processes and HIV disease course following serostatus notification (Antoni et al., 1990). Additional work suggests that stressful life events and low social support (Leserman et al., 1997), concealing sexual orientation (Cole, Kemeny, Taylor, Visscher, & Fahey, 1996), using denial coping (Ironson et al., 1994), and rumination (Mulder, de Vroome, van Griensven, Antoni, & Sandfort, 1999) may predict faster HIV progression, whereas active coping predicts slower disease progression (Mulder, Antoni, Duivenvoorden, Kauffman, & Goodkin, 1995). Next we review some of the major studies relating psychosocial factors, immune function, and HIV disease progression.

Depression

HIV-infected individuals often encounter a considerable number of stressors, which may result in a wide array of emotional responses, including depressed affect. Two substantial long-term studies have confirmed a positive relationship between depressed affect and mortality in HIV-infected men (Mayne, Vittinghoff, Chesney, Barrett, & Coates, 1996) and women (Ickovics et al., 2001). In the Mayne et al. (1996) study, data collection occurred at six-month intervals, with up to 15 waves of follow-up in 402 HIV-infected homosexual or bisexual men. The more frequently a participant had elevated depressed affect, the greater his risk of mortality. Although the relationship between depressed affect and mortality was not related to a decline in CD4 number, a previous report based on the same cohort observed a depression–CD4 relationship in men with initially high CD4 counts (Barrett et al., 1994). More recently, Ickovics et al. (2001) studied 765 HIV-seropositive women every six months, for up to seven years. The results indicated that depressive symptoms among women with HIV were associated with significantly greater decline in CD4 cell counts, disease progression, and mortality.

Stressful Life Events

The impact of life stressors has also been studied in the context of HIV disease. Leserman et al. (2000) followed 82 gay men with HIV-infection every six months for up to seven and a half years. Cox regression models with time-dependent covariates were used, adjusting for race, baseline CD4, and viral load as well as cumulative average antiretroviral medications.

Faster progression to AIDS was associated with higher cumulative average stressful life events, use of denial as a coping mechanism, lower satisfaction with social support, and elevated serum cortisol.

Cognitive–affective processing of stressors may also affect immunity during HIV-infection. Antoni et al. (1991) examined how HIV-infected individuals process the stress of seropositivity notification and whether this predicted immunologic status during the early period of adjustment to this stressor. Changes in cognitive processing style were significantly correlated with changes in affective and immunological functioning over time (Lutgendorf et al., 1998). Benight et al. (1997) also compared HIV-infected gay men and healthy male control participants who were affected by Hurricane Andrew. Greater coping self-efficacy was related to lower emotional distress and posttraumatic stress disorder symptoms in both groups and lower norepinephrine to cortisol ratios in the HIV-infected group.

Coping

Studies have found that active coping is associated with a lower likelihood of symptom development in HIV-infected gay men (N. Mulder et al., 1995). Another study observed that a "fighting spirit" type coping style also predicted less symptom development over a one-year period (Solano et al., 1993). This study also reported that denial coping was predictive of a greater number of HIV-related symptoms. Specific aspects of coping such as denial have been negatively associated with CD4 cells and lymphocyte proliferative response to phytohemagglutinin (PHA; Ironson et al., 1994), whereas active coping has been positively related to NKCC (Goodkin, Blaney, Feaster, & Fletcher, 1992).

Several studies have also examined immunological correlates of coping responses to HIV-specific stressors (e.g., HIV antibody testing and serostatus notification). Antoni et al. (1995) prospectively related coping strategies and immunological measures in HIV-seropositive (and HIV-seronegative) homosexual men over the three-week and one-year period following notification of their antibody test results. Disengagement coping strategies (e.g., denial, behavioral/mental disengagement) were significantly related to lower T-helper/suppressor (CD4/CD8) cell ratios, T-inducer subset % values, and lymphocyte proliferative responses to PHA. Greater disengagement coping responses also predicted poorer proliferative response to PHA at the one-year follow-up. Ironson et al. (1994) found that increases in the use of denial surrounding notification of HIV-serostatus predicted faster progression to full-blown AIDS over a two-year period. Use of denial to deal with test results was also associated with lower CD4 cell counts one year after notification. Other maladaptive coping styles have been associated with poor immunity and survival. Reed, Kemeny, Taylor, Wang, and Visscher

(1994) reported that men with AIDS scoring high on a coping measure called "realistic acceptance" or fatalism showed a shorter survival time. This coping style has also been related to poorer immune function in HIV groups (Kemeny et al., 1994). Thus, how an individual copes with stressors may have a profound impact on immune function during HIV disease.

Social Support

The role of social support has also been examined in the context of HIV disease. Stigmatization, alienation from friends and family, major life events and readjustments, increased reliance on medical personnel, loss of social ties, and gradual deterioration of physical health status and immune function are among the many psychosocial challenges faced by people living with HIV (Zuckerman & Antoni, 1995). Theorell et al. (1995) found that low social support availability predicted a faster decline in CD4 counts over a five-year period among HIV-infected men with hemophilia. Good social support may also be associated with improved clinical markers of disease. Cruess et al. (2000) examined a sample of HIV-positive individuals exposed to Hurricane Andrew and found that social integration and reliable alliance, both important aspects of social support, independently predicted lower antibody titers to HHV-6, an indicator of greater control over the virus. Furthermore, greater levels of these same supportive elements also predicted lower mood disturbance scores.

Health Behavior

A variety of health behaviors are relevant to the health status of HIV positive individuals. Substance use is associated with a wide array of immunological effects that may have direct health implications for HIV-infected individuals. Alcohol use is related to decreased lymphocyte number and proliferative responses, and alcoholism and related liver disease are also associated with impaired NKCC and decreased NK cell numbers. Alcohol abuse may also amplify the suppressive effects of depression on NKCC. The use of substances ranging from injected drugs to cigarettes has been associated with accelerated HIV disease progression. Therefore, substance abuse may contribute to the decline in immunological status, possibly causing faster disease progression (Pillar, Nair & Watson, 1991) in this diverse group. Less is known about the direct immune effects of specific sexual behaviors. However, repeated exposure to different strains of HIV and to other sexually transmitted pathogens (e.g., herpes viruses) may contribute directly to the development of opportunistic infections (e.g., systemic HSV-2 infections) and cancers (e.g., HPV-associated cervical and anal intraepithelial neoplasias).

Maintaining positive health behaviors such as adequate sleep, nutrition, exercise, and adherence to HIV medications are a central part of managing HIV disease. Combination antiretroviral therapy with protease inhibitors offer some hope that viral replication can be slowed, with a lower likelihood of resistance or undue side effects than earlier antiretroviral regimens. However, failure to adhere to the demanding medication regimens can substantially increase the risk of developing drug-resistant strains of the virus. The resulting treatment philosophy views HIV infection as a chronic disease in which patient management is critical (Schneiderman, 1999). The key is consistent adherence to a demanding medication schedule in the context of an already stressful daily existence. Because depressed affect, substance use, risky sexual behaviors, and poor adherence to HIV medications may all contribute to adverse health outcomes among HIV-infected individuals, it is also important to understand the underlying physiological factors that intervene on these phenomena. The stressors that encompass HIV and AIDS affect the way infected individuals appraise day-to-day situations, choose coping strategies, acquire support, and deal emotionally with stressful events, which may in turn alter stress hormones and the ability to engage in healthy behaviors. These underlying processes can subsequently lead to alterations in immune system functioning.

Stress–Endocrine–Immune Processes in HIV Infection

An individual's perception of the nature of a stressor or the availability of an adequate coping response to that stressor has been shown to accompany a series of physiological events resulting in specific autonomic, neuroendocrine, and neuropeptide changes (Schneiderman & McCabe, 1989). As mentioned earlier, these physiological changes are an adaptive part of the normal stress response. For example, the SNS secretes norepinephrine and epinephrine to prepare an individual to either confront or flee a stressful situation (Axelrod & Reisine, 1984). However, chronic elevations in stress hormones, which also include corticosteroids, may lead to decrements in immune system functioning and may affect HIV (McEwen, 1998).

Research has shown that the ability of HIV to infect healthy lymphocytes is enhanced in vitro by supplementing the cell culture with corticosteroids (Markham, Salahuddin, Veren, Orndorff, & Gallo, 1986), which suggests that adrenal stress hormones may affect HIV pathogenesis. Viral susceptibility may also be related to the efficacy of lymphocyte or NK cell cytotoxicity, which is likely compromised by increased glucocorticoid secretions resulting from psychosocial stress. In a study of AIDS patients treated with met-enkephalin three times per week for 21 days, increases in T-lymphocyte percentage, T-helper-inducer (CD4) cell number, NKCC, IL-2 production, and PHA mitogen response were observed, as well as improvements in mitogen responsivity and recession of Kaposi's sarcoma lesions (Wybran et al., 1987).

Elevations in glucocorticoids such as cortisol, a product of the HPA axis, enhance HIV replication, are immunosuppressive, and also accompany affective disorder and stressful experiences. Elevated levels of cortisol are associated with impaired immunity. Furthermore, HIV-infected individuals display elevated resting levels of cortisol, which are thus associated with lower CD4 cell counts and decreased NKCC thus favoring HIV replication (Markham et al., 1986). Thus, the endocrine system represents a potential underlying mechanism through which stress affects immune function in HIV disease.

Through exposure to multiple psychosocial stressors, HIV-infected individuals may become tense and sympathetically activated for extended periods of time. Those undergoing chronic SNS arousal with subsequent release of norepinephrine may experience health decrements, because these endocrines may down-regulate the proliferation of naive (uncommitted) T-lymphocytes (Felton, 1996). These cells are already significantly depleted in HIV infection and can also further alter functions such as lymphocyte trafficking, adhesion, cytokine production, and cytotoxicity (Cole, Korin, Fahey, & Zack, 1998; Webster, Elenkov, & Chrousos, 1997). Diminished naive T-lymphocyte proliferation may render HIV-infected individuals less able to respond to novel pathogens, opening the door to opportunistic infections (Maher et al., 1997). Depletions in cytotoxic T-lymphocytes may decrease the ability to regulate HIV replication and the ability to respond to other pathogens (Musey et al., 1997).

In summary, elevated levels of cortisol and catecholamines are associated with impaired immunity. Distress-associated neuroendocrine changes may affect immune function in HIV-infected individuals, and such changes could relate to HIV disease progression by way of impaired surveillance of latent and novel pathogens, which once reactivated can stimulate HIV proliferation. Stressful events interpreted as being uncontrollable might lead to social isolation, loneliness, anxiety, and depression, which can be accompanied by alterations in some neurohormones (e.g., catecholamines and cortisol) as a result of SNS activation and dysregulation of the HPA axis. These neuroendocrine changes may also be accompanied by changes in the immune system (redistribution of lymphocytes, decrements in lymphocyte proliferation and NKCC) via interactions among neural and neuroendocrine signals at the immune cell membrane, intracellular cyclic nucleotide activation, and altered production of cytokines such as IL-I and IL-II, and IFN-γ. Because these specific components of the immune system are known to decline across the course of HIV infection (Pantaleo, Graziosi, & Fauci, 1993), it can be further hypothesized that superimposing stressor-induced changes in the functioning of the immune system may increase the rate at which infected persons develop clinical symptoms caused by opportunistic infections and neoplasias.

There are far fewer studies of these types of mechanisms in HIV-infected women than in men. Byrnes et al. (1999), however, found that greater pessimism was associated with lower NKCC in HIV-infected women. Recently, depression was associated with impaired NKCC among women with HIV disease (Evans et al., 2002). There is also a growing literature on characteristics of long-term survivors of AIDS that suggests that factors such as life engagement, finding meaning, and social support may be important (Ironson, Solomon, Cruess, Barroso, & Stivers, 1995). Future work is needed to help clarify the underlying mechanisms relating psychosocial factors, immune function, and disease progression.

STRESS AND CANCER

A diagnosis of cancer and subsequent adjuvant treatments are sources of considerable emotional distress among patients. The psychosocial issues these patients deal with appear to be specific to different phases of the disease experience, changing somewhat across the prediagnostic, diagnostic, treatment, recurrence, and terminal phases (Fawzy, Fawzy, Hyun, & Wheeler, 1997). During the treatment phase, which is usually initiated by curative intervention such as surgery and other adjuvant therapies, the predominant reactions often include fear and grief (Gordon et al., 1980; Meyerowitz, 1980; Pozo et al., 1992). During this challenging period, maladaptive responses may include avoidance, postoperative reactive depression, and prolonged postoperative grief (Fawzy et al., 1997).

Confrontation with a life-threatening cancer diagnosis, surgery, and postoperative side-effects may also result in increased levels of psychological distress, anxiety, and depression that persist long after surgery. In some cancer patients, more pronounced distress reactions and psychiatric symptoms may appear, especially in those who do not use effective coping strategies (Irvine, Brown, Crooks, Roberts, & Browne, 1991). Therefore, psychosocial factors may affect quality of life and health outcomes of cancer patients.

Psychosocial Factors Related to Cancer Progression

There is growing evidence that several psychosocial factors can mediate distress reactions and quality of life after treatment for cancer, including the patient's cognitive appraisals, use of adaptive coping strategies, and sense of social support. For example, optimism–pessimism (assessed before surgery) predicts the degree of emotional distress experienced during the period after surgery for breast cancer and over the next year (Carver et al., 1994). Thus, breast cancer patients' distress in the months after surgery is related to their use of cognitive coping strategies. Denial and disengagement responses also prospectively predicted future distress, even when controlling for prior distress, whereas acceptance (an effort to accommodate to the situation's reality) and positive reframing were strongly linked with lower distress during the period surrounding surgery and afterward. Several studies have also shown that women with breast cancer who perceive that they have adequate social support resources do better than women who perceive themselves as having inadequate resources (Helgeson & Cohen, 1996).

Breast cancer patients often report significantly more life stressors before discovery of the primary breast tumor (Forsen, 1991; Funch & Marshall, 1983; Geyer, 1991) or recurrence (Ramirez et al., 1989), as compared to healthy women controls. Those with greater cumulative stressors may be at risk for relapse or shortened survival time (Ramirez et al., 1989), although contradictory evidence of this effect also exists (Barraclough et al., 1992). Some work suggests that breast cancer patients' reactions to diagnosis may predict the course of disease (Greer, Morris, Pettingale, & Haybittle, 1990), although other work fails to find a link between depression and cancer prognosis (Barraclough et al., 1992; Jamison, Burish, & Wallston, 1987). It seems likely that the discrepancies among these studies may have resulted from methodological differences (Mulder, Pompe, Speigel, Antoni, & Vries, 1992; Watson & Ramirez, 1991), and future work is needed in this area.

Temoshok et al. (1985) examined psychological reactions surrounding the treatment of patients with malignant melanoma and found that patient delay in seeking medical attention had the strongest relationship with tumor thickness, suggesting that denial and avoidance coping strategies may have an impact on disease status. In a separate report, Temoshok (1985) also found that the emotional expression of either sadness or anger was positively related to tumor-specific host-response factors. Furthermore, patients with an unfavorable outcome (e.g., either death or disease progression) reported greater dysphoric mood and distress one to three years earlier. Overall, these findings suggest that psychosocial factors, such as emotionality or mood, may relate to disease progression in melanoma patients.

Based on these observed relationships, Fawzy et al. (1990) examined the effects of a time-limited stress-reduction intervention among patients with stage I or II malignant melanoma shortly after surgery. This intervention was a closed group format with 7 to 10 patients over a six-week period and focused on (a) health education, (b) stress awareness building, (c) cognitive restructuring, (d) coping skills training, and (e) anxiety reduction skills such as progressive muscle relaxation and imagery. The investigators found that patients assigned to the intervention group reported higher levels of vigor and greater use of active–behavioral coping than the controls at postintervention. At six-month follow-up, the patients assigned to the intervention group showed lower depression, fatigue, confusion, and total mood distur-bance as well as more active–behavioral and active–cognitive coping than the controls. This randomized study showed the efficacy of a brief psychologi-cal intervention in concurrently attenuating distress and improving mood among melanoma patients. In addition, they found that after controlling for relevant demographic and medical variables, there was a significantly greater death rate among the control patients than among those who had partici-pated in the group intervention and that enhancement of active–behavioral coping over time also predicted lower rates of recurrence and death (Fawzy et al., 1993).

Psychosocial factors such as active coping have been shown to predict greater survival time, and repressive coping has been related to poorer survival in malignant melanoma patients (Rogentine et al., 1979). Further-more, elevated negative life events and other psychosocial factors such as passive coping, emotional inhibition, and pessimistic appraisals have been associated with greater promotion of cervical neoplasia (Antoni & Goodkin, 1989). Poor expression of anger (Pettingale, Morris, Greer, & Haybittle, 1985), stoicism (Greer, 1991), repressiveness (Jensen, 1987), and lack of social support (Levy, Herberman, Lippman, D'Angelo, & Lee, 1991) have all been related to poorer prognosis in breast cancer patients as well. Al-though the effects of these types of psychosocial phenomena have been widely studied among cancer patients, less is known about some of the potential underlying biological changes resulting from these effects.

Important Immune Parameters in Cancer

The exact role of the immune system in the initiation, promotion, and recurrence of cancer is an area of considerable debate (Bovbjerg, 1991). Some cancers frequently studied in psycho-oncology research that have known immune involvement include malignant melanoma (Fonteneau et al., 1997), breast cancer (Miller et al., 1997), and cervical cancer (Clerici, Shearer, & Clerici, 1998). Although extensive reviews within the context of some specific cancers are available (Anderson, Kiecolt-Glaser, & Glaser, 1994), consensus on the role of the immune system in the course of human cancers overall is still uncertain.

Immunological Processes in Cancer

The cytolytic activity of NK cells and cytotoxic T-cells is believed to play an important role in the host response against spontaneous tumors, especially when dealing with shed tumor cells, thus preventing metastases (Gorelik & Herberman, 1989). Among patients with solid tumors, higher NKCC predicted longer survival time without metastases over a 13-year period (Pross & Baines, 1988). Lower NKCC also predicted development of distant metastases in those patients untreated for head and neck tumors (Schantz & Goephert, 1987). Breast cancer patients have been shown to display significantly lower NKCC, even among stages I to III patients, and NKCC appears to be even lower in more advanced stage IV patients (Baxevanis et al., 1993) and in those with liver metastases (Yamasaki et al., 1993). Thus, these specific immune components may play a role in cancer disease progression.

Role of Cell-Signaling Cytokines in Immunotherapy of Cancer

The discovery of the potential role of the immune system in cancer progression has led to the development of a number of immunological treatments. The past decade has seen significant work in immunotherapy with response modifiers, such as the cytokines IL-2 and IFN-γ in the treatment of different cancers (DeVita, Hellman, & Rosenberg, 1997). Lymphokine-activated killer (LAK) cells, NK-like cells that have been stimulated with substances such as IL-2 or IFN-γ, may be more cytotoxic than resting NK cells against a wider range of tumor cells, including those of breast cancer patients (Baxevanis et al., 1993). Peri-lesional delivery of IL-2 with the appropriate subsets of NK cells (e.g., adherent NK cells) resulted in shrinking of established human squamous cell carcinomas of the head and neck growing in immunosuppressed mice (Vujanovic et al., 1995). A similar combination also led to reduced established hepatic metastases and prolonged survival in mice with human gastric cancer metastasized to the liver (Vujanovic et al., 1995). Patients with liver metastases from breast cancer showed increases in lymphoproliferative responses to IL-2 and autologous tumor extract antigen in mixed culture after adoptive cell transfer, and these increases correlated with survival after treatment (Yamasaki et al., 1993). In this study, lymphocyte count and proliferation rate of cultured lymphocytes was also significantly associated with prognosis. Therefore, immunotherapy seems at least to some extent effective in modulating cancer disease progression.

Stress–Immune Relationships in Cancer

Researchers have also examined whether or not psychosocial factors play a role in the relationship between immune function and cancer progression. Growing evidence suggests that behavioral and psychosocial factors related to stress responses and distress states may influence many of the aforementioned immunological variables in breast cancer patients (Andersen et al., 1998). The confrontation with a life-threatening cancer diagnosis, surgery itself, and postoperative pain may result in increased levels of psychological distress, anxiety, and depression that persist long after surgery, especially in patients who do not use effective coping strategies (Irvine et al., 1991). One study found that women at familial risk for breast cancer showed significant associations between heightened emotional distress and decreased NKCC (Bovbjerg & Valdimarsdottir, 1993). Among early-stage cancer patients receiving adjuvant therapy, greater psychological distress levels are associated with decrements in immune cells (neutrophils) important in surveying bacterial pathogens, and an increased incidence of infectious disease symptoms (Bovbjerg, 1996). Other work has also found a relationship between lower social support and greater decrements in NKCC and lymphocyte proliferative responses to mitogens in an older sample of spouses of urological cancer patients (Baron et al., 1990).

Fawzy et al. (1990) evaluated the effects of their short-term group intervention for melanoma patients on immune system functioning. They found that patients assigned to the group intervention developed significant increases in the percentage of large granular lymphocytes (e.g., CD57 with Leu-7) when compared to control participants. These patients also revealed significant increases in NK cells (e.g., CD16 with Leu-11 and CD56 with NKH1) along with an increase in cytokine (e.g., IFN-γ) enhanced NKCC at six-month follow-up. Reductions in distress were also related to enhancements in NK cell number and activity. These results demonstrate that a short-term psychological intervention led to an enhancement in the immune system's ability to fight tumor growth and that these changes paralleled distress reductions observed during the intervention.

Among women at increased risk for cervical carcinoma because of coinfection with HIV and human papillomavirus (HPV), a promoter of cervical cancer, greater pessimism was associated with lower NKCC (Byrnes et al., 1999). Poorer social support (Levy et al., 1991) and greater distress levels (Anderson et al., 1998) have also been related to decrements in NKCC among patients with early-stage breast cancer. Early-stage breast cancer patients with greater distress after surgery also had lower NKCC by 15 months after surgery, and lower NKCC at this point predicted a shorter time to recurrence over a five- to eight-year follow-up (Levy et al., 1991). In another study with early-stage breast cancer patients, greater NKCC was associated with patients' perceptions of emotional support from their spouses, greater perceived support from their physicians, and seeking social support as a coping strategy (Levy et al., 1990). It appears that distress, certain coping strategies, and inadequate social support experienced by breast cancer patients during the period following surgery could contribute to persistent decrements in immune function, possibly increasing the risk of regional and distant metastases over longer periods.

Another study demonstrated an association between distress levels and decrements in immune system functioning in breast cancer patients

(Andersen et al., 1998). Higher distress related to lower NKCC, lower IFN-γ-stimulated NKCC, and lower lymphocyte proliferative responses to plant lectins and to anti-CD3 monoclonal antibody among 116 stage II and III breast cancer patients in the period after surgery but before the start of adjuvant therapy. These findings held even after controlling for the patient's age, disease stage, and recovery time since surgery. It seems that physiological effects of stress inhibit cellular immune responses that are relevant to cancer prognosis in women with breast cancer. These findings highlight the need for longitudinal studies to determine the duration of these effects, their ability to predict health consequences in breast cancer patients, and perhaps their underlying biological and behavioral mechanisms.

CONCLUSION

This chapter has provided an overview of the biobehavioral bases of some disease processes. Although the story is incomplete, it is clear that psychosocial factors may potentially influence disease outcomes for some medical conditions, including CHD, infectious illness, HIV/AIDS, and some cancers.

There is strong evidence that psychosocial factors can influence the development and course of disease. In large epidemiological studies, depression has been associated with an 80% increase in hypertension incidence (Jonas, Franks, & Ingram, 1997) and a 50% increase in CHD incidence (Anda et al., 1993). In patients with established CHD, there is a five- to six-fold increase in mortality after myocardial infarction as a function of depression. Epidemiological studies have also linked anxiety (Kawachi, Sparrow, Vokonas, & Weiss, 1994) and hostility (Shekell, Gale, Ostfeld, & Paul, 1983) to CHD mortality. In terms of HIV disease, large-scale epidemiological studies have found robust links between depression and mortality in men (Mayne et al., 1996) and women (Ickovics et al., 2001). Similarly, faster progression to AIDS has been associated with higher cumulative stressful life events, use of denial as a coping mechanism, and lower satisfaction with social support (Leserman et al., 2000). In studies of cancer patients, women with established breast cancer have been reported to have a three- to four-fold increase in mortality if they have high depression scores (Watson, Haviland, Greer, Davidson, & Bliss, 1999). Similarly, men who perceived themselves as being moderately or highly hopeless have an 80% greater chance of dying from cancer (Everson et al., 1996).

A main goal of this chapter was to show that the relationships between psychosocial and behavioral factors, on the one hand, and increased morbidity and mortality, on the other, occur through plausible biological mechanisms. In the case of CHD the means by which diet, smoking, and sedentary lifestyle adversely affect health was reviewed, and the role of the insulin metabolic syndrome in the development of CHD was explored. Potential stress mechanisms involved in CHD, such as low levels of brain serotonin and psychosocial factors and behaviors associated with elevated SNS and HPA axis activation were also discussed.

We also described some of the major putative neural–endocrine–immune pathways that have related psychosocial stress and infectious diseases, including HIV/AIDS. The most prominent links between perceived stress, depressed affect, and stressful life events on the one hand and adverse health effects of infectious diseases on the other have been changes in SNS and HPA axis activation and their impact on cellular immunity. In their review of the literature, Herbert and Cohen (1993) found that stressors were consistently associated with decreases in NKCC, increases in herpes virus antibody titers, and increases in circulating white blood cells. Studies of HIV/AIDS have identified potent psychosocial factors (depressed affect, stressful life events, use of denial coping, lack of perceived social support), neuroendocrine variables (catecholamines, cortisol), and immune factors (decreases in NKCC and increases in herpesvirus antibody titers) as important variables involved in disease progression.

There is also evidence that some cancers, such as breast cancer and malignant melanomas, may be influenced by psychosocial variables. Furthermore, psychosocial factors such as active coping have been shown to predict greater survival time in melanoma patients (Fawzy et al., 1993), whereas repressive coping has been related to poorer survival in such patients (Rogentine et al., 1979). Similarly, lack of social support (Levy et al., 1991) has been related to poorer prognosis in breast cancer patients. Although the immune system's exact role in the initiation, promotion, and recurrence of cancer is an area of debate (Bovbjerg, 1991), immune system involvement has been shown for malignant melanoma (Fonteneau et al., 1997), breast cancer (Miller et al., 1997), and cervical cancer (Clerici et al., 1998). In terms of stress–immune relationships in the context of cancer, women at familial risk for breast cancer have shown significant associations between elevated emotional distress and decreased NKCC (Bovbjerg & Valdimarsdottir, 1993). Similarly, women with early-stage breast cancer have shown relationships between poorer social support (Levy et al., 1991) and greater distress levels (Andersen et al., 1998) with decrements in NKCC.

In conclusion, the effects of psychosocial and behavioral variables in the development and progression of some organic diseases are fairly well-established. Health research spanning the past several decades has helped shed some light on these processes. However, the biobehavioral pathways linking psychosocial and behavioral factors and disease outcomes are complex, and just beginning to be understood. The mounting evidence linking psychosocial and behavioral mechanisms across a number of medical conditions clearly solidifies the role of health psychology researchers within the medical arena; future research delineating the biobehavioral processes mediating these relationships is clearly warranted.

REFERENCES

Anda, R., Williamson, D., Jones, D., Macera, C., Eaker, E., Glassman, A., et al. (1993). Depressed affect, hopelessness, and the risk of ischemic heart disease in a cohort of U.S. adults. *Epidemiology, 4,* 285–294.

Andersen, B., Farrar, W., Golden-Kreutz, D., Kutz, L., MacCallum, R., Courtney, M., et al. (1998). Stress and immune responses after surgical treatment for regional breast cancer. *Journal of the National Cancer Institute, 90,* 30–36.

Andersen, B. L., Kiecolt-Glaser, J. K., & Glaser, R. (1994). A biobehavioral model of cancer stress and disease course. *American Psychologist, 49,* 389–404.

Anderson, E. A., Balon, T. W., Hoffman, R. P., & Sinkey, M. A. (1992). Insulin increases sympathetic activity but not blood pressure in borderline hypertensive humans. *Hypertension, 19,* 621–627.

Antoni, M. H., Baggett, L., Ironson, G., August, S., LaPerriere, A., Klimas, N., et al. (1991). Cognitive behavioral stress management intervention buffers distress responses and immunologic changes following notification of HIV-1 seropositivity. *Journal of Consulting and Clinical Psychology, 59,* 906–915.

Antoni, M. H., Goldstein, D., Ironson, G., LaPerriere, A., Fletcher, M. A., & Schneiderman, N. (1995). Coping responses to HIV-1 serostatus notification predict concurrent and prospective immunologic status. *Clinical Psychology and Psychotherapy, 2,* 234–248.

Antoni, M. H., & Goodkin, K. (1989). Life stress and moderator variables in the promotion of cervical neoplasia. II: Life event dimensions. *Journal of Psychosomatic Research, 33,* 457–467.

Antoni, M. H., Schneiderman, N., Fletcher, M., Goldstein, D., LaPerriere, A., & Ironson, G. (1990). Psychoneuroimmunology and HIV-1. *Journal of Consulting and Clinical Psychology, 58,* 38–49.

Appels, A., Bär, F. W., Bär, J., Bruggeman, C., & de Baets, M. (2000). Inflammation, depressive symptomatology, and coronary artery disease. *Psychosomatic Medicine, 62,* 601–605.

Ardlie, N. G., Glew, G., & Schwartz, C. J. (1966). Influence of catecholamines on nucleotide-induced platelet aggregation. *Nature, 212,* 415–417.

Armstrong, D. B., Dublin, L. I., & Wheatley, G. M. (1951). Obesity and the relation to health and disease. *Journal of the American Medical Association, 147,* 1007–1014.

Arntzenius, A. C., Kromhout, D., Barth, J. D., Reiber, J. H. C., Bruschke, A. V. G., Buis, B., et al. (1985). Diet, lipoproteins, and the progression of coronary atherosclerosis. *New England Journal of Medicine, 312,* 805–811.

Axelrod, J., & Reisine, T. (1984). Stress hormones: Their interaction and regulation. *Science, 224*, 452–459.

Ballenger, J. C., Goodwin, F. K., Major, L. F., & Brown, G. L. (1979). Alcohol and central serotonergic metabolism in man. *Archives of General Psychiatry, 36*, 224–227.

Barefoot, J., Dahlstrom, W. G., & Williams, R. B. (1983). Hostility, CHD incidence, and total mortality: A 25-year follow-up study of 225 physicians. *Psychosomatic Medicine, 45*, 50–63.

Baron, R., Cutrona, C., Hicklin, D., Russel, D., & Lubaroff, D. (1990). Social support and immune function among spouses of cancer patients. *Journal of Personality and Social Psychology, 59*, 344–352.

Barraclough, J., Pinder, P., Cruddas, M., Osmond, C., Taylor, I., & Perry, M. (1992). Life events and breast cancer prognosis. *British Medical Journal, 304*, 1078–1081.

Barrett, D. C., Chesney, M. A., Burack, I. N., Stall, R. D., Ekstrand, M. L., & Coates, T. J. (1994). Depression and CD4 decline. (Letter to the Editor). *Journal of the American Medical Association, 271*, 1743.

Barrett-Connor, E., & Khaw, K. T. (1989). Cigarette smoking and increased central adiposity. *Annals of Internal Medicine, 111*, 783–787.

Baxevanis, C., Reclos, G., Gritzapis, A., Dedousis, G., Missitzis, I., & Papamichail, M. (1993). Elevated prostaglandin E2 production by monocytes is responsible for the depressed levels of natural killer and lymphokine-activated killer cell function in patients with breast cancer. *Cancer, 72*, 491–501.

Benight, C. C., Antoni, M. H., Kilbourn, K., Ironson, G., Kumar, M. A., Fletcher, M. A., et al. (1997). Coping self-efficacy buffers psychological and physiological disturbances in HIV-infected men following a natural disaster. *Health Psychology, 16*, 248–255.

Benowitz, N. L., Kuyt, F., & Jacob, P. (1984). Influence of nicotine on cardiovascular and hormonal effects of cigarette smoking. *Clinical Pharmacology, 36*, 74–81.

Berliner, J., Leitinger, N., & Watson, A. (1997). Oxidized lipids in ahterogensis: Formation, destruction, and action. *Thrombosis and Haemostatis, 78*, 195–199.

Blair, D., Habicht, J. P., Sims, E. A. H., Sylvester, D., & Abraham, S. (1984). Evidence for an increased risk for hypertension with centrally located body fat and the effect of race and sex on this risk. *American Journal of Epidemiology, 119*, 526–540.

Bosma, H., Peter, R., Siegrist, J., & Marmot, M. (1998). Two alternative job stress models and the risk of coronary heart disease. *American Journal of Public Health, 88*, 68–74.

Bovbjerg, D. (1991). Psychoneuroimmunology: Implications for oncology? *Cancer, 67*, 828–832.

Bovbjerg, D. (1996, March). *Stress, psychoneuroimmunology and cancer.* Symposium presented at the Fourth International Congress of Behavioral Medicine, Washington, DC.

Bovbjerg, D., & Valdimoarsdottir, H. (1993). Familial cancer, emotional distress, and low natural cytotoxic activity in healthy women. *Annals of Oncology, 4,* 745–752.

Breslow, J. L. (1991). Lipoprotein transport gene abnormalities underlying coronary heart disease susceptibility. *Annual Review of Medicine, 42,* 357–371.

Brindley, D. N., McCann, B. S., Niaura, R., Stoney, C. M., & Suarez, E. C. (1993). Stress and lipoprotein metabolism: Modulators and mechanism. *Metabolism, 42*(Suppl.), 3–15.

Brischetto, C. S., Connor, W. E., Connor, S. L., & Matarazzo, J. D. (1983). Plasma lipid and lipoprotein profiles of cigarette smokers from randomly selected families: Enhancement of hyperlipidemia and depression of high-density lipoprotein. *American Journal of Cardiology, 52,* 675–680.

Burke, G. L., Webber, L. S., & Srinivasan, S. R. (1986). Fasting plasma glucose and insulin levels and their relationship to cardiovascular risk factors in children: The Bogalusa heart study. *Metabolism, 35,* 441–446.

Byrnes, D., Antoni, M., Goodkin, K., Efantis-Potter, J., Simon, T., Munajj, J., et al. (1999). Stressful events, pessimism, natural killer cell cytotoxicity and cytotoxic/suppressor T-cells in HIV+ black women at risk for cervical cancer. *Psychosomatic Medicine, 60,* 714–722.

Calabrese, J., Kling, M., & Gold, P. (1987). Alterations in immunocompetence during stress, bereavement, and depression: Focus on neuroendocrine regulation. *American Journal of Psychiatry, 144,* 1123–1134.

Carney, R. M., McMahon, R. P., Freedland, K. E., Becker, L., Krantz, D. S., Proschan, M. A., et al. (1998). Reproducibility of mental stress-induced myocardial ischemia in the psychophysiological investigations of myocardial ischemia (PIMI). *Psychosomatic Medicine, 60,* 64–70.

Carney, R. M., Rich, M. W., Freedland, K. E., Saini, J., teVelde, A., Simeone, C., et al. (1988). Major depressive disorder predicts cardiac events in patients with coronary artery disease. *Psychosomatic Medicine, 50,* 627–633.

Carver, C. S., Pozo-Kaderman, C., Harris, S. D., Noriega, V., Scheier, M. F., Robinson, D. S., et al. (1994). Optimism vs. pessimism predicts the quality of women's adjustment to early stage breast cancer. *Cancer, 73,* 1213–1220.

Castelli, W. P., Doyle, J., Gordon, T., Hames, C. G., Hjortland, M., Hulley, S. B., et al. (1977). Alcohol and blood lipids: The cooperative lipoprotein phenotyping study. *Lancet, 2,* 153–155.

Clerici, M., Shearer, G., & Clerici, E. (1998). Cytokine dysregulation in invasive cervical carcinoma and other human neoplasias: Time to consider the TH1/TH2 paradigm. *Journal of the National Cancer Institute, 90,* 261–263.

Coccaro, E. F., Siever, L. J., Klar, H. M., Maurer, G., Cochrane, K., Cooper, T. B., et al. (1989). Serotonergic studies in patients with affective and personality disorders. *Archives of General Psychiatry, 46,* 587–599.

Cohen, S., Tyrrell, D. A., & Smith, A. P. (1991). Psychological stress in humans and susceptibility to the common cold. *New England Journal of Medicine, 325,* 606–612.

Cohen, S., Tyrrell, D. A., & Smith, A. P. (1993). Negative life events, perceived stress, negative affect, and susceptibility to the common cold. *Journal of Personality and Social Psychology, 64*, 131–140.

Cole, S., Kemeny, M., Taylor, S., Visscher, B., & Fahey, J. (1996). Accelerated course of HIV infection in gay men who conceal their homosexuality. *Psychosomatic Medicine, 58*, 219–231.

Cole, S., Korin, Y., Fahey, J., & Zack, J. (1998). Norepinephrine accelerates HIV replication via protein kinase-A dependent effects on cytokine production. *Journal of Immunology, 161*, 610–616.

Conway, T. L., Vickers, Jr., R. R., & Ward, H. W. (1981). Occupational stress and variation in cigarette, coffee, and alcohol consumption. *Journal of Health and Social Behavior, 22*, 155–161.

Craig, W. Y., Palomaki, G. E., & Haddow, J. E. (1989). Cigarette smoking and serum lipid and lipoprotein concentrations: An analysis of published data. *British Medical Journal, 298*, 784–788.

Cruess, S. E., Antoni, M. H., Cruess, D. G., Fletcher, M. A., Ironson, G., Kumar, M., et al. (2000). Reductions in HSV-2 antibody titers during cognitive behavioral stress management and relationships with neuroendocrine function, relaxation skills and social support in HIV+ men. *Psychosomatic Medicine, 7*, 160–182.

Cullen, P., Schulte, H., & Assmann, G. (1998). Smoking, lipoproteins and coronary heart disease risk: Data from the Munster heart study (PROCAM). *European Heart Journal, 19*, 1632–1641.

Dahan, P., Haettich, B., Le Parc, J. M., & Paolaggi, J. B. (1988). Meningoradiculitis due to herpes simplex virus disclosing HIV infection. *Annals of the Rheumatic Diseases, 47*, 440.

Danesh, J., Collins, R., & Peto, R. (1997). Chronic infections and coronary heart disease: Is there a link? *Lancet, 350*, 430–436.

Danzer, R. (2001). Cytokine-induced sickness behavior: Where do we stand? *Brain, Behavior, and Immunity, 15*, 7–24.

de Padua Mansur, A., Caramelli, B., Vianna, C. B., Chamone, D., & Ramires, J. A. (1997). Smoking and lipoprotein abnormalities on platelet aggregation in coronary heart disease. *International Journal of Cardiology, 62*, 151–154.

DeFronzo, R. A., Sherwin, R. S., & Kraemer, N. (1987). Effect of physical training on insulin action in obesity. *Diabetes, 36*, 1379–1385.

DeMartini, J. C., Brodie, S. J., de la Concha-Bermejillo, A., Ellis, J. A., & Larimore, M. D. (1993). Pathogenesis of lymphoid interstitial pneumonia in natural and experimental ovine lentivirus infection. *Clinical Infectious Diseases, 17*, S236–S242.

DeVita, V., Hellman, S., & Rosenberg, S. (Eds.). (1997). *Cancer: Principles and practice of oncology* (5th ed.). Philadelphia: Lippincott-Raven.

Doll, D. C., & List, A. E. (1982). Burkitt's lymphoma in a homosexual. *Lancet, 1*, 1026–1027.

Epstein, L. H., & Perkins, K. A. (1988). Smoking, stress, and coronary heart disease. *Journal of Consulting and Clinical Psychology, 56*, 342–349.

Erikssen, J., Forfang, K., & Jervell, J. (1981). Coronary risk factors and physical fitness in healthy middle-aged men. *Acta Medica Scandinavica, 645*(Suppl.), 57–64.

Esler, M., Julius, S., Zweifler, A., Randall, O., Harburg, E., Gardiner, H., et al. (1997). Mild high-renin essential hypertension: Neurogenic human hypertension? *New England Journal of Medicine, 296*, 405–411.

Esterling, B., Antoni, M. H., Kumar, M., & Schneiderman, N. (1990). Emotional repression, trauma disclosure responses and Epstein-Barr viral capsid antigen titers. *Psychosomatic Medicine, 52*, 397–410.

Esterling, B., Kiecolt-Glaser, J., & Glaser, R. (1996). Psychosocial modulation of cytokine-induced natural killer cell activity in older adults. *Psychosomatic Medicine, 58*, 264–272.

Evans, D. L., Ten Have, T., Douglas, S. D., Gettes, D. R., Morrison, M., Chiappini, M. S., et al. (2002). Depression in women with HIV-infection is associated with viral load, CD8 T cells and natural killer lymphocytes. *American Journal of Psychiatry, 159*, 1752–1759.

Evans, P., & Edgerton, N. (1991). Life events and mood as predictors of the common cold. *British Journal of Medical Psychology, 64*, 35.

Eversole, L., Stone, C., & Beckman, A. (1988). Detection of EBV and HPV DNA sequences in oral "hairy" leukoplakia by in situ hybridization. *Journal of Medical Virology, 26*, 271.

Everson, S. A., Goldberg, D. E., Kaplan, G. A., Cohen, R. D., Pukkala, E., Tuomi-lehto, J., et al. (1996). Hopelessness and risk of mortality and incidence of myocardial infarction and cancer. *Psychosomatic Medicine, 58*, 113–121.

Fawzy, F. I., Cousins, N., Fawzy, N., Kemeny, M. E., Elashoff, R., & Morton, D. (1990). A structured psychiatric intervention for cancer patients. I. Changes over time in methods of coping and affective disturbance. *Archives of General Psychiatry, 47*, 720–728.

Fawzy, F. I., Fawzy, N., Hyun, C. S., Elashoff, R., Guthrie, D., Fahey, J. L., et al. (1993). Malignant melanoma: Effects of an early structured psychiatric intervention, coping, and affective state on recurrence and survival 6 years later. *Archives of General Psychiatry, 50*, 681–689.

Fawzy, F. I., Fawzy, N. W., Hyun, C. S., & Wheeler, J. G. (1997). Brief coping-oriented therapy for patients with malignant melanoma. In J. L. Spira (Ed.), *Group therapy for medically ill patients* (pp. 133–164). New York: Guilford Press.

Fawzy, F. I., Kemeny, M. E., Fawzy, N. W., Elashoff, R., Morton, D., Cousins, N., et al. (1990). A structured psychiatric intervention for cancer patients. II. Changes over time in immunological measures. *Archives of General Psychiatry, 47*, 729–735.

Feldt-Rasmussen, B., Mathiesen, E. R., Deckert, T., Fiese, J., Christensen, N. J., Bent-Hansen, L., et al. (1987). Central role for sodium in the pathogenesis of blood pressure changes independent of angiotensin, aldosterone and cate-cholamines in type 1 (insulin-dependent) diabetes mellitus. *Diabetologia, 30,* 610–617.

Felton, D. (1996). Changes in the neural innervation of lymphoid tissues with age. In N. Hall, F. Altman, & S. Blumental (Eds.), *Mind–body interactions and disease and psychoneuroimmunological aspects of health and disease* (pp. 157–164). Washington, DC: Health Dateline Press.

Folkow, B. (1978). Cardiovascular structural adaptation: Its role in the inhibition and maintenance of primary hypertension: Volhard lecture. *Clinical Science, 55,* 3s–22s.

Fonteneau, J., Le Drean, E., Le Guiner, S., Gervois, N., Diez, E., & Jotereau, F. (1997). Heterogeneity of biologic responses of melanoma-specific CTL. *Journal of Immunology, 159,* 2831–2839.

Forsen, A. (1991). Psychosocial stress as a risk for breast cancer. *Psychotherapy and Psychosomatics, 55,* 176–185.

Fournier, A. M., Gadia, M. T., Kubrusly, D. B., Skyler, J. S., & Sosenko, J. M. (1986). Blood pressure, insulin, and glycemia in nondiabetic subjects. *American Journal of Medicine, 80,* 861–864.

Fournier, R. D., Chiueh, C. C., & Kopin, I. J. (1986). Refined carbohydrate increases blood pressure and catecholamine excretion in SHR and WKY. *American Journal of Physiology, 250,* E381–E385.

Frasure-Smith, N., Lesperance, F., & Talajic, M. (1995). Depression and 18-month prognosis after myocardial infarction. *Circulation, 91,* 999–1005.

Friedman, G. D., Klatsky, A. L., & Siegelaub, A. B. (1982). Alcohol, tobacco and hypertension. *Hypertension, 4*(Suppl. 3), 143–150.

Fuller, R. W., Holland, D. R., Yen, T. T., Bemis, K. G., & Stamm, N. B. (1979). Antihypertensive effects of fluoxetine and 1-5 hydroxytryptophan in rats. *Life Sciences, 25,* 1237–1242.

Funch, D., & Marshall, J. (1983). The role of stress, social support and age in survival from breast cancer. *Journal of Psychosomatic Research, 27,* 77–83.

Garvey, W. T., & Hermayer, K. L. (1998). Clinical implications of the insulin resistance syndrome. *Clinical Cornerstone, 1,* 13–28.

Gawin, F. H., Compton, M., & Dych, R. (1989). Buspirone reduces smoking. *Archives of General Psychiatry, 46,* 288–289.

Geyer, S. (1991). Life events prior to manifestation of breast cancer: A limited prospective study covering eight years before diagnosis. *Journal of Psychosomatic Research, 35,* 355–363.

Glaser, R., & Gotlieb-Stematsky, T. (Eds.). (1982). *Human herpes virus infections: Clinical aspects.* New York: Marcel Dekker.

Glaser, R., Kennedy, S., Lafuse, W. P., Bonneau, R. H., Speicher, C. E., & Kiecolt-Glaser, J. K. (1990). Psychological stress-induced modulation of IL-2 receptor gene expression and IL-2 production in peripheral blood leukocytes. *Archives of General Psychiatry, 47,* 707–712.

Glaser, R., & Kiecolt-Glaser, J. (1987). Stress-associated depression in cellular immunity: Implications for acquired immune deficiency syndrome (AIDS). *Brain, Behavior and Immunity, 1,* 107–112.

Glaser, R., & Kiecolt-Glaser, J. (1997). Chronic stress modulates the virus-specific immune response to latent herpes simplex virus Type 1. *Annals of Behavioral Medicine, 19,* 78–82.

Glaser, R., Kiecolt-Glaser, J. K., Speicher, C. E., & Holliday, J. E. (1985). Stress, loneliness, and changes in herpesvirus latency. *Journal of Behavioral Medicine, 8,* 249–260.

Glaser, R., Pearson, G. R., Bonneau, R. H., Esterling, B. A., Atkinson, C., & Kiecolt-Glaser, J. K. (1993). Stress and the memory T-cell response to the Epstein-Barr virus in healthy medical students. *Health Psychology, 12,* 435–442.

Glaser, R., Rice, J., Sheridan, J., Fertel, R., Stout, J., Speicher, C., et al. (1987). Stress-related immune suppression: Health implications. *Brain, Behavior and Immunity, 1,* 7–20.

Glaser, R., Rice, J., Speicher, C., Stout, J., & Kiecolt-Glaser, J. (1986). Stress depresses interferon production and natural killer cell activity in humans. *Behavioral Neurosciences, 100,* 675–678.

Golay, A., Felber, J. P., & Dusmet, M. (1985). Effect of weight loss on glucose disposal in obese and obese diabetic patients. *International Journal of Obesity, 9,* 181–190.

Goldberg, D. M., Soleas, G. J., & Levesque, M. (1999). Moderate alcohol consumption: The gentle face of Janus. *Clinical Biochemistry, 32,* 505–518.

Goodell, S. E., Quinn, T. C., Mkrtichian, E., Schuffler, M. D., Holmes, K. K., & Corey, L. (1983). Herpes simplex virus proctitis in homosexual men. Clinical, sigmoidoscopic, and histopathological features. *New England Journal of Medicine, 308,* 868–871.

Goodkin, K., Blaney, N., Feaster, D., & Fletcher, M. A. (1992). Active coping is associated with natural killer cell cytotoxicity in asymptomatic HIV-1 seropositive homosexual men. *Journal of Psychosomatic Research, 36,* 635–650.

Gordon, W. A., Freidenbergs, I., Diller, L., Hibbard, M., Wolf, C., Levine, L., et al. (1980). Efficacy of psychosocial intervention with cancer patients. *Journal of Consulting and Clinical Psychology, 48,* 743–759.

Gorelik, E., & Herberman, R. (1989). Immunological control of tumor metastases. In R. Goldfarb (Ed.), *Fundamental aspects of cancer* (pp. 383–399). Dordrecht, Netherlands: Kluwer Academic.

Greeno, C. G., & Wing, R. R. (1994). Stress-induced eating. *Psychological Bulletin, 115,* 444–464.

Greer, S. (1991). Psychological responses to cancer and survival. *Psychological Medicine, 21,* 43–49.

Greer, S., Morris, T., Pettingale, K., & Haybittle, J. (1990). Psychological response to breast cancer and 15-year outcome. *Lancet, 335*(8680), 49–50.

Griffith, P. D., & Grundy, J. E. (1987). Molecular biology and immunology of cytomegalovirus. *Journal of Biochemistry, 241,* 313–324.

Hart, C. L., Smith, G. D., Hole, D. J., & Hawthorne, V. M. (1999). Alcohol consumption and mortality from all causes, coronary heart disease, and stroke: Results from a prospective cohort study of Scottish men with 21 years of follow up. *British Medical Journal, 318,* 1725–1729.

Hart, M. N., Heistad, D. D., & Brody, M. J. (1980). Effect of chronic hypertension and sympathetic denervation on wall/lumen ratio of cerebral vessels. *Hypertension, 2,* 419–428.

Heath, G. W., Gavin, J. R. III, & Hinderliter, J. M. (1983). Effects of exercise and lack of exercise on glucose tolerance and insulin sensitivity. *Journal of Applied Physiology, 55,* 512–517.

Heindel, J. J., Orci, L., & Jeanrenaud, B. (1975). Fat mobilization and its regulation by hormones and drugs in white adipose tissue. In D. Masoro (Ed.), *International encyclopedia of pharmacology and therapeutics. Pharmacology of lipid transport and atherosclerotic processes* (pp. 175–373). Oxford, England: Pergamon Press.

Helgeson, V. S., & Cohen, S. (1996). Social support and adjustment to cancer: Reconciling descriptive, correlational, and intervention research. *Health Psychology, 15,* 135–148.

Herberman, R. (1991). Principles of tumor immunology. In A. Holleb, D. Fink, & G. Murphy (Eds.), *American Cancer Society textbook of clinical oncology* (pp. 69–79). Atlanta, GA: American Cancer Society.

Herbert, T., & Cohen, S. (1993). Depression and immunity: A meta-analytic review. *Psychological Bulletin, 113,* 472–486.

Hickey, N., Mulcahy, R., Bourke, G. J., Graham, I., & Wilson-Davis, K. (1975). Study of coronary risk factors related to physical activity in 15,171 men. *British Medical Journal, 3,* 507–509.

Hollenbeck, C., Haskell, W., & Rosenthal, M. (1985). Effect of habitual physical activity on regulation of insulin-stimulated glucose disposal in older males. *Journal of the American Geriatric Society, 33,* 273–277.

Hwang, I. S., Ho, H., Hoffman, B. B., & Reaven, G. M. (1987). Fructose-induced insulin resistance and hypertension in rats. *Hypertension, 10,* 512–516.

Ickovics, J. R., Hamburger, M. E., Vlahov, D., Schoenbaum, E. E., Schuman, P., Boland, R. J., et al. (2001). Mortality, CD4 cell count decline, and depressive symptoms among HIV-seropositive women. *Journal of the American Medical Association, 285,* 1466–1474.

Ironson, G., Balbin, E., Solomon, G., Fletcher, M. A., Fahey, J., Klimas, N., et al. (2001). Relative preservation of natural killer cell cytoxity in healthy AIDS patients with low CD4 counts. *AIDS, 15,* 2065–2073.

Ironson, G., Friedman, A., Klimas, N., Antoni, M., Fletcher, M. A., LaPerriere, A., et al. (1994). Distress, denial, and low adherence to behavioral intervention predict faster disease progression in gay men infected with HIV. *International Journal of Behavioral Medicine, 1,* 90–105.

Ironson, G., Solomon, G., Cruess, D., Barroso, J., & Stivers, M. (1995). Psychosocial factors related to long-term survival in HIV/AIDS. *Clinical Psychology and Psychotherapy, 2,* 249–266.

Ironson, G., Wynings, C., Schneiderman, N., Baum, A., Rodriguez, M., Greenwood, D., et al.(1997). Post traumatic stress symptoms, intrusive thoughts, loss and immune function after Hurricane Andrew. *Psychosomatic Medicine, 59,* 128–141.

Irvine, D., Brown, B., Crooks, D., Roberts, J., & Browne, G. (1991). Psychosocial adjustment in women with breast cancer. *Cancer, 67,* 1097–1117.

Irwin, M., Daniels, M., Smith, T., Bloom, E., & Weiner, H. (1987). Impaired natural killer cell activity during bereavement. *Brain Behavior and Immunity, 1,* 98–104.

Irwin, M., & Gillin, J. (1987). Impaired natural killer cell activity in depressed patients. *Psychiatry Research, 20,* 181–182.

Irwin, M., Hauger, R., Patterson, T., Semple, S., Ziegler, M., & Grant, I. (1997). Alzheimer caregiver stress: Basal natural killer cell activity, pituitary-adrenal cortical function, and sympathetic tone. *Annals of Behavioral Medicine, 19,* 83–90.

Jamison, R., Burish, T., & Wallston, K. (1987). Psychogenic factors in predicting survival of breast cancer patients. *Journal of Clinical Oncology, 5,* 768–772.

Jennings, G. L., Deakin, G., Dewar, E., Lanfer, E., & Nelson, L. (1989). Exercise, cardiovascular disease and blood pressure. *Clinical and Experimental Hypertension: Theory and Practice, 11,* 1035–1052.

Jensen, M. (1987). Psychobiological factors predicting the course of breast cancer. *Journal of Personality, 55,* 317–342.

Jonas, B. S., Franks, P., & Ingram, D. D. (1997). Are symptoms of anxiety and depression risk factors for hypertension?: Longitudinal evidence from the National Health and Nutrition Examination Survey I epidemiologic follow-up study. *Archives of Family Medicine, 6,* 43–49.

Julius, S. (1993). Sympathetic hyperactivity and coronary risk in hypertension: Corcoran lecture. *Hypertension, 21,* 886–893.

Julius, S., Pascual, A. V., & London, R. (1971). Role of parasympathetic inhibition in the hyperkinetic type of borderline hypertension. *Circulation, 44,* 413–418.

Kaplan, J. R., Manuck, S. B., Clarkson, T. B., Lusso, F., & Taub, D. M. (1982). Social stress and atherosclerosis in normocholesterolemic monkeys. *Science, 220,* 733–735.

Kaplan, J. R., Manuck, S. B., Clarkson, T. B., Lusso, F., Taub, D. M., & Miller, E. W. (1982). Social stress, environment and atherosclerosis in cynomolgus monkeys. *Arteriosclerosis, 2,* 359–368.

Kawachi, I., Sparrow, D., Vokonas, P. S., & Weiss, S. T. (1994). Symptoms of anxiety and risk of coronary heart disease: The normative aging study. *Circulation, 90,* 2225–2229.

Kawachi, I., Sparrow, D., Spiro, A., Vokonas, P., & Weiss, S. T. (1996). A prospective study of anger and coronary heart disease. The normative aging study. *Circulation, 94,* 2090–2095.

Kaysen, G., & Noth, R. H. (1984). The effects of alcohol on blood pressure and electrolytes. *Medical Clinics of North America, 68,* 221–246.

Kemeny, M. E., Weiner, H., Duran, R., Taylor, S. E., Visscher, B., & Fahey, J. L. (1995). Immune system changes after the death of a partner in HIV-positive gay men. *Psychosomatic Medicine, 57,* 547–554.

Kemeny, M. E., Weiner, H., Taylor, S. E., Schneider, S., Visscher, B., & Fahey, J. L. (1994). Repeated bereavement, depressed mood, and immune parameters in HIV seropositive and seronegative gay men. *Health Psychology, 13,* 1424.

Kerschbaum, A., Pappajohn, D. J., & Bellet, S. (1968). Effect of smoking and nicotine on adrenocortical secretion. *Journal of the American Medical Association, 203,* 275–278.

Kiecolt-Glaser, J. K., Dura, J. R., Speicher, C. E., Trask, O. J., & Glaser, R. (1991). Spousal caregivers of dementia victims: Longitudinal changes in immunity and health. *Psychosomatic Medicine, 53,* 345–362.

Kiecolt-Glaser, J., Fisher, L., Ogrocki, P., Stout, J., Speicher, C., & Glaser, R. (1987). Marital quality, marital disruption, and immune function. *Psychosomatic Medicine, 49,* 13–34.

Kiecolt-Glaser, J. K., Kennedy, S., Malkoff, S., Fisher, L., Speicher, C. E., & Glaser, R. (1988). Marital discord and immunity in males. *Psychosomatic Medicine, 50,* 213–229.

Kiecolt-Glaser, J., Malarkey, W., Cacioppo, J., & Glaser, R. (1994). Stressful personal relationships: Endocrine and immune function. In R. Glaser & J. Kiecolt-Glaser (Eds.), *Handbook of human stress and immunity* (pp. 321–339). San Diego, CA: Academic Press.

King, D. S., Dalsky, G. P., & Clutter, W. E. (1988). Effects of exercise and lack of exercise on insulin sensitivity and responsiveness. *Journal of Applied Physiology, 64,* 1942–1946.

Kiyonaga, A., Arakawa, K., Tanaka, H., & Shindo, M. (1985). Blood pressure and hormonal responses to aerobic exercise. *Hypertension, 7,* 125–131.

Klatsky, A. L., Friedman, G. D., Siegelaub, A. B., & Gerard, M. J. (1977). Alcohol consumption and blood pressure: Kaiser-Permanente multiphasic health examination data. *New England Journal of Medicine, 296,* 1194–1200.

Kleinman, K. S., & Fine, L. G. (1988). Prognostic implications of renal hypertrophy in diabetes mellitus. *Diabetes and Metabolism Reviews, 4,* 179–189.

Kol, A., Bourcier, T., & Lichtman, A. H. (1999). Chlamydial and human heat shock proteins activate human vascular endothelium, smooth muscle cells, and macrophages. *Journal of Clinical Investigation, 103,* 571–577.

Krantz, D. S., & Manuck, S. B. (1984). Acute psychophysiologic reactivity and risk of cardiovascular disease: A review and methodological critique. *Psychological Bulletin, 96,* 435–464.

Krotkiewski, M., Mandroukas, K., Sjö, L., Sullivan, L., Wetterqvist, H., & Björntorp, P. (1979). Effects of long-term physical training on body fat, metabolism and blood pressure in obesity. *Metabolism, 28,* 650–658.

Kyes, R. C., Botchin, M. B., Kaplan, J. R., Manuck, S. B., & Mann, J. J. (1995). Aggression and brain serotonergic responsivity: Response to slides in male macaques. *Physiology & Behavior, 57,* 205–208.

Landsberg, L. (1992). Hyperinsulinemia: Possible role in obesity-induced hypertension. *Hypertension, 19*(Suppl.), I61–I65.

Landsberg, L., & Young, J. B. (1985). Insulin-mediated glucose metabolism in the relationship between dietary intake and sympathetic nervous system activity. *International Journal of Obesity, 9,* 63–68.

Leith, L. M., & Taylor, A. H. (1990). Psychological aspects of exercise: A decade literature review. *Journal of Sport Behavior, 13,* 219–239.

Leserman, J., Petitto, J. M., Golden, R. N., Gaynes, B. N., Gu, H., Perkins, D. O., et al. (2000). Impact of stressful life events, depression, social support, coping, and cortisol on progression to AIDS. *American Journal of Psychiatry, 157,* 1221–1228.

Leserman, J., Petitto, J., Perkins, D., Folds, J., Golden, R., & Evans, D. (1997). Severe stress, depressive symptoms, and changes in lymphocyte subsets in Human Immunodeficiency Virus-infected men. *Archives of General Psychiatry, 54,* 279–285.

Levine, L. R., Enas, G. G., Thompson, W. L., Byyny, R. L., Dauer, A. D., Kirby, R. W., et al. (1989). Use of fluoxetine, a selective serotonin uptake inhibitor, in the treatment of obesity: A dose-response study. *International Journal of Obesity, 13,* 635–645.

Levine, M. S., Woldenberg, R., Herlinger, H., & Laufer, I. (1987). Opportunistic esophagitis in AIDS: Radiographic diagnosis. *Radiology, 165,* 815–820.

Levy, S., Herberman, R., Lippman, M., D'Angelo, T., & Lee, J. (1991). Immunological and psychosocial predictors of disease recurrence in patients with early-stage breast cancer. *Journal of Behavioral Medicine, 17,* 67–75.

Levy, S. M., Herberman, R. B., Whiteside, T., Sanzo, K., Lee, J., & Kirkwood, J. (1990). Perceived social support and tumor estrogen/progesterone receptor status as predictors of natural killer cell activity in breast cancer patients. *Psychosomatic Medicine, 52,* 73–85.

Libby, P., Ridker, P. M., & Maseri, A. (2002). Inflammation and atheroschlerosis. *Circulation, 105,* 1135–1143.

Lutgendorf, S. K., Antoni, M. H., Ironson, G., Starr, K., Costello, N., Zuckerman, M., et al. (1998). Changes in cognitive coping skills and social support during cognitive behavioral stress management intervention and distress outcomes in symptomatic human immunodeficiency virus (HIV)-seropositive gay men. *Psychosomatic Medicine, 60,* 204–214.

Lutgendorf, S., Antoni, M., Kumar, M., & Schneiderman, N. (1994). Changes in cognitive coping strategies predict EBV-antibody titer change following a stressor disclosure induction. *Journal of Psychosomatic Research, 38,* 63–78.

Maher, K., Klimas, N., Dickinson, G., Triplett, J., Maggio, C., Valenzuela, R., et al. (1997). T-lymphocyte subsets and highly active antiretriviral therapy (HAART) of HIV infection. *Cytometry, 30,* 345.

Maheswaran, R., Gill, J. S., Davies, P., & Beevers, D. G. (1991). High blood pressure due to alcohol: A rapidly reversible effect. *Hypertension, 17,* 787–792.

Maier, S., Watkins, L., & Fleshner, M. (1994). Psychoneuroimmunology: The interface between brain, behavior and immunity. *American Psychologist, 49,* 1004–1017.

Manttari, M., Tenkanen, L., Alikoski, T., & Manninen, V. (1997). Alcohol and coronary heart disease: The roles of HDL-cholesterol and smoking. *Journal of Internal Medicine, 241,* 157–163.

Markham, P., Salahuddin, S., Veren, K., Orndorff, S., & Gallo, R. (1986). Hydrocortisone and some other hormones enhance the expression of HTLV-III. *International Journal of Cancer, 37,* 67–72.

Mayne, T. J., Vittinghoff, E., Chesney, M. A., Barrett, D. C., & Coates, T. J. (1996). Depressive affect and survival among gay and bisexual men infected with HIV. *Archives of Internal Medicine, 156,* 2233–2238.

McCann, B. S., Warnick, G. R., & Knopp, R. H. (1990). Changes in plasma lipids and dietary intake accompanying shifts in perceived workload and stress. *Psychosomatic Medicine, 52,* 97–108.

McEwen, B. S. (1998). Protective and damaging effects of stress mediators. *New England Journal of Medicine, 338,* 171–179.

McGinnis, J. M., & Foege, W. H. (1993). Actual causes of death in the United States. *Journal of the American Medical Association, 270,* 2207–2212.

McKinnon, W., Weisse, C. S., Reynolds, C. P., Bowles, C. A., & Baum, A. (1989). Chronic stress, leukocyte subpopulations, and humoral response to latent viruses. *Health Psychology, 8,* 399–402.

Menotti, A. (1999). Diet, cholesterol and coronary heart disease: A perspective. *Acta Cardiology, 54,* 169–172.

Meyerowitz, B. E. (1980). Psychosocial correlates of breast cancer and its treatments. *Psychological Bulletin, 87,* 108–131.

Miller, G. J. (1980). High density lipoproteins and atherosclerosis. *Annual Review of Medicine, 31,* 97–108.

Miller, J., Tessmer-Tuck, J., Pierson, B., Weisdorf, D., McGlave, P., Blazar, B., et al. (1997). Low dose subcutaneous interleukin-2 after autologous transplantation generates sustained in vivo natural killer cell activity. *Biological Blood Marrow Transplantation, 3,* 34–44.

Modan, M., Halkin, H., Almog, S., Lusky, A., Eshkol, A., Shefi, M., et al. (1985). Hyperinsulinemia: A link between hypertension, obesity and glucose intolerance. *Journal of Clinical Investigation, 75,* 809–817.

Morricone, L., Ferrari, M., Enrini, R., Inglese, L., Giardini, D., Garancini, P., et al. (1999). The role of central fat distribution in coronary artery disease in obesity: Comparison of nondiabetic obese, diabetic obese and normal weight subjects. *International Journal of Obesity and Related Metabolic Disorders, 23,* 1129–1135.

Morris, J. K., Cook, D. G., & Shaper, A. G. (1992). Non-employment and changes in smoking, drinking, and body weight. *British Medical Journal, 304,* 536–541.

Mulder, C., de Vroome, E., van Griensven, G., Antoni, M. H., & Sandfort, T. (1999). Distraction as a predictor of the virological course of HIV-1 infection over a 7-year period in gay men. *Health Psychology, 18,* 107–113.

Mulder, N., Antoni, M. H., Duivenvoorden, H., Kauffman, R., & Goodkin, K. (1995). Active confrontational coping predicts decreased clinical progression over a one-year period in HIV-infected homosexual men. *Journal of Psychosomatic Research, 39,* 957–965.

Mulder, N., Pompe, G., Speigel, D., Antoni, M., & Vries, M. (1992). Do psychosocial factors influence the course of breast cancer? *Psycho-Oncology, 1,* 155–167.

Mulvany, M. J. (1984). Pathophysiology of vascular smooth muscle in hypertension. *Journal of Hypertension, 2*(Suppl. III), 413–420.

Musey, L., Hughes, J., Schacker, T., Shea, T., Corey, L., & McElrath, M. J. (1997). Cytotoxic-T-cell responses, viral load, and disease progression in early human immunodeficiency virus type 1 infection. *New England Journal of Medicine, 337,* 1267–1274.

Naranjo, C. A., & Sellers, E. M. (1986). *Recent developments in alcoholism* (pp. 265–281). New York: Plenum Press.

Nelson, L., Jennings, G. L., Esler, M. D., & Korner, P. I. (1986). Effect of changing levels of physical activity on blood-pressure and haemodynamics in essential hypertension. *Lancet, 2,* 473–476.

O'Neill, B., & Leonard, B. (1986). Is there an abnormality in neutrophil phagocytosis in depression? *IRCS Medical Science, 14,* 802–803.

Paffenbarger, R. S., Wing, A. L., Hyde, R. T., & Jung, D. L. (1983). Physical activity and incidence of hypertension in college alumni. *American Journal of Epidemiology, 117,* 245–257.

Palmblad, J., Cantrell, K., Strander, H., Froberg, J., Karlesson, C., Levi, L., et al. (1976). Stressor exposure and immunological response in man: Interferon-producing capacity and phagocytosis. *Journal of Psychosomatic Research, 20,* 193–199.

Pantaleo, G., Graziosi, C., & Fauci, A. S. (1993). The immunopathogenesis of human immunodeficiency virus infection. *New England Journal of Medicine, 328,* 327–335.

Pettingale, K. W., Morris, T., Greer, S., & Haybittle, J. L. (1985). Mental attitudes to cancer: An additional prognostic factor. *Lancet, 1,* 750.

Pillar, R., Nair, B. S., & Watson, R. R. (1991). AIDS, drugs of abuse and the immune system: A complex immunotoxicological network. *Archives of Toxicology, 65,* 609–617.

Pozo, C., Carver, C. S., Noriega, V., Harris, S. D., Robinson, D. S., Ketcham, A. S., et al. (1992). Effects of mastectomy versus lumpectomy on emotional adjustment to breast cancer: A prospective study of the first year post surgery. *Journal of Clinical Oncology, 10*, 1292–1298.

Pross, H., & Baines, M. (1988). *Low natural killer cell activity in the peripheral blood of metastasis free cancer patients is associated with reduced metastasis free survival time*. 19th International Leukocyte Conference, Alberta, Canada.

Pykallsto, O. J., Smith, P. H., & Brunzell, J. D. (1975). Determinants of human adipose tissue lipoprotein lipase: Effect of diabetes and obesity on basal and diet induced activity. *Journal of Clinical Investigation, 56*, 1108–1117.

Ramirez, A., Craig, T., Watson, J., Fentiman, I., North, W., & Rubens, R. (1989). Stress and relapse of breast cancer. *British Medical Journal, 298*, 291–293.

Reaven, G. M. (1988). Role of insulin resistance in human disease: Banting lecture. *Diabetes, 37*, 1595–1607.

Reed, G. M., Kemeny, M. E., Taylor, S. E., Wang, H. J., & Visscher, B. (1994). Realistic acceptance as a predictor of decreased survival time in gay men with AIDS. *Health Psychology, 13*, 299–307.

Reisin, E., Frohlich, E. D., & Messerli, F. H. (1983). Cardiovascular changes in obesity after weight reduction. *Annals of Medicine, 98*, 315–319.

Rimm, E. B., Williams, P., Fosher, K., Criqui, M., & Stampfer, M. J. (1999). Moderate alcohol intake and lower risk of coronary heart disease: Meta-analysis of effects on lipids and haemostatic factors. *British Medical Journal, 319*, 1523–1528.

Rinaldo, C. R. (1990). Immune suppression by herpes viruses. *Annual Reviews of Medicine, 41*, 331–338.

Risch, S. C., & Nemeroff, C. B. (1992). Neurochemical alterations of serotonergic neuronal systems in depression. *Journal of Clinical Psychiatry, 53*, 3–7.

Robbins, T. W., Everitt, B. J., & Sahakian, B. J. (1981). Stress-induced eating in animals. In L. A. Cioffi, W. P. T. James, & T. B. Van Etallie (Eds.), *The body weight regulatory system: Normal and disturbed mechanisms* (pp. 289–297). New York: Raven.

Robbins, T. W., & Fray, P. J. (1980). Stress-induced eating: Fact, fiction or misunderstanding? *Appetite, 1*, 103–133.

Robertson, D., Tseng, C. J., & Appalsamy, M. (1988). Smoking and mechanisms of cardiovascular control. *American Heart Journal, 115*, 258–263.

Rogentine, G., Van Krammen, D., Fox, B., Docherty, J., Rosenblatt, J., Boyd, S., et al. (1979). Psychological factors in the prognosis of malignant melanoma: A perspective study. *Psychosomatic Medicine, 4*, 647–655.

Roghman, K., & Haggerty, R. (1973). Daily stress, illness, and use of health services in young families. *Journal of Pediatric Research*, 520–526.

Rosenberg, Z. F., & Fauci, A. S. (1991). Activation of latent HIV infection. *Journal of the National Institutes of Health Research, 2*, 41–45.

Rostad, F. G., & Long, B. C. (1996). Exercise as a coping strategy for stress: A review. *International Journal of Sports Psychology, 27*, 197–222.

Rowe, J. W., Young, J. B., Minaker, K. L., Stevens, A. L., Pallotta, J., & Landsberg, L. (1981). Effect of insulin and glucose infusions on sympathetic nervous system activity in normal man. *Diabetes, 30,* 219–225.

Ruf, J. C. (1999). Wine and polyphenols related to platelet aggregation and atherosclerosis. *Drugs and Experimental Clinical Research, 25,* 125–131.

Sacks, F. M., & Dzau, V. J. (1986). Adrenergic effects on plasma lipoprotein metabolism: Speculation on mechanisms of action. *American Journal of Medicine, 80*(Suppl. 2A), 71–81.

Schantz, S., & Goephert, H. (1987). Multimodal therapy and distant metastasis: The impact of NK cell activity. *Archives of Otolaryngology, Head and Neck Surgery, 113,* 1207–1213.

Scherwitz, L. W., Perkins, L. L., & Chesney, M. A. (1992). Hostility and health behaviors in young adults: The CARDIA study. *American Journal of Epidemiology, 136,* 136–145.

Schleifer, S. J., Macari-Hinson, M. M., Coyle, D. A., William, W. R., Kahn, M., & Gorlin, R. (1989). The nature and course of depression following myocardial infarction. *Archives of Internal Medicine, 149,* 1785–1789.

Schneiderman, N. (1999). Behavioral medicine and the management of HIV/AIDS. *International Journal of Behavioral Medicine, 6,* 3–12.

Schneiderman, N., Antoni, M. H., & Ironson, G. (1997). Cognitive behavioral stress management and secondary prevention in HIV/AIDS. *Psychology & AIDS Exchange, 22,* 1–8.

Schneiderman, N., Antoni, M. H., Ironson, G., Fletcher, M. A., Klimas, N., & LaPerriere, A. (1994). HIV-1, immunity and behavior. In R. Glaser (Ed.), *Handbook of human stress and immunity* (pp. 267–300). New York: Academic Press.

Schneiderman, N., & McCabe, P. (1989). Psychophysiologic strategies in laboratory research. In N. Schneiderman & S. M. Weiss (Eds.), *Handbook of research methods in cardiovascular behavioral medicine. Plenum series in behavioral psychophysiology and medicine* (pp. 349–364). New York: Plenum Press.

Schonfeld, G., & Pfleger, B. (1971). Utilization of exogenous free fatty acids for the production of very low density lipoprotein triglyceride by livers of carbohydrate-fed rats. *Journal of Lipid Research, 12,* 614–621.

Schooley, R. T. (1990). Cytomegalovirus in the setting of infection with human immunodeficiency virus. *Reviews of Infectious Diseases, 12*(Suppl. 7), S811–S819.

Shaper, A. G., & Wannamethee, S. G. (2000). Alcohol intake and mortality in middle aged men with diagnosed coronary heart disease. *Heart, 83,* 394–399.

Shekell, R. B., Gale, M., Ostfeld, A. M., & Paul, O. (1983). Hostility, risk of coronary disease, and mortality. *Psychosomatic Medicine, 45,* 219–228.

Shively, C. A., Kaplan, J. R., & Adams, M. R. (1986). Effects of ovariectomy, social instability and social status on female *Macaca fascicularis* social behavior. *Physiology and Behavior, 36,* 1147–1153.

Siegman, A. W., Townsend, S. T., Civelek, A. C., & Blumenthal, R. S. (2000). Antagonistic behavior, dominance, hostility, and coronary heart disease. *Psychosomatic Medicine*, *62*, 248–257.

Simpson, P. (1983). Norepinephrine-stimulated hypertrophy of cultured rat myocardial cells is an alpha-1 adrenergic response. *Journal of Clinical Investigation*, *72*, 732–738.

Sims, E. A. H. (1982). Mechanisms of hypertension in the overweight. *Hypertension*, *4*(Suppl.), III4.1–III4.9.

Solano, L., Costa, M., Salvati, S., Coda, R., Aiuta, F., Mezzaroma, I., et al. (1993). Psychosocial factors and clinical evolution in HIV-1 infection: A longitudinal study. *Journal of Psychosomatic Research*, *37*(1), 39–51.

Solomon, G. F., Benton, D., Harker, J. O., Bonavida, B., & Fletcher, M. A. (1993). Prolonged asymptomatic states in HIV-seropositive persons with 50 CD4+ T-cells/mm3: Preliminary psychoimmunologic findings. *Journal of Acquired Immune Deficiency Syndrome*, *6*, 1172–1173.

Temoshok, L. (1985). Biopsychosocial studies on cutaneous malignant melanoma: Psychosocial factors associated with prognostic indicators, progression, psychophysiology and tumor-host response. *Social Science Medicine*, *20*, 833–840.

Temoshok, L., Heller, B. W., Sagebiel, R. W., Blois, M. S., Sweet, D. M., DiClemente, R. J., et al. (1985). The relationship of psychosocial factors to prognostic indicators in cutaneous malignant melanoma. *Journal of Psychosomatic Research*, *29*, 139–153.

Theorell, T., Blomkvist, V., Jonsson, H., Schulman, S., Berntorp, E., & Stigendal, L. (1995). Social support and the development of immune function in human immunodeficiency virus infection. *Psychosomatic Medicine*, *57*, 32–36.

Thompson, P. D., Cullinane, E. M., & Sady, S. P. (1988). Modest changes in high-density lipoprotein concentration and metabolism with prolonged exercise training. *Circulation*, *78*, 25–34.

Tobian, L. (1983). Salt and hypertension. *American Journal of Nephrology*, *3*(2), 80–87.

Tompkins, E. L., Clementa, A. J., & Taylor, D. P. (1980). Inhibition of aggressive behavior in rhesus monkeys by buspirone. *Research Communications in Psychology, Psychiatry, and Behavior*, *4*, 337–352.

Troisi, R. J., Weiss, S. T., Parker, D. R., Sparrow D., Young J. B., & Landsberg, L. (1991). Relation of obesity and diet to sympathetic nervous system activity. *Hypertension*, *17*, 669–677.

Twisk, J. W., Snel, J., Kemper, H. C., & van Mechelen, W. (1999). Changes in daily hassles and life events and the relationship with coronary heart disease risk factors: A 2-year longitudinal study in 27–29-year-old males and females. *Journal of Psychosomatic Research*, *46*, 229–240.

Verrier, R. L., & Mittelman, M. A. (1996). Life-threatening cardiovascular consequences of anger in patients with coronary heart disease. *Cardiology Clinics*, *14*, 289–307.

Vitaliano, P. P., Scanlan, J. M., Siegler, I. C., McCormick, W. C., & Knopp, R. H. (1998). Coronary heart disease moderates the relationship of chronic stress with the metabolic syndrome. *Health Psychology, 17,* 520–529.

Vujanovic, N., Yasumura, S., Hirabayashi, H., Lin, W., Watkins, S., Herberman, R., et al. (1995). Antitumor activities of subsets of human IL-2-activated natural killer cells in solid tissues. *Journal of Immunology, 154,* 281–289.

Watson, M., Haviland, J. S., Greer, S., Davidson, J., & Bliss, J. M. (1999). Influence of psychological response on survival in breast cancer: A population based cohort study. *Lancet, 354,* 1331–1336.

Watson, M., & Ramirez, A. (1991). Life events, personality, behavior and cancer. In M. Watson & C. Cooper (Eds.), *Cancer and stress: Recent research.* London: Wiley.

Webster, A. (1991). Cytomegalovirus as a possible co-factor in HIV disease progression. *Journal of Acquired Immune Deficiency Syndrome, 4*(Suppl.), S47–S52.

Webster, E. L., Elenkov, I. J., & Chrousos, G. P. (1997). The role of corticotropin-releasing hormone in neuroendocrine-immune interactions. *Molecular Psychiatry, 2,* 368–372.

Weisse C. (1992). Depression and immunocompetence: A review of the literature. *Psychological Bulletin, 111,* 475–489.

Wiedenfeld, S. A., O'Leary, A., Bandura, A., Brown, S., Levine, S., & Raska, K. (1990). Impact of perceived self-efficacy in coping with stressors on components of the immune system. *Journal of Personality and Social Psychology, 59,* 1082–1094.

Williams, J. E., Paton, C. C., Siegler, L. C., Eigenbrodt, M. L., Nieto, F. J., & Tyroler, H. A. (2000). Anger proneness predicts coronary heart disease risk: Prospective analysis from the Atherosclerosis Risk Communities (ARIC) Study. *Circulation, 101,* 2034–2039.

Wybran, J., Schandene, L., Van Vooren, J. P., Vandermoten, G., Latinne, D., Sonnet, J., et al. (1987). Immunologic properties of methionine-enkephalin, and therapeutic implications in AIDS, ARC, and cancer. *Annals of the New York Academy of Science, 496,* 108–114.

Yamasaki, S., Kan, N., Harada, T., Ichinose, Y., Morigichi, Y., Li, L., et al. (1993). Relationship between immunological parameters and survival of patients with liver metastases from breast cancer given immuno-chemotherapy. *Breast Cancer Research and Treatment, 26,* 55–65.

Young, J. B., & Landsberg, L. (1977a). Stimulation of the sympathetic nervous system during sucrose feeding. *Nature, 269,* 615–617.

Young, J. B., & Landsberg, L. (1977b). Suppression of sympathetic nervous system during fasting. *Science, 196,* 1473–1475.

Yudkin, J. S., Kumari, M., Humphries, S. E., & Mohamed-Ali, V. (1999). Inflammation, obesity, stress and coronary heart disease: Is interleukin-6 the link? *Atherosclerosis, 148,* 209–214.

Zieler, K. L., Maseri, A., Klassen, D., Rabinowitz, D., & Burgess, J. (1968). Muscle metabolism during exercise in man. *Transactions of the Association of American Physiologists, 81*, 266–268.

Zuckerman, M., & Antoni, M. H. (1995). Social support and its relationship to psychological physical and immune variables in HIV infection. *Clinical Psychology and Psychotherapy, 2*, 210–219.

3

PSYCHONEUROIMMUNOLOGY

MICHAEL J. FORLENZA AND ANDREW BAUM

Psychoneuroimmunology (PNI) is the basic science examining structural and functional links between behavioral, nervous, endocrine, and immune systems. This includes not only brain-to-immune networks but also neural and chemical pathways by which the immune system feeds information to the brain. These networks include brain and brainstem nuclei, sympathetic and parasympathetic neurons, neuroendocrine pathways, numerous immune cells, neurotransmitters, hormones, peptides, and cytokines. An increasing body of research demonstrates not only that the brain influences immune reactivity but that an activated immune system alters behavior. PNI is also a clinical science studying relationships between mood states and immunity as well as the impact of psychologically mediated immune system changes and health outcomes. There are considerable data suggesting that conditions such as depression affect immune activity, but it is less clear how these alterations influence susceptibility and resistance to infectious and inflammatory disease. However, a thorough understanding of the bidirectional nature of these interactions as well as health consequences of perturbations to these systems will ultimately inform sophisticated behavioral interventions designed to prevent and treat medical illness.

This chapter provides a broad overview of the field of PNI, including basic concepts, hypotheses, and findings. It is not intended as an exhaustive review but rather as a general introduction for clinicians, psychologists, and other scientists interested in a summary of PNI. As such, it introduces fundamental theories and relevant issues in PNI, beginning with an outline of the basic components and processes of immunity as well as a discussion of common in vitro and in vivo measurement systems used in PNI research. A thorough understanding of basic immunology is important for anyone interested in pursuing PNI research, but this summary will permit the reader to follow and interpret research reported later in the chapter. This section also includes discussion of timing of immune measurements.

This chapter also summarizes data pertaining to the structural relationships between the CNS, endocrine, and immune systems as well as immune system effects on behavior, highlighting promising psychological interventions that show the potential either to improve indexes of immunity or to decrease stress. Finally, this chapter addresses important issues related to the design and interpretation of PNI research, particularly with regard to studies in clinical populations. For example, does the pathophysiology of the disease in question involve disruption, dysregulation, or alteration of the immune system? Does the assay system used relate to appropriate or relevant immune processes?

Data accumulating from PNI researchers and laboratories are extensive and cover diverse arrays of experimental and quasi-experimental research. As a consequence, an exhaustive review of this literature is beyond the scope and space limitations of this chapter. Although the majority of data relevant to PNI are animal studies, this chapter will focus primarily on PNI research that has been carried out with adult humans (see Moyniham & Ader, 1996, for a review of animal models in PNI). This is not to suggest that animal work is unimportant or that it has not guided research with human populations. Rather, the addition of the large animal literature in PNI would make the chapter unwieldy and the different focus of researchers studying animals from that of researchers studying humans will add several layers of complexity to it. Human PNI research places relatively more emphasis on whether psychological factors alter immune system function and if those alterations influence susceptibility to disease.

WHAT IS THE IMMUNE SYSTEM?

Immune system generally refers to the vast system of cells, organs, lymphatics, and other bodily structures or agents that participate in defense of the body and homeostasis. It is complex and difficult for several reasons, including the inherent complexity of its organization. The immune system is layered, and many of its functions are redundant or reciprocal. Alteration of one aspect of immunity is often compensated for by another. Failure to appreciate the enormous complexity of the immune system makes understanding and interpreting the results from PNI research difficult at best. We refer the reader to Playfair (1995) or Rabin (1999) for more detailed information.

The immune system comprises many specialized organs, cells, and molecules that facilitate the process of protecting and defending against infectious agents such as bacteria, viruses, fungi, and parasites. Each of these structures interacts in complex networks; no part of the immune system acts in isolation. The unique ability of the immune system to recognize and distinguish host cells from nonhost cells (self vs. nonself) allows it to begin this protective function. Once foreign cells are recognized, they must be rendered inactive or destroyed and multiple mechanisms such as phagocytosis (literally "cell-eating") neutralize and eliminate these pathogens. To coordinate the complex processes of recognition and destruction, all of the cells of the immune system communicate with each other by way of secreted molecules termed cytokines. Cytokines are produced by immune cells and act as chemical messengers between cells or among other components of the immune system and the brain. Particular patterns of cytokine signals determine subsequent responses. Intercellular communication is not limited to the immune system; information concerning infection or tissue damage is carried to the CNS, which in turn sends regulatory signals back to the immune system. The immune system may therefore be considered a major participant in the maintenance of homeostasis along with the endocrine and nervous systems.

Appropriate functioning of the immune system dramatically reduces likelihood of infection and subsequent dysfunction, reducing the probability of infection or minimizing the duration or intensity of infections that do occur. Failures of immune defenses or of systemic resistance to infection reflect important sources of disability and premature mortality. Although many people understand that failures of the immune system lead to acute or chronic infection, there are additional disease states associated with overactivity or dysregulation of immune processes. Freedom from immune-mediated disease results from a controlled balance between immunity and tolerance of self-antigens. This has important implications when designing PNI interventions aimed at attenuating stress effects on immune function, suggesting that immune enhancement should be directed primarily at buffering suppressive effects or maintaining desirable levels of activity.

The immune system has traditionally been subdivided into several subsystems, each with its own characteristic mechanisms, processes, and effector cells. The *natural* or *innate immune system* is phylogentically very old; all multicellular organisms appear to have some analogous components of this system. The *acquired* or *adaptive immune system* emerged later in evolution and is present only in cartilaginous and bony fish, amphibians, reptiles, birds, and mammals (Thompson, 1995). The primary difference between the innate and acquired immune systems is in how they recognize microorganisms (Fearon & Locksley, 1996). Recent research also indicates that the immune response and the stress response may have common evolutionary origins (Ottaviani & Franceschi, 1995). Appreciation of the evolutionary history of stress and immunity fosters better understanding of the complex layering and seeming redundancy in stress and immune processes as well as vulnerability to disease (Henderson, Forlenza, & Baum, 2003). It also underscores the tremendous importance of host abilities to detect and protect itself from threatening infectious agents.

This chapter uses the traditional categorizations of innate and acquired immunity, but it should be emphasized that many if not most components of the immune system interact in a complex coordinated network of events that are not yet fully understood. In fact, many aspects of innate and acquired immunity are complementary (Fearon & Locksley, 1996), and dysregulation in one system often results in dysregulation in the other, increasing host vulnerability to disease. The designation of immune cells or processes as part of the innate immune system or the acquired immune system may best be viewed as heuristic devices used to classify and organize the tremendous complexity of immunity.

Innate Immunity

In general, aspects of innate immune responses are less often studied than acquired immune responses in PNI. Innate immunity is present at birth and functions rapidly (often within minutes) to protect the host from infection and tissue injury. Components of innate immunity are nonspecific and do not distinguish between different types of foreign molecules. That is, they need not recognize specific antigens (proteins on foreign cells that are capable of generating an immune response) and do not learn from previous exposures to particular pathogens. Rather, innate immunity functions more generically by providing physical and chemical barriers that discriminate only between self and nonself and by launching attacks by effectors that pursue nonself targets indiscriminately. Barriers include skin and mucous membranes as well as bactericidal chemicals in tears and saliva and gastrointestinal tract secretions. These barriers represent the first line of defense against infection by preventing access to internal tissue. When these barriers are breached and pathogens enter the body, other defenses are brought to bear on nascent infections. These innate defenses include numerous cells and molecules responsible for recognizing and destroying foreign antigens. As previously stated, the optimum functioning of these cells and proteins does not depend on previous exposure and sensitization by antigen.

The effector cells of innate immunity include *neutrophils, mast cells, monocytes, macrophages,* and *dendritic cells. Neutrophils* and *macrophages* act as primary phagocytes, and macrophages and *dendritic cells* function as antigen presenting cells (APC). Phagocytic activity involves entrapping and engulfing foreign elements with the cell body or extensions of it. APCs are responsible for presenting phagocytosed foreign antigens to T-cells and B-cells of the acquired immune system. Activity of APCs constitutes one example of the many interactions between innate and acquired immune systems and will be described in more detail later.

Neutrophils, or polymorphonuclear leukocytes (PMN), are the largest cellular component of the immune system, comprising approximately 60% of circulating white blood cells (WBC). PMNs function as phagocytes and are the first line of host defense against infectious agents that enter the body. Their targets consist of bacteria, viruses, and virally infected cells, protozoa, fungi, and tumor cells (Smith, 1994). They are capable of secreting a variety of regulatory cytokines and act as principle components of acute inflammation. PMNs can exist in several states of activation, from dormant to fully activated, and may be primed or activated by various extracellular signals that facilitate a more powerful antimicrobial response once the cells encounter microorganisms. Following phagocytosis of microorganisms, neutrophils kill these cells by oxidative processes such as the formation of reactive oxygen species (ROS). ROS such as superoxide (O_2^-) and hydrogen peroxide (H_2O_2) are very effective cell-killing mechanisms, but are also capable of generating extensive tissue damage in the host (Smith, 1994). Chronically activated PMNs have been implicated in a number of inflammatory diseases (Weiss, 1989).

The monocyte–macrophage system is made up of large mononucleated phagocytes with multiple functions. These cells develop from pluripotent stem cells in the bone marrow. As long as they remain in the peripheral circulation, they are termed *monocytes*. However, once they are summoned by chemical stimuli and migrate into tissue spaces, they are termed *macrophages*. Microglia, Kupffer cells, and Langerhans cells are macrophage-derived cells found in the CNS, liver, and the skin, respectively. Macrophages are similar to PMNs and may engulf microbes, kill tumor cells, process and present antigen to T- and B-cells, and participate in control of blood concentrations of lipids (Adams, 1994). Dysregulation of this lipid-controlling function has been implicated in the development of atherosclerotic plaques (Berliner et al., 1995; Wick, Perschinka, & Xu, 1999).

Natural killer cells (NK) are perhaps the most studied cells in PNI. NK cells are a subset of large granular lymphocytes and make up approximately 15% of the lymphocyte population. Unlike T-lymphocytes and B-lymphocytes, NK are capable of recognizing and destroying foreign antigens without previous sensitization. This nonspecific recognition allows NK to be categorized as part of innate immunity. NK cells appear to play a crucial role in defense against infectious agents and virally infected cells (Whiteside &

Herberman, 1989). Cytotoxicity is accomplished through several mechanisms, including the secretion of perforins or proteins that create pores in target cell membranes and cause osmotic lysis. They also contain granule of lytic enzymes that can destroy or damage pathogens or disrupt their protective membranes. NK cytotoxic activity may be upregulated (termed *lymphokine activated killer* cells, LAK) if stimulated with the cytokines interleukin-2 or interferon γ (Whiteside & Herberman, 1989). NK also secrete a host of regulatory cytokines that help coordinate immune responses (Whiteside & Herberman, 1989).

Other white blood cells that function as part of innate immunity include *basophils, eosinophils*, and *mast cells*. Basophils and the closely related mast cells play a role in Type 1 immediate hypersensitivity reactions (tissue-damaging immune responses to allergens) and acute inflammatory responses. Antigens or certain antibodies cause basophils and mast cells to release stored molecules such as histamine that increases vascular permeability and attracts PMLs and macrophages (Playfair, 1995). Eosinophils also function in Type 1 allergic reactions and are further specialized for destruction of parasites (Huston, 1997).

In addition to the effector cells of the innate immune system, there are a series of soluble proteins found in serum that are capable of initiating and assisting in innate immune responses. The complement system consists of approximately 20 proteins produced by the liver that function prominently in bacterial and fungal infections (Playfair, 1995). These proteins are activated by microbial surface markers as well as by circulating antibody. Activation of complement results in a cascade of enzymes, leading to opsonization (coating of antigens with complement proteins) and osmotic lysis of microbes (through creation of cytolytic membrane attack complexes) as well as by summoning other phagocytic or inflammatory cells (Huston, 1997). This latter function results from the fact that some soluble proteins attract cells that are responsive to chemotaxis. Complement proteins also function to enhance the acquired immune response through the promotion of antigen processing and presentation by B-cells to T-cells and by direct activation of B-cells (Nielsen, Fischer, & Leslie, 2000).

Acute phase proteins (e.g., C-reactive protein, haptoglobin, fibrinogen) constitute additional systemic mechanisms against infection and tissue damage. Plasma concentrations of these proteins increase dramatically as an early response to infection, and their production and secretion from the liver is controlled by various cytokines (e.g., IL-6, TNF-a, INF-γ) and growth factors (Suffredini, Fantuzzi, Badolata, Oppenheim, & O'Grady, 1999). These proteins enhance immune resistance by facilitating opsonization, complement activation, leukocyte activation, protein and ion transport, and phagocytosis (Suffredini et al., 1999). Although the pattern of cytokine stimulation and acute phase response differs in different conditions, it is generally thought that acute phase proteins help to regulate the inflammation, and as with many immune-related phenomena, the response is not always beneficial (Gabay & Kushner, 1999).

Finally, the major histocompatibility complex (MHC) refers to a series of genes that code for cell surface proteins termed human leukocyte antigens (HLA). MHC molecules are subdivided into two types. Class I are found on all nucleated cells and class II are found on monocytes, macrophages, B-cells, and dendritic cells (Huston, 1997). The HLA form the molecular basis for self- non–self-discrimination and are responsible for presenting foreign antigens to various subclasses of T-cells. Cytotoxic T-cells (CD8$^+$) will recognize foreign antigen only if it is bound to class I HLA, and helper T-cells (CD4$^+$) will recognize foreign antigen only if bound to class II HLA.

Acquired Immunity

Similar to the innate immune system, the acquired or adaptive immune system is made up of both cellular and molecular components. Lymphocytes are the primary cells of acquired immunity and are divided into two broad classes: T-cells and B-cells. T-cells are responsible for what has been called cellular immunity and can destroy antigen-bearing cells directly. B-cells produce circulating antibodies and confer humoral immunity. Together, these classes of effector mount stronger, more sharply focused attacks on antigens surviving innate immune system actions. Although innate and acquired immunity overlap somewhat, these two systems are not redundant. The primary distinction between the acquired and innate immune systems is the formers' ability to recognize and remember specific antigens. The acquired immune system allows the host to develop immunity against specific individual infectious agents and mount more effective, targeted defenses against them.

T-lymphocytes make up approximately 60 to 70% of peripheral blood lymphocytes, and each T-cell is genetically programmed to recognize and respond to specific antigens. It has been estimated that there are 10^9 different types of basic T-cell clones, developing in the bone marrow and migrating to the thymus for further maturation and differentiation. It is in the thymus that the T-cells take on characteristic cell surface markers. T-cells with the marker CD4$^+$ generally have a helper function (activating and coordinating the immune response), and T-cells with the marker CD8$^+$ generally have cytotoxic (along with CD28$^+$) or suppressor functions (along with CD11$^+$; Huston, 1997).

Naive CD4$^+$ cells secrete IL-2 when initially activated by antigen and differentiate into subpopulations of cells designated T_H1 or T_H2. The difference between the subsets of T-cells concerns the predominant pattern of cytokines secreted by further stimulation. T_H1 cells primarily secrete IL-2, interferon gamma (INF-γ), and tumor necrosis factor beta (TNF-ß), whereas

T_H2 cells primarily secrete IL-4, IL-5, IL-9, IL-10, and IL-13. T_H1 cytokines tend to generate cell-mediated inflammation and T_H2 cytokines mediate humeral allergic reactions (Huston, 1997). It is important to note that T_H1 and T_H2 responses will inhibit each other (Vedhara, Fox, & Wang, 1999). Once activated, cytokines from $CD4^+$ cells may stimulate B-cells to generate an antibody response and may stimulate macrophages to become tumoricidal (Adams, 1994). In addition, $CD8^+$ cells become cytotoxic, killing virally infected cells.

B-cells ($CD19^+$) normally make up 10 to 20% of circulating lymphocytes. Like T-cells, B-cells recognize specific antigens that bind to receptors on the cell surface. Antigenic binding causes B-cells to rapidly divide and differentiate into plasma cells that in turn begin to synthesize and secrete antibodies (immunoglobulins), proteins that bind to the antigen. Antibodies participate in opsonization (similar to complement proteins), prevent antigens from infecting host cells, and facilitate phagocytosis by PMLs and macrophages. There are five general classes of antibodies, and each can be divided into several subclasses. IgM is produced as part of a primary response from exposure to a novel antigen, and several days are needed for this antibody response to develop. If this antigen is encountered in the future, the secondary response will develop more rapidly, will last longer, and the new antibodies (IgG) will have a much greater binding affinity for the antigen (Ahmed & Gray, 1996). A unique feature of the acquired immune system is immunologic memory. As part of the primary immune response, subclasses of both T-cells and B-cells develop into memory cells and may lie dormant for years until they are re-exposed to the same antigen. Re-exposure will activate the memory cells to produce a larger and much more rapid secondary response.

HOW IS IMMUNITY MEASURED IN PNI RESEARCH?

Many important methodological issues must be addressed when conducting PNI research. Some of these relate to important aspects of stress (i.e., timing, duration, intensity, see Baum, Cohen, & Hall, 1993, for a detailed discussion) while others concern assessment of important variables such as smoking, diet, physical activity, sleep, and alcohol consumption. For example, both tobacco smoke and nicotine are known to alter many aspects of immune function (McAllister-Sistilli et al., 1998) and smoking and tobacco withdrawal alter hypothalamic-pituitary axis (HPA) hormones in ways similar to acute stress (Pickworth & Fant, 1998). Nutritional status and dietary lipids are related to alterations in immunity (De Pablo & Alvarez De Cienfuegos, 2000) and exercise has been shown to modify several aspects of innate immunity (Simon, 1991; Woods, Davis, Smith, & Nieman, 1999).

Finally, sleep has been suggested as one mechanism mediating the stress immune relationship (Hall et al., 1998). Of particular importance is the fact that distressed people often act in ways that can both potentiate distress and alter their immune function (Kiecolt-Glaser & Glaser, 1988). For valid conclusions to be drawn, it is necessary that researchers measure and control for these host variables.

Perhaps one of the most important issues related to measurement in PNI are the relationships among the timing of putative immunomodulators (e.g., stress), subsequent alterations in measures of immune processes, and disease. Studies involving naturalistic stressors become problematic when trying to determine the relationship between stress, pathogen exposure, and immune changes. For example, it is unclear when stress is most likely to increase susceptibility to infection relative to pathogen exposure (Cohen & Williamson, 1991). Laboratory studies examining the impact of short-term distress on immune indexes may clarify the nature and timing of immune changes over time, but most of these changes are transient and clinical relevance is uncertain. Results from these kinds of studies may best be used to understand basic mechanisms in PNI rather than in making assertions concerning susceptibility to disease or progression of existing disease.

In addition to difficulties inherent in validly and reliably measuring psychological and behavioral factors in humans, measurement in PNI is further complicated by the need for both descriptive measurement of the immune system and more functional assessment of immune system responsiveness. There are several assay systems available, each of which provides different information about the state of the immune system at any given moment. Each assay technique carries inherent advantages and disadvantages (see Vedhara, Fox, & Wang, 1999 for detailed discussion). A clear understanding of these will help clarify the relevance and significance of PNI research. Importantly, no single assay provides information about the immune system as a whole (Kiecolt-Glaser & Glaser, 1995). No measurement currently exists that will fully characterize the state of host immunity in its entirety. Because of this, statements concerning immunosuppression and susceptibility to disease based on single measurements are difficult to interpret. Many researchers now routinely measure several different aspects of the immune system simultaneously in an effort to examine patterns of immune responsiveness.

Cytokines

Cytokines are soluble proteins synthesized and secreted by immune cells of the innate and acquired immune systems and are vital for the normal regulation of immunity. These proteins act as chemical messengers between immune cells and can have wide-ranging effects. Cytokines can activate immune cells, direct them to proliferate, influence the movement of immune cells to sites of infection or injury, and cause them to differentiate into different classes of effector cells (Maier & Watkins, 1998). Cytokines may act on the cell that secreted them (autocrine) or may bind to other immune cells (paracrine). Important to PNI, cytokines also signal the CNS about the state of the immune system and engender alteration of neural and endocrine activity as well as behavior. Although detailed mechanisms are not fully understood, there appear to be several ways for the immune system to communicate with the CNS (Maier & Watkins, 1998). Research has shown that there are specialized transport mechanisms that actively bring cytokines across the blood–brain barrier (Banks, Oritz, Plotkin, & Kastin, 1991) and that cytokines enter the CNS at sites where the blood–brain barrier is weak (Saper & Bredr, 1994). In addition, Maier, Goehler, Fleshner, and Watkins (1998) reported a series of studies detailing the binding of certain cytokines to receptors on the vagus nerve, which in turn rapidly carries the signal to the CNS.

Enumerative Assays

Enumerative tests describe the status of the immune system by counting the number of cells, cytokines, or antibodies in a given blood sample. These measures can be used as both baseline values and to assess changes over time. Absolute cell counts and percentages provide basic information about the state of the immune system, and values can be obtained by flow cytometry for the total number of leukocytes as well as subpopulations such as PML, $CD4^+$, or NK cells. It is important to note that transient alterations in the number or percentages of cells are most often interpreted as reflecting immune cell mobilization and trafficking (the movement of cells to and from stored reservoirs) rather than a change in actual cell number (Kiecolt-Glaser & Glaser, 1995). This is because these measures are typically derived from blood samples and reflect only numbers of cells in peripheral circulation. Most cells remain in tissues, lymphatics, or immune organs such as the spleen. In addition, the health consequences of these changes in healthy people, especially when modest in magnitude, are unknown. Simply enumerating the total number of antibodies does not necessarily provide information about immune status or responsiveness because antibodies respond to specific pathogens, and it is impossible to know from cell counts if specific antibodies are responding to a specific pathogen (Miller & Cohen, 2001). This problem can be addressed by measuring antibodies to specific known pathogens.

Enzyme-Linked Immunosorbent Assay

The enzyme-linked immunosorbent assay (ELISA) is one of the more common techniques for the detection and quantification of antibodies. The

ELISA techniques are versatile, and procedures can be adapted to measure levels of total antibody in a sample as well as levels of specific antibodies. The assay is based on principles of specificity characteristic of antigen–antibody binding. The basic procedure involves coating a plastic plate with antigens and then introducing the test sample containing the antibodies. Antibodies specific to the antigens on the plate will bind to the antigens and all other antibodies are washed off. This is referred to as *antibody capture*. A second antibody specific for the captured antibodies is then introduced. This second antibody is linked to an enzyme that changes color when a chemical substrate is added in the final step. The amount of color change is associated with the amount of enzyme in the sample, which in turn is associated with the amount of captured antibody.

The ELISA can also be used to measure concentrations of cytokines in plasma or serum. Procedures are similar to those used to measure antibody except that the plates are coated with antibodies specific for specific cytokines.

Functional Assays

In contrast to enumerative assays, functional assays measure basic immunological responses to challenge or stimulation. Tests may be in vitro, in which immune cells are removed from the host, placed into culture, and then aspects of immune function are measured. Assays may also measure in vivo responses to challenges such as vaccinations in the natural context of the body. The combination of enumerative and functional assays is most informative in that it allows the determination of the functional relevance of alterations in cell numbers (Vedhara et al., 1999).

Mitogenic Proliferation

One of the more common functional assays used in PNI is termed the lymphocyte proliferation or blastogenesis assay. This assay is important in that it measures the nonspecific proliferative response of lymphocytes to mitogenic stimulation (a mitogen is a substance capable of nonspecifically activating lymphocytes), and it is assumed that individuals demonstrating poor proliferation would be more susceptible to infectious disease. Common mitogens used in PNI research include phytohemagglutinin (PHA, stimulates T-cells), conconavalin A (Con A, stimulates T-cells), and pokeweed mitogen (PWM, stimulates T- and B-cells). The basic procedure involves isolation of lymphocytes from a sample of blood in culture with mitogen in various concentrations and a radioactive label. As the cells replicate because of mitogenic stimulation, they incorporate the radioactive label into their own DNA. The amount of radioactivity emitted (quantified as counts per minute; cpm) is proportional to the amount of proliferation.

Although the proliferation assay is clearly a step forward from basic enumeration of cells, it has been criticized because of its nonspecific nature. In vivo, T-cells and B-cells proliferate in response to interactions with specific antigens, and therefore only a small subset of cells will divide on exposure. However, the mitogen stimulation used in the assay induces massive nonspecific proliferation, and it is unclear how these actions relate to each other.

Natural Killer Cells Cytotoxicity

Another common assay used in PNI is the NK cytotoxicity assay. This assay measures the capacity of nonactivated NK cells to kill cancer cells in vitro. Isolated NK cells are incubated for three to four hours at various concentrations with K562, an NK-sensitive cancer cell line, that have been labeled with radioactive chromium. The more efficient NK cells are at lysing target cells, the more radioactive material is released into fluid media around the cells. Radioactivity in the media is measured and cytotoxicity expressed in lytic units (the quantity of effector cells needed to kill a set number of target cells; Whiteside, Bryant, Day, & Herberman, 1990). NK cytotoxicity assays are commonly used because of the known sensitivity of NK cells to psychological stress.

Simulated Antibody and Cytokine Assays

As mentioned, concentrations of antibodies or cytokines can be detected and quantitated in plasma samples. More commonly, antibody and cytokine concentrations are measured in supernatant following in vitro mitogen or antigen stimulation of immune cells. This procedure provides functional information about the immunoreactivity of immune cells. In addition, cytokine bioassays provide information on the bioactivity of the cytokines being measured. These assays measure concentration of cytokines as a function of its role in immune cell activation.

Measures of Innate Immunity

Less common in PNI than the previously discussed functional assays for cellular and humoral immunity are assays measuring activity of the innate immune system. These assays include measurement of neutrophil or monocyte *chemotaxis* (the ability of cells to move toward a microbial target by flowing chemoattractant chemicals), phagocytosis of *staphylococcus aureas* bacteria, and neutrophil *oxidative burst* (the ability of activated neutrophils to produce microbial-reactive oxygen radicals when stimulated in vitro).

In Vivo Assays

In addition to the in vitro assays described, immune processes can be measured in vivo. The assumption is that in vivo measurement will more closely mimic natural responses to antigen exposure. Typically, research participants are inoculated with a common antigen or a vaccine and a response is measured. These may include the time it takes to develop an antibody response or the extent to which people demonstrate hypersensitivity. There are two types of skin tests used to assess hypersensitivity to antigens: Immediate hypersensitivity (type I) is antibodymediated and delayed hypersensitivity (type IV) is T-cell (CD4[+]) mediated.

ORIGINS OF PNI AND ITS ROLE IN MIND–BODY RELATIONSHIPS

Modern PNI research began with serendipitous findings from studies involving conditioned taste aversion (Ader, 1974). Laboratory rats were conditioned by pairing cyclophosphamide (the unconditional stimulus that produces nausea) with saccharin-flavored water (the conditional stimulus). It was expected that animals conditioned with the saccharin–cyclophosphamide combination would subsequently avoid drinking when given saccharin alone. However, the investigators discovered that many of the animals died due to infection. A detailed analysis revealed that in addition to nausea, cyclophosphamide was a potent immunosuppressant, and it was hypothesized that the heightened mortality was a result of the conditioned immunosuppression. Ader and Cohen (1975) subsequently designed a taste-aversion conditioning paradigm in which this hypothesis was specifically tested. As before, taste aversion was conditioned in rats by pairing saccharin with cyclophosphamide. Three days after conditioning, all animals were injected with sheep red blood cells that were expected to elicit an immune response. When antibody titers where measured six days later, no antisheep red blood cell antibody was detected in conditioned animals or in those treated with cyclophosphamide. In contrast, high antibody titers were observed in placebo-treated rats, unconditioned rats, and in conditioned rats that were not reexposed to saccharin. They concluded that conditioned animals reexposed to saccharin were significantly immunosuppressed (Ader & Cohen, 1975). Much of the subsequent work in conditioning and immune function focused on conditioned immunosuppression in rats and mice (for review, see Ader & Cohen, 1993).

The importance of these early findings cannot be overstated. Traditionally, the immune system was considered an autonomous, self-regulating system with no interactions between it and other homeostatic or regulatory systems. The conditioned alteration of an immune system response by a previously neutral stimulus not capable of altering the immune response on its own implied that the immune system and the nervous system were linked.

Although this may not seem surprising today, in the mid-1970s this was revolutionary.

Early studies of stress and immunity in humans examined a wide range of experimental and naturally occurring stress, including space flight and recovery (Fischer et al., 1972; Kimzey, 1975), sleep deprivation (Palmblad et al., 1976, 1979), life change stress (Cohen-Cole et al., 1981; Locke & Heisel, 1977), bereavement (Bartrop et al., 1977), academic stress (Kasl, Evans, & Niederman, 1979), and examination stress (Dorian et al., 1981). Immune outcomes included numbers of WBC and subsets, phagocytosis and lymphocyte cytotoxicity, stimulated cytokine and antibody production, and seroconversion and antibody response to vaccine challenge. These studies established that psychosocial stressors have reliable effects on a number of immune system parameters in humans and that, in general, the effects tend toward immune suppression (Locke, 1982). In addition, evidence suggested differential effects of acute and chronic stress on immune function and differential responsiveness of cellular and humoral immune systems to stress (Locke, 1982).

Since the first publication of the edited book *Psychoneuroimmunology* in 1981 (Ader, 1981), the field of PNI has expanded rapidly. At the basic level, research continues to shed light on neuro–immune mechanisms, including detailed studies on the immune modulation of behavior. Laboratory work with humans has also clarified the importance of individual differences such as stress reactivity for immune outcomes. PNI research has begun to understand some of the clinical implications of stress-induced immune dysregulation by examining disease outcomes in stressed people.

Underlying Models in PNI

Many biobehavioral models of health and illness postulate that neuro-endocrine and immune systems are proximate biological pathways mediating the impact of psychosocial variables on health and suggest that stress-induced alterations of these systems are important mechanisms in the etiology or progression of physical disease states (Reichlin, 1993). An extensive body of basic research exists along with numerous reviews (Biondi & Picardi, 1999; Cohen & Herbert, 1996) and meta-analyses (Herbert & Cohen, 1993) evaluating immediate and long-term stress effects on immune or endocrine system function. Although individual studies will vary in the details of their specific hypotheses, all human PNI research is based to some extent on models that feature mood or stress as causes of suppression or dysregulation in the immune system, which in turn lead to poor health. This may be considered a mediational model whereby alterations in the immune system mediate the influence of psychological or social factors on health. This model has been referred to as the S→ I→ H model, where S is stress, I is immune dysregulation, and H is health (Keller, Shiflett, Schleifer, & Bartlett, 1994). Although this is considered the direct path between stress and health, models also suggest indirect pathways whereby stress alters important health behaviors (e.g., diet, physical activity, sleep) known to influence immunity, and it is likely that there are complex reciprocal interactions between direct and indirect paths. Moreover, methodological difficulties inherent in PNI research preclude most studies from examining the entire model. Rather, studies focus on either links between psychosocial factors and immune function or psychosocial factors in health.

The first path on the general PNI model asserts that psychological factors alter or influence immune function, and there is clear evidence for this assertion. Moreover, many studies test hypotheses concerning the autonomic or neuroendocrine mediation of stress effects on immunity. For clear interpretations, psychological factors should be independent of specific health behaviors such as smoking, diet, or exercise known to influence immunity. Most often, hypotheses being tested concern negative influences of acute or chronic stressful experience, poor coping, lack of social support, or traits such as negative affect on the immune system. That is, these negative events or traits are assumed to lead to immunosuppression. In contrast, most intervention studies are designed to either increase coping or support or to decrease negative affect and distress, which in turn should improve indexes of immunity.

The implication of these immune alterations is that immunosuppression (resulting from stress or some other psychological or behavioral factor) should leave the host more vulnerable to disease, and Cohen and Williamson (1991) summarized evidence for associations among stress, increases in illness behaviors, and infectious pathology. However, it is not clear how suppressed the immune system must be to increase susceptibility to infection, when windows of "opportunity" exist for infectious agents to gain a foothold, or how often or long these opportunities last. This model also fails to explain the impact of stress and distress on autoimmune and inflammatory diseases that result from overactivity of the immune system. For PNI to move forward, newer models must be proposed that specify instances in which stress inhibits or enhances aspects of immune function.

Connections Between the Nervous and Immune Systems

Regulation of the immune system is partly a function of internal systemic activity but also appears to be affected by the brain and regulatory systems such as the nervous and endocrine systems. Several structures are located in the hypothalamus (paraventricular nuclei) and the brain stem (paragigantocellular nuclei, parabranchial nuclei, and locus ceruleus; Chrousos, 1998), which may be influenced in this process, and nuclei in the limbic forebrain and cerebral cortex play a role in immunoregulation (Felton et al., 1991). Activities in these central systems are carried to the periphery via the hypothalamic–pituitary–adrenal axis (HPA) and the sympathetic nervous system (SNS) that in turn cause release of hormones that stimulate or restrain specific immune system functions.

Research has shown that there is extensive innervation of both primary and secondary lymphoid tissues such as the spleen, liver, and lymph nodes (Felton & Felton, 1991). These observations provided an anatomical link between the brain and the immune system. In addition, immune cells have receptors for, and respond to, hormones and neurotransmitters released by the nervous and endocrine systems. The binding of hormones and neuro-transmitters influences activation, trafficking, and functioning of immune cells. For example, cortisol is broadly immunosuppressive and inhibits lym-phocyte proliferation and phagocytosis, as well as production of antibodies and various cytokines in humans and rodents (Munck & Guyer, 1991). Cortisol also has a counter-regulatory role in suppressing inflammation as part of the acute-phase response to infection (Chrousos, 1995). The cate-cholamines epinephrine and norepinephrine also play important roles in modulation of the immune response. When bound to adrenergic receptors on immune cells, these hormones have been shown to alter cellular migration, lymphocyte proliferation, antibody secretion, and cell lysis by macrophages and NK cells (Madden & Livnat, 1991). The combination of stress-induced cortisol and catecholamines alters the balance between T_H1 and T_H2 cells by inhibiting the secretion of IL-12 and increasing the secretion of IL-10 from macrophages. Increasing levels of Il-10 inhibits T_H1 cells and cell-mediated immunity while stimulating B-cells and humoral immunity (Elenkov, Papanicolaou, Wilder, & Chrousos, 1996).

Communication between brain and immune systems is bidirectional. Not only can the CNS exert influence over the immune system, the immune system is also capable of signaling the brain and affecting responses. Acti-vated immune cells secrete cytokines (e.g., TNF-a, IL-1, IL-6) that activate CNS stress-response systems alerting the brain to ongoing immune responses to foreign antigens and host tissue damage (Besodovsky et al., 1992). As noted, these signals likely reach the CNS through several mechanisms, and this is an area of active research (for more detailed discussions of possible pathways, see Chrousos, 1998; Maier & Watkins, 1998). The concept of a bidirectional feedback loop between the CNS and the immune system implies that perturbations at any point in the loop will be reflected in subsequent responses. Both physical and psychological stressors activate these biobehavioral pathways, although their entry into the feedback loop will be in different places.

An activated immune system also has consequences for behavior. The constellation of common signs and symptoms of infection (e.g., fever, fatigue, lethargy, loss of appetite) are not the direct result of infectious agents, but rather result from the actions of cytokines in the brain (Dantzer et al., 1998). For example, IL-1 produced by activated monocytes and macrophages stimulates neutrophil leukocytosis, synthesis of acute phase proteins, activates the HPA axis, and induces fever and sleep while suppressing appetite and thirst (Kennedy & Jones, 1990). Resulting patterns of behaviors are experienced as illness and can be distinguished from actual verified infection (Cohen & Williamson, 1991). In addition, although most people consider these symptoms distressing, they indicate that the immune system is operating. Research has found it useful to separate verified infection from these symptoms of illness that often reflect immune system resistance (e.g., Cohen, Tyrrell, & Smith, 1991).

Stress and Immune Function

Of particular interest in PNI research are stress effects on immune function, and this review will highlight several areas of important research. However, classifying stress and stressful events is difficult, and researchers have debated definitions of stress for some time. For our purposes, stress may be defined as a negative experience that is associated with threat, harm, or excessive demand (Baum, 1990). Stressors may be considered thoughts or events that connote threat or cause loss or harm. The psychological and physiological responses that follow stressor exposure are generally considered adaptive in that they support coping directed toward adjustment and control.

Stress is commonly characterized as acute or chronic. Although this may provide a useful heuristic, it is problematic in that it lacks precision, and the terms are meaningful only in relation to each other. Also, it does not distinguish between durations of events, threats, or responses. A more useful categorization of stress may be laboratory stress as distinguished from naturalistic stress. For both ethical and logistical reasons, human laboratory research studying stress and immunity most often involve short-term exposure to stressful or challenging tasks such as mental arithmetic or giving a speech. This allows for more precise measurement of stressor exposure, stress experience, and immune responding.

Laboratory Stress

Laboratory research in PNI typically requires research participants to be involved in one or more sessions in a laboratory setting. Following arrival at the lab, most participants are fitted with an in-dwelling catheter that is placed in a vein in the anticubital fossa. This allows researchers to draw blood from participants several times without the need for additional stressful needle sticks. Following an acclimation period that allows for any immediate neuroendocrine responses to the needle stick to dissipate, participants are exposed to one or more demanding or challenging tasks. The tasks usually range from 5 to 20 minutes in length. Mental arithmetic tasks often involve serial subtraction of odd numbers from larger four- or five-digit numbers. Participants are prodded to maintain a rapid, error-free pace. Speech tasks demand that participants prepare and deliver a short speech defending themselves against a fictitious accusation. Often these speeches are video-taped and played back to the participants. A third common laboratory stressor requires married couples to discuss important marital problems for a specified length of time. Each of these tasks requires that participants engage in tasks that they may perceive as demanding or threatening. Multiple blood draws are taken to assess immune system changes in response to the stress task. Initial or baseline blood draws allow researchers to control for any prestress interindividual differences in the status of the immune system. Blood is taken during the performance of the task, and four or five draws may subsequently be taken over various time intervals to determine the time course of immune system responses following the termination of the task.

Exposure to acute laboratory stress alters the number and percentages of lymphocyte subsets as well as some aspects of cellular immunity. Common findings include increases in the number of NK cells (Bachen et al., 1992; Cacioppo et al., 1995; Delahanty et al., 1996; Herbert et al., 1994; Naliboff et al., 1991; Sgoutas-Emch et al., 1994), increases in NK cytotoxicity (Bachen et al., 1992; Cacioppo et al., 1995; Delahanty et al., 1996; Naliboff et al., 1991; Sgoutas-Emch et al., 1994), and increases in the number of $CD8^+$ cells (Bachen et al., 1992; Cacioppo et al., 1995; Herbert et al., 1994; Manuck, Cohen, Rabin, Muldoan, & Bachen, 1991; Naliboff et al., 1991; Sgoutas-Emch et al., 1994). The functional significance of this latter finding is uncertain because other markers are needed in addition to $CD8^+$ to determine how the cell is acting. Studies have also found decreases in lymphocyte proliferation to Con A (Bachen et al., 1992; Cacioppo et al., 1995; Delahanty et al., 1996; Sgoutas-Emch et al., 1994; Zakowski, Cohen, Hall, Wollman, & Baum, 1994) and PHA (Bachen et al., 1992; Delahanty et al., 1996; Herbert et al., 1994; Manuck et al., 1991). Numbers of WBC, $CD3^+$, $CD4^+$, and $CD19^+$ cells were often unchanged by laboratory stress. It is interesting to note that many researchers found that immune changes were most pronounced in people demonstrating high cardiovascular reactivity to stress and were either small or nonexistent in people classified as low reactors (Cacioppo et al., 1995; Herbert et al., 1994; Manuck et al., 1991; Sgoutas-Emch et al., 1994; Zakowski, McAllister, Deal, & Baum, 1992). The observed immune changes likely reflect combinations of sympathetic activation and parasympathetic withdrawal (Kiecolt-Glaser, Cacioppo, Malarkey, & Glaser, 1992). These effects are abolished by adrenergic block-ade (Bachen et al., 1995). The psychological and neurobiological substrates of high cardiovascular reactivity are currently not known. Immune changes associated with high reactivity imply that these people may experience a greater magnitude and frequency of immune disruption in their daily lives.

Naturalistic Stress

A common criticism of PNI laboratory studies concerns their external validity. The stressors used may not reflect actual experiences (most people are not asked to perform serial subtraction by sevens while someone prods them to go faster) and issues of timing and control of other influences also affect the generalizability of those findings. Researchers have addressed this problem by examining immune changes in people during naturally stressful situations. For example, Schedlowski et al. (1993) evaluated immune changes resulting from first-time tandem parachutists. Consistent with laboratory data, results showed increases in NK numbers and cytotoxic activity and increases in number of $CD8^+$ cells. In contrast, Schedlowski et al. found increases in $CD2^+$, $CD3^+$, and $CD4^+$ cell numbers. Although these immune changes showed rapid increases immediately after the jump, all of the immune parameters were decreased one hour after the jump. Delahanty et al. (1996) also found evidence of this NK cell activity in the lab, concluding that NK show a biphasic response: Immediate increases are followed by decreases to below baseline across time.

One of the more commonly studied naturalistic stressors is academic exam stress. An early example of this was reported by Dorian et al. (1981), in which immune function was studied in Canadian psychiatric residents taking the Oral Fellowship Examination, a major qualifying exam that allows successful candidates to bill the National Health care system. Lymphoblast transformation in the psychiatric residents was significantly lower during the high stress period when compared to age- and sex-matched controls. This type of stressor may be considered relatively short-term, although preparations for and distress about the exam may be extended. Most people experience exam stress at some point in their lives, which makes studying exam stress a valuable tool in understanding how common everyday stressors affect immune function. In addition, this research design allows for prospective examination of *changes* in immune function before and after taking academic exams.

Psychosocial and immune data are usually collected at two time points: Baseline data are collected weeks or months before the exam at a time that is presumably less stressful than immediately before the exam. The second time point may be immediately before or after taking the exam. Researchers can then analyze changes in immune parameters in response to testing. In a series of exam stress studies, Glaser, Kiecolt-Glaser, and colleagues have shown that exam stress leads to increases in antibody titers to latent

Epstein-Barr virus (Glaser, Kiecolt-Glaser, Speicher, & Holliday, 1985; Glaser, Pearl, Kiecolt-Glaser, & Malarkey, 1994; Glaser, Rice, Sheridan, et al., 1987; Glaser et al., 1999) and herpes simplex virus type 1 and cytomegalovirus (Glaser et al., 1985), as well as increases in circulating IgG, IgM, and IgA (Glaser et al., 1986). Exam stress also leads to decreases in stimulated INF-gamma production (Glaser et al., 1986, 1987) NKCA (Glaser et al., 1986), B-cell transformation (Kiecolt-Glaser, Speicher, Holliday, & Glaser, 1984), and memory T-cell proliferative response to EBV particles (Glaser et al., 1993). Interpreting these alterations becomes problematic if one looks only for unidirectional (i.e., suppressive) effects of stress on immunity. Instead, results are interpreted as suppression of cellular immune responses requiring a compensatory upregulation of humoral immunity. This perspective is supported by Marshall et al. (1998), who have shown that stress associated with medical school exams leads to a shift in $T_H1:T_H2$ cytokine ratio that favors the development of humoral immune responses. This may be interpreted as dysregulation rather than immunosuppression.

Immune responses to chronic stress are also important in PNI, because it is often assumed that chronicity of stress is key in understanding the negative impact of stress on health. Spousal caregivers of Alzheimer's disease patients report high levels of chronic stress, depression, and anxiety resulting from the demands of long-term care of their spouses (Schultz, O'Brien, Bookwala, & Fleissner, 1995). Because caregivers also report more days of infectious illness (Kiecolt-Glaser, Dura, Speicher, Trask, & Glaser, 1991), studies have assessed immune functioning in these caregivers. When compared to sociodemographically matched controls, caregivers had significantly lower percentages of T-cells and $CD4^+$ cells, significantly lower $CD4^+:CD8^+$ ratios, and significantly greater antibody titers to Epstein-Barr virus (Kiecolt-Glaser et al., 1987). Caregivers also show decreased lymphocyte proliferation (Kiecolt-Glaser et al., 1991), decreased stimulated NK cytotoxicity (Esterling, Kiecolt-Glaser, Bodnar, & Glaser, 1994), decreased memory T-cell proliferation to HSV-1 antigens, and increased antibody titers to HSV-1 (Glaser & Kiecolt-Glaser, 1997). Irwin et al. (1997) found no differences in NK cytotoxicity or basal levels of neuroendocrine hormones between caregivers and controls. Cacioppo et al. (1998) found that although caregivers have decreased baseline cellular immune responses, caregiving has little effect on responses to or recovery from acute laboratory challenge.

Stress and Infectious Disease

Although studies examining basic relationships among behavior, the CNS, and the immune system provide valuable insight, evidence that psychological factors alter aspects of immune function do not yield information about susceptibility to disease. As mentioned, most documented immune changes resulting from stress are transient, and it is unclear if they are of sufficient magnitude to increase host vulnerability. To gain this type of information, it is necessary to gather information about verifiable disease outcomes (as opposed to self-report data about symptoms) in addition to psychological and immune data. Viral-challenge studies involve exposing research participants to active viruses and then measuring who becomes ill. Psychological, behavioral, or biobehavioral factors can be assessed to determine if they are related to infection or symptoms. These designs control for pathogen exposure and enable researchers to rule out alternative explanations such as the possibility that stress increases exposure to infectious agents by increasing social contact (Cohen, 1996). In addition, distinctions can be made between infection with a specific pathogen and the emergence of clinical symptoms. Close monitoring of participants enables researchers to confirm infection and symptomology.

In a series of viral-challenge studies, Cohen and colleagues (Cohen et al., 1991; Cohen, Tyrrell, & Smith, 1993) found that rates of viral infection and clinical colds increased with increases in negative life events, negative affect, and level of psychological stress. Perceived stress and negative affect predicted infection, and increasing numbers of negative life events predicted the development of clinical symptoms after infection. These findings suggest that the association between life events and disease risk were independent of the association between perceived stress or negative affect and disease risk. In addition, none of the relationships between stress and illness could be explained by differences in important health behaviors (e.g., smoking, alcohol, diet, exercise, or sleep) or the measured immune responses (e.g., numbers of WBC and nonspecific antibodies). These data have been replicated in a similar study by Stone et al. (1992). In an effort to clarify immune mechanisms responsible for symptom severity in stressed people, Cohen, Doyle, and Skoner (1999) demonstrated that severity of upper respiratory illness as measured by reported symptoms of mucous weights was mediated by stress-induced increases in local levels of IL-6, a pro-inflammatory cytokine. In addition, local concentrations of IL-6 varied in phase with both symptoms and mucous production (Cohen et al., 1999). These data provide the strongest evidence that psychological stress alters immune responses in such a way as to influence disease outcomes.

Researchers have also examined whether psychosocial or behavioral variables influence the immune system in such a way as to contribute to disease progression in persons infected with the human immunodeficiency virus (HIV). These variables have included stressful events, bereavement, general distress, specific responses to HIV infection, depression, and social support. The large variability in disease course offers PNI researchers the opportunity to understand interactions between the psychology, immunology, and virology of HIV infection and AIDS.

The complex nature of PNI research in humans combined with problems inherent in studying HIV infection has made progresses in this area difficult. Despite a large number of cross-sectional and prospective natural history studies, results are equivocal, and no firm conclusions can be drawn. Many studies suffer from methodological flaws such as small homogenous samples, insufficient follow-up time, and lack of immune system and other controls, making interpretation problematic. For example, studies may not control for baseline levels of $CD4^+$ cells, viral strain, or stage of disease. As with other PNI studies, research designs are strongest when they prospectively examine relationships among psychosocial variables, immune parameters, and clinical or disease endpoints.

A number of well-controlled studies have shown that psychosocial factors are associated with decreases in $CD4^+$ cell levels. Kemeny and Dean (1995) found that HIV-positive gay men experiencing bereavement showed a more rapid loss of $CD4^+$ cells over time than nonbereaved HIV-positive gay men. Also, self-reproach was predictive of $CD4^+$ loss whereas grief was not. However, $CD4^+$ levels were not related to symptom onset, AIDS onset, or HIV mortality. Similarly, Segerstrom, Taylor, Kemeny, Reed, and Visscher (1996) found that self-blaming attributions for negative events were associated with the slope of $CD4^+$ decline of HIV-positive gay men over an 18-month period but not related on AIDS onset. Vedhara et al. (1997) found that emotional distress was related to a significant decrease in $CD4^+$ levels and increased HIV progression in HIV positive gay men and Cole, Kemeny, Taylor, Visscher, and Fahey (1996) showed that gay men who concealed their homosexual identity reached critically low levels of $CD4^+$ T cells, AIDS diagnosis, and AIDS mortality faster than those men who were mostly or completely open about their gay identity. Miller, Kemeny, Taylor, Cole, and Visscher (1997) found that lower levels of loneliness at baseline were predictive of more rapid declines in $CD4^+$ cells over the follow-up period, pointing out that social relationships may not be uniformly positive on immune or heath outcomes.

Although these studies were designed with sufficient statistical power and appropriate controls, these data must be viewed in the context of equally well-designed studies with negative findings. For example, Kessler et al. (1991) found no relationship between serious stressful events and either a drop in $CD4^+$ or onset of fever or thrush. Neither Lyketsos et al. (1993) nor Vedhara, Schifitto, and McDermott (1999) found any associations between depressive symptoms as measured by the Center for Epidemiologic Studies Depression Scale (CES–D; Radloff, 1977) rate of change in $CD4^+$ levels across time. Vedhara et al. (1999) assessed symptoms and immunological status in HIV-infected women. Finally, Burack et al. (1993) reported a marginal association ($p = .10$) between CES–D scores and rate of $CD4^+$ decline that was not related to AIDS onset or mortality.

FINDINGS FROM PSYCHOSOCIAL INTERVENTION STUDIES

The research we have discussed is only a sample of published research in PNI. There is wealth of strong evidence that psychological and behavioral factors can influence immune function, and convincing evidence is emerging showing that variables such as stress influence susceptibility to some disease. However, much of this research is correlational, making inferences about causality problematic. In addition, as already stated, data supporting PNI models must show that associations between psychological and behavioral variables and disease outcomes are reliably mediated by immune mechanisms. Psychological interventions investigating the possibility of immune system modulation offer attractive research alternatives that allow for causal interpretations.

Enthusiasm for experimental intervention of immune modulation is driven by potential clinical benefits. That is, if people can reliably manipulate their immune system, especially under stressful conditions, they may be able to prevent infection, suppress autoimmune or chronic inflammation, and decrease excess morbidity. Studied interventions include stress management training, relaxation, disclosure of traumatic events, hypnosis, and classical conditioning. A recent meta-analysis of 59 intervention trials examined the evidence for psychological modulation of immune function in humans (Miller & Cohen, 2001), and results are briefly summarized. Taken together, psychological interventions were inconsistent at modulating immune system responses, and those immune changes that were evident occurred in the context of specific interventions.

Interventions induced reliable increases in B-cells and salivary IgA and reliable decreases in antibodies to Epstein-Barr virus. A small positive effect was also shown for proliferative responses to PHA. No other consistent relationships between psychological interventions and immune modulation emerged. Despite a theoretically compelling rationale, the meta-analysis showed no reliable evidence that stress-management interventions could reliably alter immune outcomes. Relaxation interventions similarly did not produce reliable immune changes except for an increase in total salivary IgA. Disclosure interventions yielded evidence of reduction of antibodies to Epstein-Barr (indicative of an indirect increase in cellular immunity) and a reliable decline in T_H cells. Hypnosis also showed evidence of immune modulation, including reliable increases in salivary IgA and neutrophil adherence. People were also able to reliably suppress their immediate (type I) hypersensitivity responses but not their delayed (type IV) hypersensitivity responses. Finally, classical conditioning trials enhanced NK cytotoxicity. Miller and Cohen (2001) cautioned that many of these data must be considered preliminary because most of the interventions in the meta-analysis suffer from a "file drawer" problem. That is, the bias toward publishing positive findings will yield overestimates of effect sizes in meta-analyses because an unknown number of null findings are never published.

Intervention research with HIV/AIDS patients shows more promise than interventions involving healthy individuals. This may be a result of ceiling effects for immune system improvement in people without disease and the fact that HIV infection and AIDS are clearly mediated by failures of the immune system. Research in this area focuses on cognitive–behavioral stress management (CBSM) interventions and hypothesizes that decreases in illness-related distress or improvements in coping should prevent decreases in CD4$^+$ counts or other immune measures. For example, Antoni et al. (1991) found that a five-week multicomponent CBSM intervention before stressful notification of HIV status significantly buffered postnotification depression levels. Also, among seropositive participants there were significant increases in CD4$^+$, NK cell counts, and proliferative responses to PHA. NK cell cytotoxicity and proliferative responses to PWM were unaffected. In additional analyses from this intervention, Esterling et al. (1992) showed that Epstein-Barr virus—viral capsid antigens (EBV-VCA) and human herpes virus–6 (HHV-6) were significantly decreased in the participants assigned to the CBSM intervention regardless of HIV status. This decrease is often interpreted as indicative of greater cellular control of viral reactivation and replication. Eller (1995) found that HIV-positive men practicing six weeks of progressive muscle relaxation via audiotape had significant decreases in depression and significant increases in CD4$^+$ cells compared to no-treatment controls. Those men in the guided imagery group showed decreases in depression and fatigue but no changes in immune function. In contrast, Lutgendorf et al. (1997) found no changes in CD4$^+$ cell numbers, CD8$^+$ cell numbers, or titers of antibodies against HSV-1 after a 10-week group CBSM intervention, although there was a significant decrease in titers of antibodies against HSV-2 but not HSV-1. Finally, Goodkin et al. (1998) found that CD4+ cell counts, total T-cell counts, and total lymphocyte counts of HIV-positive men decreased less following participation in a brief (10 week) bereavement-support group compared to HIV-positive men not participating in the support group. These findings persisted at six-month follow-up.

CONCLUSION

The field defined by PNI research has promise for better understanding the fundamental relationships between the mind and body. Clear evidence detailing the many neuroanatomical, neurochemical, and neuroendocrine connections between the brain and the immune systems has established the notion that they are closely related. In addition, it is clear that perturbations in one system lead to reliable alterations in the other. Stressful experiences, lack of sleep, depression, poor social support, marital discord, and other psychosocial factors all affect measures of immune function. One of the most attractive implications of this work is that psychosocial variables affect disease processes through their effects on the immune system, but support for hypotheses about the impact of these immune changes on pathophysiology is equivocal (Cohen & Herbert, 1996). More research is needed to determine the specific pathways and immune mechanisms involved, specifically address-ing questions such as what type of stressors affect immunity, how changes in immunity and vulnerability are timed one relative to the other, and whether there are individual differences in susceptibility to immune system variability. These answers will help us to identify those who are the most vulnerable to psychosocially induced perturbations in immunity and to determine how long they must experience stress before their risk is increased.

Although it is clear that psychosocial interventions aimed at reducing stress and improving coping skills improves quality of life, we are still learning about the extent of these effects and their influence on physical health outcomes. Interventions may improve functioning and distress, thereby re-ducing symptom salience or reporting without actually altering physical health. Given the current state of knowledge, it would be premature to suggest that psychosocial or behavioral interventions are capable of altering immune system function in such a way as to protect against disease. Although stress alters immunity and seems to heighten vulnerability to infection by viruses, the converse (that relieving stress prevents immune alteration and disease) is not necessarily true. The fact that naturally occurring disease in general is a rare event makes studying relevant health outcomes difficult.

Studies concerning the clinical implications of PNI should be based on disease models in which the origins of disease are clearly immune-mediated. In HIV disease and AIDS, the immune system is a clear and central player in both defense against the virus and in assessing the impact of the disease. In contrast, there is still considerable controversy about the role of the immune system in immune surveillance against tumor cells, and therefore alterations of immune function in cancer patients are difficult to interpret (Bovbjerg & Valdimarsdottir, 1998). Furthermore, the reported alternations in immune function are often within normal ranges, and studies of stress and immunity seem to explain normal variance in a small aspect of immune responsiveness (Cohen & Rabin, 1998).

These considerations suggest several directions of PNI and frame several goals for this research. Considering the importance of innate immunity in the overall immune response, it is somewhat surprising that relatively little attention has been focused on this point. Few studies have been carried out examining stress-induced alterations in neutrophil or macrophage function in humans and how these alterations may influence susceptibility to infection. Similarly, little work has been done investigating changes in complement or acute phase proteins resulting from stress.

As previously described, most PNI models work from the assumption that stress leads to immunosuppression, which in turn leads to illness. Although this model may be valid for infectious diseases, it does not account for instances of inflammatory or autoimmune diseases. These diseases result not from immunosuppression but from overactivity of immune processes. Future PNI models will need to address these issues by delineating the differing mechanisms involved.

To date, research examining hypotheses about the capacity of psychological interventions to modulate the immune system in humans is equivocal. Miller and Cohen (2001) suggested several reasons for this and proposed that future trials need to enroll appropriate participant populations, choose appropriate immune measures, use designs that are more methodologically rigorous, increase numbers of participants to increase statistical power, and analyze mediational pathways. Future PNI researchers will need to thoroughly educate themselves in immunology and disease pathology as well as all areas of behavioral medicine if they are to address the many pressing problems that PNI aims to solve.

REFERENCES

Adams, D. O. (1994). Molecular biology of macrophage activation: A pathway whereby psychosocial factors can potentially affect health. *Psychosomatic Medicine, 56*, 316–327.

Ader, R. (1974). Letter to the editor. *Psychosomatic Medicine, 36*, 183–184.

Ader, R. (Ed.). (1981). *Psychoneuroimmunology.* New York: Academic Press.

Ader, R., & Cohen, N. (1975). Behaviorally conditioned immunosuppression. *Psychosomatic Medicine, 37*, 333–340.

Ader, R., & Cohen, N. (1993). Psychoneuroimmunology: Conditioning and stress. *Annual Review of Psychology, 44*, 53–85.

Ahmed, R., & Gray, D. (1996). Immunological memory and protective immunity: Understanding their relation. *Science, 272*, 54–59.

Antoni, M. H., Baget, L., Ironson, G., LaPerriere, A., August, S., Klimas, N., et al. (1991). Cognitive–behavioral stress management intervention buffers distress responses and immunologic changes following notification of HIV-1 seropositivity. *Journal of Consulting and Clinical Psychology, 59*(6), 906–915.

Bachen, E. A., Manuck, S. B., Cohen, S., Muldoon, M. F., Raible, B. S., Herber, T. B., et al. (1995). Adrenergic blockade ameliorates cellular immune responses to mental stress in humans. *Psychosomatic Medicine, 57*, 366–372.

Bachen, E. A., Manuck, S. B., Marsland, A. L., Cohen, S., Malkoff, S. B., Muldoon, M. F., et al. (1992). Lymphocyte subset and cellular immune responses to a brief experimental stressor. *Psychosomatic Medicine, 54,* 673–679.

Banks, W. A., Oritz, L., Plotkin, S. R., & Kastin, A. J. (1991). Human interleukin (IL) 1 alpha, murine IL-1 alpha, and murine IL-1 beta are transported from blood to brain in the mouse by a shared saturable mechanism. *Journal of Pharmacology and Experimental Therapeutics, 259,* 988–996.

Bartrop, R. W., Luckhurst, E., Lazarus, L., Kilch L. G., & Penny, R. (1977). Depressed lymphocyte function after bereavement. *Lancet, 1,* 834–836.

Baum, A. (1990). Stress, intrusive imagery, and chronic stress. *Health Psychology, 9*(6), 653–675.

Baum, A., Cohen, L., & Hall, M. (1993). Control and intrusive memories as possible determinants of chronic stress. *Psychosomatic Medicine, 55,* 274–286.

Berliner, J. A., Navab, M., Fogelman, A. M., Frank, J. S., Demer, L. L., Edwards, P. A., et al. (1995). Atherosclerosis: Basic mechanisms: Oxidation, inflammation, and genetics. *Circulation, 91*(9), 2488–2496.

Besedovsky, H. O., del Rey, A., Klusman, I., Furukawa, H., Monge Arditi, G., & Kabiersch, A. (1992). Cytokines as modulators of the hypothalamus-pituitary-adrenal axis. *Journal of Steroid Biochemistry & Molecular Biology, 40*(4–6), 613–618.

Biondi, M., & Picardi, A. (1999). Psychological stress and neuroendocrine function in humans: The last two decades of research. *Psychotherapy & Psychosomatics, 68*(3), 114–150.

Bovbjerg, D. H., & Valdimarsdottir, H. B. (1998). Psychoneuroimmunology: Implications for psycho-oncology. In J. C. Holland (Ed.), *Psycho-Oncology* (pp. 125–134). New York: Oxford University Press.

Burack, J. H., Barrett, D. C., Stall, R. D., Chesney, M. A., Ekstrand, M. L., & Coates, T. J. (1993). Depressive symptoms and CD4 lymphocyte decline among HIV-infected men. *Journal of the American Medical Association, 270*(21), 2568–2573.

Cacioppo, J. T., Malarkey, W. B., Kiecolt-Glaser, J. K., Uchino, B. N., Sgoutas-Emch, S. A., Sheridan, J. F., et al. (1995). Heterogeneity in neuroendocrine and immune response to brief psychological stressors as a function of autonomic cardiac activation. *Psychosomatic Medicine, 57,* 154–164.

Cacioppo, J. T., Poehlmann, K. M., Kiecolt–Glaser, J. K., Malarkey, W. B., Burleson, M. H., Berntson, G. G., et al. (1998). Cellular immune response to acute stress in female caregivers of dementia patients and matched controls. *Health Psychology, 17*(2), 182–189.

Chrousos, G. P. (1995). Seminars in medicine of the Beth Israel Hospital, Boston: The hypothalamic-pituitary-adrenal axis and immune-mediated inflammation. *New England Journal of Medicine, 332*(20), 1351–1362.

Chrousos, G. P. (1998). Stressors, stress, and neuroendocrine integration of the adaptive response: The 1997 Hans Selye memorial lecture. *Annals of the New York Academy of Science, 851,* 311–335.

Cohen, S. (1996). Psychological stress, immunity, and upper respiratory infections. *Current Directions in Psychological Science, 5*(3), 86–89.

Cohen, S., Doyle, W., & Skoner, D. P. (1999). Psychological stress, cytokine production, and severity of upper respiratory infection. *Psychosomatic Medicine, 61*(2), 175–180.

Cohen, S., & Herbert, T. B. (1996). Health Psychology: Psychological factors and physical disease from the perspective of human psychoneuroimmunology. *Annual Review of Psychology, 47*, 113–142.

Cohen, S., & Rabin, B. S. (1998). Psychologic stress, immunity, and cancer. *Journal of the National Cancer Institute, 90*(1), 3–4.

Cohen, S., Tyrrell, D. A. J., & Smith, A. P. (1991). Psychological stress and susceptibility to the common cold. *New England Journal of Medicine, 325*, 606–612.

Cohen, S., Tyrrell, D. A. J., & Smith, A. P. (1993). Life events, perceived stress, negative affect and susceptibility to the common cold. *Journal of Personality and Social Psychology, 64*, 131–401.

Cohen, S., & Williamson, G. M. (1991). Stress and infectious disease in humans. *Psychological Bulletin, 109*(1), 5–24.

Cohen-Cole, S., Cogen, R., Stevens, A., Kirk, K., Gartan, E., Hain, J., et al. (1981). Psychosocial, endocrine, and immune factors in acute necrotizing ulcerative gingivitis ("trenchmounth"). *Psychosomatic Medicine, 43*, 91.

Cole, S. W., Kemeny, M. E., Taylor, S. E., Visscher, B. R., & Fahey, J. L. (1996). Accelerated course of human immunodeficiency virus infection in gay men who conceal their homosexual identity. *Psychosomatic medicine, 58*(3), 219–231.

Dantzer, R,. Bluthe, R., Laye, S., Bret-Dibat, J., Parnet, P., & Kelley, K. W. (1998). *Cytokines and sickness behavior.* In S. M. McCann, & J. M. Lipton (Eds.), *Annals of the New York Academy of Sciences, 840*, 586–590.

Delahanty, D. L., Dougall, A. L., Hawken, L., Trakowski, J. H., Schmitz, J., Jenkins, F. J., et al. (1996). Time Course of natural killer cell activity and lymphocyte proliferation in response to two acute stressors in healthy men. *Journal of Applied Biobehavioral Research, 1*(2), 120–132.

De Pablo, M. A., & Alvarez De Cienfuegos, G. A. (2000). Modulatory effects of dietary lipids on immune system functions. *Immunology & Cell Biology, 78*(1), 31–39.

Dorian, B. J., Keystone, E., Garfinkel, P. E., & Brown, G. M. (1981). Immune mechanisms in acute psychological stress. *Psychosomatic Medicine, 43*, 84.

Elenkov, I. J., Papanicolaou, D. A., Wilder, R. L., & Chrousos, G. P. (1996). Modulatory effects of glucocorticoids and catecholamines on human interleukin-12 and interleukin-10 production: Clinical implications. *Proceedings of the Association of American Physicians, 108*(5), 374–381.

Eller, L. S. (1995). Effects of two cognitive–behavioral interventions on immunity and symptoms in person with HIV. *Annals of Behavioral Medicine, 17*(4), 339–348.

Esterling, B. A., Antoni, M. H., Schneiderman, N., Carver, C. S., LaPerriere, A., Ironson, G., et al. (1992). Psychological modulation of antibody to Epstein-Barr viral capsid antigen and human herpesvirus type-6 in HIV-1-infected and at-risk gay men. *Psychosomatic Medicine, 54*, 354–371.

Esterling, B. A., Kiecolt-Glaser, J. K., Bodnar, J. C., & Glaser, R. (1994). Chronic stress, social support, and persistent alterations in the natural killer cell response to cytokines in older adults. *Health Psychology, 13*(4), 291–298.

Fearon, D. T., & Locksley, R. M. (1996). The instructive role of innate immunity in the acquired immune response. *Science, 272*, 50–53.

Felton, D. L., Cohen, N., Ader, R., Felton, S. Y., Carlson, S. L., & Roszman, T. L. (1991). Central neural circuits involved in neural-immune interactions. In R. Ader, D. L. Felton, & N. Cohen (Eds.), *Psychoneuroimmunology* (2nd ed.). San Diego, CA: Academic Press.

Felton, S. Y., & Felton, D. L. (1991). Innervation of lymphoid tissue. In R. Ader, D. L. Felton, & N. Cohen (Eds.), *Psychoneuroimmunology* (2nd ed.). San Diego, CA: Academic Press.

Fischer, C. L., Daniels, J. C., Levin, W. C., Kimzey, S. L., Cobb, E. K., Ritzmann, S. E., et al. (1972). Effects of the space flight environment on man's immune system: II. Lymphocyte counts and reactivity. *Aerospace Medicine, 43*, 1122–1125.

Gabay, C., & Kushner, I. (1999). Mechanisms of disease: Acute-phase proteins and other systemic responses to inflammation. *New England Journal of Medicine, 340*(6), 448–454.

Glaser, R., Freidman, S. B., Smyth, J., Ader, R., Bijur, P., Brunell, P., et al. (1999). The differential impact of training stress and final examination stress on herpesvirus latency at the United States Military Academy at West Point. *Brain, Behavior, and Immunity, 13*(3), 240–251.

Glaser, R., & Kiecolt-Glaser, J. K. (1997). Chronic stress modulates the virus-specific immune response to latent herpes simplex virus type 1. *Annals of Behavioral Medicine, 19*(2), 78–82.

Glaser, R., Kiecolt-Glaser, J. K., Bonneau, R. H., Malarkey, W. B., & Hughes, J. (1992). Stress-induced modulation of the immune response to recombinant hepatitis B vaccine. *Psychosomatic Medicine, 54*(1), 22–29.

Glaser, R., Kiecolt-Glaser, J. K., Speicher, C. E., & Holliday, J. E. (1985). Stress, loneliness, and changes in herpesvirus latency. *Journal of Behavioral Medicine, 8*(3), 249–260.

Glaser, R., Mehl, V. S., Penn, G., Speicher, C. E., & Kiecolt-Glaser, J. (1986). Stress-associated changes in plasma immunoglobulin levels. *International Journal of Psychosomatics, 33*(2), 41–42.

Glaser, R., Pearl, D. K., Kiecolt-Glaser, J. K., & Malarkey, W. B. (1994). Plasma cortisol levels and reactivation of latent Epstein-Barr virus in response to examination stress. *Psychoneuroendocrinology, 19*(8), 765–772.

Glaser, R., Pearson, G. R., Bonneau, R. H., Esterling, B. A., Atkinson, C., Kiecolt-Glaser, J. K., et al. (1993). Stress and memory T-cell response to the Epstein-Barr virus in healthy medical students. *Health Psychology, 12*(6), 435–442.

Glaser, R., Rice, J., Sheridan, J., Fertel, R., Stout, J., Speicher, C., et al. (1987). Stress-related immune suppression: Health implications. *Brain, Behavior, & Immunity, 1*(1), 7–20.

Glaser, R., Rice, J., Speicher, C. E., & Kiecolt-Glaser, J. K. (1986). Stress depresses interferon production by leukocytes concomitant with a decrease in natural killer cell activity. *Behavioral Neuroscience, 100*(5), 675–678.

Goodkin, K., Feaster, D. J., Deshratn, A., Blaney, N. T., Kumar, M., Baldewicz, T., et al. (1998). A bereavement support group intervention is longitudinally associated with salutary effects on the CD4 count and number of physician visits. *Clinical and Diagnostic Laboratory Immunology, 5*(3), 382–391.

Hall, M., Baum, A., Buysse, D. J., Prigerson, H. G., Kupfer, D. J., & Reynolds, C. F. (1998). Sleep as a mediator of the stress-immune relationship. *Psychosomatic Medicine, 60*(1), 48–51.

Henderson, B. N., Forlenza, M., & Baum, A. (2003). *An evolutionary framework for biobehavioral contributions to health and disease.* Unfinished manuscript.

Herbert, T. B., & Cohen, S. (1993). Stress and immunity in humans: A meta-analytic review. *Psychosomatic Medicine, 55,* 364–379.

Herbert, T. B., Cohen, S., Marsland, A. L., Bachen, E. A., Rabin, B. S., Muldoon, M. F., et al. (1994). Cardiovascular reactivity and the course of immune response to an acute psychological stressor. *Psychosomatic Medicine, 56,* 337–344.

Huston, D. P. (1997). The biology of the immune system. *Journal of the American Medical Association, 278*(22), 1804–1814.

Irwin, M., Hauger, R., Patterson, T. L., Semple, S., Ziegler, M., & Grant, I. (1997). Alzheimer caregiver stress: Basal natural killer cell activity, pituitary-adrenal cortical function, and sympathetic tone. *Annals of Behavioral Medicine, 19*(2), 83–90.

Kasl, S. V., Evans, A. S., & Niederman, J. C. (1979). Psychosocial risk factors in the development of infectious mononucleosis. *Psychosomatic Medicine, 41,* 445–466.

Keller, S. E., Shiflett, S. C., Schleifer, S. J., & Bartlett, J. A. (1994). Stress, immunity, and health. In R. Glaser & J. K. Kiecolt-Glaser (Eds.), *Handbook of human stress and immunity* (pp. 217–244). San Diego, CA: Academic Press.

Kemeny, M. E., & Dean, L. (1995). Effects of AIDS-related bereavement on HIV progression among New York City gay men. *AIDS Education and Prevention, 7*(5 Suppl.), 36–47.

Kennedy, R. L., & Jones, T. H. (1990). Cytokines in endocrinology: Their roles in health and in disease. *Journal of Endocrinology, 129,* 167–178.

Kessler, R. C., Foster, C., Joseph, J., Ostrow, D., Wortman, C., Phair, J., et al. (1991). Stressful life events and symptom onset in HIV infection. *American Journal of Psychiatry, 148*(6), 733–738.

Kiecolt-Glaser, J. K., Cacioppo, J. T., Malarkey, W. B., & Glaser, R. (1992). Acute psychological stressors and short-term immune changes: What, why, for whom, and to what extent? *Psychosomatic Medicine, 54,* 680–685.

Kiecolt-Glaser, J. K., Dura, J. R., Speicher, C. E., Trask, O. J., & Glaser, R. (1991). Spousal caregivers of dementia victims: Longitudinal changes in immunity and health. *Psychosomatic Medicine, 53*(4), 345–362.

Kiecolt-Glaser, J. K., & Glaser, R. (1988). Methodological issues in behavioral immunology research with humans. *Brain, Behavior, and Immunity, 2,* 67–78.

Kiecolt-Glaser, J. K., & Glaser, R. (1995). Psychoneuroimmunology and health consequences: Data and shared mechanisms. *Psychosomatic Medicine, 57,* 269–274.

Kiecolt-Glaser, J. K., Glaser, R., Shuttleworth, E. C., Dyer, C. S., Ogrocki, B. S., & Speicher, C. E. (1987). Chronic stress and immunity in family caregivers of Alzheimer's disease victims. *Psychosomatic Medicine, 49*(5), 523–535.

Kiecolt-Glaser, J. K., Speicher, C. E., Holliday, J. E., & Glaser, R. (1984). Stress and the transformation of lymphocytes by Epstein-Barr virus. *Journal of Behavioral Medicine, 17*(1), 1–12.

Kimzey, S. L. (1975). The effects of extended space flight on hematologic and immunologic systems. *Journal of the American Medical Women's Association, 30,* 218–232.

Locke, S. E. (1982). Stress, adaptation, and immunity: Studies in humans. *General Hospital Psychiatry, 4*(1), 49–58.

Locke, S. E., & Heisel, J. S. (1977). The influence of stress and emotions on human immunity. *Biofeedback and Self-Regulation, 2,* 320.

Lutgendorf, S. K., Antoni, M. H., Ironson, G., Klimas, N., Kumar, M., Starr, K., et al. (1997). Cognitive-behavioral stress management decreases dysphoric mood and herpes simplex virus-type2 antibody titers in symptomatic HIV-seropositive gay men. *Journal of Consulting and Clinical Psychology, 65*(1), 31–43.

Lyketsos, C. G., Hoover, D. R., Guccione, M., Senterfitt, W., Dew, M. A., Wesch, J., et al. (1993). Depressive symptoms as predictors of medical outcomes in HIV progression. *Journal of the American Medical Association, 270*(21), 2563–2567.

Madden, K. S., & Livnat, S. (1991). Catecholamine action and immunologic reactivity. In R. Ader, D. L. Felton, & N. Cohen (Eds.), *Psychoneuroimmunology* (2nd ed.). San Diego, CA: Academic Press.

Maier, S. F., Goehler, L. E., Fleshner, M., & Watkins, L. R. (1998). The role of the vagus nerve in cytokine-to-brain communication. *Annals of the New York Academy of Sciences, 840,* 289–300.

Maier, S. F., & Watkins, L. R. (1998). Cytokines for psychologists: Implications of bidirectional immune-to-brain communication for understanding behavior, mood, and cognition. *Psychological Review, 105*(1), 83–107.

Manuck, S. B., Cohen, S., Rabin, B. S., Muldoon, M. F., & Bachen, E. A. (1991). Individual differences in cellular immune responses to stress. *Psychological Science, 2*(2), 111–115.

Marshall, G. D., Agarwal, S. K., Lloyd, C., Cohen, L., Henninger, E. M., & Morris, G. J. (1998). Cytokine dysregulation associated with exam stress in healthy medical students. *Brain, Behavior, and Immunity, 12*(4), 297–307.

McAllister-Sistilli, C. G., Cagguila, A. R., Knopf, S., Rose, C. A., Miller, A. L., & Donny, E. C. (1998). The effects of nicotine on the immune system. *Psychoneuroendocrinology, 23*(2), 175–187.

Miller, G. E., & Cohen, S. (2001). Psychological interventions and the immune system: A meta-analytic review and critique. *Health Psychology, 20*(1), 47–63.

Miller, G. E., Kemeny, M. E., Taylor, S. E., Cole, S. W., & Visscher, B. R. (1997). Social relationships and immune processes in HIV seropositive gay and bisexual men. *Annals of Behavioral Medicine, 19*(2), 139–151.

Moyniham, J. A., & Ader, R. (1996). Psychoneuroimmunology: Animal models of disease. *Psychosomatic Medicine, 58*(6), 546–598.

Munck, A., & Guyer, P. M. (1991). Glucocorticoids and immune function. In R. Ader, D. L. Felton, & N. Cohen (Eds.), *Psychoneuroimmunology* (2nd ed.). San Diego, CA: Academic Press.

Naliboff, B. D., Benton, D., Solomon, G. F., Morley, J. E., Fahey, J. L., Bloom, E. T., et al. (1991). Immunological changes in young and old adults during brief laboratory stress. *Psychosomatic Medicine, 53*(2), 121–132.

Nielsen, C. H., Fischer, E. M., & Leslie, R. G. Q. (2000). The role of complement in the acquired immune response. *Immunology, 100*(1), 4–12.

Ottaviani, E., & Franceschi, C. (1995). The neuroimmunology of stress from invertebrates to man. *Progress in Neurobiology, 48*, 421–440.

Palmblad, J., Cantell, K., Strander, H., Frobert, J., Claes-Goran, K., Lennart, L., et al. (1976). Stressor exposure and immunological response in man: Interferon-producing capacity and phagocytosis. *Journal of Psychosomatic Research, 20*, 193–199.

Palmblad, J., Petrini, B., Wasserman, J., & Akerstedt, T. (1979). Lymphocyte and granulocyte reactions during sleep deprivation. *Psychosomatic Medicine 41*, 273–278.

Pickworth, W. B., & Fant, R. V. (1998). Endocrine effects of nicotine administration, tobacco and other drug withdrawal in humans. *Psychoneuroendocrinology, 23*(2), 131–141.

Playfair, J. (1995). *Infection and immunity*. New York: Oxford University Press.

Rabin, B. S. (1999). *Stress, immune function, and health*. New York: John Wiley & Sons.

Radloff, L. S. (1977). The CES-D scale: A self-report depression scale for research in the general population. *Applied Psychological Measurement, 1*, 385–401.

Reichlin, S. (1993). Neuroendocrine-immune interactions. *New England Journal of Medicine, 329*, 1246–1253.

Saper, C. B., & Bredr, C. D. (1994). The neurologic basis of fever. *New England Journal of Medicine, 330*, 1880–1886.

Schedlowski, M., Jacobs, R., Stratmann, G., Richter, S., Hadicke, A., Tewew, U., et al. (1993). Changes in natural killer cells during acute psychological stress. *Journal of Clinical Immunology, 13*(2), 119–128.

Schultz, R., O'Brien, A. T., Bookwala, J., & Fleissner, K. (1995). Psychiatric and physical morbidity effects of dementia caregiving: Prevalence, correlates, and causes. *Gerontologist, 35*(6), 771–791.

Segerstrom, S. C., Taylor, S. E., Kemeny, M. E., Reed G. M., & Visscher, B. R. (1996). Causal attributions predict rate of immune decline in HIV-seropositive gay men. *Health Psychology, 15*(6), 485–493.

Sgoutas-Emch, S. A., Cacioppo, J. T., Uchino, B. N., Malarkey, W. B., Pearl, D., Kiecolt-Glaser, J. K., et al. (1994). The effects of an acute psychological stressor on cardiovascular, endocrine, and cellular immune response: A prospective study of individuals high and low in heart rate reactivity. *Psychophysiology, 31*, 264–271.

Simon, H. B. (1991). Exercise and human immune function. In R. Ader, D. L. Fenton, & N. Cohen (Eds.), *Psychoneuroimmunology* (2nd ed., pp. 869–895). San Diego, CA: Academic Press.

Smith, J. A. (1994). Neutrophils, host defense, and inflammation: A double-edged sword. *Journal of Leukocyte Biology, 56*, 672–686.

Stone, A. A., Bovbjerg, D. H., Neale, J. M., Napoli, A., Valdimarsdottir, H., Cox, D., et al. (1992). Development of common cold symptoms following experimental rhinovirus infection is related to prior stressful life events. *Behavioral Medicine, 18*(3), 115–120.

Suffredini, A. F., Fantuzzi, G., Badolata, R., Oppenheim, J., & O'Grady, N. (1999). New insights into the biology of the acute phase response. *Journal of Clinical Immunology, 19*(4), 203–214.

Thompson, C. B. (1995). New insights into V(D)J recombination and its role in the evolution of the immune system. *Immunity, 3*(5), 531–539.

Vedhara, K., Fox, J. D., & Wang, E. C. Y. (1999). The measurement of immune dysfunction in psychoneuroimmunology. *Neuroscience and Biobehavioral Reviews, 23*, 699–715.

Vedhara, K., Nott, K. H., Bradbeer, C. S., Davidson, E. A., Ong, E. L., Snow, M. H., et al. (1997). Greater emotional distress is associated with accelerated CD4+ cell decline in HIV infection. *Journal of Psychosomatic Research, 42*(4), 379–390.

Vedhara, K., Schifitto, G., & McDermott, M. (1999). Disease progression in HIV-positive women with moderate to severe immunosuppression: The role of depression. *Behavioral Medicine, 25*(1), 43–47.

Weiss, S. J. (1989). Tissue destruction by neutrophils. *New England Journal of Medicine, 320*, 365–376.

Whiteside, T. L., Bryant, J., Day, R., & Herberman, R. B. (1990). Natural killer cytotoxicity in the diagnosis of immune dysfunction: Criteria for a reproducible assay. *Journal of Clinical Laboratory Analysis, 4*, 102–114.

Whiteside, T. L., & Herberman, R. B. (1989). The role of natural killer cells in human disease. *Clinical Immunology and Immunopathology, 53*, 1–23.

Wick, G., Perschinka, H., & Xu, Q. (1999). Autoimmunity and atherosclerosis. *American Heart Journal, 138*(5), S444–S449.

Woods, J. A., Davis, J. M., Smith, J. A., & Nieman, D. C. (1999). Exercise and cellular innate immune function. *Medicine and Science in Sports and Exercise, 31*(1), 57–66.

Zakowski, S. G., Cohen L., Hall, M. H., Wollman, K., & Baum, A. (1994). Differential effects of active and passive laboratory stressors on immune function in healthy men. *International Journal of Behavioral Medicine, 1*(2), 163–184.

Zakowski, S., McAllister, C. G., Deal, M., & Baum A. (1992). *Health Psychology, 11*(4), 223–232.

4

BEHAVIORAL ASPECTS OF GENETIC RISK FOR DISEASE: CANCER GENETICS AS A PROTOTYPE FOR COMPLEX ISSUES IN HEALTH PSYCHOLOGY

LARI WENZEL AND KAREN GLANZ

The years 2000 and 2001 heralded the announcement that the vast majority of the human genome had been sequenced, with an analysis suggesting that there are about 32,000 genes in the human genome (Lander et al., 2001). The ability to analyze entire genomes has accelerated gene discovery and revolutionized the breadth and depth of biological questions that can be addressed. "These exciting successes confirm the view that acquisition of a comprehensive, high-quality human genome sequence will have unprecedented impact and long-lasting value for basic biology, biomedical research, biotechnology, and health care" (Collins et al., 1998).

For many, the goal now is to develop the tools to make sense of sequence data and move into the study of gene function. Emerging tools and technologies for genetic analysis are setting the stage for a new era of gene identification and functional studies, with a transition to sequence-based biology. This transition will advance progress in understanding gene–environment interactions and development of DNA-based medical diagnostics and therapeutics (Collins et al., 1998). It is useful to remember, however, that the sequence of the human genome is only a starting point. The next step involves "annotation"—documenting all there is to know about every gene, including where and how it works and interacts.

Genetic factors influence virtually every human disorder, determining disease susceptibility or resistance and interactions with environmental factors. Availability of the human genome sequence presents unique scientific opportunities, chief among them the study of natural genetic variations in humans and identification of disease-related genes. As a result, tests for genetic components of risk in the majority of common illnesses will lead to new treatments.

Knowledge of all the human genes and their functions may allow effective preventive measures and change drug research strategy and drug discovery development processes. The potential implication of genomics and pharmacogenomics in clinical research and clinical medicine is that disease could be treated according to genetic and specific individual markers, selecting medications and dosages that are optimized for individual patients. In short, this genomic medicine holds promise of revolutionizing the diagnosis and treatment of many illnesses (Collins & McKusick, 2001).

Due to the seminal accomplishment of the completion of the human genome sequence, attention will shift to more complex and more prevalent genetic disorders and traits that involve multiple genes and environmental effects. In addition, the possibility of defining patient populations genetically may improve outcomes by predicting individual responses to drugs, and it also could improve safety and efficacy in therapeutic areas such as neuropsychiatry, cardiovascular medicine, rheumatoid arthritis, endocrinology (diabetes and obesity), and oncology. There is, however, no immediate solution to the genetics of complex traits.

As articulated by Plomin (1998), "It is crucial for the field [of health psychology] that we be prepared to use genes as they are found" (p. 54). As genes are identified for increasing numbers of adult onset conditions, it is expected that the demand for genetic counseling and testing will increase (Collins, 1999). During this period, there will be a concomitant need to provide cost-effective educational and counseling adjuncts to the genetic counseling and testing process. The discipline of health psychology can provide a pivotal contribution as genetic conditions are elucidated and future health care recommendations are advanced. However, the field needs to be prepared to develop and test new theoretical models, measures, and interventions most likely to apply to diverse and complex areas of genetic research.

This chapter illuminate burgeoning research areas in which health psychologists provide an important contribution as the sciences of genetics, epidemiology, and public health unite toward common goals. First, we highlight the complexities involved in polygene disorders where genetics, environment, and behavior converge. In this discussion, the distinction between genetics of behavior and mood (e.g., addiction, smoking, anxiety) and genetics of physical conditions (e.g., obesity, hypertension) are briefly addressed. These contrasting polygenic disorders challenge health psychologists to develop clinical research strategies that can integrate complementary conceptual approaches across disorders while simultaneously addressing conceptual differences. We then detail how health psychology and other professions have contributed to examination of single gene disorders (e.g., Huntington's disease, BRCA1/2 mutations). Additional discussion elaborates on the utility of several conceptual models that have guided research related to risk perception, screening behavior, risk reduction, decision making, psychosocial distress and family communication.

POLYGENE DISORDERS: BEHAVIORAL GENOMICS

Most types of behavior depend on an interplay between environmental factors and multiple genes (McGuffin & Martin, 1999), although each gene accounts for only a small percentage of the variance (Comings & Blum, 2000). Genes in such multiple-gene systems are called quantitative trait loci (QTLs), because they are likely to result in continuous (quantitative) distributions of phenotypes that underlie susceptibility to common disorders. The most solid genetic findings about individual differences in human behavior come from quantitative genetic research such as twin and adoption studies that consistently converge on the conclusion that genetic variation makes a substantial contribution to phenotypic variation for all behavioral domains. Nearly all behaviors that have been studied show moderate to high heritability—usually, to a somewhat greater degree than do many common physical diseases (Plomin, Owen, & McGuffin, 1994).

Addiction

About 50% of the risk for addiction in humans is genetic. Recent analyses revealed new candidate members of several gene families involved in signal transduction pathways that may have a role in addiction (Nestler & Landsman, 2001). By targeting medications to the biological and genetic causes of addiction, it will in theory be possible to counteract the powerful biological forces that drive drug craving and relapse. Such medications would then make social and psychological interventions more effective.

Posttraumatic Stress Disorder and the Anxiety Disorders

A recent investigation was undertaken to examine whether and to what degree genetic and environmental contributions overlapped among posttraumatic stress disorder (PTSD), alcohol dependence (AD), and drug dependence (DD) individuals. The results suggest that PTSD, AD, and DD each have etiologically distinct components and also have significant genetic and unique environmental contributions in common (Xian et al., 2000). To test for distinction between generalized anxiety disorder (GAD) and panic disorder (PD), a study of 6,724 male–male monozygotic and dizygotic twin pair members of the Vietnam Era Twin Registry was conducted. These data suggest a distinction in liability for GAD versus PD, where the common genetic influence to GAD and PD may account partially for the risk of the co-occurrence of these disorders in a lifetime (Scherrer et al., 2000).

Smoking

Twin studies suggest that propensity to smoke and ability to quit smoking are influenced by genetic factors (Carmelli, Swan, Robinette, & Fabsitz, 1992; Heath & Martin, 1993; Sabol et al., 1999). A role of dopaminergic or other genes in smoking cessation is of particular potential importance, because research in this area may lead to the identification of subgroups of individuals for whom pharmacological cessation aids may be most effective (Rossing, 1998). Recent preliminary evidence suggests that the SLC6A3 gene may influence smoking risk, age at smoking initiation, and ability to quit smoking (Lerman et al., 1999). In addition, individual differences in propensity to nicotine dependence appear to be mediated, in part, by genetic factors. For example, neuroticism was positively associated with smoking practices among smokers with 5-HTTLPR S genotypes but not among smokers with the L genotype (Lerman, Caporaso, et al., 2000). Assessment of the 5-HTTLPR genotype and neuroticism may help to identify smokers who are more responsive to psychotropic medications, such as selective serotonin reuptake inhibitors (SSRIs), which are being used in smoking cessation treatment (Lerman, Caporaso, et al., 2000). Because smoking-related factors are extremely complex, studies of diverse populations and of many aspects of smoking behavior—including initiation, maintenance, cessation, relapse, and influence of environmental factors—are needed to identify smoking-associated genes (Arinami, Ishiguro, & Onaivi, 2000). A better understanding of genetic, neuropharmacological, and environmental determinants can lead to the development of improved prevention and treatment strategies tailored to the needs of individual smokers (Plomin, 1998).

Obesity

Genetic studies of families and populations have generated useful information on genes and mutations associated with or linked to obesity, body fat distribution, and other relevant phenotypes. This information, combined with knowledge of the chromosomal location of genes identified from animal studies, has made it possible to identify specific mutations that contribute to the development of obesity in humans (York & Bouchard, 2000). There is increasing evidence that shared genetic factors could play a role in determining the covariation between obesity and its major comorbidities, including high blood pressure, insulin resistance, diabetes, and dyslipidemia.

Evidence from both genetic epidemiology and molecular epidemiology studies suggests that genetic factors are involved in determining the susceptibility to gaining or losing fat in response to diet or the risk of developing some of the comorbidities generally observed in obese individuals (Pérusse & Bouchard, 2000). In addition, our knowledge of a growing number of genes and molecules implicated in biochemical processes associated with obesity (feeding control, energy efficiency, adipogenesis) is leading toward a molecular understanding of the body weight regulatory system, thus paving the way for new methods of obesity control, to include pharmacological and nutritional methods (Palou, Serra, Bonet, & Picó, 2000).

Hypertension

The emerging genomics fields, together with the behavioral sciences, are well-positioned to collaboratively address the complexities of a number of diseases influenced by activity–inactivity and obesity. The study of hypertension can serve as a promising example of this future collaboration. Primary hypertension makes up approximately 95% of hypertensives and is a major risk factor for coronary heart disease, stroke, and renal disease in the United States. Hypertension represents a multifactorial and polygenic disease with incremental contributions from genetic and environmental determinants.

Advances in knowledge and technology associated with the Human Genome Project, combined with continuing basic research on the physiological and biochemical causes of hypertension, offer promise for improved diagnosis and therapy of this prevalent disease (Ambler & Brown, 1999). Over time, genetic testing may be more predictive of predisposition to CAD than current conventional testing of known risk factors. The understanding of one's genetic predisposition to CAD may enable targeted environmental modification strategies aimed at individuals at greatest risk. In addition, genotyping to tailor therapy might become a routine part of risk management (Jukema & Kastelein, 2000).

SINGLE GENE DISORDERS: HUNTINGTON'S DISEASE

As discussed earlier, single genes do not determine most human behaviors. Only certain rare disorders, such as Huntington's disease, have a simple mode of transmission in which a specific mutation confers the certainty of developing the disorder. Understandably, news of this mutation can have potentially profound effects on individual probands and their families. Because Huntington's disease is currently incurable, the potential benefits of a positive genetic test primarily include some relief from uncertainty, the chance to avoid passing on the mutation, and prudent future planning. However, receipt of this information can also engender considerable distress for the carrier and his or her partner, with partners following the same course of distress as the carrier (Tibben, Timman, Bannink, & Duivenvoorden, 1997). Those who have undergone predictive testing identify subsequent difficulties in family communication as well as the uncertainties inherent in being at risk (Binedell, Soldan, & Harper, 1998). This information recognizes the trade-off between relieving uncertainty about *whether* one has the mutation but replaces it with the arguably greater uncertainty related to *when* the disease will manifest. The stress potentially induced by this genetic information must be carefully considered as we examine interventions targeted at communicating sensitive information and subsequently assisting people as they attempt to manage the uncertainty.

In the discussion that follows, the field of cancer genetic research will serve as a prototype for applying psychological models to behavioral aspects of genetic risk for disease. We focus on the cancer area because it has already begun to apply psychological models and methods to the complex issues of risk communication, screening adherence, decision making, emotional responses to testing, and familial implications of a potentially inherited disorder.

SINGLE GENE DISORDERS: BRCA1 AND BRCA2 MUTATIONS

It is estimated that between 7 to 10% of breast and ovarian cancers are attributable to an inherited susceptibility (Claus, Schildkraut, Thompson, & Risch, 1996). Mutations in the BRCA1 and BRCA2 genes are implicated in the majority of high-risk families (Ford et al., 1998). As a consequence, cancer risk counseling is an essential component of overall care for women in high-risk families.

Cancer Risk Counseling

One of the first, and hence most advanced, applications of psychology to cancer genetics has been in the area of inherited breast–ovarian cancer risk. Recent work is also focusing on risk for heritable forms of colorectal cancer (Glanz, Grove, Lerman, Gotay, & Le Marchand, 1999); however, research on inherited breast–ovarian cancer risk is several years more advanced. Genetic testing and genetic counseling for inherited breast–ovarian cancer risk are increasingly being integrated into the clinical management of women at high risk for developing these cancers. Although testing is now available through commercial biotechnology companies, it is generally recommended that genetic testing for inherited BRCA1 and BRCA2 alterations be provided within the context of institutionally approved genetic testing research programs.

Genetic counseling is an important component of the genetic testing process, both before women pursue testing and after results are available. Key elements of genetic counseling include standardized pretest education and counseling to facilitate informed decision making about genetic testing, postdisclosure counseling to provide information about risk status, recommendations for cancer surveillance, and options for breast and ovarian cancer prevention (Biesecker et al., 1993; Schneider & Marnane, 1997; Schneider et al., 1998). The genetic counseling process provides a forum through which concerns specific to the BRCA1/2 mutation can be addressed. The goals of this process include providing the client with an assessment of individual cancer risk, providing accurate information as a basis for decision making about testing or posttesting actions, and offering the emotional support needed to understand and cope with this information (Kelly, 1992).

Cancer Genetic Risk and Risk Management

From the work in genetic–environmental exposure has come the widely accepted estimate that 80 to 90% of human cancer is a result of environmental factors (Lichtenstein et al., 2000). Yet in the past 15 years, the explosion of molecular genetics has sometimes overshadowed environmental explanations by revealing genetic mechanisms underlying cancer (Hoover, 2000). We now know, for example, that women who carry an alteration in the BRCA1 or BRCA2 genes face significantly elevated risks for developing breast and ovarian cancer, often at ages much earlier than those observed in the general population (Breast Cancer Linkage Consortium, 1999; Easton, Ford, Bishop, & the Breast Cancer Linkage Consortium, 1995).

Women who are found to have a BRCA1 or BRCA2 alteration are estimated to have a lifetime risk of breast cancer of 55 to 85% (Easton et al., 1995; Ford et al., 1998; Struewing et al., 1997) and a significantly elevated risk of ovarian cancer, ranging from 15 to 65% (Easton et al., 1995; Ford et al., 1998; Struewing et al., 1997). In addition, carriers have been estimated to have a 38% 10-year risk and up to a 65% cumulative risk of contralateral breast cancer (Easton et al., 1995; Marcus et al., 1996). The risks are high and the details are complex and still emerging.

Among women affected with breast cancer who were treated with mastectomy, studies have consistently demonstrated a substantially elevated risk of contralateral breast cancer among BRCA 1/2 carriers (Breast Cancer Linkage Consortium, 1999; Easton et al., 1995). It is also likely that long-term follow-up of carriers who were treated with breast conservation therapy will reveal an increased risk for ipsilateral breast cancer (Hellman, 1999; Turner et al., 1999). Some studies also have demonstrated an increased risk for colon cancer associated with BRCA1/2 carriers (with onset at an average age; Ford et al., 1994; Phelan et al., 1996), although later studies did not confirm these findings (Struewing et al., 1997).

Recommendations for the clinical management of women with BRCA1/2 mutations were developed by members of the Cancer Genetics Studies Consortium, convened through the National Human Genome Research Institute (Burke et al., 1997). The panel based its recommendations primarily on expert opinion, because of the paucity of evidence or outcome-based data (Burke et al., 1997). For women without a previous history of cancer, the suggested guidelines for surveillance include monthly breast self-exams (BSE) and beginning at age 25 to 35, annual or semiannual clinician-performed exams and annual mammography (Burke et al., 1997). Although the value of screening mammography in women under age 50 has not been established in this high-risk population, the potential benefit of early detection for mutation carriers is thought to outweigh possible adverse effects (Burke et al., 1997). Ovarian screening consists of pelvic exam, CA-125 blood tests, and transvaginal ultrasound every 6 to 12 months, beginning at ages 25 to 35 (Burke et al., 1997). However, these tests have limited sensitivity and specificity (Burke et al., 1997).

Risk Perception

Several health benefits can be derived from genetic testing and risk evaluation. For example, the knowledge of one's elevated risk for a disease can motivate vigilance for disease symptoms, as well as participation in disease surveillance programs. Depending on the characteristics of the disease, risk status evaluation can also promote active disease prevention strategies. Prevention strategies, such as prophylactic surgeries, may be selected to reduce breast or ovarian cancer risk. However, there are no known prevention strategies for Huntington's disease. By contrasting these two diseases, one might speculate that the extent to which risk information is stressful is determined not only by how one copes with stress and uses available resources but also by the actual and perceived threat associated with the disease characteristics, as well as the family's experience with the disease. Therefore, when contrasting diseases with a heritable component, it is important to recognize those that are known to have a gene–environment interaction versus those specifically associated with a genetic mutation. As we plan risk counseling interventions, it is essential to recognize that the benefits of reducing uncertainty and motivating increased surveillance may be offset or greatly diminished by the threat of disease and sequelae of stress (Baum, Friedman, & Zakowski, 1997).

Heightened perception of breast cancer risk seems to be associated with increased screening behavior for logical and theoretical reasons. First, physicians are more likely to advise women with a family history or those who report breast symptoms about early detection, and such physician advice is an excellent predictor of whether women will obtain a mammogram. In addition, it appears that moderate levels of cancer worry facilitate and motivate interest in genetic testing (Durfy, Bowen, McTiernan, Sporleder, & Burke, 1999; Glanz et al., 1999) and adherence behaviors. A meta-analytical review of the literature describing the relationship between breast cancer risk and mammography screening found that screening adherence was greater for women with a family history, a history of breast problems, and those feeling vulnerable to and worried about cancer (McCaul, Schroeder, & Reid, 1996).

From this viewpoint, it would make sense to counsel genetically predisposed women by acknowledging personal vulnerability to disease and constructing messages designed to recognize feelings of cancer-specific worry while simultaneously providing guidance in practicing health protective behaviors. There is suggestive evidence that this may be effective. Results from a recent coping skills intervention study showed that women with a family history of breast cancer who have high levels of distress may be most likely to benefit from a behavioral coping skills intervention to promote adherence to breast cancer screening (Audrain et al., 1999).

Little is known, however, about the mutation carrier population specific to long-term screening adherence, barriers to screening, or decision making. Perhaps similar constructs of risk perception and vulnerability motivate this group to adherence. Data do suggest that although higher risk generally motivates more screening or preventive behavior, high distress or anxiety about one's risk may also interfere with this behavior (e.g., Kash, Holland, Halper, & Miller, 1992). This may be a result of the anxiety produced during screening activities (e.g., Valdimarsdottir et al., 1995).

One recent study suggested that rates of adherence to breast cancer screening did not change following genetic testing among BRCA1/2 mutation carriers, and only 21% of mutation carriers obtained a CA125 screening test and 15% obtained a transvaginal ultrasound (Lerman et al., 2000). This information raises concerns that this extremely high-risk population is neglecting some of the benefits of early detection. It is critical to identify potential barriers that appear to be hindering recommended screening regimens for this very high-risk population. As suggested by Croyle and Lerman (1999), there may be a need for new theoretical models, measures of risk perception, stress associated with risk, and interventions to address issues of screening adherence that are unique to the mutation carrier group.

Psychological Models for Enhancing Screening Among People With Genetic Disorders

Three psychological models, the stress-response theory, the health belief model and the precaution adoption process model, are particularly useful in understanding and developing strategies for improving screening adherence among those with genetic disorders. Because early detection of cancer is the most powerful available tool for improving prognosis and survival, these models are of both heuristic and practical value.

Stress measurement and stress theory is a particularly useful way to explore the sequelae of genetic risk evaluation. The model of stress theory suggests that stressors are interpreted within the context of exposure variables and personal factors, which in turn makes threats or demands more or less salient and stress more or less likely. Stressor characteristics (test outcome, uncertainty, and disease severity) and appraisal of these characteristics (such as prevention options) determines a stress response. In the case of a positive test result that confirms risk for disease, this outcome provokes a potential cascade of potentially adaptive or threatening or intrusive thoughts. These stress responses can in turn determine a series of psychological, biological, and health behavior changes (Baum et al., 1997). This model allows us to construct interventions that can address cognitions that may drive a high-risk person either toward or away from necessary screening and surveillance. Through application of this model and the transactional model (discussed later), we are encouraged to tailor interventions toward cognitive and behavioral responses most indicative of the individual's personal variables.

The health belief model provides guidance from which to investigate the interrelated constructs of cancer susceptibility via heritability, perceptions of risk, and screening adherence (Strecher & Rosenstock, 1997). The health belief model (HBM) addresses people's reactions to potential health threats. Although threats of disease and injury lurk anywhere, most such threats remain out of mind, so it may be difficult to motivate health-promoting and disease-preventive behaviors. For example, a cancer threat in the context of an unaffected, asymptomatic person with a strong family history may still be viewed as remote. In fact, depending on a person's age, lifestyle, and significant family cancer experiences, he or she may continue to perceive him- or herself as at lower or higher risk for cancer than is actually the case.

Specific to genetic disorders, an extended conceptualization and empirical definition of the conditions that connect disease threats to the self could be applied. This extension is consistent with a related model, the precaution adoption process model (PAPM), which proposes that one's experience with a risk may make it more salient and embed it in a cultural context (Weinstein, 1988). For example, the HBM assumes that motivation is the product of the scale value of responses to questions of the perceived vulnerability to a disease (e.g., how likely is it that you will get breast cancer?) and of the perceived severity of the disease (e.g., how serious would it be if you were to get breast cancer?). In the case of genetic disorders, perhaps the perceived severity of the disease may be shaped by the respondent's experience with cancer in the family (i.e., deaths versus survivors of particular cancers), as well as the developmental stage of the respondent when these experiences occurred (i.e., adolescence versus adulthood). Conceivably this additional information could contribute to the HBM by providing some evidence of respondents' judgments related to perceived vulnerability, which in turn would affect their motivation to take part in screening. Perhaps the model could be extended to identify a respondent's weighted value of his or her experience with cancer (personal and familial) and how these experiences shaped their beliefs and perceptions of vulnerability. These values could then be tested within the high-risk family to identify potential shared risk perceptions and subsequent screening or risk-reduction practices.

CANCER RISK REDUCTION

In addition to options for early detection, carriers may also face risk-reduction options. This, too, is an area of ongoing biomedical research and is replete with uncertainties. Thus, women and their families who are faced with these decisions are quite limited in the informational basis for selecting among them. Some women may consider prophylactic mastectomy or prophylactic oophorectomy to reduce their risks, although there are residual risks after these surgeries (Hartmann et al., 1999; Piver, Jishi, Tsukada, & Nava, 1993; Struewing et al., 1995). Additional options include chemoprevention with Tamoxifen to reduce breast cancer risk (although there are no data about the efficacy in carriers), or oral contraceptives to reduce ovarian cancer risk (Narod et al., 1998). Risk reduction options such as these may also have side effects or risks for other medical conditions, as well as other potential benefits, all of which need to be weighed carefully. For women who have already had breast or ovarian cancer, these options need to be considered in the context of their general health (Isaacs, Peshkin, & Lerman, 2000). In addition, these guidelines should be individualized for each patient, with recognition that a woman's approach to medical management may change over time (Isaacs et al., 2000).

The options of risk reduction versus screening represent some of the most challenging questions facing carriers who have completed the genetic testing and counseling process (e.g., Karp, Brown, Sullivan, & Massie, 1999). As alluded to earlier, BRCA1/2 mutation carriers may be in a position to decide between prophylactic mastectomy or close surveillance (i.e., clinical breast exam and mammography) or prophylactic oophorectomy or close surveillance (i.e., CA125 or transvaginal ultrasound). In this position, they must make subjective judgments about the likelihood of benefits relative to risks for each option. For example, is the risk reduction associated with prophylactic mastectomy worth the potential impact of the surgery on one's body image and sexual function? Is the risk reduction associated with prophylactic oophorectomy worth the potential impact on hormonal changes that may have negative ramifications for related health concerns? A theoretical foundation guided by decision theory and empirical literature provides a foundation from which to assist people at genetically high risk for cancer to examine options and use strategies most suitable to their personal values.

DECISION-MAKING MODELS TO ENHANCE SATISFACTION WITH PERSONAL CHOICES FOR BREAST–OVARIAN CANCER PREVENTION AND SURVEILLANCE

Genetic testing and detailed risk analysis raise fundamental issues for risk management and preventive care. As these issues are articulated, very personal decisions are contemplated. Ideally, these choices are addressed within the context of solid medical information provided in a timely but thoughtful manner. Even under ideal risk communication conditions, these potential choices may provoke conflict and anxiety. Decisional conflict is a state of uncertainty about the course of action to take (O'Connor, 1995). This state is likely when making choices involving risk or uncertainty of outcomes (e.g., Will I avoid cancer risk if I have prophylactic surgeries?), high stakes in terms of potential gains and losses (e.g., What will happen to my body, sex life, and general health if I choose surgery?), the need to make value tradeoffs in selecting a course of action (e.g., I may prolong my life by choosing surgery), and anticipated regret over the positive aspects of rejected options (e.g., With screening, my body would not undergo these radical changes) (Kasper, Mulley, & Weinberg, 1992; Levine, Gafni, Markham, & MacFarlane, 1992; O'Connor, 1993, 1995; O'Connor & D'Amico, 1990). Major defining characteristics of decisional conflict include verbalization of uncertainty, vacillation between choices, delayed decision making, and questioning personal values and beliefs while attempting decision making (O'Connor, 1995). Decision aids have the potential to reduce decisional conflict by tackling the hypothesized cause of the conflict, thereby leading to effective decision making through informed choices that are consistent with personal values (Kasper et al., 1992; Levine et al., 1992; O'Connor,

1995). A decision aid can help an individual explicitly consider the relative value of various outcomes in light of her beliefs about the chances of a course of action preventing cancer or improving the prognosis after diagnosis.

The efficacy of an interactive decision aid designed to help BRCA1/2 mutation carriers make optimal personal decisions about breast cancer prevention/surveillance is currently being evaluated (Schwartz et al., 2000). The theoretical foundation for this tool is subjective expected utility (SEU) theory, which as an extension of classical expected utility theory allows for the use of subjective probabilities of outcomes when the objective probability is unknown. From the standpoint of SEU theory (Savage, 1954), an effective decision aid would ensure greater concordance between SEUs and actual decisions. This is important as mutation carriers are faced with complex probabilistic risk data and significantly different options for managing this risk.

PSYCHOSOCIAL FACTORS IN CANCER GENETICS: DISTRESS RELATED TO TESTING

Given the information described, it is reasonable to hypothesize that BRCA1/2 mutation carriers experience significant levels of cancer-related distress (e.g., Watson et al., 1996). Surprisingly, available data do not provide evidence for clinically significant or persistent global distress related to BRCA1/2 testing (Croyle, Smith, Bodkin, Baty, & Nash, 1997; Lerman et al., 1996). There may be subgroups of participants, however, who are more vulnerable. For example, one study identified that women diagnosed with cancer less than one year before genetic testing appeared to be particularly vulnerable to potential genetic testing stress (Wood, Mullineaux, Rahm, Fairclough, & Wenzel, 2000). Identification of vulnerable subgroups can provide the basis for future studies of the relative benefits of educational and counseling interventions.

Recent work examining distress after cancer genetic testing supports the stress-response theory. The Multidimensional Impact of Cancer Risk Assessment (MICRA) questionnaire (Cella et al., 2002) along with standard measures of general distress was administered to 175 people one month after they received genetic test results. Study participants were divided into four standard clinical test result groups: (a) BRCA1/2 positive; (b) BRCA1/2 negative; (c) panel negative/uninformative; and (d) true negative. Unlike the general distress questionnaires that did not significantly distinguish the four groups, the genetic testing distress measure was able to differentiate participants who were BRCA1/2 positive from the other groups (Cella et al., 2002). This promising measure provides some confirmation to earlier hypotheses that notification of a genetic risk for cancer may potentiate a stress response for those at highest risk.

FAMILIAL IMPLICATIONS OF GENETIC TESTING

Familial concerns and implications often surface after genetic testing. This may be especially true in the context of "cascade testing," which starts with the initial proband, or affected individual, and then branches out to other relatives if a known risk-conferring mutation is identified. As previously mentioned, most clinical genetic research settings discuss implications of the test result for other family members (Biesecker et al., 1993). The tested person is then given the option to contact his or her relatives directly or have the health care provider contact the relatives. Even if family members themselves do not participate in testing, they may be profoundly affected by the genetic diagnosis of another family member (Thompson, Gustafson, Hamlett, & Spock, 1992; Thompson et al., 1994). In addition, knowledge of their relatives' test results may help to clarify their own personal risk status, even without testing.

Because inherited risk is shared within families, the risk status of one family member has clear implications for others. Familial risk communication patterns and outcomes, particularly related to determinants of decision making and testing, could be considered one of the most pressing and least studied aspects of genetic testing (Bowen, Patenaude, & Vernon, 1999). Several studies have begun to elucidate family risk communication patterns and potential conflicts. For example, factors that may influence the extent to which probands are willing to discuss their BRCA1/2 test results with their relatives include the proband's test result and gender, with greater test results disclosure to female relatives (Green, Richards, Murton, Statham, & Hallowell, 1997; Hughes et al., 1999). Although disclosure to a sister may have positive effects on quality of life among BRCA1/2 carriers (Lerman, Peshkin, Hughes, & Isaacs, 1998), probands with higher levels of anxiety and depression may be less likely to disclose their test results to relatives because of anticipated negative reactions (Julian-Reynier et al., 1996). Although family communication is important to make other family members aware of their risk status and the availability of testing, it can also generate distress and conflict among probands and within families (Lerman et al., 1998; Ponder & Green, 1996).

Despite the potential importance of communicating test results to relatives, we know very little about the communication processes used and their implications or impact on relationships. For example, the impact of genetic testing for Huntington disease on the family system suggests that family functioning was affected through membership, patterns of communication, and caregiving concerns (Sobel & Cowan, 2000). Genetic testing for hereditary nonpolyposis colorectal cancer (HNPCC) mutations has also been associated with increasing levels of family expressiveness among mutation carriers, although possibly also adversely affecting family cohesion among younger mutation carriers (Hughes, Lerman, Tercyak, Lynch, & Harty, 2000). Information on communication patterns of BRCA1/2 female carriers and their sisters indicates that although the most important reason for communicating results was to provide genetic risk information, carriers also communicated their results to obtain emotional support (74%) and to get advice about medical decisions (42%). They also discussed the possibility of discrimination and recommendations for cancer management with significantly more sisters. Among sisters to whom test results were not communicated, the most important reason for not sharing test results was because of emotionally distant relationships (Hughes et al., 2002). These studies support the conclusion that genetic testing is most often a family, and not only an individual, matter. As a family matter, we are challenged to develop or adapt conceptual models that address risk communication and social support within the context of family interactions and relationships.

SYSTEMS THEORY AS A CONCEPTUAL MODEL FOR EXAMINING GENETIC TESTING IN FAMILIES

The family functioning domain is perhaps the most dynamic and least understood of all psychosocial aspects of cancer genetics. Yet familial psychosocial facts and situations can be important to the genetic testing process (Daly et al., 1999). Systems theory could be invaluable in conceptual model development and hypothesis generation.

For example, one might expect that family factors and individual adjustment are interrelated, linking positive family factors such as support and cohesion with better adjustment (e.g., Klemp & La Greca, 1987). Conversely, family conflict and disruption may be associated with poor adjustment and regret over genetic testing. In some families, conflicting views of the usefulness of knowledge gained from genetic testing might isolate the proband and create future medical decision-making challenges. Supportive family interactions may be associated with more comfort and confidence in decision making and communication. In addition, the stress-buffering effects of supportive interpersonal relationships could promote satisfaction with decision making.

These are important considerations when recognizing that, typically, the proband's motivation for genetic testing is the expressed desire to support the health and well-being of their children (Geller, Doksum, Bornhardt, & Metz, 1999; Glanz et al., 1999; Vernon et al., 1999). To this end, supportive families may facilitate the proband's proactive discussion and planning related to genetics as a family issue. We can begin to generate hypotheses related to how and why familial interactions influence testing decisions and subsequent planning. Green and colleagues (1997) have offered interesting family dynamic insights from which hypotheses can be derived. For example, although genetic communication is most prominent among female relatives, if mothers are alive, they appear to be the key figures in supplying family information. It also appears that tested individuals may view themselves as the family gatekeeper, perceiving themselves as balancing the obligation of passing on information with that of not causing alarm. It has also been noted that communication is impeded by such family factors as adoption, divorce, remarriage, family rifts, and large age gaps between siblings (Green et al., 1997).

Family systems research could be a particularly useful paradigm as genetic studies evolve. The use of a family systems genogram, for example, specific to family functioning related to disease, could unlock some of the answers to how and why people perceive themselves at more or less risk for disease. A family systems genogram could accompany the traditional family pedigree generated by the genetic counselor and function as a "road map" of the on-going life in a family across generations (Pendagast & Sherman, 1977).

Within this systems genogram, many pertinent questions could be addressed. Is there a central clearinghouse or gatekeeper from whom family information flows? How do people handle family business? Who contacts whom? In what way? The quality of relationships can be evaluated by such criteria as the frequency of contact between various members of the extended family; type of contact; closest and most distant relationships; characteristics of the relationships that have been formed; emotional cut-offs; ethnic, religious, and socioeconomic differences; as well as issues with intense emotional charge for each nuclear family household (e.g., money). In hereditary cancer families, important events include cancer diagnoses and deaths, which all have emotional impacts and can create social reorganization within the family system. Such an instrument could yield valuable information about how people cope with illness and threatening information such as an inherited disorder.

It is important to note, however, that a potential conflict may exist in the area of genetics in which a basic belief of individualism and privacy may be challenged if we delve too deeply into the family structure. This concept has been supported by cultural, professional, and technological progress, in which families often moved toward emotional and geographical distance as generations grow up. To a certain extent, this practice has resulted in a separation of the generations, and the belief that each generation starts a new life with the establishment of a new nuclear family unit. The researcher seeking to understand the family psychodynamics may be seen as intruding—in contrast to a family who seeks out counseling or therapy, where a psychologist is invited to analyze the family's functioning.

Despite the dilemmas inherent in conducting this type of research, genetic studies of families indicate that family patterns tend to repeat themselves over generations. It is therefore essential to begin developing new models and measures to examine how family variables interact with constructs such as risk communication, decisions about genetic testing, and the quality of life of persons in the family, while being sensitive to the inherent pitfalls of assessing multiple family members across generations.

THE TRANSACTIONAL MODEL OF STRESS AND COPING TO ADDRESS PSYCHOSOCIAL CONCERNS FOR MUTATION CARRIERS

The previous section has addressed some of the most salient psychosocial factors in genetic testing. The transactional model of stress and coping (Chesney, Folkman, & Chambers, 1996; Folkman & Chesney, 1995; Lazarus & Folkman, 1984) has been particularly useful in guiding the study of these factors (Baum et al., 1997; Lerman & Glanz, 1997). This model posits that an individual's response to a stressful event or situation (e.g., disclosure of positive test results) is dependent on three factors: (a) primary appraisal, which refers to an individual's perceptions of the level of risk and threat associated with the situation; (b) secondary appraisal, which refers to an individual's evaluation of his or her ability to exert control over the event and to manage emotional reactions; and (c) coping efforts, which refer to the strategies one uses to manage the event or one's feelings. Based on this theoretical framework, a psychosocial telephone counseling intervention is currently being tested (Lerman, Hughes, et al., 2000). (See Figure 4.1.)

The overall goal of the study is to evaluate the efficacy of psychosocial telephone counseling (PTC) delivered in conjunction with standard genetic counseling (SGC) to carriers of BRCA1/2 mutations compared to SGC alone. In addition, the mechanisms by which PTC affects psychosocial and behavioral outcomes are investigated, as well as the subgroups of carriers most and least likely to benefit from PTC.

The transactional model has directed the process through which the intervention targets three key areas affected by the genetic testing result: emotional reactions, family concerns, and medical decision making. Through this process the intervention fosters an accurate understanding of personal risk (primary appraisal). If, for example, an unaffected carrier underestimates her cancer risk, she may not initiate coping efforts and may be less motivated to obtain recommended screening tests. By contrast, if she overestimates

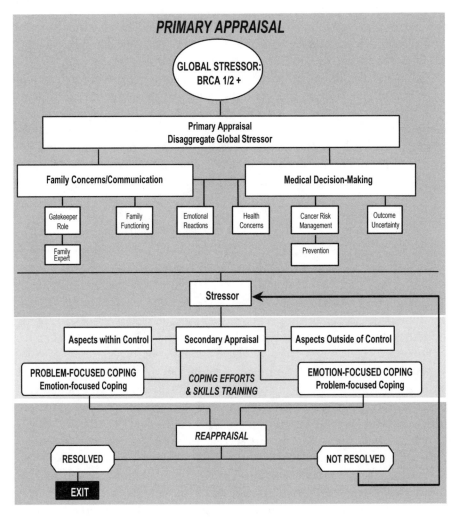

Figure 4.1. Transactional model applied to the BRCA plus experience.

her risk, this could lead to increased distress and decreased adherence. Second, the intervention targets a carrier's appraisals of her ability to reduce her risk of developing and dying from cancer and her ability to manage her distress (secondary appraisal). A carrier who does not feel equipped to deal with her risk status or her feelings about it may be more likely to experience distress and difficulty communicating with family members. Third, to minimize long-term distress and maximize satisfaction with medical decision making and family concerns, this intervention fosters adaptive coping efforts (those that fit best with the woman's needs and resources).

A critical component of the PTC process is the application of specific coping strategies best suited to address concerns and promote adaptive coping. These concerns have broadly been defined in domains of medical decision making (e.g., exploring options for risk reduction or planning a screening program), managing family concerns (e.g., examining whether to tell family members), and managing emotions (e.g., understanding and addressing uncertainty; Wenzel et al., 2003). Several of the coping strategies were chosen from Coping Effectiveness Training (Chesney et al., 1996) and were altered to fit with the needs and resources of this clientele. For example, active coping efforts were aimed either at problem management (e.g., problem solving to obtain a mammogram) or emotional regulation (e.g., seeking social support). These strategies included identifying the stressor, identifying changeable and unchangeable aspects of the stressor, problem-solving, communication, decision making, enhancing social support, and thought changing.

If effective, results of this investigation could make important clinical, scientific, and policy contributions. This structured intervention could, for example, be adopted in the clinical setting for implementation by genetic counselors or other health professionals. Subgroups of carriers most likely to benefit would help clinicians to target this intervention to their clients who are most in need. Finally, the exploration of mechanisms by which PTC affects key outcomes will contribute to the understanding of the processes of stress and coping after genetic testing, thereby informing future research.

A MULTIVARIATE FRAMEWORK FOR HEALTH PSYCHOLOGY RESEARCH IN GENETICS OF ADULT ONSET DISEASES

In view of the multiple and complex factors delineated in this chapter, we have developed an initial framework for conceptualizing the role of psychosocial and familial factors in adult genetic disorders. In this framework, each factor should be viewed in a multivariate manner within the context of the other model components. Assessment could begin at genetic-specific levels (knowledge of risk, knowledge of pedigree), before proceeding systematically to more complex psychological levels (perception of risk, stress, and adjustment). This resembles the transactional model in that when gaps in knowledge exist, intervention should begin at an educational level. (See Figure 4.2.)

This model also depicts likely pathways between personal knowledge of risk, psychosocial variables associated with risk, and ultimately health behaviors and activities for stress management related to risk (for self and family). Two pathways—personal experience with genetic illness (i.e.,

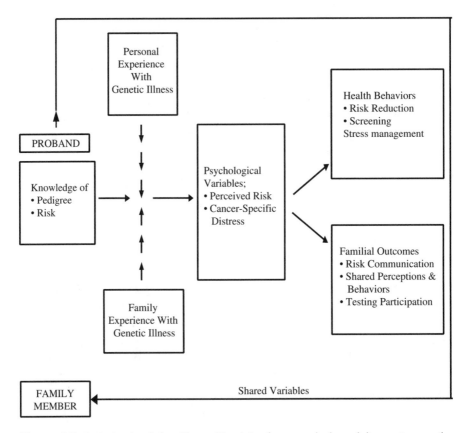

Figure 4.2. A behavioral health multivariate framework in adult-onset genetic disorders.

affected) and family experience with genetic illness (i.e., number and severity of diagnoses)—are hypothesized as mediators between knowledge of risk and psychological variables. This conceptualization could augment information derived from the health belief model and precaution adoption process model, where experience with a genetic illness may affect perceived vulnerability and perceived severity of a given disorder. These mechanisms could be assessed as potential mediating variables in future research.

This type of framework may also allow us to build on genetic research by exploring intrafamilial variables thought to influence risk perception, communication, and decisions related to genetic risk. As illustrated in Figure 4.2, all information gleaned from family member 1 (the proband) should prove fruitful in examining shared and divergent perceptions of risk and associated outcomes. This presumes that not only is inherited risk shared, so too are cultural, social, and perhaps psychological variables that affect coping and adjustment to genetic risk.

CONCLUSION

The Human Genome Project has been considered by many to be the most important project in biology and the biomedical sciences, and one that will permanently change biology and medicine. Advances in the understanding of human genetics and genomics will have important implications for individuals and society, where soon we may be able to ask how effects of specific genes unfold in behavioral development and how they interact and correlate with experience. This top-down, behavioral genomic level of analysis will complement current functional approaches (Plomin & Crabbe, 2000). However, we are challenged to develop and evaluate optimal strategies for conveying and evaluating risk and susceptibility. Future research should be directed at assisting individuals and families in attaining maximum benefits from the genetic information, which may translate into improvements in physical and psychological well-being. Multiple modalities can be explored to achieve these benefits. These will likely include combinations of educational and counseling efforts through printed material, videos, CD-ROM, decision-making aids, and structured counseling interventions. Health psychology is poised to contribute to the goals set forth by the Human Genome Project, in which examination of the ethical, legal, and social implications of genome research is an integral and essential component of the project (Collins et al., 1998).

REFERENCES

Ambler, S. K., & Brown, R. D. (1999). Genetic determinants of blood pressure regulation. *Journal of Cardiovascular Nursing, 13,* 59–77.

Arinami, T., Ishiguro, H., & Onaivi, E. S. (2000). Polymorphisms in genes involved in neurotransmission in relation to smoking. *European Journal of Pharmacology, 410,* 215–226.

Audrain, J., Rimer, B., Cella, D., Stefanek, M., Garber, J., Pennanen, M., et al. (1999). The impact of a brief coping skills intervention on adherence to breast self-examination among first-degree relatives of newly diagnosed breast cancer patients. *Psycho-Oncology, 8,* 220–229.

Baum, A., Friedman, A. L., & Zakowski, S. G. (1997). Stress and genetic testing for disease risk. *Health Psychology, 16,* 8–19.

Biesecker, B. B., Boehnke, M., Calzone, K., Markel, D. S., Garber, J. E., Collins, F. S., et al. (1993). Genetic counseling for families with inherited susceptibility to breast and ovarian cancer. *Journal of the American Medical Association, 269,* 1970–1974.

Binedell, J., Soldan, J. R., & Harper, P. S. (1998). Predictive testing for Huntington's disease: II. Qualitative findings from a study of uptake in South Wales. *Clinical Genetics, 54,* 489–496.

Bowen, D. J., Patenaude, A. F., & Vernon, S. W. (1999). Psychosocial issues in cancer genetics: From the laboratory to the public. *Cancer, Epidemiology Biomarkers, and Prevention, 8*, 326–328.

Breast Cancer Linkage Consortium. (1999). Cancer risks in BRCA2 mutation carriers. *Journal of the National Cancer Institute, 91*, 1310–1316.

Burke, W., Daly, M., Garber, J., Bodkin, J., Kahn, M. J., Lynch, P., et al. (1997). Recommendations for follow-up care of individuals with an inherited predisposition to cancer: II. BRCA1 and BRCA2. *Journal of the American Medical Association, 277*, 997–1003.

Carmelli, D., Swan, G. E., Robinette, D., & Fabsitz, R. (1992). Genetic influence on smoking—A study of male twins. *New England Journal of Medicine, 327*, 829–833.

Cella, D., Hughes, C., Peterman, A., Chang, C., Peshkin, B., Schwartz, L., et al. (2002). A brief assessment of concerns associated with genetic testing for cancer: The multidimensional impact of cancer risk assessment (MICRA) questionnaire. *Healthy Psychology, 21*, 564–572.

Chesney, M. A., Folkman, S., & Chambers, D. (1996). Coping effectiveness training for men living with HIV disease: Preliminary findings. *International Journal of STD and AIDS, 7*, 75–82.

Claus, E. B., Schildkraut, J. M., Thompson, W. D., & Risch, N. J. (1996). The genetic attributable risk of breast and ovarian cancer. *Cancer, 77*, 2318–2324.

Collins, F. S. (1999). Shattuck lecture—Medical and societal consequences of the human genome project. *New England Journal of Medicine, 341*, 28–37.

Collins, F. S., & McKusick, V. A. (2001). Implications of the Human Genome Project for medical science. *JAMA, 285*, 540–544.

Collins, F. S., Patrinos, A., Jordan, E., Chakravarti, A., Gesteland, R., Walters, L., et al. (1998). New goals for the U.S. Human Genome Project: 1998–2003. *Science, 282*, 682–689.

Comings, D. E., & Blum, K. (2000). Reward deficiency syndrome: Genetic aspects of behavioral disorders. *Progress in Brain Research, 126*, 325–341.

Croyle, R. T., & Lerman, C. (1999). Risk communication in genetic testing for cancer susceptibility. *Journal of the National Cancer Institute, 25*, 59–66.

Croyle, R. T., Smith, K. R., Bodkin, J. R., Baty, B., & Nash, J. (1997). Psychological responses to BRCA1 mutation testing: Preliminary findings. *Health Psychology, 16*, 63–72.

Daly, M., Famer, J., Harrop-Stein, C., Montgomery, S., Itzen, M. Costalas, J. V., et al. (1999). Exploring family relationships in cancer risk counseling using the genogram. *Cancer, Epidemiology, Biomarkers, and Prevention, 8*, 393–398.

Durfy, S. J., Bowen, D. J., McTiernan, A., Sporleder, J., & Burke, W. (1999). Attitudes and interest in genetic testing for breast and ovarian cancer susceptibility in diverse groups of women in western Washington. *Cancer, Epidemiology, Biomarkers, and Prevention, 8*, 369–375.

Easton, D. F., Ford, D., Bishop, T., & the Breast Cancer Linkage Consortium. (1995). Breast and ovarian cancer incidence in BRCA1-mutation carriers. *American Journal of Human Genetics, 56*, 265–271.

Folkman, S., & Chesney, M. A. (1995). Coping with HIV infection. In M. Stein & A. Baum (Eds.), *Perspectives on Behavioral Medicine* (pp. 115–134). Hillsdale, NJ: Erlbaum.

Ford, D., Easton, D. F., Bishop, D. T., Narod, S. A., Goldgar, D. E., & the Breast Cancer Linkage Consortium. (1994). Risks of cancer in BRCA1-mutation carriers. *Lancet, 343*, 692–695.

Ford, D., Easton, D. F., Stratton, M., Narod, S., Goldgar, D., Devilee, P., et al. (1998). Genetic heterogeneity and penetrance analysis of the BRCA1 and BRCA2 genes in breast cancer families. *American Journal of Human Genetics, 62*, 676–689.

Geller, G., Doksum, T., Bernhardt, B. A., & Metz, S. A. (1999). Participation in breast cancer susceptibility testing protocols: Influence of recruitment source, altruism, and family involvement on women's decisions. *Cancer, Epidemiology, Biomarkers, and Prevention, 8*, 377–383.

Glanz, K., Grove, J., Lerman, C., Gotay, C., & Le Marchand, L. (1999). Correlates of intentions to obtain genetic counseling and colorectal cancer gene testing among at-risk relatives from three ethnic groups. *Cancer, Epidemiology, Biomarkers, and Prevention, 8*, 329–336.

Green, J., Richards, M., Murton, F., Statham, H., & Hallowell, N. (1997). Family communication and genetic counseling: The case of hereditary breast and ovarian cancer. *Journal of Genetic Counseling, 6*, 45–60.

Hartmann, L. C., Schaid, D. J., Woods, J. E., Crotty, T. P., Myers, J. L., Arnold, P. G., et al. (1999). Efficacy of bilateral prophylactic mastectomy in women with a family history of breast cancer. *New England Journal of Medicine, 340*, 77–84.

Heath, A. C., & Martin, N. G. (1993). Genetic models for the natural history of smoking: Evidence for a genetic influence on smoking persistence. *Addictive Behaviors, 18*, 19–34.

Hellman, S. (1999). The key and the lamppost. *Journal of Clinical Oncology, 17*, 3007–3008.

Hoover, R. N. (2000). Cancer—nature, nurture, or both. *New England Journal of Medicine, 343*, 135–136.

Hughes, C., Lerman, C., Schwartz, M., Peshkin, B. N., Wenzel, L., Narod, S., et al. (2002). All in the family: An evaluation of the process and content of family communication about BRCA1/2 genetic test results. *American Journal of Medical Genetics, 107*, 143–150.

Hughes, C., Lerman, C., Tercyak, K., Lynch, H., & Harty, A. (2000, April). *Familial impact of genetic testing for HNPCC mutations.* Paper presented at the annual meeting of the Society of Behavioral Medicine, Nashville, TN.

Hughes, C., Lynch, H., Durham, C., Snyder, C., Lemon, S., Narod, S., et al. (1999). Communication of BRCA1/2 test result in hereditary breast cancer families. *Cancer Research Therapy Control, 8,* 51–59.

Isaacs, C., Peshkin, B. N., & Lerman, C. (2000). Evaluation and management of women with a strong family history of breast cancer. In J. R. Harris, M. E. Lippman, M. Morrow, & C. K. Osborne (Eds.), *Diseases of the breast* (2nd ed., pp. 237–254). Philadelphia: J.B. Lippincott.

Jukema, J. W., & Kastelein, J. J. (2000). Tailored therapy to fit individual profiles. Genetics and coronary artery disease. *Annals of the New York Academy of Sciences, 902,* 17–24.

Julian-Reynier, C., Eisinger, F., Vennin, P., Chabal, F., Aurran, Y., Nogues, C., et al. (1996). Attitudes toward cancer predictive testing and transmission of information to the family. *Journal of Medical Genetics, 33,* 731–736.

Karp, J., Brown, K. L., Sullivan, M. D., & Massie, M. J. (1999). The prophylactic mastectomy dilemma: A support group for women at high genetic risk for breast cancer. *Journal of Genetic Counseling, 8,* 163–173.

Kash, K. M., Holland, J. C., Halper, M. S., & Miller, D. G. (1992). Psychological distress and surveillance behaviors of women with a family history of breast cancer. *Journal of the National Cancer Institute, 84,* 24–30.

Kasper, J. F., Mulley, A. G., & Wennberg, J. E. (1992). Developing shared decision-making programs to improve the quality of health care. *Quality Review Bulletin, 18,* 183–190.

Kelly, P. T. (1992). Informational needs of individuals and families with hereditary cancers. *Seminars in Oncology Nursing, 8,* 288–292.

Klemp, S. B., & La Greca, A. M. (1987). Adolescents with IDDM: The role of family cohesion and conflict. *Diabetes, 36,* 18A.

Lander, E. S., Linton, L. M., Birren, B., Nusbaum, C., Zody, M. C., Baldwin, J., et al. (2001). Initial sequencing and analysis of the human genome. *Nature, 409,* 860–921.

Lazarus, R. S., & Folkman, S. (1984). *Stress, appraisal, & coping.* New York: Springer.

Lerman, C., Caporaso, N. E., Audrain, J., Main, D., Bowman, E. D., Lockshin, B., et al. (1999). Evidence suggesting the role of specific genetic factors in cigarette smoking. *Health Psychology, 18,* 14–20.

Lerman, C., Caporaso, N. E., Audrain, J., Main, D., Boyd, N. R., & Shields, P. G. (2000). Interacting effects of the serotonin transporter gene and neuroticism in smoking practices and nicotine dependence. *Molecular Psychiatry, 5,* 189–192.

Lerman, C., Daly, M., Sands, C., Balshem, A., Lustbader, E., Heggan, T., et al. (1993). Mammography adherence and psychological distress among women at risk for breast cancer. *Journal of the National Cancer Institute, 85,* 1074–1080.

Lerman, C., & Glanz, K. (1997). Stress, coping, and health behavior. In K. Glanz, F. M. Lewis, & B. K. Rimer (Eds.), *Health behavior and health education: Theory, research, and practice* (2nd ed., pp. 113–138). San Francisco: Jossey-Bass.

Lerman, C., Hughes, C., Croyle, R. T., Main, D., Durham, C., Snyder, C., et al. (2000). Prophylactic surgery decisions and surveillance practices one year following BRCA1/2 testing. *Preventive Medicine, 31*, 75–80.

Lerman, C., Narod, S., Schulman, K., Hughes, C., Gomez-Caminero, A., Bonney, G., et al. (1996). BRCA1 testing in families with hereditary breast–ovarian cancer: A prospective study of patient decision-making and outcomes. *JAMA, 275*, 1885–1892.

Lerman, C., Peshkin, B. N., Hughes, C., & Isaacs, C. (1998). Family disclosure in genetic testing for cancer susceptibility: Determinants and consequences. *Journal of Health Care Law and Policy, 1*, 353–372.

Lerman, C., Trock, B., Rimer, B. K., Jepson, C., Brody, D., & Boyce, A. (1991). Psychological side effects of breast cancer screening. *Health Psychology, 10*, 259–267.

Levine, M. N., Gafni, A., Markham, B., & MacFarlane, D. (1992). A bedside decision instrument to elicit a patient's preference concerning adjuvant chemotherapy for breast cancer. *Annals of Internal Medicine, 117*, 53.

Lichtenstein, P., Holm, N. V., Verkasalo, P. K., Iliadou, A., Kaprio, J., Koskenvuo, M., et al. (2000). Environmental and heritable factors in the causation of cancer—Analyses of cohorts of twins from Sweden, Denmark, and Finland. *New England Journal of Medicine, 343*, 78–85.

Marcus, J. N., Watson, P., Page, D. L., Narod, S. A., Lenoir, G. M., Tonin, P., et al. (1996). Hereditary breast cancer: Pathobiology, prognosis, and BRAC1 and BRAC2 gene linkage. *Cancer, 77*, 697–709.

McCaul, K. D., Schroeder, D. M., & Reid, P. A. (1996). Breast cancer worry and screening: Some prospective data. *Health Psychology, 15*, 430–433.

McGuffin, P., & Martin, N. (1999). Science, medicine, and the future. Behaviour and genes. *British Medical Journal, 319*, 37–40.

Narod, S. A., Risch, H., Moslehi, R., Dorum, A., Neuhausen, S., Olsson, H., et al. (1998). Oral contraceptives and the risk of hereditary ovarian cancer. *New England Journal of Medicine, 339*, 424–428.

Nestler, E. J., & Landsman, D. (2001). Learning about addiction from the genome. *Nature, 409*, 834–835.

O'Connor, A. M. (1993). Decisional conflict. In G. K. McFarland & E. A. McFarlane (Eds.), *Nursing diagnosis and intervention* (2nd ed., p. 468). St. Louis, MO: CV Mosby.

O'Connor, A. M. (1995). Validation of a decisional conflict scale. *Medical Decision Making, 15*, 25–30.

O'Connor, A. M., & D'Amico, M. (1990). Decisional conflict. In G. K. McFarland & M. D. Thomas (Eds.), *Psychiatric mental health nursing: Application of the nursing process* (p. 192). Philadelphia: J.B. Lippincott.

O'Connor, A. M., Tugwell, P., Wells, G., & Elmslie, T. (1995). Do decision aids help post-menopausal women considering preventive hormone replacement therapy (HRT)? *Medical Decision Making, 15*, 33.

Palou, A., Serra, F., Bonet, M. L., & Picó, C. (2000). Obesity: Molecular bases of a multifactorial problem. *European Journal of Nutrition, 39,* 127–144.

Pendagast, E. G., & Sherman, C. O. (1977). A guide to the genogram: Family systems training. *The Family, 5,* 3–14.

Pérusse, L., & Bouchard, C. (2000). Gene-diet interactions in obesity. *American Journal of Clinical Nutrition, 72,* 1285S–1290S.

Phelan, C. M., Rebeck, T. R., Weber, B. L., Devilee, P. Ruttledge, M. H., Lynch, H. T., et al. (1996). Ovarian cancer risk in BRCA1 carriers is modified by the HRAS1 variable number of tandem repeat (VNTR) locus. *Nature Genetics, 12,* 309–311.

Piver, M. S., Jishi, M. F., Tsukada, Y., & Nava, G. (1993). Primary peritoneal carcinoma after prophylactic oophorectomy in women with a family history of ovarian cancer. *Cancer, 71,* 2751–2755.

Plomin, R. (1998). Using DNA in health psychology. *Health Psychology, 17,* 53–55.

Plomin, R., & Crabbe, J. (2000). DNA. *Psychological Bulletin, 126,* 806–28.

Plomin, R., Owen, M. J., & McGuffin, P. (1994). The genetic basis of complex human behaviors. *Science, 264,* 1733–1739.

Ponder, M., & Green, J. M. (1996). BRCA1 testing: Some issues in moving from research to service. *Psycho-Oncology, 5,* 223–232.

Rossing, M. A. (1998). Genetic influences on smoking: Candidate gene. *Environmental Health Perspectives, 106,* 231–238.

Sabol, S. Z., Nelson, M. L., Fisher, C., Gunzerath, L., Brody, C. L., Hu, S., et al. (1999). A genetic association for cigarette smoking behavior. *Health Psychology, 18,* 7–13.

Savage, L. J. (1954). *The foundations of statistics.* New York: Wiley.

Scherrer, J. F., True, W. R., Xian, H., Lyons, M. J., Eisen, S. A., Goldberg, J., et al. (2000). Evidence for genetic influences common and specific to symptoms of generalized anxiety and panic. *Journal of Affective Disorders, 57,* 25–35.

Schneider, K. A., & Marnane, D. (1997). Cancer risk counseling: How is it different? *Journal of Genetic Counseling, 6,* 97–109.

Schneider, K. A., Schrag, D., Kieffer, S. A,. Shannon, K. E., Light, T., DiGianni, L., et al. (1998). Decisions about prophylactic surgery following BRCA1/2 results (abstract). *Journal of Genetic Counseling, 7,* 467–468.

Schwartz, M. D., Lerman, C., Peshkin, B., Main, D., Kavanagh, C., & Isaacs, C. (2000, April). *Psychological outcomes of genetic testing for breast-ovarian cancer susceptibility.* Paper presented at the annual meeting of the Society of Behavioral Medicine, Nashville, TN.

Sobel, S. K., & Cowan, D. B. (2000). Impact of genetic testing for Huntington Disease on the family system. *American Journal of Medical Genetics, 90,* 49–59.

Strecher, V. J., & Rosenstock, I. M. (1997). The Health Belief Model. In K. Glanz, F. M. Lewis, & B. K. Rimer (Eds.), *Health behavior and health education: Theory, research, and practice* (2nd ed., pp. 41–59). San Francisco: Jossey-Bass.

Struewing, J. P., Hartge, P., Wacholder, S., Baker, S. M., Berlin, M., McAdams, M., et al. (1997). The risk of cancer associated with specific mutations of BRCA1 and BRCA2 among Ashkenazi Jews. *New England Journal of Medicine, 336*, 1401–1408.

Struewing, J. P., Lerman, C., Kase, R. G., Giambarresi, T. R., & Tucker, M. A. (1995). Anticipated uptake and impact of genetic testing in hereditary breast and ovarian cancer families. *Cancer, Epidemiology, Biomarkers, and Prevention, 4*, 169–173.

Thompson, R. J., Jr., Gil, K. M., Gustafson, K. E., George, L. K., Keith, B. R., Spock, A., et al. (1994). Stability and change in the psychological adjustment of mothers of children and adolescents with cystic fibrosis and sickle cell disease. *Journal of Pediatric Psychology, 19*, 171–188.

Thompson, R. J., Jr., Gustafson, K. E., Hamlett, K. W., & Spock, A. (1992). Stress, coping, and family functioning in the psychological adjustment of mothers and children and adolescents with cystic fibrosis. *Journal of Pediatric Psychology, 17*, 573–585.

Tibben, A., Timman, R., Bannink, E. C., & Duivenvoorden, H. J. (1997). Three-year follow-up after presymptomatic testing for Huntington's disease in tested individuals and partners. *Health Psychology, 16*, 20–35.

Turner, B. C., Harrold, E., Matloff, E., Smith, T., Gumbs, A. A., Beinfield, M., et al. (1999). BRCA1/BRCA2 germline mutations in locally recurrent breast cancer patients after lumpectomy and radiation therapy: Implications for breast-conserving management in patients with BRCA1/BRCA2 mutations. *Journal of Clinical Oncology, 17*, 3017–3024.

Valdimarsdottir, H. B., Bovbjerg, D. H., Kash, K. M., Holland, J. C., Osborne, M. P., & Miller, D. G. (1995). Psychological distress in women with a familial risk of breast cancer. *Psycho-Oncology, 4*, 133–141.

Vernon, S. W., Gritz, E. R., Peterson, S. K., Perz, C. A., Marani, S., Amos, C. I., et al. (1999). Intention to learn results of genetic testing for hereditary colon cancer. *Cancer, Epidemiology, Biomarkers, and Prevention, 8*, 353–360.

Watson, M., Lloyd, S. M., Eeles, R., Ponder, B., Easton, D., Seal, S., et al. (1996). Psychosocial impact of testing (by linkage) for the BRCA1 breast cancer gene: An investigation of two families in the research setting. *Psycho-Oncology, 5*, 233–239.

Weinstein, N. D. (1988). The Precaution Adoption Process Model. *Health Psychology, 7*, 355–386.

Wenzel, L. B., Hughes, C., Peshkin, B. N., Powell-Emsbo, S., Benkendorf, J., & Lerman, C. (2003). *Development of a cancer genetic psychosocial telephone counseling intervention.* Unpublished manuscript.

Wood, M. E., Mullineaux, L., Rahm, A. K., Fairclough, D., & Wenzel, L. B. (2000). Impact of BRAC1 testing on women with cancer: A pilot study. *Genetic Testing, 4*, 265–272.

Xian, H., Chantarujikapong, S. I., Scherrer, J. F., Eisen, S. A., Lyons, M. J., Goldberg, J., et al. (2000). Genetic and environmental influences on posttraumatic stress disorder, alcohol and drug dependence in twin pairs. *Drug and Alcohol Dependence, 61*, 95–102

York, D., & Bouchard, C. (2000). How obesity develops: Insights from the new biology. *Endocrine, 13*, 143–154.

5

PERSONALITY THEORY AND RESEARCH IN THE STUDY OF HEALTH AND BEHAVIOR

TIMOTHY W. SMITH AND JOHN M. RUIZ

The effect of personality characteristics on physical health has been a central topic in health psychology and behavioral medicine since the inception of these fields (Stone, Cohen, & Adler, 1980; Weiss, Herd, & Fox, 1981). The influence of stable patterns of emotion, cognition, and action on the development, course, and impact of illness has actually been a recurring theme throughout the history of medicine since the writings of Hippocrates (McMahon, 1976). A hundred years ago, a leading figure in the development of modern medicine, Sir William Osler, anticipated later theories about the impact of personality on cardiovascular illnesses when he suggested that coronary heart disease was typically found among "not the neurotic, delicate person . . . but the robust, the vigorous in mind and body, the keen and ambitious man, the indicators of whose engine is always at full speed ahead" (Osler, 1910, p. 839). Similarly anticipating research on the role of personality in the presentation of disease and the process of adaptation to illness, Osler (1910) suggested that it is not only important to know which disease the patient has, but also psychological characteristics of the patient who has the disease. Recent reviews indicate that personality traits reliably predict the development of serious illnesses and moderate their impact (Contrada, Cather, & O'Leary, 1999; Smith & Gallo, 2001). These reviews also indicate that the study of personality and health continues to be an important topic not only in health psychology and behavioral medicine (Smith & Gallo, 2001) but in personality psychology as well (Contrada et al., 1999; Smith & Williams, 1992; Wiebe & Smith, 1997).

Personality traits and processes have been examined in each of the three major areas in health psychology and behavioral medicine (Smith & Ruiz, 1999): health behavior and prevention; psychosomatics, or the impact of stress and emotion on the development of disease; and psychosocial aspects of acute and chronic illness and care. In this chapter, we review examples of research in each of these areas, focusing in more depth on psychosomatics, where personality characteristics have been studied most extensively. Before presenting these topics, we discuss central issues in current personality theory and research, as well as the basic models of the association between personality and health. Finally, we conclude with a discussion of future issues in research and clinical practice.

CURRENT CONCEPTS IN PERSONALITY RESEARCH

In a seminal discussion of personality psychology, Allport (1937) stated that "personality *is* something and personality *does* something" (p. 48, emphasis added). The former meaning refers to personality *traits*—stable patterns of thought, emotion, and behavior, presumably based in biological or psychological structures, which characterize the person over time and across situations. In this sense, personality is something that people "have" (Cantor, 1990). The latter meaning refers to the psychological *processes* or *mechanisms* through which the person's thoughts, feelings, and actions are organized and influence adaptation. Current theory and research reflect both the having and doing views of personality, as well as attempts to integrate them (Cantor, 1990; Mischel & Shoda, 1998, 1999).

Trait Psychology

For 30 years following Allport's (1937) description of the field, personality theory and research focused primarily on traits. Many assessment devices were developed to assess these constructs, ranging from self-report questionnaires to projective tests. In a landmark critique, Walter Mischel (1968) posed a serious challenge to traditional trait models by noting the limited evidence of validity and predictive utility of personality assessments. It was not always clear that these measures assessed the intended constructs, and there was little indication that they provided unique information in the description of individuals or predictions about future behavior. He and others also argued that the behavioral consistency typically attributed to personality traits is more apparent than real, reflecting observers' exaggerated perceptions of consistencies in their own and others' behavior. In contrast, situations rather than personality traits were seen as the more important influence on behavior and emotional response. Mischel (1973) further argued that to the extent that personality characteristics were important determinants of behavior, they took the form of specific cognitive processes or mechanisms, such as encodings or appraisals of other people and situations, expectancies, goals, and behavioral competencies, and strategies.

Mischel's critique lessened enthusiasm for traditional trait research for nearly 20 years, and such research returned to its previous level of activity only within the past decade (John & Srivastava, 1999). Research on personality and health may have contributed to the fading influence of Mischel's critique (Smith & Gallo, 2001), because it is difficult to reconcile the view that personality traits have weak scientific status with the mounting empirical evidence that they predict illness and premature mortality over the expanse of several decades. However, a more obvious source of renewed interest in trait approaches has been the emergence and growing acceptance of the five factor model (Digman, 1990; McCrae & John, 1992) as an adequate taxonomy of personality traits. For many years before the emergence of this model, research on personality traits seemed like a disorderly proliferation of traits and assessment procedures, developed and studied with little reference to previous descriptions of closely related characteristics. In contrast, the five factor model posits that five broad traits and their components provide a sufficient, integrative framework for the description of personality.

The five factor model traits and their facets are listed in Table 5.1. Although not without compelling critics (e.g., Block, 1995; McAdams, 1995; Westen, 1995), this taxonomy has proved to be useful in many research areas, including personality and health (Marshall, Wortman, Vickers, Kusulas, & Hervig, 1994; Smith & Williams, 1992). These concepts and related assessment tools provide an opportunity to compare, contrast, organize, and integrate—both conceptually and empirically—personality characteristics hypothesized to influence health. In this way, the five factor model can facilitate cumulative and systematic progress and prevent the accumulation of otherwise scattered and unintegrated studies of various traits.

An important variant of the five factor model (Trapnell & Wiggins, 1990) replaces the traits of agreeableness (versus antagonism) and extraversion (versus introversion) with the main dimensions of the interpersonal circumplex (Kiesler, 1983; Wiggins, 1979), permitting the integration of the five factor and interpersonal approaches to personality (Carson, 1969; Kiesler, 1996; Leary, 1957). In the interpersonal perspective, personality is reflected in or even consists of recurring patterns of the individual's transactions with others, including both actual or overt interactions and imagined or internal interactions (Kiesler, 1996; Sullivan, 1953). Also, transactions vary along

TABLE 5.1
Elements of the Five Factor Model of Personality

Trait	Opposite pole	Facts or components
Neuroticism	Emotional stability	Anxiety, depression, angry hostility, self-consciousness, vulnerability, impulsiveness
Agreeableness	Antagonism	Trust, altruism, modesty, straightforwardness, compliance, tender-mindedness
Extraversion	Introversion	Warmth, gregariousness, assertiveness, activity, excitement-seeking, positive emotions.
Conscientiousness	Unreliability	Competence, order, self-discipline, dutifulness, achievement striving, deliberation
Openness to experience	Closed-mindedness	Fantasy, aesthetics, introspection, curiosity, novelty-seeking, low dogmatism

Note. Reproduced by special permission of the Publisher, Psychological Assessment Resources, Inc., 16204 North Florida Avenue, Lutz, Florida 33549, from the *NEO Personality Inventory–Revised Professional Manual* by Paul Costa and Robert McCrae, Copyright 1985, 1989, 1992 by PAR, Inc. Further reproduction is prohibited without permission of PAR, Inc.

two primary dimensions of social behavior—dominance (versus submissiveness) and friendliness (versus hostility).

As depicted in Figure 5.1, social behavior and related individual differences can be described as blends of these dimensions, reflected as locations around the interpersonal circumplex. This version of the five factor model is useful in clarifying the similarities and differences among closely related personality characteristics linked to health. For example, as discussed next, a set of characteristics referred to as hostility confer increased risk of serious illness (T. Miller et al., 1996). Although these traits share the cold, unfriendly interpersonal style of the left half of the circumplex, they vary in dominance versus submissiveness. Verbal aggressiveness is associated with hostile dominance, whereas resentment, cynicism, and mistrust are associated with hostile submissiveness (Gallo & Smith, 1998; Ruiz, Smith, & Rhodewalt, 2001). Hence, the circumplex version of the five factor model is particularly useful for comparing, contrasting, and integrating traits involving social behavior. Because the circumplex can also be used to describe social stimuli or contexts, this approach also facilitates the integration of personality characteristics and other risk factors typically construed as features of the social environment, such as social support (Gallo & Smith, 1999). Social motives corresponding to the main dimensions of the interpersonal circumplex have been labeled agency and communion (Bakan, 1966; Wiggins & Trapnell, 1996). *Agency* refers to strivings for separateness,

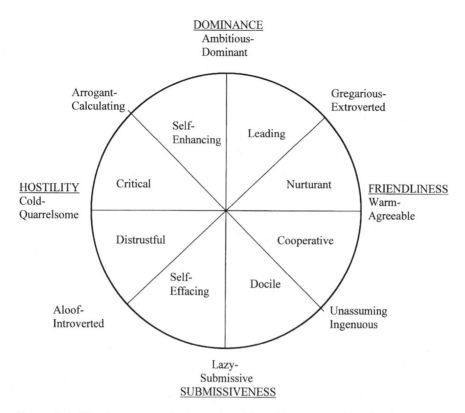

Figure 5.1. The interpersonal circumplex. From "Patterns of Hostility and Social Support: Conceptualizing Psychosocial Risk as a Characteristic of the Person and the Environment," by L. C. Gallo and T. W. Smith, 1999, *Journal of Research in Personality, 33,* pp. 281–310. Copyright 1999 by Academic Press. Adapted with permission from Elsevier and authors. See also Wiggins (1977).

individuality, achievement, and power. In contrast, communion refers to strivings for connection and closeness, concern for others, and fostering relationships. These motivational dimensions are closely related to the masculine and feminine sex roles, respectively. In addition, Helgeson (1994; Helgeson & Fritz, 1998) has argued that excessive pursuit of either motivational orientation has negative health consequences.

The Cognitive–Social Perspective

Despite the value of the five factor model in the organization and integration of research on personality and health, this approach is largely descriptive. That is, until recently (e.g., McCrae & Costa, 1996), the five factor model has not included discussions of the processes or mechanisms through which these broad traits influence the individual's thoughts, feelings, or behaviors in the course of responding and adapting to everyday events

(Mischel & Shoda, 1998). Hence, the second meaning of personality in Allport's description—personality as "doing," or the cognitive–social approach (Cantor, 1990)—is an essential complement to trait approaches. To date, there is no consensus emerging around an "adequate taxonomy" of these cognitive–social personality units (McAdams, 1995), but Mischel's (1973) original presentation of these variables (described earlier) has been valuable, as have been his extensions and refinements (Mischel & Shoda, 1995). Examples of these personality processes and mechanisms from his work and others (Cantor, 1990; McAdams, 1995; Westen, 1995) include mental representations (i.e., schemas) of the self, others, relationships, and social interaction sequences (i.e., scripts); current concerns, goals, motives, and life tasks; encoding or appraisals of situations and people; coping and self-regulation; and strategies, tactics, and competencies in goal-directed behavior. These constructs have been labeled middle units of personality, because they provide more specific and detailed accounts of behavior than do broader trait dimensions (McAdams, 1995).

In this view, individual differences in personality comprise the specific content of these elements (e.g., positive versus negative representations of the self and others), their relative degree of chronic activation or accessibility (e.g., readily activated expectations or appraisals of others as threatening versus less accessible construals of social threat), and the unique organization among them (e.g., association of perceptions of rebuke with responses of anger versus guilt). Such characteristics obviously come closer to providing an explanation of an individual's thought, feeling, or behavior in a given situation, as compared to the more descriptive function of the five factor model. These more specific and mechanistic middle units provide a sequential description of how events, situations, and other inputs affect the individual, and in combination with specific individual differences determine subsequent emotional and behavioral responses. Although theorists have cautioned against equating these middle units of personality with the mechanisms through which broad traits influence behavior (McAdams, 1995), these levels of analysis in personality theory and research are complementary (McCrae & Costa, 1996; Mischel & Shoda, 1998). Empirical efforts to combine them have illustrated cognitive and affective mechanisms through which traits influence behavior (e.g., Graziano, Jensen-Campbell, & Hair, 1996).

VIEWS OF THE SITUATION IN TRAIT, COGNITIVE–SOCIAL, AND INTERPERSONAL APPROACHES

These approaches differ not only in their conceptualization of the key units of personality but also in the conceptualization of the role of situations as determinants of behaviors. Given the emphasis on temporal and cross-situational stability in thought, feeling, and behavior, classic trait approaches view the impact of situations either as "error variance" in tests of the impact of personality or as an independent class of influences on responses. This person-versus-situation dichotomy has resulted in a variety of studies and debates about their relative importance as influences on behavior (Bem & Allen, 1974; Bowers, 1973; Funder & Ozer, 1983; Mischel, 1973). This dichotomy also prompted one of the most important attempts to reconcile trait psychology and views of situational primacy: interactional approaches to personality (Ekehammer, 1974; Endler & Magnusson, 1976). In this view, the outcomes of common concern to both personality psychologists studying traits and social psychologists interested in the impact of situations (e.g., on thoughts, feelings, and overt behavior) are seen as reflecting the influence of three factors—characteristics of the person, characteristics of the situation, and the statistical interaction between the person and situation factors. The impact of the situation depends on (i.e., is moderated by; Baron & Kenney, 1986) the individual's personality characteristics, and the association between personality traits and specific responses depends on the situation. For example, the degree of anger and irritation expressed by an individual in a conversation involves the interaction of his or her level of trait hostility and the friendliness versus hostility of the remarks made by the interaction partner. Both characteristically hostile and friendly persons are unlikely to be irritated while interacting with friendly conversation partners. However, when interacting with an unfriendly partner, an antagonistic or hostile person is quite likely to respond in kind with anger and irritation, whereas highly agreeable individuals might manage to avoid this complementary response. This person-by-situation statistical interaction approach is central in many applications of personality theory to the study of health.

In a recent refinement and extension of this concept, Mischel and Shoda (1995, 1998) suggested that behavioral stabilities attributed to personality traits actually reflect stable patterns of differing responses (i.e., profiles) across specific types of situations. Further, this patterning of behavior across situations provides a more accurate and informative description of personality. For example, two individuals with the same mean level of aroused anger and expressed hostility during a typical week could have very different situational patterns or "behavioral signatures"(Mischel & Shoda, 1998). One individual might respond to dominant or controlling actions of coworkers with anger and hostility but respond in a more even-tempered or even aloof manner to perceived rejection or criticism from a romantic partner. In contrast, a second person might respond to controlling actions of coworkers with even-tempered assertiveness but react with anger and hostility to perceived slights from a spouse. If the two classes of evoking situations occur with roughly equal frequency for these two individuals, they would appear to have similar standing on the trait of hostility. However, the situational analysis suggests different personality characteristics. The first individual may display antagonistic defensiveness in response to threats to status, whereas the second appears to display sensitivity to rejection (Downey, Freitas, Michaels, & Khour, 1998) by loved ones. Hence, two similar levels of trait hostility reflect very different patterns of situationally specific responding. In this view, stable "if, then" conditional patterns of situation-specific responses are more informative than traditional traits as units of analysis in personality (Mischel & Shoda, 1998).

In both the traditional and newer models of the interaction between the person and situation, these factors interact statistically but do not affect each other. However, a basic assumption of the cognitive–social approach is the reciprocal determinism (Bandura, 1978) of persons and situations. That is, people both shape and are shaped by the environments they encounter. Through the situations they choose to enter or avoid, their appraisals or encoding of those situations, the goals they pursue there, and the related behavior they display, people influence the internal reactions and overt behavior of others (Buss, 1987). In addition, these selected, evoked, and intentionally manipulated features of the environment impinge on the individual, influencing his or her subsequent thoughts, feelings, and actions (Ickes, Snyder, & Garcia, 1997). Through the recurrence of these reciprocal influences, individuals tend to create environments that maintain distinguishing features of their personality (Caspi, Bem, & Elder, 1989; Wagner, Kiesler, & Schmidt, 1995). Intentionally or not, competitive people create contests, and agreeable persons foster pleasant interactions. That is, personality is reflected not only in differential *reactions* to classes of situations but to differing levels of *exposure* to those classes of situations as well (Bolger & Schilling, 1991; Bolger & Zuckerman, 1995). This differential exposure to some types of situations reflects the impact of personality characteristics on situations, and is a potentially important source of the continuity of individual differences in personality characteristics. This tenet of the cognitive–social approach is articulated by Mischel and Shoda (1999) as follows:

> Thus people select, influence, and even generate their own interpersonal situations and are influenced by them in an interactive process. . . . Ultimately this results in a degree of stability or equilibrium in the situations the person characteristically experiences. Such stability 'belongs' neither to the person nor to the situation in isolation, but is a reflection of the enduring pattern of reciprocal interactions between the individual and his or her distinctive interpersonal world that dynamically influence each other. (Mischel & Shoda, 1999, pp. 211–212)

This view is similar to another tenet of the interpersonal approach: the transactional cycle (Carson, 1969; Kiesler, 1996). As depicted in Figure 5.2, the individual's beliefs, appraisals, goals, and other internal middle units

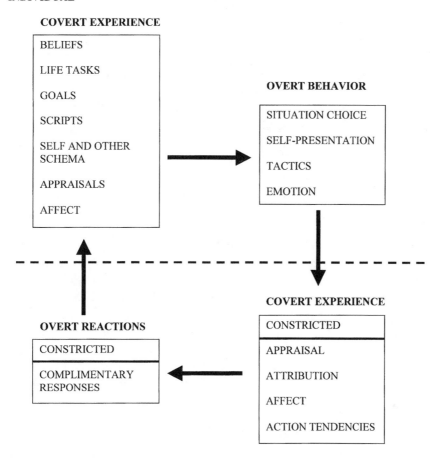

INDIVIDUAL

COVERT EXPERIENCE

| BELIEFS |
| LIFE TASKS |
| GOALS |
| SCRIPTS |
| SELF AND OTHER SCHEMA |
| APPRAISALS |
| AFFECT |

OVERT BEHAVIOR

| SITUATION CHOICE |
| SELF-PRESENTATION |
| TACTICS |
| EMOTION |

COVERT EXPERIENCE

| CONSTRICTED |
| APPRAISAL |
| ATTRIBUTION |
| AFFECT |
| ACTION TENDENCIES |

OVERT REACTIONS

| CONSTRICTED |
| COMPLIMENTARY RESPONSES |

OTHERS IN THE SOCIAL ENVIRONMENT

Figure 5.2. The transactional cycle. From "Patterns of Hostility and Social Support: Conceptualizing Psychosocial Risk as a Characteristic of the Person and the Environment," by L. C. Gallo and T. W. Smith, 1999, *Journal of Research in Personality, 33,* pp. 281–310. Copyright 1999 by Academic Press. Adapted with permission from Elsevier and authors. See also Kiesler (1996).

of personality direct his or her overt behavior. This overt behavior, in turn, influences or constricts the internal or covert reactions of others, as when overt expressions of warmth and friendliness evoke positive appraisals and affects in interaction partners. These evoked internal experiences guide the overt reactions of the interaction partner. In this way, the responses of interaction partners tend to be consistent with or complement the initial internal state of the original actor. Hence, over brief interaction cycles and those patterns recurring over longer periods of time and even across multiple relationships, the individual shapes and is shaped by social environments consistent with his or her personality. In fact, classic statements of the interpersonal approach (e.g., Sullivan, 1953) maintain that these "enduring patterns of reciprocal interaction" between individuals and their interpersonal worlds *are* personality. Applications of personality theory and research to health typically have not emphasized these more dynamic assumptions of the relationship between characteristics of the person and the surrounding social context, but these approaches have much to offer in the conceptualization of personality influences on health and the design of related interventions (Revenson, 1990; Smith & Christensen, 1992; Smith & Gallo, 2001).

ISSUES IN PERSONALITY ASSESSMENT

Inclusion of personality characteristics in research and clinical practice in health psychology and behavioral medicine requires reliable and valid assessments of these constructs. More than 50 years of progress in personality assessment has produced a valuable set of conceptual, methodological, and quantitative tools (Ozer & Reiss, 1994; West & Finch, 1997). However, these established standards have been inconsistently applied in the study of personality and health (Smith & Gallo, 2001; Wiebe & Smith, 1997). Adequate measurement of personality characteristics in health research must follow from a theory or model of the construct to be assessed. Similarly, evaluations of the strengths and weaknesses of a particular assessment instrument can be made only in reference to that conceptual model (Ozer & Reise, 1994). This essential step is often given insufficient attention in research on personality and health. In addition to clear definitions of the construct, key issues to be addressed are the following: (a) What is the *structure* of the construct (e.g., unidimensional vs. multidimensional, hierarchical), and what is the expected degree of relationship among items or indicators tapping the construct? (b) What is the *stability* of the construct over time? and (c) What is the expected *pattern of relationships* with measures of other constructs and other measures of the same construct? (See West & Finch, 1997). Answers to these questions help identify the relative importance of various forms of psychometric evidence and provide specific hypotheses to be tested in measurement research. Without such models, psychometric analysis of measures can be misleading.

Reliability is an important concern in personality and health research, as the reproducibility or dependability of measurement of personality characteristics is essential for tests of their association with any health outcome. Without adequate reliability, the power to detect hypothesized effects suffers. Differing degrees of reliability across measures in multivariate analyses can produce erroneous conclusions about differential predictive utility. For example, if smoking can be measured quite reliably but the personality trait of hostility is assessed less reliably, a multivariate prediction of the incidence of heart disease would be biased to detect the relative importance of the former risk factor. Similarly, if in a study of subsequent health outcomes one personality characteristic is measured to rule it out as a confounding factor that would otherwise provide an alternative explanation for the health effects of a second personality characteristic, an unreliable assessment of the confounding trait will result in an undercorrection of its potential contribution to the effects of the second trait.

The relevance of specific types of reliability depends on the model of the construct (Ozer & Reise, 1994). For most personality characteristics, internal consistency and at least short-term stability would be expected. One common problem in personality and health research is that traits are often assessed with small, modestly intercorrelated sets of items. This threat to the reliability of test scores limits their potential predictive utility, and this limitation is compounded by the fact that the association between personality traits and subsequent objective health outcomes can be statistically small, especially when examined over long periods of time.

Reliability is necessary but not sufficient for the establishment of validity. Validity is the degree to which theoretical rationales and empirical evidence support the adequacy of interpretations based on measures of a construct (Messick, 1989). It is a property of an interpretation rather than a measurement device, because different uses of a measure can dramatically alter validity. No single index provides a summary of validity, because the evaluations of inferences are made in reference to a model of the construct and a related, evolving body of evidence (Ozer, 1999; West & Finch, 1997). At the simplest level, the content of items or ratings is an important determinant of validity. If key aspects of the concepts to be assessed are underrepresented in an item pool, then validity will suffer. Similarly, overrepresentation of items reflecting one feature of a multicomponent construct will compromise validity, as will the inclusion of item content outside of the conceptual definition of the construct to be assessed (e.g., social desirability). Psychometric evaluations of personality assessment devices should also determine if the set of items or ratings has the hypothesized structure, a process that has often revealed limitations of scales used in personality and health research (e.g., Contrada & Jussim, 1992; Marshall, Wortman, Kusulas, Herrig, & Vickers, 1992). Multifaceted constructs pose important interpretive challenges, as scale components can have different associations with health outcomes (Carver, 1989; Hull, Lehn, & Tedlie, 1991). Indicators of internal consistency (e.g., Cronbach's alpha) are not good indicators of unidimensionality versus multidimensionality, and theory-driven techniques such as confirmatory factor analysis should be used instead to evaluate this aspect of the measurement model (Ozer & Reise, 1994; West & Finch, 1997).

Strong tests of the validity of personality assessments examine patterns of association with other scales or criteria, again based on a conceptual model of the relative degree of association with other measures and constructs. The convergent and divergent (i.e., discriminant) validity of personality scales must be evaluated through such conceptually guided analyses (Campbell & Fiske, 1959; Fiske & Campbell, 1992). It is important to demonstrate that measures are closely related to scales assessing similar constructs, and less closely related to scales assessing conceptually more distinct constructs. Evidence of divergent or discriminant validity is stronger to the extent that it involves comparisons with conceptually related but not interchangeable dimensions (Ozer & Reise, 1994; West & Finch, 1997). Thus, measures of constructs that are plausible alternative interpretations of the characteristic assessed by a candidate scale under evaluation should be included in psychometric evaluations to provide strong tests of discriminant validity. Positive results of such theory-driven comparisons, in turn, provide stronger evidence of construct validity.

As noted, the five factor model and its variants provide a conceptual taxonomy for the convergent and discriminant validation of traits assessed in personality and health research, and systematic use of such frameworks can help identify similarities among supposedly distinct scales (Gallo & Smith, 1998; Smith & Williams, 1992). In several areas of personality and health research, inadequate attention to the construct validity of trait measures has been problematic (Funk, 1992; Rhodewalt & Smith, 1991). Assessment research not only strengthens the scientific foundations of the study of personality and health, but can also suggest refinements of the guiding conceptual models and substantive research questions (Marshall et al., 1992; Schultz, Bookwala, Knapp, Scheier, & Williamson, 1996). Attention to psychometric strengths and weaknesses of specific assessment devices is an invaluable tradition in both trait psychology and the interpersonal approach. These methodological issues have received less attention in the development and use of measures in the social–cognitive tradition. Although the relevance of social–cognitive constructs to the research and practice agenda in health psychology and behavioral medicine is clear, careful consideration of these psychometric issues is necessary to ensure that this potential contribution is maximized.

MODELS OF PERSONALITY AND HEALTH

A variety of models have been proposed describing the impact of personality traits and processes on health (for reviews, see Contrada et al., 1999; Smith & Gallo, 2001; Suls & Sanders, 1989; Wiebe & Smith, 1997). These models describe influences of personality on actual illness through behavioral mechanisms such as diet, smoking, exercise, and other lifestyle factors, as well as through more direct psychobiological mechanisms such as the physiology of stress. Other models have been proposed to describe the effects of personality on responses to illness and potentially stressful aspects of medical care. In these latter instances, the outcomes of interest include emotional adaptation to acute or chronic illness, the level of functional activity (i.e., disability or limited functioning), and even the patient's adherence to treatment recommendations. The following review is based on our previous description of these models (Smith & Gallo, 2001). It is not exhaustive, but it does illustrate the variety of ways in which personality characteristics affect health.

Health Behavior Models

As presented in Figure 5.3, personality characteristics could influence health through their intervening effects on a variety of health behaviors, such as smoking, activity or exercise levels, diet, and engagement in preventive practices (e.g., sun screen and seatbelt use, drinking and driving, participation in medical screening). The simplest version of this model (panel I in Figure 5.3) suggests that personality characteristics (e.g., sensation seeking, impulsiveness) are directly related to the frequency or severity of health-relevant behaviors (e.g., drinking and driving), which in turn are directly related to health outcomes. In the most prominent models of health behavior, individual factors presumed to guide health behaviors—such as locus of control, self-efficacy, and health beliefs (Armitage & Conner, 1999; Bandura, 1989; Lau, 1988; Strickland, 1978)—do not resemble personality traits as they are typically conceptualized. However, these factors could easily be construed as personality characteristics in the social–cognitive framework (Miller, Shoda, & Hurley, 1996). In addition, broader personality traits might influence these middle unit determinants of health behavior.

In a more complex model (panel II in Figure 5.3), personality characteristics may moderate the effects of stressful life events on health behaviors. That is, stressful life circumstances may have a negative impact on health behaviors, and personality characteristics may alter the magnitude of this

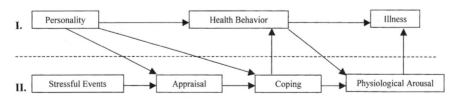

Figure 5.3. The health behavior model.

effect. For example, persons high in neuroticism might respond to stressful life circumstances with a decrease in exercise and an increase in the consumption of high-calorie, high-fat foods, thereby increasing their risk of subsequent illness. Hence, personality characteristics might influence engagement in varying degrees or types of health behavior as adaptive or maladaptive coping responses during times of stress.

Some changes in health behavior in response to stressful events may moderate the physiological effects of stress. For example, stressful life events can disrupt the quality of sleep, and disrupted sleep can impair the immune system, leaving the individual more susceptible to infectious illness. Other health behaviors (e.g., smoking, physical inactivity, consumption of caffeine) can potentiate physiological stress responses (Blumenthal et al., 1990; Davis & Matthews, 1990; MacDougall, Musante, Castilo, & Acevedo, 1988). In such cases, personality characteristics could render the individual more or less likely to respond to stressful life circumstances with changes in health behaviors, and those changes in health behaviors could influence the physiological effects of those stressors and the subsequent risk of disease.

Stress Moderation Models: Interactions and Transactions

Stress moderation models of the effects of personality on health are based on the assumption that the physiological effects of psychological stress affect the development and course of physical illness. Large, frequent, and enduring increases in sympathetic–adrenomedullary (SAM) and hypothalamic–pituitary–adrenocortical (HPAC) system activity in response to environmental stressors are believed to foster the development and progression of a variety of illnesses from the common cold to coronary heart disease (Lovallo, 1997). These effects of stress are most thoroughly documented in the case of psychophysiological influences on cardiovascular disease (Manuck, 1994; Rozanski, Blumenthal, & Kaplan, 1999) and illnesses otherwise controlled by the immune system (Cohen & Herbert, 1996; Kiecolt-Glaser & Glaser, 1995; Smith & Ruiz, 2002). These pathways are biologically plausible, and a growing body of research provides at least preliminary support for the effects of stress on pathophysiology in these systems. In addition, personality variables have been related to both cardiovascular responses (Houston, 1989) and immune system parameters (Segerstrom, 2000).

Stress moderation models of the effects of personality on health suggest that individuals vary in the extent of their psychophysiological responses to environmental stressors, and that these differences are—at least in part—effects of personality characteristics. Hence, these models are closely tied to the person-by-situation, statistical interaction models described earlier. The level of environmental stress in a given situation interacts with personality characteristics to determine psychophysiological responses and ultimately

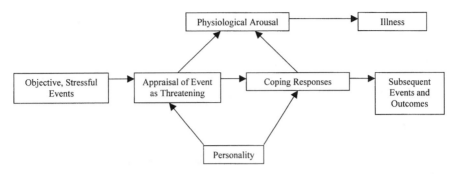

Figure 5.4. The interactional stress moderation model.

the risk of disease. As depicted in Figure 5.4, personality characteristics could moderate the effects of environmental stressors on pathophysiological stress responses by influencing how an event is appraised and the type or effectiveness of coping responses. Both appraisals and coping responses would, in turn, alter physiological responses (Lazarus & Folkman, 1984).

As in the general person-by-situation, statistical interaction model of personality, this view implicitly conceptualizes the person and situation as independent influences on stress responses. As described earlier, interpersonal or transactional views of personality assume that individuals and the situations they encounter are reciprocally related (Bandura, 1978). That is, individuals shape and are shaped by the situations they encounter. This extension of the interactional stress moderational model is depicted in Figure 5.5. As in the previous model, personality characteristics can influence the appraisal of potentially stressful events, as well as the individual's selection of coping strategies and the effectiveness of their implementation. However, this transactional model includes an additional pathway of personality effects on illness—the impact of personality processes on the individual's exposure to potential stressors. Through the processes depicted in Figure 5.2,

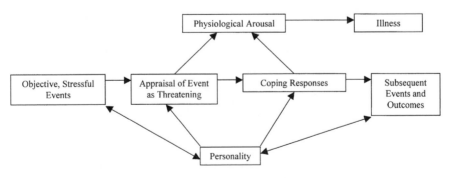

Figure 5.5. The transactional stress moderation model.

individuals influence the frequency, severity, and duration of the stressors they encounter during daily life (Smith & Anderson, 1986; Smith & Rhodewalt, 1986). These effects of personality on exposure to stressors, appraisal of stressors, and coping influence the development of illness through the common pathway of physiological reactivity to those events.

Constitutional Predisposition Models

In the health behavior and stress moderation models, personality characteristics have substantial effects on health, albeit through very different pathways. However, it is possible that statistical associations between personality characteristics and subsequent health actually reflect a noncausal, third-variable association. Several theorists have proposed models of this type (Krantz & Durel, 1983; Suls & Sanders, 1989; R. Williams, 1994). As depicted in Figure 5.6, such models are based on the assumption that a constitutional predisposition—determined by genetic factors, early experience, or their joint effects—contributes to individual differences in physiological reactivity. This constitutionally based individual difference in reactivity in turn has two effects; it renders the individual more or less susceptible to illness and it influences the development and expression of certain personality characteristics. Hence, statistical associations between personality traits and illness do not reflect a causal association, but instead are both coeffects of the underlying constitutional factor.

A growing body of evidence from behavioral genetics research indicates that many of the personality characteristics identified as risk factors for disease are, in fact, at least partially heritable (Plomin & Caspi, 1999), as is the overlap among conceptual distinct dimensions of psychosocial risk (Raynor, Pogue-Geil, Kamarcky, McCaffery, & Manuck, 2002). In addition, some evidence also suggests that individual differences in the magnitude of physiological responses to stressors are also at least somewhat heritable (Smith et al., 1987; Turner & Hewitt, 1992). Hence, there is preliminary

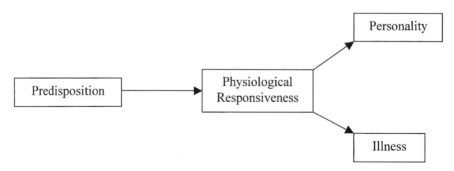

Figure 5.6. Constitutional vulnerability model.

support for this model. However, even if personality characteristics and physiological reactivity are heritable, psychosocial processes may still play a role in the effects of constitutional vulnerabilities on health. For example, through the transactional processes described, the personality processes (i.e., behavioral phenotypes) associated with reactive constitutions may contribute to increased exposure to stressors. In this way, the most reactive and vulnerable individuals may be exposed recurrently to what is for them an especially unhealthy environment.

Illness Behavior Model

Each of the models described thus far depicts associations of personality characteristics with actual health. Personality characteristics can also influence illness behavior that is independent or in excess of actual illness. Objective indicators of health and illness (e.g., physician evaluations, laboratory tests, etc.) are correlated with illness behaviors such as symptom reports, self-assessments of health, health care utilization, and work absenteeism. In many cases this association between illness and illness behavior is quite substantial. However, it is far from perfect (G. Kaplan & Camacho, 1983; Maddox & Douglas, 1973), and the discrepancy between illness and illness behavior can itself be related to personality characteristics (Cioffi, 1991; Cohen, 1979; Watson & Pennebaker, 1989).

Personality characteristics could influence the portion of variance in illness behavior that is independent of actual illness through a variety of mechanisms, as depicted in Figure 5.7. For example, personality traits and processes could influence the extent to which individuals attend to physical sensations, construe such sensations as symptoms of ill health, give voice to these symptoms, and seek some sort of medical care. Illness behavior in excess of actual illness is an important clinical and economic challenge in health care. In addition, many important components of health are not reducible to the simple presence or severity of disease (Ryff & Singer, 1998).

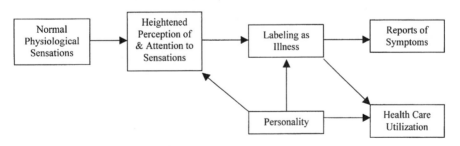

Figure 5.7. Illness behavior model.

Hence, the role of personality in these processes potentially has considerable practical importance. However, this association between personality and illness behavior raises a critical methodological concern for studies seeking to examine the influence of personality on actual health and illness. If operational definitions of illness outcomes are used that could conceivably reflect illness behavior rather than actual illness, then the interpretation of associations between personality and subsequent health is in doubt. Hence, the construct validity of measures of health is no less critical than the construct validity of personality predictors.

Personality and Adaptation to Illness and Medical Care

Personality traits and processes are also important moderators of the individual's adjustment to acute and chronic disease and to the medical procedures used to diagnose and treat those conditions. Serious illness can have significant impact on emotional adjustment, levels of functional activity, physical comfort, and personal relationships. However, individuals with similar medical conditions and prognoses can have widely varying responses on these dimensions. This individual variability in the psychosocial impact of illness could reflect the moderating effects of personality. Similarly, many illnesses involve demands on the patient to adhere to sometimes complex medical regimens, and again patients vary widely in the extent in their compliance (Dunbar-Jacob, Schlenk, & Caruthers, 2002). Personality characteristics could affect this aspect of medical illness and care, as well.

Possible influences of personality on adaptation to medical illness and care are depicted in Figure 5.8. In this view, objective characteristics of the illness or condition, as well as features of the typical medical assessment

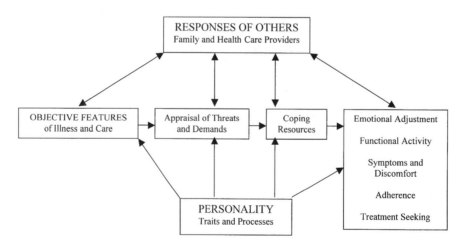

Figure 5.8. Personality and social influences on adaptation to illness and care.

and treatment, are depicted as potential stressors, and outcomes of interest include the patient's emotional adjustment, level of functional activity (versus disability), the level of subjective physical distress or symptoms (e.g., pain, fatigue), adherence to the prescribed medical regimen, and the seeking of additional medical care. As in the stress moderation model, personality processes could influence the individual's appraisal of objective features of the illness and related medical care, as well as the type and effectiveness of coping responses. Through the behavioral and psychophysiological mechanisms, personality characteristics could also affect the overall severity and temporary exacerbations of the illness itself. Personality factors may also influence the outcomes of emotional adjustment, functional activity, and physical symptoms independently of the impact of illness. For example, individuals high in neuroticism are likely to report more emotional distress and physical symptoms regardless of the actual severity of illness and the stressfulness of medical care.

A large and growing body of research demonstrates that social relationships and interactions have an important impact on adjustment to acute and chronic illness (Wills, 1997). Personal relationships are an essential source of social support, and this support can influence adjustment to illness and stressful medical care through pathways depicted in Figure 5.8 (Schmalling & Sher, 2000). Support can affect the course and severity of disease itself, the individual's appraisal of the illness and key features of care, coping responses, and even "steady states" or premorbid levels of functioning on outcome variables. Social interactions and relationships with health care providers are another important influence on adaptation.

Although social effects on patient adaptation are typically conceptualized and studied as separate from personality factors, the interpersonal and transactional approaches to personality call attention to the fact that these are likely to be interrelated influences. The earlier quality of on-going relationships represents an important context that can shape the impact of stressful illness and demanding medical care, and as described earlier those relationships are likely to reflect—at least in part—the patient's personality characteristics. The patient's specific responses to the medical condition are also likely to be influenced by personality factors, and those responses are likely to affect the patient's social context. For example, patients who express anger at the unfairness of their condition may eventually undermine important sources of support in close relationships, perhaps furthering their sense of resentment. Patients who respond to objectively worrisome aspects of their illness with minimization or denial to reduce their own emotional distress may evoke intrusive care from family members, as concerned support providers attempt to convince the patient of the seriousness of the situation. Finally, patients who respond with passivity and helplessness may evoke care that undermines the patient's independence and functional activity level more, thereby perpetuating the sense of helplessness. Hence, personality and social mechanisms in adaptation to disease could easily reflect two sides of a single process.

PERSONALITY CHARACTERISTICS AS RISK FACTORS FOR DISEASE

Most of the research on personality factors in health has focused on stress moderation models of the effects of traits on subsequent health. That is, personality traits are examined as potential risk factors for illness, and the mechanisms underlying such associations are presumed to involve the psychophysiological processes described earlier. In this approach, health behavior correlates of personality (e.g., smoking, activity level, diet, etc.) are seen as alternative mechanisms potentially accounting for the effects of personality on health, and therefore are typically controlled in statistical tests. There are literally dozens of personality characteristics that have been discussed as possible risk factors for serious illness. In the following section, we review those that have received the most attention and accumulated the most compelling evidence of a robust prospective association with objective indications of illness.

Type A Behavior

Undoubtedly, the most well-known personality characteristic identified as a risk factor for subsequent disease is the Type A behavior pattern, originally described by Friedman and Rosenman (1959). Although they intentionally referred to the Type A pattern as an "action-emotion complex" rather than a personality characteristic or type, Friedman and Rosenman clearly described stable individual differences in emotional and behavioral responses—specifically, achievement striving, competitiveness, time urgency, impatience, excessive job involvement, and easily provoked hostility. The Type A pattern (and the relative absence of these characteristics, or Type B pattern) has been assessed with a variety of methods, although three have been widely used. The Type A Structured Interview (SI; Rosenman, 1978) consists of a semistandardized set of questions and probes, generally addressing characteristics in the conceptual description of the pattern. However, the individual's style of responding is given primary importance in scoring, rather than the content of answers. The Jenkins Activity Survey (JAS; Jenkins, Rosenman, & Zyzanski, 1974) is a self-report questionnaire, with items mostly tapping competitiveness, achievement striving, and impatience. Finally, the Framingham Type A Scale (FTAS: Haynes, Feinleib, & Kannel, 1980) is a brief self-report scale mostly assessing competitiveness and impatience. These measures are only weakly correlated, and they demonstrate differing associations with other personality characteristics (Rhodewalt & Smith, 1991). Hence, a basic issue in personality assessment—convergent validity—has been a significant problem in Type A research.

Over the first two decades of research on the topic, prospective studies demonstrated an association between Type A behavior and the development of coronary heart disease (CHD), leading a panel of experts to conclude that this pattern was an independent risk factor equal in importance to other "standard" CHD risk factors (Cooper, Detre, & Weiss, 1981). However, shortly after this consensus report, several failures to replicate the association between Type A behavior and CHD incidence were published (Ragland & Brand, 1988; Shekelle, Gale, & Norusis, 1985; Shekelle, Hulley, et al., 1985), prompting a waning of enthusiasm for the Type A construct. However, a subsequent quantitative review found that the inconsistencies across studies could be accounted for by assessment methods and characteristics of study samples. Briefly, Type A behavior as assessed by the SI was a reliable predictor of subsequent CHD, but this effect was severely attenuated in samples with high levels of preexisting coronary disease (Miller, Turner, Tindale, Posavac, & Dugoni, 1991).

Stress moderation models have been the most influential accounts of the mechanisms linking Type A behavior and CHD (Glass, 1977; Price, 1982). Related research has demonstrated that Type A and B individuals have similar resting levels of blood pressure, heart rate, and plasma neuroendocrine concentrations. However, in response to psychological challenges and demands, Type As demonstrate larger increases in these parameters (Houston, 1988; Lyness, 1993). This physiological reactivity, in turn, could account for the effects of Type A behavior on CHD (Manuck, 1994; Rozanski et al, 1999). Constitutional predisposition models have also been proposed. In this view, the overt manifestations of the Type A pattern (e.g., loud, rapid speech) and the physiological reactivity described both reflect an underlying constitutional predisposition toward sympathetic nervous system responsivity, and this constitutionally based reactivity could influence CHD development. Hence, the behavioral characteristics are not necessarily causally related to CHD (Krantz & Durel, 1983).

Transactional models of Type A behavior and disease have also been proposed. In this view, Type A individuals are exposed to more frequent, severe, and prolonged challenges and demands in everyday life, compared to Type Bs. This greater stress exposure reflects several challenge-and-demand engendering responses of Type As. Compared to their more easygoing counterparts, Type As select more demanding tasks, appraise tasks as requiring a greater level of achievement, elicit competitive and disagreeable behavior from others, and evaluate their own performances harshly (Smith & Anderson, 1986). In this view, the heightened cardiovascular reactivity believed to link Type A behavior to disease arises from two distinct sources—greater reactivity to stressors encountered by both Type As and Bs, and reactivity to the additional stressors Type As create through their thoughts and actions. Also, this more challenging and demanding environment would also tend to sustain the Type A style.

Hostility

One valuable consequence of the inconsistency in the literature on the health consequences of the Type A pattern has been an effort to examine the individual components of this complex set of characteristics. Such efforts quickly identified hostility as the aspect of the Type A pattern most closely and consistently related to CHD (Dembroski, MacDougall, Costa, & Grandits, 1989; Hecker, Chesney, Black, & Frautchi, 1988; Matthews, Glass, Rosenman, & Bortner, 1977). Although the term *hostility* is frequently used to describe a set of related concepts examined in this literature, it is more appropriately applied only to cognitive processes such as cynicism, suspiciousness, mistrust, and attributions or interpretations of others' actions as reflecting hostile intent (Smith, 1994). Individual differences in trait anger are a closely related construct, referring to frequent and pronounced episodes of anger arousal and a low threshold for the elicitation of anger. Individual differences in overt aggressive behavior reflect a third dimension and include a variety of verbal and physical actions sharing the intent to inflict emotional or physical harm. Finally, characteristic styles of expressing or coping with anger (e.g., "anger-in" and "anger-out") have also been the focus of considerable research in this area. Hence, clear conceptual definitions of the constructs of interest are essential given the obvious similarities, likely intercorrelations, and conceptual distinctions among these personality characteristics.

As with the Type A pattern, the broad construct of hostility has been assessed with behavioral ratings from the Type A SI and a series of self-report questionnaires (Barefoot & Lipkus, 1994). Again, these measures demonstrate modest intercorrelations at best, and have unique associations with other personality characteristics (Barefoot & Lipkus, 1994; Gallo & Smith, 1998; Martin, Watson, & Wan, 2000; Ruiz et al., 2001). Some of the more widely used measures (e.g., Cook & Medley, 1954) have psychometric limitations, such as complex internal structures and overlap with conceptually distinct personality characteristics (Contrada & Jussim, 1992; Steinberg & Jorgensen, 1996). Refinements in the measurement of hostility could facilitate more definitive estimates of the magnitude of the association between this set of personality characteristics and subsequent health, as well as greater resolution as to the specific traits involved.

As in the literature on the Type A pattern, the results of prospective studies of hostility and health have been somewhat inconsistent. However, a quantitative review demonstrated that behavioral ratings and self-reports of hostility are reliably associated with the incidence of CHD and premature mortality (Miller, Smith, et al., 1996). Subsequent prospective studies have confirmed the association of anger and hostility with the incidence of CHD (e.g., Chang, Ford, Meoni, Wang, & Klag, 2002; Everson, Kaplan, Goldberg, Salonen, & Salonen, 1997; Kawachi, Sparrow, Spiro, Vokonas, & Weiss, 1996; Williams et al., 2000). The development of CHD involves a decades-long process in which the endothelial lining of the coronary artery is injured and subclinical coronary artery disease (CAD) progresses in the absence of symptoms. Relatively late in this process, the severity and complexity of coronary artery lesions become sufficient to produce myocardial ischemia, arrhythmias, myocardial infarction, or even sudden coronary death (Kop, 1999). The pathophysiology of CAD and the emergence of clinical manifestations of CHD are both complex processes, with unique underlying physiological mechanisms (Kamarck & Jennings, 1991; Rozanski et al., 1999; Smith & Ruiz, 2002). Associations between hostility initially assessed in healthy individuals and the later development of CHD could reflect the impact of this personality characteristic on the initiation of CAD, its progression, the acute emergence of CHD symptoms (e.g., ischemia), or some combination of these phases of the disease. Recent evidence suggests hostility affects multiple phases of disease development. For example, in some studies hostility is associated with the extent of subclinical (i.e., presymptomatic) levels of atherosclerosis (Iribarren et al., 2000; Matthews, Owens, Kuller, Sutton-Tyrrell, & Jansen-McWilliams, 1998), although some negative findings have also been reported (O'Malley, Jones, Feuerstein, & Taylor, 2000). Among individuals with established, clinically apparent CHD, anger and hostility are associated with transient ischemia and other acute manifestations of the disease (Rosenberg et al., 2001; Rozanski et al., 1999). Additional research is needed to identify the specific stages of CHD development affected by hostility, because such information could identify the contributing pathophysiological mechanisms and suggest optimal timing of interventions (Cohen, Kaplan, & Manuck, 1994). Recently, trait anger has been found to predict the incidence of stroke (Williams et al., 2000), and this association may reflect the impact of this trait on atherosclerosis in the carotid, rather than coronary arteries.

Models of the effects of hostility on health are generally based on the person-by-situation statistical interaction or stress moderation approach. Briefly, hostile persons are seen as responding to potential stressors with larger and more prolonged increases in blood pressure, heart rate, and neuroendocrines (e.g., catecholamines, cortisol), as compared to their more agreeable counterparts (Williams, Barefoot, & Shekelle, 1985). This reactivity, in turn, is hypothesized to initiate and hasten the development of CAD, precipitate manifestations of CHD among persons with significant CAD, and could contribute to other types of illness through stress-induced impairments in immune functioning (Rabin, 1999; Rozanski et al., 1999). A variety of studies support the hypothesis that hostility is associated with enhanced physiological reactivity to interpersonal stressors (e.g., Smith & Gallo, 1999; Suarez, Kuhn, Schanberg, Williams, & Zimmermann, 1998) and with greater reactivity during daily life (Benotsch, Christensen, & McKelvey, 1997; Guyll & Contrada, 1998; Pope & Smith, 1991). Hostility is also associated with high levels of interpersonal conflict and low levels of social support at home and at work (Smith & Gallo, 2001), and this psychosocial vulnerability (Smith & Frohm, 1985; Smith, Pope, Sanders, Allred, & O'Keefe, 1988) could account for some of the negative health consequences of hostility. A pervasive pattern of conflict and low support could also reflect a transactional process in which hostile individuals engender disagreements and animosity (Smith, 1995; Smith & Pope, 1990). As a result, they would be exposed to greater levels of physiologically taxing social stressors, undermine the availability of otherwise stress-buffering social support, and accumulate interpersonal experiences that promote continuing hostility.

Other models of the health effects of hostility have been proposed. For example, hostility is associated with negative heath behaviors, such as smoking, excessive alcohol intake, and inactivity (Siegler, 1994). In most studies controlling the effects of health behavior, hostility still has a significant effect on subsequent health (Miller et al., 1996). However, in others, negative health behavior seems to account for the health consequences of hostility (e.g., Everson et al., 1997). Individual differences in hostility are at least partially heritable (e.g., Smith et al., 1991) and candidate genes have been identified (Jang et al., 2001; Manuck et al., 1999). This provides indirect support for constitutional models asserting that brain mechanisms contribute to the expression of hostile personality characteristics and the physiological reactivity that affects disease development (Kaplan, Botchin, & Manuck, 1994; Williams, 1994). Again, in this approach, personality characteristics may be epiphenomenal rather than causally linked to disease development.

Dominance as Coronary-Prone Behavior

Studies of components of the Type A pattern suggest that hostility is not the only unhealthy element. A combination of loud, rapid, and vigorous speech during the SI and a tendency to "talk over" the interviewer has been associated with increased risk of CHD and premature death (Houston, Chesney, Black, Cates, & Hecker, 1992; Houston, Babyak, Chesney, Black,

& Ragland, 1997). This interpersonal style clearly reflects the personality characteristic of dominance (versus submissiveness). Other studies have found that self-report measures of dominance are associated with increased risk CHD (Siegman et al., 2000; Whiteman, Deary, Lee, & Fowkes, 1997).

A well-developed nonhuman primate model of CAD has established that social dominance is a significant risk factor among male animals (J. Kaplan & Manuck, 1998). Specifically, male animals that tend to occupy the top (i.e., dominant) half of group hierarchies develop much more severe CAD than do subordinate male animals, but only if they are exposed to the chronic stress of being housed with a new set of cage mates every few weeks. Both dominant and subordinate animals develop low levels of CAD when housed in stable living groups. Also, this susceptibility to CAD among dominant monkeys housed in unstable conditions can be prevented through pharmacological blockade of sympathetic nervous system input to the heart, suggesting that the physiological effects of recurring assertion of social dominance account for the interactive effects of dominance and chronic stress on CAD. Hence, this nonhuman primate analogue illustrates a person-by-situation statistical interaction model of disease development. In a series of psychophysiological studies of humans, the act of asserting influence or dominance over others is associated with heightened cardiovascular reactivity (Smith, Allred, Morrison, & Carlson, 1989; Smith, Nealey, Kircher, & Limon, 1997; Smith, Ruiz, & Uchino, 2000). When considered along with studies of hostility, these studies suggest that personality characteristics associated with both dimensions of the interpersonal circumplex could be important influences on health.

Neuroticism and Negative Affectivity

Individual differences in the tendency to experience negative emotions such as anxiety and sadness have long been suspected as important influences on health (Alexander, 1950; Dunbar, 1943). A variety of closely related constructs have been discussed in this role. Negative affectivity (Watson & Clark, 1984) refers to the tendency to experience frequent, pronounced, and prolonged episodes of negative emotions (e.g., anxiety or fear, sadness or depression, etc.), especially in response to negative events. As described in Table 5.1, the five factor trait of neuroticism (versus emotional stability) includes these characteristics, as well as related cognitive factors such as low self-esteem and a sense of vulnerability. These traits reflect the disposition to experience negative moods within the range of normal emotional adjustment and do not imply the presence of a clinically significant emotional disorder. Individuals with such disorders do score high on measures of neuroticism and negative affectivity (Clark, Watson, & Mineka, 1994), and high levels of these normal personality traits do pose a significant risk for the future development of mood or anxiety disorders (Hirschfeld et al., 1989; Zonderman, Herbst, Schmidt, Costa, & McCrae, 1993). However, there are many potential differences between chronic negative emotion within the normal range and emotional disorders, and their associations with health may differ as well (Cohen & Rodriguez, 1995; Coyne, 1994; Watson, Clark, & Harkness, 1994).

Many psychometrically sound measures are available for assessing neuroticism, negative affectivity, and their components (Watson et al., 1994), and two issues are important when using them. First, dimensions within the broad traits of neuroticism and negative affectivity are closely intercorrelated. For example, a measure of depressed mood may correlate as closely with a measure of trait anxiety as it does with a second measure of depression. Thus, although the component constructs can be distinguished conceptually and sometimes empirically, scale labels within this trait domain often imply a greater degree of specificity or discriminant validity than can be documented (Watson et al., 1994). Second, because clinical emotional disorders are associated with elevated scores on these measures, associations with health outcomes could reflect the effects of either or both normal and pathological emotional processes. That is, in any large sample, there may be individuals with clinically significant emotional disorders, and they could contribute to an association with health outcomes.

Neuroticism and negative affectivity are also associated with symptom reports and other illness behaviors that are in excess of actual illness (Costa & McCrae, 1987a; Watson & Pennebaker, 1989). Hence, associations between such scales and operational definitions of health that include illness behavior could reflect an association with actual health, the discrepancy between illness and illness behavior (e.g., excessive somatic complaints), or some combination of these outcome constructs. Therefore, to estimate the effects of this personality characteristic—or any trait closely related to it—on actual health, objective measures of health that are relatively uncontaminated with illness behavior must be used.

For many years, the clear evidence that neuroticism was associated with illness behavior in the absence of actual illness was combined with some evidence that it did not predict more objective indications of illness (e.g., mortality, diagnosis of cancer, or CHD) to support the additional conclusion that this personality trait was not a risk factor for actual illness (Costa & McCrae, 1987b; Stone & Costa, 1990; Wiebe & Smith, 1997). A growing body of subsequent research has challenged this conclusion. For example, prospective studies have indicated that self-reported fear, anxiety, and depression are associated with rising levels of blood pressure over time and increased incidence of diagnosed hypertension (Davidson, Jonas, Dixon, & Markovitz, 2000; Jones, Franks, & Ingram, 1997; Markovitz, Matthews, Wing, Kuller, & Meilahn, 1991; Spiro, Aldwin, Ward, & Mroczek, 1995).

Among individuals with hypertension, negative affectivity is associated with increased risk of stroke and death from cardiovascular causes (Simonsick, Wallace, Blaser, & Gerkman, 1995). Among initially healthy persons, symptoms of anxiety and depression have been found to predict the later development of CHD (Anda et al., 1993; Barefoot & Schroll, 1996; Eaker, Pinsky, & Castelli, 1992; Ford et al., 1998; Kawachi, Sparow, Vokonas, & Weiss, 1994; Kubzansky et al., 1997; Pennix et al., 2001), heart failure (Williams, Kasl, et al., 2002), stroke (May et al., 2002), and early death (Hermann et al., 1998; Martin et al., 1995; Somerevill et al., 1989). Among individuals with established CHD, measures of neuroticism and negative affectivity predict recurrent coronary events and longevity (Ahern et al., 1990; Barefoot et al., 1996; Denollet, Sys, & Brutsaert, 1995; Follick et al., 1988; Frasure-Smith, Lespérance, & Talajic, 1995a; Horsten et al., 2000; Lespérance, Frasure-Smith, Talajic, & Bourassa, 2002; Moser & Dracup, 1996), as do depressive disorders (Carney, Rich, & Freedland, 1988; Frasure-Smith, Lespérance, & Talajic, 1993, 1995b; Januzzi, Stern, Pasternak, & DeSanctis, 2000). Similarly, depressive symptoms have been found to predict mortality among initial survivors of stroke (House et al., 2001).

Such studies challenge the earlier conclusion that neuroticism and negative affectivity are associated with illness behavior but not actual illness. However, it is important to note that some large, well-controlled studies do not find an association between neuroticism and objective health outcomes (G. Kaplan & Reynolds, 1988; Lane, Carroll, Ring, Beevers, & Lip, 2001; Shekelle, Vernon, & Ostfeld, 1991; Zonderman, Costa, & McCrae, 1989). Nonetheless, the more recent evidence would seem to suggest that this personality characteristic is associated with both actual illness and illness behavior in excess of actual illness. Given that neuroticism and negative affectivity are broad, multifaceted personality traits, it may be that some of their components are associated with illness behavior, whereas others are related to actual illness (Barefoot, Bechkham, Peterson, Haney, & Williams, 1992; Cohen, Tyrell, & Smith, 1991; Cohen et al., 1995).

Neuroticism and negative affectivity could influence actual health through several of the mechanisms discussed earlier (Cohen & Rodriquez, 1995). Anxiety and depressive symptoms are associated with suppressed immune functioning (Cohen & Herbert, 1996; Herbert & Cohen, 1993; Kiecolt-Glaser & Glaser, 1995; McGuire, Kiecolt-Glaser, & Glaser, 2002), increasing the likelihood of infectious illnesses and possibly cancer (Rabin, 1999). Chronic anxiety and depressive symptoms have also been associated with alterations in autonomic influences on the cardiovascular system (Berntson, Sarter, & Cacioppo, 1998; Carney, Freedland, Rich, & Jaffe, 1995; Watkins, Grossman, Krishnan, & Sherwood, 1998). Heightened sympathetic and reduced parasympathetic inputs to this system could contribute to the development and progression of CAD and the emergence of symptomatic CHD at later stages of disease development (Kop, 1999; Rozanski et al., 1999). Hence, stress moderation models provide a plausible account of the health effects on neuroticism.

Transactional mechanisms are also possible, as chronic negative emotions such as depression are associated with increased future exposure to stressful life experiences (Daley & Hammen, 2002; Daley et al., 1997; Davila, Bradbury, Cohan, & Tochluk, 1997; Gunthert, Cohen, & Armeli, 1999; Hammen, 1991; Neyer & Asendorpf, 2001; Potthoff, Holahan, & Joiner, 1995; Smith & Zautra, 2002). For example, through negative expectations about others and ineffective interpersonal problem solving or coping skills, depressed persons may undermine potential sources of social support and engender conflict in their personal relationships (Joiner & Coyne, 1999). Similarly, neuroticism is associated with both increased exposure and emotional reactivity to negative events during everyday life (Bolger & Schilling, 1991; Bolger & Zuckerman, 1995). Finally, some of the negative health consequences of neuroticism and negative affectivity may be a result of health behavior mechanisms, because these traits have been found to be associated with inactivity, smoking, and problematic adherence to prescribed medical regimens (Booth-Kewley & Vickers, 1994; Carney et al., 1995; Wiebe, Alderfer, Palmer, Lindsay, & Jarrett, 1994). It is important to note that in most of the studies described, neuroticism and negative affectivity predicted subsequent health even when health behaviors were statistically controlled. Hence, it is unlikely that this model provides a complete account of the health effects of this personality trait.

Optimism, Pessimism, and Hopelessness

Individual differences in optimistic, as opposed to pessimistic or even hopeless, expectations about the future have also been found to predict subsequent health. Research on this topic is based on a variety of conceptual models and uses several different measurement procedures (Scheier, Carver, & Bridges, 2001; Peterson & Bossio, 2001). For example, the generalized expectancy model of Scheier and Carver (1985) defined optimism as the tendency to "expect good experiences in the future" (Carver & Scheier, 2001, p. 31), and a brief self-report scale is used to assess this expectancy. In contrast, the explanatory style approach of Seligman and his colleagues defines optimism as the tendency to attribute problems in one's life to "temporary, specific, and external (as opposed to permanent, pervasive, and internal) causes" (Gillham, Shatte, Reivich, & Seligman, 2001, p. 54). This later version of the construct can be assessed with either self-report inventories or expert coding of written or spoken material.

As in other research areas discussed, the various measures of optimism, pessimism, and hopelessness correlate only modestly (Norem & Chang,

2001). They also have differing patterns of association with measures of other concepts, and substantial overlap with other traits studied in the literature on personality and health. For example, some optimism measures correlate substantially with neuroticism (Marshall et al., 1992; Scheier, Carver, & Bridges, 1994; Smith, Pope, Rhodewalt, & Poulton, 1989), raising concerns about the extent to which associations between optimism and measures of illness behavior could reflect shared variance with this five factor model trait. Formal studies of the structure of these scales and their convergent and discriminant validity have suggested that optimism and pessimism may be most accurately considered as inversely related but distinct dimensions, and that overlap with measures of neuroticism and other traits explains some but certainly not all of the health correlates of optimism and pessimism (Chang, 1998; Chang, D'Zurilla, & Maydeu-Olivares, 1994; Chang, Maydeu-Olivares, & D'Zurilla, 1997; Scheier et al., 1994).

In recent years, several studies have provided prospective evidence that optimism and pessimism predict future, objectively defined health outcomes. Generalized optimistic expectancies have been found to predict reduced incidence of medical complications following coronary artery bypass graft surgery (Scheier et al., 1989, 1999), and pessimism has been associated with decreased survival among breast cancer patients (Schultz et al., 1996). When combined with measures of closely related cognitive–social personality traits (e.g., self-esteem, mastery), optimism has also been associated with reduced likelihood of recurrent coronary events following angioplasty (Helgeson & Fritz, 1999). Optimism assessed in expectant mothers has been found to predict the delivery of healthier newborns (Lobel & DeVincent, 2000), and content codings of optimistic explanatory style have been associated with physician ratings of health (Peterson, Seligman, & Vaillant, 1988) and longevity (Peterson, Seligman, Yurko, Martin, & Friedman, 1998) over long follow-up intervals. Other measures of optimism have also been found to predict CHD incidence (Kubzansky, Sparrow, Vokonas, & Kawachi, 2001), survival following stroke (Lewis, Dennis, O'Rourke, & Sharpe, 2001), and longevity (Maruta, Colligan, Malinchoc, & Offord, 2000). Responses to brief hopelessness scales have been associated with the development of hypertension (Everson, Kaplan, Goldberg, & Salonen, 2000), cardiovascular and cancer deaths (Everson et al., 1996), progression of atherosclerosis (Everson et al., 1997), myocardial infarction (Anda et al., 1993; Everson et al., 1996), and longevity (Stern, Dhanda, & Hazuda, 2001). Hence, across a variety of assessment devices, populations, and medical outcomes, high levels of optimism—and low levels of pessimism and hopelessness—are associated with better health over time. However, some failures to replicate this association have been reported (e.g., Cassileth, Lusk, & Miller, 1985), and in at least one case optimism was associated with reduced longevity (Friedman et al., 1993). In addition, in only some of the supportive studies was the potential overlap of optimism–pessimism and neuroticism ruled out as an alternative explanation. Nonetheless, there is growing support for the health relevance of this cognitive–social personality characteristic.

The basic model of the health consequences of optimism is a stress moderation approach. Through their positive appraisals and sustained adaptive coping, optimists are presumed to experience less potentially unhealthy physiological stress responses. Some evidence supports this hypothesis. For example, optimism is associated with more robust immune functioning (Segerstrom, Taylor, Kemeny, & Fahey, 1998), and pessimism is associated with higher levels of ambulatory blood pressure (Raikkonen, Matthews, Flory, Owens, & Gump, 1999). Health behavior mechanisms are also possible, because optimism is associated with more effective participation in health care (Lin & Peterson, 1990; Strack, Carver, & Blaney, 1987). Recent observations of greater social support and reduced interpersonal conflict among optimists has led to the suggestion that transactional mechanisms may also contribute to the salubrious effects of this trait (Brissette, Scheier, & Carver, 2002; Smith et al., 2003). In the conceptual space defined by the interpersonal circumplex, optimism is associated with friendly dominance, and this interpersonal style could tend to evoke positive reactions from others. Recurring positive responses from others, in turn, could sustain an optimistic outlook (Smith et al., 2003).

Other Traits as Risk Factors

Many other personality characteristics have been examined as influences on health and illness. Repressive or defensive coping (Jorgensen et al., 2001; Weinberger, Schwartz, & Davison, 1979), hardiness (Kobasa, 1979), conscientiousness (Friedman et al., 1993), and curiosity (Swan & Carmelli, 1996) have all been studied. In some cases, such as hardiness, the related theoretical models and early empirical research had a critical influence on the development of interest in personality and health (Suls & Rittenhouse, 1987), but subsequent research failed to provide substantial evidence of prospective associations with objectively defined health and illness (Funk, 1992; Smith & Gallo, 2001). In other cases, such as repressive coping, evidence is more promising and may yet become as convincing as the research on traits such as hostility and negative affectivity (Contrada et al., 1999; Smith & Gallo, 2001). Preliminary evidence suggests that constructs from the cognitive–social perspective (e.g., social goals) are related to physiological reactivity to interpersonal stressors, and therefore may be related to vulnerability to disease (Chen, Matthews, Salomon, & Ewart, 2002; Sauro et al., 2001). In all cases, attention to the conceptual and methodological issues reviewed will be important in future research.

PERSONALITY CHARACTERISTICS AND HEALTH BEHAVIOR

Virtually all of the traits discussed as predictors of health and illness have also been examined as predictors of health behavior. In some cases, this research has been directed toward alternatives to the prevailing psychobiological (i.e., stress moderation) explanations of the effects of personality on health. As noted, hostility (Siegler, 1994), neuroticism, and negative affectivity (Booth-Kewley & Vickers, 1994; Carney et al., 1995) and optimism (Lin & Peterson, 1990; Strack et al., 1987) have all been examined in this context. Although these personality characteristics certainly are related to health behavior and these correlates may contribute to their health effects, these associations between traits and subsequent illness cannot be adequately accounted for by this mechanism. In other cases, personality variables have been examined in an effort to construct comprehensive accounts of the development and determinants of health behavior or "lifestyle" contributions to health.

Within the traditional view of personality traits, some constructs have been found to predict the development of unhealthy behaviors. For example, high levels of negative emotionality and low levels of restraint are associated with subsequent unhealthy behaviors such as alcohol and other substance abuse, dangerous driving habits, and unsafe sexual practices (Caspi et al., 1997; Sher, Bartholow, & Wood, 2000). Low restraint reflects impulsivity and excitement-seeking, and hence likely involves elements or facets of both (low) conscientiousness and extraversion. In addition, this trait, like negative affectivity, can be seen as developing from early childhood differences in temperament dimensions such as irritability, low self-control and persistence, and emotional lability (Caspi et al., 1997).

Although these associations are useful for developmental models of health behavior and the identification of high risk groups, the implications for risk-reducing interventions are not always clear. Traditional trait theory and the concept of temperament as a developmental precursor of traits typically do not emphasize the mechanisms through which traits affect specific behaviors, and these approaches often emphasize the genetic origins and temporal stability of personality. Hence, such views are limited as guides to risk-reducing interventions. They may be useful in describing who is at risk, but are less useful in suggesting what might be done about it.

Models of personality factors in health behavior more closely tied to the cognitive–social perspective have more obvious implications for interventions. For example, individual differences in self-control skills, competence in peer relations, and self-esteem are potentially more readily modifiable individual difference predictors of the development of problematic health behaviors (Chassin, Presson, Pitts, & Sherman, 2000; Wills, Gibbons,

Gerrard, & Brody, 2000). The cognitive and social aspects of self-regulation, problem solving, and coping identified as risk factors for unhealthy behaviors can serve as a menu of targets for risk reducing interventions, even if these personality processes are seen as evolving from differences in temperament (Caspi et al., 1997; Wills et al., 2000).

The cognitive–social approach has also been applied to other health behaviors in adulthood. S. Miller and her colleagues (1996) have argued that health-relevant versions of the cognitive and social variables discussed earlier can explain individual differences in the enactment of health protective behavior. Examples of these variables are listed in Table 5.2. In this model, individuals differ in their style of attending to, encoding, and processing health-relevant information. For example, some individuals scan for and amplify health-relevant information, whereas others may avoid or attenuate information about possible health threats. Individuals also differ in their beliefs about the impact of specific behaviors and behavior changes on health (i.e., outcome expectancies), as well as their specific ability to enact and maintain health behavior changes (self-efficacy expectations). A similar process or mechanistic view of the effects of individual differences in optimism/pessimism has been described by Aspinwall, Richter, and Hoffman (2001). The favorable expectations of optimists lead them to gather more extensive and complete information about potential health threats and to develop and implement more flexible and effective coping strategies. These and other cognitive–social constructs listed in Table 5.2 can provide mechanistic explanations of the impact of personality processes on health behavior, as well as guide the development and implementation of preventive interventions.

Application of the cognitive–social perspective in personality to issues of health behavior creates links to other concepts that are not typically construed as personality characteristics. The literature on relapse prevention illustrates this issue. For most health behavior changes, maintenance of initial positive changes is a critical concern. In smoking cessation, reductions in problematic drinking, diet and weight loss, and interventions to promote increased exercise and activity levels, beneficial initial treatment effects are often followed by a return to earlier, undesirable behaviors. Relapse-prevention training (Collier & Marlatt, 1995; Marlatt & Gordon, 1985) is an attempt to address this problem by including in the latter stages of treatment specific interventions directed toward the cognitive, behavioral, and interpersonal determinants of relapse. In this view, planning for the very likely event of at least temporary relapses or slips is a key component of treatment. The intervention targets addressed in relapse-prevention training bear a clear resemblance to the middle units of personality identified in the cognitive–social approach. For example, individuals are helped to identify high risk situations and associated emotional states (e.g., sadness, loneliness, anxiety), skills for managing social pressure to engage in undesirable behavior

TABLE 5.2

Personality Influences on Protective Behaviors in the Cognitive–Social
Approach to Health Information Processing

Person variable	Example
Health relevant encodings	Internal representations of health and risk Attentional strategies in processing health information
Health beliefs and expectations	Outcome expectancies for health behaviors Self-efficacy for health behaviors
Affects	Emotional impact of health information Feelings about the self
Health goals and values	Desired health outcomes and their subjective importance Health-relevant goals and life tasks

Self-regulatory competencies and skills	Knowledge and strategies for overcoming
	   barriers to change
	Planning and problem-solving for relapse
	   and maintenance.

Note. From "Applying Cognitive–Social Theory to Health-Protective Behavior: Breast Self-Examination in Cancer Screening," by S. M. Miller, Y. Shoda, and K. Hurley, 1996, *Psychological Bulletin, 119*, p. 73. Copyright 1996 by the American Psychological Association. Originally appeared in "A Cognitive–Affective System Theory of Personality: Reconceptualizing Situations, Dispositions, Dynamics, and Invariance in Personality Structures," by W. Mischel and Y. Shoda, 1995, *Psychological Review, 102*, p. 253. Adapted with permission by the publisher and authors.

are assessed and refined, self-control strategies are developed for managing cravings or impulses to return to earlier patterns, and maladaptive appraisals of slips (e.g., catastrophizing and the abstinence violation effect) are modified. These approaches clearly overlap with the cognitive–social description of appraisals, self-regulation strategies, and behavioral competencies.

As described, the cognitive–social perspective also addresses the reciprocal relationship between these person variables and aspects of the social context. Health behaviors are related to interpersonal processes, such as the health behavior patterns of peers and family members and the level of supportiveness for health behavior change available from these sources. As a result, this view can provide a more comprehensive account of the determinants of health behavior and targets for risk reduction by calling attention to recurring features of the social context that may combine with personality processes to support or undermine healthier lifestyles.

PERSONALITY AND ADJUSTMENT TO MEDICAL
ILLNESS AND CARE

Many personality variables have been studied as influences on patients' responses to illness and medical care. As a group, these studies support the long-standing notion that it is indeed important to know which patient has the disease (Osler, 1910). Traditional personality traits have been examined, although less frequently than constructs within the cognitive–social perspective. For example, among patients with end-stage renal disease undergoing hemodialysis, high levels of hostility are associated with poor adherence to dietary restrictions and medication regimens (Christensen, Wiebe, & Lawton, 1997). Conscientiousness has also been associated with adherence in this population in some (Christensen & Smith, 1995) but not all studies (Moran, Christensen, & Lawton, 1997). Personality traits have also been consistently associated with a variety of outcomes (e.g., disability or functional activity levels, emotional adaptation, subjective pain levels) among patients with various forms of chronic pain (Gatchel & Weisberg, 2000).

Personality constructs in the cognitive–social approach have been found to predict adjustment in several acute medical and chronic illness contexts. For example, optimism assessed in pregnant women has been found to be associated with more positive emotional adjustment during pregnancy and following childbirth (Carver & Gaines, 1987; Park, Moore, Turner, & Adler, 1997), and with better adjustment among women following an abortion (Cozzarelli, 1993; Major, Richards, Cooper, Cozzarelli, & Zubek, 1998). Among patients undergoing coronary angioplasty, optimism and related cognitive traits (i.e., mastery, positive self-concept) are associated with better emotional adjustment over time (Helgeson, 1999). Similar positive effects of optimism on emotional adjustment following coronary-artery bypass surgery have been reported (Fitzgerald, Tennen, Affleck, & Pransky, 1993; King, Rowe, Kimble, & Zerwic, 1998; Scheier et al., 1999). Optimism has also been found to predict better emotional adjustment and more adaptive coping among patients with cancer (Carver et al., 1993) and rheumatoid arthritis (Affleck, Tennen, & Apter, 2001). Hence, generalized positive expectancies seem to be associated with better adaptation in a variety of medical contexts (Scheier et al., 2001).

Other middle-units of personality have also been found to influence adaptation in chronic disease. In a daily experience sampling study of patients with fibromyalgia, perceived progress toward personal goals for relationships and health was an important predictor of subsequent emotional adjustment (Affleck et al., 1998). Among patients awaiting kidney transplantation, those characterized by a high level of interest in and attention to health-related information demonstrated a decrease in depressive symptoms following transplantation. In contrast, patients who displayed the opposite encoding or attentional strategy showed increasing levels of depression following transplantation (Christensen, Ehlers, Raichle, Bertolatus, & Lawton, 2000). This cognitive personality trait was unrelated to changes in depression among similar patients who do not undergo transplant. Hence, the experience of receiving the donor organ and the related surgical procedure and medical regimen interacted with this personality characteristic to influence adjustment.

Person-by-situation statistical interaction models have been particularly useful in understanding various aspects of patients' adaptation to chronic illness. Individual differences in encoding styles, preferences for information about health, and personal involvement in medical care are not related to emotional adaptation, disability levels, and adherence to medical regimens in the same manner across all situations. Rather, the match between such individual differences and characteristics of the specific medical situation are the more important determinant (Christensen, 2000). For example, among patients undergoing dialysis for ESRD, strong preferences for health information and participation in care are associated with better outcomes when individuals are undergoing home dialysis or peritoneal dialysis—two forms of treatment in which self-care requirements are substantial and essential. In contrast, low levels of this encoding style and preference are associated with better psychological and behavioral outcomes among patients undergoing in-center dialysis, in which passive reliance on treatment center staff is required (Christensen, 2000; Christensen et al., 1997). These patient-by-situation statistical interactions are often more important determinants of adaptation than are main effects for either the personality characteristics or the central dimensions of the medical situation.

Concepts from the interpersonal approach have also been found to predict adaptation to illness. The social motives associated with the two primary dimensions of the circumplex (i.e., agency and communion) appear to be important. High levels of agency are generally associated with beneficial emotional outcomes in chronic illness (Helgeson, 1993; Helgeson & Lepore, 1997), unless agency is extreme and accompanied by very low levels of communion (Helgeson & Lepore, 1997). High levels of communion are generally not associated with adaptation, unless they are unaccompanied by offsetting or mitigating levels of agency. Such unmitigated communion (Helgeson & Fritz, 1998) has been found to predict poor adaptation to coronary heart disease (Fritz, 2000; Helgeson, 1993; Helgeson & Fritz, 1999). Hence, a balance of these motivations appears to facilitate adaptation to chronic disease.

Other research supports the interpersonal view that cognitive personality characteristics and aspects of the patient's social context combine to influence adaptation. For example, unsupportive spouse behavior contributes to poor emotional adjustment among cancer patients, apparently by fostering maladaptive coping by the patient (Manne, 1999; Manne & Glassman, 2000). Cognitive and social factors are typically conceptualized and studied as separate influences on patient adjustment. Yet, as suggested by the findings of such research and the tenets of the interpersonal approach, these factors may reflect multiple features of a single transactional process that influences patients' adaptation. That is, the traditionally intraindividual perspective on the patient's coping and adaptation may be usefully placed within a broader view of the surrounding social context (Coyne & Smith, 1991). Again, an important component of that social context involves health care providers. This is illustrated by a recent study in which individual differences in neuroticism were associated with differing patient presentations of similar illnesses, and those differing presentations of symptoms, in turn, prompted physicians to recommend different medical tests and procedures (Ellington & Wiebe, 1999).

CONCLUSION

Personality characteristics are clearly relevant to the three broad topics in health psychology and behavioral medicine. Personality is related to health behaviors that confer risk of illness and premature mortality. Personality traits are also reliable risk factors for disease even when health behavior is controlled, suggesting that these characteristics play a role in the psychosomatic pathways through which stress and emotion affect the pathophysiology of disease. Finally, personality characteristics affect the experience of and response to acute and chronic illness and medical care. Hence, the concepts and methods of personality psychology are integral elements of these fields.

Future research testing models of these influences of personality on health behavior and outcomes must be clearly grounded in theory. This process begins with an adequate conceptual description of the personality characteristic under consideration, as only then can measurements be developed, evaluated, and refined optimally. Clear conceptualization and valid measurement of the health endpoints is equally important, to capture the outcomes of greatest importance and to avoid confusing personality effects on illness behavior with effects on illness itself. Finally, a clear and comprehensive description of the mechanisms through which personality processes influence health outcomes is needed. Such models should be informed by an appreciation for the pathophysiology of the disease across specific phases of development and course. Attention to this issue will ensure that studies of personality and health address medically plausible associations. Similarly, models of personality influences on adaptation to illness and medical care should be based on comprehensive descriptions of the nature and impact of the condition and its usual medical management. In this way, responses to essential features of illness and care will be the primary focus of research.

It is also clear that future research on personality and health should take full advantage of the range of current and emerging perspectives in personality psychology. The five factor model provides valuable conceptual benchmarks for the comparison and integration of personality concepts and measures used in the study of health. An integrated science of personality and health founded on carefully validated measures of personality constructs has much more value than an alternative based on a proliferation of isolated and insufficiently validated scales. However, the largely descriptive and atheoretical nature of the five factor taxonomy creates the necessity of complementary research based in the more process- and mechanistic-oriented approach of the cognitive–social perspective. Trait models may describe who is a risk, but are less helpful in guiding explanations of that risk and suggesting targets for health-promoting interventions. Finally, the interpersonal tradition in personality may facilitate the integration of these efforts with related effort focused on social risk factors.

The preceding discussion also highlights the value of considering personality processes in the clinical evaluation and management of individual patients. In the application of theory and research on personality and health to individual patients, the differing contributions and limitations of the major traditions in the field of personality again become quite salient. A wide variety of psychometrically sound assessment devices are available for the assessment of personality traits as typically defined. However, standardized assessments of the central constructs in the cognitive–social approach have not been developed. Hence, these models are likely to guide the clinician's interviewing and case conceptualization, rather than be the focus of more formal psychological assessment. A major challenge for the future is the development of reliable and valid assessments of the health-relevant constructs within the cognitive–social approach for use in clinical practice. Finally, although consideration of personality characteristics in clinical assessment and intervention implicitly calls attention to the individual patient, interpersonal and transactional concepts in personality underscore the importance of the patient's network of social relations and recurring patterns of social interaction. The interpersonal tradition does include a variety of psychometrically sound assessment procedures for use in clinical practice (Kiesler, 1996). The interpersonal perspective should also facilitate better integration of personality traits and processes with other elements in the biopsychosocial perspective underlying application in clinical health psychology and behavioral medicine. The application of these diverse concepts and methods of modern personality psychology may foster more compelling and useful evidence regarding age-old hypotheses about the impact of personality on health.

REFERENCES

Affleck, G., Tennen, H., & Apter, A. (2001). Optimism, pessimism, and daily life with chronic illness. In E. C. Chang (Ed.), *Optimism and pessimism: Implications for theory, research, and practice* (pp. 147–168). Washington, DC: American Psychological Association.

Affleck, G., Tennen, H., Urrows, S., Higgins, P., Abeles, M., Hall, C., et al. (1998). Fibromyalgia and women's pursuit of personal goals: A daily process analysis. *Health Psychology, 17,* 40–47.

Ahern, D. K., Gorkin, L., Anderson, J. L., Tierney, C., Hallstrom, A., Ewart, C., et al. (1990). Biobehavioral variables and mortality or cardiac arrest in the Cardiac Arrhthmia Pilot Study (CAPS). *American Journal of Cardiology, 66,* 59–62.

Alexander, F. (1950). *Psychosomatic medicine.* New York: Norton.

Allport, G. W. (1937). *Personality: A psychological interpretation.* New York: Holt.

Anda, R., Wiliamson, D., Jones, D., Macera, C., Eaker, E., Glassman, A., et al. (1993). Depressed affect, hopelessness, and the risk of ischemic heart disease in a cohort of U.S. adults. *Epidemiology, 4,* 285–294.

Armitage C. J., & Conner, M. (1999). Social cognition models and health behaviour: A structured review. *Psychology and Health, 15,* 1–17.

Aspinwall, L. G., Richter, L., & Hoffman, R. R. (2001). Understanding how optimism works: An examination of optimists' adaptive moderation of belief and behavior. In E. C. Chang (Ed.), *Optimism and pessimism: Implications for theory, research, and practice* (pp. 217–238). Washington, DC: American Psychological Association.

Bakan, D. (1966). *The duality of human existence: Isolation and communion in Western man.* Boston: Beacon.

Bandura, A. (1978). The self-system in reciprocal determinism. *American Psychologist, 33,* 1175–1184.

Bandura, A. (1989). Human agency in social cognitive theory. *American Psychologist, 44,* 1175–1184.

Barefoot, J. C., Beckham, J., Peterson, B., Haney, T., & Williams, R. B. (1992). Measures of neuroticism and disease status in coronary angiography patients. *Journal of Consulting and Clinical Psychology, 60,* 127–132.

Barefoot, J. C., Helms, M. S., Mark, D. B., Blumenthal, J. A., Califf, R. M., Haney, T. L., et al. (1996). Depression and long-term mortality risk in patients with coronary artery disease. *American Journal of Cardiology, 78,* 613–617.

Barefoot, J. C., & Lipkus, I. M. (1994). The assessment of anger and hostility. In A. W. Siegman & T. W. Smith (Eds.), *Anger, hostility, and the heart* (pp. 43–66). Hillsdale, NJ: Erlbaum.

Barefoot, J. C., & Schroll, M. (1996). Symptoms of depression, acute myocardial infarction, and total mortality in a community sample. *Circulation, 93,* 1976–1980.

Baron, R. M., & Kenney, D. A. (1986). The moderator–mediator variable distinction in social psychological research: Conceptual, strategic, and statistical considerations. *Journal of Personality and Social Psychology, 51,* 1173–1182.

Bem, D. J., & Allen, A. (1974). On predicting some of the people some of the time: The search for cross-situational consistencies in behavior. *Psychological Review, 81,* 506–520.

Benotsch, E. G., Christensen, A. J., & McKelvey, L. (1997). Hostility, social support and ambulatory cardiovascular activity. *Journal of Behavioral Medicine, 20,* 163–176.

Berntson, G. G., Sarter, M., & Cacioppo, J. T. (1998). Anxiety and cardiovascular reactivity: The basal forebrain cholinergic link. *Behavioral Brain Research, 94,* 225–248.

Block, J. (1995). A contrarian view of the five-factor approach to personality description. *Psychological Bulletin, 117,* 182–215.

Blumenthal, J. A., Fredrikson, M., Kuhn, C. M., Ulmer, R. A., Walsh-Riddle, S., & Appelbaum, M. (1990). Aeorbic exercise reduces levels of cardiovascular and sympathoadrenal responses to mental stress in subjects without prior evidence of myocardial ischemia. *American Journal of Cardiology, 65,* 93–98.

Bolger, N., & Schilling, E. A. (1991). Personality and the problems of everyday life: The role of neuroticism in exposure and reactivity to daily stressors. *Journal of Personality, 59,* 355–386.

Bolger, N., & Zuckerman, A. (1995). A framework for studying personality in the stress process. *Journal of Personality and Social Psychology, 69,* 890–902.

Booth-Kewley, S., & Vickers, R. R. (1994). Associations between major domains of personality and health behavior. *Journal of Personality, 62,* 281–298.

Bowers, K. S. (1973). Situationism in psychology: An analysis and a critique. *Psychological Review, 80,* 307–336.

Brissette, I., Scheier, M. F., & Carver, C. S. (2002). The role of optimism in social network development, coping, and psychological adjustment during a life transition. *Journal of Personality and Social Psychology, 82,* 102–111.

Buss, D. M. (1987). Selection, evocation, and manipulation. *Journal of Personality and Social Psychology, 53,* 1214–1221.

Campbell, D. T., & Fiske, D. W. (1959). Convergent and discriminant validity by the multitrait-multimethod matrix. *Psychological Bulletin, 56,* 81–105.

Cantor, N. (1990). From thought to behavior: "Having" and "doing" in the study of personality and cognition. *American Psychologist, 45,* 735–750.

Carney, R. M., Freedland, K., Rich, M., & Jaffe, A. S. (1995). Depression as a risk factor for cardiac events in established coronary heart disease: A review of possible mechanisms. *Annals of Behavioral Medicine, 17,* 142–149.

Carney, R. M., Rich, M. W., & Freedland, K. E. (1988). Major depressive disorder predicts cardiac events in patients with coronary artery disease. *Psychosomatic Medicine, 50,* 627–633.

Carson, R. C. (1969). *Interaction concepts in personality.* Chicago: Aldine.

Carver, C. S. (1989). How should multifaceted personality constructs be tested? Issues illustrated by self-monitoring, attributional style, and hardiness. *Journal of Personality and Social Psychology, 65,* 375–406.

Carver, C. S., & Gaines, J. G. (1987). Optimism, pessimism, and post-partum depression. *Cognitive Therapy and Research, 11*, 449–462.

Carver, C. S., Pozo, C., Harris, S. D., Noriega, V., Scheier, M. F., Robinson, D. S., et al. (1993). How coping mediates the effects of optimism on distress: A study of women with early stage breast cancer. *Journal of Personality and Social Psychology, 65*, 375–391.

Carver, C. S., & Scheier, M. F. (2001). Optimism, pessimism, and self-regulation. In E. C. Chang (Ed.), *Optimism and pessimism: Implications for theory, research, and practice* (pp. 31–52). Washington, DC: American Psychological Association.

Caspi, A., Begg, D., Dickson, N., Harrington, H., Langley, J., Moffitt, T. E., et al. (1997). Personality differences predict health-risk behaviors in young adulthood: Evidence from a longitudinal study. *Journal of Personality and Social Psychology, 73*, 1052–1063.

Caspi, A., Bem, D. J., & Elder, G. H. (1989). Continuities and consequences of interactional styles across the life course. *Journal of Personality, 57*, 375–406.

Cassileth, B. R., Lusk, E. J., & Miller, D. S. (1985). Psychosocial correlates of survival in advanced malignant disease. *New England Journal of Medicine, 312*, 1551–1555.

Chang, E. C. (1998). Distinguishing between optimism and pessimism: A second look at the "optimism–neuroticism hypothesis." In R. R. Hoffman, M. F. Sherrik, & J. S. Warm (Eds.), *Viewing psychology as a whole: The integrative science of William N. Dember* (pp. 415–432). Washington, DC: American Psychological Association.

Chang, E. C., D'Zurilla, T. J., & Maydeu-Olivares, A. (1994). Assessing the dimensionality of optimism and pessimism using a multimeasure approach. *Cognitive Therapy and Research, 18*, 143–160.

Chang, E. C., Maydeu-Olivares, A., & D'Zurilla, T. J. (1997). Optimism and pessimism as partially independent constructs: Relationship to positive and negative affectivity and psychological well-being. *Personality and Individual Differences, 23*, 433–440.

Chang, P. P., Ford, D. E., Meoni, L. A., Wang, N., & Klag, M. (2002). Anger in young men and subsequent premature cardiovascular disease. *Archives of Internal Medicine, 162*, 901–906.

Chassin, L., Presson, C. C., Pitts, S. C., & Sherman, S. J. (2000). A natural history of cigarette smoking from adolescence to adulthood in a Midwestern community sample: Multiple trajectories and their psychosocial correlates. *Health Psychology, 19*, 223–231.

Chen, E., Matthews, K. A., Salomon, K., & Ewart, C. K. (2002). Cardiovascular reactivity during social and nonsocial stressors: Do children's personal goals and expressive skills matter? *Health Psychology, 21*, 16–24.

Christensen, A. J. (2000). Patient X treatment context interaction in chronic disease: A conceptual framework for the study of patient adherence. *Psychosomatic Medicine, 62*, 435–443.

Christensen, A. J., Ehlers, S. L., Raichle, K. A., Bertolatus, J. A., & Lawton, W. J. (2000). Predicting change in depression following renal transplantation: Effects of patient coping preferences. *Health Psychology, 19,* 348–353.

Christensen, A. J., & Smith, T. W. (1995). Personality and patient adherence: Correlates of the Five Factor Model in renal dialysis. *Journal of Behavioral Medicine, 18,* 305–313.

Christensen, A. J., Wiebe, J. S., & Lawton, W. J. (1997). Cynical hostility, powerful others control expectancies, and patient adherence in hemodialysis. *Psychosomatic Medicine, 59,* 307–312.

Cioffi, D. (1991). Beyond attentional strategies: A cognitive–perceptual model of somatic interpretation. *Psychological Bulletin, 109,* 25–41.

Clark, L. A., Watson, D., & Mineka, S. (1994). Temperament, personality, and the mood and anxiety disorders. *Journal of Abnormal Psychology, 103,* 103–116.

Cohen, F. (1979). Personality, stress, and the development of physical illness. In G. C. Stone, F. Cohen, & N. E. Adler (Eds.), *Health psychology: A handbook* (pp. 77–111). San Francisco: Jossey-Bass.

Cohen, S., Doyle, W. J., Skoner, D. P., Fireman, P., Gwaltney, J. M., & Newsom, J. T. (1995). State and trait negative affect as predictors of objective and subjective symptoms of respiratory viral infections. *Journal of Personality and Social Psychology, 68,* 159–169.

Cohen, S., & Herbert, T. (1996). Health psychology: Psychological factors and disease from the perspective of human pschoneuro-immunology. *Annual Review of Psychology, 47,* 113–142.

Cohen, S., Kaplan, J. R., & Manuck, S. B. (1994). Social support and coronary heart disease: Underlying psychological and biological mechanisms. In S. A. Shumaker & S. M. Czajowski (Eds.), *Social support and cardiovascular disease* (pp. 195–221). New York: Plenum Press.

Cohen, S., & Rodriguez, M. (1995). Pathways linking affective disturbances and physical disorders. *Health Psychology, 14,* 374–380.

Cohen, S., Tyrell, D., & Smith, A. (1991). Psychological stress and susceptibility to the common cold. *New England Journal of Medicine, 325,* 606–612.

Collier, C. W., & Marlatt, G. A. (1995). Relapse prevention. In A. J. Goreczny (Ed.), *Handbook of health and rehabilitation psychology* (pp. 307–321). New York: Plenum Press.

Contrada, R. J., Cather, C., & O'Leary, A. (1999). Personality and health: Dispositions and processes in disease susceptibility and adaptation to illness. In L. A. Pervin & O. P. John (Eds.), *Handbook of personality: Theory and research* (2nd ed., pp. 31–56). New York: Guilford Press.

Contrada, R. J., & Jussim, L. (1992). What does the Cook and Medley Hostility Scale measure? In search of an adequate measurement model. *Journal of Applied Social Psychology, 22,* 615–627.

Cook, W., & Medley, D. (1954). Proposed hostility and pharisaic virtue scales for the MMPI. *Journal of Applied Psychology, 38,* 414–418.

Cooper, T., Detre, T., & Weiss, S. M. (1981). Coronary-prone behavior and coronary heart disease: A critical review. *Circulation, 63,* 1199–1215.

Costa, P. T., Jr., & McCrae, R. R. (1987a). Neuroticism, somatic complaints, and disease: Is the bark worse than the bite? *Journal of Personality, 55,* 299–316.

Costa, P. T., Jr., & McCrae, R. R. (1987b). Personality assessment in psychosomatic medicine. In T. M. Wise (Ed.), *Advances in psychosomatic medicine* (pp. 71–82). Basel, Switzerland: Karger.

Costa, P. T., Jr., & Widiger, T. A. (Eds.). (1994). *Personality disorders and the five factor model of personality.* Washington, DC: American Psychological Association.

Coyne, J. C. (1994). Self-reported distress: Analog or ersatz depression? *Psychological Bulletin, 116,* 29–45.

Coyne, J. C., & Smith, D. A. F. (1991). Couples coping with myocardial infarction: A contextual perspective on wives' distress. *Journal of Personality and Social Psychology, 61,* 404–412.

Cozzarelli, C. (1993). Personality and self-efficacy as predictors of coping with abortion. *Journal of Personality and Social Psychology, 65,* 1224–1236.

Daley, S. E., & Hammen, C. (2002). Depressive symptoms and close relationships during the transition to adulthood: Perspectives from dysphoric women. Their best friends, and their romantic partners. *Journal of Consulting and Clinical Psychology, 70,* 129–141.

Daley, S. E., Hammen, C., Burge, D., Davila, J., Paley, B., Lindberg, N., et al. (1997). Predictors of the generation of episodic stress: A longitudinal study of late adolescent women. *Journal of Abnormal Psychology, 106,* 251–259.

Davidson, K., Jonas, B. S., Dixon, K. E., & Markovitz, J. H. (2000). Do depression symptoms predict early hypertension incidence in young adults in the CARDIA study? Coronary artery risk development in young adults. *Archives of Internal Medicine, 22,* 1495–1500.

Davila, J., Bradbury, T. N., Cohan, C. L., & Tochluk, S. (1997). Marital functions and depressive symptoms: Evidence for a stress generation model. *Journal of Personality and Social Psychology, 73,* 849–861.

Davis, M. D., & Matthews, K. A. (1990). Cigarette smoking and oral contraceptive use influence women's lipid lipoprotein, and cardiovascular responses during stress. *Health Psychology, 9,* 717–736.

Dembroski, T. M., MacDougall, J. M., Costa, P. T., Jr., & Grandits, G. A. (1989). Components of hostility as predictors of sudden death and myocardial infarction in the Multiple Risk Factor Intervention Trial. *Psychosomatic Medicine, 51,* 514–522.

Denollet, J., Sys, S., & Brutsaert, D. L. (1995). Personality and mortality after myocardial infarction. *Psychosomatic Medicine, 57,* 582–591.

Digman, J. M. (1990). Personality structure: Emergence of the five-factor model. *Annual Review of Psychology, 41,* 417–440.

Downey, G., Freitas, A. L., Michaels, B., & Khouri, H. (1998). The self-fulfilling prophecy in close relationships: Rejection sensitivity and rejection by romantic partners. *Journal of Personality and Social Psychology, 75*, 545–560.

Dunbar, H. F. (1943). *Psychosomatic diagnosis.* New York: Hoeber.

Dunbar-Jacob, J., Schlenk, E. A., & Caruthers, D. (2002). Adherence in the management of chronic disorders. In A. J. Christensen & M. H. Anton, (Eds.), *Chronic physical disorders: Behavioral medicine's perspective* (pp. 69–82). Oxford, England: Blackwell.

Eaker, E. D., Pinsky, J., & Castelli, W. P. (1992). Myocardial infarction and coronary death among women: Psychosocial predictors from a 20-year follow-up of women in the Framingham study. *American Journal of Epidemiology, 135*, 854–864.

Ekehammer, B. (1974). Interactionism in personality from a historical perspective. *Psychological Bulletin, 81*, 1026–1048.

Ellington, L., & Wiebe, D. J. (1999). Neuroticism, symptom presentation and medical decision making. *Health Psychology, 18*, 634–643.

Endler, N. S., & Magnusson, D. (1976). Toward an interactional psychology of personality. *Psychological Bulletin, 83*, 956–979.

Everson, S. A., Goldberg, D. E., Kaplan, G. A., Cohen, R. D., Pukkala, E., Tuomilehto, J., et al. (1996). Hopelessness and risk of mortality and incidence of myocardial infarction and cancer. *Psychosomatic Medicine, 58*, 113–121.

Everson, S. A., Kaplan, G. A., Goldberg, D. E., Salonen, R., & Salonen, J. T. (1997). Hopelessness and 4-year progression of carotid atherosclerosis. *Arteriosclerosis, Thrombosis, and Vascular Biology, 17*, 1490–1495.

Everson, S. A., Kaplan, G. A., Goldberg, D. E., & Salonen, J. T. (2000). Hypertension incidence is predicted by high levels of hopelessness in Finnish men. *Hypertension, 35*, 561–567.

Everson, S. A., Kauhanen, J., Kaplan, G., Goldberg, D., Julkunen, J., Tuomilehto, J., et al. (1997). Hostility and increased risk of mortality and myocardial infarction: The mediating role of behavioral risk factors. *American Journal of Epidemiology, 146*, 142–152.

Fiske, D. W., & Campbell, D. T. (1992). Citations do not solve problems. *Psychological Bulletin, 112*, 393–395.

Fitzgerald, T. E., Tennen, H., Affleck, G., & Pransky, G. S. (1993). The relative importance of dispositional optimism and control appraisals in quality of life after coronary artery bypass surgery. *Journal of Behavioral Medicine, 16*, 25–43.

Follick, M. J., Gorkin, L., Capone, R. J., Smith, T. W., Ahern, D. K., Stablein, D., et al. (1988). Psychological distress as a predictor of ventricular arrhythmias in a post-myocardial infarction population. *American Heart Journal, 116*, 32–36.

Ford, D. E., Mead, L. A., Chang, P. P., Cooper-Patrick, L., Wang, N., et al. (1998). Depression is a risk factor for coronary artery disease in men. *Archives of Internal Medicine, 158*, 1422–1426.

Frasure-Smith, N., Lespérance, F., & Talajic, M. (1993). Depression following myocardial infarction. *Journal of the American Medical Association, 270,* 1819–1825.

Frasure-Smith, N., Lespérance, F., & Talajic, M. (1995a). Depression and 18-month prognosis after myocardial infarction. *Circulation, 91,* 999–1005.

Frasure-Smith, N., Lespérance, F., & Talajic, M. (1995b). The impact of negative emotions on prognosis following myocardial infarction: Is it more than depression? *Health Psychology, 14,* 388–398.

Friedman, H. S., Tucker, J. S., Tomlinson-Keasey, C., Schwartz, J. E., Wingard, D. L., & Criqui, M. H. (1993). Does childhood personality predict longevity? *Journal of Personality and Social Psychology, 65,* 176–185.

Friedman, M., & Rosenman, R. H. (1959). Association of a specific overt behavior pattern with increases in blood cholesterol, blood clotting time, incidence of arcus senilis and clinical coronary artery disease. *Journal of the American Medical Association, 169,* 1286–1296.

Fritz, H. L. (2000). Gender-linked personality traits predict mental health and functional status following a first coronary event. *Health Psychology, 19,* 420–428.

Funder, D. C., & Ozer, D. J. (1983). Behavior as a function of the situation. *Journal of Personality and Social Psychology, 44,* 107–112.

Funk, S. (1992). Hardiness: A review of theory and research. *Health Psychology, 11,* 335–345.

Gallo, L. C., & Smith, T. W. (1998). Construct validation of health-relevant personality traits: Interpersonal circumplex and Five-Factor Model analyses of the Aggression Questionnaire. *International Journal of Behavioral Medicine, 5,* 129–147.

Gallo, L. C., & Smith, T. W. (1999). Patterns of hostility and social support: Conceptualizing psychosocial risk as a characteristic of the person and the environment. *Journal of Research in Personality, 33,* 281–310.

Gatchel, R. J., & Weisberg, J. N. (2000). *Personality characteristics of patients with pain.* Washington, DC: American Psychological Association.

Gillham, J. E., Shatte, A. J., Reivich, K. J., & Seligman, M. E. P. (2001). Optimism, pessimism, and explanatory style. In E. C. Chang (Ed.), *Optimism and pessimism: Implications for theory, research, and practice* (pp. 53–76). Washington, DC: American Psychological Association.

Glass, D. C. (1977). *Behavior patterns, stress, and coronary disease.* Hillsdale, NJ: Erlbaum.

Graziano, W. G., Jensen-Campbell, L. A., & Hair, E. C. (1996). Perceiving interpersonal conflict and reacting to it: The case for agreeableness. *Journal of Personality and Social Psychology, 70,* 820–835.

Gunthert, K. C., Cohen, L. H., & Armeli, S. (1999). The role of neuroticism in daily stress and coping. *Journal of Personality and Social Psychology, 7,* 1087–1100.

Guyll, M., & Contrada, R. J. (1998). Trait hostility and ambulatory cardiovascular activity: Responses to social interaction. *Health Psychology, 17*, 30–39.

Hammen, C. (1991). Generation of stress in the course of unipolar depression. *Journal of Abnormal Psychology, 100*, 48–61.

Haynes, S. G., Feinleib, M., & Kannel, W. B. (1980). The relationship of psychosocial factors to coronary heart disease in the Framingham Study: III. Eight-year incidence of coronary heart disease. *American Journal of Epidemiology, 111*, 37–58.

Hecker, M. H. L., Chesney, M. A., Black, G. W., & Frautchi, N. (1988). Coronary-prone behaviors in the Western Collaborative Group Study. *Psychosomatic Medicine, 50*, 153–164.

Helgeson, V. S. (1993). Implications of agency and communion for patient and spouse adjustment to a first coronary event. *Journal of Personality and Social Psychology, 64*, 807–816.

Helgeson, V. S. (1994). Relation of agency and communion to well-being: Evidence and potential explanations. *Psychological Bulletin, 116*, 412–428.

Helgeson, V. S. (1999). Applicability of cognitive-adaptation theory to predicting adjustment to heart disease after coronary angioplasty. *Health Psychology, 18*, 561–569.

Helgeson, V. S., & Fritz, H. L. (1998). A theory of unmitigated communion. *Personality and Social Psychology Review, 2*, 173–183.

Helgeson, V. S., & Fritz, H. L. (1999). Cognitive adaptation as a predictor of new coronary events after percutaneous transluminal coronary angioplasty. *Psychosomatic Medicine, 61*, 488–495.

Helgeson, V. S., & Lepore, S. (1997). Men's adjustment to prostate cancer: The role of agency and unmitigated agency. *Sex Roles, 37*, 251–267.

Herbert, T. B., & Cohen, S. (1993). Depression and immunity: A meta-analytic review. *Psychological Bulletin, 113*, 472–486.

Hermann, C., Brano-Driehorst, S., Kaminsky, B., Leibring, E., Staats, H., & Ruger, U. (1998). Diagnostic groups and depressed mood as predictors of 22-month mortality in medical inpatients. *Archives of General Psychiatry, 46*, 345–350.

Hirschfeld, R., Klerman, G., Lavori, P., Keller, M., Griffith, P., & Corywell, W. (1989). Premorbid personality assessments of first onset of major depression. *Archives of General Psychiatry, 46*, 345–350.

Horsten, M., Mittleman, M. A., Wamala, S. P., Schenck-Gustafsson, K., & Orth-Gomer, K. (2000). Depressive symptoms and lack of social integration in relation to prognosis of CHD in middle-aged women. The Stockholm Female Coronary Risk Study. *European Heart Journal, 21*, 1043–1045.

House, A., Knapp, P., Bamford, J., & Vail, A. (2001). Mortality at 12 and 24 months after stroke may be associated with depressive symptoms at 1 month. *Stroke, 32*, 696–701.

Houston, B. K. (1988). Cardiovascular and neuroendocrine reactivity, global Type A, and components of Type A behavior. In B. K. Houston & C. R. Snyder

(Eds.), *Type A behavior pattern: Research, theory, and intervention* (pp. 212–253). New York: Wiley.

Houston, B. K. (1989). Personality dimensions in reactivity and cardiovascular disease. In N. Schneiderman, S. M. Weiss, & P. G. Kaufmann (Eds.), *Handbook of research methods in cardiovascular behavioral medicine* (pp. 495–510). New York: Plenum Press.

Houston, B. K., Babyak, M. A., Chesney, M., Black, G., & Ragland, D. (1997). Social dominance and 22-year all cause mortality in men. *Psychosomatic Medicine, 59*, 5–12.

Houston, B. K., Chesney, M. A., Black, G. W., Cates, D. S., & Hecker, M. L. (1992). Behavioral clusters and coronary heart disease risk. *Psychosomatic Medicine, 54*, 447–461.

Hull, J. G., Lehn, D. A., & Tedlie, J. C. (1991). A general approach to testing multifaceted personality constructs. *Journal of Personality and Social Psychology, 61*, 932–945.

Ickes, W., Snyder, M., & Garcia, S. (1997). Personality influences on the choice of situations. In R. Hogan, J. Johnson, & S. Briggs (Eds.), *Handbook of personality psychology* (pp. 165–195). San Diego, CA: Academic Press.

Iribarren, C., Sidney, S., Bild, D. E., Liu, K., Markovitz, J. H., Roseman, J. M., et al. (2000). Association of hostility with coronary artery calcification in young adults: The CARDIA study. *Journal of the American Medical Association, 283*, 2546–2551.

Jang, K. L., Hu, S., Livelsy, W. J., Angleitner, A., Riemann, R., Ando, J., et al. (2001). Covariance structure of neuroticism and agreeableness: A twin and molecular genetic analysis of the role of the serotonin transporter gene. *Journal of Personality and Social Psychology, 81*, 295–304.

Januzzi, J. L., Stern, T. A., Pasternak, R. C., & DeSanctis, R. W. (2000). The influence of anxiety and depression on outcomes of patients with coronary artery disease. *Archives of Internal Medicine, 160*, 1913–1921.

Jenkins, C. D., Rosenman, R. H., & Zyzanski, S. J. (1974). Prediction of clinical coronary heart disease by a test for the coronary-prone behavior pattern. *New England Journal of Medicine, 23*, 1271–1275.

John, O. P., & Srivastava, S. (1999). The big five trait taxonomy: History, measurement, and theoretical perspectives. In L. A. Pervin & O. P. John (Eds.), *Handbook of personality: Theory and research* (2nd ed., pp. 102–138). New York: Guilford Press.

Joiner, T., & Coyne, J. C. (1999). *The interactional nature of depression: Advances in interpersonal approaches.* Washington, DC: American Psychological Association.

Jones, B. S., Franks, P., & Ingram, D. D. (1997). Are symptoms of anxiety and depression risk factors for hypertension? *Archives of Family Medicine, 6*, 43–49.

Jorgensen, R. S., Frankowski, J. J., Lantinga, L. J., Phadke, K., Sprafkin, R. P., & Abdul-Karim, K. W. (2001). Defensive hostility and coronary heart disease:

A preliminary investigation of male veterans. *Psychosomatic Medicine, 63*, 463–469.

Kamarck, T. W., & Jennings, J. R. (1991). Biobehavioral factors in sudden cardiac death. *Psychological Bulletin, 109*, 42–75.

Kaplan, G. A., & Camacho, T., (1983). Perceived health and mortality: A nine-year follow-up of the Human Population Laboratory cohort. *American Journal of Epidemiology, 117*, 292–304.

Kaplan, G. A., & Reynolds, P. (1988). Depression and cancer mortality and morbidity: Prospective evidence from the Alameda County study. *Journal of Behavioral Medicine, 11*, 1–13.

Kaplan, J. R., Botchin, M. B., & Manuck, S. B. (1994). Animal models of aggression and cardiovascular disease. In A. W. Siegman & T. W. Smith (Eds.), *Anger, hostility, and the heart* (pp. 127–148). Hillsdale, NJ: Erlbaum.

Kaplan, J. R., & Manuck, S. B. (1998). Monkeys, aggression, and the pathobiology of atherosclerosis. *Aggressive Behavior, 24*, 323–334.

Kawachi, I., Sparrow, D., Spiro, A., Vokonas, P., & Weiss, S. T. (1996). A prospective study of anger and coronary heart disease. The Normative Aging Study. *Circulation, 94*, 2090–2095.

Kawachi, I., Sparrow, D., Vokonas, P. S., & Weiss, S. T. (1994). Symptoms of anxiety and risk of coronary heart disease: The normative aging study. *Circulation, 90*, 2225–2229.

Kiecolt-Glaser, J. K., & Glaser, R. (1995). Psychoneuroimmunology and health consequences: Data and shared mechanisms. *Psychosomatic Medicine, 57*, 269–274.

Kiesler, D. J. (1983). The 1982 interpersonal circle: A taxonomy for complementarity in human transactions. *Psychological Review, 90*, 185–214.

Kiesler, D. J. (1996). *Contemporary interpersonal theory and research: Personality, psychopathology, and psychotherapy.* New York: Wiley.

King, K. B., Rowe, M., Kimble, L., & Zerwic, J. (1998). Optimism, coping, and long-term recovery from coronary artery bypass surgery in women. *Research in Nursing and Health, 21*, 15–26.

Kobasa, S. C. (1979). Stressful life events, personality and health: An inquiry into hardiness. *Journal of Personality and Social Psychology, 37*, 1–11.

Kop, W. J. (1999). Chronic and acute psychological risk factors for clinical manifestations of coronary artery disease. *Psychosomatic Medicine, 61*, 476–487.

Krantz, D. S., & Durel, L. A. (1983). Psychobiological substrates of the Type A behavior pattern. *Health Psychology, 2*, 393–411.

Kubzansky, L. D., Kawachi, I., Spiro, A., Weiss, S. T., Vokonas, P. S., & Sparrow, D. (1997). Is worrying bad for your heart? A prospective study of worry and coronary heart disease in the Normative Aging Study. *Circulation, 95*, 818–824.

Kubzanksy, L. D., Sparrow, D., Vokonas, P., & Kawachi, I. (2001). Is the glass half empty or half full: A prospective study of optimism and coronary heart disease in the normative aging study. *Psychosomatic Medicine, 63*, 910–916.

Lane, D., Carroll, D., Ring, C., Beevers, D. G., & Lip, G. Y. H. (2001). Mortality and quality of life 12 months after myocardial infarction: Effects of depression and anxiety. *Psychosomatic Medicine, 63,* 221–230.

Lau, R. R. (1988). Beliefs about control and health behavior. In D. S. Gochman (Ed.), *Health behavior: Emerging research perspectives* (pp. 43–63). New York: Plenum Press.

Lazarus, R. S., & Folkman, S. (1984). *Stress, appraisal, and coping.* New York: Springer.

Leary, T. (1957). *Interpersonal diagnosis of personality.* New York: Ronald.

Lespérance, F., Frasure-Smith, N., Talajic, M., & Bourassa, M. G. (2002). Five-year risk of cardiac mortality in relation to initial severity and one-year changes in depression symptoms after myocardial infarction. *Circulation, 105,* 1049–1053.

Lewis, S. C., Dennis, M. S., O'Rourke, S. J., & Sharpe, M. (2001). Negative attitudes among short-term stroke survivors predict worse long-term survival. *Stroke, 32,* 1640–1645.

Lin, E. H., & Peterson, C. (1990). Pessimistic explanatory style and response to illness. *Behaviour Research and Therapy, 28,* 243–248.

Lobel, M., & DeVincent, C. J. (2000). The impact of prenatal maternal stress and optimistic disposition on birth outcomes in medically high-risk women. *Health Psychology, 19,* 544–553.

Lovallo, W. (1997). *Stress and health.* Thousand Oaks, CA: Sage.

Lyness, S. A. (1993). Predictors of differences between Type A and B individuals in heart rate and blood pressure reactivity. *Psychological Bulletin, 114,* 266–295.

MacDougall, J. M., Musante, L., Castilo, S., & Acevedo, M. C. (1988). Smoking, caffeine, and stress: Effects on blood pressure and heart rate I male and female college students. *Health Psychology, 7,* 461–478.

Maddox, G. L., & Douglas, E. B. (1973). Self-assessment and health: A longitudinal study of elderly subjects. *Journal of Health and Social Behavior, 14,* 87–93.

Major, B., Richards, C., Cooper, M. L., Cozzarelli, C., & Zubek, J. (1998). Personal resilience, cognitive appraisals, and coping: An integrative model of adjustment to abortion. *Journal of Personality and Social Psychology, 74,* 735–752.

Manne, S. (1999). Intrusive thoughts and psychological distress among cancer patients: The role of spouse avoidance and criticism. *Journal of Consulting and Clinical Psychology, 67,* 539–542.

Manne, S., & Glassman, M. (2000). Perceived control, coping efficacy, and avoidance coping as mediators between spouses' unsupportive behaviors and cancer patients' psychological distress. *Health Psychology, 19,* 155–164.

Manuck, S. B. (1994). Cardiovascular reactivity in cardiovascular disease: "Once more unto the breach." *International Journal of Behavioral Medicine, 1,* 4–31.

Manuck, S. B., Flory, J. D., Ferrell, R. E., Dent, K. M., Mann, J. J., & Muldoon, M. F. (1999). Aggression and anger-related traits associated with a polymorphism of the tryptophan hydroxylase gene. *Biological Psychiatry, 45,* 603–614.

Markovitz, J. H., Matthews, K. A., Wing, R. R., Kuller, L. H., & Meilahn, E. N. (1991). Psychological, biological, and health behavior predictors of blood pressure change in middle-aged women. *Journal of Hypertension, 9*, 399–406.

Marlatt, G. A., & Gordon, J. J. (1985). *Relapse prevention.* New York: Guilford Press.

Marshall, G. N., Wortman, C. B., Kusulas, J. W., Hervig, L. K., & Vickers, R. R., Jr. (1992). Distinguishing optimism from pessimism: Relations to fundamental dimensions of mood and personality. *Journal of Personality and Social Psychology, 62*, 1067–1074.

Marshall, G. N., Wortman, C. B., Vickers, R. R., Kusulas, J. W., & Hervig, L. K. (1994). The five-factor model of personality as a framework for personality-health research. *Journal of Personality and Social Psychology, 67*, 278–286.

Martin, L. R., Friedman, H. S., Tucker, J. S., Schwartz, J. E., Criqui, M. H., Wingard, D. L., et al. (1995). An archival prospective study of mental health and longevity. *Health Psychology, 14*, 381–387.

Martin, R., Watson, D., & Wan, C. K. (2000). A three-factor model of trait anger: Dimensions of affect, behavior, and cognition. *Journal of Personality, 68*, 869–897.

Maruta, T., Colligan, R. C., Malinchoc, M., & Offord, K. P. (2000). Optimists vs. pessimists: Survival rate among medical patients over a 30-year period. *Mayo Clinic Proceedings, 75*, 140–143.

Matthews, K. A., Glass, D. C., Rosenman, R. H., & Bortner, R. W. (1977). Competitive drive, Pattern A, and coronary disease: A further analysis of some data from the Western Collaborative Group Study. *Journal of Personality and Social Psychology, 42*, 303–313.

Matthews, K. A., Owens, J. F., Kuller, L. H., Sutton-Tyrrell, K., & Jansen-McWilliams, L. (1998). Are hostility and anxiety associated with carotid atherosclerosis in healthy post-menopausal women? *Psychosomatic Medicine, 60*, 633–638.

May, M., McCarron, P., Stansfeld, S., Ben-Shlomo, Y., Gallacher, J., Yarnell, J., et al. (2002). Does psychological distress predict the risk of ischemic stroke and transient ischemic attack? The Caerphilly Study. *Stroke, 33*, 7–12.

McAdams, D. P. (1995). What do we know when we know a person? *Journal of Personality, 63*, 365–396.

McCrae, R. R., & Costa, P. T., Jr. (1996). Toward a new generation of personality theories: Theoretical contexts for the five-factor model. In J. S. Wiggins (Ed.), *The five-factor model of personality* (pp. 51–87). New York: Guilford Press.

McCrae, R. R., & John, O. P. (1992). An introduction to the Five-Factor Model and its applications. *Journal of Research in Personality, 60*, 175–216.

McGuire, L, Kiecolt-Glaser, J. K., & Glaser, R. (2002). Depressive symptoms and lymphocyte proliferation in older adults. *Journal of Abnormal Psychology, 111*, 192–197.

McMahon, C. E. (1976). The role of imagination in the disease process: Pre-Cartesian medical history. *Psychological Medicine, 6*, 1179–1184.

Messick, S. (1989). Validity. In R. L. Linn (Ed.), *Educational measurement* (3rd ed., pp. 13–104). New York: MacMillan.

Miller, S. M., Shoda, Y., Hurley, K. (1996). Applying cognitive–social theory to health-protective behavior: Breast self-examination in cancer screening. *Psychological Bulletin, 119,* 70–94.

Miller, T. Q., Smith, T. W., Turner, C. W., Guijarro, M. L., & Hallet, A. J. (1996). A meta-analytic review of research on hostility and physical health. *Psychological Bulletin, 119,* 322–348.

Miller, T. Q., Turner, C. W., Tindale, R. S., Posavac, E. J., & Dugoni, B. L. (1991). Reasons for the trend toward null findings in research on Type A behavior. *Psychological Bulletin, 110,* 469–485.

Mischel, W. (1968). *Personality and assessment.* New York: Wiley.

Mischel, W. (1973). Toward a cognitive social learning reconceptualization of personality. *Psychological Review, 80,* 252–283.

Mischel, W., & Shoda, Y. (1995). A cognitive–affective system theory of personality: Reconceptualizing situations, dispositions, dynamic, and invariance in personality structure. *Psychological Review, 102,* 246–268.

Mischel, W., & Shoda, Y. (1998). Reconciling processing dynamics and personality dispositions. *Annual Review of Psychology, 49,* 229–258.

Mischel, W., & Shoda, Y. (1999). Integrating dispositions and processing dynamics within a unified theory of personality: The cognitive–affective personality system. In L. A. Pervin & O. P. John (Eds.), *Handbook of personality: Theory and research* (2nd ed., pp. 197–218). New York: Guilford Press.

Moran, P. J., Christensen, A. J., & Lawton, W. J. (1997). Social support and conscientiousness in hemodialysis adherence. *Annals of Behavioral Medicine, 19,* 333–338.

Moser, D. K., & Dracup, K. (1996). Is anxiety early after myocardial infarction associated with subsequent ischemic and arrhythmic events? *Psychosomatic Medicine, 58,* 395–401.

Neyer, F. J., & Asendorpf, J. B. (2001). Personality-relationship transaction in young adulthood. *Journal of Personality and Social Psychology, 81,* 1190–1204.

Norem, J. K., & Chang, E. C. (2001). A very full glass: Adding complexity to our applications of optimism and pessimism research. In E. C. Chang (Ed.), *Optimism and pessimism: Implications for theory, research and practice* (pp. 347–367). Washington, DC: American Psychological Association.

O'Malley, P. G., Jones, D. L., Feuerstein, I. M., & Taylor, A. J. (2000). Lack of correlation between psychological factors and subclinical coronary artery disease. *New England Journal of Medicine, 343,* 1298–1304.

Osler, W. (1910). The Lumelin lectures on angina pectoris. *Lancet, 1,* 839–844.

Ozer, D. J. (1999). Four principles for personality assessment. In L. A. Pervin & O. P. John (Eds.), *Handbook of personality: Theory and research* (2nd ed., pp. 671–686). New York: Guilford Press.

Ozer, D. J., & Reise, S. P. (1994). Personality assessment. *Annual Review of Psychology*, 45, 357–388.

Park, C. L., Moore, P. J., Turner, R. A., & Adler, N. E. (1997). The roles of constructive thinking and optimism in psychological and behavioral adjustment during pregnancy. *Journal of Personality and Social Psychology*, 73, 584–592.

Penninx, B. W., Beckman, A. T. F., Honig, A., Deeg, D. J. H., Schoevers, R. A., van Eijk, T. M., et al. (2001). Depression and cardiac mortality: Results from a community-based longitudinal study. *Archives of General Psychiatry*, 58, 221–227.

Peterson, C., & Bossio, L. M. (2001). Optimism and physical well-being. In E. C. Chang (Ed.), *Optimism and pessimism: Implications for theory, research, and practice* (pp. 127–146). Washington, DC: American Psychological Association.

Peterson, C., Seligman, M., & Vaillant, G. E. (1988). Pessimistic explanatory style is a risk factor for physical illness: A thirty-five-year longitudinal study. *Journal of Personality and Social Psychology*, 55, 23–27.

Peterson, C., Seligman, M., Yurko, K., Martin, L. R., & Friedman, H. (1998). Catastrophizing and untimely death. *Psychological Science*, 9, 127–130.

Plomin, R., & Caspi, A. (1999). Behavioral genetics and personality. In L. A. Pervin & O. P. John (Eds.), *Handbook of personality: Theory and research* (2nd ed., pp. 251–276). New York: Guilford Press.

Pope, M. K., & Smith, T. W. (1991). Cortisol excretion in high and low cynically hostile men. *Psychosomatic Medicine*, 53, 386–392.

Potthoff, J. G., Holahan, C. J., & Joiner, T. E. (1995). Reassurance seeking, stress generation, and depressive symptoms: An integrative model. *Journal of personality and social psychology*, 68, 664–670.

Price, V. (1982). *Type A behavior pattern: A model for research and practice*. New York: Academic Press.

Rabin, B. S. (1999). *Stress, immune function, and health: The connection*. New York: Wiley-Liss & Sons.

Ragland, D. R., & Brand, R. J. (1988). Type A behavior and mortality from coronary heart disease. *New England Journal of Medicine*, 318, 65–69.

Raikkonen, K., Matthews, K. A., Flory, J. D., Owens, J. F., & Gump, B. (1999). Effects of optimism, pessimism, and trait anxiety on ambulatory blood pressure and mood during everyday life. *Journal of Personality and Social Psychology*, 76, 104–113.

Raynor, D. A., Pogue-Geile, M. F., Kamarck, T. W., McCaffery, J. M., & Manuck, S. B. (2002). Covariation of psychosocial characteristics associated with cardiovascular disease: Genetic and environmental influences. *Psychosomatic Medicine*, 64, 191–203.

Revenson, T. A. (1990). All other things are not equal: An ecological approach to personality and disease. In H. S. Friedman (Ed.), *Personality and disease* (pp. 65–96). New York: Wiley.

Rhodewalt, F., & Smith, T. W. (1991). Current issues in Type A behavior, coronary proneness, and coronary heart disease. In C. R. Snyder & D. R. Forsyth (Eds.), *Handbook of social and clinical psychology* (pp. 197–220). New York: Pergamon.

Rosenberg, E. L., Ekman, P., Jiang, W., Babyak, M., Coleman, R. E., Hanson, M., et al. (2001). Linkages between facial expressions of anger and transient myocardial ischemia in men with coronary artery disease. *Emotion, 1,* 1067–1115.

Rosenman, R. H. (1978). The interview method of assessment of the coronary-prone behavior pattern. In T. M. Dembroski, S. M. Weiss, J. L. Shields, S. G. Haynes, & M. Feinleig (Eds.), *Coronary-prone behavior* (pp. 55–70). New York: Springer-Verlag.

Rozanski, A., Blumenthal, J. A., & Kaplan, J. (1999). Impact of psychological factors on the pathogenesis of cardiovascular disease and implications for therapy. *Circulation, 99,* 2192–2217.

Ruiz, J. M., Smith, T. W., & Rhodewalt, F. (2001). Distinguishing narcissism and hostility: Similarities and differences in interpersonal circumplex and five-factor correlates. *Journal of Personality Assessment, 76,* 537–555.

Ryff, C. D., & Singer, B. (1998). The contours of positive human health. *Psychological Inquiry, 9,* 1–28.

Sauro, M. D., Jorgensen, R. S., Larson, C. A., Frankowski, J. J., Ewart, C. K., & White, J. (2001). Sociotropic cognition moderates stress-induced cardiovascular responsiveness in college women. *Journal of Behavioral Medicine, 24,* 423–439.

Scheier, M. F., & Carver, C. S. (1985). Optimism, coping, and health: Assessment and implications of generalized outcome expectancies. *Health Psychology, 4,* 219–247.

Scheier, M. F., Carver, C. S., & Bridges, M. W. (1994). Distinguishing optimism from neuroticism (and trait anxiety, self-mastery, and self-esteem): A reevaluation of the Life Orientation Test. *Journal of Personality and Social Psychology, 67,* 1063–1078.

Scheier, M. F., Carver, C. S., & Bridges, M. W. (2001). Optimism, pessimism, and psychological well-being. In E. C. Chang (Ed.), *Optimism and pessimism: Implications for theory, research, and practice* (pp. 189–216). Washington, DC: American Psychological Association.

Scheier, M. F., Matthews, K. A., Owens, J., Magovern, G., Lefebre, R., Abbott, R., et al. (1989). Dispositional optimism and recovery from coronary artery bypass surgery: The beneficial effects of physical and psychological well-being. *Journal of Personality and Social Psychology, 57,* 1024–1040.

Scheier, M. F., Matthews, K. A., Owens, J. F., Schulz, R., Bridges, M. W., Magovern, G. J., et al. (1999). Optimism and rehospitalization after coronary artery bypass graft surgery. *Archives of Internal Medicine, 159,* 829–835.

Schmaling, K. B., & Sher, T. G. (2000). *The psychology of couples and illness: Theory, research, and practice.* Washington, DC: American Psychological Association.

Schultz, R., Bookwala, J., Knapp, J. E., Scheier, M., & Williamson, G. M. (1996). Pessimism, age, and cancer mortality. *Psychology and Aging, 11,* 304–309.

Segerstrom, S. C. (2000). Personality and the immune system: Models, methods, and mechanisms. *Annals of Behavioral Medicine, 22,* 180–190.

Segerstrom, S. C., Taylor, S. E., Kemeny, M. E., & Fahey, J. L. (1998). Optimism is associated with mood, coping, and immune change in response to stress. *Journal of Personality and Social Psychology, 74,* 1646–1655.

Shekelle, R. B., Gale, M., & Norusis, M. (1985). Type A score (Jenkins Activity Survey) and risk of recurrent coronary heart disease in the Aspirin Myocardial Infarction Study. *American Journal of Cardiology, 56,* 221–225.

Shekelle, R. B., Hulley, S., Neaton, J., Billings, J., Borhani, N., Gerace, T., et al. (1985). MRFIT Research Group: The MRFIT behavior pattern study II. Type A behavior pattern and incidence of coronary heart disease. *American Journal of Epidemiology, 122,* 559–570.

Shekelle, R. B., Vernon, S. W., & Ostfeld, A. M. (1991). Personality and coronary heart disease. *Psychosomatic Medicine, 53,* 176–184.

Sher, K. J., Bartholow, B. D., & Wood, M. D. (2000). Personality and substance use disorders: A prospective study. *Journal of Consulting and Clinical Psychology, 68,* 818–829.

Siegler, I. C. (1994). Hostility and risk: Demographics and lifestyle variables. In A. W. Siegman & T. W. Smith (Eds.), *Anger, hostility, and the heart* (pp. 199–214). Hillsdale, NJ: Erlbaum.

Siegman, A. W., Kubzansky, L. D., Kawachi, I., Boyle, S., Vokonas, P. S., & Sparrow, D. (2000). A prospective study of dominance and coronary heart disease in the normative aging study. *American Journal of Cardiology, 86,* 145–149.

Simonsick, E. M., Wallace, R. B., Blaser, D. G., & Gerkman, L. F. (1995). Depressive symptomatology and hypertension-associated morbidity and mortality in older adults. *Psychosomatic Medicine, 57,* 427–435.

Smith, B. W. & Zautra, A. J. (2002). The role of personality in exposure and reactivity to interpersonal stress in relation to arthritis disease activity and negative affect in women. *Health Psychology, 21,* 81–88.

Smith, T. W. (1994). Concepts and methods in the study of anger, hostility, and health. In A. W. Siegman & T. W. Smith (Eds.), *Anger, hostility, and the heart* (pp. 23–42). Hillsdale, NJ: Erlbaum.

Smith, T. W. (1995). Assessment and modification of coronary-prone behavior: A transactional view of the person in social context. In A. J. Goreczny (Ed.), *Handbook of health and rehabilitation psychology* (pp. 197–217). New York: Plenum Press.

Smith, T. W., Allred, K. D., Morrison, C., & Carlson, S. (1989). Cardiovascular reactivity and interpersonal influence: Active coping in a social context. *Journal of Personality and Social Psychology, 56,* 209–218.

Smith, T. W., & Anderson, N. B. (1986). Models of personality and disease: An interactional approach to Type A behavior and cardiovascular risk. *Journal of Personality and Social Psychology, 50*, 1166–1173.

Smith, T. W., & Christensen, A. J. (1992). Cardiovascular reactivity and interpersonal relations: Psychosomatic processes in social context. *Journal of Social and Clinical Psychology, 11*, 279–301.

Smith, T. W., & Frohm, K. D. (1985). What's so unhealthy about hostility? Construct validity and psychosocial correlates of the Cook and Medley Ho Scale. *Health Psychology, 4*, 503–520.

Smith, T. W., & Gallo, L. C. (1999). Hostility and cardiovascular reactivity during marital interaction. *Psychosomatic Medicine, 61*, 436–445.

Smith, T. W., & Gallo, L. C. (2001). Personality traits as risk factors for physical illness. In A. Baum, T. Revenson, & J. Singer (Eds.), *Handbook of health psychology* (pp. 139–172). Hillsdale, NJ: Erlbaum.

Smith, T. W., McGongile, M., Turner, C. W., Ford, M. H., & Slattery, M. L. (1991). Cynical hostility in adult male twins. *Psychosomatic Medicine, 53*, 684–692.

Smith, T. W., Nealey, J. B., Kircher, J. C., & Limon, J. P. (1997). Social determinants of cardiovascular reactivity: Effects of incentive to exert influence and evaluative threat. *Psychophysiology, 34*, 65–73.

Smith, T. W., & Pope, M. K. (1990). Cynical hostility as a health risk: Current status and future directions. *Journal of Social Behavior and Personality, 5*, 77–88.

Smith, T. W., Pope, M. K., Rhodewalt, F., & Poulton, J. L. (1989). Optimism, neuroticism, coping, and symptom reports: An alternative interpretation of the Life Orientation Test. *Journal of Personality and Social Psychology, 56*, 640–648.

Smith, T. W., Pope, M. K., Sanders, J. D., Allred, K. D., & O'Keefe, J. L. (1988). Cynical hostility at home and work: Psychosocial vulnerability across domains. *Journal of Research in Personality, 22*, 525–548.

Smith, T. W., & Rhodewalt, F. (1986). On states, traits, and processes: A transactional alternative to individual difference assumptions in Type A behavior and physiological reactivity. *Journal of Research in Personality, 20*, 229–251.

Smith, T. W., & Ruiz, J. M. (1999). Methodological issues in adult health psychology. In P. C. Kendall, J. N. Butcher, & G. N. Holmbeck (Eds.), *Handbook of research methods in clinical psychology* (2nd ed., pp. 499–536). New York: Wiley.

Smith, T. W., & Ruiz, J. M. (2002). Psychosocial influences on the development and course of coronary heart disease: Current status and implications for research and practice. *Journal of Consulting and Clinical Psychology, 70*, 548–568.

Smith, T. W., Ruiz, J. M., Glazer, K., Nealey, J., Hawkins, M., & Uchino, B. (2003). *On the bright side of social life: Optimism in interpersonal context.* Unpublished manuscript.

Smith, T. W., Ruiz, J. M., & Uchino, B. N. (2000). Vigilance, active coping, and cardiovascular reactivity during social interaction in young men. *Healthy Psychology, 19*, 382–392.

Smith, T. W., Turner, C. W., Ford, M. H., Hunt, S. C., Barlow, G. K., Stults, B. M., et al. (1987). Blood pressure reactivity in adult male twins. *Health Psychology, 6,* 209–220.

Smith, T. W., & Williams, P. G. (1992). Personality and health: Advantages and limitations of the five factor model. *Journal of Personality, 60,* 395–423.

Somervell, P. D., Kaplan, B. H., Heiss, G., Tyroler, H. A., Kleinbaum, D. G., & Obrist, P. A. (1989). Psychologic distress as a predictor of mortality. *American Journal of Epidemiology, 130,* 1013–1023.

Spiro, A., Aldwin, C. M., Ward, K. D., & Mroczek, D. K. (1995). Personality and the incidence of hypertension among older men: Longitudinal findings from the normative aging study. *Health Psychology, 14,* 563–569.

Steinberg, L., & Jorgensen, R. S. (1996). Assessing the MMPI-based Cook-Medley Hostility Scale: The implications of dimensionality. *Journal of Personality and Social Psychology, 70,* 1281–1287.

Stern, S. L., Dhanda, R., & Hazuda, H. P. (2001). Hopelessness predicts mortality in older Mexican and European Americans. *Psychosomatic Medicine, 63,* 344–351.

Stone, G. C., Cohen, F., & Adler, N. E. (1980). *Health psychology.* San Francisco: Jossey-Bass.

Stone, S. V., & Costa, P. T., Jr. (1990). Disease-prone personality or distress-prone personality? The role of neuroticism in coronary heart disease. In H. S. Friedman (Ed.), *Personality and disease* (pp. 178–200). New York: Wiley.

Strack, S., Carver, C., & Blaney, P. (1987). Predicting successful completion of an aftercare program following treatment for alcoholism: The role of dispositional optimism. *Journal of Personality and Social Psychology, 53,* 579–584.

Strickland, B. R. (1978). Internal–external expectancies and health-related behaviors. *Journal of Consulting and Clinical Psychology, 46,* 1192–1211.

Suarez, E. C., Kuhn, C. M., Schanberg, S. M., Williams, R. B., & Zimmermann, E. A. (1998). Neuroendocrine, cardiovascular, and emotional responses of hostile men: The role of interpersonal challenge. *Psychosomatic Medicine, 60,* 78–88.

Sullivan, H. S. (1953). *The interpersonal theory of psychiatry.* New York: Norton.

Suls, J., & Rittenhouse, J. D. (1987). Personality and health: An introduction. *Journal of Personality, 55,* 155–167.

Suls, J., & Sanders, G. S. (1989). Why do some behavioral styles place people at coronary risk? In A. W. Siegman & T. M. Dembroski (Eds.), *In search of coronary-prone behavior* (pp. 1–20). Hillsdale, NJ: Erlbaum.

Swan, G. E., & Carmelli, D. (1996). Curiosity and mortality in aging adults: A five-year follow-up of the Western Collaborative Group Study. *Psychology and Aging, 11,* 449–453.

Trapnell, P. D., & Wiggins, J. S. (1990). Extension of the Interpersonal Adjective Scales to include the big five dimensions of personality. *Journal of Personality and Social Psychology, 59,* 781–790.

Turner, J. R., & Hewitt, J. K. (1992). Twin studies of cardiovascular response to psychological challenge: A review and suggested future directions. *Annals of Behavioral Medicine, 14,* 12–20.

Wagner, C. C., Kiesler, D. J., & Schmidt, J. A. (1995). Assessing the interpersonal transaction cycle: Convergence of action and reaction interpersonal circumplex measures. *Journal of Personality and Social Psychology, 69,* 938–949.

Watkins, L. L., Grossman, P., Krishnan, R., & Sherwood, A. (1998). Anxiety and vagal control of heart rate. *Psychosomatic Medicine, 60,* 498–502.

Watson, D., & Clark, L. A., (1984). Negative affectivity: The disposition to experience aversive emotional states. *Psychological Bulletin, 96,* 465–490.

Watson, D., Clark, L. A., & Harkness, A. R. (1994). Structures of personality and their relevance to psychopathology. *Journal of Abnormal Psychology, 103,* 18–31.

Watson, D., & Pennebaker, J. W. (1989). Health complaints, stress, and distress: Exploring the central role of negative affectivity. *Psychological Review, 96,* 234–254.

Weinberger, D. A., Schwartz, G. E., & Davison, R. J. (1979). Low anxious, high anxious, and repressive coping styles: Psychometric patterns and behavioral and physiological responses to stress. *Journal of Abnormal Psychology, 58,* 369–380.

Weiss, S. M., Herd, J. A., & Fox, B. H. (1981). *Perspectives on behavioral medicine.* New York: Academic Press.

West, S. G., & Finch, J. F. (1997). Personality measurement: Reliability and validity issues. In R. Hogan, J. Johnson, & S. Briggs (Eds.), *Handbook of personality psychology* (pp. 143–164). San Diego, CA: Academic Press.

Westen, D. (1995). A clinical–empirical model of personality: Life after the Mischelian ice age and the Neolithic age. *Journal of Personality, 63,* 495–524.

Whiteman, M. C., Deary, I. J., Lee, A. J., & Fowkes, F. G. R. (1997). Submissiveness and protection from coronary heart disease in the general population: Edinburgh Artery Study. *Lancet, 350,* 541–545.

Wiebe, D. J., Alderfer, M. A., Palmer, S. C., Lindsay, R., & Jarrett, L. (1994). Behavioral self-regulation in adolescents with Type I diabetes: Negative affectivity and blood glucose symptom perception. *Journal of Consulting and Clinical Psychology, 62,* 1204–1212.

Wiebe, D. J., & Smith, T. W. (1997). Personality and health: Progress and problems in psychosomatic's. In R. Hogan, J. Johnson, & S. Briggs (Eds.), *Handbook of personality psychology* (pp. 891–918). San Diego, CA: Academic Press.

Wiggins, J. S. (1979). A psychological taxonomy of trait-descriptive terms: The interpersonal domain. *Journal of Personality and Social Psychology, 37,* 395–412.

Wiggins, J. S., & Trapnell, P. D. (1996). A dyadic-interactional perspective on the five-factor model. In J. S. Wiggins (Ed.), *The five-factor model of personality* (pp. 88–162). New York: Guilford Press.

Williams, J. E., Nieto, F. J., Sanford, C. P., Couper, D. J., & Tyroler, H. A. (2002). The association between trait anger and incident stroke risk. The Atherosclerosis Risk in Communities (ARIC) Study. *Stoke, 33*, 13–20.

Williams, J. E., Paton, C. C., Siegler, I. C., Eigenbrodt, M. L., Nieto, F. J., Tyroler, H. A. (2000). Anger proneness predicts coronary heart disease risk: Prospective analysis from the atherosclerosis risk in communities (ARIC) study. *Circulation, 101*, 2034–2039.

Williams, R. B., Jr. (1994). Basic biological mechanisms. In A. W. Siegman & T. W. Smith (Eds.), *Anger, hostility, and the heart* (pp. 117–125). Hillsdale, NJ: Erlbaum.

Williams, R. B., Jr., Barefoot, J. C., & Shekelle, R. B. (1985). The health consequences of hostility. In M. A. Chesney & R. H. Rosenman (Eds.), *Anger and hostility in cardiovascular and behavioral disorders* (pp. 173–185). New York: Hemisphere.

Williams, S. A., Kasl, S. V., Heiat, A., Abramson, J. L., Krumholz, H. M., & Vaccarino, V. (2002). Depression and risk of heart failure among the elderly: A prospective community-based study. *Psychosomatic Medicine, 64*, 6–12.

Wills, T. A. (1997). Social support and health. In A. Baum, S. Newman, J. Weinman, R. West, & C. McManus (Eds.), *Cambridge handbook of psychology, health, and medicine* (pp. 168–171). New York: Cambridge University Press.

Wills, T. A., Gibbons, F. X., Gerrard, M., & Brody, G. H. (2000). Protection and vulnerability processes relevant for early onset of substance use: A test among African American children. *Health Psychology, 19*, 253–263.

Zonderman, A. B., Costa, P. T., & McCrae, R. R. (1989). Depression as a risk factor for cancer morbidity and mortality in a nationally representative sample. *Journal of the American Medical Association, 262*, 1191–1215.

Zonderman, A. B., Herbst, J., Schmidt, C., Costa, P. T., & McCrae, R. R. (1993). Depressive symptoms as a non-specific graded risk for psychiatric diagnoses. *Journal of Abnormal Psychology, 102*, 544–552.

6

PSYCHOSOCIAL MODELS

LAURA M. BOGART AND DOUGLAS L. DELAHANTY

During the 19th century, the major threats to the lives and health of Americans stemmed from infectious diseases such as tuberculosis, poliomyelitis, influenza, rubella, and smallpox (Matarazzo, 1982). Improved personal hygiene and sanitation combined with the advent of antibiotics and vaccinations led to changes in the patterns of illness in the United States. The death rate from infectious agents continues to decrease, and diseases of lifestyle and behavior are the major threats to health today (Matarazzo, 1982). Heart disease, cancers, HIV infection, obesity, and atherosclerosis are associated with behavioral factors such as diet, exercise, smoking, alcohol and substance use, and sexual practices. Recent advances in the treatment of these diseases stem largely from altering behavior of at-risk individuals and not from medical advances in therapy or pharmacology. Healthy People 2010 (U.S. Department of Health & Human Services, 2000) recognized that health promotion is largely dependent on changing peoples' behavior, and that it was primarily through altering high risk behaviors that disease morbidity and mortality could be reduced. However, high risk behaviors

Preparation of this chapter was partially supported by grant R03MH#62283 (L. M. Bogart, principal investigator) and grant R01MH#62042 (D. L. Delahanty, principal investigator), both from the National Institute of Mental Health.

have been repeatedly found to be resistant to change. Social psychologists have conducted extensive empirical and theoretical research examining barriers and facilitators to behavior change. Social psychological theories have integrated the findings of empirical studies and provided a testable framework that provides researchers with a means by which they can systematically examine variables involved in the health behavior decision-making process. These theories guide new research and often reveal points at which interventions would be most appropriate. This chapter reviews the most commonly examined social psychological theories of health behavior, focusing on the theory of reasoned action, the theory of planned behavior, the health belief model, and the transtheoretical model, or stages of change model. After briefly describing each of these theories, we review studies that have examined the effectiveness of these models at predicting behavior change and the limitations of each model. Because the efficacy of a model depends on the health behavior being examined, the theories will be presented as they apply to each of the most commonly examined health behaviors (diet, exercise, smoking cessation, safer sex).

THEORY OF REASONED ACTION AND THEORY OF PLANNED BEHAVIOR

According to the theory of reasoned action (TRA; Ajzen & Fishbein, 1980), intentions to engage in a behavior are a proximal predictor of that behavior. An individual's intentions are in turn influenced by two factors: attitudes toward the behavior and the perceived attitudes of important others (subjective norms). The relative influence of each of these factors on intentions may differ depending on the particular behavior and population studied (Ajzen & Fishbein, 1980; Fishbein & Ajzen, 1975). Furthermore, attitudes are a function of beliefs about the consequences of engaging in the behavior and the subjective evaluations of those consequences. For example, an individual who believes that smoking causes cancer and who also believes that cancer is an undesirable consequence may be less likely to smoke. Subjective norms are a function of the likelihood that important others (e.g., family, friends, spouses/partners) think an individual should engage in a particular behavior, as well as the individual's motivation to comply with the desires of important others. For example, if a woman believes that her main sex partner would like her to use condoms, and she values his opinion, she would be more likely to use condoms.

Despite the relative success of the TRA model as a predictor of health behavior, it was designed to explain behaviors directly under an individual's control. Many health behaviors, however, are not under individuals' control, either because of intrinsic factors, such as lack of innate abilities, or extrinsic factors, such as the need for assistance or consent from others to perform the behaviors. In particular, most safer sex behaviors require not only ability and knowledge about proper condom use but also cooperation from sexual partners (Fisher & Fisher, 1992). To address this consideration, Ajzen (1985) posited the theory of planned behavior (TPB), which expanded the TRA model to include perceived behavioral control.

Perceived behavioral control is defined as how easy or difficult it is to perform a behavior. This construct is conceptually similar to self-efficacy (Bandura, 1977a, 1977b, 1986, 1992), which is a person's beliefs concerning how capable he or she is of performing specific actions that result in desired outcomes. Although some theorists have debated whether the two constructs are equivalent (Terry & O'Leary, 1995; White, Terry, & Hogg, 1994), little work has been able to make a strong distinction. Therefore, in this review, we discuss under the general rubric of the TPB those studies that have added either perceived behavioral control or self-efficacy to the TRA model.

Health Belief Model

The health belief model (HBM) was developed by a group of social psychologists at the U.S. Public Health Service in the 1950s, and therefore represents a public health approach to predicting and explaining behavior. The model was designed to explain why people generally failed to take part in disease prevention or detection programs even when these programs were offered for free or minimal cost. The major premise of the model was that the odds of a person engaging in behaviors necessary to avoid a disease depended on that person's perceived susceptibility to the disease, the perceived seriousness of the disease (perceived susceptibility and seriousness are often combined into perceived threat), and a weighing of the perceived benefits to taking action against perceived barriers to taking action (Rosenstock, 1974). For a person to engage in a healthy behavior (e.g., quitting smoking), the individual must perceive a high risk of contracting a disease (e.g., lung cancer) and must perceive that the disease will have a moderately severe impact on his or her life. In addition, the perceived benefits of the healthy behavior (e.g., anticipated positive effects on health) and effectiveness of the behavior at decreasing illness must outweigh the perceived barriers to engaging in the healthy behavior (e.g., expense, pain, inconvenience, unpleasantness). The HBM also stipulates that these factors may not be enough to lead an individual to engage in healthy behaviors, but that a cue to action is often necessary to instigate the healthy behavior. Cues to action can be internal (e.g., perceived body states) or external (e.g., advertisements, social pressure). However, cues are difficult to study as they can be fleeting, barely consciously recognized, and quickly forgotten (Strecher & Rosenstock, 1997). For these reasons, research has rarely examined the role of cues in leading to behavior change, and therefore, cues will not be covered in this chapter.

Stages of Change

The stages of change (SOC) or transtheoretical model (Prochaska & DiClemente, 1983, 1986; Prochaska, DiClemente, & Norcross, 1992) describes the process by which individuals make changes in their behaviors. Although the model has been more recently applied to other health risk behaviors (Burke et al., 2000; Prochaska et al., 1994), it was originally developed to explain the relative failure of smoking cessation interventions. The model posits that individuals move through a series of stages of change: precontemplation, contemplation, preparation for action, action, and maintenance. Individuals in the precontemplation stage have no intention to change their behavior in the next six months. Individuals in the contemplation stage plan to change their behavior in the next six months but not in the next month. Individuals in the preparation stage intend to change their behavior in the next month. Individuals in the action stage have changed their behavior but have only been engaging in the new behavior for less than six months; and individuals in the maintenance stage have been engaging in the new behavior for more than six months.

Two social–cognitive constructs have been associated with the stages of change model: decisional balance and self-efficacy (e.g., DiClemente, 1986; Diclemente et al., 1991; Prochaska et al., 1994). Decisional balance is defined as the balance between comparative gains and losses, or pros and cons, from taking a course of action. The construct was taken from Janis and Mann's (1977) decision-making model and is similar to the perceived benefits and perceived barriers construct in the HBM. Decisional balance tends to change as individuals move through the stages of change (Prochaska et al., 1994). Individuals at earlier stages (i.e., precontemplation or contemplation) perceive more disadvantages than advantages to undertaking a behavior, whereas individuals at later stages (i.e., action or maintenance) perceive more advantages than disadvantages. The cross-over in decisional balance tends to occur in the contemplation or preparation stage. Bandura's (1986) concept of self-efficacy has also been incorporated in the transtheoretical model. Individuals with higher levels of self-efficacy tend to be in higher stages (e.g., DiClemente, 1986; DiClemente et al., 1991).

Initially, it was proposed that individuals would move in a linear fashion through the stages of change (Prochaska et al., 1992). However, consistent findings that relapse and recycling through stages are the norm for individuals trying to modify addictions led to a modification of this model. The model now posits that people move through the stages of change in a spiral fashion, oftentimes relapsing back to earlier stages such as precontemplation or contemplation, but then recycling back to preparation or action (Prochaska & DiClemente, 1984; Prochaska et al., 1992). By suggesting that change is not a continuum but rather is static and allows for regression and recycling, the transtheoretical model appears well-suited for predicting changes in addictive and other health behaviors.

PREDICTION OF CONDOM USE BY SOCIAL PSYCHOLOGICAL MODELS

As of 2001, more than 774,000 individuals contracted AIDS in the United States (CDC, 2001), and about 15 million people become infected with a sexually transmitted disease or infection (STD or STI) per year (CDC, 2000). Untreated STDs can eventually result in severe decreases in quality of life and in some cases, premature death. Moreover, the public health costs of HIV and other STDs are staggering. The total estimated cost of all STDs in the United States was almost 17 billion dollars in 1994 (Eng & Butler, 1997). Although correct and consistent condom use remains the most effective way to reduce the risk of STDs (CDC, 1993), most sexually active American adults and adolescents do not use condoms consistently (e.g., Catania et al., 1992). Clearly, understanding the reasons why individuals choose to forego condom use is an essential step for prevention researchers and practitioners. Thus, a great deal of research has examined the social cognitive predictors of condom use.

Theory of Reasoned Action and Theory of Planned Behavior

The effectiveness of the TRA and TPB models in predicting condom use intentions and behaviors have been tested among a variety of populations, including college students (Boyd & Wandersman, 1991; Chan & Fishbein, 1993; Conner, Graham, & Moore, 1999; Fisher, Fisher, & Rye, 1995; Kashima, Gallois, & McCamish, 1993; Serovich & Greene, 1997), men who have sex with men (MSM; Boldero, Sanitioso, & Brain, 1999; Fisher et al., 1995; Ross & McLaws, 1992), injection drug users (Corby, Schneider-Jamner, & Wolitski, 1996), clients of public STD clinics (Baker, Morrison, Carter, & Verdon, 1996; Morrison, Gilmore, & Bakker, 1995), sex workers (Sneed & Morisky, 1998), adolescents (Adler, Kegeles, Irwin, & Wibbelsman, 1990; Krahe & Reiss, 1995; Rannie & Craig, 1997; Reinecke, Schmidt, & Ajzen, 1996), urban African Americans (Jemmott & Jemmott, 1991; Stevenson, Davis, Weber, Weiman, & Abdul-Kabir, 1995), and young adults (Lugoe & Rise, 1999; Serovich & Greene, 1997; Sutton, McVey & Glanz, 1999). In general, results of this research provide strong empirical support for the prediction of condom use intentions and behaviors using the TRA and TPB models.

Three recent meta-analyses have tested the hypothesized relationships of the TRA and TPB models. Albarracin, Johnson, Fishbein, and Mueller-leile (2001) and Sheeran and Orbell (1998) both found robust associations between condom use intentions and behavior (sample-weighted average correlations = .45 and .44, respectively). In addition, Albarracin et al. and Sheeran and Taylor (1999) found support for a number of the TPB variables as predictors of condom use intentions. Albarracin and colleagues found attitudes ($r = .58$) to have a stronger relation to intentions than did norms ($r = .39$) or perceived behavioral control ($r = .45$), and perceived behavioral control was not as highly related to condom use behavior ($r = .25$) than as to intentions. Sheeran and Taylor noted large effect sizes for both attitudes ($r = .45$) and subjective norms ($r = .42$) for the prediction of intentions, and a medium effect size was observed for self-efficacy/perceived behavioral control ($r = .35$). A separate test of the effect of sexual partner norms on intentions yielded a correlation of .50, suggesting that perceptions about the desire of one's partner to use condoms are of greater importance than are perceptions of the desires of other significant others, such as friends and family members. In addition, both Albarracin et al. and Sheeran and Taylor found support for the full model when all variables were considered simultaneously, although Albarracin et al. did not find support for a direct pathway from perceived behavioral control to behavior.

Recent narrative reviews have supported the conclusions of these meta-analyses (Abraham, Sheeran, & Orbell, 1998; Bennett & Bozionelos, 2000; Fisher & Fisher, 2000; Godin & Kok, 1996). Moreover, tests of the TPB have generally found that including self-efficacy or perceived behavioral control as a predictor increases the utility of the TRA model in predicting condom use intentions (Basen-Engquist & Parcel, 1992; Cates, 1991; Jemmott, Jemmott, Spears, Hewitt, & Cruz-Collins, 1992; Kowalewski, Longshore, & Anglin, 1994; Richard & van der Plight, 1991; Schaalma, Kok, & Peters, 1993; Walter, Vaughan, Gladis, & Ragin, 1993) and behavior (Brien, Thombs, Mahoney, & Wallnau, 1994; Goldman & Harlow, 1993; Heinrich, 1993; Mahoney, Thombs, & Ford, 1995; Malow, Corrigan, Cunningham, & West, 1993; Wulfert & Wan, 1993). Additional research has supported the relation of self-efficacy to other kinds of safer sexual behaviors, such as talking to partners about contraception (Basen-Engquist, 1992; Joffe & Radius, 1993; Malow et al., 1993), refusing intercourse unless contraception is used (Kasen, Vaughan, & Walter, 1992), and using female condoms (Bogart, Cecil, & Pinkerton, 2000). The relationship of self-efficacy to safer sex intentions and behaviors is not surprising, given that condom use requires the effort and consent of more than one person. Individuals who feel that they are of lower status in their sexual relationships may believe that they do not have the necessary control to initiate condom use.

Despite the number of empirical studies supporting the TRA and TPB models, several inconsistencies in the literature remain. The relative importance of attitudes and social norms for the prediction of condom use and intentions varies across studies, with some investigations finding attitudes to be a stronger predictor (Basen-Engquist & Parcel, 1992; Chan & Fishbein, 1993; Jemmott & Jemmott, 1991; Richard & van der Plight, 1991; Wilson, Zenda, & Lavelle, 1991), some finding norms to be more important (Fishbein, Middlestadt, & Trafimow, 1993; Kashima et al., 1993; Lugoe & Rise, 1999; Ross & McLaws, 1992; White et al., 1994), and others finding relatively equal weights for attitudes and subjective norms (Sheeran & Taylor, 1999).

Several characteristics of the samples examined may account for differences among the findings. For example, differences in sexual orientation between samples may be one reason for conflicting results. In several studies with gay samples, attitude was not a significant predictor of intention (Godin, Savard, Kok, Fortin, & Boyer, 1996; Ross & McLaws, 1992; Wulfert, Wan, & Backus, 1996; see Fisher et al., 1995, for an exception). In addition, the prediction of condom use may differ by partner type. Both Morrison et al. (1995) and Richard and van der Plight (1991) found that the TRA was a better predictor with a steady partner than with casual partners. Additional research is needed to uncover reasons for these findings.

Empirical work also has observed gender differences in the prediction of the TRA/TPB (Adler et al., 1990; Morrison et al., 1995; Richard & van der Plight, 1991; Terry, 1993; Wilson, Zenda, McMaster, & Lavelle, 1992). Sheeran and Taylor's (1999) meta-analysis found that women report greater intentions to use condoms than men on average, despite being less likely to buy, carry, and keep condoms than men (Sacco, Rickman, Thompson, Levine, & Reed, 1993). This research and other similar work (Baldwin & Baldwin, 1988; Linden et al., 1990) suggests that researchers should evaluate the TRA/TPB model for men and women separately, and that other variables, such as relationship factors and condom preparatory behaviors, may need to be included as separate constructs in the model. In addition, condom use behavior is primarily under the male partner's control. Thus, beliefs about perceived behavioral control over condom use and self-efficacy to enact condom use have very different meanings among men and women. Because little research has directly examined gender differences in the utility of the models, no conclusions can be made at this time.

Despite the general support found for the TRA/TPB models in predicting condom use intentions and behaviors, the model has been found to account for less than 50% of the variance (e.g., Sheeran & Taylor, 1999).

Accordingly, some researchers have argued for the inclusion of other variables in the model. Most notably, some researchers have argued for the inclusion of past condom use behavior (e.g., Ross & McLaws, 1992). In their recent meta-analysis, however, Albarracin et al. (2001) found that relations between attitudes, norms, and intentions remained strong, beyond the effects of past behavior. Thus, past behavior may be important for the prediction of condom use but the effectiveness of the TRA/TPB model is not compromised by its inclusion.

Health Belief Model

Research on the HBM and condom use has rarely examined the model as a whole. Rather, researchers tend to focus on one aspect or component of the model, such as perceived benefits or perceived risk. Although less researched than the TPB in the condom use literature, components of the HBM also have been examined in diverse samples, such as college students (Basen-Engquist, 1992; Lollis, Johnson, & Antoni, 1997; Rosenthal, Hall, & Moore, 1992; Steers, Elliot, Nemiro, Ditman, & Oskamp, 1996; Yep, 1993), men who have sex with men (Aspinwall, Kemeny, Taylor, Schneider, & Dudley, 1991; Bakker, Buunk, Siero, & Van Den Eijnden, 1997; McCusker, Zapka, Stoddard, & Mayer, 1989; Mongomery et al., 1989), adolescents (Abraham, Sheeran, Spears, & Abrams, 1992; Adih & Alexander, 1999; Laraque et al., 1997; Petosa & Jackson, 1991; Wilson & Lavelle, 1992), Latinas (Ford & Norris, 1995; Neff & Crawford, 1998; Newcomb et al., 1998), and African Americans (Brunswick & Banaszak-Holl, 1996; Ford & Norris, 1995; Neff & Crawford, 1998).

Perceived susceptibility, as applied to sexual risk behavior, is an individual's subjective perception of the risk of contracting HIV or other STDs. The HBM predicts that greater perceived risk for HIV will lead to greater condom use intentions. Accordingly, a recent meta-analysis (Sheeran & Taylor, 1999) noted a small but significant relationship between perceived vulnerability and intentions to use condoms ($r = .13$), providing some support for the HBM hypothesis.

The results are less clear, however, for the relationship between perceived susceptibility and actual condom use behavior. Although the HBM predicts that greater perceived risk would lead to greater condom use, the majority of studies have not examined this hypothesis prospectively. Moreover, findings from the small amount of longitudinal work that has been done have not supported the utility of perceived susceptibility in predicting condom use. Although McBride, Weatherby, Inciardi, and Gillespie (1999) found that migrant workers who perceived themselves to be at higher risk for HIV at baseline were more likely to report sexual abstinence or 100%

condom use six months later (rs = .20 or less), several studies have found no significant relationship between the two variables (Lollis et al., 1997; Richard & van der Pligt, 1991; Rosenthal et al., 1992; Sibthorpe, Fleming, Tesselaar, & Gould, 1991).

Another way in which the relationship between susceptibility and risk behaviors has been tested is by examining perceived changes in behaviors as a result of the threat of HIV/AIDS. For example, Steers et al. (1996) asked participants whether they had increased condom use and decreased sexual behavior and numbers of partners because of the threat of HIV/AIDS. Perceived susceptibility was a significant and moderate predictor of multiple changes in risk behavior among Whites in the sample. A similar finding has been demonstrated among Latinas (Newcomb et al., 1998), and a meta-analysis by Gerrard, Gibbons, and Bushman (1996) provided support for this relationship. However, these studies may be limited by retrospective bias. Participants were typically asked whether they had changed their behavior as a result of HIV infection, and this perception was correlated with risk perceptions at the same time point. Because individuals' perceptions of behavior change can be colored by their current risk perceptions, such results must be viewed with caution.

Perceived severity of HIV also has been examined in tests of the HBM model's predictions. However, researchers have argued that the severity of HIV, which is fatal and incurable, is widely acknowledged and understood by most individuals (see Aspinwall et al., 1991; Bakker et al., 1997; Lollis et al., 1997). Thus, perceived severity may not have a sufficient amount of variability to be used as a predictor in the HBM model. This may be the reason for weak or nonsignificant results for this variable (e.g., Rosenthal et al., 1992), as well as the relative lack of attention given to this variable in the condom use literature. Some researchers have instead included other variables related to severity in the HBM model. Bakker et al. (1997) asked MSM to estimate the extent to which HIV is prevalent among their peers (i.e., "people you could have sex with"). Results indicated that this variable, in combination with perceived HIV risk, was a unique predictor of intention to use condoms among older, but not younger, MSM. Thus, the prevalence of HIV may be more salient among older MSM, who have observed the epidemic since its inception.

The most common perceived benefit examined has been the effectiveness of condoms in preventing pregnancy, HIV, and other STDs (e.g., Adih & Alexander, 1999; Bakker et al., 1997; Neff & Crawford, 1998; Newcomb et al., 1998). Other research has examined the benefit of condoms as adding to sexual excitement (Lollis et al., 1997). A variety of perceived barriers have been investigated, including reduction in sexual pleasure, breakage, inconvenience, discomfort, and embarrassment associated with condom use, the cost of condoms, the inability to use condoms or discuss condoms with one's partner, and the perception that alcohol increases risky sexual behavior (e.g., Adih & Alexander, 1999; Basen-Engquist, 1992; Ford & Norris, 1995; Lollis et al., 1997; Neff & Crawford, 1998; Nyamathi, Stein, & Brecht, 1995; Wilson & LaVelle, 1992).

In line with Janz and Becker's (1984) review of the HBM for preventive behaviors, perceived barriers have received strong support as predictors of sexual risk intentions and behavior (e.g., Basen-Engquist, 1992; Nyamathi et al., 1995), and greater support has been found for perceived barriers than for perceived benefits (e.g., Adih & Alexander, 1999 Wulfert et al., 1996; Yep, 1993). This may be partially because of a ceiling effect in the measurement of benefits. Because most people tend to agree that condoms are effective devices against HIV and other STDs, there is little variability in benefits as a predictor. Moreover, benefits tend to be measured in terms of "cold" cognitions and beliefs about condoms. Barriers, on the other hand, tend to be operationalized as motivational/emotional aspects of condom use, such as perceived lack of pleasure and spontaneity associated with condoms, which may be more relevant to the immediate context of condom use.

Several studies have found ethnic (Neff & Crawford, 1998; Steers et al., 1996) and gender (e.g., Lollis et al., 1997; Rosenthal et al., 1992; Wilson & LaVelle, 1992) differences in the utility of the HBM in predicting condom use. Steers et al. (1996) examined the HBM in White, Hispanic American, African American, and Asian American college students. Although perceived susceptibility was a significant predictor of behavior change among Whites, this relationship was considerably weaker among individuals in the other ethnic groups. Lollis and colleagues (1997) investigated gender differences in the predictive value of HBM components for various HIV-relevant behaviors. Although the HBM components did not significantly predict condom use, greater perceived risk was a reliable predictor of multiple sexual partners for men but not for women, and higher perceived costs and lower perceived benefits of condom use were reliable predictors of multiple sexual partners and numbers of risky sexual practices for women but not for men. The reasons for these ethnic and gender differences are unclear. However, because the same measures were used for all groups examined within each study, the researchers failed to account for culture and gender differences in the qualitative nature of the HBM constructs. For example, men are likely to have different perceptions about condoms than are women, but research investigating men's and women's perceptions tends to ask men and women to rate the same barriers and benefits. More research is needed to determine whether conflicting findings by ethnicity and gender is an artifact of the measurement used or a result of true differences in the HBM constructs among the groups.

Stages of Change Model

The stages of change model has been applied to condom use in a variety of populations, including college students (Grimley, Prochaska, Velicer, & Prochaska, 1995; Grimley, Riley, Bellis, & Prochaska, 1993; Prochaska et al., 1994), adolescents (Grimley & Lee, 1997), men and women at high or moderate risk for HIV (Evers, Harlow, Redding, & LaForge, 1998; Galavotti et al., 1995; Harlow et al., 1999; Lauby et al., 1998; Prochaska et al., 1994; Stark et al., 1998), and substance users (Anderson et al., 1996; Bowen & Trotter, 1995; Collins, Kohler, DiClemente, & Wang, 1999; Rhodes & Malotte, 1996; Schneider-Jamner, Wolitski, & Corby, 1997). This research has demonstrated that individuals can be reliably and validly placed into one of the stages (e.g., Bowen & Trotter, 1995; Evers et al., 1998). Not surprisingly, individuals who report no condom use (e.g., Bowen & Trotter, 1995) and having had an STD in the past year (Collins et al., 1999) tend to be in earlier stages. This suggests that the stages are accurately assessing individuals' motivations and behaviors regarding condom use.

In most investigations, a significant proportion of participants are in the precontemplation stage (e.g., Bowen & Trotter, 1995; Collins et al., 1999; Grimley et al., 1993). Moreover, individuals tend to be in higher stages of change for condom use with casual partners than with main/primary partners (Anderson et al., 1996; Collins et al., 1999; Galavotti et al., 1995; Grimley & Lee, 1997; Grimley et al., 1995; Harlow et al., 1999; Lauby et al., 1998). For example, Harlow et al. (1999) found in a sample of at-risk individuals that more than twice as many participants were in the precontemplation stage for condom use with main partners versus condom use with casual partners. This is consistent with previous research, which has found that condom use is more likely with casual than with main partners (e.g., Lansky, Thomas, & Earp, 1998), most likely because individuals tend to perceive higher risk for disease from unprotected intercourse with casual partners (e.g., Grimley et al., 1995). In one investigation individuals who had been with their main partners less than one year versus one year or more were at a higher stage (Collins et al., 1999), indicating that condom use with main partners decreases over time.

Although the majority of research on the stages of change and condom use has been cross-sectional (e.g., Anderson et al., 1996; Galavotti et al., 1995; Grimley & Lee, 1997; Grimley et al., 1993, 1995; Harlow et al., 1999; Lauby et al., 1998; Prochaska et al., 1994; Stark et al., 1998), some intervention and longitudinal research has been conducted (Collins et al., 1999; Evers et al., 1998; Rhodes & Malotte, 1996; Schneider-Jamner et al., 1997). Evers and colleagues (1998) assessed female participants' stage at two time points, two years apart, allowing an examination of the natural course of stages. Although the proportion of women at each stage was relatively stable over time, women were likely to have changed stages over the two-year period, and movement between stages was not linear. In addition, although some women improved, some relapsed. The probability of relapse from condom use was high, suggesting that individuals who have been using condoms regularly may benefit from intervention.

The stages have been reliably and validly distinguished using the decisional balance and self-efficacy constructs of the model. Decisional balance for condom use reflects the perception that condoms are an effective means of preventing HIV and STDs on the one hand but are costly to use in terms of partner concerns, embarrassment, and pleasure reduction. Overall, individuals in the precontemplation stage report perceiving more barriers than benefits to condom use, and individuals in later stages, such as maintenance, report perceiving more benefits than barriers (Grimley et al., 1993, 1995; Lauby et al., 1998). Moreover, as individuals progress through the stages, they gradually increase their belief in the advantages of condom use, but their beliefs about the disadvantages remain relatively stable (Grimley et al., 1993, 1995). Because the crossover into perceiving greater benefits tends to take place before or during the preparation stage (Prochaska et al., 1994), researchers have suggested that interventions should focus on increasing individuals' perceptions of the benefits of condom use to move individuals into a later stage (e.g., Grimley, Prochaska, & Prochaska, 1997). However, the causal relationship between perceived advantages of condom use and movement through the stages has yet to be tested directly.

Research has generally found that self-efficacy for using condoms increases as individuals progress through the stages (Galavotti et al., 1995; Grimley et al., 1995; Lauby et al., 1998). The lowest levels of self-efficacy have been observed in the precontemplation stage, when individuals are not using condoms and are not motivated to change their behavior in the near future. The highest levels have been found at the action and maintenance stages, when individuals are using condoms 100% of the time (Grimley et al., 1993).

Determining interventions that lead to stage progression is important for understanding how to change risk behavior. Thus, this line of work holds promise for testing the validity of, as well as applying, the model. However, this research has suffered from some limitations, including the inability to identify the effective aspects of a multicomponent intervention (Schneider-Jamner et al., 1997; Rhodes & Malotte, 1996) or relatively weak results (Collins et al., 1999). For example, Collins et al. (1999) conducted an intervention for drug users based on the transtheoretical model of change. Baseline and follow-up surveys were administered to individuals in intervention and comparison communities. Results indicated that individuals in the intervention community were less likely to be in the precontemplation stage for casual sex partners than were individuals in the control community.

However, the intervention did not appear to have an effect on condom use with main sex partners, suggesting that different interventions are needed to address condom use concerns with main and other types of sexual partners.

Combination Models

Because the social cognitive theories reviewed have significant overlap among the constructs, researchers have attempted to combine or compare models to determine the components from each model that work best in predicting condom use (e.g., Ford & Norris, 1995; Richard & van der Pligt, 1991; Wulfert & Wan, 1995; Wulfert et al., 1996). In general, this research indicates that the TRA and TPB are more useful for predicting condom use than is the HBM. For instance, two studies tested regression models incorporating TRA and HBM components (Ford & Norris, 1995; Richard & van der Pligt, 1991). In both studies, attitudes (from the TRA) were a significant predictor of condom use beyond other TRA and HBM components. Perceived susceptibility was a significant unique predictor in one study (Ford & Norris, 1995) but not the other (Richard & van der Pligt, 1991).

Other work has pointed to the need for an integrated model with self-efficacy as a central construct. Wulfert and colleagues compared the predictive value of the HBM, TRA, and self-efficacy among college students, single adults, and gay men (Wulfert & Wan, 1995; Wulfert et al., 1996). Their research demonstrated that a combination model subsuming constructs from TRA and HBM, with self-efficacy as a central construct, has superior predictive validity to any of the models by themselves. In their model, self-efficacy was a function of attitudes and subjective norms and attitudes, which were operationalized as barriers to safer sex (i.e., pleasure reduction and interpersonal partner-related barriers). Self-efficacy in turn was related to greater intentions and condom use. Similarly, a study of injection drug and crack cocaine users found that sexual assertiveness, a construct related to self-efficacy, was directly related to changes in condom use behavior and was determined by stage of change (Bowen, 1996).

Summary of Research Predicting Condom Use With Social Cognitive Constructs

As awareness and concern about the AIDS epidemic has increased, a great deal of research has focused on the prediction of condom use from social cognitive theories. In general, attitudes, intentions, and beliefs about condoms; perceived ability to use condoms; and beliefs about HIV are likely to influence condom use. However, condom use behavior is qualitatively different from other health behaviors, such as smoking, exercise, and nutritional behavior, in that it has a strong social component: A condom is used by two people within the context of a social interaction. Thus, a significant proportion of the variance in condom use behavior may be explained by the negotiations between sexual partners rather than the cognitions of only one partner. Future research combining data from both members of a couple is needed to address this issue. Furthermore, researchers have rarely focused on partner type when evaluating individuals' condom use. Yet research has demonstrated that individuals are more likely to use condoms with casual than with main–primary partners (e.g., Lansky et al., 1998). The dynamics between long-term primary partners and occasional, casual, or one-time partners are likely to be qualitatively different, especially by gender. Thus, it seems likely that different social cognitive constructs will predict condom use behavior for main and casual partners.

PREDICTION OF EXERCISE BY SOCIAL PSYCHOLOGICAL MODELS

Engaging in regular moderate physical activity has been repeatedly shown to be associated with a reduction in all-cause mortality rates and increased longevity (Blair et al., 1989; Paffenbarger, Hyde, Wing, & Hsieh, 1986). In addition, exercise is inversely related to incidence of coronary heart disease (Berlin & Colditz, 1990) and has been shown to be beneficial in preventing and treating hypertension (American College of Sports Medicine, 1993; Paffenberger et al., 1993). Although somewhat mixed, research has suggested an inverse relationship between physical activity and incidence of breast and colon cancers (Sternfield, 1992; Thune, Brenn, Olund, & Gaard, 1997), and exercise interventions have been beneficial in treating depression and anxiety (see Phillips, Kiernan, & King, 2001, for a review). Despite the noted benefits to exercising, the majority of the U.S. population leads relatively sedentary lifestyles (National Centers for Chronic Disease Prevention and Health Promotion, 1996). Therefore, a great deal of research on the social cognitive predictors of exercise exists, primarily focusing on the TRA, TPB, and the SOC. Only a small amount of research has examined the HBM and exercise behavior (e.g., Corwyn & Benda, 1999; O'Connell, Price, Roberts, Jurs, & McKinley, 1985). Thus, this review focuses on the TRA, TPB, and SOC as tools for describing and predicting exercise behavior.

Theory of Reasoned Action and Theory of Planned Behavior

The utility of the TPB in predicting exercise behavior has been examined in a number of studies (Bozionelos & Bennett, 1999; Brenes, Strube, & Storandt, 1998; Courneya, Bobick, & Schinke, 1999; Courneya & Friedenreich, 1997, 1999; Courneya, Friedenreich, Arthur, & Bobick, 1999;

Courneya, Keats, & Turner, 2000; Courneya, Plotnikoff, Hotz, & Birkett, 2000; Craig, Goldberg, & Dietz, 1996; Kerner & Grossman, 1998; Smith & Biddle, 1999; Trafimow & Trafimow, 1998), reviews (e.g., Biddle & Nigg, 2000; Blue, 1995; Godin, 1993; Godin & Kok, 1996), and one meta-analysis (Hausenblas, Carron, & Mack, 1997). Across diverse samples of healthy (e.g., college students; Bozionelos & Bennett, 1999) and nonhealthy populations (e.g., patients with cancer; Courneya et al. 2000), research has consistently found attitudes and perceived behavioral control to be strongly predictive of intentions, and intentions and perceived behavioral control to significantly predict behavior. In the majority of studies, subjective norm has had a negligible or nonsignificant effect, suggesting that social pressure does not have much of an effect on individuals' intentions to exercise. A meta-analysis by Hausenblas and colleagues (1997) was performed on 162 effect sizes from 31 studies, and large effect sizes were obtained for the relationships between attitudes and intention, perceived behavioral control and intention, perceived behavioral control and behavior, and intention and behavior. Moreover, the effect size for the prediction of intention from attitudes was more than two times the effect size for the corresponding relationship between subjective norm and behavior. However, the researchers did not have enough power to estimate the full TRA or TPB models in the meta-analysis. Thus, the interrelationships among variables and the hierarchical nature of the model could not be examined. As a consequence, their results may overestimate the true effect sizes and must be viewed with some caution.

Despite the support found for the TRA/TPB in the exercise domain, the current body of literature on the TRA/TPB and exercise contains a heterogeneous set of studies with diverse samples, operationalizations, and methodologies, making comparisons between studies difficult. Some research has failed to include the behavioral component of the model (e.g., Trafimow & Trafimow, 1998), whereas other research has examined the model cross-sectionally (Courneya, Bobick, & Schnicke, 1999; Courneya & Friedenreich, 1999; Courneya et al., 2000; Trafimow & Trafimow, 1998) rather than prospectively. Although a growing number of studies have used longitudinal methodologies (e.g., Bozionelos & Bennett, 1999; Brenes et al., 1998; Courneya, Bobick, & Schnicke, 1999; Courneya, Friedenreich, et al., 1999; Courneya et al., 2000; Kerner & Grossman, 1998; Norman, Conner, & Bell, 2000; Smith & Biddle, 1999), stronger results have been obtained from cross-sectional research. For example, Courneya, Bobick, et al. (1999) conducted two studies of the TPB and exercise behavior. The first study, which was cross-sectional in design, assessed exercise behavior among healthy female undergraduates and found that the TPB explained 42% of the variance in intentions and 40% of the variance in self-reported exercise behavior. In the second study, which was prospective, the percentages decreased to 27% of the variance in intentions to attend an exercise class and 19% of the variance in actual attendance behavior over an 11-week period.

Most studies have used self-reports of exercise behavior, although a few studies have used other methods, such as attendance at an exercise program (Smith & Biddle, 1999) or cycling duration, as measured by a computerized ergonometer (Courneya, Keats, et al., 2000). In addition, Kerner and Grossman (1998) asked attendees of a health club to keep a daily log of exercise over a five-month period; intent and perceived behavioral control at baseline accounted for 29% of the variance in exercise behavior. Courneya and colleagues have used the Leisure Score Index (LSI) of the Godin Leisure Time Exercise Questionnaire (Godin, Jobin, & Bouillon, 1986; Godin & Shepard, 1985) to assess the frequency of mild, moderate, and strenuous exercise done during free time for at least 20 minutes in a typical week. In general, research has found that the TPB accounts for a moderate to large proportion of the variance in LSI scores (e.g., 36% in Courneya, Bobick, et al., 1999; but see Courneya & Friedenreich, 1999).

In sum, there is strong support for using the theory of planned behavior to predict exercise intentions and behavior. Clearly, however, there are several directions for future research that would address gaps in the literature. Research testing the efficacy of the model among those of different sociodemographic groups, such as those of diverse ethnicities, as well as older adults and children, is needed for a more complete understanding of the conditions under which the model operates for exercise behavior. In addition, the use of standardized and longitudinal measures of exercise behavior in future research would greatly enhance the validity and reliability of conclusions about the TRA/TPB and exercise behavior.

Stages of Change Model

In general, research on exercise and the SOC has demonstrated that individuals can be validly distinguished based on their stage of exercise behavior (Burke et al., 2000; Cardinal, 1997; Ingledew, Markland, & Medley, 1998; Marcus & Simkin, 1993; Miilunpalo, Nupponen, Laitakari, Marttila, & Paronen, 2000; Mullan & Markland, 1997; Myers & Roth, 1997). Individuals in later stages report more exercise, as measured by the Leisure Score Index (Cardinal, 1997), and greater amounts of physical activity (Burke et al., 2000; Rosen, 2000). Individuals in later stages are also more likely to have a lower body mass index (BMI), better cardiovascular fitness, and a healthier diet (Burke et al., 2000; Burn, Naylor, & Page, 1999; Cardinal, 1997). In addition, those in later stages tend to report greater self-efficacy, greater intentions, and more intrinsic motivation for exercise behavior than those in earlier stages of the model (e.g., Burn et al., 1999; Ingledew et al., 1998; Mullan & Markland, 1997; Rosen, 2000).

The stages also have been differentiated based on constructs from the HBM. Individuals in precontemplation have been found to perceive lower severity for physical inactivity, suggesting that severity may be a motivator of behavior for later stages (Courneya, 1995). In addition, Prochaska (1994) found that individuals in the precontemplation stage perceived more barriers than benefits, whereas individuals in the action stage perceived more benefits than barriers. Thus, individuals in earlier stages are more likely to perceive barriers, and individuals in later stages are more likely to perceive benefits of exercise (see also Myers & Roth, 1997).

Although some research has noted differences in stages by race and ethnicity (Cardinal, 1997) and gender (Miilunpalo et al., 2000), the majority of work in this domain has not examined such differences or has not been able to do so because of sample limitations. However, age has been investigated as a possible determinant or correlate of stage. Exercise activity appears to be less prevalent among older people (Burke et al., 2000; Cardinal, 1997; Miilunpalo et al., 2000). Burke et al. (2000) surveyed a cohort of 18 year olds and found most individuals in the sample were in either the action or maintenance stage. Campbell and colleagues (2000), however, found that the distribution of individuals older than 75 years of age was bimodal, with 39% in precontemplation and 41% in maintenance.

Despite the success of the model in distinguishing stages of exercise activity, much of the research has examined healthy populations (e.g., Burke et al., 2000; Burn et al., 1999; Campbell et al., 2000; Cardinal, 1997; Ingledew et al., 1998; Mullan & Markland, 1997; Myers & Roth, 1997; Peterson & Aldana, 1999; Pinto & Marcus, 1995). Results of these studies may not generalize to individuals suffering from mental or physical disorders. In addition, the majority of research in this area has been cross-sectional (e.g., Burn et al., 1999; Campbell et al., 2000; Cardinal, 1997; Miilunpalo et al., 2000; Mullan & Markland, 1997; Myers & Roth, 1997; Nigg et al., 1999; Pinto & Marcus, 1995), making examination of the predictive value of the theory impossible. Finally, research has been largely descriptive, summarizing the distribution of stages for different samples, without explaining why individuals fall in different categories. Future research improving on these limitations is needed to design effective, theory-based interventions.

Summary of Research Predicting Exercise Behavior With Social Cognitive Constructs

Research has indicated support for both the TRA/TPB and SOC with respect to exercise behavior. However, because the majority of work has been cross-sectional and has not tested interventions, the body of literature serves largely to describe and identify correlates of exercise intentions and behavior, rather than to predict behavior change. In addition to designing prospective and intervention studies, future research should concentrate on examining exercise behavior among members of diverse and nonhealthy populations, as well as predicting several different kinds of exercise behavior. Because exercise behavior encompasses a variety of activities, examination of a breadth of behaviors across several time points is needed for a comprehensive evaluation of individuals' exercise programs.

PREDICTION OF DIETARY BEHAVIORS BY SOCIAL PSYCHOLOGICAL MODELS

Diet can serve as a direct risk factor for the development of cardiovascular disease and several kinds of cancer and indirectly increases risk for these diseases and others (e.g., diabetes) through obesity (Greenwald, Sondik, & Lynch, 1986; Rimer, McBride, & Crump, 2001; Turpeinen, 1979). Consumption of a high-fat diet increases levels of low density lipoproteins (LDLs), which appear to serve as a mechanism in the development of atherosclerosis (Rich-Edwards, Manson, Hennekens, & Buring, 1995). In addition, a recent meta-analysis concluded that interventions geared toward decreasing fat consumption result in a lowering of cholesterol levels (Brunner et al., 1997), and increased dietary fiber consumption may be important in the prevention and control of cancer (Jacobs, Slavin, & Marquart, 1995). As diet modifications have demonstrated significant effects on health, social psychological models have attempted to predict individuals most likely to change their dieting behaviors.

Theory of Reasoned Action and Theory of Planned Behavior

Research on the theory of planned behavior has generally provided support for the model as a predictor of dietary behavior, although, as with the other reviewed behaviors, the effects of attitudes and perceived behavioral control tend to be larger than the effects of subjective norms. In a review of the TRA/TPB and health behavior, Godin and Kok (1996) compiled results from five studies of eating behavior. Across 10 eating behaviors, an average of 32% of the variance in intention was explained by the TPB constructs. Of the two behaviors for which behavioral data were available, an average of 25% of the variance in behavior was explained by intention and perceived behavioral control. Across the other eight behaviors, the average correlation between attitude and intention was .34, the average correlation between subjective norm and intention was .16, and the average correlation between perceived behavioral control and intention was .32. Other more recent studies have produced similar findings (e.g., Conner & Armitage, 1998; Povey, Conner, Sparks, James, & Shepherd, 2000), reinforcing the strength of the TRA/TPB in predicting dietary behavior.

Despite findings supporting the TRA/TPB, a number of issues remain. The majority of studies have examined the components of the model at one time point (e.g., Conner, Martin, Silverdale, & Grogan, 1996) rather than prospectively, and therefore no firm conclusions can be made about the longitudinal relationship of intentions to eating behavior. In addition, the amount of variance explained by the model is relatively low, and it has been argued that other variables, such as the perceived need to eat a healthy diet (e.g., Povey et al., 2000), self-identification as someone concerned about the health consequences of diet (Sparks, Shepherd, Wieringa, & Zimmermans, 1995), or media pressure to diet (Conner et al., 1996) ought to be added to the model to increase its predictive utility.

Health Belief Model

A limited amount of research has applied the HBM to dietary behaviors, with mixed results (e.g., Becker, Maiman, Kirscht, Haefner, & Drachman, 1977; Contento & Murphy, 1990; Dittus, Hilers, & Beerman, 1993; Hagdrup, Simoes, & Brownson, 1998; Hayes & Ross, 1987; Kelly, Zyzanski, & Alemagno, 1991; O'Connell et al., 1985; Ransford, 1986; Sapp & Jensen, 1998). Using a cross-sectional design, greater consumption of high fat foods was related to perceived susceptibility to heart disease, weight gain, and "feeling unwell" in a British sample (Sparks et al., 1995). In addition, more perceived barriers to eating a healthy diet were associated with lower fruit and vegetable intake, and greater perceived benefit of reducing the risk of cancer was related to higher fruit and vegetable consumption, in a statewide phone survey (Hagdrup et al., 1998). Other research has also indicated that perceived barriers (Sands, Archer, & Puleo, 1998) and perceived benefits (Contento & Murphy, 1990) are important predictors of nutritional behavior. In contrast, only perceived barriers, and not perceived susceptibility, severity, or benefits, predicted intention to follow a healthy diet among individuals with elevated cholesterol levels (Norman, Edwards, Fitter, & Gray, 1992).

No definitive conclusions can be made about the efficacy of the HBM for dietary behaviors, because most earlier research in this area has failed to test the full model of the HBM. Sapp and Jensen (1998), however, applied structural equation modeling techniques to test the full model for "eating a quality diet" using data from a national survey of adults in the United States. A variety of food behaviors were examined over three days. The

HBM was a good predictor of perceived nutritional behavior, but only a moderate to weak predictor of actual food intake. In another study using structural equation modeling, different components of the HBM were related to eating behavior for men and women (Schafer, Keith, & Schafer, 1995). For men, percentage of calories from fat was predicted by perceived threat, self-efficacy, and perceived benefits. Barriers and benefits were predictive of fat intake in women.

Some research has combined aspects of the HBM with other social psychological models to predict food intake. For example, Steptoe and colleagues (Steptoe, Doherty, Kerry, Rink, & Hilton, 2000) used constructs from the HBM and social cognitive theory to test an intervention based on the SOC for increasing consumption of low-fat foods among individuals with high cholesterol. Greater self-efficacy and perceived benefits of maintaining a low-fat diet were significant multivariate predictors of lower fat consumption at baseline, as well as behavior changes over time. Across both intervention and control groups, patients who made larger reductions in fat intake reported increases in self-efficacy and increases in perceived benefits. However, these two variables only accounted for 4% of the variance in dietary changes.

Stages of Change Model

The SOC has been used as a framework for understanding healthy eating across several populations and dietary behaviors (Brug, Glanz, & Kok, 1997; Steptoe et al., 2000). Some researchers have examined at-risk populations (e.g., patients with high cholesterol; Steptoe et al., 2000) or older adults (Nigg et al., 1999), whereas others have looked at members of the general population (e.g., survey of Dutch adults; Brug et al., 1997) or college students (e.g., Prochaska et al., 1994). In addition, some have chosen to examine increasing healthy eating (e.g., fruit and vegetable consumption; Brug, Hospers, et al., 1997; Ling & Horwath, 1999), whereas others have focused on decreasing unhealthy eating (e.g., reducing fat; Prochaska et al., 1994; see also Nigg et al., 1999; Read, Auld, Bock, & Bruhn, 1996). Across studies, the stages have been shown to be a valid representation of behavior, such that individuals in higher stages are more likely to report eating fruit and vegetables (Brug, Glanz, & Kok, 1997) and to have a low fat consumption (Brug, Hospers, et al., 1997; Curry, Kristal, & Bowen, 1992).

Consistent with research on other health behaviors, self-efficacy and attitudinal variables are associated with the stages for dietary behavior. Individuals with higher self-efficacy to maintain a healthy diet tend to be in a later stage than individuals with lower self-efficacy (Brug, Glanz, et al., 1997; Brug, Hospers, et al., 1997; Glanz et al., 1994; Ling & Horwath,

1999). In addition, individuals in precontemplation tend to perceive more disadvantages than advantages to healthy eating, whereas individuals in later stages (i.e., action and maintenance) tend to perceive the reverse (Prochaska et al., 1994).

Another correlate of the stages is age (e.g., Curry et al., 1992; Nigg et al., 1999; Read et al., 1996). Read et al. (1996) found that older individuals (aged 55–64) were more likely to be at the action or maintenance stage than were individuals younger than 55 years old. This suggests that, as individuals grow older, they may become more aware of cardiovascular disease and the need to change their diet. Although a healthy diet would benefit younger individuals as well, they are often not targeted for dietary health promotion messages.

As a whole, research on the transtheoretical model and dietary behavior is still in its infancy. Little research has been conducted, and the majority of studies have been cross-sectional in design (e.g., Bowen, Meischke, & Tomoyasu, 1994; Brug, Glanz, et al., 1997; Brug, Hospers, et al., 1997; Nigg et al., 1999; Prochaska et al., 1994). Thus, the causal influence of variables such as self-efficacy on stage progression has not been tested. Moreover, the transtheoretical model, which was originally formulated for addictive behavior, may not be applicable to dietary behavior. Addictive behaviors, such as smoking, are more discrete and specific, and the endpoint of the model would be complete abstinence from smoking. Dietary behaviors, however, are more complex and encompass a range of behaviors, both general and specific, such as maintaining a generally healthy diet or reducing unhealthy foods (e.g., fat) and increasing healthy foods (e.g., fruits and vegetables). The end stage of the model is less defined, because one can make some dietary changes but not others, so a person can simultaneously be in several stages for several different dietary behaviors.

Research is therefore needed that measures the stages for more than one dietary behavior for each participant. Povey et al. (2000) began to address this concern by measuring stages of change for three dietary behaviors that differed in specificity: eating a healthy diet, which was the most general, eating a low-fat diet, which was moderately specific, and eating five portions of fruits and vegetables per day, which was the most specific. The highest proportion of individuals for each behavior were in maintenance, and the lowest proportion were in preparation. However, participants were less likely to be in the action or maintenance stage for specific, as opposed to more general, eating behavior. Hence, people may inaccurately perceive that they are maintaining a healthy diet—they may believe they are eating healthy, but they may not actually be reducing fat or increasing fruit and vegetable consumption. This points to a need to measure dietary behaviors at the highest level of specificity for valid assessment of the stages of change.

Summary of Research Predicting Dietary Behavior With Social Cognitive Constructs

Relatively little research has tested the effectiveness of social psychological models in predicting dietary behaviors, and the research that has been performed has examined only one behavior or set of behaviors at a single time point. Thus, any conclusions in this area would be premature until more research is conducted. Because the realm of diet encompasses many different behaviors, such as increasing vegetable intake and reducing fat intake, future research needs to examine a variety of eating behaviors at varying levels of specificity across several time points. Moreover, interventions based on the models also would need to have multiple components to address a range of eating behaviors.

PREDICTION OF SMOKING BEHAVIOR BY SOCIAL PSYCHOLOGICAL MODELS

Cigarette smoking is arguably the single most preventable cause of death and illness in the United States (Grunberg, Faraday, & Rahman, 2001), with tobacco use accounting for nearly one in five deaths (American Cancer Society, 1998) and more than 85% of lung cancer cases (Bartecchi, Mackenzie, & Schrier, 1994). Smoking is associated with numerous other cancers (e.g., mouth, larynx, esophagus, pancreas) as well as a major cause of heart disease. The total economic cost of smoking exceeds $100 billion per year (Office of Technology Assessment, 1993). Approximately 69% of current smokers interviewed in 1994 reported wanting to quit smoking completely, and approximately 46% had attempted to quit (Office on Smoking and Health, 1996). Despite the obvious risk to health and personal interest in quitting, approximately 21% of adults in the United States smoke every day (Office on Smoking and Health, 1996). Because of the prevalence of and difficulty in altering smoking behavior, much research has been conducted examining the utility of the social theories of behavior change in predicting who is most likely to change his or her smoking behavior.

Theory of Reasoned Action and Theory of Planned Behavior

The initiation of smoking has been investigated in the context of the TRA and TPB in a number of diverse samples, including preadolescents (Morrison, Gillmore, Simpson, Wells, & Hoppe, 1996) and adolescents (Chassin et al., 1981; Chassin, Presson, Sherman, Corty, & Olshavsky, 1984; Chassin, Presson, Sherman, Montello, & McGrew, 1986; Grube, Morgan, & McGee, 1986; Hanson, 1997; Maher & Rickwood, 1997;

O'Callagan, Callan, & Baglioni, 1999). In addition, research has tested whether the TRA/TPB adequately predicts smoking cessation among pregnant women (Bennett & Clatworthy, 1999; Godin & Lepage, 1988; Godin, Valois, Lepage, & Desharnais, 1992) and current smokers (Godin et al., 1992; Hu & Lanese, 1998; Marin, Marin, Perez-Stable, Otero-Sabogal, & Sabogal, 1990; Nguyet, Beland, & Otis, 1998; Norman et al., 1999).

In general, the TRA model has received support (e.g., Budd, 1986; Chassin et al., 1984; Godin & Lepage, 1988; Gottlieb, Gingliss, & Weinstein, 1992; Grube et al., 1986; Maher & Rickwood, 1997; Morrison, Gillmore, Simpson, Wells, & Hoppe, 1996; Nguyet et al., 1998; O'Callagan et al., 1999), explaining a reported 17% to 52% of the variance in intentions across studies. However, the attitudinal component has displayed more consistent and robust results than the subjective norms component. Compared to attitudes, the relationship between subjective norms and intentions tends to be weaker (e.g., Budd, 1986; Chassin et al., 1981; Gottlieb et al., 1992; Grube et al., 1986) or nonsignificant (e.g., Godin & Lepage, 1988; Hanson, 1997; Marin et al., 1990). On the other hand, a smaller amount of research has found norms to be as strong as, or stronger than, attitudes in the prediction of intention (Maher & Rickwood, 1997; Morrison et al., 1996; O'Callagan et al., 1999). For example, Morrison et al. (1996) found attitudes and norms to be equally weighted in the prediction of intentions to smoke among preadolescents, possibly because peer pressure is strong in this age group.

Consistent with the tenets of the TPB, the addition of perceived behavioral control or self-efficacy to the TRA model has usually, but not always (O'Callagan et al., 1999), led to an increase in the predictive value of the model (Godin et al., 1992; Grube et al., 1986; Hanson, 1997; Hu & Lanese, 1998; Maher & Rickwood, 1997; Norman et al., 1999). For instance, a longitudinal study of smokers attending health promotion clinics found that perceived behavioral control predicted 49% of the variance in intentions to quit smoking, and intentions in turn were associated with making an attempt to quit smoking (Norman et al., 1999). The effects of attitudes and subjective norms on intentions were not significant. In contrast, a longitudinal study of adolescents found the basic TRA model to predict intentions to smoke in the next month but not behavior one month later; perceived behavioral control was not significantly related to intentions or actual behavior (O'Callagan et al., 1999). Because studies of the TPB and smoking differ markedly in terms of sample type and design, it is difficult to draw conclusions concerning the varying results. However, it is possible that attitudes and subjective norms are better predictors than perceived behavioral control for adolescents, who are just beginning to make decisions about smoking, as compared to long-term smokers, who may feel that their behavior is beyond their control.

At least three studies have found the model to vary by ethnicity (Hanson, 1997; Marin et al., 1990; Morrison et al., 1996). In a sample of female adolescents attending a family planning clinic, attitudes, subjective norms, and perceived behavioral control were all significant predictors of intention to smoke in the next month for African American participants, but only attitudes and perceived behavioral control predicted intentions for Hispanic and White participants (Hanson, 1997). Similarly, attitudes have been shown to be stronger predictors of intention to quit than norms for both Hispanic and White smokers (Marin et al., 1990). These findings support Ajzen and Fishbein's (1980) contention that the TPB components are likely to vary by the specific population studied, suggesting that formative research must be conducted to adapt assessments of the TPB constructs to sample characteristics.

Aside from ethnicity, the variability in findings across some studies may partially be related to differences in study design. Many studies in this realm are cross-sectional and examine intentions rather than actual behavior (e.g., Bennett & Clatworthy, 1999; Chassin et al., 1981; Godin & Lepage, 1988; Hanson, 1997; Hu & Lanese, 1998; Maher & Rickwood, 1997; Nguyet et al., 1998), although some researchers have assessed behavior prospectively (e.g., Chassin et al., 1984; Godin et al., 1992; Grube et al., 1986; Marin et al., 1990; O'Callagan et al., 1999). Generally, intentions are moderately to highly correlated with later smoking behavior (e.g., Chassin et al., 1984; Morrison et al., 1996; O'Callagan et al., 1999). Stronger results have been obtained for the cross-sectional relationships of attitudes and subjective norms with intentions (e.g., Nguyet et al., 1998), versus the longitudinal prediction of behavior (e.g., Grube et al., 1996; O'Callagan et al., 1999).

Other research has investigated the utility of augmenting the TRA/TPB with a number of other variables related to smoking behavior. In particular, some researchers have called for the addition of perceived norms, or perceived prevalence of smoking behavior among peers and family, to the TRA/TPB model (Chassin et al., 1981, 1984; Grube et al., 1986). In a study of adolescents (Grube et al., 1986), the predictive ability of the TRA was significantly improved with the addition of a measure of perceived amount of peer and parental smoking (i.e., how many cigarettes, on average, friends and parents were perceived to smoke per day). Thus, peer models of smoking behavior may have as much of an influence as the perceived pressure to smoke by peers (i.e., subjective norms).

Several studies have demonstrated that the inclusion of past behavior also adds to the predictive utility of the TPB for both adolescents and current smokers (Hu & Lanese, 1998; Nguyet et al., 1998; Norman et al., 1999; O'Callagan et al., 1999). Past behavior has been operalizationed as frequency of smoking (Nguyet et al., 1998; O'Callagan et al., 1999) and number of previous quit attempts (Hu & Lanese, 1998; Nguyet et al., 1998). For example, in a Canadian mail survey, individuals who smoked more cigarettes per day and who had made a fewer number of attempts to quit were more likely to intend to quit smoking (Nguyet et al., 1998). Thus, it seems that earlier smoking behavior gives individuals the skills and experiences necessary for future smoking behavior, such as the ability to obtain cigarettes and find opportunities to smoke them. However, the TPB components—favorable attitudes toward quitting, perceived pressure of important others to quit, and the perceived ability to quit—are still necessary for enacting successful smoking cessation.

A construct related to earlier smoking behavior, nicotine addiction, also has been tested as an addition to the TPB, with somewhat mixed findings (Bennett & Clatworthy, 1999; Hu & Lanese, 1998). Hu and Lanese observed nonsignificant results for the addition of nicotine addiction to the TPB model, and nicotine addiction was not related to intentions in univariate tests. Bennett and Clatworthy found that the TPB variables did not add to the prediction of quitting smoking above the unique effects of nicotine addiction, which was strongly related to quitting in univariate tests. Although more research is needed, it appears that the TPB may be a better predictor of smoking intentions and behaviors among individuals who are not strongly addicted to nicotine. In individuals with strong nicotine addiction, a rational model such as the TPB may not be able to describe smoking behavior adequately.

In general, the TRA/TPB provides a useful framework for predicting and describing smoking behavior. However, the model is unable to account for the majority of the variance in intentions and behavior, and other variables, such as norms, past behavior, and nicotine addiction, show promise for increasing the explanatory power of the model. In addition, more research is needed with different ethnic groups to test the cross-cultural applicability of the model and the reasons for previously observed differences between groups.

Health Belief Model

As with the other health behaviors reviewed, the majority of studies examining smoking using the HBM have examined components of the HBM without examining the entire model. Moreover, the HBM, although effective at predicting one-time health behaviors such as mammograms and immunizations, has been less successful at predicting habitual behaviors such as smoking (Kaufert, Rabkin, Syrotuik, Boyko, & Shane, 1986; Kirscht, 1988; Mullen, Hersey, & Iverson, 1987). However, some research has found significant effects. For example, Manfredi, Lacey, Warnecke, and Petraitis (1998) found that generalized concern about the effects of smoking on one's health was a strong predictor of desire and plans to quit smoking in a sample of 248 young, low socioeconomic-status African American women.

Regular smokers also have been found to report less self-efficacy to quit and perceive greater benefits and lower risk from smoking (Hamilton,

Cross, & Resnicow, 2000). Perceived susceptibility to disease, severity of smoking risk, and belief in harm from smoking have also been associated with success in quitting smoking (Marshall, 1990; Warnecke, Graham, Rosenthal, & Manfred, 1975), although negative findings have been reported (Croog & Richards, 1977). In addition, a study examining the efficacy of the HBM in predicting adherence to physicians' advice to quit smoking (Pederson, Wanklin, & Baskruilk, 1984) found that the entire model considered together was related to smoking cessation, despite perceived severity, efficacy, and perceived health effects not being related to adherence behavior.

Researchers have also tested the effectiveness of smoking interventions based on components of the HBM model. Lerman and colleagues (1997) conducted an intervention study in which biomarker feedback and genetic susceptibility information was incorporated into a quit-smoking counseling session. The genetic susceptibility group reported immediate increases in perceived risk to smoking and benefits to quitting, but, two months later, there were no differences in cessation rates between groups, suggesting that interventions targeting health beliefs are not effective in enhancing quitting in smokers.

Conrad and colleagues conducted a prospective study in which they examined the role of worksite cues in decreasing smoking behavior (Conrad, Campbell, Edington, Faust, & Vilnius, 1996). In this study, exposure to a health-promoting worksite was directly related to decreased smoking at follow-up and was indirectly related to smoking behavior through decreasing participants' perceived barriers to quitting smoking.

The predictive ability of the HBM has been shown to differ based on demographic characteristics of the samples examined. In particular, the HBM has been used to explain gender differences in smoking behavior, with research suggesting that women may perceive fewer benefits to quitting, greater benefits to continuing smoking, and may have less knowledge of or perceive less threat of negative consequences (Brownson et al., 1992; Rose, Chassin, Presson, & Sherman, 1996; Sorensen & Pechacek, 1987).

As with other social psychological models and smoking behavior, researchers have tested whether the HBM is effective in predicting smoking beyond the effects of addiction. Kanvil and Umeh (2000) found that past cigarette use accounted for 70% of the variance in intentions to smoke. When perceived susceptibility and barriers were added to the model, they only accounted for a marginal percentage of the variance in intentions to smoke beyond that accounted for by earlier cigarette use (Kanvil & Umeh, 2000), suggesting that HBM variables do not add much to the predictive strength of addiction variables.

Overall, the HBM has shown limited utility in predicting smoking behavior or cessation, possibly because the HBM, unlike the SOC, does not account for fluctuations in readiness to change and variations in the cost–benefit analysis that occurs in smokers (Mermelstein, 1997). In addition, interventions effective at altering components of the HBM are not effective at altering smoking behaviors. Although perceived health risks and susceptibility to disease have been related to increased cessation, results have been mixed, and examination of all components of the HBM have not consistently been associated with smoking behavior.

Stages of Change

The theory most examined in relation to predicting or explaining changes in smoking behavior is the transtheoretical or stages of change theory (DiClemente et al., 1991; Prochaska & DiClemente, 1983). Several studies have shown that stages of change can be used to predict smoking cessation (DiClemente et al., 1991; Prochaska, DiClemente, Velicer, & Rossi, 1993; Schmid & Gmel, 1999; Velicer, Norman, Fava, & Prochaska, 1999). Schmid and Gmel examined 953 nonsmokers, current smokers, and former smokers at two time points eight years apart. They found that progression through the stages of change was more likely than regression over time, although, as previously found (Prochaska & DiClemente, 1984), the modal response was for individuals to remain in the same stage. In addition, stage membership at time 1 was strongly predictive of smoking status at time 2; the odds of being a smoker at time 2 clearly decreased as one progressed through the stage hierarchy at time 1. Although univariate analyses using stage of change to predict cessation have largely produced positive findings, multivariate analyses including addiction variables (e.g., age of smoking onset, number of cigarettes smoked daily, duration of smoking) have found that stage membership no longer predicts or greatly decreases the ability to predict cessation (Farkas, Pierce, Zhu, et al., 1996; Schmid & Gmel, 1999). These findings have led researchers to question the usefulness of the stages of change model at predicting cessation as other predictive factors (e.g., addiction variables) are better at predicting who will quit smoking (Farkas, Pierce, Zhu, et al., 1996; Farcas, Pierce, Gilpin, et al., 1996).

Cross-sectional research has largely supported the hypothesis that perceived cons of smoking would increase as one progresses through the stages of change from precontemplation through preparation (DiClemente et al., 1991; Etter & Perneger, 1999; Fava, Velicer, & Prochaska, 1995; Herzog, Abrams, Emmons, Linnan, & Shadel, 1999; Velicer et al., 1999). Herzog and colleagues (1999), in a study of 1,535 smokers, found a nearly linear pattern of increasing means for reports of cons of smoking from precontemplation to contemplation to preparation (effect sizes ranged from .17 to .46). Similarly, precontemplators have been shown to report significantly fewer negative effects of smoking than later-stage smokers (Ahijevych &

Parsley, 1999), and progressing from precontemplation to contemplation and from contemplation to preparation has been associated with significant increases in the reporting of cons of smoking (Etter & Perneger, 1999). However, prospective research has suggested that the weighing of pros and cons largely fail to predict progressive movement through the stages of change (Etter & Perneger, 1999; Herzog et al., 1999; Prochaska, DiClemente, Velicer, Ginpil, & Norcross, 1985).

One of the primary implications of the transtheoretical model is the need to assess the stage of readiness for change for individuals engaging in health risk behaviors and to tailor interventions accordingly (Prochaska et al., 1992). Although theoretically supported, empirical studies examining the efficacy of stage-matched and -mismatched interventions at altering smoking behavior have produced mixed results (Dijkstra, DeVries, Roijackers, & van Breukelen, 1998; Prochaska et al., 1993; Quinlan & McCaul, 2000). Whereas stage-matched interventions appear effective for individuals who are ready to change their smoking behavior (Dijkstra et al., 1998; Prochaska et al., 1993), equivalent results are often found between stage-matched, stage-mismatched, and control interventions for individuals who are not ready to quit (Dijkstra et al., 1998; Prochaska et al., 1993; Quinlan & McCaul, 2000).

Summary of Research Predicting Smoking Behavior With Social Cognitive Constructs

Because of the prevalence of and difficulty in altering smoking behavior, social theories of behavior change have focused on predicting who may be most likely to change their smoking behavior. However, these theories have shown limited efficacy in predicting smoking cessation. The transtheoretical model has demonstrated the greatest effectiveness at predicting readiness to change and smoking cessation, largely because the model was designed to account for changes or lack of changes in smoking behavior. The other psychosocial models are limited in their ability to predict change in smoking because they were originally devised to explain nonaddictive behaviors that progress in a more linear fashion. Largely because of the addictive nature of smoking, cessation is a relatively rare outcome of a change attempt. Multiple attempts to quit are the norm, and theories must take into account relapse when dealing with smoking behavior.

DISCUSSION

This chapter examines the effectiveness of the most commonly researched social psychological models at predicting a number of health behaviors. In general, the models display a moderate ability to predict health behavior, although the efficacy of each model depends on the behavior examined. In general, the TPB appears to be the strongest model with respect to the health behaviors summarized, oftentimes predicting the highest percentage of the variance in behavior. In addition, because the largest amount of research has tested the TRA/TPB compared to the other models reviewed, social psychologists have developed a clearer picture of the conditions under which the model is and is not effective.

Limitations of studies testing the models and limitations of the models themselves make it difficult to determine the overall usefulness of social models of health behavior. The majority of studies are cross-sectional in nature, and findings of prospective studies tend to be much weaker than findings of cross-sectional research. In addition, the ability to draw conclusions concerning overall effectiveness of the models is hindered by inconsistencies between studies in the way that health behaviors are operationalized and by the lack of relevant control groups. The models are too narrow to sufficiently account for the complex interplay in social, biological, and psychological factors involved in most health behaviors. In particular, a number of variables have been shown to be stronger predictors of behavior than those included in the health models. With regard to smoking, addiction variables appear to account for the majority of the variance in smoking behavior (Farkas, Pierce, Zhu, et al., 1996; Schmid & Gmel, 1999), with social psychological variables accounting for relatively little variance in addition to addiction variables. Similarly, controlling for past condom use greatly decreases the relations between the components of the models and current or future condom use (e.g., Ross & McLaws, 1992).

Shortcomings of each model also limit their effectiveness at predicting behavior. Although the TPB appears to be the most appropriate model for predicting condom use, exercise, and diet, it is limited in its ability to predict addictive behaviors, such as smoking. In addition, although the relative importance of each of the key variables of the TPB varies between studies and behaviors, attitudes and perceived behavioral control typically account for a larger amount of health behaviors than do subjective norms. Several researchers have called for an expansion in the conceptualization of norms, for example, to include peer pressure as well as the traditional operationalization of perceived desire of important others (e.g., Grube et al., 1986). Moreover, some specific subjective norms, such as those of one's sex partner, may be more appropriate to study than others for some health behaviors, such as condom use. Thus, researchers who break down the subjective norms construct into its specific parts may find greater predictive success with this variable.

The majority of studies examining dimensions of the HBM have found it consistently useful for explaining and predicting health behaviors. With regard to predicting both preventive health and sick role behaviors, comparisons across studies have suggested that perceived barriers are the most powerful predictors of health behaviors, followed by perceived benefits, perceived susceptibility, and perceived severity (Janz & Becker, 1984). However, there are a number of conditions that may not be accounted for by the model. The HBM is a psychosocial model and therefore is limited in its ability to explain behaviors that are not associated with people's attitudes and beliefs (Janz & Becker, 1984). The habitual aspects of some health behaviors (e.g., smoking) may overshadow the influence of attitudes and beliefs, making the HBM less effective at predicting habitual behaviors. In addition, the model is based on the idea that health is highly valued and that health-related behaviors are undertaken to improve health. However, a number of health-related behaviors may be undertaken for nonhealth reasons (e.g., appearance, peer pressure), and health may not be equally valued by all persons. One difficulty in assessing the usefulness of the HBM at predicting behavior stems from the fact that most studies do not examine the effectiveness of the entire HBM but rather examine individual components of the HBM.

The transtheoretical model most adequately predicts smoking cessation behavior versus the other health behaviors reviewed. When used as a singular predictor it accounts for a large amount of variance in smoking behavior, but adding measures of addiction into the model greatly decreases or eliminates its predictive ability. A number of other predictions of the model are not consistently supported, and critics have noted limitations that may explain some of the contradictory findings. Sutton (1996) has suggested that the SOC model imposes artificial categorization on what is actually a continuous process. In addition, the time frames (e.g., six months) stated in the definitions of the stages appear arbitrary (Herzog et al., 1999). A number of investigators have criticized the precontemplative category as including too wide a range of individuals (Dijkstra, Bakker, & De Vries, 1997; Farkas, Pierce, Zhu, et al., 1996). Because the behavior of someone who never intends to change differs dramatically from that of someone who might consider quitting changing a behavior, these investigators have suggested breaking down the precontemplative stage into substages.

Given that even successful applications of the models have not been able to explain more than 50% of the variance in health behavior, there are a number of directions for future research. Most important, researchers need to focus on developing valid measures of health behavior and on using these measures to test the efficacy of the models over time, to take into account the complex and longitudinal nature of health behavior. With the recent advent of more sophisticated multilevel approaches to statistical analysis, such as hierarchical linear modeling (HLM; Bryk & Raudenbush, 1992; Raudenbush, Bryk, Cheong, & Congdon, 2000), researchers can analyze large amounts of longitudinal data, gleaned for example, from coital, exercise, food intake, and smoking logs. Unlike ordinary least-squares regression and repeated-measures analysis of variance, HLM can handle unbalanced designs, such as diary data, in which there are unequal numbers of observations per participant. Thus, researchers using this technique can test whether the models sufficiently account for repeated health behaviors at more than one or two time points, and thus can test the utility of the model in predicting a more realistic and valid set of behaviors.

Researchers also need to expand their definitions of the health behaviors reviewed to include preparatory behaviors, as well as several different manifestations of each type of behavior. For example, it has been argued that preparatory behaviors—condom buying, condom availability, and discussion of condom use with sexual partners—are mediators of the effects of psychosocial variables (e.g., attitudes) on condom use behavior (Sheeran, Abraham, & Orbell, 1999). Thus, individuals who are too embarrassed to buy condoms may never be able to actually use condoms; however, this construct is missing from most models of health behavior. In addition, all of the health behaviors discussed can be operationalized in different ways, and researchers should include more than one operationalization when testing models. Food intake behavior can be thought of, for instance, as the decision to eat low fat foods, the decision to avoid certain kinds of high fat foods, or the decision to eat more vegetables. An individual may practice all three of these behaviors or may practice only one or two, and researchers will miss key food intake behaviors by focusing only on one of them. Likewise, safer sex encompasses a range of behaviors such as increasing condom use, decreasing numbers of sexual partners, practicing abstinence, or engaging in less risky behaviors. A breadth of behaviors, as well as the choices that individuals make among behaviors, must be examined for a valid assessment of each model in predicting health behavior and, ultimately, health outcomes.

Finally, to more fully understand and predict behavior, it is necessary to take a broader view of behavior and incorporate environmental and biological–genetic factors into health models. The interplay of situational, environmental, and person factors has been examined in a number of more recently developed models such as the theory of triadic influence (Flay & Petraitis, 1994) and the biopsychosocial models reviewed in chapter 2. However, more research is needed to determine whether interactionist models incorporating a number of variables are more effective at predicting behavior and whether they provide a better means of devising interventions than the social psychological models reviewed in this chapter.

REFERENCES

Abraham, C., Sheeran, P., & Orbell, S. (1998). Can social cognitive models contribute to the effectiveness of HIV-preventive behavioural interventions? A brief review of the literature and a reply to Joffe (1996; 1997) and Fife-Schaw (1997) [comment]. *British Journal of Medical Psychology, 71*, 297–310.

Abraham, C., Sheeran, P., Spears, R., & Abrams, D. (1992). Health beliefs and promotion of HIV-preventive intentions among teenagers: A Scottish perspective. *Health Psychology, 11*, 363–370.

Adih, W. K., & Alexander, C. S. (1999). Determinants of condom use to prevent HIV infection among youth in Ghana. *Journal of Adolescent Health, 24*, 63–72.

Adler, N. E., Kegeles, S. M., Irwin, C. E., Jr., & Wibbelsman, C. (1990). Adolescent contraceptive behavior: An assessment of decision processes. *Journal of Pediatrics, 116*, 463–471.

Ahijevych, K., & Parsley, L. A. (1999). Smoke constituent exposure and stage of change in black and white women cigarette smokers. *Addictive Behaviors, 24*, 115–120.

Ajzen, I. (1985). From intentions to actions: A theory of planned behavior. In J. Kuhl & J. Beckman (Eds.), *Action-control: From cognition to behavior* (pp. 11–31). Heidelberg, Germany: Springer.

Ajzen, I., & Fishbein, M. (1980). *Understanding attitudes and predicting social behavior*. Englewood Cliffs, NJ: Prentice-Hall.

Albarracin, D., Johnson, B. T., Fishbein, M., & Muellerleile, P. A. (2001). Theories of reasoned action and planned behavior as models of condom use: A meta-analysis. *Psychological Bulletin, 127*, 142–161.

American Cancer Society. (1998). *Cancer facts and figures 1998: Tobacco use*. Atlanta, GA: Author.

American College of Sports Medicine. (1993). Physical activity, physical fitness, and hypertension. *Medicine and Science in Sport and Exercise, 25*, i–x.

Anderson, J. E., Cheney, R., Faruque, S., Long, A., Toomey, K., & Wiebel, W. (1996). Stages of change for HIV risk behavior: Injecting drug users in five cities. In R. T. Trotter II (Ed.), *Multicultural AIDS prevention programs* (pp. 1–17). New York: Hayworth Press.

Aspinwall, L. G., Kemeny, M. E., Taylor, S. E., Schneider, S. G., & Dudley, W. N. (1991). Psychosocial predictors of gay men's AIDS risk-reduction behavior. *Health Psychology, 10*, 432–444.

Baker, S. A., Morrison, D. M., Carter, W. B., & Verdon, M. S. (1996). Using the theory of reasoned action (TRA) to understand the decision to use condoms in an STD clinic population. *Health Education Quarterly, 23*, 528–542.

Bakker, A. B., Buunk, B. P., Siero, F. W., & Van Den Eijnden, R. J. J. M. (1997). Application of a modified health belief model to HIV preventive behavioral intentions among gay and bisexual men. *Psychology and Health, 12*, 481–492.

Baldwin, J. D., & Baldwin, J. I. (1988). Factors affecting AIDS-related sexual risk-taking behavior among college students. *Journal of Sex Research, 25,* 181–196.

Bandura, A. (1977a). Self-efficacy: Toward a unifying theory of behavioral change. *Psychological Review, 84,* 191–215.

Bandura, A. (1977b). *Social learning theory.* Englewood Cliffs, NJ: Prentice-Hall.

Bandura, A. (1986). *Social foundations of thought and action: A social cognitive theory.* Englewood Cliffs, NJ: Prentice-Hall.

Bandura, A. (1992). A social cognitive approach to the exercise of control over AIDS infection. In R. J. DiClemente (Ed.), *Adolescents and AIDS: A generation in jeopardy* (pp. 89–116). London: Sage.

Bartecchi, C., Mackenzie, T., & Schrier, R. (1994). The human cost of tobacco use. *New England Journal of Medicine, 330,* 907–913.

Basen-Engquist, K. (1992). Psychosocial predictors of "safer sex" behaviors in young adults. *AIDS Education and Prevention, 4,* 120–134.

Basen-Engquist, K., & Parcel, G. S. (1992). Attitudes, norms, and self-efficacy: A model of adolescents' HIV-related sexual risk behavior. *Health Education Quarterly, 19,* 263–277.

Becker, M. H., Maiman, L. A., Kirscht, J. P., Haefner, D. P., & Drachman, R. H. (1977). The health belief model and prediction of dietary compliance: A field experiment. *Journal of Health and Social Behavior, 18,* 348–366.

Bennett, P., & Bozionelos, G. (2000). The theory of planned behavior as predictor of condom use: A narrative review. *Psychology, Health, and Medicine, 5,* 307–326.

Bennett, P., & Clatworthy, J. (1999). Smoking cessation during pregnancy: Testing a psycho-biological model. *Psychology, Health, and Medicine, 4,* 319–326.

Berlin, J. A., & Colditz, G. A. (1990). A meta-analysis of physical activity in the prevention of coronary heart disease. *American Journal of Epidemiology, 132,* 612–628.

Biddle, S. J. H., & Nigg, C. R. (2000). Theories of exercise behavior. *International Journal of Sports Psychology, 31,* 290–304.

Blair, S. N., Kohl, H. W., Paffenbarger, R. S., Clark, D. G., Cooper, K. H., & Gibbons, L. W. (1989). Physical fitness and all-cause mortality: A prospective study in healthy men and women. *Journal of the American Medical Association, 262,* 2395–2401.

Blue, C. L. (1995). The predictive capacity of the theory of reasoned action and the theory of planned behavior in exercise research: An integrated literature review. *Research in Nursing and Health, 18,* 105–121.

Bogart, L. M., Cecil, H., & Pinkerton, S. D. (2000). Intentions to use the female condom among African American women. *Journal of Applied Social Psychology, 30,* 1923–1953.

Boldero, J., Sanitioso, R., & Brain, B. (1999). Gay Asian Australians' safer-sex behavior and behavioral skills: The predictive utility of the theory of planned behavior and cultural factors. *Journal of Applied Social Psychology, 29,* 2143–2163

Bowen, A. M. (1996). Predicting increased condom use with main partners: Potential approaches to intervention. In R. T. Trotter II (Ed.), *Multicultural AIDS prevention programs* (pp. 57–74). New York: Hayworth Press.

Bowen, A. M., & Trotter, R. II. (1995). HIV risk in intravenous drug use and crack cocaine smokers: Predicting stages of change for condom use. *Journal of Consulting and Clinical Psychology, 63,* 238–248.

Bowen, D. J., Meischke, H., & Tomoyasu, N. (1994). Preliminary evaluation of the process of changing to a low-fat diet. *Health Education Research, 9,* 85–94.

Boyd, B., & Wandersman, A. (1991). Predicting undergraduate condom use with the Fishbein and Ajzen and Triandis attitude–behavior models: Implications for public health interventions. *Journal of Applied Social Psychology, 21,* 1810–1830.

Bozionelos, G., & Bennett, P. (1999). The theory of planned behavior as predictor of exercise. *Journal of Health Psychology, 4,* 517–529.

Brenes, G. A., Strube, M. J., & Storandt, M. (1998). An application of the theory of planned behavior to exercise among older adults. *Journal of Applied Social Psychology, 28,* 2274–2290.

Brien, T. M., Thombs, D. L., Mahoney, C. A., & Wallnau, L. (1994). Dimensions of self-efficacy among three distinct groups of condom users. *Journal of American College Health, 42,* 167–174.

Brownson, R. C., Jackson-Thompson, J., Wilkerson, J. C., Davis, J. R., Owens, N. W., & Fisher, E. B. (1992). Demographic and socioeconomic differences in beliefs about the health effects of smoking. *American Journal of Public Health, 82,* 99–103.

Brug, J., Glanz, K., & Kok, G. (1997). The relationship between self-efficacy, attitudes, intake compared to others, consumption, and stages of change related to fruit and vegetables. *American Journal of Health Promotion, 12,* 25–30.

Brug, J., Hospers, H. J., & Kok, G. (1997). Differences in psychosocial factors and fat consumption between stages of change for fat reduction. *Psychology and Health, 12,* 719–727.

Brunner, E., White, I., Thorogood, M., Bristow, A., Curle, D., & Marmot, M. (1997). Can dietary interventions change diet and cardiovascular risk factors? A meta-analysis of randomized controlled trials. *American Journal of Public Health, 87,* 1415–1422.

Brunswick, A. F., & Banaszak-Holl, J. (1996). HIV risk behavior and the health belief model: An empirical test in an African American community sample. *Journal of Community Psychology, 24,* 44–65.

Bryk, A. S., & Raudenbush, S. W. (1992). *Hierarchical linear models: Applications and data analysis methods.* Newbury Park, CA: Sage.

Budd, R. J. (1986). Predicting cigarette use: The need to incorporate measures of salience in the theory of reasoned action. *Journal of Applied Social Psychology, 16,* 663–685.

Burke, B., Richards, J., Milligan, R. A. K., Beilin, L. J., Dunbar, D., & Gracey, M. P. (2000). Stages of change for health-related behaviours in 18-year-old Australians. *Psychology and Health, 14,* 1061–1075.

Burn, G. E., Naylor, P., & Page, A. (1999). Assessment of stages of change for exercise within a worksite lifestyle screening program. *American Journal of Health Promotion, 13,* 143–145.

Campbell, M. K., Tessaro, I., DeVellis, B., Benedict, S., Kelsey, K., Belton, L., et al. (2000). Tailoring and targeting a worksite health promotion program to address multiple health behaviors among blue-collar women. *American Journal of Health Promotion, 14,* 306–313.

Cardinal, B. J., (1997). Construct validity of stages of change for exercise behavior. *American Journal of Health Promotion, 12,* 68–74.

Catania, J. A., Coates, T. J., Kegeles, S. Fulilove, M. T., Peterson, J., Marin, B., et al. (1992). Condom use in multi-ethnic neighborhoods of San Francisco: The population-based AMEN (AIDS in multi-ethnic neighborhoods) study. *American Journal of Public Health, 82,* 284–287.

Cates, W., Jr. (1991). Teenagers and sexual risk taking: The best of times and the worst of times. *Journal of Adolescent Health, 12,* 84–94.

Centers for Disease Control and Prevention (CDC). (1993). Update: Barrier protection against HIV infection and other sexually transmitted diseases. *Morbidity and Mortality Weekly Report, 42,* 589–596.

Centers for Disease Control and Prevention (CDC). (2000). *Sexually transmitted disease surveillance, 1999.* Atlanta: Department of Health and Human Services, Division of STD Prevention.

Centers for Disease Control and Prevention (CDC). (2001). *HIV/AIDS surveillance report, 12*(2), 1–48.

Chan, K. S., & Fishbein, M. (1993). Determinants of college women's intentions to tell their partners to use condoms. *Journal of Applied Social Psychology, 23,* 1455–1470.

Chassin, L., Corty, E., Presson, C. C., Olshavsky, R. W., Bensenberg, M., & Sherman, R. J. (1981). Predicting adolescents' intentions to smoke cigarettes. *Journal of Health and Social Behavior, 22,* 445–455.

Chassin, L., Presson C. C., Sherman, S., Corty, E., & Olshavsky, R. W. (1984). Predicting the onset of cigarette smoking: A longitudinal study. *Journal of Applied Social Psychology, 14,* 224–243.

Chassin, L., Presson, C. C., Sherman, S. J., Montello, D., & McGrew, J. (1986). Changes in peer and parent influence during adolescence: Longitudinal versus cross-sectional perspectives on smoking intention. *Developmental Psychology, 22,* 327–324.

Collins, C., Kohler, C., DiClemente, R. & Wang, M. Q. (1999). Evaluation of the exposure effects of a theory-based street outreach HIV intervention on African American drug users. *Evaluation and Program Planning, 22,* 279–293.

Conner, M., & Armitage, C. J. (1998). Extending the theory of planned behavior: A review and avenues for future research. *Journal of Applied Social Psychology, 28,* 1429–1464.

Conner, M., Graham, S., & Moore, B. (1999). Alcohol and intentions to use condoms: Applying the theory of planned behaviour. *Psychology and Health, 14,* 795–812.

Conner, M., Martin, E., Silverdale, N., & Grogan, S. (1996). Dieting in adolescence: An application of the theory of planned behavior. *British Journal of Health Psychology, 1,* 315–325.

Conrad, K. M., Campbell, R. T., Edington, D. W., Faust, H. S., & Vilnius, D. (1996). The worksite environment as a cue to smoking reduction. *Research in Nursing and Health, 19,* 21–31.

Contento, I. R., & Murphy, B. M. (1990). Psycho-social factors differentiating people who reported making desirable changes in their diets from those who did not. *Journal of Nutrition Education, 22,* 6–13.

Corby, N. H., Schneider-Jamner, M., & Wolitski, R. J. (1996). Using the theory of planned behavior to predict intention to use condoms among male and female injecting drug users. *Journal of Applied Social Psychology, 26,* 52–75.

Corwyn, R. F., & Benda, B. B. (1999). Examination of an integrated theoretical model of exercise behavior. *American Journal of Health Behavior, 23,* 381–392.

Courneya, K. S. (1995). Understanding readiness for regular physical activity in older individuals: An application of the theory of planned behavior. *Health Psychology, 14,* 80–87.

Courneya, K. S., Bobick, T. M., & Schinke, R. J. (1999). Does the theory of planned behavior mediate the relation between personality and exercise behavior? *Basic and Applied Social Psychology, 21,* 317–324.

Courneya, K. S., & Friedenrich, C. M. (1997). Determinants of exercise during colorectal cancer treatment: An application of the theory of planned behavior. *Oncology Nursing Forum, 24,* 1715–1723.

Courneya, K. S., & Friedenrich, C. M. (1999). Utility of the theory of planned behavior for understanding exercise during breast cancer treatment. *Psycho-oncology, 8,* 112–122.

Courneya, K. S., Friedenrich, C. M., Arthur, K., & Bobick, T. M. (1999). Understanding exercise motivation in colorectal cancer patients: A prospective study using the theory of planned behavior. *Rehabilitation Psychology, 44,* 68–84.

Courneya, K. S., Keats, M. R., & Turner, R. (2000). Social cognitive determinants of hospital-based exercise following high-dose chemotherapy and bone marrow transplant. *International Journal of Behavioral Medicine, 7,* 189–203.

Courneya, K. S., Plotnikoff, R. C., Hotz, S. B., & Birkett, N. J. (2000). Social support and the theory of planned behavior in the exercise domain. *American Journal of Health Behavior, 24,* 300–308.

Craig, S., Goldberg, J., & Dietz, W. H. (1996). Psychosocial correlates of physical activity among fifth and eight graders. *Preventive Medicine, 25,* 506–513.

Croog, S. H., & Richards, N . (1977). Health beliefs and smoking patterns in heart patients and their wives: A longitudinal study. *American Journal of Public Health, 67,* 921–930.

Curry, S. J., Kristal, A. R., & Bowen, D. J. (1992). An application of the stage model of behavior change to dietary fat reduction. *Health Education Research, 7,* 97–105.

DiClemente, C. C. (1986). Self-efficacy and the addictive behaviors. *Journal of Social and Clinical Psychology, 4,* 302–315.

DiClemente, C. C., Prochaska, J. O., Fairhurst, S. K., Velicer, W. F., Velasquez, M. M., & Rossi, J. S. (1991). The process of smoking cessation: An analysis of precontemplation, contemplation, and preparation stages of change. *Journal of Consulting and Clinical Psychology, 59,* 295–304.

Dijkstra, A., Bakker, M., & De Vries, H. (1997). Subtypes within a sample of precontemplating smokers: A preliminary extension of the stages of change. *Addictive Behaviors, 22,* 327–337.

Dijkstra, A., De Vries, H., Roijackers, J., & van Breukelen, G. (1998). Tailored interventions to communicate stage-matched information to smokers in different motivational stages. *Journal of Consulting and Clinical Psychology, 66,* 549–557.

Dittus, K. L., Hilers, V. N., & Beerman, K. A. (1993). Attitudes and behaviors about pesticide residues, susceptibility to cancer, and consumption of fruits and vegetables. *Journal of Nutrition Education, 25,* 245–250.

Eng, T. R., & Butler, W. T. (Eds.). (1997). *The hidden epidemic: Confronting sexually transmitted diseases.* Washington, DC: Institute of Medicine, National Academy Press.

Etter, J., & Perneger, T. V. (1999). Associations between the stages of change and the pros and cons of smoking in a longitudinal study of Swiss smokers. *Addictive Behaviors, 24,* 419–424.

Evers, K. E., Harlow, L. L., Redding, C. A., & LaForge, R. G. (1998). Longitudinal changes in stages of change for condom use in women. *American Journal of Health Promotion, 13,* 19–25.

Farkas, A. J., Pierce, J. P., Gilpin, E. A., Zhu, S. H., Rosbrook, B., Berry, C., et al. (1996). Is stage of change a useful measure of the likelihood of smoking cessation? *Annals of Behavioral Medicine, 18,* 79–86.

Farkas, A. J., Pierce, J. P., Zhu, S. H., Rosbrook, B., Gilpin, E. A., Berry, C., et al. (1996). Addiction versus stages of change models in predicting smoking cessation. *Addiction, 91,* 1271–1280.

Fava, J. L., Velicer, W. F., & Prochaska, J. O. (1995). Applying the transtheoretical model to a representative sample of smokers. *Addictive Behaviors, 20,* 189–203.

Fishbein, M., & Ajzen, I. (1975). *Belief, attitude, intention, and behavior: An introduction to theory and research.* Reading, MA: Addison-Wesley.

Fishbein, M., Middlestadt, S. E., & Trafimow, D. (1993). Social norms for condom use: Implications for HIV prevention intervention of a KABP survey with heterosexuals in the eastern Caribbean. *Advances in Consumer Research, 20,* 292–296.

Fisher, J. D., & Fisher, W. A. (1992). Changing AIDS-risk behavior. *Psychological Bulletin, 111,* 455–474.

Fisher, J. D., & Fisher, W. A. (2000). Theoretical approaches to individual-level change in HIV risk behavior. In J. L. Peterson & R. J. DiClemente (Eds.), *Handbook of HIV prevention* (pp. 3–55). New York: Plenum Press.

Fisher, W. A., Fisher, J. D., & Rye, B. J. (1995). Understanding and promoting AIDS-preventive behavior: Attitude-behavior correspondence. *Health Psychology, 14,* 255–264.

Flay, B. R., & Petraitis, J. (1994). The theory of triadic influences: A new theory of health behavior with implications for preventive interventions. *Advances in Medical Sociology, 4,* 19–44.

Ford, K., & Norris, A. E. (1995). Factors related to condom use with casual partners among urban African-American and Hispanic males. *AIDS Education & Prevention, 7,* 494–503.

Galavotti, C., Cabral, R. J., Lansky, A., Grimley, D. M., Riley, G. E., & Prochaska, J. O. (1995). Validation of measures of condom and other contraceptive use among women at high risk for HIV infection and unintended pregnancy. *Health Psychology, 14,* 570–578.

Gerrard, M., Gibbons, F. X., & Bushman, B. J. (1996). Relation between perceived vulnerability to HIV and precautionary sexual behavior. *Psychological Bulletin, 119,* 390–409.

Glanz, K., Patterson, R. E., Kristal, A. R., DiClemente, C. C., Heimendinger, J., Linnan, L., et al. (1994). Stages of change in adopting healthy diets: Fat, fiber, and correlates of nutrient intake. *Health Education Quarterly, 21,* 499–519.

Godin, G. (1993). The theories of reasoned action and planned behavior: Overview of findings, emerging research problems and usefulness for exercise promotion. *Journal of Applied Sport Psychology, 5,* 141–157.

Godin, G., Jobin, J., & Bouillon, J. (1986). Assessment of leisure time exercise behavior by self-report: A concurrent validity study. *Canadian Journal of Public Health, 77,* 359–361.

Godin, G., & Kok, G. (1996). The theory of planned behavior: A review of its application to health-related behaviors. *American Journal of Health Promotion, 11,* 87–98.

Godin, G., & LePage, L. (1988). Understanding the intentions of pregnant nullipara to not smoke cigarettes after childbirth. *Journal of Drug Education, 18,* 115–124.

Godin, G., Savard, J., Kok, G., Fortin, C., & Boyer, R. (1996). HIV seropositive gay men: Understanding adoption of safe sexual practices. *AIDS Education and Prevention, 8,* 529–545.

Godin, G., & Shepard, R. J. (1985). A simple method to assess exercise behavior in the community. *Canadian Journal of Applied Sport Science, 10,* 141–146.

Godin, G., Valois, P., Lepage, L., & Desharnais, R. (1992). Predictors of smoking behaviour: An application of Ajzen's theory of planned behaviour. *British Journal of Addiction, 87*, 1335–1343.

Goldman, J. A., & Harlow, L. L. (1993). Self-perception variables that mediate AIDS-preventive behavior in college students. *Health Psychology, 12*, 489–498.

Gottlieb, N. H., Gingliss, P. L., & Weinstein, R. P. (1992). Attitudes, subjective norms and models of use for smokeless tobacco among college athletes: Implications for prevention and cessation programming. *Health Education Research, 7*, 359–368.

Greenwald, P., Sondik, E., & Lynch, B. S. (1986). Diet and chemoprevention in NCI's research strategy to achieve national cancer control objectives. *Annual Review of Public Health, 14*, 515–543.

Grimley, D. M., & Lee, P. A. (1997). Condom and other contraceptive use among a random sample of female adolescents: A snapshot in time. *Adolescence, 32*, 771–779.

Grimley, D. M., Prochaska, G. E., & Prochaska, J. O. (1997). Condom use adoption and continuation: A transtheoretical approach. *Health Education Research, 12*, 61–75.

Grimley, D. M., Prochaska, J. O., Velicer, W. F., & Prochaska, G. E. (1995). Contraceptive and condom use adoption and maintenance: A stage paradigm approach. *Health Education Quarterly, 22*, 20–35.

Grimley, D. M., Riley, G. E., Bellis, J. M., & Prochaska, J. O. (1993). Assessing the stages of change and decision-making for contraceptive use for the prevention of pregnancy, sexually transmitted diseases, and acquired immunodeficiency syndrome. *Health Education Quarterly, 20*, 455–470.

Grube, J. W., Morgan, M., & McGee, S. T. (1986). Attitudes and normative beliefs as predictors of smoking intentions and behaviours: A test of three models. *British Journal of Social Psychology, 25*, 81–93.

Grunberg, N. E., Faraday, M. M., & Rahman, M. A. (2001). The psychobiology of nicotine self-administration. In A. Baum, T. Revenson, & J. Singer (Eds.), *Handbook of health psychology*. Mahwah, NJ: Erlbaum.

Hagdrup, N. A., Simoes, E. J., & Brownson, R. C. (1998). Fruit and vegetable consumption in Missouri: Knowledge, barriers, and benefits. *American Journal of Health Behavior, 22*, 90–100.

Hamilton, G., Cross, D., & Resnicow, K. (2000). Occasional cigarette smokers: Cue for harm reduction smoking education. *Addiction Research, 8*, 419–437.

Hanson, M. J. S. (1997). The theory of planned behavior applied to cigarette smoking in African-American, Puerto Rican, and non-Hispanic White teenage females. *Nursing Research, 46*, 155–162.

Harlow, L. L., Prochaska, J. O., Redding, C. A., Rossi, J. S., Velicer, W. F., Snow, M. G., et al. (1999). Stages of condom use in a high HIV-risk sample. *Psychology and Health, 14*, 143–157.

Hausenblas, H. A., Carron, A. V., & Mack, D. E. (1997). Application of the theories of reasoned action and planned behavior to exercise behavior: A meta-analysis. *Journal of Sport and Exercise Psychology, 19,* 36–51.

Hayes, D., & Ross, D. E. (1987). Concern with appearance, health beliefs, and eating habits. *Journal of Health and Social Behavior, 28,* 120–130.

Heinrich, L. B. (1993). Contraceptive self-efficacy in college women. *Journal of Adolescent Health, 14,* 269–276.

Herzog, T. A., Abrams, D. B., Emmons, K. M., Linnan, L. A., & Shadel, W. G. (1999). Do processes of change predict smoking stage movements? A prospective analysis of the transtheoretical model. *Health Psychology, 18,* 369–375.

Hu, S., & Lanese, R. R. (1998). The applicability of the theory of planned behavior to the intention to quit smoking across workplaces in southern Taiwan. *Addictive Behaviors, 23,* 225–237.

Ingledew, D. K., Markland, D., & Medley, A. R. (1998). Exercise motives and stages of change. *Journal of Health Psychology, 3,* 477–489.

Jacobs, D. R., Slavin, J., & Marquart, L. (1995). Whole grain intake and cancer: A review of the literature. *Nutrition and Cancer, 24,* 221–229.

Janis, I. L., & Mann, L. (1977). *Decision-making: A psychological analysis of conflict, choice, and commitment.* London: Cassel & Collier Macmillan.

Janz, N. K., & Becker, M. H. (1984). The health belief model: A decade later. *Health Education Quarterly, 11,* 1–47.

Jemmott, J. B. III., Jemmott, L. S., Spears, H., Hewitt, N., & Cruz-Collins, M. (1992). Self-efficacy, hedonistic expectancies, and condom-use intentions among inner-city black adolescent women: A social cognitive approach to AIDS risk behavior. *Journal of Adolescent Health, 13,* 512–519.

Jemmott, L. S., & Jemmott, J. B. III. (1991). Applying the theory of reasoned action to AIDS risk behavior: Condom use among black women. *Nursing Research, 40,* 228–234.

Joffe, A., & Radius, S. M. (1993). Self-efficacy and intent to use condoms among entering college freshmen. *Journal of Adolescent Health, 14,* 262–268.

Kanvil, N., & Umeh, K. F. (2000). Lung cancer and cigarette use: Cognitive factors, protection motivation and past behavior. *British Journal of Health Psychology, 5,* 235–248.

Kasen, S., Vaughan, R. D., & Walter, H. J. (1992). Self-efficacy for AIDS preventive behaviors among tenth grade students. *Health Education Quarterly, 19,* 187–202.

Kashima, Y., Gallois, C., & McCamish, M. (1993). The theory of reasoned action and cooperative behavior: It takes two to use a condom. *British Journal of Social Psychology, 32,* 227–239.

Kaufert, J. M., Rabkin, S. W., Syrotuik, J., Boyko, E., & Shane, F. (1986). Health beliefs as predictors of success of alternate modalities of smoking cessation: Results of a controlled trial. *Journal of Behavioral Medicine, 9,* 475–489.

Kelly, R. B., Zyzanski, S. J., & Alemagno, S. A. (1991). Prediction of motivation and behavior change following health promotion: Role of health beliefs, social support, and self-efficacy. *Social Science and Medicine, 32,* 311–320.

Kerner, M. S., & Grossman, A. H. (1998). Attitudinal, social, and practical correlates to fitness behavior: A test of the theory of planned behavior. *Perceptual and Motor Skills, 87,* 1139–1154.

Kirscht, J. P. (1988). The health belief model and predictions of health actions. In D. S. Gochman (Ed.), *Health behavior: Emerging research perspectives* (pp. 27–42). New York: Plenum Press.

Kowalewski, M. R., Longshore, D., & Anglin, M. D. (1994). The AIDS risk reduction model: Examining intentions to use condoms among injection drug users. *Journal of Applied Social Psychology, 24,* 2002–2027.

Krahe, B., & Reiss, C. (1995). Predicting intentions of AIDS-preventive behavior among adolescents. *Journal of Applied Social Psychology, 25,* 2118–2140.

Lansky, A., Thomas, J. C., & Earp, J. A. (1998). Partner-specific sexual behaviors among persons with both main and other partners. *AIDS, 30,* 93–96.

Laraque, D., McLean, D. E., Brown-Peterside, P., Ashton, D., & Diamond, B. (1997). Predictors of reported condom use in central Harlem youth as conceptualized by the health belief model. *Journal of Adolescent Health, 21,* 318–327.

Lauby, J. L., Semaan, S., Cohen, A., Leviton, L., Gielen, A., Pulley, L., et al. (1998). Self-efficacy, decisional balance and stages of change for condom use among women at risk for HIV infection. *Health Education Research, 13,* 343–356.

Lerman, C., Gold, K., Audrain, J., Lin, T. H., Boyd, N. R., Orleans, C. T., et al. (1997). Incorporating biomarkers of exposure and genetic susceptibility into smoking cessation treatment: Effects on smoking-related cognitions, emotions, and behavior change. *Health Psychology, 16,* 87–99.

Linden, C., Kegeles, S., Hearst, N., Grant, P., Johnson, D., Bolan, G., et al. (1990). Heterosexual behaviors and factors that influence condom use among patients attending a sexually transmitted disease clinic—San Francisco. *Morbidity and Mortality Weekly Report, 39,* 685–689.

Ling, A. M., & Horwath, C. (1999). Self-efficacy and consumption of fruit and vegetables: Validation of a summated scale. *American Journal of Health Promotion, 13,* 290–298.

Lollis, C. M., Johnson, E. H., & Antoni, M. H. (1997). The efficacy of the health belief model for predicting condom usage and risky sexual practices in university students. *AIDS Education and Prevention, 9,* 551–563.

Lugoe, W., & Rise, J. (1999). Predicting intended condom use among Tanzanian students using the theory of planned behaviour. *Journal of Health Psychology, 4,* 497–506.

Maher, R. A., & Rickwood, D. (1997). The theory of planned behavior, domain-specific self-efficacy and adolescent smoking. *Journal of Child and Adolescent Substance Abuse, 6,* 57–76.

Mahoney, C. A, Thombs, D. L., & Ford, O. J. (1995). Health belief and self-efficacy models: Their utility in explaining college student condom use. *AIDS Education & Prevention, 7*, 32–49.

Malow, R. M., Corrigan, S. A., Cunningham, S. C., & West, J. A. (1993). Psychosocial factors associated with condom use among African-American drug abusers in treatment. *AIDS Education and Prevention, 5*, 244–253.

Manfredi, C., Lacey, L. P., Warnecke, R., & Petraitis, J. (1998). Sociopsychological correlates of motivation to quit smoking among low-SES African American women. *Health Education and Behavior, 25*, 304–318.

Marcus, B. H., & Simkin, L. R. (1993). The stages of exercise behavior. *Journal of Sports Medicine and Physical Fitness, 33*, 83–88.

Marin, B. V., Marin, G., Perez-Stable, E. J., Otero-Sabogal, R., & Sabogal, F. (1990). Cultural differences in attitudes toward smoking: Developing messages using the theory of reasoned action. *Journal of Applied Social Psychology, 20*, 478–493.

Marshall, P. (1990). "Just one more . . . !" A study into the smoking attitudes and behavior of patients following first myocardial infarction. *International Journal of Nursing Studies, 4*, 375–387.

Matarazzo, J. D. (1982). Behavioral health's challenge to academic, scientific, and professional psychology. *American Psychologist, 37*, 1–14.

McBride, D. C., Weatherby, N. L., Inciardi, J. A., & Gillespie, S. A. (1999). AIDS susceptibility in a migrant population: Perception and behavior. *Substance Use and Misuse, 34*, 633–652.

McCusker, J., Zapka, J. G., Stoddard, A. M., & Mayer, K. H. (1989). Responses to the AIDS epidemic among homosexually active men: Factors associated with preventive behavior. *Patient Education and Counseling, 13*, 15–30.

Mermelstein, R. J. (1997). Individual interventions: Stages of change and other health behavior models—The example of smoking cessation. In S. J. Gallant & G. P. Keita (Eds.), *Health care for women: Psychological, social, and behavioral influences* (pp. 387–403). Washington, DC: American Psychological Association.

Miilunpalo, S., Nupponen, R., Laitakari, J., Marttila, J., & Paronen, O. (2000). Stages of change in two modes of health-enhancing activity: Methodological aspects and promotional implications. *Health Education Research, 15*, 435–448.

Montgomery, S. B., Joseph, J. G., Becker, M. H., Ostrow, D. G., Kessler, R. C., & Kirschti, J. P. (1989). The health belief model in understanding compliance with preventive recommendations for AIDS: How useful? *AIDS Education and Prevention, 1*, 303–323.

Morrison, D. M., Gillmore, M. R., & Baker, S. A. (1995). Determinants of condom use among high-risk heterosexual adults: A test of the theory of reasoned action. *Journal of Applied Social Psychology, 25*, 651–676.

Morrison, D. M., Gillmore, M. R., Simpson, E. E., Wells, E. A., & Hoppe, M. J. (1996). Children's decisions about substance use: An application and extension of the theory of reasoned action. *Journal of Applied Social Psychology, 26*, 1658–1679.

Mullan, E., & Markland, D. (1997). Variations in self-determination across the stages of change for exercise in adults. *Motivation and Emotion, 21*, 349–362.

Mullen, P. D., Hersey, J. C., & Iverson, D. C. (1987). Health behavior models compared. *Social Science and Medicine, 24*, 973–981.

Myers, R. S., & Roth, D. L. (1997). Perceived benefits of and barriers to exercise and stage of exercise adoption in young adults. *Health Psychology, 16*, 277–283.

National Centers for Chronic Disease Prevention and Health Promotion. (1996). *Physical activity and health: A report of the surgeon general* (S/N 017-023-00196-5). Atlanta, GA: Author.

Neff, J. A., & Crawford, S. L. (1998). The health belief model and HIV risk behaviors: A causal model analysis among Anglos, African-Americans, and Mexican-Americans. *Ethnicity and Health, 3*, 283–299.

Newcomb, M. D., Wyatt, G. E., Romero, G. J., Tucker, M. B., Wayment, H. A., Carmona, J. V., et al. (1998). Acculturation, sexual risk taking, and HIV health promotion among Latinas. *Journal of Counseling Psychology, 45*, 454–467.

Nguyet, N. M., Beland, F., & Otis, J. (1998). Is the intention to quit smoking influenced by other heart-healthy lifestyle habits in 30- to 60-year-old men? *Addictive Behaviors, 23*, 23–30.

Nigg, C. R., Burbank, P. M., Padula, C., Dufresne, R., Rossi, J. S., Velicer, W. F., et al. (1999). Stages of change across ten health risk behaviors for older adults. *Gerontologist, 39*, 473–482.

Norman, P., Conner, M., & Bell, R. (1999). The theory of planned behavior and smoking cessation. *Health Psychology, 18*, 89–94.

Norman, P., Conner, M., & Bell, R. (2000). The theory of planned behavior and exercise: Evidence for the moderating role of past behavior. *British Journal of Health Psychology, 5*, 249–261.

Norman, P., Edwards, M., Fitter, M., & Gray, W. (1992). "Healthy eating" clinics in primary care: Programme intensity and patients' health beliefs. *Counseling Psychology Quarterly, 5*, 135–148.

Nyamathi, A., Stein, J. A., & Brecht, M. (1995). Psychosocial predictors of AIDS risk behavior and drug use behavior in homeless and drug addicted women of color. *Health Psychology, 14*, 265–273.

O'Callagan, F. V., Callan, V. J., & Baglioni, A. (1999). Cigarette use by adolescents: Attitude–behavior relationships. *Substance Use and Misuse, 34*, 455–468.

O'Connell, J. K., Price, J. H., Roberts, S. M., Jurs, S. G., & McKinley, R. (1985). Utilizing the health belief model to predict dieting and exercising behavior of obese and nonobese adolescents. *Health Education Quarterly, 12*, 343–351.

Office on Smoking and Health, National Center for Chronic Disease Prevention and Health Promotion, CDC. (1996). Cigarette smoking among adults— United States, 1994. *Mortality and Morbidity Weekly Report, 45*(27), 588–590.

Office of Technology Assessment. (1993). *Statement on smoking-related deaths and financial costs.* Washington, DC: U.S. Government Printing Office.

Paffenbarger, R. S., Hyde, R. T., Wing, A. L., & Hsieh, C. C. (1986). Physical activity, all-cause mortality, and longevity of college alumni. *New England Journal of Medicine, 314,* 605–613.

Paffenbarger, R. S., Hyde, R. T., Wing, A. L., Lee, I., Jung, D. L., & Kampert, J. B. (1993). The association of changes in physical-activity level and other lifestyle characteristics with mortality among men. *New England Journal of Medicine, 328,* 538–545.

Pederson, L., Wanklin, J., & Baskruilk, J. (1984). The role of health beliefs in compliance with physicians' advice to quit smoking. *Social Science and Medicine, 19,* 573–580.

Peterson, T. R., & Aldana, S. G. (1999). Improving exercise behavior: An application of the stages of change model in a worksite setting. *American Journal of Health Promotion, 13,* 229–232.

Petosa, R., & Jackson, K. (1991). Using the health belief model to predict safer sex intentions among adolescents. *Health Education Quarterly, 18,* 463–476.

Phillips, W. T., Kiernan, M., & King, A. C. (2001). The effects of physical activity on physical and mental health. In A. Baum, T. Revenson, & J. Singer (Eds.), *Handbook of health psychology.* Mahwah, NJ: Erlbaum.

Pinto, B. M., & Marcus, B. H. (1995). A stages of change approach to understanding college students' physical activity. *Journal of American College Health, 44,* 27–31.

Povey, R., Conner, M., Sparks, P., James, R., & Shepherd, R. (2000). Application of the theory of planned behaviour to dietary behaviours: Roles of perceived control and self-efficacy. *British Journal of Health Psychology, 5,* 121–139.

Prochaska, J. O. (1994). Strong and weak principles for progressing from precontemplation to action on the basis of twelve problem behaviors. *Health Psychology, 13,* 47–51.

Prochaska, J. O., & DiClemente, C. C. (1983). Stages and processes of self-change in smoking: Toward an integrative model of change. *Journal of Consulting and Clinical Psychology, 51,* 390–395.

Prochaska, J. O., & DiClemente, C. C. (1984). *The transtheoretical approach: Crossing traditional boundaries of change.* Homewood, IL: Dorsey Press.

Prochaska, J. O., & DiClemente, C. C. (1986). Toward a comprehensive model of change. In W. R. Miller & N. Heather (Eds.), *Treating addictive behaviors: Processes of change* (pp. 3–27). New York: Plenum Press.

Prochaska, J. O., DiClemente, C. C., & Norcross, J. C. (1992). In search of how people cope: Applications to addictive behaviors. *American Psychologist, 47,* 1102–1114.

Prochaska, J. O., DiClemente, C. C., Velicer, W. F., Ginpil, S. E., & Norcross, J. C. (1985). Predicting change in smoking status for self-changers. *Addictive Behaviors, 10,* 396–406.

Prochaska, J. O., DiClemente, C. C., Velicer, W. F., & Rossi, J. S. (1993). Standardized, individualized, interactive, and personalized self-help programs for smoking cessation. *Health Psychology, 12,* 399–405.

Prochaska, J. O., Velicer, W. F., Rossi, J. S., Goldstein, M. G., Marcus, B. H., Rakowski, W., et al. (1994). Stages of change and decisional balance for 12 problem behaviors. *Health Psychology, 13,* 39–46.

Quinlan, K. B., & McCaul, K. D. (2000). Matched and mismatched interventions with young adult smokers: Testing a stage theory. *Health Psychology, 19,* 165–171.

Rannie, K., & Craig, D. M. (1997). Adolescent females' attitudes, subjective norms, perceived behavioral control and intentions to use latex condoms. *Public Health Nursing, 14,* 51–57.

Ransford, H. E. (1986). Race, heart disease worry, and health protective behavior. *Social Science and Medicine, 22,* 1355–1362.

Raudenbush, S., Bryk, A., Cheong, Y. F., & Congdon, R. (2000). *HLM 5: Hierarchical linear and nonlinear modeling.* Lincolnwood, IL: Scientific Software International.

Read, M. H., Auld, G., Bock, M. A., & Bruhn, C. M. (1996). Age, dietary behaviors, and the stages of change model. *American Journal of Health Behavior, 20,* 417–424.

Reinecke, J., Schmidt, P., & Ajzen, I. (1996). Birth control versus AIDS prevention: A hierarchical model of condom use among young people. *Journal of Applied Social Psychology, 27,* 743–759.

Rhodes, F., & Malotte, C. K. (1996). Using stages of change to assess intervention readiness and outcome in modifying drug-related and sexual HIV risk behaviors of IDUs and crack users. In R. T. Trotter II (Ed.), *Multicultural AIDS prevention programs* (pp. 109–136). New York: Hayworth Press.

Richard, R., & van der Plight, J. (1991). Factors affecting condom use among adolescents. *Journal of Community and Applied Social Psychology, 1,* 105–116.

Rich-Edwards, J. W., Manson, J. E., Hennekens, C. H., & Buring, J. E. (1995). The primary prevention of coronary heart disease in women. *New England Journal of Medicine, 332,* 1758–1766.

Rimer, B. K., McBride, C. M., & Crump, C. (2001). Women's health promotion. In A. Baum, T. Revenson, & J. Singer (Eds.), *Handbook of health psychology* (519–540). Mahwah, NJ: Erlbaum.

Rose, J. S., Chassin, L., Presson, C. C., & Sherman, S. J. (1996). Demographic factors in adult smoking status: Mediating and moderating influences. *Psychology of Addictive Behaviors, 10,* 28–37.

Rosen, C. S. (2000). Integrating stage and continuum models to explain processing of exercise messages and exercise initiation among sedentary college students. *Health Psychology, 19,* 172–180.

Rosenstock, I. M. (1974). Historical origins of the health belief model. *Health Education Monographs, 2,* 328–335.

Rosenthal, D. A., Hall, C., & Moore, S. M. (1992). AIDS, adolescents, and sexual risk taking: A test of the health belief model. *Australian Psychologist, 27,* 166–171.

Ross, M. W., & McLaws, M. L. (1992). Subjective norms about condoms are better predictors of use and intentions than attitudes. *Health Education Research, 7,* 335–339.

Sacco, W. P., Rickman, R. L., Thompson, K., Levine, B., & Reed, D. L. (1993). Gender differences in AIDS-relevant condom attitudes and condom use. *AIDS Education and Prevention, 5,* 311–326.

Sands, T., Archer, J., Jr., & Puleo, S. (1998). Prevention of health risk behaviors in college students: Evaluating seven variables. *Journal of College Student Development, 39,* 331–342.

Sapp, S. G., & Jensen, H. H. (1998). An evaluation of the health belief model for predicting perceived and actual dietary quality. *Journal of Applied Social Psychology, 28,* 235–248.

Schaalma, H., Kok, G., & Peters, L. (1993). Determinants of consistent condom use by adolescents: The impact of experience of sexual intercourse. *Health Education Research, 8,* 255–269.

Schafer, R. B., Keith, P. M., & Schafer, E. (1995). Predicting fat in diets of marital partners using the health belief model. *Journal of Behavioral Medicine, 18,* 419–433.

Schmid, H., & Gmel, G. (1999). Predictors of smoking status after eight years: The interaction of stages of change and addiction variables. *Psychology and Health, 14,* 731–746.

Schneider-Jamner, M., Wolitski, R. J., & Corby, N. H. (1997). Impact of a longitudinal community HIV intervention targeting injecting drug users' stage of change for condom and bleach use. *American Journal of Health Promotion, 12,* 15–24.

Serovich, J. M., & Greene, K. (1997). Predictors of adolescent sexual risk taking behaviors which put them at risk for contracting HIV. *Journal of Youth & Adolescence, 26,* 429–444.

Sheeran, P., Abraham, C., & Orbell, S. (1999). Psychosocial correlates of heterosexual condom use: A meta-analysis. *Psychological Bulletin, 125,* 90–132.

Sheeran, P., & Orbell, S. (1998). Do intentions predict condom use? Meta-analysis and examination of six moderator variables. *British Journal of Social Psychology, 37,* 231–250.

Sheeran, P., & Taylor, S. (1999). Predicting intentions to use condoms: A meta-analysis and comparison of the theories of reasoned action and planned behavior. *Journal of Applied Social Psychology, 29,* 1624–1675.

Sibthorpe, B., Fleming, D., Tesselaar, H., & Gould, J. (1991). Needle use and sexual practices: Differences in perception of personal risk of HIV among intravenous drug users. *Journal of Drug Issues, 21,* 699–712.

Smith, R. A., & Biddle, S. J. H. (1999). Attitudes and exercise adherence: Test of the theories of reasoned action and planned behavior. *Journal of Sports Sciences, 17,* 269–281.

Sneed, C. D., & Morisky, D. E. (1998). Applying the Theory of Reasoned Action to condom use among sex workers. *Social Behavior & Personality*, *26*, 317–327.

Sorensen, G., & Pechacek, T. F. (1987). Attitudes toward smoking cessation among men and women. *Journal of Behavioral Medicine*, *10*, 129–137.

Sparks, P., Shepherd, R., Wieringa, N., & Zimmermans, N. (1995). Perceived behavioral control, unrealistic optimism, and dietary change: An exploratory study. *Appetite*, *24*, 243–255.

Stark, M. J., Tesselaar, H. M., O'Connell, A. A., Person, B., Galavotti, C., Cohen, A., et al. (1998). Psychosocial factors associated with the stages of change for condom use among women at risk for HIV and STDs: Implications for intervention development. *Journal of Consulting and Clinical Psychology*, *66*, 967–978.

Steers, W. N., Elliot, E., Nemiro, J., Ditman, D., & Oskamp, S. (1996). Health beliefs as predictors of HIV-preventive behavior and ethnic differences in prediction. *Journal of Social Psychology*, *136*, 99–110.

Steptoe, A., Doherty, S., Kerry, S., Rink, E., & Hilton, S. (2000). Sociodemographic and psychological predictors of changes in dietary fat consumption in adults with high blood cholesterol following counseling in primary care. *Health Psychology*, *19*, 411–419.

Sternfield, B. (1992). Cancer and the protective effect of physical activity: The epidemiological evidence. *Medicine and Science in Sports and Exercise*, *24*, 1195–1209.

Stevenson, H. C., Davis, G., Weber, E., Weiman, D., & Abdul-Kabir, S. (1995). HIV prevention beliefs among urban African-American youth. *Journal of Adolescent Health*, *16*, 316–323.

Strecher, V. J. & Rosenstock, I. M. (1997). The health belief model. In A. Baum, S. Newman, J. Weinman, R. West, & C. McManus (Eds.), *Cambridge handbook of psychology, health, and medicine* (pp. 113–116). New York: Cambridge University Press.

Sutton, S. (1996). Can "stages of change" provide guidance in the treatment of addictions? A critical examination of Prochaska and DiClemente's model. In G. Edwards & C. Dare (Eds.), *Psychotherapy, psychological treatments and the addictions* (pp. 189–205). New York: Cambridge University Press.

Sutton S., McVey D., & Glanz, A. (1999). A comparative test of the theory of reasoned action and the theory of planned behavior in the prediction of condom use intentions in a national sample of English young people. *Health Psychology*, *18*, 72–81.

Terry, D. (1993). Self-efficacy expectancies and the theory of reasoned action. In D. J. Terry, C. Gallois, & M. McCamish (Eds.), *The theory of reasoned action: Its application to AIDS–preventive behaviour* (pp. 135–151). New York: Pergamon Press.

Terry, D. J., & O'Leary, J. E. (1995). The theory of planned behaviour: The effects of perceived behavioural control and self-efficacy. *British Journal of Social Psychology*, *34*, 199–220.

Thune, I., Brenn, T., Olund, E., & Gaard, M. (1997). Physical activity and the risk of breast cancer. *New England Journal of Medicine, 336*, 1269–1275.

Trafimow, D., & Trafimow, J. H. (1998). Predicting back pain sufferers' intentions to exercise. *Journal of Psychology, 132*, 581–592.

Turpeinen, O. (1979). Effect of cholesterol-lowering diet on mortality from coronary heart disease and other causes. *Circulation, 59*, 1–7.

U.S. Department of Health & Human Services. (2000). *Healthy people 2010: Understanding and improving health* (2nd ed.). Washington, DC: U.S. Government Printing Office.

Velicer, W. F., Norman, G. J., Fava, J. L., & Prochaska, J. O. (1999). Testing 40 predictions from the transtheoretical model. *Addictive Behaviors, 24*, 455–469.

Walter, H. J., Vaughan, R. D., Gladis, M. M., & Ragin, D. F. (1993). Factors associated with AIDS-related behavioral intentions among high school students in an AIDS epicenter. *Health Education Quarterly, 20*, 409–420.

Warnecke, R., Graham, S., Rosenthal, S. F., & Manfred, C. (1975). Social and psychological correlates of smoking behaviour in black women. *Journal of Health and Social Behavior, 19*, 397–410.

White, K. M., Terry, D. J., & Hogg, M. A. (1994). Safer sex behavior: The role of attitudes, norms, and control factors. *Journal of Applied Social Psychology, 24*, 2164–2192.

Wilson, D., & Lavelle, S. (1992). Psychosocial predictors of intended condom use among Zimbabwean adolescents. *Health Education Research, 7*, 55–68.

Wilson, D., Zenda, A., & Lavelle, S. (1991). Predicting Zimbabwean women's ability to tell their partners to use condoms. *Journal of Social Psychology, 132*, 261–263.

Wilson, D., Zenda, A., McMaster, J., & Lavelle, S. (1992). Factors predicting Zimbabwean students' intentions to use condoms. *Psychology and Health, 7*, 99–114.

Wulfert, E., & Wan, C. K. (1995). Safer sex intentions and condom use viewed from a health belief, reasoned action, and social cognitive perspective. *Journal of Sex Research, 32*, 299–311.

Wulfert, E., Wan, C. K., & Backus, C. A. (1996). Gay men's safer sex behavior: An integration of three models. *Journal of Behavioral Medicine, 19*, 345–367.

Yep, G. A. (1993). Health beliefs and HIV prevention: Do they predict monogamy and condom use? *Journal of Social Behavior and Personality, 8*, 507–520.

7

HOW INTEGRATIVE BEHAVIORAL THEORY CAN IMPROVE HEALTH PROMOTION AND DISEASE PREVENTION

CRAIG K. EWART

Health problems and their causes are complex. The origins of most illnesses can be traced to a variety of behavioral, social, biological, and environmental sources. But which of these should preventive intervention target? How do we measure a given causal influence, and how might we manipulate it to protect health? Such questions call for conceptual models that identify the critical variables and explain how to orchestrate and apply information from many disciplines with relevant expertise, disciplines as diverse as epidemiology, sociology, psychology, anthropology, physiology, microbiology, and genetics.

Portions of this chapter were developed originally in a paper presented at the Institute of Medicine's Workshop on the Social and Behavioral Science Base for HIV/AIDS Prevention and Intervention, National Academy of Sciences, Washington, DC, June 12, 1995. Preparation of this manuscript was supported in part by National Institutes of Health Grant HL52080. I would like to thank Dr. Michael P. Carey, who commented on an earlier draft.

The construction of guiding models and organizing frameworks is the task of theory. In the field of health promotion, theories are needed to guide efforts to encourage "self-protective action"—that is, to help people develop and sustain patterns of behavior that enhance health and reduce the risk of illness. Two kinds of theorizing are needed. One approach models causal processes at a particular level of analysis, such as the level of the individual, or of the social network, or of the society. The other kind of theory-building is *integrative*: It strives to create a multileveled theoretical architecture that places the individual in broader environmental context, organizes important social and individual mechanisms of behavior change, indicates how these components interact with one another, and thereby suggests how they might be activated and coordinated to support health-protective activity.

This chapter examines ways in which integrative theory can improve health promotion and disease prevention interventions. Social action theory (SAT), a recent example of such theorizing, is used to illustrate the possibilities and challenges of integrative theory-building. It is argued that, in addition to identifying and coordinating important behavioral and social mechanisms of change, the integrative framework provided by a meta-theory such as SAT can help disclose strengths and shortcomings of popular health promotion models, identify gaps in present knowledge, and suggest priorities for future research.

ROLE OF BEHAVIORAL THEORY IN ILLNESS PREVENTION

A scientific theory is an invented set of concepts that helps us organize, interpret, and control our environment (Pedhazur & Schmelking, 1991). It is an explanation that connects a group of facts. A "fact," in science, is a *reproducible phenomenon*, an event or relationship that has been observed repeatedly and that is deemed sufficiently important to need explaining. In health promotion, theory guides intervention planning by providing explanatory concepts, or "theoretical constructs," that tell which facts or phenomena to look for when trying to understand, predict, or influence a health outcome. A theory also tells how to identify and measure the important causal factors, how to modify them, what to expect when doing so, and how to interpret the results.

Consider the challenge of trying to curb adolescent smoking. A theory's explanatory constructs might draw our attention to causal processes such as social modeling, mass communication, and tobacco marketing practices, as well as to specific ways in which these factors function as interrelated variables—meaning that variations in one factor may cause other related factors to vary in predictable ways. A useful theory should specify indicators that can be used to uncover and measure the key variables, such as indexes of adolescent exposure to cigarette ads, and also specify operations by which the presumed causal variables can be manipulated to effect desired changes in other variables, such as lower smoking rates. The theory will provide a basis for predicting the degree to which variation in one variable (television watching) is likely to influence variations in others (perceiving smoking as attractive). When efforts to predict or influence behavior fail, a useful theory can suggest why; perhaps there was a failure to define, identify, or measure key variables, for example, or to use appropriate procedures to manipulate causal processes. Good theories help us learn from failures by revealing critical errors.

Theories are most useful when they are viewed as tentative approximations of reality, to be held only until a better approximation is found. One theory replaces another, not because the newer theory is "true" and the other "false" but because the newer theory is found to be more useful in "offering a more comprehensive, more parsimonious, and more integrative explanation of phenomena" (Wallander, 1992). Often, a new theory is preferred because it enhances prediction and control, or because the newer theory poses more interesting or more informative questions. In the field of health behavior, the central questions involve patterns of personal behavior that make people vulnerable to illness or injury. Theories of health behavior, therefore, are judged according to their ability to help us to understand the conditions under which people engage in activities conducive to good health and to influence causal processes that lead to effective action.

Defining Health Promotion and Illness Prevention

Definitions of illness and health are central to any theory of health promotion or disease prevention. A recent definition of illness characterizes disease as "a state that places individuals at increased risk of adverse consequences" (Temple, McLeod, Gallinger, & Wright, 2001). Key to this broad but useful definition is the notion of risk, which in medicine is typically defined in terms of overt symptoms (nominalist tradition) or in terms of underlying mechanisms or dispositions (essentialist tradition). The authors of this definition argue that either tradition is appropriate for characterizing disease as long as the state in question (symptom cluster or disposition) is associated with increased risk of adverse outcomes.

Conversely, health or wellness can be described in terms of states that place individuals at *reduced* risk of adverse consequences. Such states would include the absence of disease symptoms (nominalist view), as well as the presence of underlying mechanisms or dispositions that function to keep one from becoming ill (essentialist view). People in whom disease symptoms or processes are not evident are generally considered to be "well." In the 1980s, the term *wellness* came into widespread use as a way to describe prevention programs designed to help people who are not ill remain free of disease by exercising, eating a proper diet, and managing stress. Yet it is widely acknowledged (Glanz, Lewis, & Rimer, 1997) that being well—in the sense of not having symptoms or identifiable pathology—is not necessarily the same thing as being "healthy." Consider, for example, a person without an immune response who, to avoid infection, must remain within a sealed and sterile environment. Assume that, within this germ-free living space, the unfortunate individual's risk of becoming sick is no greater than anyone else's and that he or she is able to remain free of infection, and hence "well," indefinitely. Would it be appropriate to pronounce such an individual "healthy?" Surely not. The notion of health clearly includes a judgment about an organism's *health potential*, defined as the ability to actively resist or avoid illness threats in daily life.

These two conceptions of health—as absence of disease and as resistive potential—are reflected in two distinctly different traditional approaches to combating illness (Ewart, 1991a, 1991b). One tradition focuses on *prevention*, whereas the other tradition focuses on *health promotion*. People can be kept free of illness—that is, kept well—if health threats are prevented from entering their environments. Preventive interventions keep people well by cleansing the environment of agents that could make them ill or of hazards that might cause injury. The classic prevention paradigm is exemplified in the public health tradition of sanitation. Sanitary (preventive) approaches range from purifying the water supply to designing safer cars that are less likely to injure their occupants in a crash. Some of the greatest improvements in health in modern times are attributable to preventive, sanitary intervention.

Yet keeping people well, in the sense of illness-free, is not necessarily the same thing as making them healthier. Promoting health involves enhancing a person's ability to avoid, resist, or overcome a health threat. This approach to health is exemplified in the tradition of inoculation, which improves the immune system's ability to identify and resist a pathogen. Inoculation is associated historically with the development of vaccines to enhance an individual's resistance to infectious agents. "Behavioral" inoculation (i.e., health promotion) can be said to involve enabling people to recognize health threats and to take protective action (Ewart, 1991a, 1991b).

Note that the two strategies also differ in their stance in terms of individual behavior. Illness prevention strategies try to sanitize the environment so that self-protective behavior by individuals will be rendered unnecessary. Preventive environmental approaches thus are said to be passive with respect to the individual. Health promotion, in contrast, targets the individual directly. Health promotion strategies try to empower people against disease or injury threats by enhancing their personal capabilities and altering their habits, and therefore are active with respect to individual behavior. Thus, in the view presented, theories of health behavior belong to the domain of health promotion.

Despite fundamental differences in conception and focus, environmentally oriented prevention strategies and behaviorally oriented health promotion strategies are generally agreed to be most effective when applied in combination (Jeffery, 1989). Separating human waste from the public water supply can dramatically lower the incidence of infectious diseases. Yet teaching people to practice safe food handling techniques can reduce the infection rate even further. And although individual behavior change remains the first line of defense against the spread of HIV, for example, needle exchange programs that remove infected injection equipment from a drug user's environment can play a vital preventive role. Even purely environmental strategies are more effective when informed by a scientific understanding of individual behavior, as the history of efforts to design passive restraint systems for automobiles can attest.

Challenges

The task of developing useful theoretical frameworks to guide health promotion faces several challenges. One challenge is to define precisely what one means by *health behavior*, and to specify how the behaviors of individuals are related to their environmental contexts. The fact that behavior change typically takes place gradually over time, in a developmental sequence, poses another challenge. And the need to specify procedures by which behaviors actually can be altered—and not merely predicted—poses yet another.

Defining Health Behavior and Its Context

Behavior, a word used to describe the activities of organisms, also can be used to describe any set of actions and reactions within a system, whether the entities involved are people, galaxies, or subatomic particles (Schwartz, 1981, 1982). In this sense, behavior is the subject of all health science disciplines, which include the study of molecules (biochemistry), organs (physiology), individual persons (psychology, anthropology), groups (sociology), and social–political systems (political science, economics). Many contemporary health problems require analysis at all of these levels. Theories of health behavior analyze systems of behavior at the level of the individual person, although they often draw on social analyses that explain disease incidence in populations as a function of group-level phenomena, as well as on biological analyses that explain disease susceptibility in terms of organ systems or biochemical processes.

Theories in the behavioral sciences usually are designed to explain a limited set of phenomena at the individual level of analysis (e.g., Pavlovian conditioning, self-efficacy theory, cognitive dissonance theory). Yet health problems call for conceptual frameworks that can integrate theories at different levels of analysis. In older natural sciences such as chemistry or physics, theories explaining specific phenomena are subsumed under higher order explanations or laws; the theory of relativity, for example, provides a parsimonious explanation for a variety of seemingly unrelated phenomena. We should not exclude the possibility that a theory of similar breadth and parsimony may emerge someday in the behavioral and social sciences. But in the field of health promotion, the phenomena that must be addressed are too numerous and too varied to be encompassed by any one theory now at hand.

Theories of health behavior differ in their range or scope. A theory may focus on a cognitive process or group of processes within an individual (e.g., decision theory, self-efficacy theory, health belief models) or may strive to integrate processes that occur at different levels of analysis (e.g., alcohol "myopia" models, group influence theories). In the context of health, theories of behavior that focus only on the individual are limited to the extent that they fail to consider the role of social–political influences or underlying biological processes. Health problems generally result from a variety of causal factors, and their treatment thus requires a multileveled approach.

This complexity creates a need for integrative frameworks or models, designed to connect multiple phenomena, on different levels of analysis, within a more encompassing conceptual structure. Such a view can be described broadly as *holistic*, a term used to suggest a complex system of interacting parts, each one of which influences and is influenced by the others, and therefore should be viewed in a wider context. Such theories may be used to generate structural models showing how diverse social, cognitive, and physiological mechanisms may combine in causal pathways that may be affected by moderator variables.

Developmental Perspective

Causal processes that facilitate the development of a desired self-protective behavior pattern often differ from those that help sustain it over time. Different principles may be needed to explain why some patients with diabetes fail to acquire the ability to monitor their glucose levels initially (e.g., persuasion, social modeling) and why those who do learn this skill may succeed or fail in continuing to do so regularly over time (e.g., stimulus control). Process models of change, of which stage theories are an example, acknowledge that health behavior change often occurs gradually, in a developmental sequence (Prochaska, DiClemente, & Norcross, 1992). Different theories may focus on different elements or phases of this process.

Manipulating Causal Mechanisms

It was noted earlier that a good theory enables us both to predict and control, or influence, important phenomena. Some theories in the health field do an adequate job of predicting rates of health behaviors in populations but, when faced with the challenge of altering health behaviors, their prescriptions for change are vague. Identifying the correlates of a health behavior can improve our ability to predict its occurrence, just as knowing a person's zip code can be useful in predicting his or her income or as knowing his or her body temperature can help determine if an individual is ill. But changing the postal code system will not alter income discrepancies, nor will reducing a fever by cooling the body eliminate an infection. More powerful—and more useful—are theories that predict behavior while also specifying precisely the modifiable causal processes or mechanisms that can be manipulated to effect change. In the health field, modest success in predicting behavioral outcomes such as smoking cessation or weight loss can ensure that a theory will win acceptance initially. But the critical test of the theory's utility, as well as its explanatory power, comes later, after repeated attempts to use the theory in designing applied behavioral interventions have disclosed its strengths and limitations.

Themes and Variations

Familiar theories of health behavior differ in the ways they confront the challenges described. Some of the more important differences involve the role of social influences on individual behavior and the manner in which these influences are presumed to operate, the role of cognition in health behavior change, the nature of temporal relationships between variables in the causal model, and the influence of moderating variables on relationships between causal processes and their behavioral effects. It is important to remain alert to these differences when trying to select a theoretical framework that will be well-suited to a particular health promotion objective.

Social Influence

Many models of health behavior change draw heavily on theories of social influence (Schneiderman & Speers, 2001). A number of applied intervention strategies derive from work in behavioral counseling, persuasive communication, community organization, and social activation and control. But the various health behavior models differ widely with respect to the manner in which social influence processes are presumed to operate. Understanding these differences is important when trying to appraise the strengths and weaknesses of different theoretical perspectives. In *social exchange* theories, for example, social influence is a function of the diverse benefits people derive from interacting with others (Kelley et al., 1983). Interpersonal encounters are analyzed carefully to identify specific outcomes—desired and undesired—that people experience in a given type of transaction. Health behavior theories that emphasize the importance of social support draw on the social exchange tradition when they define support in terms of the type and quality of emotional and instrumental assistance people provide each other, the frequency with which various forms of support are given, and the number and characteristics of people from whom support is available. From the perspective of social exchange theory, behaviors that protect or undermine health are components of social transactions that provide emotional support, practical aid, money, or other forms of assistance.

Health behavior models that draw on social learning theory define social–contextual influences largely in terms of *social modeling* processes, emphasizing observational learning and reinforcement for adopting behaviors and attitudes of respected individuals (Bandura, 1986). Young people may start smoking or engage in unsafe sex, for example, because they believe that people who do so gain status, acceptance, or other social rewards. A rather different view is found in health behavior models based on *social attachment* theories, in which influence operates through emotional bonding and identification. People want to be like those to whom they are attached emotionally, and emulating another person's behavior can provide a way to feel connected (Hawkins, Catalano, & Miller, 1992). People may engage in a risky activity if doing so helps them feel closer to someone to whom they formed an attachment, as when emotional bonds to drug-abusing peers presumably make an adolescent want to use drugs (Jessor & Jessor, 1977).

Models that emphasize the role of community environments in shaping health often draw on theories of social control, in which social influences operate through various institutional structures (e.g., family, work group, school) and social roles (e.g., spouse, parent, student, employee) that hold peoples' unhealthy impulses in check (Shoemaker, 1990). Should family or community structures break down, people will have fewer incentives to comply with social roles and norms, and hence will be more likely to engage in risky behavior. In this view, health-damaging behavior patterns among the urban poor reflect the disintegration of family and community networks, which has led to poor socialization of children, produced schools where students are not rewarded for learning, decreased respect for community norms, and eroded the work ethic, leaving people defenseless in the face of their hedonistic impulses (Elliott, Huizinga, & Menard, 1989).

Yet another dimension on which theoretical approaches differ is the degree to which the acquisition or maintenance of self-protective behavior patterns are mediated by cognition. In social control theory, the removal of external restraints or imposition of unwanted control weakens ability to resist deviant impulses and thereby leads directly to risk-taking. In attachment theory, the weakening of bonds to conventional authority figures in the family makes it possible to develop attachments to deviant peers, which leads to deviant behavior. In neither case are cognitive processes of individuals assigned a necessary role, although they are not excluded. Social exchange theorists emphasize the benefits people receive and the costs they incur as they interact with others; these positive and negative experiences may affect risky behavior directly without intervening cognition, or they may involve appraisal processes—depending on the theorist's point of view. Only the modeling processes envisioned in social learning theory rely extensively on reflective thought. Observers do not merely imitate models, they use information supplied by the model to formulate rules about behavior-outcome contingencies and appraise their personal capabilities.

Cognitive mediation is emphasized heavily in models based on expectancy-value theory, such as the theory of reasoned action (Ajzen & Fishbein, 1980), the theory of planned behavior (Ajzen, 1985), the health belief model (Kirscht, 1974), and behavioral decision theory (Fischoff, Bostrom, & Quadrel, 1993). In these and similar models, behavior change is driven by deliberate appraisals of the perceived costs and the benefits of changing one's habits.

Temporal Relationships

A third dimension on which theories of health behavior differ involves the temporal proximity of causal influences to behavioral outcomes. Theories based on social exchange models, for example, highlight the immediate, proximal impact of one person's actions on another's. As, for example, when a couple engages in unsafe love making because one partner fears that the other will react negatively to a condom. Each person's responses in the situation directly influences—from moment to moment—the actions of the other.

In health behavior models based on social control and attachment concepts, however, social influences are less immediate. In social control theory, the breakdown of communities and families removes the conventional social restraints and inducements that hold deviant impulses in check. In attachment theory, the weakening of emotional bonds to family members creates conditions for developing bonds to deviant others, which may lead eventually to risky activity. In both perspectives, social influence operates through the gradual alteration of social norms and restrictions, with the result that people are left defenseless against unsafe impulses. In theories based on models of social exchange, in contrast, social influence is more immediate; people engage in a risky activity because it causes partners to give them something they need or desire. Social learning theories derived from social modeling hold that social influence may be both immediate and delayed: Modeling may have a proximal influence by prompting immediate imitative action (as when the presence of another drinker facilitates heavy drinking) or may affect behavior more distally by teaching general rules that the observer later may enact at a different time and place.

Moderating Factors

A final dimension on which theories often differ is in the conditions that limit or *moderate* the behavioral impact of social modeling, exchange, attachment, or rational decision making. Some theoretical models posit risk or resilience variables that increase or reduce susceptibility to social influence (Luthar & Zigler, 1991). Emotional stress, especially depression, is thought to make people more susceptible to being influenced in ways that may prove detrimental, as is a history of academic and relationship failures and low self-esteem—all of which may covary with depression (Coie, 1991). Temperamental traits of impulsivity, sensation seeking, irritability, and rebelliousness are thought to increase the likelihood that people will imitate deviant social models, experience disrupted ties to conventional attachment figures, or resist social controls or fail to consider the risks rationally (Sher, 1991). On the other hand, interpersonal skills, social problem-solving competencies, academic capabilities, and positive self-evaluations (self-esteem) may render people less susceptible to negative influences (Garmezy, Masten, Nordstrom, & Farrarese, 1979). Some theories of social influence posit the influence of one or more influence modes interacting with these moderating variables.

Implications for Behavioral Risk Reduction

Differences in the ways theories treat social influence, cognitive mediation of behavior, temporal relationships between causes and outcomes, and moderating factors have direct, practical implications for interventions to promote health and reduce risk. Resources for intervention are not limitless. The multifaceted nature of health problems demands that behavioral interventions target specifically those elements of the problem that will yield the greatest benefit. If health-protective behavior is affected by distal influences such as the erosion of community structures and the weakening of family ties, then preventive intervention should take the form of efforts to rebuild or strengthen communities and families. On the other hand, if risky behavior is determined by the nature of social networks and the types of exchanges that take place within them, these transactions should be a major focus. Important also is the question of cognition's role in behavior change. Do the various social–environmental influences affect risky behavior directly? Or do the presumed causal processes operate indirectly, by causing some individuals to appraise risky activities more favorably? If the latter is the case, then interventions designed to alter more distal factors in the environment, such as community characteristics or social networks, seem likely to fail unless they target individuals' perceptions and appraisals of activities known to convey risk. Finally, if emotional stress, lack of social skills, or the absence of other personal resources increase the ease with which people are persuaded to engage in risky activities, then prevention efforts will not succeed unless they include interventions specifically designed to reduce stress, build needed skills, enhance self-esteem, or supply other necessary resources to those in need.

SOCIAL ACTION THEORY PERSPECTIVE

The diverse challenges and conceptual themes discussed underscore the need for multileveled, integrative thinking on the part of those responsible for designing behavioral interventions to enhance health. A recent example of this conceptual approach, SAT (Ewart, 1991a, 1991b), offers a useful illustration of this kind of thinking. In the remaining portions of this chapter, SAT is used to show how a multileveled conceptual framework can enhance planners' ability to analyze health-related behavior patterns, develop appropriate intervention goals, and design effective behavior change strategies. Some implications of this integrative perspective will be considered.

Most familiar models of health behavior grew out of efforts to apply the expertise of a single discipline to a single health problem. Principles of behavior analysis, attitude change, decision theory, social cognition, and network analysis, for example, have been applied extensively in research on smoking cessation, weight loss, diet change, HIV exposure, and substance abuse (Glanz et al., 1997). Although this work identified a variety of behavioral phenomena that can affect health, it became apparent that these phenomena were influenced by other processes (often at other levels of analysis) that were not envisaged in the original theoretical scheme. Applications to health revealed that the theories that originally gave rise to specific behavioral intervention approaches had not been designed to integrate all of the relevant causal factors, nor to indicate how they might be coordinated to achieve desired health outcomes.

What might integrative, multilevel theorizing look like, and how might it improve our ability to encourage self-protective activities that enhance health? The example of such thinking, presented—SAT—was constructed explicitly to function as an architectural schema, indicating how lower order phenomena studied in various social science disciplines are interrelated and how they can be orchestrated to achieve a desired health promotion or illness prevention goal. SAT identifies important causal constructs and indicates how they interact. Derived from systems theory (deRosnay, 1979; Schwartz, 1981) the SAT framework represents behaviors, persons, and environments as interacting systems; this approach can disclose potential causal pathways and moderating effects that are not apparent when behavioral, personal, and environmental factors are viewed as isolated phenomena. It may become evident, for example, that social environmental forces constrain an individuals' self-protective activities, or that individual differences shape peoples' responses to social interventions. This multilayered architecture provides a conceptual map that can be used to coordinate proximal and distal determinants of action, to determine which factors should be targeted for change, and to identify conditions that, although difficult or even impossible to alter, can be used to identify vulnerable subgroups who need special attention and resources.

Following SAT's systems approach, development of a behavioral intervention advances in three stages, each of which is represented by a separate subcomponent of the SAT model, as depicted in Figures 7.1, 7.2, and 7.3. These subcomponents allow intervention planners to (a) analyze health habits as systems and thereby discern their critical elements and interrelationships; (b) integrate individual self-change processes that must be activated to generate desired behavior patterns; and (c) identify the contextual factors that support or disrupt self-protective activity. The first step in planning a health promotion intervention is to envision the end goal, which SAT defines in terms of sustained behavioral routines or action states that enhance or protect health. The next step is to identify and activate cognitive and social mechanisms that support self-change. The final step is to address biological influences and social environmental structures that facilitate or constrain (i.e., that moderate) the self-change mechanisms. These steps are outlined in the figures.

Health Habits as Action States

An action theory perspective emphasizes the value of treating health behaviors or "habits" as organized systems, comprising highly routinized sequences of actions, consequences, and reactions that lead to a predictable outcome. For example, drinking habits that contribute to alcohol abuse involve frequently practiced drinking routines, each of which consists of a predictable sequence of behaviors, such as leaving work and driving to a familiar bar, meeting friends, ordering a favorite beverage, socializing, and so on. These routines can be viewed as functional feedback loops in which each event in the sequence is reinforced by the consequences it generates and, in turn, sets the stage for the next event in the series. In this example, the act of leaving work and driving to the bar is reinforced by the pleasant

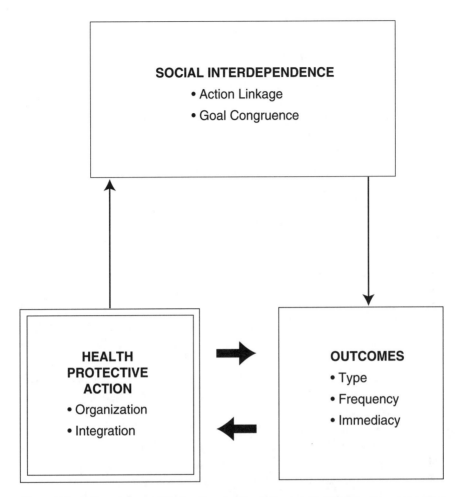

Figure 7.1. Action state model of self-protective behavior. Habitual routines represent action–outcome feedback loops that may be interconnected with the routines of important others. From "Social Action Theory for a Public Health Psychology," by C. K. Ewart, 1991, *American Psychologist, 46,* p. 933. Copyright 1991 by the American Psychological Association. Reprinted with permission.

feeling of arriving in a relaxing setting and seeing familiar faces. These reinforcing feelings increase the desire to order a drink, the drink eases social inhibitions and facilitates conversation, and convivial interaction sets occasion for additional drinking. Interventions to curb alcohol consumption, therefore, must identify new actions and new outcomes to replace this health-endangering behavior sequence. Intervention planning begins by identifying habitual routines (action systems) that endanger health and specifying alternative health routines (such as exercising, using stress management techniques, or involvement with friends who do not hang out in bars) that could help the person avoid situations where drinking is likely to occur.

The action state model of a desired health habit is depicted in Figure 7.1. It depicts the end goal of health promotion: to replace a health-endangering behavior pattern with a new routine (action state) that will prevent, disrupt, or replace behaviors that threaten health. The model in Figure 7.1 indicates that a desired health routine (health protective action) will become habitual only if it generates positive effects (outcomes) that are experienced immediately and frequently, and are congruent with the routines of other persons with whom the individual interacts (social interdependence). The end goal of intervention is to establish this protective system. Planning begins by identifying the components of the problematic habit system that need to be replaced and then specifying the components of the desired alternative health habit system (e.g., exercise, stress management) that must be established for lasting change to occur.

Figure 7.1 indicates that habitual action states (systems) have several important characteristics. First, they are functional in that they produce a desired result. Second, although they are composed of voluntary behaviors (as distinguished from Pavlovian reflexes), habitual routines usually do not involve much self-reflective thought (indeed, the ability to perform the sequence without attending carefully to one's actions indicates that the sequence has become highly routinized, or habitual). Third, the disruption of a habitual action sequence often is felt to be unpleasant or annoying. Fourth, many action sequences that endanger health are interlinked with the routines of important others. Habitual routines involved in eating, substance use, and sexual activities typically are shared with other people; that is, these behavior patterns are characterized by social interdependence.

The analysis of health habits as action states has several important practical implications for theories of health behavior. First, it encourages the intervention planner to "begin with the end in view" by envisioning the desired action system that the intervention should promote. Second, the action state perspective urges planners to think of habits in terms of interlinked sequences of events rather than as isolated acts and to focus on causal relationships that tie the events together. Third, this view forces one to think seriously about the behavioral consequences, or outcomes, that would be needed to reinforce desired health-protective routines. If reinforcing consequences will not be present to support the behavior, the intervention may be doomed to fail. Thus, the action state model poses health promotion's greatest challenge: how to ensure that supportive consequences will be experienced, immediately and often, whenever and wherever the desired behavior occurs.

Fourth, the action state model encourages a holistic view of health habits by highlighting the role of social influence in behavior change. To the extent that health-endangering action scripts are socially interlinked with action scripts of another person, trying to change them is likely to disrupt the other's activities. Negative reactions by friends or family members can make it difficult to establish new health-protective patterns. The degree of action linkage, or the degree to which two people's routines are interconnected (interdependent), determines how disruptive the behavior change will be, and thus how difficult it may be to sustain the routine over time. This implies that unhappiness in a relationship may not be a barrier to health-habit change if partners' routines are not tightly interlinked, and happiness in a relationship may not guarantee success when routines are highly interdependent. It is a mistake, for example, to assume that measures of relationship satisfaction (e.g., marital satisfaction scales) define the ability to change.

Finally, the emphasis on action sequences in SAT (Figure 7.1) underscores the need to study interpersonal interaction sequences in subgroups at risk before intervening. This feature of the model calls attention to the influence of cultural factors in behavior change; for example, social interaction in "collectivist" cultures that emphasize interdependence may differ considerably from interaction patterns that typify more "individualistic" cultures in which personal independence is emphasized (Han & Shavitt, 1994; Landrine & Klonoff, 2001; Markus & Kitayama, 1991; Wheeler, Reis, & Bond, 1989). Where and when do risky behaviors occur? What are the action sequences that lead up to and follow unsafe activities? Who is involved in these situations? What consequences do the participants experience, and how soon and how often do they experience them? What social and structural influences shape these situations and consequences? SAT suggests that the best way to answer these questions is by directly observing people in situations that may pose risk. Where direct observation is not feasible, those at risk can be asked to record their experiences in structured diaries or reconstruct them in individual interviews or focus group settings. Experience sampling methods, in which participants carry beepers that signal them to record their experiences with electronic diaries, or to report them by telephone, can be helpful (Smyth et al., 2001; Stone & Schiffman, 1994).

Self-Change Processes

The action state model suggests goals for preventive intervention but does not represent mechanisms that must be coordinated to alter behavior. Drawing on health behavior research, SAT integrates critical self-change processes that must be activated and resources that must be mobilized to create new health behavior patterns. A systems view implies that these processes may interact in ways that are not often examined in health behavior research. Central are cognitive processes of appraisal and problem solving that shape people's motivation and ability to change.

Interrelationships among these self-change processes are depicted in Figure 7.2.

Self-change activities are influenced by the effects they generate: The consequences people experience when engaging in new self-protective routines affect their willingness to persevere in health protective action. This relationship is represented by the feedback function indicated by the broken line in Figure 7.2. Self-change processes comprise motivational appraisals, problem-solving activities, generative capabilities, and social interaction processes.

Motivational Appraisal

People do not achieve sustained health-habit change unless they believe that change is beneficial, are capable of taking the necessary actions, and view habit change as compatible with important personal strivings or projects. Decades of research within the framework of expectancy-value theory and social–cognitive theory have generated models of motivation relevant to health. Perhaps the most widely investigated appraisal process in health behavior is represented in SAT by the notion of outcome expectancies, which refer to people's beliefs about the consequences of changing (Fischoff, 1995; Fischoff et al., 1993). Outcome expectancies typically are measured by questions that ask the extent to which the respondent agrees with the proposition that "in situation A, doing behavior B causes consequence C," and the corresponding proposition that "causing consequence C is good/bad." These judgments may be altered through social modeling and exposure techniques. In the former, people are exposed to models similar to themselves who are shown enjoying the benefits of healthy behavior or suffering the ill effects of unhealthy habits. Direct exposure involves having the individual experience an outcome directly, as when cardiac patients who have suffered acute myocardial infarction develop new confidence by exercising on a graded treadmill protocol (Ewart, Stewart, Gillilan, & Kelemen, 1986; Ewart, Taylor, Reese, & DeBusk, 1983).

In addition to believing that a behavior change would be beneficial, people must feel capable of taking steps needed to achieve change. *Self-efficacy* refers to a person's level of confidence that he or she can take the necessary steps (Bandura, 1997). Self-efficacy scales have been developed for a variety of health behaviors; research with these instruments shows that they indicate the likelihood that the person will change. The relative importance of outcome expectancy and self-efficacy judgments varies with

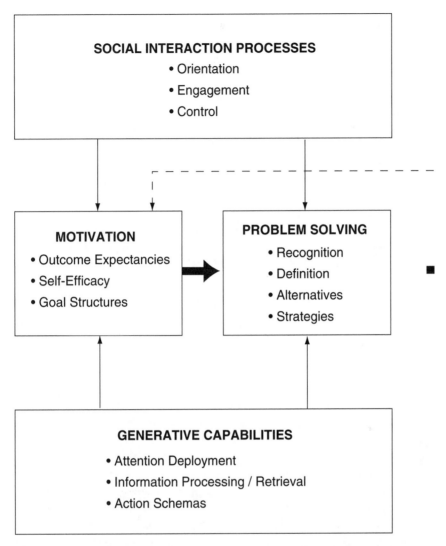

Figure 7.2. Self-change (process) model of health-protective action. Habit change occurs only to the extent that motivational appraisal processes lead to effective problem solving; motivation and problem solving both depend on the availability of personal generative capabilities and supportive social exchanges. From "Self-Change (Process) Model of Health-Protective Action," by C. K. Ewart, 1991, *American Psychologist, 46,* p. 934. Copyright 1991 by the American Psychological Association. Reprinted with permission.

the behavior in question. Self-efficacy explains little when the behavior is easy to perform (e.g., selecting the fluoridated rather than the unfluoridated version of one's favorite toothpaste) but accounts for more variance than outcome expectancies when the benefits of changing are evident but the changes are difficult to make (e.g., weight loss). Self-efficacy can be increased by having the person perform an unfamiliar or difficult activity in gradually increasing doses, by allowing him or her to observe people like themselves successfully perform the behavior, by verbal persuasion, and through interventions designed to modulate physiological arousal (Bandura, 1997).

Personal *goal* appraisals influence how strongly self-efficacy or outcome expectancies affect motivation to alter health behavior. People channel their resources toward valued projects or strivings that serve developmentally relevant life tasks such as achieving independence, establishing supportive relationships, pursuing a career, caring for children, maintaining a given life style, or coping with debility in old age (Diener, Suh, Lucas, & Smith, 1999). Projects can be characterized in a variety of ways, including the extent to which they serve goals of agency (achievement, independence, social competition) as opposed to communion (affiliation, nurturance, acceptance; Helgeson, 1993, 1994). People are more likely to view a health behavior as desirable (outcome expectancy) and feasible (self-efficacy) if the behavior is compatible with valued personal projects and strivings than if it appears to be incompatible with these strivings. People who value agency may prefer to set challenging self-goals, the achievement of which can bring a strong sense of self-efficacy, whereas those who focus their attention on communal strivings may sometimes choose to set less demanding behavioral goals that, being easier to attain, will enable them to please the friends or family members who want them to change (Ewart, 1991a, 1991b).

Strivings can be assessed by giving people a few examples of typical personal projects (e.g., trying to improve a relationship, lose weight, get more sleep, save money) and then asking them to describe their own personal projects and preoccupations. People can be asked to rate the importance of their projects, the degree to which these projects conflict with health-behavior change goals, and the extent to which the projects are supported by other important people in their lives. This information helps tailor interventions. Barriers to self-change can be lowered by helping people modify their projects or readjust their priorities. This may be accomplished through value-clarification procedures that involve identifying valued strivings, clarifying ways in which different strivings or projects may conflict with one another, and considering means by which projects and self-protective behavior changes might be made to support or enhance each other. For example, the use of condoms during sex can be construed both as a means of protection against HIV and a means to advance affiliative (communal) strivings for a more meaningful relationship.

266   CRAIG K. EWART

Problem Solving

Even highly motivated people are unlikely to succeed in changing health habits if they do not formulate appropriate goals and plans. Effective planning and goal setting are a function of problem solving, which in Figure 7.2 is shown to mediate the connection between motivation and sustained action (Figure 7.2). SAT does not assert that all health behaviors are the result of goal setting, planning, or problem solving, but holds instead that motivational appraisals often fail to generate long-term change because people do not take the time to think through what they are trying to accomplish, anticipate difficulties, devise solutions, create plans, and set attainable goals. In this view, intervention must do more than persuade people to think more positively about changing their habits. It must also activate planning, problem solving, and goal-setting processes that constitute the fulcrum of the change process. An important practical implication of this perspective is that behavioral interventions to promote health must target problem-solving capabilities in addition to altering motivational beliefs. This can be done by challenging participants in interventions to think flexibly and creatively about how to achieve change (e.g., problem definition, anticipation, brainstorming, planning, goal setting) and by continuing to emphasize the importance of a problem-solving approach throughout the change process. Much of the hard work of maintaining a new health habit over time involves sustaining continued vigilance in identifying new problems, generating solutions, making plans, and setting goals (Perri, Nezu, & Viegener, 1992).

Generative Capabilities

The ability to generate appraisals and formulate coherent plans derives from two major forms of social competence. One form of competence consists of relevant knowledge—of knowing what one should do and why—and the other form of competence consists of practical know how, or skill in executing a sequence of actions to produce a desired effect. The two types of competence correspond to the distinction in cognitive science between declarative and procedural forms of knowledge (Ewart, 1991a, 1991b). Together, they constitute generative capabilities that enable one to comprehend, organize, retrieve, and apply information needed to make appraisals and solve problems. Thus, in Figure 7.2, generative capabilities shape both the motivation and the problem-solving components of the self-change model.

Traditional health education programs emphasized the acquisition of declarative knowledge by teaching health and illness "facts" (Glanz et al., 1997). Yet these efforts typically failed to impart important procedural knowledge in the form of practical behavioral skills or action schemas that enable people to make decisions and act on their appraisals of the facts. It is important to identify the types of behavioral skills that help a person avoid health threats, and devise methods to measure these skills (e.g., role-playing of high risk situations). Also needed are ways to measure problem-solving capability. Problem solving is a skill in which people differ and that can be enhanced to support behavior change. One method that can be used to assess problem-solving competence is the open-middle story completion technique (Spivack, Platt, & Shure, 1976; Spivack & Shure, 1974). In this method, respondents are told the beginning of a problem situation and its successful ending but are not told what happened in between. The interviewer invites the person to supply a middle that will connect the problematic beginning with the successful outcome. A person's ability to propose an effective course of action provides an index of his or her ability to generate workable solutions to similar problems in everyday life (Wade, Holden, Lynn, Mitchell, & Ewart, 2000).

Social Interaction Processes

Generative capabilities represent competencies of individuals. Yet another critical form of social competence is relationally constituted. Successful appraisal and problem solving depend not only on the generative capabilities of individuals but also on the capabilities of their interpersonal relationships, represented in Figure 7.2 by the box labeled social interaction processes. These competencies are characteristics of relationship systems rather than persons; they are constituted by the interactive capabilities of the relationship. When behavior change by one partner in a relationship disrupts the interlinked routines of the other partner, the ability to handle the disruption is a function of the competence of the relationship. Like generative capabilities, social interaction processes shape both motivation and problem solving (Figure 7.2).

Research on marital and parent–child conflict resolution processes suggests that relational competence in families has several distinct components. Over the past several decades, diverse theories of interpersonal relations have shown remarkable agreement in identifying two fundamental dimensions of relationship style that have emerged repeatedly in factor analyses of interpersonal behaviors. One of these dimensions represents warmth versus hostility (also labeled acceptance–love versus rejection), whereas the other represents involvement versus detachment (also labeled dominance–control–restrictiveness versus submission–autonomy–permissiveness; Baldwin, 1955; Schaefer, 1959; Sears, 1957; Symonds, 1939). Developmental research suggests that children whose interactions with their parents exhibit high levels of warmth and involvement tend to be more successful in many areas; presumably this is because a warm and involved relationship style is a contextual variable that affects parents' ability to socialize their children (Darling & Steinberg, 1993).

More generally, SAT proposes that the level of warmth or acceptance within a close personal relationship is a function of behavioral orientation processes. This is defined as the frequency with which partners try to understand and acknowledge each other's goals and strivings and their readiness to accommodate conflicts either by coordinating their goals (e.g., taking turns), compromising (e.g., each gets part of what they want), or by resolving conflicts at a higher level (Dodge, Asher, & Parkhurst, 1989). The last strategy typically involves envisioning shared, higher order goals, as when partners agree to disagree on some issue to achieve harmony on matters of larger concern to both. The dimension of involvement versus detachment is represented in SAT by the notion of *engagement processes*, which refer to the behaviors that partners use when attempting to resolve goal conflicts. Positive engagement is typified by reflective listening, sharing of feelings, and problem solving, whereas negative engagement is typified by maneuvers designed to silence or hurt the other partner (interrupting, name-calling, put-downs) and by withdrawal (Ewart, 1993). A third relationship factor consists of *control processes*, which refer to partners' ability to collectively agree on behavioral goals and generate appropriate action plans.

The importance of relationship orientation, engagement, and control for health promotion is suggested by research indicating that the availability of a supportive partner is associated with lower vulnerability to depression (Coyne & Downey, 1991) and increased compliance with health-protective behavior (Bovbjerg et al., 1995) and that these processes predict the long-term stability of close interpersonal relationships. Moreover, studies of physiological responses to interpersonal conflict indicate that interactions characterized by hostile orientation and negative engagement processes are associated with cardiovascular hyperreactivity and immune down-regulation that, if chronic, might have implications for resistance to infection and cardiovascular diseases (Ewart, Taylor, Kraemer, & Agras, 1991; Kiecolt-Glaser et al., 1993). SAT proposes that individuals in relationships characterized by high levels of acceptance and positive engagement will be more successful in securing their partners' support in risk reduction. This effectiveness will increase their motivation by reducing negative outcome expectancies, enhancing self-efficacy, and reducing the tension between behavior change and valued personal strivings. Strong partner support also will aid them in anticipating high-risk situations and in engaging in effective problem solving and goal setting.

Although the importance of socially supportive relationships is acknowledged in the health literature, the ability to distinguish between goal coordination (orientation), problem-solving communication (engagement), and planning processes (control) allows us to move beyond social support as a global variable and examine the specific aspects of relationship functioning that underlie self-protective activity. Relationship orientation, engagement, and control processes comprise interpersonal behaviors that can be reliably measured as well as enhanced through behavioral modeling and counseling techniques. Relational competence can be assessed directly by observing communication exchanges between partners as they try to solve problems, as well as indirectly by means of self-report instruments developed for use in marital research and counseling. Within the proposed framework, we can begin to ask if relationship orientation, engagement, or control functions differentially contribute to people's success in avoiding exposure to health threats. We also can examine the impact of interventions that target these functions in efforts to strengthen involvement in health-protective activity.

This discussion of relational competence emphasizes the support available in stable, long-term relationships between adults or between parents and their children. Far less research effort has been devoted to studying support processes that may operate in other relationship systems such as, for example, peer friendships in adolescence. Information on these and other relationship systems, such as patterns found in non-Western cultures, is greatly needed.

Contextual Influences

The social interaction processes that make up relational competence affect preventive behavior indirectly by facilitating cognitive appraisal, problem solving, and action and by enabling partners to cope with relationship disruptions that result from trying to change. They therefore occupy a midpoint on the proximal–distal scale of social influences described earlier (similar to theories of social attachment and identification). At a farther remove are larger social and environmental systems that constrain or facilitate self-protective acts. These influences are represented in the contextual influences model of the SAT framework, as indicated in Figure 7.3.

Social Settings

Neighborhood and workplace environments and activities affect self-protective behavior through the material resources they provide, the social relationships they afford, and their impact on biology and emotion. Neighborhood disorder, crowding, violence, noise, temperature, and pollution have a variety of direct and indirect effects on peoples' capacity for self-protective action (Chen, Matthews, & Boyce, 2002; Ewart, in press; Ewart, Jorgensen, Suchday, Chen, & Matthews, 2002; Gallo & Matthews, 2003; Leventhal & Brooks-Gunn, 2000). Although a variety of approaches have been used to measure environmental stressors, the various definitions can be grouped into three main categories (Wandersman, 2001). Structural

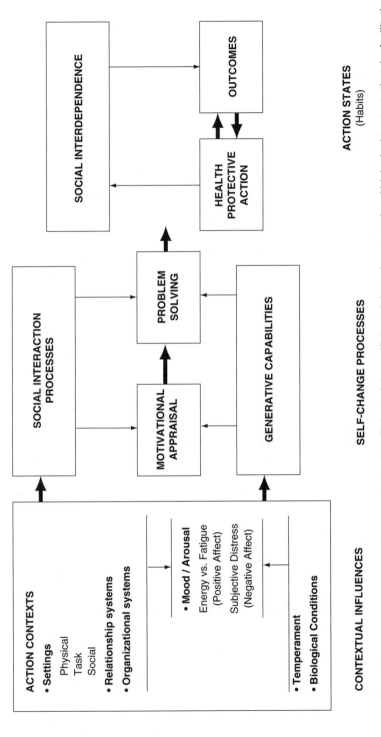

Figure 7.3. Contextual model of health-protective action. This model specifies social–environmental and biological contexts that, by facilitating or inhibiting self-change processes, tend to encourage or disrupt the development and maintenance of health-protective action states (habits). From "Contextual Model of Health-Protective Action," by C. K. Ewart, 1991, *American Psychologist, 46,* p. 939. Copyright 1991 by the American Psychological Association. Reprinted with permission.

models draw on macro scale indicators of unemployment, crime, and poverty at the census-tract level. Neighborhood disorder models emphasize neighborhood-level markers of social incivility and physical decay. Environmental stress models focus on ambient stressors such as heat, noise, or pollution. In this framework, the second and third categories represent proximal environmental stressors and barriers that threaten to disrupt the development and maintenance of self-protective health habits (Ewert & Suchday, 2002). Structural phenomena, including socioeconomic forces, represent more distal influences that help shape the proximal environments of the neighborhood, school, or workplace.

Social Networks

A person's social networks play an important role in shaping health behavior. Social norms and roles often are invoked to explain the processes by which social networks and systems influence the behavior of individuals. Social norms provide rules or standards that specify what members of a group must do or not do in specific situations, whereas a social role is a norm that specifies the behaviors required of people who occupy particular positions in the society or group. The assumption that norms or roles influence individual behavior directly is an oversimplification, because it suggests that society hands people scripts that they then enact without further thought (Giddens, 1979). Members of a social group do not simply enact roles or comply with norms, they pursue goals, using roles or norms as models to guide their actions. Norms function as rules of thumb that indicate the kinds of things one should do, or avoid doing, in pursuing one's goals. They also suggest the kinds of aversive consequences that one may experience if one chooses to flout the norm.

It is important, however, to distinguish between perceived norms and actual norms (Kuran, 1995). People often base their actions (at least actions that are publicly visible) on how they think others would behave, thereby conforming to a *perceived* norm of conduct, or public opinion. But the perception may not be accurate. Others may not support the perceived norm, or they may conform to it publicly while not endorsing it privately. This opens the possibility of influencing people's actions by altering their perceptions of publicly endorsed behavior codes, norms, and opinions.

Interventions to modify health behavior by altering social norms—or peoples' awareness of norms—have enjoyed some measure of success as components of educational programs to curb excessive alcohol use or discourage unsafe sexual activity. In programs to reduce the spread of HIV, for example, changes in laws and policies to permit clean needle exchange programs and increased availability of condoms alter perceived norms by making self-protective action easier, safer, and less susceptible to punishment. These interventions operate in part by altering perceived public norms for behavior in potentially unsafe situations. A social systems approach to HIV education can target socially mediated contingencies by encouraging group members to identify with their group and by characterizing HIV as a threat to the group's shared identity, by showing members how their transactions with one another affect their risk, by specifying safer ways to interact, and by identifying ways in which the group as well as individual members will benefit from collective behavior change (Heckathorn, 1990, 1995). Such intervention establishes new perceived norms for self-protection.

Social networks and settings also influence individual behavior by exposing people to social models whose actions convey information about behavior–outcome contingencies, by providing opportunities to develop and sustain supportive relationships (i.e., to acquire "relational" competence), and by influencing biological conditions that facilitate or constrain action. In the SAT perspective, these influences do not affect self-protective activity directly, however, but operate by enhancing or undermining generative capabilities or relational resources. Social contingencies designed to support health protective activity are likely to affect health behavior only to the degree that they enhance people's generative capabilities (action scripts) and alter their appraisals of their personal strivings (projects), their ability to act (self-efficacy), and the perceived consequences of self-protective activity (outcome expectancies). Social modeling interventions will be effective only to the extent that they, too, activate these mechanisms. The availability of supportive others will facilitate behavior change only in the degree to which interpersonal involvements achieve the needed levels of relational competence.

Biological Contexts

Biological influences also facilitate or constrain self-protective action by affecting the development of personal generative capabilities and relational competence, and thereby shaping the ways people construe their objectives, perceive contingencies, appraise their capabilities, solve problems, and set goals. Biological contexts include physiological conditions such as fatigue or illness, states induced by alcohol or other substances, as well as biologically based behavioral dispositions that are evident from birth and that affect the evolution of temperamental differences in activity, sociability, and impulsivity (Caspi, 2000; Eisenberg, Fabes, Guthrie, & Reiser, 2000; Ewart, 1991a, 1991b, 1994, in press; Kagan, 1998. Biological and social–contextual influences combine to influence mood states, which are constituted by varying combinations of energy level and positive or negative affect. Mood states may give rise to appraisals that contribute to emotions such as fear, anger, sadness, joy, or pride, and thereby enhance or impede one's ability to engage in self-protective activity. Anxiety, anger, or depression, as well as states of intoxication, may interfere with people's ability to recall information relevant to self-protection, to envision effective forms of action, to appraise the potential consequences of their actions, or to solve problems and formulate appropriate behavioral goals. Emotions of joy and pride, on the other hand, may enhance these activities. People who are emotionally distressed also have difficulty developing and maintaining close supportive interpersonal relationships that facilitate self-change.

Demographic Characteristics

Certain demographic characteristics such as race, class, gender, age, and sexual orientation often are correlated with health behavior. The SAT framework omits these terms, not because they are unimportant but because they refer to broad social categories rather than to specific mechanisms and processes of health behavior change. Social categories are not risk factors in themselves but serve as crude markers for contextual influences and constraints that limit people's ability to protect their health. Being poor, or discriminated against, may adversely affect one's material resources, social networks, and interpersonal relationships. These constraints, rather than demographic labels, are the proper targets of preventive intervention, and hence are the focus of SAT.

IMPLICATIONS FOR HEALTH BEHAVIOR CHANGE

Progress in developing more effective health promotion programs requires an improved understanding of the causal pathways by which distal social influences at the community and societal levels "act at a distance" to affect the self-protective behaviors of individuals. Also needed is a better understanding of the factors that moderate these causal influences. Consideration of causal pathways and moderators reveals gaps in current knowledge and discloses the limits of theoretical models widely used in health promotion and disease prevention research. SAT's integrative–holistic perspective suggests new ways to think about causal pathways and raises interesting questions about existing approaches.

Causal Pathways

Unlike theories that posit a direct link between social institutions and individual behaviors (e.g., problem behavior theory; Jessor & Jessor,

1977), SAT holds that social influences are mediated extensively by cognitive appraisal and problem-solving processes. Only in the case of tightly interlinked habitual routines (where one partner's action directly cues, enables, or reinforces the action of the other partner) does the social context directly affect self-protective action. For the most part, supportive relationships, as well as more distal societal and cultural contexts, facilitate personal change by fostering favorable outcome expectancies, bolstering self-efficacy, inducing health-protective strivings, building generative and relational competence, and supporting problem-solving and goal-setting behavior (Figure 7.2). This network of causal linkages implies that cognitive–behavioral interventions aimed at individuals are more likely to generate sustained self-protective action when supported by interventions designed to improve the functioning of close interpersonal relationships, to alter socially mediated contingencies (norms) that operate in groups and institutions (Kuran, 1995), to provide effective social modeling, and to restructure social networks (Wandersman, 2001). On the other hand, the latter interventions are expected to alter individual behavior in the degree to which they affect the critical cognitive mediating mechanisms of self-protective action.

The SAT model also identifies influences that moderate the impact of social and cultural factors. Impaired cognitive functioning, or biological processes (e.g., involving alcohol/ substance use), may render some people more resistant to certain forms of social influence. Temperamental impulsivity, irritability, or aggressiveness may affect acquisition of social competence in childhood, and thus alter responsiveness to social influence later in life (Ewart, in press; Ewart & Jorgensen, in press). Positive and negative affective states are known to affect susceptibility to social influence, and chronic depression may reduce people's ability to mount effective self-change efforts (Ewart, 1991a, 1991b).

The Role of Health Beliefs

Much research in health promotion has been guided by theoretical models in which motivation to adopt protective habits is driven by personal expectations about the likelihood of negative health outcomes and the value of taking action to prevent them. Familiar examples of such expectancy–value formulas include the Health Belief Model (HBM; Kirscht, 1974), the Theory of Reasoned Action (TRA; Ajzen & Fishbein, 1980), the Theory of Planned Behavior (TPB; Ajzen, 1985), and Protection Motivation Theory (PMT; Rogers, 1983). Key components of these models include concepts such as the perceived probability of a health threat, its severity, one's susceptibility to it, the costs and benefits of taking protective action, evaluations of potential outcomes, and one's "behavioral intention" to act.

Although these components may go by different names in the various theories, the constructs they represent are highly similar, if not redundant. Widespread use of these and related models has revealed several difficulties.

First, there is confusion about what certain constructs mean. Inadequate definition frustrates attempts to measure key variables needed to test the theories. A review of questionnaires used to evaluate one popular model concludes, for example, that "a disconcertingly large number did not appear to be good measures of HBM constructs" (Strecher & Rosenstock, 1997, p. 55). Variations in the methods used to test this and similar formulations have thwarted efforts to build a reliable body of knowledge.

A second concern is that effects of the major constructs appear to vary depending on the influence of other variables that are not included in a simple expectancy–value scheme. Inability to define these unknown variables, or to specify their measurement characteristics, weakens statistical tests of the theory and limits the amount of useful information that can be derived from it (Weinstein, 1993).

Finally, it is not clear that the key constructs and the algorithms used to combine them in statistical tests actually map onto people's thought processes in real situations. Efforts to improve a models' performance have focused mainly on altering questionnaire items and formats to enhance reliability, or trying out new ways to aggregate items, or combining variables differently in regression equations. Yet even in cases where such tinkering enhances correlations between questionnaire scores and health outcomes, it does not necessarily clarify the underlying social and cognitive mechanisms that cause behavior change. If the key constructs in a model are of dubious value, and if important moderator variables are undefined, fiddling with measurement and aggregation rules (e.g., to add or to multiply?) will not accomplish much (Sutton, McVey, & Glanz, 1999).

Theories of health behavior are of little help to interventionists unless the variables they specify can be manipulated, using empirically tested methods, to foster change. Widely used expectancy–value models were developed originally to *predict* rates of health behaviors in populations–not to generate *change*–so they should not be expected to include the modifiable cognitive and social processes that give rise to beliefs and intentions (Kirscht, 1974). In SAT, the components of familiar models are represented as motivational appraisal processes concerning action outcomes, self-efficacy, and personal strivings; these processes are governed by mechanisms of social modeling, graduated performance, and behavioral reinforcement. The principles by which these influence mechanisms operate have been derived from a large body of experimental research and provide specific procedural guidelines for effecting health behavior change (Bandura, 1997, pp. 283–293). Popular expectancy–value models are difficult to use when designing applied interventions because the linkage between the beliefs they specify and the causal processes that give rise to these beliefs–and to habit change– is unclear.

SAT facilitates intervention planning by offering a parsimonious set of motivational mechanisms (Figure 7.2) that can easily account for all of the varied contents of a simple expectancy–value model. Outcome expectancies, for example, incorporate constructs such as "perceived benefits" or "risks," "susceptibility," and "severity." Self-efficacy replaces less adequately specified constructs like "perceived control," and goal structures (personal strivings and specific action goals) offer both distal and proximal goal constructs in place of "behavioral intentions." Each SAT motivational component represents a well studied behavioral mechanism with explicit operational guidelines for assessment and intervention.

Moreover, SAT organizes these change mechanisms and processes within a systems framework that indicates how the parts may interrelate, thereby prompting researchers to ask more informed questions. Such organization generates a rich source of fruitful hypotheses about how to improve interventions in cases when they fail to achieve their desired effects.

The integration of social influences into the change process is another important concern. Social influence is included in the TRA and TPB theories but only as a "subjective norm" representing the strength of the belief that others want one to change multiplied by the strength of one's desire to please them. Expectations that others will approve or disapprove of one's actions are but one type of outcome expectancy among many others, and there are no strong empirical grounds for arguing that beliefs about social outcomes have to operate differently than other outcome beliefs. Separating anticipated social outcomes from other outcome expectancies, and using a different aggregation algorithm to estimate their effect, may weaken their observed correlations with behavior. This may partly explain why the subjective norm component does not consistently account for a greater share of the variance in tests of the TRA and TPB models. Moreover, in a truly integrative view, social processes would be expected to operate through a variety of influence channels, of which outcome expectancies are but one. Representing social influences as a subjective norm blurs important distinctions between behavioral *interdependence* conceived in SAT in terms of action linkage (Action State Model), capabilities of relational systems (Self-Change Model), and social structures and networks (Contextual Model). These processes suggest several causal pathways to consider.

In addition to identifying and organizing causal mechanisms, a useful theory of prevention must be able to specify factors that limit the operation of these components. Expectancy–value models have been criticized for assuming that people always think about their options and make reasoned decisions before acting. This is true for many behaviors but not for all. The SAT model identifies a variety of factors that may prevent or undermine reflective decision making. People may fail to make well-considered decisions because they lack necessary information or problem-solving skills (generative capabilities) or because they are unable to engage the support of a sympathetic partner (social interaction processes). They may fail to think before acting because of memory impairment attributable to alcohol, fatigue, or illness. They may suffer from mood disorders that bias their memories or sap their desire to solve problems and set goals. Research examining these moderating effects is needed to enable intervention planners to tailor preventive programs to the specific needs and limitations of those at risk.

When a poorly specified model fails to perform as desired, and when the persistent tweaking of questionnaire items and aggregation rules has failed to improve matters, a researcher may decide that it is time to look around for new constructs to boost the predictive formula. Such ad hoc amplification can result in what Bandura has labeled "cafeteria-style theorizing" (Bandura, 1997, p. 285), in which the choice of model components appears arbitrary and the interrelationships among the core constructs are less than compelling. Several popular health behavior models, for example, have been retrofitted with new self-efficacy modules in recent years. Although adding a self-efficacy measure may enhance prediction under some circumstances, a better solution is to rethink the behavior change problem from an integrative perspective that considers how underlying mechanisms interact with and mutually influence one another. SAT facilitates such thinking by treating self-efficacy, in this example, as an interacting process rather than a simple add-on.

Should the Change Process Be Divided Into Discrete Stages?

The perspective provided by an integrative theory such as SAT also has implications for the notion that processes of health behavior change should be subdivided into a sequence of discrete stages, as in the popular transtheoretical model (TTM; Prochaska et al., 1992). The idea that habit change is a journey of many steps is intuitively compelling; anyone who has tried to lose weight, exercise, or stop smoking knows that these goals are not accomplished quickly. Altering health habits requires one to master new knowledge, develop new skills, assemble social and material resources, and solve the seemingly endless cascade of practical problems and challenges that threaten to undermine healthy intentions. Indeed, the process of self-change can become so demanding that it is best approached by breaking it down into subtasks: Building motivation to change, acquiring necessary knowledge and skills, enlisting the help of others, coping with difficult situations, battling boredom and fatigue, and resuming one's efforts in the wake of disheartening lapses.

In the TTM, for example, behavior change unfolds in a predictable sequence of distinct phases: precontemplation, contemplation, preparation, action, and (after six months effort), maintenance, which usually is followed by relapse (Prochaska et al., 1992). This appealing scheme has drawn vigorous criticism in recent years, both on conceptual grounds (Bandura, 1997) and for the theory's empirical failures (Herzog, Abrams, Emmons, Linnan, & Shadel, 1999; Sutton, 1996). Critics have challenged the applicability and scientific value of a stage approach.

Stage theories of development clearly have been successful in biology. In many organisms (recall the humble butterfly), knowing an individual's stage of development lets one predict with considerable accuracy how long it will remain in that stage and to specify precisely the conditions needed to facilitate successive transitions from one stage to the next. This is because the organism's growth is known to unfold in a fixed number of easily identifiable stages, the sequence of the stages is irreversible, and it applies equally to all members of the same species.

Stage theories in the domain of health behavior do not enjoy these advantages. Although schemes such as the TTM presume that most individuals at a given behavioral stage share common characteristics, such as an intention to stop smoking before a certain date, it is acknowledged that many smokers who report this intention actually are not thus inclined. Progress through the hypothesized stage sequence, moreover, is held to be only *typical*–not universal; it is accepted that many people will not progress and many may revert to earlier stages. Finally, the amount of time an individual spends in a given behavioral stage is understood to be highly variable, ranging from a minute or less to many years. At best, therefore, behavioral stages of change should be viewed only as typical pathways that a number of people seem likely to follow.

Stage models like the TTM are simple descriptive classification systems that lack clear links to empirically validated mechanisms of change. The TTM holds that processes used to promote change must match a person's present behavioral stage. But therein lies a problem. The "processes of change" identified in the TTM are poorly defined; attempts to implement them to foster change have generally been disappointing. Difficult to specify also are the barriers to change and the interventions and conditions needed to overcome them.

Apart from stage theory's conceptual difficulties, most empirical studies of stage models have not used designs that test the notion that change proceeds in discrete stages as opposed to incrementally, along a more evenly graduated continuum (Weinstein, Rothman, & Sutton, 1998). Experimental studies using interventions that match or mismatch participants' stages would provide more definitive tests than do the widely prevalent cross-sectional designs. Yet such experiments face significant challenges. These include problems in assessing the stages and barriers to change, difficulties in specifying interventions that optimally match (or mismatch) one stage but not another, and the problem of controlling the precise sequence in which participants experience the stage-appropriate (or inappropriate) treatments.

It may be feasible to develop and test workable stage models for health-protective actions that consist mainly of simple decision-making processes, entail relatively little effort, are of comparatively low cost, are easy to perform, and do not need to be repeated or maintained over an extended period of time. An example is the use of a Precaution Adoption Process Model to predict a homeowner's decision to test the house for the presence of radon gas (Weinstein, Lyon, Sandman, & Cuite, 1998; Weinstein & Sandman, 1992). But many health behaviors (e.g., weight loss) require one to develop and apply complex sets of skills, and to integrate different change mechanisms, over long periods of time (Jeffery, French, & Rothman, 1999). Simple stage schemes are less likely to achieve predictive value in these instances (Quinlan & McCaul, 2000; Rosen, 2000).

The TTM and other stage models have performed a useful service in emphasizing the need to tailor interventions to people's level of readiness to change. But they are not the only tailoring options.

SAT was developed explicitly to guide behavioral tailoring, but without requiring in advance that the treatments must be presented in a preset sequence. Instead, the intervention planner develops a "readiness profile" based on dimensional assessment of the key interacting components of the system. In the SAT example, these interacting components include a person's motives, personal projects, capabilities, and resources. The profile can include an assessment of social–environmental influences as well as cognition. The analysis identifies modifiable social and individual variables that should be included in readiness profiling, and provides a framework for estimating which ones, if targeted, are more likely to facilitate sustained, self-protective activity.

PRIORITIES FOR HEALTH BEHAVIOR RESEARCH AND INTERVENTION

Integrative theory building, using the systems perspective offered by SAT, suggests priorities for theory, research, and intervention aimed at promoting self-protective behavior. Following are recommendations derived from the preceding analysis and review. Major needs include the necessity of developing approaches to health promotion that integrate social and individual levels of analysis and devising theories and models that explain how to *change* behavior, as distinct from predicting it.

Integrating Personal and Social Perspectives

A major implication of this review is that interventions to foster health-protective behavior should be guided by an integrative model that organizes relevant theories and phenomena, indicates how they may interact, and provides a coherent agenda for intervention. Models that consider only one level of analysis (e.g., individual, group, community), and programs that try to combine many theories and techniques in ad hoc fashion, are less likely to succeed than programs that are guided by a coherent conceptual framework (Bandura, 1997). This does not mean that all interventions must address all aspects of a problem simultaneously. Rather, intervention planning should be guided by an internally consistent, multileveled perspective. Interdisciplinary collaboration, as opposed to segmentation and polarization, is needed (Schneiderman & Speers, 2001).

Psychologists, by virtue of their interests and expertise, tend to favor health promotion theories and strategies that target individuals. Yet individually oriented theories are inadequate in circumstances in which people cannot control their exposure to a health threat (e.g., violence, rape, ambient smoke). Health promotion strategies aimed at individuals also are deficient when they ignore the important role the social contexts, networks, and organizations play in shaping health behavior (Wandersman, 2001). The need to be included in a group or network creates powerful incentives to engage in risky behaviors if others are doing so (Friedman, 1995). This means that intervention must target social linkages and strive to alter network norms.

Yet social theories that ignore individuals also are inadequate. Individual-level theories do help explain why social disruption renders some people more vulnerable to illness or injury than others. Individuals differ in how they cope with challenges such as chronic poverty, unemployment, unsafe neighborhoods, or domestic violence. Ethnographic research in impoverished urban communities shows that many people manage to acquire a fund of practical knowledge, interpersonal skill, and social ties that allows them to avoid exposure to threats such as HIV/AIDS (Fullilove, 1995). Community-oriented prevention is more likely to be effective if planners can identify these "resilient" individuals, ascertain how they cope, and develop supportive interventions (e.g., styled on self-help programs) that help the effective copers communicate their strategies and skills to others. Victims of poverty, drug dependence, and spousal abuse may all benefit from learning situationally relevant coping strategies, especially if their efforts can be supported by others in their milieu. Attempts to promote social and structural changes will achieve greater impact if they include interventions to support and enhance personal resilience in members of threatened groups.

Ignorance of individual cognitive and behavioral processes also may undermine attempts to alter social networks or to use them to channel education to hard-to-reach subgroups. Social networks are sustained by the needs and wants of the individuals who make up the network. These needs and wants give the network's members the power to influence each other's behavior. Individuals' motives for belonging to a network are likely to influence how strongly they will adhere to network norms and how they will react to peer-led network interventions (Prestby, Wandersman, Florin, Rich, & Chavis, 1990). Prevention programs targeting peer leaders will accomplish little if they fail to consider the motives and skills of the identified leaders and of the peers they are supposed to influence. Critical to their success is an accurate understanding of how people process and respond to social influence attempts by their peers. Social–cognitive theories of individual behavior can guide the training of peer leaders by suggesting models of effective peer communication and persuasion. Although many people eventually change when their friends change, many others may seek out different networks (Broadhead & Heckathorn, 1994; Friedman, 1995; Heckathorn, 1990, 1995).

An integrated perspective indicates that a better understanding of relationships between group-level processes and individual behavior is greatly needed. It is important, for example, to understand how young people come to participate in vulnerable subgroups, so that interventions to reduce risk in young people can be effectively tailored and timed. Also needed is research to develop methods to alter social reinforcement and punishment contingencies that operate at the group level, especially through persuasive communications, modeling, and changes in laws and policies. Research examining how changes at the level of groups and networks affect personal relational competence, generative capabilities, motivational appraisals, and problem-solving activities should be a priority. Also, we need to understand how the motives and competencies of individuals affect their reactions to network interventions by peers. It is important to determine how these processes may vary with culture, race, social class, gender, age, and sexual orientation.

Emphasis on Behavior Change

Theories of health behavior should be evaluated on the basis of the degree to which they facilitate the control of self-endangering and protective behavior—that is, they should be judged not only on their ability to predict behavior but on their usefulness in explaining how to change it. Interrelationships among mechanisms of change should be specified in the form of causal pathways and interactions (moderators). Causal studies of social influence that examine the connections between distal (e.g., group), intermediate (e.g., relationship), and proximal (e.g., interdependent action sequence) levels are needed. Methods developed in the fields of behavioral analysis and qualitative research may prove helpful. It is important to note that theories based on an integrative understanding of causal processes may not always surpass present expectancy–value models at predicting health behavior change in populations, yet they are likely to be much more useful to intervention planners.

CONCLUSION

The challenge of fostering sustained health-protective activity is too complex to be encompassed by a single theory or intervention technique. Models of health promotion and disease prevention must be able to integrate processes by which social–environmental mechanisms on different levels of analysis influence the behavior of individuals. SAT facilitates this task by providing a multileveled architecture in which health habits are analyzed as action states (functional feedback loops) shaped by individual-level self-change processes operating within a matrix of biological and social–contextual influences. This systems perspective offers a useful basis for appraising models of health promotion and illness prevention. It suggests that a major challenge facing the field is to move beyond theories that predict behavioral outcomes but fail to identify the causal mechanisms that can be activated to promote change, as well as models that address a single level of analysis. SAT proposes that health promotion is best regarded as a process of helping people acquire, orchestrate, and repeatedly activate the complex skill sets and environmental supports needed to achieve long-term health habit change.

REFERENCES

Ajzen, I. (1985). From decisions to actions: A theory of planned behavior. In J. Kuhl & J. Beckmann (Eds.), *Action-control: From cognition to behavior* (pp. 11–39). New York: Springer.

Ajzen, I., & Fishbein, M. (1980). *Understanding attitudes and predicting social behavior.* Homewood, IL: Dorsey Press.

Baldwin, A. L. (1955). *Behavior and development in childhood.* New York: Dryden Press.

Bandura, A. (1986). *Social foundations of thought and action: A social cognitive theory.* Englewood Cliffs, NJ: Prentice-Hall.

Bandura, A. (1997). *Self-Efficacy: The exercise of control*. New York: W. H. Freeman.

Bovbjerg, V. E., McCann, B. S., Brief, D. J., Follette, W. C., Retzlaff, B. M., Dowdy, A. A., et al. (1995). Spouse support and long-term adherence to lipid-lowering diets. *American Journal of Epidemiology, 141*, 451–460.

Broadhead, R. S., & Heckathorn, D. D. (1994). AIDS prevention outreach among injection drug users: Agency problems and new approaches. *Social Problems, 41*, 473 – 495.

Caspi, A. (2000). The child is father of the man: Personality continuities from childhood to adulthood. *Journal of Personality and Social Psychology, 78*(1), 158–172.

Chen, E., Matthews, K. A., & Boyce, W. T. (2002). Socioeconomic differences in children's health: How and why do these relationships change with age? *Psychological Bulletin, 128*, 295–329.

Coie, D. A. (1991). Preliminary support for a competency-based model of depression in children. *Journal of Abnormal Psychology, 100*, 181–190.

Coyne, J. C., & Downey, G. (1991). Social factors and psychopathology: Stress, social support, and coping processes. *Annual Review of Psychology, 42*, 401–425.

Darling, N., & Steinberg, L. (1993). Parenting style as context: An integrative model. *Psychological Bulletin, 113*, 487–496.

deRosnay, J. (1979). *The macroscope*. New York: Harper & Row.

Diener, E., Suh, E. M., Lucas, R. E., & Smith, H. L. (1999). Subjective well-being: Three decades of progress. *Psychological Bulletin, 125*(2), 276–302.

Dodge, K. A., Asher, S. R., & Parkhurst, J. T. (1989). Social life as a goal-coordination task. *Research on motivation in education (Vol. 3: Goals and cognitions)* (Vol. 3, pp. 107–135). New York: Academic Press.

Eisenberg, N., Fabes, R. A., Guthrie, I. K., & Reiser, M. (2000). Dispositional emotionality and regulation: Their role in predicting quality of social functioning. *Journal of Personality and Social Psychology, 78*(1), 136–157.

Elliott, D. S., Huizinga, D., & Menard, S. (1989). *Multiple problem youth: Delinquency, substance use, and mental health problems*. New York: Springer-Verlag.

Ewart, C. K. (1991a). Familial transmission of essential hypertension: Genes, environments, and chronic anger. *Annals of Behavioral Medicine, 13*, 40–47.

Ewart, C. K. (1991b). Social action theory for a public health psychology. *American Psychologist, 46*, 931–946.

Ewart, C. K. (1993). Editorial comment: Marital interaction—The context for psychosomatic research. *Psychosomatic Medicine, 55*, 410–412.

Ewart, C. K. (1994). Nonshared environments and heart disease risk: Concepts and data for a model of coronary-prone behavior. In E. Hetherington, D. Reiss, & R. Plomin (Eds.), *The separate social worlds of siblings* (pp. 175–203). Hillsdale, NJ: Erlbaum.

Ewart, C. K. (in press). Social environments, agonistic stress, and elevated blood pressure in urban youth. In R. Portman, J. Sorof, & J. Ingelfinger (Eds.), *Pediatric hypertension*. Totowa, NJ: Humana Press.

Ewart, C. K., & Jorgensen, R. S. (in press). Agonistic interpersonal striving: Social–cognitive mechanism of cardiovascular risk in youth? *Health Psychology*.

Ewart, C. K., Jorgensen, R. S., Suchday, S., Chen, E., & Matthews, K. A. (2002). Measuring stress resilience and coping in vulnerable youth: The Social Competence Interview. *Psychological Assessment, 14*(3), 339–352.

Ewart, C. K., Stewart, K. J., Gillilan, R. E., & Kelemen, M. H. (1986). Self-efficacy mediates strength gains during circuit weight training in men with coronary artery disease. *Medicine and Science in Sports and Exercise, 18*, 531–540.

Ewart, C. K., & Suchday, S. (2002). Discovering how urban poverty and violence affect health: Development and validation of a neighborhood stress index. *Health Psychology, 21*(3), 254–262.

Ewart, C. K., Taylor, C. B., Kraemer, C. H., & Agras, W. S. (1991). High blood pressure and marital discord: Not being nasty matters more than being nice. *Health Psychology, 10*, 155–163.

Ewart, C. K., Taylor, C. B., Reese, L. B., & DeBusk, R. F. (1983). The effects of early post myocardial infarction exercise testing on self perception and subsequent physical activity. *American Journal of Cardiology, 51*, 1076–1080.

Fischoff, B. (1995). *What do people need to know about AIDS?* Paper presented at the workshop on the social and behavioral science base for HIV/AIDS prevention and intervention, Washington, DC.

Fischoff, B., Bostrom, A., & Quadrel, M. J. (1993). Risk perception and communication. *Annual Review of Public Health, 14*, 183–203.

Friedman, S. R. (1995, June). *Social science intervention models*. Paper presented at the workshop on the social and behavioral science base for HIV/AIDS prevention and intervention, Institute of Medicine, Washington, DC.

Fullilove, R. E. (1995, June). *Community disintegration and public health: An American inner city case study*. Paper presented at the workshop on the social and behavioral science base for HIV/AIDS prevention and intervention, Institute of Medicine, Washington, DC.

Gallo, L. C., & Matthews, K. A. (2003). Understanding the association between socioeconomic status and physical health: Do negative emotions play a role? *Psychological Bulletin, 129*, 10–51.

Garmezy, N., Masten, A. S., Nordstrom, L., & Farrarese, M. (1979). The nature of competence in normal and deviant children. In M. W. Kent & J. E. Rolf (Eds.), *Social competence in children* (pp. 23–43). Hanover, NH: University Press of New England.

Giddens, A. (1979). *Central problems in social theory: Action, structure, and contradiction in social analysis*. Berkeley: University of California Press.

Glanz, K., Lewis, F. M., & Rimer, B. K. (1997). *Health behavior and health education: Theory, research, and practice*. San Francisco: Jossey-Bass.

Han, S. P., & Shavitt, S. (1994). Persuasion and culture: Advertising appeals in individualistic and collectivistic societies. *Journal of Experimental Social Psychology, 30,* 326–350.

Hawkins, J. D., Catalano, R. F., & Miller, J. Y. (1992). Risk and protective factors for alcohol and other drug problems in adolescence and early adulthood: Implications for substance abuse prevention. *Psychological Bulletin, 112,* 64–105.

Heckathorn, D. D. (1990). Collective sanctions and compliance norms: A formal theory of group-mediated social control. *American Sociological Review, 55,* 366–384.

Heckathorn, D. D. (1995, June). *Cognitive psychology, social networks, and AIDS.* Paper presented at the workshop on the social and behavioral science base for HIV/AIDS prevention and intervention, Washington, DC.

Helgeson, V. S. (1993). Implications of agency and communion for patient and spouse adjustment to a first coronary event. *Journal of Personality and Social Psychology, 64*(5), 807–816.

Helgeson, V. (1994). Relation of agency and communion to well-being: Evidence and potential explanations. *Journal of Personality and Social Psychology, 116,* 412–428.

Herzog, T. A., Abrams, D. B., Emmons, K. M., Linnan, L. A., & Shadel, W. G. (1999). Do processes of change predict smoking stage movements? A prospective analysis of the transtheoretical model. *Health Psychology, 18,* 369–375.

Jeffery, R. W. (1989). Risk behaviors and health: Contrasting individual and population perspectives. *American Psychologist, 44,* 1194–1202.

Jeffery, R. W., French, S. A., & Rothman, A. J. (1999). Stage of change as a predictor of success in weight control in adult women. *Health Psychology, 18,* 543–546.

Jessor, R., & Jessor, S. L. (1977). *Problem behavior and psychosocial development.* New York: Academic Press.

Kagan, J. (1998). *Galen's prophecy: Temperament in human nature.* Boulder, CO: Westview Press.

Kelley, H., Berscheid, E., Christensen, A., Harvey, J. H., Huston, T. L., Levinger, G., et al. (1983). *Close relationships.* New York: Freeman.

Kiecolt-Glaser, J. K., Malarkey, W. B., Chee, M. A., Newton, T., Cacioppo, J. T., Mao, H. Y., et al. (1993). Negative behavior during marital conflict is associated with immunological down-regulation. *Psychosomatic Medicine, 55,* 395–409.

Kirscht, J. P. (1974). The health belief model and illness behavior. *Health Education Monographs, 2,* 387–408.

Kuran, T. (1995). *Private truths, public lies: The social consequences of preference falsification.* Cambridge, MA: Harvard University Press.

Landrine, H., & Klonoff, E. A. (2001). Cultural diversity and health psychology. In A. Baum, T. Revenson, & J. Singer (Eds.), *Handbook of health psychology* (pp. 851–891). Mahwah, NJ: Erlbaum.

Leventhal, T., & Brooks-Gunn, J. (2000). The neighborhoods they live in: The effects of neighborhood residence on child and adolescent outcomes. *Psychological Bulletin, 126*, 309–337.

Luthar, S. S., & Zigler, E. (1991). Vulnerability and competence: A review of research on resilience in childhood. *American Journal of Orthopsychiatry, 61*, 6–22.

Markus, H. R., & Kitayama, S. (1991). Culture and the self: Implications for cognition, emotion, and motivation. *Psychological Review, 98*, 224–253.

Pedhazur, E. J., & Schmelking, L. P. (1991). *Measurement, design, and analysis: An integrative approach.* Hillsdale, NJ: Erlbaum.

Perri, M. G., Nezu, A. M., & Viegener, B. J. (1992). *Improving the long-term management of obesity: Theory, research, and clinical guidelines.* New York: John Wiley & Sons.

Prestby, J., Wandersman, A., Florin, P., Rich, R., & Chavis, D. (1990). Benefits, costs, incentive management and participation in voluntary organizations: A means to understanding and promoting empowerment. *American Journal of Community Psychology, 18*, 111–149.

Prochaska, J. C., DiClemente, C. C., & Norcross, J. (1992). In search of how people change. *American Psychologist, 47*, 1102–1114.

Quinlan, K. B., & McCaul, K. D. (2000). Matched and mismatched interventions with young adult smokers: Testing a stage theory. *Health Psychology, 19*, 165–171.

Rogers, R. W. (1983). Cognitive and psychological processes in fear appeals and attitude change: A revised theory of protection motivation. In J. T. Cacioppo & R. E. Petty (Eds.), *Social–psychophysiology* (pp. 153–176). New York: Guilford Press.

Rosen, C. S. (2000). Is the sequencing of change processes by stage consistent across health problems? A meta-analysis. *Health Psychology, 19*, 593–604.

Schaefer, E. S. (1959). The circumplex model for maternal behavior. *Journal of Abnormal and Social Psychology, 59*, 226–235.

Schneiderman, N., & Speers, M. A. (2001). Behavioral science, social science, and public health in the 21st century. In N. Schneiderman, M. A. Speers, J. M. Silva, H. Tomes, & J. H. Gentry (Eds.), *Integrating behavioral and social sciences with public health* (pp. 3–28.). Washington, DC: American Psychological Association.

Schwartz, G. E. (1981). A systems analysis of psychobiology and behavior therapy: Implications for behavioral medicine. *Psychotherapy and Psychosomatics, 36*, 159–184.

Schwartz, G. E. (1982). Testing the biopsychosocial model: The ultimate challenge facing behavioral medicine? *Journal of Consulting and Clinical Psychology, 50*(6), 1040–1053.

Sears, R. R. (1957). Identification as a form of behavior development. In D. B. Harris (Ed.), *The concept of development* (pp. 149–161). Minneapolis: University of Minnesota Press.

Sher, K. J. (1991). *Children of alcoholics*. Chicago: University of Chicago Press.

Shoemaker, D. J. (1990). *Theories of delinquency: An examination of explanations of delinquent behavior* (2nd ed.). New York: Oxford University Press.

Smyth, J., Wonderlich, S., Crosby, R., Miltenberger, R., Mitchell, J., & Rorty, M. (2001). The use of ecological momentary assessment approaches in eating disorder research. *International Journal of Eating Disorders, 30,* 83–95.

Spivack, G., Platt, J. J., & Shure, M. B. (1976). *The problem-solving approach to adjustment*. San Francisco: Jossey-Bass.

Spivack, G., & Shure, M. B. (1974). *Social adjustment in young children: A cognitive approach to solving real life problems*. San Francisco: Jossey-Bass.

Stone, A. A., & Schiffman, S. (1994). Ecological Momentary Assessment (EMA) in behavioral medicine. *Annals of Behavioral Medicine, 16,* 199–202.

Strecher, V. J., & Rosenstock, I. M. (1997). The health belief model. In K. Glanz, F. M. Lewis, & B. K. Rimer (Eds.), *Health behavior and health education: Theory, research, and practice* (pp. 41–59). San Fancisco: Jossey-Bass.

Sutton, S. (1996). Can "stages of change" provide guidance in the treatment of addictions? A critical examination of Prochaska and DiClemente's model. In G. Edwards & C. Dare (Eds.), *Psychotherapy, psychological treatments and the addictions* (pp. 189–205). Cambridge, England: Cambridge University Press.

Sutton, S. R., McVey, D., & Glanz, A. (1999). A comparative test of the Theory of Reasoned Action and the Theory of Planned Behavior in the prediction of condom use intentions in a national sample of English young people. *Health Psychology, 18,* 72–81.

Symonds, P. M. (1939). *The psychology of parent–child relationships*. New York: Appleton-Century-Crofts.

Temple, L. K. F., McLeod, R. S., Gallinger, S., & Wright, J. G. (2001). Defining disease in the genomics era. *Science, 293*(3), 807–808.

Wade, S. L., Holden, G., Lynn, H., Mitchell, H., & Ewart, C. (2000). Cognitive–behavioral predictors of asthma morbidity in inner-city children. *Journal of Developmental and Behavioral Pediatrics, 21*(5), 340–346.

Wallander, J. L. (1992). Theory-driven research in pediatric psychology: A little bit on why and how. *Journal of Pediatric Psychology, 17*(5), 521–535.

Wallander, J. L. (2000). *Social–emotional competence and physical health*. Washington, DC: Center for the Advancement of Health.

Wandersman, A. (2001). Community mobilization for prevention and health promotion can work. In N. Schneiderman, M. A. Speers, J. M. Silva, H. Tomes, & J. H. Gentry (Eds.), *Integrating behavioral and social sciences with public health* (pp. 231–247). Washington, DC: American Psychological Association.

Weinstein, N. D. (1993). Testing four competing theories of health-protective behavior. *Health Psychology, 12,* 324–333.

Weinstein, N. D., Lyon, J. E., Sandman, P. M., & Cuite, C. L. (1998). Experimental evidence for stages of health behavior change: The Precaution Adoption Process Model applied to home radon testing. *Health Psychology, 17,* 445–453.

Weinstein, N. D., Rothman, A. J., & Sutton, S. R. (1998). Stage theories of health behavior: Conceptual and methodological issues. *Health Psychology, 17,* 290–299.

Weinstein, N. D., & Sandman, P. M. (1992). A model of the precaution adoption process: Evidence from home radon testing. *Health Psychology, 11,* 170–180.

Wheeler, L., Reis, H. T., & Bond, M. H. (1989). Collectivism—Individualism in everyday social life: The middle kingdom and the melting pot. *Journal of Personality and Social Psychology, 57,* 79–86.

III

CLINICAL ISSUES

8

THE PRACTICE OF CLINICAL HEALTH PSYCHOLOGY: PROFESSIONAL ISSUES

REBECCA K. PAPAS, CYNTHIA D. BELAR, AND RONALD H. ROZENSKY

Although practice in clinical health psychology dates back to the time of Hippocrates, practice *as* clinical health psychology is relatively new in the health care professions.

> The specialty of Clinical Health Psychology applies scientific knowledge of the interrelationships among behavioral, emotional, cognitive, social and biological components in health and disease to the promotion and maintenance of health; the prevention, treatment and rehabilitation of illness and disability; and the improvement of the health care system. (American Psychological Association Council of Representatives, 1997)

Practitioners of various disciplines have for many years used psychological principles and interventions in attempts to improve health. In fact, curiosity about, and beliefs concerning, mind–body relationships have been with us throughout recorded history. Yet within the past two decades there have been significant developments in the science and practice of clinical health psychology. In addition to significant expansion, it has become increasingly formalized and recognized as a distinct specialty in the professional practice of psychology. In synergism with the growth of scientific knowledge, the roles and functions of its practitioners have multiplied; education and training guidelines have been developed; credentialing procedures have been created; and new professional, ethical, and legal issues have been confronted. It is these aspects of clinical health psychology that this chapter will address, with due respect for the indebtedness of the specialty to its historical roots.

The term *clinical health psychology* was perhaps first used by Millon, Green, and Meagher (1982), who edited the first *Handbook of Clinical Health Psychology*. Soon thereafter the first practice primer, *The Practice of Clinical Health Psychology*, was published (Belar, Deardorff, & Kelly, 1987; later updated by Belar & Deardorff, 1995). A second edited handbook with substantial content relevant to clinical health psychology appeared in 1991 (Sweet, Rozensky, & Tovian), with another *Clinical Handbook of Health Psychology* appearing in 1998 (Camic & Knight). Suffice it to say that in the past decade there has been an explosion of journals, textbooks, handbooks, and clinical guides that provide an extensive knowledge base for practice within the specialty. Many of these are referenced throughout the three volumes of this handbook. The culmination of this process has been (a) recognition by the American Board of Professional Psychology (ABPP) of board certification for practitioners through the American Board of Clinical Health Psychology (Belar & Jeffrey, 1995); and (b) recognition by the American Psychological Association (APA) Council of Representatives as a distinct specialty in the professional practice of psychology. It is noted that the specialty was designated clinical health psychology rather than health psychology to clearly communicate to the public that this is the part of the field that is related to the provision of health care services. It is important to remember that there are numerous scholars, scientists, and teachers who make significant contributions to health psychology who are neither trained nor self-identify as health service providers. In addition to the definition noted, the APA archival definition includes the following:

> The distinct focus of Clinical Health Psychology is on physical health problems. The specialty is dedicated to the development of knowledge regarding the interface between behavior and health, and to the delivery of high quality services based on that knowledge to individuals, families, and health care systems. (APA Council of Representatives, 1997)

The archival description continues with a description of populations, problems and issues addressed, and procedures used, much of which will be described in more detail in other volumes of this series, although a full text of the definition is provided in the appendix at the end of this chapter. Of special significance is the fact that the biopsychosocial model and the ability to work in a broad range of health care settings with other health care professions are fundamental aspects of the specialty. This means that biological, psychological, and sociocultural components of health and disease, and their interactions, are integral to practice, and that skills in interprofessional practice are critical. The purpose of this chapter is to focus on some of the cross-cutting professional issues particularly relevant to clinical health psychology, many of which have been addressed in previous work, but that are briefly summarized. These include issues related to settings, ethics, malpractice, education and training, credentialing, and changes in the health care system. However, we shall first address a critical issue for the specialty and for health care: mind–body dualism. [Note: Because this chapter is intended to highlight aspects of ethical, legal, and other professional issues that pertain to the practice of clinical health psychology, the reader interested in a broad overview of issues relevant to clinical psychology practice may refer to Bennett, Bryant, VandenBos, and Greenwood (1990); Bersoff (1999); Doverspike (1999); Koocher and Keith-Spiegel (1998); Lowman and Resnick (1994); APA's *Law and Mental Health Professionals* state-by-state series—for example, *Arizona* (Miller & Sales, 1986)].

THE PERILS OF MIND–BODY DUALISM

Many of the critical issues facing clinical health psychology can be traced to the fact that mind–body dualism has been firmly entrenched in Western society, the health care system, and the discipline itself. This dualism has made it difficult for consumers to access relevant services for a variety of reasons that are briefly addressed in this section. First, with the exception of primary care providers, physician training has been dominated by a biomedical versus biopsychosocial model; thus medication is often viewed as the treatment of choice. In addition, medical school curricula include psychiatry and mental health as core components but often lack curricular components that integrate behavior and health. Psychologists in medical schools have strived to change this, with a number of successes noted with both advances in psychological science and professional groups such as the Association for the Behavioral Sciences and Medical Education. At the residency training level, psychological science has been considered part of the core curriculum for family practitioners and pediatricians for several decades now; thus it is no surprise that these practitioners have systematically welcomed close collaboration with psychologists. Nevertheless, the importance of the role of psychology in the education and training of other health care disciplines, not just medicine, has often been underestimated and is still underdeveloped.

Second, physicians are often hesitant to refer patients for psychological services unless significant psychopathology is present, because patients can often seem insulted by the suggestion that psychological services are relevant when they view their problem as primarily medical–surgical. Either/or thinking is prevalent in physicians and patients, although less so now than two decades ago, in our experience. In practice we have developed materials for physicians to facilitate referrals to clinical health psychologists. Yet organized psychology has not systematically approached the postgraduate education of other health professions. In addition to other professionals, educating the public about the integration of behavior and health is critical. Historically psychology has presented itself as a "mental health profession," an image that could deter a consumer not viewing him- or herself as having a "mental health problem." Although this stance on the part of organized psychology has changed, it will require a sustained approach to advocacy and public information for a broader view of the profession to be accepted.

Another impact of dualism is that most practitioners of psychology have been trained primarily as mental health service providers. Thus the public does not have access to a large cadre of broadly trained clinical health psychologists; even board certification in the specialty is less than a decade old. Although behavioral medicine has been found to be the modal content area in clinical psychology doctoral programs (Sayette & Mayne, 1990), many programs have only one or two faculty with expertise in the area. Moreover, they often lack access to multidisciplinary health care settings where their faculty can serve as role models for the integration of science and practice in clinical health psychology. Broader opportunities are often available at the internship level, with training in behavioral medicine offered in about 36% of programs; however, only 2% offered a major rotation in primary care, an increasingly important arena for psychological services in the evolving health care system (American Psychological Association, 1998a).

With the pressure on practitioners to expand their scope of practice to remain financially viable, there is risk that insufficiently trained providers could provide substandard care, be unable to work well with other health care professions and thus damage the credibility of the profession. There needs to be an increased focus on respecialization and standards for practice in clinical health psychology, and the development of user-friendly continuing professional education for professional psychologists. In the context of increasing the cadre of psychologists with skills for practice in this area, we also reemphasize the importance of integration of science and practice in education and training. The scientist–practitioner model has been a generative one; it has resulted in both the advancement of knowledge and the expansion of practice in clinical health psychology. In fact one could argue it actually created the specialty itself. Our present state of knowledge is not sufficient for the training of practitioners without clinical research skills; when it is, we anticipate that other professions will be applying the knowledge and skills developed by psychology as well.

An unfortunate consequence of dualism is that in ambulatory care, psychological services are often geographically separated from medical–surgical services, even in large health care systems. This is a significant barrier to integrated care and can hinder patient follow-through with referrals as well as interprofessional collaboration in practice and clinical research. Although many clinical health psychologists practice side-by-side with pediatricians or family practitioners in primary care settings, specialists in tertiary care settings, and multidisciplinary teams in rehabilitation settings, academic and health policy decisions often tend to support discipline-based silos or clinics that hinder access to services.

Perhaps the most significant consequence of mind–body dualism has been that in fee-for-service systems, psychologists are reimbursed for services rendered to patients meeting criteria for diagnosis in the *DSM–IV* (American Psychiatric Association, 1994), a system that is not relevant to many services of clinical health psychologists. In fact, insurance coding restrictions are a major, prohibitive factor to growth of psychological services in health and rehabilitation (Glueckauf, 1999). In addition, the development of "behavioral health carveouts" has been antithetical to the fundamental tenets of clinical health psychology. Despite considerable evidence that health psychology services result in significant medical cost offset, their growth will be impeded by the specialty managed behavioral (mental) health care industry, which views such cost savings as accruing to "others."

The Interdivisional Healthcare Committee (IHC), a coalition of APA health-oriented divisions, has undertaken a project to expand current insurance procedure codes to ensure that psychologists have the option of being reimbursed as primary health care providers. The use of such insurance codes promotes consumer access to psychological services in health care by minimizing referral-related barriers. Code implementation also enhances the integration of psychological services within the financial structure of the health care system, a fundamental marker for the growth of psychology as a health care profession (Tovian, 1999). Effective in January 2002, six new current procedural terminology (CPT) codes for health and behavior assessment and intervention services were approved for behavioral, social, and psychophysiological procedures for the prevention, treatment, or management of physical health problems. The new behavioral health codes are reimbursable by Medicare in most states, using medical rather than psychiatric funding dollars. For reimbursement to occur, services must be associated with the patient's medical condition, as documented by an *International Classification of Disease (ICD–9;* Practice Management Information Corporation, 1998) code, rather than with any existing mental health diagnoses (American Psychological Association, 2002a). The creation of truly integrated capitated health care delivery systems could also serve to address this problem, because systems will be more motivated to design cost-effective services most relevant to their members rather than being driven by a process of external review of codes or staying within the boundaries of their specialty.

PROFESSIONAL ROLE ISSUES IN CLINICAL HEALTH PSYCHOLOGY

In general, psychologists can become part of an integrated health care system (APA Practice Directorate, 1996) in primary care, secondary care, tertiary care, prevention, or rehabilitation. As noted in volume 1 of this series, psychologists have contributed to health care research and service for each of the *ICD–9* categories of disorders. As Resnick and Rozensky (1996) have noted, given that disease is a natural component of the human condition, there are unlimited opportunities to be part of the health care team no matter how the changes in the health system evolve. As part of the team in any of these settings, the clinical health psychologist should understand the culture of the organization as well as know the specific techniques and procedures necessary to function effectively on behalf of the patient. Historically, the culture in many health care settings has been based on the biomedical model, which emphasizes quick decisions for the control of disease. The biopsychosocial model, in contrast, is patient-centered and encourages the patient to take an active role in controlling illness. Each model has implications for both collaborative relationships with physicians and for patient care.

Understanding referral procedures in health care settings is important (Rozensky, Sweet, & Tovian, 1997). Each hospital's policies and procedures manual provides guidelines for referral procedures, as well as a many other procedures. A summary of referral customs follows: (a) in hospital-based collaborative care, psychologists generally do not see a patient under the care of an attending physician unless requested by that physician; (b) psychologists should provide inpatient consultations within 24 hours, making reports available immediately; (c) psychologists should clarify with the referring physician and the health care team as to how the results of consultations will be communicated to the patient; (d) psychologists should not refer a patient to a medical or dental colleague for consultation without first discussing with the original referral source or until the case is discharged to the psychologist's care; and (e) psychologists should not leave the attending physician without specific directions or proper follow-up after providing a consultation. Many consultations may require more than one contact.

As referrals provide the basis for collaborative relationships in health care settings, educating physicians about psychological referral criteria may be very useful. Indeed, many physicians or other professionals may not understand the nature of clinical health psychologist training or areas of competency, thinking of psychology in its heretofore traditional mental health role. The clinical health psychologist should educate other professionals in the health care setting in a manner that is neither defensive nor arrogant. Providing a handout or brochure with some criteria for consultation may be helpful (for example, if complaints seem out of proportion to organic pathology, if treatment does not yield expected results despite an improved organic status, or when new symptoms arise as old symptoms resolve; see Belar & Deardorff, 1995, for a more complete list). Specific scientific or clinical journal articles on specific areas of clinical practice, assessment, or treatment can be forwarded to referring physicians or an offer of providing grand rounds in a particular area are methods of peer education. Referrals can be premature; for example, a request for a mental status evaluation just hours after trauma, or extensively delayed beyond optimal opportunity for psychological intervention such as consulting psychology after staff have consistently confronted an agitated patient. Another common occurrence is that a request for consultation be made to administer a specific psychological test rather than to answer a referral question. Educating physicians about appropriate methods of phrasing the referral may also be warranted. Explaining the referral in an appropriate manner can minimize the possibilities that the patient will hear an inappropriate message—for example, "the pain must be all in my head." (See Belar & Deardorff, 1995, for suggested referral phrases.) Patients who are not told of the reason for the referral (68% of patients referred to psychiatry, according to Bagheri, Lane, Kline, & Araujo, 1981), furthermore, may arrive in a somewhat hostile fashion, making the assessment more difficult. Even with appropriate referral information, many medical–surgical patients may have initial difficulty with obtaining psychological services because they are expected to play a more active role in self-care than in the biomedical model. Thus, educating the patient about the biopsychosocial model may also be important in promoting active participation. In addition, many patients are mind–body dualists and have not been educated to understand the reciprocal influences of mind and body. For patients who are not psychologically minded, providing something concrete may be helpful in easing the transition, such as offering an explanation of psychophysiological aspects of the medical problem or a diary for self-monitoring troublesome symptoms (Belar & Deardorff, 1995).

Primary Care Settings

Primary care is defined by Bray (1996) as first contact care at the point of entry for the patient into the health care system. Primary care providers coordinate care over time with continuing responsibility for the patient. Given that 60% of visits to primary care physicians have some mental health component (Cummings & VandenBos, 1981), opportunities for psychologists in primary care are increasing, a trend that is expected to continue through the next decade. Clinical health psychologists who work in primary care must be competent in recognizing and treating a broad range of behavioral and mental health problems over the lifespan (Resnick & Rozensky, 1996). Often the illnesses are not as debilitating as would be seen in other clinical settings. The clinical health psychologist working in primary care must also learn to diagnose and treat during shorter sessions for a greater volume of patients per day. Whether working in a clinic, group practice, or with an individual family medicine practitioner, the clinical health psychologist must learn the culture of the primary care setting just as she or he would the hospital setting. Establishing and maintaining a good collaborative relationship with the primary care physician is essential. In one pilot study of collaboration in primary care, clinical health psychologists who had regular meetings with other providers or who practiced in the same building were most successful in establishing a collaborative relationship. Factors interfering with collaboration included managed care and reimbursement issues, as well as not being on hospital staffs where physicians practice (Bray & Rogers, 1995). Thus, it would be beneficial for clinical health psychologists to take the lead in arranging regular contact such as scheduled telephone conferences, lunch or breakfast appointments, use of faxes to make referrals, or shared hospital rounds. Where a collaborative structure has not been established, it may be especially important to educate the physician about making psychology referrals in primary care.

Increased Responsibility for Physical Health

Because of the unique role played by clinical health psychologists in health care settings, having an adequate understanding of medical problems and relevant treatments is imperative. Responsibilities for clinical health psychologists could include, for example, determining whether expectations are realistic for penile prosthesis surgery, knowing whether a patient can withstand the rigors of heart transplant surgery and its sequelae, or promoting lifestyle changes to enhance medical management. In addition, because psychological treatment is typically associated with longer sessions, more frequent contact, and a well-developed rapport with the patient, the medical–surgical patient may report new, important details related to medical conditions to the clinical health psychologist. When the clinician suspects that the patient is behaving in a manner or describing symptoms suggestive of organic disease, it is his or her responsibility to refer the patient for medical evaluation. Such information should be documented and passed on to other health care providers. In general, clinical health psychologists frequently have more responsibility for physical health than anticipated— for example, by having to assess whether previous medical work-ups have been adequate, without having extensive training in that area. Thus, it is essential that the clinical health psychologist has established relationships with specialty physicians in whom the clinician has confidence to enable "curbside" consultations to determine the proper avenue for medical treatment (Belar & Deardorff, 1995).

ETHICS

Because goals of treatment are related to physical illness, the practice of clinical health psychology is typically accompanied by unique ethical challenges. Maintaining competence may be the most challenging aspect of practice, because clinical health psychologists must not only keep pace with constant changes in the field but also keep tabs on the ever-changing American health care delivery system and on medical treatment issues relevant to psychology. Adequate knowledge of the biological domain is necessary because clinical health psychologists are frequently called to alert physicians to relevant changes in patient's physical status during treatment as well as to promote patient lifestyle changes relevant to medical management. Besides competence, ethical concerns related to the multidisciplinary medical setting include issues of confidentiality and the proper use of psychological information. Finally, today's managed care milieu may necessitate economic informed consent and increased patient advocacy.

ASSESSMENT IN THE MEDICAL SETTING

Common mistakes in assessment in the medical setting include failing to consider the impact of the hospital environment and situational events (e.g., upheaval related to illness) on the patient's mood, which can lead to erroneous conclusions about causality and the permanence of a patient's condition. Conversely, underestimating the impact of psychopathology on the medical–surgical patient's problem is also a potential problem. For example, an estimated 30 to 54% of chronic pain patients seen in clinics meet criteria for major depressive disorder at any given point in time (Banks & Kerns, 1996). Thus, the clinical health psychologist must have a thorough understanding of how anxiety and depression as well as personality disorders interact with various medical–surgical problems and treatment.

Because many standardized psychological tests have been normed on a psychiatric population, the inappropriate generalization of results to specific medical–surgical populations can be unethical without proper caveats. For example, test norms for depression based on psychiatric patients may overestimate prevalence in pain patients, because endorsement of somatic items may reflect illness experience rather than mental health status (Banks & Kerns, 1996). Inappropriate misuse of psychological information may also occur in a multidisciplinary setting if results are not thoroughly explained to other professionals without relevant expertise. For example, it is imperative that clinical health psychologists convey that psychological tests cannot rule out organic problems or confirm that problems are functional in origin.

Confidentiality

Another issue related to the health care setting is patient confidentiality. Of course, the practicing health psychologist should be aware of both state laws pertaining to issues of confidentiality and APA ethical standards dictating confidential communication (see Section 4, "Privacy and Confidentiality" of *Ethical Principles of Psychologists and Code of Conduct*; American Psychological Association, 2002b). In particular in health care settings, the psychologist should make certain that the patient understands what the psychologists will be putting into the patient chart. Because patient functioning is often discussed by multidisciplinary teams and documented accordingly in widely circulated medical records, maintaining appropriate patient confidentiality may be difficult. Although many organizations maintain separate psychological records, it is essential that informed-consent procedures include notifying the patient of procedures for documenting psychological information and of the release of information to the managed care organization (MCO) or insurer. Rozensky et al. (1997) suggest that the consulting psychologist should include in the medical record a note indicating what information was given to insurance companies and with whom the psychologist has spoken to facilitate additional conversations with third-party payers as needed. Other unique challenges to confidentiality derive from seeing patients in multibed patients' rooms, which frequently do not ensure privacy. If a time or location cannot be arranged for seeing the patient privately, the clinical health psychologist should give the patient the explicit option of declining psychological services. In addition, because many medical management issues such as compliance are closely related to family-systems issues, family members often seek information about patient status. The clinical health psychologist should obtain written consent to provide confidential information to the family unless the patient is unable to make informed decisions.

Patient Welfare

Because the clinical health psychologist interfaces with the patient, the hospital and the health care delivery system, she or he may often be called on to act as patient advocate. One example may be in the domain of patient compliance, where a clinical health psychologist must decide if the medical system is intolerant of deviations from treatment that clearly represent the patient's values, or, similarly, if staff frustrations are the true reason for referral. Similarly, conflicting pressures related to medical decision making may test the psychologist's commitment to integrity. For example, the clinical health psychologist may be pressured to endorse an otherwise unfit candidate for organ transplantation to please the patient's physician, the referral source, or to satisfy hospital's malpractice risk assurance.

Trends in managed care and in capitation have created new aspects of contractual arrangements that may also heighten the need for patient advocacy. It is telling that a recent literature review of the most frequently published ethical concerns related to the MCO role included discontinuing treatment when still indicated, misleading advertising, treatment delays or denials, loss of consumer choice, and promoting inadequate treatment for the neediest populations. Issues related to the practitioner in organized health care delivery include issues of abandonment and divided loyalties, as well as patient confidentiality, informed consent, competence, appropriate diagnoses, and technology use (American Psychological Association, 1997). Thus, the clinical health psychologist must take care to protect a patient's autonomy rather than allow devaluation in the face of health care system or provider values.

Understanding how to negotiate through the maze of managed care is an ethical issue related to competence. In an APA committee report on health care delivery (1997), recommendations for provider competence include (a) brief treatment modalities; (b) time-limited service delivery; (c) taking an active, directive role in therapy; (d) patient advocacy; (e) interactions with staff and providers on behalf of the patient; and (f) working within plan limits. Haas and Cummings (1991) also suggested that the practitioner may have an ethical obligation to ensure that managed care plans with which they are associated have mechanisms with which to receive feedback and to give recommendations for change.

With the advent of managed care, the practitioner may also be ethically obligated to obtain economic informed consent by exposing contract obligations, fiduciary duties, or other financial limitations of the client's insurance or managed care plan that may affect treatment (Substance Abuse and Mental Health Services Administration [SAMHSA], 1998). The responsibility for economic informed consent may rest with the clinical health psychologist rather than the payer because of the changing nature of treatment relationships. Although traditional relationships existed exclusively between practitioner and client, on one hand, and between client and insurer on the other hand, many MCOs may today contract directly with the clinical health psychologist. Thus, the limitations of treatment may be a result of the clinical health psychologist's desire to maintain a good relationship with the MCO (SAMHSA, 1998).

MALPRACTICE RISKS

Malpractice as a legal term involves a complaint of professional negligence within the context of the professional relationship. Although psychologists as a group have been relatively immune from malpractice suits, clinical health psychologists may potentially be at greater risk than traditional mental health providers for malpractice suits because of their role in physical disease management (Belar & Deardorff, 1995; Knapp & VandeCreek, 1981). And, although several categories of risk may place a clinical health psychologist at the center of a malpractice lawsuit, the possibility of a successful suit is potentially greater because demonstration of physical harm is more easily verifiable than emotional harm.

Standard 2.01 of the *Ethical Principles of Psychologists and Code of Conduct* (American Psychological Association, 2002b) states that "psychologists provide services, teach, and conduct research with populations and in areas only within the boundaries of their competence, based on their education, training, supervised experience, consultation, study, or professional experience." Clearly the easiest route to follow to avoid malpractice entanglements is to practice within one's area of competency and training. Thus, those working in medical settings and with medical patients should first and foremost have completed the requisite training to work with those patients and those with specific medical disorders. (Education and training issues are discussed later in this chapter, beginning with the discussion of the Arden House conference.)

To prove that professional malpractice has occurred, several determinations must be made. First, a professional relationship must be established between psychologist and client. When a practitioner agrees to treat, diagnose, assess, or provide psychological services to a client, a professional relationship has been established (Bennett et al., 1990). Second, when the practitioner fails to deliver services using a requisite standard of care, the duty of care has been breached. Third, for a successful malpractice claim, the plaintiff must demonstrate that this breach in care directly resulted in demonstrable harm to the client. Fourth, plaintiffs must prove that this breach in care was the cause of harm to the client (Deardorff, Cross, & Hupprich, 1984).

Clinical health psychologists may be more vulnerable than traditional mental health providers in the determination of malpractice because physical harm is less difficult to prove than emotional harm and is often irreversible. It is also much easier to determine the cause of physical harm. Moreover, although traditionally lawsuits have been relatively scarce because of the reluctance of mental health patients to discuss problems in public court, psychological treatment for medical–surgical patients is typically associated with goals of physical health. Such treatment is often abbreviated in a medical setting and thus may not afford the closer professional relationships with patients that tend to buffer traditional mental health practitioners from being the defendant in lawsuits. Finally, because clinical health psychologists are typically involved in physical disease management, they are more likely than traditional mental health practitioners to be at risk for being accused of practicing medicine without a license (Knapp & VandeCreek, 1981).

Clinical health psychologists should be aware that risks are not only related to physical illness but also improper and unethical behavior. The most frequent claim by far in successful malpractice suits in 1991 was sexual misconduct, followed by incorrect treatment, evaluation, and breach of confidentiality (VandeCreek & Stout, 1993). A discussion of each area as it relates to clinical health psychology follows.

Each year, a majority of complaints filed with the APA allege sexual misconduct, typically against male psychologists by adult female clients (e.g., APA Ethics Committee, 1999). In almost every complaint of sexual misconduct, there are other boundary violations as well (Doverspike, 1999). Clinical health psychologists who work in multidisciplinary settings should be aware that ethical and legal guidelines for other disciplines with whom they collaborate may be different, and not always prohibitive of sexual relationships with patients. In addition, because venues of practice for clinical health psychologists are different from traditional mental health practice, entering a medical or surgical room, where the patient is in a hospital bed, gowned, and in less control of his or her appearance is common. Because most therapists who become sexually involved with clients are divorced, separated, or unhappily married and feel vulnerable or lonely when the relationship begins (Harvard Mental Health Letter, 1985), increased self-attention and vigilance of unique boundary issues can reduce the potential for ethical and legal infractions.

Another malpractice risk, breach of confidentiality, may also have special relevance to clinical health psychologists working in medical settings. Although an improper breach of confidentiality may prompt an ethical or legal claim, breaking confidentiality is warranted to prevent suicide or harm to others. The stipulation regarding harm to others, also called duty to protect, was prompted by the *Tarasoff v. Regents of the University of California* (1976) ruling and is required by law in some states (Koocher & Keith-Spiegel, 1998). When a client makes such a threat, a psychologist is not immediately required to warn the intended party. Duty to warn is an option of last resort after medications, bringing the intended victim into therapy and possible commitment have been suggested or have failed (Roswell, 1988). Making a determination of harm to self or others may be particularly difficult for clinical health psychologists who often have little or no previous contact with a patient in the emergency room or after being admitted (Belar & Deardorff, 1995). Using suicidality assessment procedures that are commensurate with community standards, documented accordingly, can protect from legal risk. In addition, although incorrect diagnosis related to malpractice occurs when the misclassification is the proximate cause of injury, if another well-trained psychologist would have made the same error, malpractice cannot be established (Roswell, 1988). Because medical staff are not psychiatric staff and thus not necessarily familiar with suicide-related precautions, the clinical health psychologist may want to introduce an intervention for educating and discussing with staff the preventive measures and resulting procedures if an attempt were made.

Clinical health psychologists working with medical–surgical patients should clarify roles and provide proper documentation about the sources of information (Belar & Deardorff, 1995). For example, when treating patients with medical disorders, the clinical health psychologist can avoid any confusion about who made the medical diagnosis by clearly stating in a report, under the *DSM–IV*'s Axis III category, e.g., "ulcerative colitis per S. Smith's, MD, diagnosis." In addition, psychologists are often asked about psychopharmacology issues by primary care physicians and other nonpsychiatric physicians. Completing level II psychopharmacological training (American Psychological Association, 1992b) will clearly prepare the psychologist for collaborative practice and knowledgeable discussion of medication issues.

Malpractice claims related to psychological evaluation may also be relevant for clinical health psychologists who are often called on to assess candidates for medical treatment such as transplantation as well as for disability or other legal issues such as workers' compensation or competency. In such cases, the lawsuit may be filed in response to not receiving the expected gain as a result of the psychologist's conclusion. In these, like any other cases, following proper procedures with appropriate documentation can protect against legal risk.

Finally, in academic settings, the relationship between clinical trainee and supervisor has great legal significance because the trainee is essentially operating as an extension of the professional's license (Cohen, 1979). Thus, in addition to conforming to proper record-keeping guidelines, the psychologist must document in the patient's chart agreement with the trainee's diagnostic and treatment plan and follow the procedures of the facility, including cosignature and amount of supervisory time to be spent.

EDUCATION AND TRAINING FOR CLINICAL HEALTH PSYCHOLOGY

Education and training as a clinical psychologist or as a health psychologist is insufficient for practice as a clinical health psychologist. The APA archival description of the specialty clearly articulates a distinctive knowledge base that must be integrated with professional practice training for preparation as a clinical health psychologist:

> Clinical Health Psychology has evolved as a specialty area of knowledge and practice with extensive intradiscipline as well as interdisciplinary foundations in the health sciences. Biological, cognitive, affective, social and psychological bases of health and disease are bodies of knowledge that, when integrated with knowledge of biological, cognitive–affective, social and psychological bases of behavior, constitute the distinctive knowledge base of Clinical Health Psychology. This includes broad understanding of biology, pharmacology, anatomy, human physiology and pathophysiology, and psychoneuroimmunology. Health psychologists also have knowledge of how learning, memory, perception, cognition, and motivation influence health behaviors, are affected by physical illness/injury/disability, and can affect response to illness/injury/disability. Knowledge of the impact of social support, culture, physician–patient relationships, health policy and the organization of health care delivery systems on health and help-seeking is also fundamental, as is knowledge of diversity and minority health issues, individual differences in coping, emotional and behavioral risk factors for disease/injury/disability, human development issues in health and illness, and the impact of psychopathology on disease, injury, disability and treatment. The specialty also includes special expertise in health research methods and awareness of the distinctive ethical and legal issues associated with practice in Clinical Health Psychology. (APA Council of Representatives, 1997)

In 1983, delegates to the Arden House Working Conference on Education and Training in Health Psychology (Stone, 1983) articulated a set of guidelines that have continued to be supported by the field. Simply put, one must be trained first as a psychologist and then as a clinical health psychologist. In addition to generic psychology education and training, the core curriculum for clinical health psychologists is to include the domains listed next.[1]

---

[1] In earlier years it was argued that general training in clinical skills and content such as psychopathology was not required, but this view did not prevail given the demands for such knowledge and skill in practice. At the present time, students entering clinical health psychology come from APA-accredited programs in clinical, counseling, or school psychology. As yet there are no accredited doctoral programs in clinical health psychology.

1. Research methods specific to health psychology;
2. Biological bases of health and disease;
3. Social bases of health and disease;
4. Cognitive–affective bases of health and disease;
5. Psychological bases of health and disease;
6. Health policy and organization;
7. Clinical health psychology assessment;
8. Clinical health psychology intervention;
9. Interdisciplinary collaboration;
10. Clinical health psychology practica (assessment, intervention, consultation, program evaluation) in a variety of health care settings;
11. Ethical, legal, and professional issues in clinical health psychology;
12. Supervised health psychology research;
13. Clinical health psychology internship; and
14. Doctoral dissertation.

Programs offering such education and training are to have experienced clinical health psychology mentors, a multidisciplinary faculty, and access to a variety of health care settings. In addition, a commitment to integration in two specific areas is important. First, there must be an emphasis on the integration of science and practice. Education in science or practice or concurrently in both is *not* sufficient. These educational processes must be inextricably intertwined for this generative model to expand both knowledge and practice in clinical health psychology. Second, and in light of the fact that the biopsychosocial model is fundamental to the specialty, there must be a commitment to integration of the biological, psychological, and social aspects of health and disease with behavior. Consideration of these components as parallel processes serves only to perpetuate the mind–body dualism so prevalent in Western thought and health policy.

There are numerous pathways to becoming a clinical health psychologist. As in other areas, education and training must include a focus on the knowledge, skills, and attitudes required. Yet didactic experiences are insufficient, as the *sine qua non* of training in research and practice involves experiential components under the tutelage of masters. The APA's Division of Health Psychology (Division 38) maintains directories of relevant education and training at the doctoral, internship, and postdoctoral levels. Among these training programs are two postdoctoral residencies that have been accredited in the specialty of clinical health psychology by the APA Committee on Accreditation.

Despite extensive education, training, and experience, clinical health psychologists will encounter novel problems in practice. Because "learning how to learn" is the hallmark of PhD education, lifelong learning is an expected core activity for all clinical health psychologists. In addition, there are many professional psychologists who, although they do not wish to become specialists, will have opportunities to provide related services. In fact, given changes in the marketplace, many practitioners are seeking to expand their practice from that of more traditional mental health services to those related to clinical health psychology. Although there are no specific standards for "respecialization" within areas of professional practice, the true scope of practice for all psychologists is as specified in Standards 2.01a and c of the APA *Ethical Principles and Code of Conduct* (2002b):

> Psychologists provide services, teach, and conduct research with populations and in areas only within the boundaries of their competence, based on their education, training, supervised experience, consultation, study, or professional experience. Psychologists planning to provide services, teach, or conduct research involving populations, areas, techniques, or technologies new to them undertake relevant education, training, supervised experience, consultation, or study.

To facilitate an individual practitioner's determination of readiness for practice in a specific situation, the reader may refer to Belar et al. (2001) for a template for self-assessment in clinical health psychology. Using a series of questions based on core domains of science and practice, clinicians can gauge their knowledge and needs for additional study or experience.

CREDENTIALING

Credentialing can be personally based, like board certification for the psychologist, or within an organized health care system, like credentialing and privileges in hospitals.

Board Certification

Board certification is intended to serve the public and the profession by recognizing education, training, experience, and competence in specialty areas of professional psychology. Belar and Jeffrey (1995) proposed that diplomate status, or board certification, soon will be the standard for psychologists just as it is in the medical profession. Indeed, such a direction parallels the evolution of the structure and function of the American Board of Professional Psychology (ABPP) in the 1990s, now positioned to become part of the mainstream of credentialing for all specialists, rather than for the exceptional specialist (Bent, Packard, & Goldberg, 1999). To date, more than 3,600 specialists have been certified by ABPP in 11 specialties (Bent et al., 1999).

The establishment of board certification in clinical health psychology in 1993, along with the recognition of clinical health psychology as a distinct specialty by the APA Council of Representatives, follow almost two decades of expansion in this area. Clinical health psychologists who want recognition of advanced competence in the science and practice of psychology related to health, including the prevention, treatment, and rehabilitation of illness, may apply for board certification for practitioners through the American Board of Clinical Health Psychology. Because the process is somewhat parallel to physician credentialing, board certification may also aid physicians in understanding established areas of competency and specialization of clinical health psychologists working in medical settings. To qualify for board certification in clinical health psychology, the following minimum criteria are needed (ABPP, 1999):

1. A doctoral degree in psychology awarded from a college or university with concurrent APA accreditation;
2. An APA-accredited internship, which is defined as a minimum of 1,500 hours over a two-year period. Training must have occurred in an organized psychological health service setting;
3. Five years of qualifying experience, four years of which are postdoctoral level. Some experience in clinical health psychology is required in addition to
   a. The equivalent of at least one year full-time supervised health psychology experience at the postdoctoral level (a predoctoral specialty internship in health psychology is valued at six months) and
   b. The equivalent of one year of additional experience as a health psychologist.
4. Current professional work in clinical health psychology;
5. Evidence of continuing education in psychology;
6. Demonstration of professional commitment; and
7. State licensure or certification as a psychologist.

In addition, the board reviews all applications, seeking demonstration of (a) adequacy and extent of basic training; (b) amount, breadth, and quality of professional experience; (c) special competence; and (d) professional reputation for irreproachable standards of personal integrity (Belar & Jeffrey, 1995). Once these requirements are met, the candidate may then register to take the clinical health psychology qualifying exam. Requirements for registration include submission of two work samples representative of professional practice such as a report of interactions with accompanying video or audiotape. Once accepted, the candidate may take the exam, which covers the following topic areas: (a) effectiveness of candidate's efforts toward constructive intervention based on realistic assessment of presenting problem, (b) awareness of relevance of research and theory, and (c) sensitivity to ethical implications of professional practice (ABPP, 1999).

Gaining Hospital Privileges

For primary care psychologists as well as those delivering secondary and tertiary hospital-based services, the need for obtaining hospital privileges is essential. Besides the right to admit or discharge patients, clinical health psychologists may need to effectively manage patient care by having privileges to conduct a wide range of clinical assessment and treatment, patient management, and scientific and consulting activities, including program and organizational development (American Psychological Association, 1998a).

There are several influences on the granting of admitting privileges at the state, federal, and local levels. For example, the guidelines of the Joint Commission on Accreditation of Healthcare Organizations (JCAHO), a private, nonprofit corporation, were developed for the purpose of setting standards in hospitals. In 1984 the JCAHO permitted medical staff membership—previously granted to only physicians—to be granted to "other licensed individuals permitted by law and by the hospital to provide patient care services independently in the hospital" (American Psychological Association, 1998b, p. 4). JCAHO standards are limited by state law relevant to the scope of the psychologist's practice. Although hospital-based practice is clearly included in the education and clinical training of licensed psychologists, state statute or regulation may limit the scope of practice. State law may further determine hospital procedures, frequently by mandating hospitals to permit psychologists to become staff members. In 1997, such a law existed in 16 states and the District of Columbia (Rozensky, 1997). Finally, psychologists are recognized as independent Medicaid providers on both inpatient and outpatient bases in many states, in accordance with federal law (Rozensky, 1997).

The scope of clinical privileges obtained by a psychologist are defined by ethical standards in psychology, psychology guidelines for education and training, as well as legal regulations controlling the health care environment (Rozensky, 1997). In addition, medical staff membership is defined by hospital bylaws. In general, psychologists must meet the following requirements to obtain privileges (American Psychological Association, 1998b):

1. A doctoral degree in psychology from an accredited educational institution, which meets the criteria for licensure or certification in the state;

2. At least two years of supervised clinical experience in an organized multidisciplinary facility licensed to provide care; and
3. A license (or certificate wherever this is used) to practice in the state.

Important distinctions are made between the categories of responsibilities granted to medical staff. *Active staff* have the highest level of responsibilities and privileges, including eligibility to vote and hold office and to serve on organized staff committees. *Courtesy staff* are permitted to admit a limited number of patients each year and are not eligible to vote or hold office. *Consulting staff* act as consultants in their field of specialty, cannot vote or hold office, but may be asked to serve on committees. *Honorary staff* are not necessarily active in the hospital but are honored by delineation in hospital bylaws. *Affiliate staff* are limited to performing patient care under direct and continued supervision and cannot vote or hold office. Affiliate staff privileges are typically granted to psychologists in states without laws mandating greater privileges (American Psychological Association, 1998b).

Gaining staff membership, however, does not guarantee adequate staff privileges: Psychologists should attempt to gain explicit approval for specific services rather than allowing an informal status in the organization. (For a list of possible hospital privileges for psychologists, see American Psychological Association, 1998b.)

Applications for membership may be turned down for a variety of reasons. Candidates should be notified in writing of reasons for denial, which should be based on applicant's knowledge, experience, and demonstrated competence. If any of the following six factors are considered in evaluating a psychologist's application, or provide the basis for denial, the psychologist should appeal the decision and take appropriate administrative and legal action (American Psychological Association, 1998b): (a) membership or lack of membership in a professional society or association; (b) decision to advertise, lower fees, or engage in other competitive acts intended to solicit business; (c) participation in prepaid group health plans, salaried employment, or any other manner of delivering health services on other than a fee-for-service basis; (d) support for, training of, or participation in a private group practice with members of a particular class of health professionals; (e) practices with respect to testifying in malpractice suits, disciplinary actions, or any other type of proceeding; or (f) willingness to send a certain number of patients or clients to a particular hospital.

In summary, clinical health psychologists who demonstrate advanced competence in clinical health psychology may apply for board certification, soon to become the standard in the field. When applying for hospital membership, clinical health psychologists should request specific privileges to secure widest clinical opportunities within the setting.

CONCLUSION

If leaders in the field attend to the issues described throughout the chapter, we are optimistic about the future of clinical health psychology. With changes in the health care system and increases in the scientific knowledge base we anticipate an expansion of psychological practice across the spectrum of health care problems, but especially in primary care, genetic counseling, reproductive endocrinology, and organ transplantation. In addition, we anticipate more reliance on nontraditional sites for the delivery of health care services, such as worksites and school-based health care clinics, with a concomitant growth in areas of focus such as occupational health psychology and pediatric psychology. Our prescriptions for a healthy future include

1. Increased focus on the education and training of other health care disciplines at all levels;
2. Continued advocacy for psychology as a health care profession, and not solely as a mental health profession;
3. Development of curricular materials for education and training in clinical health psychology;
4. Increased focus on education and training in primary care;
5. Increased opportunities for continuing education in clinical health psychology (including incorporation of new models and technologies);
6. Increased emphasis on the integration of research and practice in the education and training of clinical health psychologists to ensure the continued development of a scientific knowledge base relevant to practice;
7. Continued focus on development of a knowledge base regarding utility of psychological interventions in (a) ameliorating health problems, (b) contributing to quality of life, and (c) offsetting medical–surgical costs;
8. Development of practice standards to inform consumers about usual and customary care relevant to specific health care problems;
9. Increased advocacy for integrated health care services, which would entail a reallocation of resources from current support of the behavioral health carve-out industry and opposition to other aspects of the health care system that promote mind–body dualism in the design and delivery of health care services; and

10. Clear education of students and practitioners alike concerning survival of practice within the changing financial landscape of the modern health care industry.

REFERENCES

American Board of Professional Psychology (ABPP). (1999, April). *American Board of Clinical Health Psychology certification procedures.* Columbia, MO: Author.

American Psychiatric Association. (1994). *Diagnostic and statistical manual of mental disorders.* Washington, DC: Author.

American Psychological Association. (1992a). Ethical principles of psychologists and code of conduct. *American Psychologist, 47,* 1597–1611.

American Psychological Association. (1992b). *Report of the Ad Hoc Task Force on Psychopharmacology of the American Psychological Association.* Washington, DC: Author.

American Psychological Association. (1997). *Final report of the American Psychological Association Working Group on the Implications of Changes in the Health Care Delivery System for the Education, Training and Continuing Professional Education of Psychologists.* Washington, DC: Author.

American Psychological Association. (1998a). *Interprofessional health care services in primary care settings: Implications for the education and training of psychologists.* Rockville, MD: Substance Abuse and Mental Health Services Administration/ Health Resources and Services Administration.

American Psychological Association. (1998b). *Practicing psychology in hospitals and other health care facilities.* Washington, DC: Author.

American Psychological Association, Ethics Committee. (1999). Report of the Ethics Committee, 1998. *American Psychologist, 54,* 701–710.

American Psychological Association. (2002a). APA *practice directorate announces new health and behavior CPT codes.* Retrieved December 2002 from http:// www.apa.org/practice/cpt—2002.html

American Psychological Association. (2002b). Ethical principles of psychologists and code of conduct. *American Psychologist, 57,* 1060–1073.

APA Council of Representatives. (1997). Archival description of clinical health psychology as a specialty in professional psychology. *Minutes of the Council of Representatives Meeting, August 1997.* Washington, DC: Author.

APA Practice Directorate. (1996). *Developing an integrated delivery system: Organizing a seamless system of care.* Washington, DC: American Psychological Association.

Bagheri, A. S., Lane, L. S., Kline, F. M., & Araujo, D. M. (1981). Why physicians fail to tell patients a psychiatrist is coming. *Psychosomatics, 22,* 407–419.

Banks, S. M., & Kerns, R. D. (1996). Explaining high rates of depression in chronic pain: A diathesis–stress framework. *Psychological Bulletin, 119,* 95–110.

Belar, C. D., Brown, R., Hersch, L. E., Hornyak, L., Reed, G., Rozensky, R. H., et al. (2001). Self-assessment in clinical health psychology: A model for ethical expansion of practice. *Professional Psychology: Research and Practice, 32,* 135–141.

Belar, C. D., & Deardorff, W. W. (1995). *Clinical health psychology in medical settings: A practitioner's guidebook.* Washington, DC: American Psychological Association.

Belar, C. D., Deardorff, W. W., & Kelly, K. E. (1987). *The practice of clinical health psychology.* New York: Pergamon Press.

Belar, C. D., & Jeffrey, T. B. (1995). Board certification in health psychology. *Journal of Clinical Psychology, 2,* 129–132.

Bennett, B. E., Bryant, B. K., VandenBos, G. R., & Greenwood, A. (1990). *Professional liability and risk management.* Washington, DC: American Psychological Association.

Bent, R. J., Packard, R. E., & Goldberg, R. W. (1999). The American Board of Professional Psychology, 1947 to 1997: A historical perspective. *Professional Psychology: Research and Practice, 30,* 65–73.

Bersoff, D. N. (1999). *Ethical conflicts in psychology: second edition.* Washington, DC: American Psychological Association.

Bray, J. (1996). Psychologists as primary care practitioners. In R. J. Resnick & R. H. Rozensky (Eds.), *Health psychology through the lifespan: Practice and research opportunities.* Washington, DC: American Psychological Association.

Bray, J. H., & Rogers, J. C. (1995). Linking psychologists and family physicians for collaborative practice. *Professional Psychology: Research and Practice, 26,* 132–138.

Camic, P. M., & Knight, S. J. (Eds.). (1998). *Clinical handbook of health psychology: A practical guide to effective interventions.* Toronto: Hogrefe & Huber.

Cohen, R. J. (1979). *Malpractice: A guide for mental health professionals.* New York: Free Press.

Cummings, N. A., & VandenBos, G. R. (1981). The twenty year Kaiser-Permanente experience with psychotherapy and medical utilization: Implications for national health policy and national health insurance. *Health Policy Quarterly, 1,* 159–175.

Deardorff, W. W., Cross, H. J., & Hupprich, W. R. (1984). Malpractice liability in psychotherapy: Client and practitioner perspectives. *Professional Psychology: Research and Practice, 15,* 590–600.

Deterring therapist–patient sex. (1985, Dec.). *Harvard Mental Health Letter, 2,* 6–7.

Doverspike, W. F. (1999). *Ethical risk management: Guidelines for practice.* Sarasota, FL: Professional Resource Press.

Glueckauf, R. L. (1999). Interdivisional healthcare committee: Speaking with one voice on cross-cutting issues in health care psychology. *Journal of Clinical Psychology in Medical Settings, 6,* 171–181.

Haas, L. J., & Cummings, N. A. (1991). Managed outpatient mental health plans: Clinical, ethical, and practical guidelines for participation. *Professional Psychology: Research and Practice, 22,* 45–51.

Knapp, S., & VandeCreek, L. (1981). Behavioral medicine: Its malpractice risks for psychologists. *Professional Psychology, 12,* 677–683.

Koocher, G. P., & Keith-Spiegel, P. (1998). *Ethics in psychology.* New York: Oxford University Press.

Lowman, R. L., & Resnick, R. J. (Eds.). 1994. *The mental health professional's guide to managed care.* Washington, DC: American Psychological Association.

Miller, M. O., & Sales, B. D. (1986). *Law and mental health professionals: Arizona.* Washington, DC: American Psychological Association.

Millon, T., Green, C. J., & Meagher, R. B. (Eds.). (1982). *Handbook of clinical health psychology.* New York: Plenum Press.

Practice Management Information Corporation. (1998). *International classification of diseases* (9th ed.). Los Angeles: Author.

Resnick, R. J., & Rozensky, R. H. (1996). Introduction. In R. J. Resnick & R. H. Rozensky (Eds.), *Health psychology through the lifespan: Practice and research opportunities* (pp. 1–6). Washington, DC: American Psychological Association.

Roswell, V. A. (1988). Professional liability: Issues for behavior therapists in the 1980s and 1990s. *Behavior Therapist, 11,* 163–171.

Rozensky, R. H. (1997). Medical or professional staff membership and participation in rural hospitals. In J. A. Morris (Ed.), *Practicing psychology in rural settings* (pp. 19–36). Washington, DC: American Psychological Association.

Rozensky, R. H., Sweet, J. J., & Tovian, S. M. (1997). *Psychological assessment in medical settings.* New York: Plenum Press.

Sayette, M. A., & Mayne, T. J. (1990). Survey of current clinical and research trends in clinical psychology. *American Psychologist, 45,* 1263–1266.

Stone, G. C. (Ed.). (1983). National Working Conference on Education and Training in Health Psychology. *Health Psychology, 2*(Suppl. 5), 1–153.

Sweet, J. J., Rozensky, R. H., & Tovian, S. M. (1991). *Handbook of clinical psychology in medical settings.* New York: Plenum Press.

Substance Abuse and Mental Health Services Administration (SAMHSA). (1998). *Ethical issues for behavioral health care practitioners and organizations in a managed care environment.* Rockville, MD: Author.

Tarasoff v. Regents of the University of California. (1976). 551 P.2d 334, 131 *California Reporter.*

Tovian, S. (1999, Spring). Interdivisional Healthcare Committee: Background and current activities. *Health Psychologist, 21,* 14.

VandeCreek, L., & Stout, C. E. (1993). Risk management in inpatient psychiatric care. In D. Ruben, C. Stout, & M. Squire (Eds.), *Current advances in inpatient psychiatric care: A handbook* (pp. 53–67). New York: Greenwood.

APPENDIX 8.1

ARCHIVAL DESCRIPTION OF CLINICAL HEALTH PSYCHOLOGY

The specialty of clinical health psychology applies scientific knowledge of the interrelationships among behavioral, emotional, cognitive, social, and biological components in health and disease to the promotion and maintenance of health; the prevention, treatment, and rehabilitation of illness and disability; and the improvement of the health care system. The distinct focus of clinical health psychology is on physical health problems. The specialty is dedicated to the development of knowledge regarding the interface between behavior and health and to the delivery of high quality services based on that knowledge to individuals, families, and health care systems.

PARAMETERS TO DEFINE PROFESSIONAL PRACTICE IN CLINICAL HEALTH PSYCHOLOGY

Fundamental to clinical health psychology is the biopsychosocial model and the ability to work in a broad range of health care settings with other health care providers.

Populations

The client populations served by health psychologists are defined by physical symptoms or physical illness experienced by persons across the life span. Populations include (but are not limited to) persons with asthma, pain, organ failure, physical disability, irritable bowel syndrome, headache, hemophilia, Raynaud's disease, diabetes, premenstrual syndrome, pregnancy, infertility, arthritis, terminal illness, cardiovascular disease, cancer, acquired immune deficiency syndrome, sickle cell disease, injury, obesity, dental disease, osteoporosis, stroke, hypertension, as well as those individuals at risk for these problems and those who desire to develop and maintain a healthy lifestyle. Patients' family members and health care providers are also recipients of clinical health psychology services.

Problems and Issues

Problems addressed by the specialty of clinical health psychology include, but are not limited to:

The information in this appendix is from http://www/apa.org/crsppp/health/html

1. Psychological conditions secondary to diseases/injury/disability (e.g., postmyocardial infarction depression, family issues in chronic illness or death, body image concerns secondary to burns, amputation, surgery);
2. Somatic presentations of psychological dysfunction (e.g., chest pain in panic attack, somatization disorders);
3. Psychophysiological disorders (e.g., tension and migraine headache, irritable bowel syndrome);
4. Physical symptoms/conditions responsive to behavioral interventions (e.g., vasospasms, urinary and fecal incontinence, anticipatory nausea);
5. Somatic complications associated with behavioral factors (e.g., mismanagement of diabetes, noncompliance with medical regimens);
6. Psychological presentation of organic disease (e.g., hypothyroidism presenting as depression, steroid-induced psychosis);
7. Psychological and behavioral aspects of stressful medical procedures (e.g., pain, lumbar puncture, wound debridement, cardiac catheterization);
8. Behavioral risk actors for disease/injury/disability (e.g., smoking weight, substance abuse, risk-taking);
9. Problems of health care providers and health care systems (e.g., physician–patient relationships, staff burn out, care delivery systems); and
10. Preferences for learning the development and maintenance of healthy lifestyles.

Procedures

Practitioners have in-depth expertise in clinical health psychology assessment, intervention, and consultation, as well as skills in interdisciplinary collaboration with other health care providers. A broad array of specialized procedures exist (e.g., Psychosocial Adjustment to Illness scale, Type A Structured Interview, Family Environment scale, Millon Behavioral Health Inventory, Sickness Impact Profile, quality of life measures, the Multidimensional Pain Inventory, psychophysiological monitoring, biofeedback, relaxation training, crisis intervention at the time of diagnosis/change in health status, cognitive–behavioral therapies for pain, headache, improving compliance and preparing for stressful medical procedures, coping-skills training to promote adaptive coping, family therapy, group therapy, staff consultation and liaison, counseling for health promotion). Practitioners also have skills in working in a broad array of health care settings with other health care disciplines.

Knowledge Base

Clinical health psychology has evolved as a specialty area of knowledge and practice with extensive intradiscipline as well as interdisciplinary foundations in the health sciences. Biological, cognitive, affective, social, and psychological *bases of health and disease* are bodies of knowledge that, when integrated with knowledge of biological cognitive–affective, social, and psychological bases of behavior constitute the distinctive knowledge base of clinical health psychology. This includes broad understanding of biology, pharmacology, anatomy, human physiology and pathophysiology, and psychoneuroimmunology. Health psychologists also have knowledge of how learning, memory, perception, cognition, and motivation influence health behaviors, are affected by physical illness/injury/disability, and can affect response to illness/injury/disability. Knowledge of the impact of social support, culture, physician–patient relationships, health policy, and the organization of health care delivery systems on health and help-seeking is also fundamental, as is knowledge of diversity and minority health issues, individual differences in coping, emotional and behavioral risk factors for disease/injury/disability, human development issues in health and illness, and the impact of psychopathology on disease, injury, disability and treatment. The specialty also includes special expertise in health research methods and awareness of the distinctive ethical and legal issues associated with practice in clinical health psychology. Education and training for clinical health psychology has been addressed in the 1983 Working Conference on Education and Training in Health Psychology (Stone, 1983). Practitioners can be board certified in clinical health psychology by the American Board of Clinical Health Psychology, an affiliated board of the American Board of Professional Psychology.

9

PAYMENT FOR CLINICAL SERVICES: FROM FUNDAMENTALS TO PRACTICE CONSIDERATIONS

NICCIE McKAY AND ROBERT G. FRANK

The extensive changes in payment practices for health care services over the past 15 years have resulted in significant changes in the delivery of clinical health psychology services. Driven by increasing costs, inconsistent quality, excessive treatment, and an aging population, health care payers have limited or denied payment for certain types of health services, including psychological treatment (Frank, 1999; Frank & VandenBos, 1994).

Changes in payment have altered many aspects of the practice of clinical health psychology. Administratively burdensome activities such as determining eligibility for services, communicating with payers, and collecting copayments have become critical and demanding aspects of every clinical health psychology practice. Even more intrusive from the clinical perspective has been the implementation of payment systems that carve out mental health treatments. Mental health "carve-outs" divide psychological from physical treatments, thereby compromising the likelihood of integrated care.

The authors thank Patricia Myers, PhD, for her comments and input on this chapter.

Moreover, such payment systems may challenge the future ability of clinical health psychologists to provide high-quality care to their patients.

Most clinical health psychologists, educated in an era when scant attention was paid to nonclinical issues, have found it difficult to assess the potential implications of new payment methods on their practices. The focus of clinical health psychologists' education and training has been on clinical interventions and health outcomes, as it should be, but with no consideration of health care financing systems. However, recent changes in payment for health services have broadened the required foundation of knowledge in clinical health psychology. In addition to knowledge of the science and practice of clinical health psychology, it now has become important for practitioners to have a grasp of payment issues.

The method of payment determines which services will be covered and to what extent, as well as the amount of payment received for services. Thus financial factors play an important role in the practice of clinical health psychology. The objectives of this chapter are to help practitioners more fully understand the current payment system, to assess the effects of different payment methods, to explain why many insurers have begun to use carve-outs for psychological services, and to consider the case for carve-ins, which involve joint provision of (and payment for) primary care and mental health services.

PAYMENT FOR HEALTH SERVICES

A key feature of the health care sector is that typically there is a difference between who receives the services and who pays for the services. Figure 9.1 illustrates the complexities of the U.S. system of health care delivery and payment by distinguishing between flows of services and flows of payment.

Who Pays?

As shown in panel A of Figure 9.1, for individuals without insurance for a particular type of service, providers deliver health services to patients, and the patient pays the provider directly (often called self-pay or out-of-pocket payment). For most individuals using health services, however, there is a third party involved—either a private insurer or a government agency.

Panel B of Figure 9.1 shows what happens when an individual has insurance for a particular type of service. The flow of services is that providers deliver health services to individuals, third-party payers deliver insurance coverage to individuals, and providers submit claims for payment to third-party payers. The flow of payments is that individuals pay premiums (private

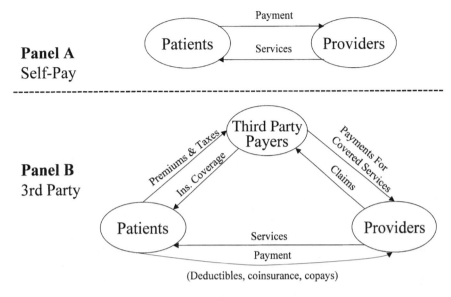

Panel A
Self-Pay

Panel B
3rd Party

Figure 9.1. Comparing self-pay and third-party payment.

insurance) or taxes (public programs) in exchange for insurance coverage. Providers receive reimbursement from third-party payers for covered services and also receive payment directly from patients (deductibles, coinsurance, and copayments). Note that, for now, managed care is just another type of third-party payer; we will discuss managed care in a later section.

Third-party payment for health services plays a key role in determining choices by patients. That is, incentives differ depending on who is paying the bill, and we have to take this into account in analyzing economic behavior of patients.

To understand this, perform a thought experiment. You go for your six-month dental check-up. Your dentist suggests additional X-rays. You say, "Didn't you do X-rays last time?" The dentist says, "Yes, but we're watching that questionable area on the lower right side, and think additional X-rays would be helpful in determining what to do." Compare your decisions in two cases. In the first case, you would pay the full charge for the X-rays out-of-pocket, whereas in the second case your insurance through your employer would pick up the full amount and you would pay nothing. Most people would have the X-rays done if they paid nothing, and considerably fewer would have them done if they had to pay out-of-pocket.

Admittedly this is a much simplified example involving a health service that is highly discretionary (in other words, you were not in pain or having other problems with your teeth). Nevertheless, the point remains that economic decisions (in this case, whether or not to purchase a particular type of health service) differ depending on who is paying the bill. Specifically, all else being equal, individuals typically will choose to consume more health services when a third party pays than when they must pay out-of-pocket for the services.

National Health Expenditures

The importance of taking who pays into account becomes apparent when examining the distribution of health expenditures according to payer. Table 9.1 presents personal health expenditures by source of payment for selected years. In 1999, consumers paid out-of-pocket for only 17.6% of personal expenditures on health services, with third-party payers accounting for the remaining 82.4%.

But the situation is even more complicated than just distinguishing between third-party and out-of-pocket payment. Third-party payers can be private (insurance companies) or public (most important, Medicare and Medicaid). As shown in Table 9.1, in 1999 public programs paid for a slightly larger share of third-party payments for personal health care than private insurers; public third-party payment accounted for approximately 53% of the total. Given the differences between private and public health insurance programs, economic incentives will differ between private and public sources of payment.

Yet another consideration is the breakdown within public programs. As Table 9.1 shows, in 1999 the federal government accounted for the bulk of public payments for personal health care in comparison to state and local governments (75.8% and 24.2%, respectively). Again, economic incentives will differ depending on the source of payment.

Expenditures on Mental Health Services

Although important, examining the distribution of personal health care expenditures can obscure differences according to type of service. For example, the percentage of expenditures paid out-of-pocket will clearly differ between dental services and hospital care. Unfortunately, there is no standard annual source of expenditures on mental health and substance abuse services comparable to the statistics for personal health expenditures. However, McKusick et al. (1998) calculated estimated expenditures on mental health and substance abuse services in 1996, which are presented in Table 9.2 by source of payment. Estimated expenditures came from the National Health Accounts (NHA) data for diagnostic groups relevant to mental health and substance abuse services.

In 1996, consumers paid out-of-pocket for 16% of total expenditures on all mental health and substance abuse services, which is about the same as for personal health expenditures as a whole. However, consumers paid a

TABLE 9.1

Personal Health Expenditures by Source of Payment: Selected Years, 1960 to 1999 (in billions of dollars)

	1960	1970	1980	1990	1995	1998	1999
	Personal health expenditures: Out-of-pocket versus third-party payment						
Personal health expenditures	23.4	63.2	214.6	609.4	865.7	1002.3	1057.7
Out-of-pocket payment	12.9	25.1	58.3	137.8	149.2	176.1	186.5
	55.1%	39.7%	27.2%	22.6%	17.2%	17.6%	17.6%
Third-party payment	10.5	38.1	156.3	471.6	716.5	826.2	871.2
	44.9%	60.3%	72.8%	77.4%	82.8%	82.4%	82.4%
	Third-party payment: Private versus public						
Third-party payment	10.5	38.1	156.3	471.6	716.5	826.2	871.2
Private	5.5	15.9	69.9	233.8	329.1	387.0	413.2
	52.4%	41.7%	44.7%	49.6%	45.9%	46.8%	47.4%
Public	5.0	22.2	86.5	237.8	387.4	439.1	458.0
	47.6%	58.3%	55.3%	50.4%	54.1%	53.1%	52.6%
	Public payment: Federal versus state and local						
Public	5.0	22.2	86.5	237.8	387.4	439.1	458.0
Federal	2.0	14.4	62.7	174.0	296.7	335.8	347.2
	40.0%	64.9%	72.5%	73.2%	76.6%	76.5%	75.8%
State and local	3.0	7.8	23.8	63.8	90.7	103.3	110.8
	60.0%	35.1%	27.5%	26.8%	23.4%	23.5%	24.2%

Note. From HealthCare Financing Administration, Office of the Actuary, National Health Statistics Group, U.S. Bureau of the Census, *Personal Health Care Expenditures Aggregate and Per Capita Amounts and Percent Distribution, by Source of Funds: Selected Calendar Years 1960–99.* In the public domain.

TABLE 9.2
Expenditures on Mental Health and Substance Abuse, 1996
(in millions of dollars)

	Mental health	Substance abuse	Total
Total MHSA expenditures: Out-of-pocket versus third-party payment			
Total expenditures	66,704	12,576	79,280
Out-of-pocket payment	11,608	1,076	12,684
	17.4%	*8.6%*	*16.0%*
Third-party payment	55,096	11,500	66,596
	82.6%	*91.4%*	*84.0%*
Third-party MHSA expenditures: Private versus public			
Third-party payment	55,096	11,500	66,596
Private	20,024	3,609	23,633
	36.3%	*31.4%*	*35.5%*
Public	35,073	7,891	42,964
	63.7%	*68.6%*	*64.5%*

larger share out-of-pocket for mental health services (17.4%) than for substance abuse services (8.6%).

Table 9.2 also shows that public payers accounted for 64.5% of all third-party payments for mental health and substance abuse services in 1996, compared to 52.6% for personal health expenditures as a whole in 1995 (Table 9.1). Of all third-party payments, public payers accounted for 63.7% for mental health services and 68.6% for substance abuse services.

Zuvekas (2001) used the 1987 National Medical Expenditure Survey (NMES) and its successor, the 1996 Medical Expenditure Panel Survey (MEPS), to estimate that out-of-pocket payment on mental health services accounted for 26.3% in 1987 and 23.0% in 1996 for the civilian, noninstitutionalized population. Third-party payment thus was more common in this study than in the McKusick et al. (1998) study, which is not surprising given that this estimate excluded all stays at long-term psychiatric facilities and acute care mental health services for institutionalized populations.

Thus we find that providers of mental health services face third-party payment more frequently than is the case for health expenditures as a whole, and that public payers account for a larger share of third-party payment for mental health and substance abuse services than for all health services. As a consequence, clinical health psychologists must pay particular attention to methods of reimbursement by third-party and public payers.

TABLE 9.3
U.S. Health Insurance Coverage, 1999

Private	7.10%	
Employment-based		(62.8%)
Public	24.1%	
Medicare		(13.2%)
Medicaid		(10.2%)
Military		(3.1%)
Uninsured	15.5%	

Note. Some individuals had more than one type of health insurance coverage. From U.S. Census Bureau, *Health Insurance Detailed Table: 1999*, 2000, Washington, DC. In the public domain.

HEALTH INSURANCE PLANS

Given that most health services are paid for by a third party, it is important to understand who these third-party payers are and the methods of payment they use to reimburse providers. In the United States, health insurance plans are the third-party payers. At the broadest level, we can categorize health insurance plans as being either public or private. Public health insurance plans include Medicare, Medicaid, and the military. For private health insurance plans, it is useful to make an additional distinction between individual plans and those that are employment-based.

As shown in Table 9.3, most individuals with health insurance in 1999 had private coverage (71%). By far the dominant type of health insurance is private, employer-sponsored, with approximately 63% of individuals in the United States having some coverage through an employer-sponsored plan in 1999. (Note that there is a difference between the proportion of individuals having private coverage and the proportion of payments by private payers.)

Employer-Sponsored Health Insurance Plans

Until the 1970s, virtually all private health insurance was what was called indemnity coverage, in which enrollees had free choice of providers and the insurer paid providers for covered services on a fee-for-service basis. Under this type of health plan, which we now call traditional fee-for-service, the patient decides which provider to visit. If the health services are covered by the patient's health plan, the provider submits a claim to the insurance company and receives payment on a per-service basis.

Today there are other types of employer-sponsored health insurance plans, in addition to traditional fee-for-service. Figure 9.2 presents information on employer-sponsored health insurance coverage in 1991, 1996, and 2000. In less than a decade, traditional fee-for-service coverage has declined

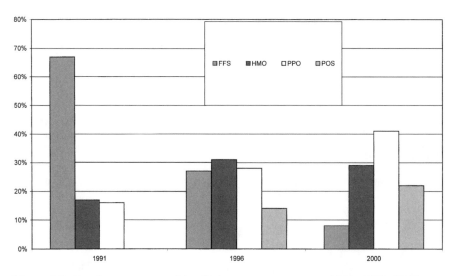

Figure 9.2. Employer-sponsored health insurance coverage: 1991, 1996, 2000.

dramatically from 67% to 8% for those with employer-sponsored health insurance. By 2000, 29% of those with employer-sponsored health insurance were covered by health maintenance organizations (HMOs), 41% were covered by preferred provider organizations (PPOs), and 22% were covered by point of service (POS) plans.

Any health plan that is not traditional fee-for-service is sometimes called managed care. Unfortunately, the term *managed care* is extremely vague and means different things to different people. For example, some would argue that any type of utilization management, such as preadmission certification, case management, or utilization review, constitutes managed care. By this definition, all health plans become managed care plans, because these days even traditional fee-for-service plans typically use some forms of utilization management. Others would argue that only HMOs should be considered managed care, because they are more likely to use capitated payment. To avoid the confusion regarding what is managed care and what is not, we will focus instead on the underlying characteristics of the health plans.

HMOs differ from traditional fee-for-service plans in that the patient's choice of provider is restricted and often the provider receives capitated payment for services. Under this type of health plan, services will be covered only if the patient visits a provider on the HMO's panel. The extent of restriction on patient choice of provider differs considerably across type of HMO, with staff model HMOs typically offering less choice among providers and independent practice association (IPA) model HMOs offering patients more choice.

The method of payment is of particular importance in analyzing economic effects of HMOs. Under capitated payment, fees are paid on a per-enrollee basis. The provider receives a set fee for each enrollee in a given health plan, with the fee being received in advance, regardless of whether or not a given enrollee receives health services. The provider is then responsible for supplying the health services covered in the contract as needed by enrollees in the plan. In such a plan, providers are termed as being "at risk," meaning that they bear the risk that expenditures may exceed revenues received.

Both PPOs and POS plans contract with independent providers at a discounted fee-for-service rate, but a POS plan also uses a primary care gatekeeper who must authorize the use of specialty services. For purposes of analyzing economic behavior, we can lump PPOs and POS plans together. Both have more restrictions on patient choice of provider than traditional fee-for-service plans and have less restrictions than HMOs. As is the case for HMOs, PPOs and POS plans have a set of panel providers. If the patient uses a panel provider, a certain coinsurance rate applies (e.g., the plan will pay for 80% of the covered services, with the patient being responsible for the remaining 20%). A patient can choose to use a nonpanel provider, but in that case the coinsurance rate is higher (e.g., the patient now might be responsible for 40% of the covered services).

With regard to method of payment, PPOs and POS plans use fee-for-service payments. As is the case for traditional fee-for-service plans, the provider submits a claim to the insurance company and receives payment on a per-service basis. However, PPOs and POS plans typically pay an amount that is discounted from the traditional fee-for-service level.

Health insurance plans thus differ primarily along two dimensions: (a) restrictions on choice of provider, and (b) method of payment for services. Although choice of provider is clearly an important consideration, method of payment is the key to understanding economic behavior of providers of health services.

Fee-for-Service Versus Capitated Payment

From the provider's perspective, what are the economic incentives associated with fee-for-service versus capitated payment? In a fee-for-service system, each time another service is supplied, the provider receives additional revenue. Thus, as long as the additional service does not harm the patient and as long as the additional revenue covers the cost of the service, the provider has an incentive to provide more services. In a capitated system, on the other hand, the provider receives a set amount of revenue in advance. Each time another service is supplied, the provider's cost increases, but revenues do not. Thus, the provider has an incentive to control the utilization of services, as long as the lack of services does not harm the patient.

Not surprisingly, providers tend to prefer fee-for-service payment, because, as long as the fee covers costs, there is no risk of losing money on services rendered. Under capitation, however, providers are at risk of earning losses if they accept a capitated rate that does not cover the cost of services rendered. From the payers' perspective, on the other hand, capitation has a built-in incentive encouraging providers to control utilization that is absent in fee-for-service payment. (Patient preferences for fee-for-service versus capitated health plans depend on trade-offs between the value placed on freedom of provider choice versus out-of-pocket cost for premiums and copayments.)

Little data exist on the extent of fee-for-service versus capitated payment for health services. For hospitals, a survey in 1994 found that nationally only about 7% of hospital revenues came from capitation contracts (*Modern Healthcare*, 1995). A survey of physicians in 1995 found that, for all physicians, 8% of patients had capitated payment, and only 5% of patients had capitated payment for medical specialists (Remler et al., 1997). Returning to Figure 9.2, 92% of individuals with employer-sponsored health insurance coverage in 2000 were in HMOs, PPOs, or POS plans. However, fee-for-service payment is by far the norm, in spite of extensive coverage in plans that could be termed managed care. And, as we have seen, method of payment is the key to understanding the economic incentives facing providers of health services.

Note that we have not addressed the linkages among utilization, payment method, and health status. If we knew the clinically appropriate level of services for a given condition, then payers could set a schedule that would pay a set amount for the appropriate level of services, and we would not have to worry about payment methods that encourage too much or too little utilization. The development of practice guidelines and clinical pathways is a first step in this direction. The problem, of course, is that it is extremely difficult to reach consensus on the appropriate level of services, and until that happens, payers will face a choice between fee-for-service and capitated payment.

IMPLICATIONS OF HEALTH CARE FINANCING SYSTEM

The U.S. financing system for health services in general and mental health services in particular has two key features: (a) typically payment is made by a third-party, and (b) most third-party payment is on a fee-for-service basis. What are the economic implications of such a health care financing system?

Individuals have an incentive to consume more health services when a third-party pays than when they must pay out-for-pocket for the services. Thus, extensive third-party payment provides an incentive for increased utilization and consequently increased expenditures. Providers paid under a fee-for-service system have an incentive to supply more services to patients

TABLE 9.4
Key Findings From Rand Health Insurance Study

Estimated spending on medical services (% of spending in free-care plan)

	Spending on					
Amount paid out-of-pocket	Acute care	Chronic care	Well care	Total outpatient	Hospital care	Total medical
None (free care)	100%	100%	100%	100%	100%	100%
25%	72%	67%	75%	71%	71%	71%
50%	56%	56%	69%	58%	68%	63%
95%	49%	51%	45%	49%	60%	55%

Estimated spending on outpatient services (% of spending in free-care plan)

	Spending on	
Amount paid out-of-pocket	Medical services	Mental health
None (free care)	100%	100%
25%	71%	70%
50%	58%	38%
95%	49%	26%

than when paid on a capitated basis. Thus, extensive use of fee-for-service payment provides an incentive for increased utilization and consequently increased expenditures.

Empirical Evidence

The landmark Rand Health Insurance Study provides empirical evidence to support these predictions (Newhouse & the Insurance Experiment Group, 1993). Beginning in 1974, the Rand Health Insurance Study enrolled participants in a range of health insurance plans requiring different levels of coinsurance for medical care, from 0 to 95%. After carefully controlling for other factors affecting utilization, the study found that patients used substantially more services when they paid a smaller proportion of the bill. For example, total spending on medical services for those who paid 25% out-of-pocket was 71% of the amount of spending by those who received free care, and those who paid 50% out-of-pocket had total spending that was 63% of spending by those with free care (see Table 9.4).

The Rand Health Insurance Study also examined effects of different levels of coinsurance across various types of services. Of particular interest are differences between outpatient mental health care and outpatient medical care. Returning to Table 9.4, the study found that total spending on outpatient medical services for those who paid 50% out-of-pocket was 58% of the spending by those who received free care. For outpatient mental health services, on the other hand, total spending for those who paid 50% out-of-pocket was 38% of the spending by those who received free care. Thus, for the same increase in percentage paid out-of-pocket, spending on outpatient mental health care decreased more than spending on outpatient medical care. That is, outpatient mental health care was more responsive to the amount of out-of-pocket payment than outpatient medical care.

The Rand Health Insurance Study also examined differences between HMO and fee-for-service plans. We will focus on results for the fee-for-service plan with 25% out-of-pocket payment, because that is close to the usual level of employer-sponsored health insurance coverage. The study found that total expenditures per participant were lower in the HMO plans than in the fee-for-service plan, with 25% out-of-pocket payment for both health services in general and for mental health services.

The findings of the Rand Health Insurance Study have been confirmed by many different studies of different populations over different time periods and for a variety of types of medical services (see review articles by Cutler & Zeckhauser, 2000; Glied, 2000; Zweifel & Manning, 2000). The empirical evidence thus supports the predictions that (a) individuals will use more services and have higher expenditures when they pay a smaller share of the bill, and (b) utilization and expenditures are lower in HMO plans than in fee-for-service plans, holding other factors constant.

Expenditures Over Time

Given the nature of the U.S. health care financing system and the empirical evidence discussed earlier, we would expect to observe increasing utilization of and increasing expenditures on health services over time. And indeed, this is what has happened. For health services as a whole, expenditures increased at an average annual rate of approximately 11% between 1980 and 1990, approximately 7% between 1990 and 1995, and approximately 5% between 1995 and 1999 (using Table 9.1). For mental health and substance abuse services, McKusick et al. (1998) estimated that expenditures increased at an average annual growth rate of 7.2% between 1986 and 1996.

Facing such a situation, payers began to search for methods of controlling the rapid growth in expenditures on health services. The increased use of capitated payment was one approach to controlling the growth in health expenditures. Medicaid programs in particular have increasingly begun to use capitated payment. According to the General Accounting Office (U.S. GAO, 1999), in June 1998 more than 40% of the Medicaid population was enrolled in a plan with either full or partial capitation.

Other approaches to reducing the rate of growth in costs have included increased out-of-pocket payment (including increased deductibles, coinsurance, and copayments) and utilization review and management programs, among others. But for mental health and substance abuse services, payers have increasingly turned to the use of carve-outs to control costs.

CARVE-OUTS

In a health insurance plan with carve-outs, a subset of health services are covered under a separate contract, with the carved-out services typically having less extensive coverage than services in the main contract. Given that a number of insurers have moved in recent years to carve-outs for mental health and substance abuse services, carve-outs are of considerable interest to clinical health psychologists.

In a carve-out program, the insurance risk for specified services or diseases is separated from the overall insurance risk and managed under a separate contract. Carve-out plans are of two types: health plan subcontract and payer carve-out (Huskamp, Azzone, & Frank, 1998). In a health plan subcontract, employees are offered a choice of health plans, with each health plan deciding whether or not to carve out certain services, such as mental health and substance abuse. The payer carve-out model also offers employees a choice of health plans, but certain services are carved out of all health plans offered and then managed under one separate contract.

Third-party payers have increasingly relied on carve-outs to control costs in the mental health and substance abuse sector. For example, Oss (1995) estimated that approximately 53 million people were enrolled in some type of plan (private or public) with mental health and substance abuse carve-outs. Medicaid programs have been particularly likely to move to the use of carve-outs. As of July 1998, 16 states had waivers for the use of carve-out programs for Medicaid mental health services for adults, often combined with substance abuse services (U.S. GAO, 1999).

Rationale for Carve-Outs

Insurers use carve-outs for two primary reasons. First, as discussed earlier, increased insurance coverage increases utilization and expenditures for covered health services. Mental health services are particularly responsive to insurance coverage in that increased coverage tends to lead to substantial increases in utilization of and expenditures on these services (Newhouse & the Insurance Experiment Group, 1993). For example, Keeler, Manning, and Wells (1988) found that individuals offered full coverage used about four times more ambulatory mental health services than those who paid for services out-of-pocket. Insurers thus have turned to carve-outs as a means of controlling expenditures on services that are likely to increase substantially as insurance coverage increases.

Insurers also use carve-outs to control adverse selection. Adverse selection occurs when an insurance plan disproportionately attracts individuals who pose a financial risk (i.e., are more likely to use services). The essence of a financially viable insurance plan is the pooling of financial risks. That is, to be financially viable, a plan must balance enrollees of low risk (i.e., those with low utilization) with enrollees of high risk (i.e., those with high utilization). A health plan sets its premiums on the basis of the actuarially expected utilization (and thus costs) across all enrollees. If the plan attracts more high-risk individuals than expected, it will lose money. If an insurer knows in advance the composition of enrollees, then premiums can be set to cover expected costs of health services used. A problem often arises, though, when insurers are competing for enrollees in that an insurer with benefits that are more comprehensive (or generous) than its competitors will be more attractive to high-risk individuals. As a consequence, insurers may carve out services that are particularly prone to adverse selection, such as mental health and substance abuse.

Effects of Carve-Outs

We have seen that the rationale for the use of carve-outs is to control utilization and thus expenditures on certain services, in this case mental health and substance abuse. The next question is whether or not it works. Because carve-outs have begun to be used only recently, there is relatively little research on this topic. However, the initial studies suggest that carve-outs often do succeed in controlling costs.

Frank and McGuire (2000) reviewed six studies of the impact of mental health carve-out programs, with the programs studied including both Medicaid and privately insured populations and with the nature of the risk-sharing arrangements varying considerably. Overall reductions in spending on mental health services for carve-out programs in comparison to fee-for-service arrangements ranged from −17% to −43%.

One of the studies reviewed was Goldman, McCulloch, and Sturm (1998), which analyzed the effect of a private-sector employer changing to a carve-out mental health plan for approximately 179,000 enrollees. During the 1980s, the employer had experienced increases in mental health costs of more than 20% annually. In response, the employer carved out mental health benefits for all employees to a single vendor in 1991. In analyzing costs over the period 1988 to 1996, the study found that costs for mental health services declined dramatically in the first year of the carve-out program and continued to decline slowly in the following five years. Factors contributing to the decrease in costs were a decrease in the number of outpatient sessions per user, a decrease in inpatient admissions, a decrease in inpatient length-of-stay, and a decrease in cost per day.

Huskamp (1999) examined the effect of a carve-out program for a public employer, the state of Massachusetts. The study compared episodes of treatment for mental health/substance abuse conditions before and after the Massachusetts Group Insurance Commission adopted a carve-out program for mental health services in 1993. The study found that adoption of the carve-out program was associated with a dramatic drop in total mental health/substance abuse costs per episode (particularly for individuals with certain severe conditions).

Drawbacks to Carve-Outs

Thus, payers have successfully used carve-outs to control utilization and expenditures on mental health and substance abuse services. However, from the providers' perspective, less utilization means fewer patients and lower revenues. Most important, though, is the effect on patients, which depends on the appropriate level of utilization.

Although many consumers and providers intuitively oppose carve-outs, there is no systematic empirical evidence that this payment method has adverse effects on health outcomes. Individuals wishing to make a case against carve-outs must demonstrate that the carve-outs ration health care utilization in such a way as to result in decreased health status for enrollees. Put another way, opponents of carve-outs must provide evidence that the increased utilization associated with not carving out certain health services results in improved health status.

Another consideration is that, although they may effectively control utilization in certain cases, carve-outs can create discontinuity of services between physical and mental health. For example, a review of Medicaid mental health carve-outs in three states found that coordination across separate systems for medical and mental health services created problems for some people (Gold & Mittler, 2000). An alternative, the "carve-in," has been proposed to address this problem.

CARVE-INS

Rather than carving out mental health services, a proposed alternative is to integrate the delivery of primary care medical services and mental health services. These plans, often labeled carve-ins, focus on integrated delivery of primary care and mental health services. Providers work in common or contiguous space, with mental health being presented as another variety of service. Carve-in plans seek cost savings associated with integrated treatment. For example, carve-in plans may utilize case funding methods to identify high utilizers as a means of containing costs and improving outcomes (Melek, 1999).

The rationale for the integration of primary care and mental health services derives from the high frequency of mental health symptoms presenting within the primary care system. According to Regier, Narrow, and Rae (1993), more than 60% of all medical visits result in no medical diagnoses, more than 50% of patients with mental health problems are seen only in the medical sector, and more than two thirds of all psychotropic prescriptions are written by nonpsychiatric physicians. When mental health services are carved out, less than 6% of covered members are seen in a year, whereas more than 15% manifest some type of psychological disorder (Melek, 1999).

Advantages of Carve-Ins

From the perspective of providers and patients, carve-ins have several advantages. First, they enhance access to mental health services. A recent report by the Center for the Advancement of Health noted that mental health and social factors contribute to 9 of 10 leading causes of death in the United States (*Mental Health Weekly*, 1999). Carve-ins also can counteract the stigma associated with traditional mental health services, and provide more convenience for consumers. In addition, by increasing interactions among providers of different types, carve-ins increase the ability of health systems to provide an integrated approach to the provision of health care.

Many proponents of carve-ins also believe the approach will enhance overall cost-effectiveness through true integration between physical and mental health treatment. Friedman, Myers, Sobel, Candell, and Benson (1995), for example, argued that if increased use of mental health services results in reduction in unnecessary or excessive use of general health services, then potential cost savings from reduced use of general health services could more than offset the increased expenditures on mental health services.

A review of the literature by Olfson, Sing, and Schlesinger (1999) indicates that three patient groups have a high potential for such a cost offset—distressed elderly medical inpatients, primary care outpatients with multiple unexplained somatic complaints, and nonelderly adults with alcoholism. In all cases, however, cost-offset effects occur only when part of what is included under medical services actually stems from psychological or psychiatric sources and when these mental health factors lead to excessive or unnecessary use of medical services.

Implementation of Carve-Ins

Effective implementation of carve-ins requires long-term commitment by payers. In the first phase of a carve-in, costs may actually rise as mental health services increase. If a short-term approach to cost control prevails, carve-ins will be seen as too expensive. Because carve-ins are most effective when addressing complex health problems, cost reductions will only be realized over the long term.

Balancing financial incentives between primary care providers and mental health providers also is essential for effective implementation of carve-ins. Primary care and mental health providers must jointly share accountability for outcomes to develop a truly integrated, collaborative practice. Joint payment rates should be used to provide an incentive for collaboration.

Implementation of carve-ins would appear to be most effective for high-risk groups such as individuals with hypertension, asthma, chronic pain, or gastrointestinal disorders. These medical diagnoses have been shown to be responsive to mental health interventions and to have effective mental health treatment result in decreased utilization of medical services (Melek, 1999).

Composition of the treatment team in a carve-in will be a key determinant of effective implementation. Carve-ins require a dedicated treatment team able to provide comprehensive care. As a consequence, the role of many disciplines is altered. For example, substantial overlap exists between services provided by psychiatrists and primary care physicians. As a result, in a carve-in model, psychiatrists might be used primarily for consultation on complex case management.

Barriers to Development of Carve-Ins

A key obstacle to the development of a carve-in is that not all primary care physicians view mental health treatments with equal enthusiasm. Clearly, primary care providers that are comfortable with psychological treatment are more likely to be effective members of an integrated carve-in team. Typically family medicine providers and advanced practice nurses tend to be the least stigmatizing toward mental health and psychological specialties. The problem is that, although there are exceptions, it can be time-consuming and costly to identify primary care team providers who are truly open and willing to participate in a carve-in team.

Another barrier to development of a carve-in is that psychologists tend to have certain expectations for individuals entering treatment. For example, psychologists may insist on individual treatment sessions, distinct from a medical visit. Psychologists may also expect that information not be shared with members of the medical staff. Although they may be useful in other situations, these types of expectations can be detrimental to the development of integrated carve-ins. If the carve-in is to succeed, assumptions regarding the culture of clinical care must be carefully evaluated by the carve-in team.

CONCLUSION

The health care financing system influences clinical practice by determining coverage levels and payment rates for psychological services. Clinical health psychologists thus must understand how different types of payment methods will affect their practices.

Although there are differences in degree according to type of service, the U.S. health care financing system is dominated by third-party payers using fee-for-service payment. Given the incentives associated with such a system, it is not surprising that expenditures on health care have risen steadily and continue to rise.

In searching for methods to control their costs, payers have begun to carve out payment for services such as mental health services that are highly responsive to insurance coverage. Although carve-outs do appear to be successful in reducing growth in mental health expenditures in isolation, many psychologists believe that carve-outs lead to a fragmented approach to the provision of health services and, in some cases, to higher total expenditures on health services as a whole.

A proposed alternative is the development of carve-ins to jointly provide primary care and mental health services. Advantages of carve-ins include the use of an integrated approach to the provision of health services and potential savings from cost offsets. However, numerous barriers exist to the development of carve-ins, such as a short-term perspective on cost savings and conflicts among clinical disciplines. Whether or not payers adopt carve-ins will ultimately depend on evidence that this approach results in long-term improvements in both health outcomes and cost savings compared with other delivery and payment systems.

REFERENCES

Cutler, D. M., & Zeckhauser, R. J. (2000). The anatomy of health insurance. In A. J. Culyer & J. P. Newhouse (Eds.), *Handbook of health economics* (pp. 563–643. Amsterdam: Elsevier Science.

Frank, R. G. (1999). We zigged when we should have zagged. *Rehabilitation Psychology, 44*(1), 36–51.

Frank, R. G., & McGuire, T. G. (2000). Economics and mental health. In A. J. Culyer & J. P. Newhouse (Eds.), *Handbook of health economics* (pp. 893–954). Amsterdam: Elsevier Science.

Frank, R. G., & VandenBos, G. R. (1994) Health care reform: The 1993–1994 evolution. *American Psychologist, 49*, 851–854.

Friedman, R., Myers, P., Sobel, D., Caudell, M., & Benson H. (1995). Behavioral medicine, clinical health psychology, and cost offset. *Health Psychology, 14*(6), 509–518.

Gabel, J., Levitt, L., Pickreign, J., Whitmore, H., Holve, E., Hawkins, S., et al. (2000). Job-based health insurance in 2000: Premiums rise sharply while coverage grows. *Health Affairs, 19*(5), 144–151.

Glied, S. (2000). Managed care. In A. J. Culyer & J. P. Newhouse (Eds.), *Handbook of health economics* (pp. 707–753). Amsterdam: Elsevier Science.

Gold, M., & Mittler, J. (2000). Medicaid's complex goals: Challenges for managed care and behavioral health. *Health Care Financing Review, 22*(2), 85–101.

Goldman, W., McCulloch, J., & Sturm, R. (1998). Costs and use of mental health services before and after managed care. *Health Affairs, 17*(2), 40–52.

Health Care Financing Administration (HCFA), Office of the Actuary, National Health Statistics Group; U.S. Bureau of the Census. (2001). Table 4: Personal health care expenditures aggregate and per capita amounts and percent distribution, by source of funds: Selected calendar years 1960–99. Retrieved June 17, 2001, from http://www.hcfa.gov/stats/nhe-pact/tables/A4/htm

Huskamp, H. A. (1999). Episodes of mental health and substance abuse treatment under a managed behavioral health care carve-out. *Inquiry, 36*, 147–161.

Huskamp, H. A., Azzone, V., & Frank, R. G. (1998). Carve-outs, women, and the treatment of depression. *Women's Health Issues, 8*(5), 267–282.

Keeler, E. B., Manning, W. G., & Wells, K. B. (1988). The demand for episodes of mental health services. *Journal of Health Economics, 7*(2): 369–392.

McKusick, D., Mark, T., King, E., Harwood, R., Buck, J., Dilonardo, J., et al. (1998). Spending for mental health and substance abuse treatment 1996. *Health Affairs, 17*(5), 147–157.

Melek, S. P. (1999). *Financial, risk and structural issues related to the integration of behavioral healthcare in primary care settings under managed care.* New York: Milliman & Robertson.

Mental Health Weekly. (1999, Dec. 6). Vol. 9(46), 5–8.

Modern Healthcare. (1995, Nov. 13). Vol. 25(42), 18.

Newhouse, J. P., & the Insurance Experiment Group. (1993). *Free for all?: Lessons from the RAND Health Insurance Experiment.* Cambridge, MA: Harvard University Press.

Olfson, M., Sing, M., & Schlesinger, H. J. (1999). Mental health/medical care cost offsets: Opportunities for managed care. *Health Affairs, 18*(2), 79–93.

Oss, M. (1995). *Managed behavioral health market share in the United States*. Gettysburg, PA: Open Minds.

Regier, D. A., Narrow, W. E., & Rae, D. S. (1993). The defacto U.S. mental and addictive disorders service system: Epidemiologic catchment area prospective one year prevalence rates of disorders and services. *Archives of General Psychiatry, 50*, 85–94.

Remler, D. K., Donelan, K., Blendon, R. J., Lundberg, G. D., Leape, L. L., Calkins, D. R., et al. (1997). What do managed care plans do to affect care? Results from a survey of physicians. *Inquiry, 34*, 196–204.

U.S. Census Bureau. (2000). *Health insurance detailed table: 1999*. Retrieved May 31, 2001, from http://www.census.gov/hhes/htthins/hlthins99/dtable1.html

U.S. General Accounting Office. (1999). *Medicaid managed care: Four states' experiences with mental health carveout programs*. Washington, DC: U.S. Government Printing Office.

Zuvekas, S. H. (2001). Trends in mental health services use and spending, 1987–1996. *Health Affairs, 20*(2), 214–224.

Zweifel, P., & Manning, W. G. (2000). Moral hazard and consumer incentives in health care. In A. J. Culyer & J. P. Newhouse (Eds.), *Handbook of health economics* (pp. 409–459). Amsterdam: Elsevier Science.

10

COMPLEMENTARY HEALTH CARE

MARGARET A. GARDEA, ROBERT J. GATCHEL,
AND RICHARD C. ROBINSON

The term *complementary health care* encompasses a heterogeneous collection of techniques, therapies, and procedures that traditionally have been considered outside of the realm of established Western medicine. These "unorthodox" techniques have been referred to by a variety of names, including *alternative medicine, integrative medicine*, and *complementary health care*. Eisenberg and his colleagues (1998) functionally defined alternative medical therapies as the range of therapeutic interventions that are "interventions neither taught widely in medical schools nor generally available in US hospitals" (p. 1569). Although this is a broad definition, the diversity of techniques that could be classified as alternative medicine is vast. For instance, acupuncture and natural herbal remedies are widely accepted as alternative medical treatments; however, prayer, exercise, and psychotherapy may also be defined as alternative by some authors. Therefore, a broad definition allows for the examination of this diverse topic. The use of the term *complementary health care* for this chapter, rather than alternative medicine, reflects the trend to integrate proven alternative practices with more conventional practices.

The writing of this chapter was supported in part by grants 2 KO2 MH01107, RO1 DE10713, and RO1 MH 46452 awarded to the second author from the National Institutes of Health.

The definitions and terms related to complementary health care have evolved over the past several years, but complementary health care has been in practice for more than two decades in clinical settings. For instance, chronic pain is a debilitating, common, and costly medical condition, and multidisciplinary pain treatment centers have been practicing what would today be considered complementary health care for years (Gatchel & Turk, 1996). At these centers, physicians, physical therapists, psychologists, and other specialists evaluate patients. Based on these evaluations, ranges of treatments are offered to the patient. An individual with chronic low back pain, for example, may be prescribed a nonsteroidal antiinflammatory from an anesthesiologist, participate in physical rehabilitation with a physical therapist, and learn self-hypnosis from a psychologist. These specialists will often be housed under one roof and conduct team conferences in which each specialist will present his or her conceptualization of the patient's difficulties so that treatments complement one another. As can be seen in this example, hypnosis complements a treatment that includes medication and physical rehabilitation.

With continued focus on lowering health care costs and rising negative sentiment from the public about current conventional health care practices (e.g., limited time spent with patients because of managed care and a lack of rationale by physicians for recommended procedures), complementary health care has received attention from consumers of health care. Eisenberg and colleagues (1993), in their landmark national telephone survey of more than 1,500 adults, found that some 34% had used one or more types of complementary/alternative medicine in 1990, with the highest frequency among relaxation, chiropractic, and massage techniques. A follow-up study found that, by 1997, this prevalence had expanded to 42%, with rising usage of herbal medicines, megavitamins, self-help groups, and folk remedies (Eisenberg et al., 1998). The primary reasons people sought such treatments included back problems, anxiety, headache, chronic pain, and cancer. Among those using complementary medicine, approximately 46% pursued direct treatment from a complementary medicine provider, up from 36% in 1990. Although few people reported relying only on complementary medicine, Eisenberg et al. extrapolated that visits to complementary medicine practitioners totaled close to $629 million in the United States for 1997, exceeding visits to conventional medicine practitioners. A parallel survey by Astin (1998) yielded similar findings, with 40% of respondents reporting use of complementary medicine, including chiropractic, lifestyle–diets, and relaxation techniques.

It was also found that complementary medicine use was more common among women compared to men, and more common among individuals with some college education compared to individuals with no college education. Use of alternative medicine was also more common among individuals who earned more than $50,000 a year (Eisenberg et al., 1998). In addition, the use of folk remedies by diverse cultural groups, such as Mexican Americans, Chinese Americans, and African Americans has been highlighted by some researchers (e.g., Becerra & Iglehart, 1995).

Not only have patients shown an interest in complementary health care, but the medical community has also responded to growing interest in these therapies. Wetzel, Eisenberg, and Kaptchuk (1998) surveyed 125 medical schools to investigate the existence and scope of courses in complementary and alternative medicine. From the 117 medical schools that responded, 64% stated that complementary health care issues were part of their curriculum, either in an elective course or in part of a required course. Although there appeared to be a diversity of content among medical schools, acupuncture, chiropractic, and herbal therapies were among the most common topics. This growing interest in complementary medicine has also now spread to scientific journals. One of the leading medical journals in the United States—*The Journal of the American Medical Association*—published a special issue on alternative medicine on November, 11, 1998.

Interest in complementary health care is no longer limited to just medical schools and scientific journals. Although physicians may be concerned about complementary health care, they are reportedly not opposed to it (Berman et al., 1995; Burg, Kosch, & Neims, 1998, as cited in Kemper, Cassileth, & Ferris, 1999). Many complementary health care practices ask that patients become active participants in the healing process, a change that might be welcomed by some primary care physicians.

There is now a great synergy developing to integrate complementary medicine with conventional medicine techniques. This can be especially seen on the national level. There is now a Center for Complementary and Alternative Medicine (CAM) within the National Institute of Health (NIH), with $50 million having been budgeted for clinical research for the fiscal year 1999 and another $50 million was budgeted for fiscal year 2000. (See Exhibit 10.1.)

Finally, as one might imagine from the demographic characteristics and trends in use for complementary health care, more and more entrepreneurs looking to take advantage of a growing market are appearing. Complementary health care is promoted by these individuals as treatments that are safer, less expensive, and have fewer side effects (Kemper et al., 1999). However, the consumer is faced with the challenge of finding effective alternative treatments without being fooled into spending hundreds and thousands of dollars on "magic beans" or "snake oil." Eisenberg has published an informative article to address this issue titled, "Advising Patients Who Seek Alternative Medical Therapies" (1997). It is an important resource for both consumers and health care professionals.

This chapter is designed to serve as a primer for those interested in complementary health care. Several different areas of complementary

EXHIBIT 10.1
NIH-Supported CAM Clinical Research Centers

- Center for Addiction and Alternative Medicine Research (University of Minnesota Medical School)
- Complementary and Alternative Medicine Program on Aging (Stanford University)
- Center for Alternative Medicine Research in Asthma and Immunology (University of California, Davis)
- Center for Alternative Medicine Research in Cancer (University of Texas Health Science Center, Houston)
- Consortium Center for Chiropractic Research (Palmer Center for Chiropractic Research, University of Iowa, and Kansas State University)
- Center for Alternative Medicine Research (Harvard Medical School)
- AIDS Research Center (Bastyr University)
- Center for the Study of Center for Complementary and Alternative Therapies for Pain Management (University of Virginia)
- Center for Alternative Medicine Pain Research and Evaluation (University of Maryland School of Medicine)
- Center for Research in Complementary and Alternative Medicine for Stroke and Neurological Disorders (Kessler Institute for Rehabilitation)
- Center for Complementary and Alternative Medicine Research in Women's Health (Columbia University)
- The NIH Center for CAM also has its own web page for general information and grant application information: http://altmed.od.nih.gov/nccam and http://altmed.od.nih.gov/nccam/research/opportunities/. Finally, there is a NIH CAM Information Clearinghouse, with the following telephone number: 888-644-6226.

Note. From "Advising Patients Who Seek Alternative Medical Therapies," by D. M. Eisenberg et al., 1997, *Annals of Internal Medicine, 127,* p. 61. Copyright 1997 by *Annals of Internal Medicine.* Reprinted with permission.

medicine are discussed briefly, and other relevant topics are introduced. When integrating complementary health care practices with conventional practices, the importance of empirical and scholarly investigation into complementary techniques cannot be understated.

COMPLEMENTARY MEDICINE TECHNIQUES

Next we describe several popular complementary medicine techniques.

Acupuncture

An increasingly important area of complementary health care is acupuncture. Beginning with the visit of President Richard Nixon to China in 1972, interest in this procedure by Western industrialized countries to address a variety of medical afflictions has grown. During that visit, President Nixon observed acupuncture while being filmed by television crews. An indication of the growing use of acupuncture is reflected in the Food and Drug

Administration's (FDA) recent decision to remove acupuncture needles from the category of experimental medical devices to a more regulated category that includes surgical scalpels and hypodermic needles (NIH Consensus Conference, 1998).

Although there are numerous theories related to acupuncture, the most common originate from China, Korea, and Japan. A form of American acupuncture has also been identified that incorporates aspects from the previously mentioned countries. According to the most common theories of acupuncture, disease arises from an imbalance of energy (qi; pronounced "chee") that might be corrected by acupuncture. This technique has been used not only by acupuncturists but also by physicians, dentists, and other clinicians for a variety of ailments. Acupuncture has been applied to nausea, pain, addictions, pulmonary disorders, hypertension, and rehabilitation from neurological damage (NIH Consensus Conference, 1998).

Vickers and Zollman (1999) provided a clear summarization of basic acupuncture concepts:

> There are 12 main meridians, and these correspond to 12 major functions or "organs" of the body. Although they have the same names (such as liver, kidney, heart, etc.), Chinese and Western concepts of the organs correlated only very loosely. Qi energy must flow in the correct strength and quality through each of these meridians and organs for health to be maintained. The acupuncture points are located along the meridians and provide one means of altering the flow of Qi. (p. 973)

Traditional Chinese acupuncturists believe that additional meridians exist, but that these meridians are not associated with an internal organ. Often, the language of complementary health care practices reflects an elegant and sophisticated theory. With acupuncture, the goal is to bring balance and harmony to the body. The notion of yin, associated with the female gender, and yang, associated with the male gender, can be thought of as opposing and integrative forces that have to be in the proper balance, quantity, and quality. As can be seen by the explanation, the language of traditional acupuncture theory is not the language of Western medical practices.

Investigation into the physiological mechanisms of acupuncture has provided interesting results. Much of the attention has been given to the activation of endogenous opioids by acupuncture. In fact, empirical evidence supports the hypothesis that opioid peptides are released during acupuncture and that the analgesic effects of acupuncture can be reversed by administering naloxone, an opioid antagonist. In addition to the release of endogenous opioids, some evidence suggests that acupuncture effects the hypothalamic–pituitary–adrenal (HPA) axis and immunofunctioning (NIH Consensus Conference, 1998).

Although there has been increased interest in the area of acupuncture, as is true for a variety of complementary health care techniques, adequate empirical evidence is just beginning to emerge with regard to its efficacy. As one can imagine, conducting truly double blind, placebo-controlled studies with acupuncture presents special challenges. Often sham acupuncture sites are used, which are sites not located along traditional meridians. When sham acupuncture sites are compared to real acupuncture sites, differences in the effect of the acupuncture can be detected for some conditions, (e.g., nausea; NIH Consensus Conference, 1998).

One such controlled study has been conducted evaluating the efficacy of a relatively new form of acupuncture, known as percutaneous electrical nerve stimulation (PENS). PENS has been found to be effective for pain-management purposes in a number of medical conditions secondary to bony metastasis, (Ahmed, Craig, White, & Huber, 1999), and the prevention and treatment of headache following electroconvulsive therapy (Ghoname, Craig & White, 1998). The fundamental basis of PENS is the systematized stimulation of the endogenous opioids through peripheral nerve stimulation. It uses acupuncture-type needle probes positioned in soft tissue to stimulate peripheral sensory nerves at the dermatonal levels corresponding to the local pathology.

In one such study of PENS, with a randomized cross-over design, 60 patients with low-back pain related to degenerative disk disease were treated with four therapeutic modalities: PENS, sham-PENS, transcutaneous electrical nerve stimulation (TENS), and spine exercise (Ghoname et al., 1999). All patients had been maintained on a stable oral analgesic treatment regimen for at least three months before entering the study. The basic PENS therapy consisted of placing 10 32-gage stainless steel acupuncture–like needle probes into the soft tissue in the low back region, to a depth of 2 to 4 centimeters. The Sham-pens therapy consisted of needle probes placed in the same pattern as PENS, except no electrical stimulation was applied. The standard TENS therapy consisted of placing four medium-sized cutaneous electrode pads in a standard dermatemal pattern. The low back spine exercise extension therapy consisted of spine flexion. Specifically, the patient was seated on a chair with full abduction of both hips and instructed to slowly touch the floor with both hands, and while remaining seated, follow this movement with a full extension.

Each of these treatments was administered for a period of 30 minutes, three times per week, for a three-week period. Pre- and posttreatment assessments of a number of variables were collected. Results of the study clearly demonstrated that PENS was significantly more effective in decreasing self-reported pain after each session than the other three therapies. It was also found the daily oral analgesic requirement was reduced with PENS by 50%, compared to sham-pens (4%), TENS (15%), and low back spine exercise (unchanged). For the overall assessment of effectiveness, 91% of the patients reported that PENS was the most effective pain-relieving modality used. PENS was also significantly more effective in improving physical activity, quality of sleep, and the sense of patient well-being than the other modalities. The Medical Outcomes Short Form 36 Health Survey (SF-36) evaluation also confirmed the superiority of PENS relative to the other treatment modalities with respect to posttreatment functioning. Finally, 81% of the patients stated that they would be willing to pay money out of pocket to receive PENS therapy compared to only 4 to 9% with the other treatment modalities.

More studies such as these are needed. Currently, according to a National Institute of Health Consensus Conference (1998), there is evidence suggesting the efficacy of acupuncture for nausea and vomiting following chemotherapy and for some pain conditions, such as postoperative dental pain and fibromyalgia. For most other conditions where acupuncture is used, there is insufficient evidence to support acupuncture's efficacy. However, the evidence for acupuncture's efficacy may be comparable to other Western medical techniques that have more adverse effects (e.g., sedating side effects from antimimetic medication for nausea and gastrointestinal side effects from nonsteroidal antiinflammatories for pain).

In addition to the more common uses for acupuncture, exploration into more nontraditional uses for acupuncture have been undertaken as we begin to unravel the physiological underpinnings of this technique. For instance, the use of acupuncture for hypertension provides an excellent example of an integrative conceptualization of Eastern and Western medicine that can be studied empirically. The use of acupuncture to treat hypertension is an acceptable practice in China, but patients will often seek care for more distressing and symptomatic problems, such as pain. However, there exists an abundance of Chinese and Russian literature that examines the use of acupuncture at the Tsu-San-Li point (anterior tibialis muscle below the knee) and the Neiguan point (forearm muscle above the wrist) for hypertension. Unfortunately, the Chinese literature requires cautious interpretation. From 1966 until 1976, China was in the midst of a cultural revolution. During this time, acupuncture was investigated, but unfavorable results were discouraged, questioning the validity of the science.

However, sound basic research has been conducted in this area. In dogs, acupuncture at the Tsu-San-Li point lowered heart rate and cardiac output but, unfortunately, had no effect on blood pressure (Lee, Lee, & Clifford, 1976). Investigations that studied rats and rabbits, however, found different results. Peter Thoren and his colleagues in Goteberg, Sweden, conducted an elaborate series of studies that examined the Tsu-San-Li point in rats. They found that when they delivered electroacupuncture at sufficient intensities to stimulate group I, II, and III muscle afferent nerves, they observed a 12-hour decrease in blood pressure. However, they did not find the same results when only the group I and II skeletal muscle afferent nerves were activated (Hoffman & Thoren, 1986; Shyu, Andersson, & Thoren, 1984; Yao, Andersson, & Thoren, 1982). This coincides with research suggesting that exercise that stimulates the group II and III skeletal muscle afferent nerves decreases blood pressure (Mitchell, 1990). Apparently, after exercise of sufficient intensity, sympathetic nerve activity decreases with an accompanying vasodepressor response (Mitchell, 1990). This model appears to represent a synergistic integration of traditional alternative medicine with conventional Western practices, empiricism, and sophisticated basic research.

Massage

Field (1999) defined massage as "the hand manipulation of body tissues to promote wellness and to reduce stress and pain. The therapeutic effects of massage are from its impact on the muscular, nervous, and circulation systems" (p. 383). There are several types of massage and, often, these types are used in conjunction with one another. Swedish massage involves stroking and kneading; Shiatsu massage involves applying pressure to pressure points; and neuromuscular massage involves applying pressure to all areas of the body (Field, 1999). In addition to these common forms of massage, other massage techniques, such as *rolfing*, a form of deep muscle massage, are touted as offering a host of benefits by their practitioners.

Although the exact physiological mechanisms of massage therapy require investigation, it may benefit patients in several ways, including possibly increasing blood circulation to certain areas (Field, 1999). Researchers have demonstrated improvements from massage related to mood, level of stress, and immune functioning (Field et al., 1992; Ironson et al., 1996). Field's use of salivary cortisol levels and measures of immune functioning again highlight the use of Western technology and empirical practices to understand the physiological determinants derived from a complementary health care practice.

Relaxation Training

One of the most commonly used procedures that can be classified as complementary health care is relaxation training. In fact, Krauss, Godfrey, Kirk, and Eisenberg (1998) investigated 401 patients with physical disabilities, ranging from paraplegia to carpal tunnel syndrome, and stated that 31.7% of these individuals reported using a relaxation technique in the past 12 months. Belar and Deardorff (1995) stated that there is empirical support for the use of relaxation training with a variety of medical conditions, including chronic pain, Raynaud's disease, and hypertension.

Although there are a variety of relaxation training techniques, most involve focusing on an individual's breathing and level of muscle tension. Diaphragmatic breathing is often part of most relaxation treatment protocols, but can be used by itself (Belar & Deardorff, 1995). This procedure involves asking an individual to begin breathing in a manner that naturally elicits relaxation. Most adults will breath with their chests instead of with their diaphragm. Patients may be asked to place a hand on their stomachs and attempt to make their hand rise and fall with each breath.

Progressive muscle relaxation is another form of relaxation training, and most people find it easy to perform. Essentially, a person is asked to tense and then relax certain muscles in his or her body (Belar & Deardorff, 1995). Jacobson (1939, as cited in Belar & Deardorff, 1995) is credited with developing this technique, which has been incorporated into many standard psychological interventions, such as systematic deconditioning. The goal is to make individuals more aware of their muscle tension so that they can quickly and easily learn to release that tension.

In 1974, Benson, Beary, and Carol developed a form of relaxation that included elements of a shortened, Westernized version of transcendental meditation. They named the technique the relaxation response, and conducted a series of controlled studies demonstrating the significant physiological change produced by this technique. These changes consisted of reduced oxygen consumption, metabolism rate, and blood pressure, all indicative of a decrease in sympathetic nervous system activities. Benson advocated the use of the relaxation response as a means of offsetting the potential harmful effects of the maladaptive chronic elicitation of the fight or flight response.

Autogenic relaxation training was initially developed by Schultz and Luthe (1969), and Belar and Deardorff (1995) described it as "a very deep state of relaxation through the use of positive self-statements suggesting such sensations as warmth, heaviness, and calmness in every body part" (p. 84). Patients are often asked to repeat a particular unique phrase to themselves, such as "my body is warm and heavy," so that the phrase becomes associated with the relaxation response. In addition, with enough practice, or conditioning trials, the phrase can begin to elicit the response quickly and easily.

Hypnosis and Imagery

Although there is a plethora of misinformation regarding hypnosis, the use of this technique by trained hypnotherapists has been proven safe and effective. It is similar to relaxation training and biofeedback in the support it has received in the research literature, and, as with relaxation training and biofeedback, the emphasis with hypnosis is on training individuals to gain greater control over their physiological functioning. Several disorders and conditions have been treated with hypnosis with varying success. These disorders include acute pain, chronic pain, smoking cessation, obesity, and sexual problems (Crasilneck & Hall, 1985).

Although controversy remains about the exact physiological mechanisms involved in hypnosis, most agree that hypnosis creates a way in which people can alter their bodily sensations. Evidence form eletroencephalograph (EEG) recordings has demonstrated that there are differences between high and low hypnotizable individuals, primarily in the frontal lobe and temporal cortex (Graffin, Ray, & Lundy, 1995). Involvement of the hippocampus, thalamus, and reticular activating system have also been implicated (Crasilneck & Hall, 1985). With the introduction of more sophisticated imaging techniques, (e.g., functional magnetic resonance imaging), additional exploration into the physiological mechanisms of hypnosis is inevitable.

Although hypnosis is a powerful and relatively safe tool, certain considerations must be made with regard to the practitioner and the patient. Crucial individual differences among patients require the application of hypnosis by a trained hypnotherapist. Ideally, the hypnotherapist is prepared to manage different manifestations of psychopathology and has been supervised for an appropriate length of time (several months to several years) by another hypnotherapist. Psychologists, psychiatrists, and social workers, when they have received additional training in hypnosis, are especially well equipped for this type of intervention.

Several factors may affect a person's level of hypnotizability, ranging from physiological individual differences to motivation. According to Wickramasekera (1999), "Hypnosis is particularly indicated if the patient has high hypnotic ability and a positive attitude toward hypnosis for treating any clinical condition in which an alteration of perception, memory, or mood can reduce the intensity of a psychological or somatic symptom and/ or provide information about the etiology of a disorder" (p. 436). In addition, Crasilneck and Hall (1985) listed motivation to be free of symptoms as one of the more crucial factors that affects hypnotizability.

Syrjala and Abrams (1996) pointed to the similarities between hypnosis and imagery. They stated that both "are states of highly focused attention during which alteration of sensations, awareness, and perceptions can occur" (p. 231). Although imagery is often incorporated into hypnosis, imagery may not be used with all individuals. Also, imagery may be used by itself or with a relaxation technique. For instance, a patient may use diaphragmatic breathing and visualize that his or her hands are covered by warm wool gloves. The line between hypnosis and imagery, or other forms of relaxation training, might become blurred at times.

Biofeedback

Biofeedback involves developing a patient's ability to alter his or her physiological response by providing the patient with feedback about the physiological response that is being elicited. For instance, patients may attempt to alter muscle tension, blood flow, or surface skin temperature. Patients are most commonly provided feedback in the form of a tone, or other auditory signal, or a visual display, such as a line that moves up or down on a computer screen (Arena & Blanchard, 1996). Electromyograph (EMG) is one of the most common types of biofeedback, which involves feedback of muscle tension. Other types of biofeedback include thermal biofeedback, which provides information on skin temperature; electroencephalograph (EEG), which provides information on brain wave activity; and electrodermal response (EDR), which provides information on sweat gland activity (Green & Shellenberger, 1999). Often, patients will receive biofeedback information from more than one of these modalities (Green & Shellenberger, 1999).

Integrating Relaxation Training, Hypnosis, and Biofeedback

Although relaxation training, hypnosis, and biofeedback are discussed separately in the preceding section, a practitioner of behavioral medicine often integrates these techniques. For instance, a patient with tension headaches may begin with EMG biofeedback that targets the frontalis or trapezius muscles. In addition, patients may be instructed in progressive muscle-relaxation training so that they may practice relaxing these, and other muscles, at home. In addition, hypnosis may be added as a helpful way to develop the patient's proficiency at relaxing frontalis muscles by visualizing, while in a hypnotic state, that sunrays are gently warming his or her forehead. As can be seen, these well-studied techniques offer multiple benefits, are relatively simple to teach, and can easily be integrated with one another and more traditional approaches.

Homeopathy

Homeopathy is a unique theoretical approach to healing that postulates dilute amounts of medicine, which create similar symptomatology in a healthy person, and will trigger a patient's innate capacity to heal. With homeopathy, the entire person is considered—the biological, mental, and spiritual aspects of a person (Chapman, 1999). Several concepts are crucial for understanding homeopathy, including the law of similars, the minute dose, and the totality of symptoms. The *law of similars* states that the same medicine that produces symptoms in a healthy person will stimulate the body's natural healing process of the ill patient and cure those similar symptoms. In homeopathy, a minute dose is used at low frequency to stimulate the body's curative processes and address the totality of the patient's condition—physical, emotional, and mental (Chapman, 1999).

Homeopathic practitioners suggest it is an effective intervention for most illnesses with the exception of irreversible tissue damage. It is also used in conjunction with more traditional Western medicine. Some of the more common ailments treated by homeopaths include asthma, depression, headaches, arthritis, and high blood pressure. Unfortunately, few empirical studies have been used to examine the efficacy of homeopathy. Critics charge it is nothing more than a placebo response because homeopathic substances are diluted beyond Avogadro's number and, therefore, no molecules from the original mixture remain (Chapman, 1999; Linde & Jonas, 1999).

Studies addressing the placebo question have been inconclusive, but recent evidence has reported an effect. Reilly, Taylor, McSharry, and Atkinson (1986) attempted to replicate two previous trials that found a significant difference between placebo and homeopathy for asthma. In a double-blind design, 28 patients suffering from allergic asthma were randomized into a homeopathic or placebo treatment group. The experimental conditions were used as a complement to their conventional medical care. Differences between the two groups were noted within one week. Overall, the homeopathic group reported improvements in respiratory function, bronchial reactivity tests, and visual analogue scores. Finally, a meta-analysis of all three trials demonstrated a significant difference between homeopathy and placebo intervention.

As can be seen, homeopathy requires additional research; however, this presents some difficult methodological challenges. Homeopathy entails a different conceptual framework than traditional Western medicine, because it suggests that each patient may receive different treatment for the same subset of symptoms. This is in line with the totality of symptoms, which may be different for each patient. Therefore, two patients with sore throats may receive different treatments if one is experiencing a general malaise and the other is not (Chapman, 1999).

Herbal Therapy

Herbal medicine is "the study and application of the therapeutic effects of plant materials within an holistic context" (Eldin & Dunford, 1999, p. 1). Ironically, this complementary intervention began as mainstream medicine. There is archaeological evidence that our nonhuman primate ancestors used herbs. Moreover, the ancient civilizations of China, Egypt,

India, Greece, and Mexico all used plants for medicinal purposes. In many cases, different cultures used the same (or chemically similar) plants for the identical purpose. The earliest written reference of plants used for healing dates back to China in 2800 B.C. with the "Great Herbal" or *Pen Ts'ao* of Shen Nung. A total of 360 species were listed, one of which—*Ma Huang* (*Ephedra sinica*)—is used today, and is also referred to as ephedrine in conventional medicine. Every culture has used plants as healing devices, although the therapeutic use and philosophy of medicinal herbs varies from culture to culture and is contingent on the ecosystem. For instance, in China the herbalist examines the client's *yin* and *yang* forces to determine the blockage of *qi* and then prescribes an assortment of herbal treatments. In contrast, in Mexico, the client or a family member may approach the *curandero/herbalista* with a specific problem. Once the practitioner determines the source of the difficulty (which may be natural, psychological, or spiritual in nature), an herbal mixture is prescribed (Eldin & Dunford, 1999; Gordon, 1996).

In the United States, most medications had an herbal origin until the advent of synthetic medications approximately 50 years ago. Since this time, botanical medicine was all but forgotten. Today, the bulk of herbal medicine research is conducted in Europe; however, a resurgence of botanical medicine is beginning to occur in the United States (Cupp, 1999; Eldin & Dunford, 1999). The motivation behind this renewed interest is monetary, as a burgeoning number of Americans are turning to herbal remedies for preventive and therapeutic care. Advertisements in print, radio, and television that saturate the media demonstrate the market is no longer limited to "naturalists." This wide acceptance of natural herbs results in a change in the political landscape and marketplace. The multi-billion-dollar pharmaceutical industry has a vested interest in herbal supplements and vitamins. The large corporations will have a powerful say in the direction of future research and the availability of products.

Most herbs are typically not classified as medications in the United States, and, therefore, are not subject to government approval for safety and efficacy requirements. As a consequence, the quality may be compromised, and this lack of regulation may lead to disastrous effects (Cupp, 1999; DeSmet, 1999). For instance, some "Paraguay Tea" imported from South America contained belladonna alkaloids instead of xanthine. This resulted in an eruption of anticholinergic poisoning. Other factors that may affect efficacy and safety of herbs include variables such as age, genetics, ethnicity, and medical conditions. In particular, the chemical make-up and pharmacodynamic properties of herbs are subject to the same pharmacokinetic principles of conventional drug chemicals. As such, factors such as interracial differences must be considered. For example, the impact of atropine on the heart rate varies among Chinese, White, and Black patients. Thus, caution should be taken when herbal remedies are given to societies different from the culture of origin (DeSmet, 1999).

Herbs are frequently a mixture of compositions rather than a single crude herb. The final pharmacological make-up creates an interaction among the bioactive constituents. As with any pharmacological substance, herbs have the danger of potentiating or neutralizing any other drug taken by the patient. Primary care physicians must make a concerted effort to inquire about the patient's use of herbs to prevent unwanted interaction.

Side-effects common to most medicinal herbs run from benign reactions, such as allergic contact dermatitis and gastrointestinal reactions, to more serious interactions such as cardiac glycocides and toxicity. One of the factors that affect the side effects is dose control. Critics point out that one problem of herbal medicine is unknown potency levels because of difficulty in measuring precise quantities (DeSmet, 1999). Variables such as soil condition, plant genotype, condition at time of harvest, and preparation methods may adulterate the product. There is also the danger of contamination as a result of substitution of one ingredient for another. For example, there was an outbreak of neuropathy in Belgium after a Chinese root was compromised either through substitution or contamination (DeSmet, 1999; Eldin & Dunford, 1999).

Other dangers of herbal medicine include the potential for abuse. For example, *Ma Huang* has been associated with a multitude of mishaps in recent years. In the United States, it has been marketed as a legal "high," an aphrodisiac, and as an energy boost. Some mixtures contained 45 mg of ephedrine and 20 mg of caffeine per tablet. News stories surfaced of truck drivers taking excessive amounts of the herb to increase their drive time and of individuals taking excessive amounts in an attempt to lose weight. Unfortunately, some serious side effects occurred, including reports of erythroderma, mania, psychosis, seizures, acute myocardial infarction, and fatal coronary artery thrombosis. Another area of concern involves attempts to manipulate interactions with Western drugs including benzodiazepines, corticosteroids, and nonsteroidal antiinflammatory drugs (DeSmet, 1999).

Sound clinical research demonstrating the efficacy of the majority of herbs has been insufficient. However, good efficacy has been demonstrated for St. John's Wort (Josey & Tackett, 1999) to treat mild to moderate forms of depression, and Ginko biloba for the memory and concentration of patients suffering from Alzheimer's disease and vascular dementia (Klejnen, & Knipschild, 1992). In fact, reference to St. John's Wort is made in textbooks used by the ancient physicians such as Hippocrates and Galen. There is evidence that it was in use throughout the Classical, Renaissance, and Victorian eras (Volz, 1997). The majority of studies have found St. John's Wort to be superior to placebo and equal in efficacy to antidepressant medication. Josey and Tackett (1999) reviewed the literature to evaluate the efficacy and possible adverse effects of St. John's Wort in comparison to tricylic antidepressants (TCAs) and monoamine oxidase inhibitors (MAOIs). The researchers selected four studies with large numbers of participants, and found St. John's Wort was significantly better than the placebo and equally effective as the TCAs and MAOIs. More important, the authors found St. John's Wort had the advantage of fewer adverse side effects. Vorbach, Arnoldt, and Hubner (1997) found similar results.

Some critics, though, have charged that much of the research governing St. John's Wort has been flawed. Kim, Streltzer, and Goebert (1999) conducted a meta-analysis in an attempt to correct the methodological shortcomings believed to mar the research. Again, St. John's Wort was found to be superior to the placebo and equivalent to TCAs. The researchers report the individuals taking TCAs were almost twice as likely to experience adverse effects and had a higher dropout rate. In another meta-analysis of randomized trials, Linde and colleagues (1996) found the same results. However, Linde et al. pointed out that many studies had problems such as a limited number of participants and heterogeneous patient populations. Differences in the content of herb substances and different herb preparation were also noted. The researchers recommended additional research on specific depressive disorders with larger participant pools. The NIH is currently funding such clinical research.

Another promising herb—Ginko biloba—is made from the leaves of the ginko tree, one of the oldest deciduous tree species. It was written about in China more than 2,000 years ago, and it has been used extensively in Europe for medicinal purposes. Among its known effects is serving as an antagonist for platelet-activating factors, improving vascular perfusion, and decreasing thrombosis. It also contains antioxidant properties that are thought to play a key role in neuroprotective and ischemia-reperfusion-protective effects (Wong, Smith, & Boon, 1998). Klejnen and Knipschild (1992) reviewed literature to evaluate the efficacy of Ginkgo biloba for "cerebral insufficiency." Of the studies deemed methodologically sound, the researchers found an improvement in 8 of 12 symptoms, including tiredness, anxiety, dizziness, tinnitus, headache, difficulties with concentration and memory, confusion, and lack of energy. Ginko has also demonstrated efficacy in treating patients suffering from Alzheimer's disease and vascular dementia. One randomized controlled study followed 309 patients suffering from Alzheimer's disease or multiinfarct dementia for a one-year period (LeBars et al., 1997). Patients given Ginko scored significantly higher on the Geriatric Evaluation by Relative's Rating Instrument (Schwartz, 1983) and the Alzheimer's Disease Assessment Scale (Mohs, Rosen, & Davis, 1983). However, no difference was reported on global measures of change. In another random controlled trial, Kanowski, Herrmann, Stephan, Wierich, and Horr (1997) reported significant improvement for patients taking Ginko. Success depended on the patients improving on two of the three outcome measures. These measures evaluated psychopathology, memory and attention, and the ability to perform daily life activities.

Side effects are uncommon for people taking Gingko biloba, and they are usually dose-related. Some of the adverse effects include headache, gastrointestinal upset, and skin allergy. A more serious concern is the possibility that Ginko may prolong bleeding. This is quite problematic given the elderly population that would most benefit from Ginko and the ease with which they normally may bruise and bleed.

Vitamins

In concert with the growing interest in herbal remedies is a movement advocating vitamin use to prevent and combat disease. Approximately 70% of the adult population in the United States takes vitamin supplements, with 100 million using them on a regular basis. Most medical experts and researchers have yet to fully endorse nutritional supplementation. There is a growing acceptance in mainstream medicine for vitamin supplements as a complementary intervention with certain kinds of disease and their prevention. Among others, some of the vitamins believed to prevent illness include vitamins C, A, and E.

Most controversial in the vitamin movement is the use of the megadose. When taken in nutritional dosage, vitamins are not harmful, but when taken in huge amounts they may cause serious side effects. The megadose is defined as "a very large dose (usually of vitamins) that surpasses the recommended daily allowance and is used therapeutically to prevent or to treat disease or in nutritional deficiency" (Jonas & Levin, 1999a, p. 581). Some of the medical conditions treated by the megadose include congestive heart failure, osteoarthritis, fatigue, kidney stones, osteoporosis, schizophrenia, depression, and dementia (Gaby, 1999). Megadosing, for the most part, has fallen out of favor. Instead, it is believed that natural products work better in moderate doses over a longer period of time versus higher doses for a quick effect (which is a common practice in conventional medicine). Aside from vitamin C and rare cases of nutrient dependency syndrome, most experts do not advocate megadosing (personal communication, C. P. Stanley, November 25, 1999). Vitamin C is believed to be effective in a megadose because of poor gastric absorption and a very short half-life. To be effective, a dose must have constant tissue availability. Esterfide vitamin C is neutral with good gastric absorption, and it slowly deesterfides by plasma esterases. However, a much lower megadose is recommended today than in the past, but experts agree more research is needed to determine the appropriate dose (Kaegi, 1998; personal communication, C. P. Stanley, November 25, 1999).

Vitamin C manufactures collagen, the primary protein substance in human beings. Proponents believe individuals with high contents of vitamin C in their diet can significantly reduce the risk of death from cardiovascular disease and cancer. More specifically in relation to cardiovascular disease, it is believed to lower LDL oxidation in addition to converting cholesterol to bile acids, inhibiting platelet aggregation and maintaining arterial wall integrity in connection with the biosynthesis of collagen healing (Halbert, 1997; Kaegi, 1998; Murray, 1996). In regard to cancer, epidemiological links have found to lower risk of stomach cancer in connection with diets high in vitamin C rich foods (Sauberlich, 1994). Laboratory experiments have demonstrated inhibited tumor growth and tumor regression (Meadows, Pierson, & Abdallah, 1991; Prasadm, 1980). Other reported benefits of increased vitamin C include enhanced immunology functioning, decreased risk for cataracts, protection from air pollutants, and improved wound healing (Halbert, 1997; Kaegi, 1998; Murray, 1996).

Vitamins A and E have also been investigated for therapeutic effects. Vitamin A plays a role in the immune system, and proponents of megadose therapy believe it affects tumors by slowing growth and decreasing the size of established tumors. The anticancer mechanism is believed to inhibit cell proliferation and promote cell differentiation (Kaegi, 1998). However, concern has been raised that vitamin A may work as a pro-oxidant and increase the risk of lung cancer in males who smoke and ingest alcohol (Omenn et al., 1996). In addition, serious terotogenic effects have occurred with pregnant women who consumed high amounts of vitamin A before the seventh week of gestation; Also, caution is required concerning megadose amounts of vitamin A because it may cause liver damage (DeSmet, 1999; Kaegi, 1998).

Vitamin E is believed to assist in protection against heart disease, cancer, and strokes (Murray, 1996). As with vitamin C, it has been found to help with cardiovascular disease by inhibiting the oxidation of LDL cholesterol, and it is recommended in primary and secondary prevention of coronary disease (Halbert, 1997; Murray, 1996). Proponents of megadose therapy believe it will assist in cardiovascular disease and cancer, but evidence regarding its efficacy in cancer is inconclusive (Kaegi, 1998).

Rigorous, random controlled research is required to better investigate the benefits of vitamin and herbal remedies. Currently, some researchers envision herbal medicine practitioners consulting with interdisciplinary medical teams. However, for a substantial shift into the mainstream biomedicine to occur, more methodologically sound research is needed. Although the investigations have been promising, there remain many unknown variables (e.g., proper dosage) and unproven claims. Without solid proof, the noteworthy and beneficial use of vitamins and herbal medication runs the risk of being dismissed as "snake oil."

Chiropractic

A distinctly American complementary medicine practice is chiropractic care. Chiropractic is the largest complementary health care profession, and chiropractors are the third largest health care provider following medical doctors and dentists. It is estimated that a staggering 70 to 80% of the adult population suffers back pain at some point in their lives. Moreover, one of three patients with low back pain seeks treatment from a chiropractor. Each year, approximately 5% of the total U.S. population uses chiropractor services. In 1990 alone, 160 million office visits were made to chiropractors. Cost estimates vary between $2.4 billion to $4 billion spent on chiropractic care annually (Frymore, 1988; Hurwitz, Coulter, Adams, Genovese, & Shekelle 1998; Kaptchuk & Eisenberg, 1998; Shekelle, Adams, Chassin, Hurwitz, & Brook, 1992).

The word *chiropractic* is derived from the Greek word meaning "hand work," and the practice began in Davenport, Iowa, on September 18, 1895. Although eyewitness accounts vary, it is said that Daniel David Palmer, the father of chiropractic, brought the field to life when he cured a janitor of his deafness by pushing a single cervical vertebra (Kaptchuk & Eisenberg, 1998; Lawrence, 1999). Palmer, who was a self-taught man, blended four distinctive health care traditions in forming chiropractic: bone setting, magnetic healing, orthodox science, and popular health reform (Kaptchuk & Eisenberg, 1998). The first two components, bone setting and magnetic healing, are rooted in folk medicine. In nineteenth-century health care, bone setters were on par with barber surgeons and midwives. Palmer likely had some training in bone setting, which entailed treating patients with "subluxations," defined as painful conditions caused by misplaced, "put out" joints. The duty of the bone setter was to "put in" a joint with a rough movement. The theory of magnetic healing during the nineteenth century defined health as an unimpeded flow of energy whereas illness was believed to be a blocked stream of energy. This philosophy is quite similar to the concept of *qi* in traditional Chinese medicine. Building on this belief, Palmer coined the phrase "innate intelligence" and asserted the nervous system, and in particular the spinal cord, was the pathway to health. As a consequence, a misaligned vertebra results in an impeded energy flow and, thus, illness. Palmer's spin on magnetic healing, woven with the bone setters' subluxation technique, initiated the chiropractic movement. In addition, Palmer described his new discipline as a science by incorporating the notion of "spinal irritation." The term was the catch-all diagnosis of the day, and it enjoyed wide acceptance in the mainstream medical community. Adopting this hypothesis accomplished two things: (a) it created an air of credibility to chiropractic; and (b) it broadened the range of subluxation and spinal irritation to encompass illness that without chiropractic may have been unscrutinized. Although traditional medicine eventually replaced spinal irritation for "neurasthenia" and, later, depression, it remained for Palmer the essential element for a comprehensive understanding of illness (Kaptchuk & Eisenberg, 1998; Lawrence, 1999; Redwood, 1999).

Popular health reform is the fourth element of chiropractic. Chiropractic became the new contender—challenging the limitations of conventional medicine and offering hope for a victory over all manifestations of disease the mainstream medical community had not yet conquered (Kaptchuk & Eisenberg, 1998). Although not rooted in scientific fact, chiropractic offered hope, along with some pain relief, and this enabled the profession to survive.

Kaptchuk and Eisenberg (1998) noted that chiropractic is "the most important example of alternative medicine in the United States and alternative medicine's greatest anomaly" (p. 2215). It has achieved mainstream acceptance from the lay community, with millions of people believing chiropractic care offers them relief that conventional medicine cannot, yet it remains on the fringe of traditional medicine. This rejection can be traced back to chiropractic's original philosophy of the "one cause one cure," monocausal theory of disease. D. D. Palmer and his son B. J. Palmer were purists who believed control of the spine was the pathway to health. As such, chiropractic was the best treatment response to most types of disease. Still others rejected the idea of innate intelligence, arguing the unscientific and speculative theory was detrimental to chiropractic by limiting it to the periphery. Some have argued that this group of individuals is diluting the true chiropractic philosophy. Today, the overwhelming majority of chiropractors see the field in this way. However, the adversarial relationship with the traditional medical community has for the most part remained and kept chiropractic on the fringe. Over the past 20 years, research has begun to advance the cause and demonstrate that chiropractic may be of some benefit to specific groups of low back pain patients (Kaptchuk & Eisenberg, 1998; Redwood, 1999).

The concept of pathology, as addressed by chiropractic care, has evolved through the years. Palmer held steadfast to the belief that manipulation of the spine was the key to health. He treated individuals suffering from subluxation, a misalignment of a single vertebra. Today, however, few chiropractors believe *simple subluxation* is the cause of disease. Rather, the term *vertebral subluxation complex* is considered to be just one of many causal agents. Moreover, the rubric of vertebral subluxation complex refers to an assortment of conditions and mechanical impediments (i.e., blood flow, mobility, muscle tone, posture, and condition of the nerve itself). Subluxation has evolved into multiple interpretations and is thought of as what a chiropractor corrects (Kaptchuk & Eisenberg, 1998).

Since its inception, advocates for chiropractic care have expanded on the virtues of spinal manipulation for a number of ailments, including back pain, lumbar rehabilitation, migraine headaches, carpal tunnel syndrome, otitis media, and asthma (Davis, Hulbert, Kassak, & Meyer, 1998; Hurwitz et al., 1998; Shekelle et al., 1992; Triano, McGregor, & Skogsbergh, 1997). The mechanisms of action for spinal manipulation are not well understood, but a multitude of maneuvers have emerged through the years. According to the Agency for Health Care Policy and Research, thrusting procedures are the most common class of techniques (Kaptchuk & Eisenberg, 1998; Triano et al., 1997). These techniques are designed to increase joint mobility beyond the normal range of motion known as "end feel"—described as an elastic barrier of resistance. Chiropractors manipulate the vertebra beyond end feel, but without harming the structure of the joint. This maneuver results in a popping sound that is believed to result in the release of synovial gases. Other purported benefits include a release of endorphins, lengthening of soft tissue, muscle relaxation, and disruption of fibrous adhesions. Vertebra movement may be executed directly on the spine with the short-lever technique or indirectly through a long-lever technique. The long-lever technique is accomplished by using a distant connection (i.e., use of the femur, shoulder, head, or pelvis) to manipulate the spine. Additional variables to this procedure include the degree of force and distance traveled (better known as amplitude) of the thrust (Kaptchuk & Eisenberg, 1998; Triano et al., 1997; Shekelle et al., 1992).

Chiropractic advocates often refer to high patient satisfaction rates. In a survey conducted by the American Chiropractic Association, the majority of patients were happy with their treatment and felt chiropractic interventions were effective for them (1993). The bulk of clinical evidence supporting chiropractic efficacy deals with acute low back pain. The chiropractic community contends spinal manipulation is an effective intervention for lumbar rehabilitation, in particular by transitioning from a passive to an active treatment modality and in controlling any exacerbation of symptoms or musculoskeletal injuries that may occur during physical therapy (Triano et al., 1997). Several studies have demonstrated manipulation is no worse, and at times better, than conventional medicine. In a review article, a meta-analysis of nine studies found short-term benefits for patients suffering from uncomplicated acute low back pain. However, the benefits for long-term effect, preventing chronicity, and for patients suffering from chronic low back pain were inconclusive (Shekelle et al., 1992). On the other hand, Triano, Skogsbergh, and McGregor (1995) conducted a randomized study of chronic low back pain patients. The researchers compared spinal manipulation to education programs. A total of 209 patients were evaluated, and patients receiving chiropractic care demonstrated greater reductions in pain and activity tolerance.

Moreover, a prospective study found chiropractic care was at least as effective as conventional medicine (Carey et al., 1995). The researchers attempted to determine any outcome and cost differences between 288 randomly selected practitioners made up of primary care physicians, orthopedic surgeons, and chiropractors. Each health care provider enrolled consecutive patients, with a total of 1,633 individuals evaluated. There were no significant outcome differences in functional recovery, return to work, and low back pain recovery. In regard to satisfaction, the chiropractic patients were more satisfied with their treatment than the physicians' patients. However, the family care physicians provided the most cost-effective interventions. This finding is consistent with a previous result evaluating low back pain that reported a preference for chiropractic care over conventional medicine (Cherkin & MacCornack, 1989).

Another study evaluated the cost-effectiveness of chiropractors compared with physiotherapy at one-year follow-up (Skargren, Carlsson, & Öberg, 1998). A total of 323 patients with neck and back pain were randomly assigned to a treatment condition. Again, no differences were found between the two interventions in regard to Oswestry scores, pain intensity, recurrence of pain, general health, and overall costs. Chiropractic was found to be most effective for patients suffering from pain that was less than one week in duration. It is also important to note that 59% of the chiropractic patients and 41% of physiotherapy patients sought additional health care.

When interpreting these data results, it may be helpful to consider Deyo's (1983) finding that the treatment modality for acute low back pain may be irrelevant to outcome, because the overwhelming majority of these cases are brief in duration. For instance, an estimated 50% of acute low back pain patients are no longer disabled two weeks from the onset of symptoms. At one month, 70% of the patients have recuperated, and at three to four months 90% have recovered. Deyo's results are preliminary and more research is necessary; however, it may mean that for an astounding number of acute low back pain patients, any intervention—chiropractic, folk, or traditional medicine—will suffice.

Although millions of Americans seek treatment with chiropractors, the profession is predominantly shunned by the medical community. Chief among the criticisms is that, aside from a smattering of back pain studies, the majority of evidence for chiropractic care is observational data. Moreover, many of the low back pain studies are either inconclusive or methodologically flawed. Defenders of chiropractic care concede rigid, controlled trials are difficult to attain and are quick to point out the assumptions of practice are similar to those of conventional medicine—namely that traditional clinical training together with common sense have guided decisions in diagnosis, treatment, and prognosis (Triano et al., 1995). However, the lack of rigorous empirical evidence is of concern. For example, low back pain studies comparing spinal manipulation to sham controls have yielded poor results. In their review of the literature, Kaptchuk and Eisenberg (1998) found only 3 of the 11 random controlled trials demonstrated a clear and significant improvement over the sham control. Three of the studies may have demonstrated some merit, but this was contingent on outcome consideration; four studies found no significant difference from the control. Moreover, there were major methodological problems with the studies, including poor outcome measures, high drop-out rates, and insufficient sample number. The authors found better results with studies comparing spinal manipulation with traditional medicine. Of the 15 low back pain trials reviewed, nine demonstrated significant benefits, one showed post-hoc improvements for a subgroup of patients, and four showed no difference between chiropractic and the comparison treatments. Two of the studies were difficult to interpret and characterize. Again, methodological problems were noted, such as insufficient control for provider-contact time, and conventional therapies may not have been adequately tested.

Koes, Assendelft, van der Heijden, and Bouter (1996) conducted a systematic review of 36 randomized clinical trials comparing chiropractic to other treatment modalities. Each study was evaluated and scored for (a) quality of method (comprising study population, interventions, measurement of effects, data presentation, and analysis); (b) researcher conclusion; and (c) results based on the main outcome measure. Overall, the studies were judged to be of poor quality, with the highest rated investigation earning a mere 60 out of a possible 100 points. Fifty-three percent of the studies demonstrated positive results for manipulation, with 14% reporting favorable results in one or more subgroups. Of the five highest rated studies, three had positive results and two reported significant results for subgroups only. The findings were inconsistent for the 11 studies with placebo control group. Moreover, follow-up information was lacking, with 16 of the studies tracking treatment effects for a minimum of three months. Although this evaluation demonstrates the possible efficacy for some subgroups of low back pain patients, more methodologically sound research is required. Specifically, future research must include randomized trials. Also, a homogenous patient population with sufficient numbers should receive standardized interventions, and they must be compared to a controlled group. Finally, valid functional outcome measures should be used.

Another concern voiced by traditional medicine against chiropractic care concerns side effects. In particular, reports of cerebral vascular accidents (CVAs), cervical epidural hematoma, cauda equina, and death have been reported in the literature. One of the most common reported accidents involve CVAs. Estimates vary tremendously from 1 in 300,000 to 1 in 1.3

million per cervical treatment session. Researchers have attempted to identify common and uncommon side effects of spinal manipulation (Klougart, Leboeuf-Yde, & Rasmussen, 1996; LeBoeuf-Yde, Hennius, Rudberg, Leufvenmark, & Thunman, 1997; Segal, Lidov, & Camins, 1996). Senstad, Leboeuf-Yde, and Borchgrevink (1997) and colleagues identified frequently reported side effects by 1,058 new patients receiving a total of 4,712 sessions. Local discomfort, headache, tiredness, and radiating discomfort were the most commonly reported side effects. Some of the less frequent side effects included dizziness, nausea, diarrhea, palpitations, and hot skin. Approximately 55% of the patients reported experiencing some kind of side effect. Of those patients, the onset of their reaction was within four hours of treatment and resolved within 24 hours. Haldeman (1997) warned of the need to conduct additional investigations on side effects, such as tiredness, nausea, and palpitations, because these may suggest a systemic effect or psychophysiological response.

Folk Medicine and Cultural Considerations

Folk medicine is a complementary medical practice that, for the most part, is viewed by biomedicine as a type of snake oil—it congers up images of psychic surgery and rituals involving eggs and prayers. However, according to the World Health Organization, 70% of the world population relies on nonallopathic health care and, as such, biomedicine must be better informed of these practices (Krippner, 1999). These patients, along with their view of health, present a unique challenge to the physician. The United States is rich in cultural diversity, and many ethnic groups continue to practice the traditional folk medicine of their homeland. Although there is a distinct philosophy and approach to each practice, there are some commonalities shared by the various folk medicines. First, in addition to the immediate disease, there is an existing causal agent. Second, this underlying cause is generally believed to be a lack of balance or harmony (Hufford, 1997). Contingent on the specific culture, the cause of illness may be biological events, experiential events, or metaphysical events.

Although metaphysical causality is mocked and dismissed by mainstream biomedicine, it is the cornerstone of most folk traditions. As Krippner (1999) noted, anthropologists have pointed out that tribal people have developed complete medical systems within a rigorous and logical framework. The difference between folk medicine and traditional biomedicine is the expression and application of that system. The spiritual philosophy of many ethnomedical traditions is that humans are a part of the environment and a broader world that goes beyond physical pragmatism into another realm that transcends ordinary reality. Maintaining balance within all realms is often a necessity, and a disruption results in illness. The cause of the imbalance can be a result of one's own fault (e.g., sinning; food balance), a result of another's wrong doing (the "evil eye"), or a result of an outside power (imbalance of dark and light forces of energy; soul loss; Baer, 1999; Hufford, 1997; Krippner, 1999).

These deeply entrenched beliefs run counter to the biomedicine tradition rooted in the enlightenment that divided the human body into three separate components—the *soma* (body), *psyche* (mind), and *pneuma* (spirit). This philosophy of elementalism assumed one could isolate and treat one division without affecting the others. As time progressed and the age of reason came to the forefront, spiritual concerns were dismissed as irrational and unnecessary (Krippner, 1999). By bringing these spiritual issues to the forefront, folk medicine fulfills a need that mainstream medicine does not. For many individuals, spiritual matters are of extreme importance and a part of their day-to-day lives. Therefore, the spiritual philosophy of folk medicines offers a type of solace difficult to attain with conventional medicine. That is, folk medicine is more comprehensive and strives to achieve a wholeness of mind, body, and emotion–spirit versus a simple cure or symptom removal. For example, the organized hierarchical goals of most folk medicine systems are often not medically related; instead, they may be along the lines of a healing of the soul (Hufford, 1997). Although there is a growing movement in mainstream medicine to discuss spirituality with patients, it has yet to gain wide-spread approval. Addressing spiritual needs is considered vital both to the practitioner and the client of folk medicine. By the same token, patients' strong faith in the efficacy of their treatments, and the hope these treatments provide, may be explained in good part by the placebo effect. Frank and Frank (1991) noted that 50% of the people taking a placebo testify to significant relief. It may be that the ethnomedicine practitioners are validating the client and his or her concerns. On the other hand, many folk medicine practices have been found to be effective. For instance, as discussed earlier, the merits of acupuncture and herbal medicine have been demonstrated. Other examples include Native American practices. In early America, Native people were more hygienic in cleaning wounds than the European invaders; the Native people successfully removed tumors, lanced boils, and treated fractures and dislocations. More recently, *curanderos* (healers) were found to treat diarrhea, simple gynecological disorders, somatic manifestations, and psychological disorders effectively (Krippner, 1999).

The scope and various types of folk medicine are too great to adequately address in this chapter. However, we will briefly discuss two of the more pervasive traditions: *curanderismo* and Chinese medicine. *Curanderismo* is a Mexican American form of health care that is a blend of ancient Indian (Aztec and Mayan), Mexican, Roman Catholic, and Mexican Arabic practices. Health is emphasized through emotional, interpersonal, and behavioral balance. Individuals seek help from *curanderos*. The focus of healing is spiritual, and religion is the center of their practice. *Curanderos* are said to possess *el don*, or "the gift," and they treat a wide variety of ailments that may be physical, natural, psychological, or spiritual in nature. Often, the illness is taken on faith because it may not be measured with medical instruments. Among the maladies treated are *empacho*, which is a clogged intestine or stomach caused by the wrong kind of food or eating too much, and *bilis*, which is psychological in nature and is a fear- or anger-induced condition. Spiritually based disorders include *susto* or loss of soul, which may be a result of shock and is the result of an accident or breaking a spiritual rule. *El mal ojo*, or the evil eye, may result in various disorders, and is caused by another staring at the victim with envy or desire. Although the practitioner's name may vary from region to region, *curanderos* include a variety of types. *Herbalistas* sell herbs, oils, perfumes, candles, spiritual artifacts, and so forth; *parteras* are midwives; *sobadores* are chiropractic-like individuals who massage, rub, and tend to misaligned bones and muscle strains; and *señoras* are similar to fortune tellers in that they read cards. All *curanderos* emphasize a balance in behavior and relationships (Baer, 1999; Krippner, 1999).

Similar to *curanderismo*, traditional Chinese medicine accentuates balance and harmony within humankind and nature. The human body is seen as being a part of nature and as a whole. When there is disharmony in body functioning or between the body and nature, disease occurs. Some traditional Chinese medicine interventions include acupuncture, Chinese herbal medicine, mind–body exercise, diet therapy, and *Tui Na*—Chinese acupressure (Krippner, 1999; Lao, 1999). Although the disruption of *Qi*, the driving force of *yin* and *yang*, has been discussed earlier in this chapter, another component of traditional Chinese medicine is *wu xing*.

The *wu xing*, or five element theory, is a philosophy describing the relationships within the human body (the physiological and pathological relationship among the body's organs) and between the human body and the external environment. The interactive relationship among the elements is dynamic, because each affects and promotes the other. The five elements are wood, fire, earth, metal, and water. In Chinese medicine, the elements represent specific body organs. For instance, the liver is symbolized by wood, the heart by fire, the spleen by earth, the lung by metal, and the kidneys by water. Illness occurs when there is an interruption in the balance or when one of the elements is destroyed (Lao, 1999).

Traditional Chinese practitioners diagnose the illness by evaluating the imbalance in the *yin* and *yang*. This is done through a variety of methods, including taking the pulse and making observations using all five of their senses. Overall, the practitioner wants to achieve harmony within the patient's body and among the family, community, and environment. The goal is a relief of pain and tension, as well as prevention of additional illness (Krippner, 1999).

As with all complementary approaches, research is needed to determine the efficacy and essential components of the given folk medicine practice. The evidence uncovered may not only elucidate our biological understanding but also enlighten the interpersonal relationship between physician and patient with regard to topics to address.

COMPLEMENTARY HEALTH CARE RESEARCH NEEDS

Complementary health care includes therapies that range from procedures with more empirical support than many traditional Western medical practices to those that have no basis in science. However, it is clear that millions of people in the United States are using complementary health care procedures, and the need to validate these often-used therapies is certain. Also, many alternative medicine procedures offer benefits with less side effects than certain medication or invasive procedures. The crucial question about these procedures relates to their safety and clinical effectiveness (Kemper et al., 1999), questions that can only be answered by sound research practices.

Associated with the need to conduct sound empirical research is the ability to recognize good research evidence when presented. Key issues for understanding and conducting clinical research have been outlined by several authors (e.g., Gatchel & Maddrey, 1998; Jonas, 1997) and include internal and external validity, validity of statistical conclusions, and functional definitions of outcome. Briefly, internal validity allows for a relationship to be inferred between two variables, either a causal relationship or a noncausal, correlational relationship. For instance, internal validity allows us to infer that a drug is more efficacious for the flu than a placebo (i.e., the medication reduced flu symptoms), or that there is a relationship between anxiety and automobile accidents (anxiety is related to accidents, but which causes the other is unclear). A causal relationship between two variables can only be determined with certain empirical designs (e.g., randomized control trials). External validity allows researchers to generalize from the experiment to the real world. Statistical validity must also be taken into account by considering concepts such as statistical power, reliability of measurements, and assumptions of statistical tests. Finally, the outcomes must be functionally defined. That is, the outcomes must be quantifiable and measurable (Gatchel & Maddrey, 1998). (For a thorough explanation, please see Gatchel & Maddrey, 1998.)

The research design that has been considered the gold standard is the randomized control trial (RCT)—more specifically, the randomized, double-blind, placebo-controlled trial. Unfortunately, not all research can be conducted using an RCT, and outcome assessment has been proposed as both an alternative and complementary method of investigation. Jonas (1997) succinctly summarized the difference between RCTs and outcomes assessment: "RCTs attempt to identify links that allow a specific intervention to be attributed to a specific outcome. Outcomes-monitoring methods attempt to assess the association between complex systems of real-life clinical situations" (p. 37). The author stressed the importance of using both methods, rather than allowing one to replace the other.

Jonas and Levin (1999b) have discussed important considerations with regard to the standards of evidence that apply to complementary health care. Nonspecific effects are often at work when treatment approaches are investigated. People appear to respond to a particular treatment, but in fact their bodies may be healing themselves with time. K. B. Thomas demonstrated this with the 80 percent rule, which states that 80% of the people who seek medical care will get better regardless of the treatment offered. Controlling for nonspecific factors requires randomized control trials; however, these are not practical for all conditions and treatments. Outcome research can be used as one acceptable alternative to examine low-risk therapies (Jonas & Levin, 1999b).

Several other authors have identified special considerations for research into complementary health care techniques. Many theories under the heading of alternative medicine have concepts that do not directly correlate to Western ideas. Therefore, diagnosis may differ between traditional alternative theories and Western theories. For example, with acupuncture, two patients with herniated discs and accompanying low back pain may be conceptualized differently by a traditional Chinese acupuncturist. One may be seen to have an excess of *yin*, whereas the other has an excess of *yang*. Another difficulty with studying complementary therapies is that some require the integration of several techniques, making it difficult to identify the "active ingredient."

Kemper, Cassileth, and Ferris (1999) make three recommendations involving prioritizing research in complementary health care: "Priority should be given to conditions and diseases that satisfy the criteria: . . . those that impose a heavy burden of suffering for which mainstream therapies are insufficient and for which CAM therapies offer a reasonable likelihood of being helpful and are already use(d) by families" (p. 908). These authors provide several examples of disorders that meet these criteria, including anxiety, asthma, attention deficit disorder, and cancer. Also, the need to examine the effectiveness of therapies that require professionals are also stressed as high priorities by these authors, because of the substantial cost related to treatment by professionals. (See Exhibit 10.2 for guidelines for physicians working with patients using complementary medicine.)

EXHIBIT 10.2
Guidelines for Physicians Working With Patients Using Complementary Medicine

- Ask patients about their CAM use in an open and non-judgmental manner. Unless questioned, most patients will not report their use of alternative therapies. An appropriate time to ask may be when inquiring about disease prevention and health practices (e.g., "Many people use chiropractic care, herbs, acupuncture, and so forth, have you ever used any of these methods or thought about using them?)
- Strive for open communication between the patient, the CAM provider and yourself.
- Work with the patient to evaluate the efficacy of the CAM modality they are using (for example, have the patient identify the primary symptom and initiate a symptom diary to monitor results; assist the patient with questions to ask the CAM provider such as their success rate in treating patient's problem and the risks involved; help the patient evaluate the cost benefits).
- Help the patient identify their expectations and choices.
- Discuss issues of safety and efficacy (review the current literature on the CAM practice).
- Help the patient assess the qualifications of the CAM provider (i.e., what are the licensing requirements; what is the extent of the service provided?).
- Follow-up and review treatment response with patient.
- Document all interactions related to CAM.

Note. From "Advising Patients Who Seek Alternative Medical Therapies," by D. M. Eisenberg et al., 1997, *Annals of Internal Medicine, 127,* p. 61. Copyright 1997 by *Annals of Internal Medicine.* Reprinted with permission.

CONCLUSION

An important distinction between theory and technique must be made when integrating alternative medicine practices with traditional Western medical practices. For instance, understanding the importance of *qi* facilitates understanding of acupuncture, but acceptance of a traditional theory is not a necessity. In fact, understanding the physiological mechanisms of a complementary health care technique may be more relevant when deciding whether to incorporate the technique with standard medical treatment. So, in our example, although it is relevant to understand that acupuncture in the Neiguan point alters the flow of *qi* according to traditional Chinese theory, it is probably more important to understand that acupuncture at the Neiguan point probably stimulates A-delta fibers of the median nerve. In addition, strange or unusual theoretical explanations that a person may receive about meditation (e.g., increase in the flow of the Kundilini, which may or may not seem out of the ordinary) should not eliminate interest in a technique if it appears to produce empirically demonstrable benefits. The first questions relate to whether there are good data to demonstrate that a procedure works and that it is safe. The second questions relate to the physiological mechanisms about how the procedure works. Both pieces of information are relevant, but the lack of sound physiological explanations does not rule out the demonstrated efficacy or effectiveness of a complementary health care technique. A traditional theory about how a technique works may not be sound, but a technique may demonstrate usefulness.

The prevalence of complementary health care use in the United States necessitates the questioning of each patient regarding his or her personal usage.

Jonas and Levin (1999b) outlined several potential risks and benefits to integrating complementary health care with more mainstream practices. The quality of care by complementary health care practitioners presents a serious set of problems. Chiropractors require licensure in all 50 states, but acupuncturists and massage therapists require licensure in only approximately 25 states. Without licensing boards, professional standards for competency cannot truly be established or monitored. In addition, as mentioned earlier in this chapter, the quality of dietary supplements and other complementary health care instruments may vary. This could produce not only fraudulent practices from companies that are only interested in making a profit but may lead to adverse reactions by individuals using these products. Not only are there short-term consequences to monitor, but the long-term effects, as well as interaction effects with other herbal remedies, must be considered. Finally, the evidence for many often practiced complementary health care practices is insufficient.

Despite the risks, with careful conceptualization and research, complementary health care offers several benefits. Most complementary health care practices require the individual to be an active observer and participant in his or her treatment, creating a sense of empowerment for the individual. In addition, complementary health care procedures offer the real possibility of reduced adverse effects that may be more acceptable to patients. Finally, complementary health care offers a way to reduce costs that are associated with conventional medicine, because alternative medicine practices rely much less on costly procedures, technologies, and drugs (Jonas & Levin, 1999b).

REFERENCES

Ahmed, H. E., Craig, W. F., White, P. F., & Huber, P. (1998). Percutaneous electrical nerve stimulation (PENS): A complementary therapy for the management of pain secondary to bony metastis. *Clinical Journal of Pain, 14*(4), 230–233.

American Chiropractic Association. (1993). Nationwide survey yields insights into the public's views of chiropractic care. *American Chiropractic Association Journal of Chiropractic, 30,* 28–31.

American Medical Association. (1998). *Journal of the American Medical Association*, *280*, 1549–1640.

Arena, J. G., & Blanchard, E. B. (1996). Biofeedback and relaxation therapy for chronic pain disorders. In R. J. Gatchel & D. C. Turk (Eds.), *Psychological approaches to pain management: A practitioner's handbook* (pp. 179–230). New York: Guilford Press.

Astin, J. A. (1998). Why patients use alternative medicine: Results of a national study. *Journal of the American Medical Association*, *279*(19), 1548–1553.

Baer, H. A. (1999). Complementary folk or ethnic approaches. In C. C. Clark (Ed.), *Encyclopedia of complementary health practice* (pp. 49–52). New York: Springer.

Becerra, R. M., & Iglehart, A. P. (1995). Folk medicine use: Diverse populations in metropolitan area. *Social Work in Health Care*, *21*, 37–58.

Belar, C. D., & Deardorff, W. W. (1995). *Clinical health psychology in health settings: A practitioner's guidebook*. Washington, DC: American Psychological Association.

Benson, H., Beary, J. F., & Carol, M. P. (1974). The relaxation response. *Psychiatry*, *37*, 37–46.

Berman, B. M., Singh, B. K., Lao, L., Singh, B. B., Ferentz, K. S., & Hartnoll, S. M. (1995). Physicians' attitudes toward complementary or alternative medicine: A regional survey. *Journal of the American Board of Family Practice*, *8*, 361–366.

Burg, M. A., Kosch, S., & Neims, A. (1998). Personal use of alternative medicine therapies by health science faculty. *Journal of the American Medical Association*, *280*, 1563.

Carey, T. S. Garrett J., Jackman, A., McLaughlin, C., Fryer, J., Smucker D. R. (1995). The outcomes and costs of care for acute low back pain among patients seen by primary care practitioners, chiropractors, and orthopedic surgeons. The North Carolina Back Pain Project. *New England Journal of Medicine*, *333*, 913–917.

Chapman, E. H. (1999). Homeopathy. In W. B. Jonas & J. S. Levin (Eds.), *Essentials of complementary and alternative medicine* (pp. 472–489). Philadelphia: Lippincott.

Cherkin, D. C., & MacCornack, F. A. (1989). Patient evaluations of low back pain care from family physicians and chiropractors. *Western Journal of Medicine*, *150*, 351–355.

Crasilneck, H. B. & Hall, J. A. (1985). *Clinical hypnosis: Principles and applications*. Boston: Allyn & Bacon.

Cupp, M. J. (1999). Herbal remedies: Adverse effects and drug interactions. *American Family Physician*, *59*(5), 1239–1245.

Davis, P. T., Hulbert, J. R., Kassak, K. M., Meyer, J. J. (1998). Comparative efficacy of conservative medical and chiropractic treatments for carpal tunnel syndrome: A randomized clinical trail. *Journal of Manipulative and Physiological Therapeutics*, *21*, 317–326.

DeSmet, P. A. G. M. (1999). The safety of herbal products. In W. B. Jonas & J. S. Levin (Eds.), *Essentials of complementary and alternative medicine* (pp. 108–147). Philadelphia: Lippincott Williams & Wilkins.

Deyo, R. (1983). Conservative therapy for low back pain: Distinguishing useful from useless therapy. *Journal of the American Medical Association, 250*, 1057–1062.

Eisenberg, D. M. (1997). Advising patients who seek alternative medical therapies. *Annals of Internal Medicine, 127*(1), 61–69.

Eisenberg, D. M., Davis, R. B., Ettner, S. L., Appel, S., Wilkey, S., Van Rompay, M., et al. (1998). Trends in alternative medicine use in the United States, 1990–1997: Results of a follow-up national survey. *Journal of the American Medical Association, 280*(18), 1569–1575.

Eisenberg, D. M., Kessler, R. C., Foster, C., Norlock, F. E., Calkins, D. R., & Delbanco, T. L. (1993). Unconventional medicine in the United States. Prevalence, costs, and patterns of use. *New England Journal of Medicine, 328*(4), 246–252.

Eldin, S., & Dunford, A. (1999). *Herbal medicine in primary care*. Oxford: Butterworth Heinemann.

Field, T. (1999). Massage therapy. In W. B. Jonas & J. S. Levin (Eds.), *Essentials of complementary and alternative medicine* (pp. 383–391). Philadelphia: Lippincott Williams & Wilkins.

Field, T., Morrow, C., Valdeon, C., Larson, S. Kuhn, C., & Schanberg, S. (1992). Massage reduces anxiety in child and adolescent psychiatric patients. *Journal of the American Academy of Child and Adolescent Psychiatry, 31*, 854–858.

Frank, J. D., & Frank, J. B. (1991). *Persuasion and healing* (3rd ed.). Baltimore: John Hopkins University Press.

Frymore, J. W. (1988). Back pain and sciatica. *New England Journal of Medicine, 318*, 291–300.

Gaby, A. R. (1999). Orthomolecular medicine and megavitamin therapy. In W. B. Jonas & J. S. Levin (Eds.), *Essentials of complementary and alternative medicine* (pp. 459–471). Philadelphia: Lippincott Williams & Wilkins.

Gatchel, R. J., & Maddrey, M. A. (1998). Clinical outcome research in complementary and alternative medicine: An overview of experimental design and analysis. *Alternative Therapies in Health and Medicine, 4*, 36–42.

Gatchel, R. J., & Turk, D. C. (1996). *Psychological approaches to pain management: A practitioner's handbook*. New York: Guilford Press.

Ghoname, E. A., Craig, W. F., & White, P. F. (1999). Use of percutaneous electrical nerve stimulation (PENS) for treating ECT-induced headaches. *Headache, 39*(7), 502–505.

Ghoname, E. A., Craig, W. F., White, P. F. Ahmed, H. E., Hamza, M. A., Henderson, B. N., et al. (1999). Percutaneous electrical nerve stimulation for low back pain: A randomized crossover study. *Journal of the American Medical Association, 281*, 818–823.

Gordon, J. S. (1996). Alternative medicine and the family physician. *American Family Physician, 54*, 2205–2212.

Graffin, N. F., Ray, W. J., & Lundy, R. (1995). EEG concomitants of hypnosis and hypnotic susceptibility. *Journal of Abnormal Psychology, 104*(1), 123–131.

Green, J. A., & Shellenberger, R. (1999). Biofeedback therapy. In W. B. Jonas & J. S. Levin (Eds.), *Essentials of complementary and alternative medicine* (pp. 410–425). Philadephia: Lippincott Williams & Wilkins.

Halbert, S. C. (1997). Diet and nutrition in primary care. *Complementary and Alternative Therapies in Primary Care, 24*, 825–843.

Halderman, S. (1997). Point of view. *Spine, 22*, 440–441.

Hoffman, P., & Thoren, P. (1986). Long-lasting cardiovascular depression induced by acupuncture-like stimulation of the sciatic nerve in unanesthetized rats: Effects of arousal and type of hypertension. *Acta Physiologica Scandinavica, 127*, 119–126.

Hufford, D. J. (1997). Folk medicine and health culture in contemporary society. *Complementary and alternative therapies in primary care, 24*, 723–741.

Hurwitz, E. L., Coulter, I. D., Adams, A. H., Genovese, B. J., & Shekelle, P. G. (1998). Use of chiropractic services from 1985 through 1991 in the United States and Canada. *American Journal of Public Health, 88*, 771–776.

Ironson, G., Field, T., Scafidi, F., Hashimoto, M., Kumar, M., Kumar, A., et al. (1996). Massage therapy is associated with enhancement of the immune systems cytotoxic capacity. *International Journal of Neuroscience, 84*, 205–218.

Jacobson, E. (1939). *Progressive relaxation*. Chicago: University of Chicago Press.

Jonas, W. B. (1997). Clinical trials for chronic disease: Randomized, controlled clinical trials are essential. *Journal of NIH Research, 9*, 33–39.

Jonas, W. B., & Levin, J. S. (Eds.). (1999a). *Essentials of complementary and alternative medicine*. Philadelphia: Lippincott Williams & Wilkins.

Jonas, W. B., & Levin, J. S. (1999b). Introduction: Models of medicine and healing. In W. B. Jonas & J. S. Levin (Eds.), *Essentials of complementary and alternative medicine* (pp. 1–15). Philadelphia: Lippincott Williams & Wilkins.

Josey, E. S., & Tackett, R. L. (1999). St. John's wort: A new alternative for depression? (1999). *International Journal of Clinical Pharmacology and Therapeutics, 37*, 111–119.

Journal of the American Medical Association. (1998, Nov. 11). Vol. *280*(18).

Kaegi, E. (1998). Unconventional therapies for cancer 5. Vitamins A, C, and E. *Canadian Medical Association Journal, 158*, 1483–1488.

Kanowski, S., Herrmann, W. M., Stephan, K, Wierich, W., & Horr, R. (1997). Proof of efficacy of the Ginkgo biloba special extract Egb761 in outpatients suffering from mild to moderate primary degenerative dementia of the Alzheimer type or multi-infarct dementia. *Phytomedicine, 4*, 3–13.

Kaptchuk, T. J., & Eisenberg, D. M. (1998). Chiropractic origins, controversies, and contributions. *Archives of Internal Medicine, 158*, 2215–2224.

Kemper, K. J., Cassileth, B., & Ferris, T. (1999). Holistic pediatrics: A research agenda. *Pediatrics, 103*(4), 902–909.

Kim, H. L., Streltzer, J., & Goebert, D. (1999). St. John's wort for depression: A meta-analysis of well defined clinical trials. *Journal of Nervous and Mental Disease, 187*, 532–538.

Klejnen, J., & Knipschild, P. (1992). Ginkgo biloba. *Lancet, 340*, 1136–1139.

Klougart, N., Leboeuf-Yde, C., & Rasmussen, L. R. (1996). Safety in chiropractic practice. Part I: The occurrence of cerebrovascular accidents after manipulation to the neck in Denmark from 1978–1988. *Journal of Manipulation and Physiological Therapeutics, 19*, 371–377.

Koes, B. W., Assendelft, W. J., van der Heijden, G. J., & Bouter, L. M. (1996). Spinal manipulation for low back pain. An updated systematic review of randomized clinical trials. *Spine, 21*, 2860–2871.

Krauss, H. H., Godfrey, C., Kirk, J., & Eisenberg, D. M. (1998). Alternative health care: Its use by individuals with physical disabilities. *Archives of Physical Medicine and Rehabilitation, 79*(11), 1440–1447.

Krippner, S. (1999). Introduction: Common aspects of traditional healing systems across cultures. In W. B. Jonas & J. S. Levin (Eds.), *Essentials of complementary and alternative medicine* (pp. 181–199). Philadelphia: Lippincott Williams & Wilkins.

Lao, L. (1999). Traditional Chinese medicine. In W. B. Jonas & J. S. Levin (Eds.), *Essentials of complementary and alternative medicine* (pp. 216–232). Philadelphia: Lippincott Williams & Wilkins.

Lawrence, D. J. (1999). Chiropractic medicine. In W. B. Jonas & J. S. Levin (Eds.), *Essentials of complementary and alternative medicine* (pp. 275–288). Philadelphia: Lippincott Williams & Wilkins.

LeBars, P. L., Katz, M. M., Berman, N., Turan, M., Freedman, A. M., & Schatzberg, A. F. (1997). A placebo-controlled, double-blind, randomized trial of an extract of Ginko biloba for dementia. *Journal of the American Medical Association, 278*, 1327–1332.

LeBoeuf-Yde, C., Hennius, B., Rudberg, E., Leufvenmark, P., & Thunman, M. (1997). Side effects of chiropractic treatment: A prospective study. *Journal of Manipulation and Physiological Therapeutics, 20*, 511–515.

Lee, D. C., Lee, M. O., & Clifford, D. H. (1976). Modification of cardiovascular function in dogs by acupuncture: A review. *American Journal of Chinese Medicine, 4*, 333–346.

Linde, K., & Jonas, W. B. (1999). Evaluating complementary and alternative medicine: The balance of rigor and relevance. In W. B. Jonas & J. S. Levin (Eds.), *Essentials of complementary and alternative medicine* (pp. 57–71). Philadelphia: Lippincott Williams & Wilkins.

Linde, K., Ramirez, G., Mulrow, C. D., Pauls, A., Weindenhammer, W., & Melchart, D. (1996). St. John's Wort for depression—An overview and meta-analysis of randomized and clinical trials. *British Journal of Medicine, 313*, 253–258.

Meadows, G. G., Pierson, H. F., & Abdallah, R. M. (1991). Ascorbate in the treatment of experimental transplanted melanoma. *American Journal of Clinical Nutrition, 54*(Suppl.), 1284S–1291S.

Mitchell, J. H. (1990). Neural control of the circulation during exercise. *Medicine and Science in Sports and Exercise, 22*(2), 141–154.

Mohs, R. C., Rosen, W. G., & Davis, K. L. (1983). The Alzheimer's disease assessment scale: An instrument for assessing treatment efficacy. *Psychopharmacology Bulletin, 19*(3), 448–450.

Murray, M. T. (1996). *Encyclopedia of nutritional supplements, the essential guide for improving your health naturally.* Rocklin, CA: Prima Publishing.

National Institutes of Health (NIH) Consensus Conference. (1998). Acupuncture. *Journal of the American Medical Association, 280*(17), 1518–1524.

Omenn, G. S., Goodman, G. E., Thornquist, M. D., Balmes, J., Cullen, M. R., Glass, A., et al. (1996). Effects of a combination of beta carotene and vitamin A on lung cancer and cardiovascular disease. *New England Journal of Medicine, 334,* 1150–1155.

Prasadm K. N. (1980). Modulation of the effects of tumor therapeutic agents by vitamin C. *Life Sciences, 27,* 275–280.

Redwood, D. (1999). Chiropractic: Definition, history, and theory. In C. C. Clark (Ed.), *Encyclopedia of complementary health practice* (pp. 337–339). New York: Springer.

Reilly, D. T., Taylor, M. A., McSharry, C., & Atkinson, T. (1986). Is homeopathy a placebo response? Controlled trial of homeopathic potency, with pollen in hayfever as model. *Lancet, 2,* 881–885.

Sauberlich, H. E.(1994). Pharmacology of vitamin C. *Annual Review of Nutrition, 14,* 371–391.

Schultz, J. H., & Luthe, W. (1969). *Autogenic therapy.* New York: Grune & Stratton.

Schwartz, G. E. (1983). Development and validation of the geriatric evaluation by relatives rating instrument (GERRI). *Psychological Reports, 53*(2), 479–488.

Segal, D. H., Lidov, M. W., & Camins, M. B. (1996). Cervical epidural hematoma after chiropractic manipulation in a healthy young woman: Case report. *Neurosurgery, 39,* 1043–1045.

Senstad, O., Leboeuf-Yde, C., & Borchgrevink, C. (1997). Frequency and characteristics of side effects of spinal manipulative therapy. *Spine, 22,* 435–441.

Shekelle, P. G., Adams, A. H., Chassin, M. R., Hurwitz, E. L., & Brook, R. H. (1992). Spinal manipulation for low-back pain. *Annals of Internal Medicine, 117,* 590–598.

Shyu, B. C., Andersson, S. A., & Thoren, P. (1984). Circulatory depression following low frequency stimulation of the sciatic nerve in anesthetized rats. *Acta Physiologica Scandinavica, 121,* 97–102.

Skargren, E. I., Carlsson, P. G., & Öberg, B. E. (1998). One year follow-up comparison of the cost and effectiveness of chiropractic and physiotherapy as primary management for back pain. Subgroup analysis, recurrence, and additional healthcare utilization. *Spine, 23,* 1875–1884.

Syrjala, K. L., & Abrams, J. R. (1996). Hypnosis and imagery in the treatment of pain. In R. J. Gatchel & D. C. Turk (Eds.), *Psychological approaches to pain management: A practitioner's handbook* (pp. 231–258). New York: Guilford Press.

Triano, J. J., McGregor, M., & Skogsbergh, D. R. (1997). Use of chiropractic manipulation in lumbar rehabilitation. *Journal of Rehabilitation Research and Development, 34,* 394–404.

Triano, J. J., Skogsbergh, D. R., & McGregor, M. (1995) Validity and basis of manipulation. In A. H. White & J. A. Schofferman (Eds.), *Spine care. Volume one. Diagnosis and conservative treatment* (pp. 437–450). St. Louis, MO: Mosby.

Vickers, A., & Zollman, C. (1999). ABC of complementary medicine acupuncture. *British Medical Journal, 319,* 973–976.

Volz, H. P. (1997). Controlled clinical trials of hypericum extracts in depressed patients: An overview. *Pharmacopsychiatry, 30,* 72–76.

Vorbach, E. U., Arnoldt, K. H., & Hubner, W. D. (1997). Efficacy and tolerability of St. John's Wort extract LI 160 versus imipramine in patients with severe depressive episodes according to ICD–10. *Pharmacopsychiatry, 30*(Suppl.), 81–85.

Wetzel, M. S., Eisenberg, D. M., & Kaptchuk, T. J. (1998). Courses involving complementary and alternative medicine at US medical schools. *Journal of the American Medical Association, 280*(9), 784–7.

Wickramasekera, I. (1999). Hypnotherapy. In W. B. Jonas & J. S. Levin (Eds.), *Essentials of complementary and alternative medicine* (pp. 426–443). Philadelphia: Lippincott Williams & Wilkins.

Wong, A. H., Smith, M., & Boon, H. S. (1998). Herbal remedies in psychiatric practice. *Archives of General Psychiatry, 55,* 1033–1044.

Yao, T., Andersson, S., & Thoren, P. (1982). Long-lasting cardiovascular depression induced by acupuncture-like stimulation of the sciatic nerve in unanesthetized spontaneously hypertensive rats. *Brain Research, 240,* 77–85.

11

TELEHEALTH AND HEALTH CARE PSYCHOLOGY: CURRENT DEVELOPMENTS IN PRACTICE AND RESEARCH

ROBERT L. GLUECKAUF, DAVID W. NICKELSON,
JEFFREY D. WHITTON, AND JEFFREY S. LOOMIS

One of the most exciting developments in health care is the burgeoning use of telecommunication technologies to provide health information, assessment, and treatment to individuals with health concerns, particularly those people with chronic disabling conditions. This new field of health care communications, known as telehealth, has expanded greatly over the past decade in the United States, Canada, Western Europe, and Australia. The promise of this technology is intuitive and straightforward: Telehealth has the potential to expand access, increase the quality of health care, and reduce the spiraling costs of specialty services (Glueckauf et al., 1999; Glueckauf, Whitton, & Nickelson, 2002).

This chapter has been supported partially by grants to the first author from the National Institute on Disability and Rehabilitation Research and the Department of Veterans Affairs. The opinions expressed in this chapter are solely those of the authors and do not reflect the policies of Florida State University, the University of Florida, or the American Psychological Association.

The recent growth of telehealth has been quite remarkable, particularly in the public sector (e.g., the armed forces and correctional systems). According to a recent survey conducted by the Association of Telehealth Service Providers (Grigsby & Brown, 2000), there are now more than 170 telehealth programs in the United States alone. Furthermore, 40% or more of these programs have been in operation for fewer than five years (Nickelson, 1998). Clinical health psychology is one of the specialty areas that stands to benefit most from the expansion of telehealth services. The crux of what is delivered in telecommunication-based health promotion interventions derives from well-established health psychology protocols. The majority of these interventions are cognitive-behavioral treatments that are grounded in years of empirical research (Glueckauf, 2002).

Although telehealth has begun to replace traditional forms of providing health information and services, there remains a substantial gap between the widespread demand for this health delivery mode and the scientific evidence supporting its efficacy and cost-effectiveness. Only a limited number of randomized controlled studies across different telecommunication modalities (e.g., Internet and automated telephone) exist to guide us in determining how and under what conditions telehealth leads to positive health outcomes. Research on consumer perceptions about the desirability of telehealth interventions and cost-effectiveness has increased both in scope and quality over the past few years, but remains underdeveloped both in terms of theory and methodological rigor. Furthermore, the need for quality assurance standards, ethical guidelines, and professional training curricula on the use of telehealth services has only recently captured the attention of health organizations and government entities (e.g., Jerome et al., 2000).

In the first portion of this chapter, we define the field of telehealth and outline the factors that have contributed to the growth of telehealth services. In the second portion, we provide a framework for categorizing the technologies used to deliver telehealth services and follow with a description of commonly used equipment and transmission networks. In the third portion, we review pertinent outcome research on telecommunication-mediated interventions in health care psychology and rehabilitation. In the fourth portion, we propose future directions for telehealth practice and research.

DEFINITION OF TELEHEALTH

Our politically charged health care and telecommunication systems continue to evolve with almost blinding speed. Any definition must be flexible enough to both accommodate technological advances and acknowledge current clinical and political realities. This is why the authors have

defined telehealth as the use of telecommunications and information technologies to provide access to health information and services across a geographical distance, including (but not limited to) consultation, assessment, intervention, and follow-up programs to ensure maintenance of treatment effects
(Glueckauf, Whitton, & Nickelson, 2002). Behavioral telehealth, a subset
of telehealth activities, is simply the use of the same technology to provide
behavioral health services (Nickelson, 1998).

This definition acknowledges that telehealth applications must meet
multiple clinical and education needs. It recognizes the broad range of health
care providers and educators who will use these applications. This definition
also makes clear the most significant way in which telehealth differs from
face-to-face encounters: It overcomes geographic limitations.

The authors also favor this definition because it does not define telehealth as a new form of practice. Telehealth is simply a tool that has the
potential for facilitating the practice of already established professional skills
across distance. It also emphasizes that telehealth is a vehicle for enhancing
maintenance of treatment effects, as well as establishing positive health
routines in home and community settings (Glueckauf, Whitton, et al., 2002).

RATIONALE FOR THE GROWTH OF TELEHEALTH

Three pervasive problems in our nation's health care system have
contributed significantly to the growth of telehealth: (a) uneven geographic
distribution of health care resources, including health care facilities and
health manpower; (b) inadequate access to health care for certain segments
of the population, such as individuals living in rural areas and those who are
physically confined; and (c) the spiraling cost of health services, particularly
specialty care.

First, most health services in the United States are centralized in
metropolitan statistical areas, leaving a sizable segment of the population
without adequate access to health services. Although a variety of outreach
programs have been implemented, they have not succeeded in closing this
resource gap. One of the most underserved constituencies are those living
in rural areas. More than 60 million people, approximately 25% of the U.S.
population, are living in rural areas (Office of Technology Assessment,
1990). For these individuals, travel to health services, particularly specialty
services, may require several hours and attendant financial loss.

Second, several populations have inadequate access to health care,
primarily as a result of geographic isolation or physical confinement. For
example, Native Americans often reside in geographic areas isolated from
adequate health services. Military personnel have access to adequate health
services while on base, but this situation can change dramatically when

they are abroad. Physical confinement also represents a significant barrier to obtaining adequate health care. In 1994, more than 1,500,000 men and women were incarcerated in prisons across the United States. This population is particularly at risk for health problems, especially infectious diseases and psychiatric disorders (Magaletta, Fagan, & Ax, 1998).

Groups who are homebound, such as geriatric populations with severe neurological and mobility disorders, older persons living in high crime areas, and those with psychiatric disorders such as agoraphobia, may encounter difficulties in obtaining adequate health care. Their medical problems make it difficult to travel even short distances. In all these cases, telehealth may offer a means for closing the gap between limited provider resources and the health care needs of the population.

Third, one of the most pressing problems in health care is the escalating cost of specialty services. This is particularly the case for persons in rural areas who may require treatment by specialists located in large metropolitan cities. Clients in rural areas frequently experience high transportation costs and concomitant loss of wages to obtain specialty health care unavailable in the rural areas. Telecommunication-mediated specialty services delivered in the home or at a local medical facility have the potential of significantly reducing the economic hardship of rural citizens. However, the key question is whether such services can be provided without significant reduction in quality of care. A recent report by Australian investigators Trott and Blignault (1998) offered preliminary support for the economic benefits of rural behavioral telehealth. They compared the costs of providing face-to-face versus telehealth-based psychiatric and psychological services to a small mining town 900 kilometers from the regional hospital in Townsville, Queensland. The findings of the investigation showed substantial cost savings primarily attributable to reduced travel expenditures by psychiatrist practitioners and by rural patients.

TELEHEALTH TECHNOLOGY AND TELECOMMUNICATION SYSTEMS

The communication technologies used to provide telehealth services fall into two broad categories: asynchronous and synchronous. *Asynchronous communication* refers to information transactions that occur among two or more persons at different points in time. Electronic mail (e-mail) is the most common form of asynchronous communication and has been used in the delivery of a variety of health care services (e.g., Gustafson et al., 1993, 1999).

Synchronous communication refers to information transactions that occur simultaneously among two or more persons. Synchronous telecommunications include computer synchronous chat systems, Telecommunications Devices for the Deaf (TDD), and telephone- and videoconferencing. Chat systems permit users to communicate instantly through typed messages. Users can "chat" in two different ways: (a) through channels or "chat rooms" in which several individuals communicate simultaneously or (b) through a direct connection in which two persons hold a private conversation. During chat room discussions, each person's contribution is displayed on screen in the order of its receipt and is read by all participants in the "room." TDDs are instruments that facilitate text-based conversations through standard telephone lines. They typically consist of a touch-typing keyboard, a single-line, moving-LED screen, text buffer, memory, and a signal light. The entire unit is approximately the size of a laptop computer (see Scherer, 2002).

The most common form of synchronous communication is the telephone. The major advantage of the telephone is its widespread availability and ease of access. The telephone has become the standard mode of communication in psychological practice for conducting preliminary screening interviews, follow-up sessions, and crisis intervention (Haas, Benedict, & Kobos, 1996). Over the past few years, innovative, low-cost automated telephone technologies have become an increasingly viable option in treating persons with chronic health conditions, such as hypertension (e.g., Friedman et al., 1996) and in providing support to their caregivers (e.g., Mahone, Tarlow, & Sandaire, 1998).

Although telephone is presently the most accessible form of communication technology, we anticipate that video teleconferencing will become *the modality of choice* for delivering telehealth services in the 21st century. Public demand for interactive videoconferencing services is expected to grow exponentially over the next decade. This surge of popularity is fueled by the declining costs of videoconferencing equipment and software, increased penetration of telecommunication services, the broadening appeal of the World Wide Web, as well as the anticipation of gigabit-speed Internet 2 (Mittman & Cain, 1999).

Three types of videoconferencing equipment currently are used to deliver telehealth services: (a) room or rollabout, (b) desktop, and (c) plug-and-play videophone systems. Although room or rollabout systems (e.g., Tandberg, Polycom, and Sony) are available in several different configurations, the basic set-up consists of a roll-about cart, a single large-screen monitor, codec (i.e., specialized computer programs and hardware that compress the video signal by reducing the number of bytes consumed by large files), microphone or speakerphone, set-top camera, and frequently an accompanying document camera. Many rollabouts use a second large-screen monitor to exhibit documents. This enables users on each end to view simultaneously both document displays and one another. Room or rollabout systems are ideal for facilitating multipoint groups (i.e., groups in various sites), as well as person-to-person videoconferencing. The cost of room or roll-about units varies from $14,000 to $50,000.

Desktop systems (e.g., Polycom, VCon, and Sony) offer a low-cost, high quality alternative to room systems in a convenient smaller package. Desktop solutions can accommodate peripheral devices (e.g., document camera and large screen monitors) and are portable. The typical desktop videoconference unit consists of a standard desktop computer (e.g., 200 MHz Pentium with PCI bus, 128 MB RAM, 100 MB free drive space, PCI SVGA Card, and a current MS Windows operating system), and a PC-based videoconferencing kit (e.g., Polycom, VCon, and Sony). These systems also are typically outfitted with a digital camera, speakerphone, and digital network interface hardware. Transmission of simultaneous audio and video signals is accomplished through the use of integrated service delivery networks (ISDN), Internet protocol (IP), and in certain cases, Switch 56 service. The current cost of a desktop videoconferencing system is $500 and up, varying with CPU speed, memory, monitor size, and the selection of peripheral devices.

Plug-and-play videophone systems (e.g., TeleVyou and Motion Media) are currently the cheapest solution among the videoconferencing systems. These devices generally use plain old telephone service (POTS), but newer models can accommodate ISDN or IP. Note, however, that the POTS-based videophones require a smaller signal size to send video and must rely on a codec to compress the video signal across the telephone network. As a result, images frequently can be jerky or grainy, and sound may be poor in quality. Furthermore, image-to-sound synchronization may be periodically inadequate, rendering verbal communications difficult to follow. The current costs of plug-and-play systems range between $500 and $2,500.

Next, three basic telecommunication networks currently are used for videoconferencing-based telehealth applications: (a) POTS, (b) Internet protocol (IP), and (c) ISDN point-to-point as well as multipoint connections. First, the POTS network is a circuit-switched service offered to private homes and businesses from the local telephone company. A switched circuit is defined as a two-way connection that exists only for the time required to make a call. When the user completes a long distance call, the circuit is broken and the individual is no longer charged for the service. This is contrasted with a permanent or "nailed-up" circuit, which is connected and usable at all times (e.g., a dedicated T1 line).

The major downfall of POTS is the local loop or the wire from the local telephone company's switch or pole to the user's facility. Transmissions within the local loop are analog in nature (i.e., electronic transmissions accomplished by adding signals of varying frequency to carrier waves of a given frequency of alternating electromagnetic current). Telephone has conventionally used analog technology. This is the reason why we use a modem (i.e., a device that converts a computer's digital signal to an analog transmission and vice versa) to connect with the Internet. This analog local loop is slowly being replaced with digital technology. As this happens, the bottleneck of slow connectivity from the home to the Internet will diminish significantly (Glueckauf et al., 1999).

To make a video call on the POTS network, the sender dials the telephone number of the recipient or end user the same way he or she would dial a regular phone call. Note that the end user must have a compatible videoconferencing device to establish a connection. Such interactions are termed "point-to-point" videoconferencing calls. Multipoint video transmissions are also possible on POTS and involve simultaneous interactions among three or more parties.

Second, the IP network is a packet, switched service where digital information (i.e., ones and zeros from the computer) is bundled into sets or groups called packets. These packets contain data in combination with transfer-formatting information to facilitate transmission from place to place on the Internet. Individuals typically gain access to the Internet at their work site (through their employer's LAN or WAN) or at home through a local Internet service provider (ISP).

ISPs connect the consumer to the Internet using a router-based network. Routers are very fast computers whose sole job is to route or transfer IP packets to their destination. These digital packets traverse the network directed by routers and bridges to the addresses contained in the packets. When the packets arrive at their destination, they are amalgamated and are then seen by the end-user as files, images, or text on the screen.

IP-based networks can experience transmission delays and sometimes lose information (i.e., data packets), particularly at times when the network is congested. This results in a degradation of image and sound quality, as well as image-to-sound synchronization. However, the future of Internet videoconferencing appears especially promising. With advancements in switched network technology, improved protocols, and low-cost, high-bandwidth next-generation Internet, IP videoconferencing is likely to become the preferred mode of communication in telehealth transactions (Glueckauf, Whitton, et al., 2002).

Third, ISDN is one of several switched digital services on the market that can support high quality, point-to-point or multipoint videoconferencing. The user pays an initial installation charge ($100 to $200), a monthly service fee ($75 to $100), a per-minute usage charge from the local provider for the service, and if applicable, long distance charges. ISDN can be obtained in several different bandwidths ranging from 128 kilobits per second (kbps) to 1.56 megabits per second (mbps). Although ISDN is currently expensive, this telecommunication mode provides an attractive high-speed (e.g., 128 kbps) alternative to slower analog transmission (56 kbps), particularly in rural areas where broadband Internet service may not be available.

LEGISLATIVE AND REGULATORY DEVELOPMENTS

Federal and state governments have recently taken a number of steps to encourage the use of telehealth. At the federal level, the congressional ad hoc Steering Committee on Telehealth—a bicameral, bipartisan, informal caucus of more than 60 legislators—for several years has sponsored technology demonstrations and a series of information sessions on current policy issues in telehealth. Often, this group brings in national experts to comment on legislative proposals. Many successful telehealth laws were first reviewed by this group (Nickelson, 1997).

The trend in federal telehealth legislation over the past five years has been to offer multiple new proposals annually. For example, 22 pieces of telehealth-related legislation were proposed in each of the 103rd, 104th, and 105th congresses (Office for the Advancement of Telehealth, 2001). In the 106th, only four legislative proposals were introduced, focusing primarily on the issue of reimbursement of telehealth services provided to rural areas (e.g., H. R. 1344, 1999; S. 770, 1999; and S. 980, 1999). A bill to expand reimbursement beyond rural areas (S. 2505) recently was introduced by Senator James Jeffords (S. 2505, 2000).

At least 35 different federal agencies or entities have been involved in the development of telehealth policy and programs, including the Department of Defense, National Aeronautics and Space Administration, Department of Veterans Affairs, and the Department of Health and Human Services (U.S. General Accounting Office, 1997). In fact, many of these agencies coordinate activities and share data through the Joint Working Group on Telehealth (JWGT), an interagency work group that coordinates federal telehealth funding and data gathering efforts.

The JWGT is continuing its efforts to implement many of the recommendations suggested by its 1997 report to Congress (U.S. Department of Commerce, 1997), such as the electronic collection and dissemination of provider credentialing information across all federal health care systems. Professional psychology plays an important role on the JWGT, particularly on the Interdisciplinary Telehealth Standards Working Group (Office for the Advancement of Telehealth, 2001).

When the JWGT began its deliberations on telehealth practice standards, spokespersons in the field of psychology successfully argued that it was premature to promulgate broad national guidelines or standards that might impede the development of innovative telehealth applications. As a result, health professions have been encouraged to use common definitions and language but are not required to follow a strict set of telehealth standards.

One particular federal agency effort merits special consideration. The Balanced Budget Act of 1997 (Pub. L. No. 105-33, 1997) mandated the Health Care Financing Administration (HCFA) to begin paying for—via the Medicare program—telehealth services provided to eligible beneficiaries in rural areas. Although psychologists were specifically included in the original legislation, they were made ineligible in the final regulation after organized psychiatry raised objections. Fortunately, this restriction was removed following the passage of the Medicare, Medicaid, and State Children's Health Insurance Program (SCHIP) Benefits Improvement and Protection Act of 2000 (H.R. 5661). In addition to expanding the range of professionals who were eligible for reimbursement, this groundbreaking legislation nullified earlier HCFA regulations that required (a) telehealth providers to split fees with the referral source (i.e., 75% of the Medicare payment to the telehealth specialist and 25% to the rural referral source) and (b) the referring rural provider to be physically present during the teleconsultation interview.

Although HCFA has not established a formal telehealth reimbursement scheme for the state-based Medicaid program, 20 U.S. states currently provide reimbursement for telehealth services. As expected, reimbursable Medicaid services must satisfy federal requirements of efficiency, economy, and quality of care. However, HCFA has encouraged individual states to be flexible in adapting federal law to create innovative payment methodologies for telehealth providers. For example, state-based Medicaid programs have the capacity to reimburse additional costs (e.g., technical support, line charges) associated with the delivery of a covered telehealth service (see http://www.hcfa.gov/medicaid/telemed.htm for more detailed information).

State politicians and agencies also have been highly involved in crafting legislation that affect citizens' access to telehealth services. A substantial number of states have pending or have passed telehealth legislation relating to reimbursement, program funding, and licensure (Office for the Advancement of Telehealth, 2001). The majority of these telehealth proposals have focused on state licensure requirements and the delivery of professional services across state lines. Some states have removed licensure restrictions (e.g., H.B. 2953, 1999, Washington State Assembly), whereas others have reaffirmed or increased them (e.g., H.B. 4073, 1998, West Virginia House). Note that there has been a significant trend toward closing state boundaries to telemedicine practitioners, particularly out-of-state licensed physicians. This trend eventually may influence psychologists' telehealth practices.

The Association of State and Provincial Psychology Boards (ASPPB) addressed this issue by altering the ASPPB Model Licensure Act to include a section on "telepractice" (Association of State and Provincial Psychology Boards, 1998). This change in the model act would allow psychologists to enter a state and practice psychology via telecommunications without obtaining a license in that state, as long as the licensure requirements of that state are equivalent to the standards where the psychologist currently holds a license. The proposed revision would permit psychologists to tele-practice up to 30 days without needing to obtain a license. A number of states are currently considering the option of incorporating this change into their psychology licensing law, but to date no state has done so.

Courts have had little to say about telehealth public policy and the legal responsibilities of health care providers, telecommunication networks, and equipment manufacturers. Similar to the trend toward using the courts to challenge unfair or harmful managed care practices (Segal, 1999), it is likely that the judicial system will in time play a role in shaping telehealth policy. The development of case law in this area bears watching, particularly case law that extends existing principles of liability to new potential rights and responsibilities.

Perhaps nowhere is there more interest and activity than in the health care and telecommunications marketplaces. Video teleconferencing (VTC) activity continues to double each year, with mental health consultations the most popular use of VTC in 1998 (American Telemedicine Service Providers, 1999). VTC units designed specifically for use in health care settings continue to be developed by such large manufacturers as Sony and Intel, signaling that the major equipment manufacturers believe the health care VTC market will continue to grow.

Even more significant, advances in Internet technology and bandwidth continue to draw more and more consumers to the World Wide Web (WWW), a great number of whom are seeking out health information—especially psychological health information. For example, a recent Harris poll reported that more than 110 million U.S. adults go online an average of three times a month for health care information (Harris Interactive, 2002). This trend is pulling many existing health care organizations—including managed care organizations—toward business models that incorporate this growing consumer comfort with the Internet. Although beyond the scope of this chapter, it is likely that VTC-based telehealth activities will migrate from closed-link telephone line technology toward open-link, packet-based Internet technology. The implications of such capabilities will likely be as significant to psychology as was the introduction of managed care technology only a little more than a decade ago (Newman, 1998).

The convergence of legislative, legal, marketplace, and consumer interest in telehealth bodes particularly well for health psychologists, who by training are well prepared to function in this next evolution of health care delivery. One helpful way to think about the activities that health psychologists will need to incorporate for successful practice is to use an integrated advocacy model—one that integrates legislative, legal and regulatory, marketplace and consumer education activities (Nickelson, 1997). Using the term *advocacy* broadly, the thrust of this model is that any activity—lobbying, regulatory rule writing, providing consultation to business, or marketing to consumers—must be accompanied by complementary activities in the other areas.

For example, leaders in psychology have a long history of pursuing legislation that serves the broad public interest (e.g., mental health parity) and that secures psychology's place in health care systems (e.g., Medicare reimbursement). In the telehealth arena this would consist of efforts to ensure that psychology is included in relevant federal and state telehealth legislation.

At the state level, psychologists can educate lawmakers about how advanced telecommunications can be used to reach populations, such as outpatient rehabilitation patients, faster, more efficiently, and for less overall cost. One caveat to consider, however, is that state governments are often strapped for resources. A possible intermediate step may be for a consortium of practitioners and researchers to propose state demonstration programs across a wide range of mental health populations who traditionally have been served by the state, such as the Medicaid population, individuals with developmental disabilities, and those requiring long-term state-sponsored rehabilitation services. A successful example of this strategy is Glueckauf and colleagues' Alzheimer's Caregiver Support Online, a Florida Department of Elder Affairs and Robert Wood Johnson Foundation-sponsored Web- and telephone-based education and support program for caregivers of individuals with progressive dementia (Glueckauf, Ketterson, Loomis, & Dages, in press; Glueckauf & Loomis, 2003).

Psychology can also work proactively to forge regulatory structures that encourage appropriate telehealth service delivery. For example, many state Medicaid program reimbursement decisions are made at the agency level. Providing evidence to the relevant regulators about the potential cost savings of rural telehealth services, such as reduced patient transportation costs to urban specialty clinics, may result in new telehealth opportunities (cf., Cheung et al., 1998). Psychologists also can work with state licensing boards to create regulatory structures that offer practitioners flexible practice options (e.g., e-health counseling), and at the same time ensure consumers suitable recourse through disciplinary or other regulatory actions. By appropriately lending expertise and support to legal actions that protect patients from potentially harmful applications of telehealth, professional psychology can ensure that the common law of telehealth develops rationally and reflects the larger public policy objectives of the profession.

In the marketplace, psychology can take steps to develop and operate behavioral telehealth systems by applying for federal and state grants, creating joint ventures or strategic partnerships with health systems, academic medical centers, and technology vendors and telecommunications providers. Psychologists can also sensitize telehealth equipment vendors to the unique needs (e.g., ease of use for rehabilitation patients, confidentiality, etc.) of mental health service patients and providers. Telehealth seems well suited to support the assessment and decision-making roles envisioned for doctoral-level psychologists in certain emerging areas of the health care marketplace. Finally, psychology can work to educate consumers about how to determine which services are appropriate for telehealth and which are not, giving consumers the power to make autonomous decisions about the services they seek and from whom they seek them. One such effort by the American Psychological Association can be found at http://www.dotcomsense.com.

BARRIERS TO THE DEVELOPMENT OF TELEHEALTH SYSTEMS

Barriers to the development of telehealth systems have been discussed in detail in a number of publications (U.S. Department of Commerce, 1997; Nickelson, 1997; Council on Competitiveness, 1994, 1996; Nickelson, 2000). Briefly, they continue to be:

- *Reimbursement*: Who will pay, how much, to whom, for what services?
- *Licensure and regulation*: How do we protect patients from substandard practice?
- *Standards, guidelines, and credentials*: Do we need them, and if so, who will develop them?
- *Evaluation*: Are telehealth services "clinically appropriate" and "cost-effective?" Who decides?
- *Privacy and confidentiality*: What information should be protected, and when might it be acceptable for the protection to be waived?

Beyond these discrete challenges, one other more diffuse but no less significant problem is the similarity between the current status of telehealth and the health care marketplace of only a few years ago. The same market forces that brought us managed care—forces that drive competition around cost, rather than quality—also support the development of telehealth. To flourish, large, for-profit managed multistate seamless "continuums of care" will likely require electronic patient records, patient accessible Internet self-help disease management models, and access to specialty care via video teleconference. Although the promise of telehealth is significant, it could potentially also be used to reduce access to care (e.g., authorizing patients only to use a self-help Web site instead of referring them to actual providers) or may further skew distribution of health services and information toward only those who can afford access via a large telecommunication provider or Internet service provider.

TELEHEALTH INTERVENTION STUDIES

Turning to telehealth outcome research, a major strength of health care psychology is its solid foundation in the scientific method, experimental design, and applied statistics. It is now the norm for health care psychologists, particularly those in health science and medical centers, to participate in program evaluation research. These efforts are typically collaborative in nature and focus on a wide variety of health problems ranging from obesity to invasive surgical interventions for uncontrolled seizures (Glueckauf, 1990, 2000). As a consequence, health care psychologists are well equipped to take advantage of emerging research opportunities in telehealth. Indeed, over the past decade or so, a small cadre of research psychologists (along with researchers from allied disciplines) has made important empirical and scholarly contributions to the field. We highlight their contributions in the telehealth research review that follows.

In keeping with the focus of the current volume, we have restricted our review of the telehealth literature to representative, controlled intervention studies involving persons at risk for or who currently have disabling health conditions. These studies broadly fall into four categories: Internet, telephone, and videoconferencing investigations, as well as comparative studies across telephone, videoconferencing, and face-to-face modalities.

Internet Studies

David Gustafson and colleagues at the University of Wisconsin have conducted several investigations (e.g., Gustafson et al., 1993, 1999) of the effects of Internet-based interventions for adults with chronic illnesses. Their program of research has focused on the development and evaluation of the Comprehensive Health Enhancement Support System (CHESS), a home-based computer system that provides a variety of interactive services to individuals with life-threatening conditions, such as women with breast cancer and persons with HIV/AIDS. CHESS users are able to communicate with others via typed messages in a discussion or chat group, type in questions for experts to answer, read articles about others with similar health concerns, monitor their health status, and gain information about coping techniques.

In their most recent investigation, Gustafson et al. (1999) randomly assigned 204 HIV-positive individuals to either CHESS plus routine medical care ($n = 107$) or routine medical care only ($n = 97$). CHESS participants consisted of three separate cohorts from two Wisconsin communities. The first cohort was administered CHESS for six months; the second and third cohorts received CHESS for three months only. HIV-positive participants were predominantly male (90%) and White (84%). Ninety percent of the sample completed all phases of the study.

Outcome measures included self-report inventories of quality of life (i.e., a modified version of the Medical Outcomes Survey consisting of eight subscales [Stewart, Hays, & Ware, 1989]) and medical service utilization. Participants completed these measures at pretreatment, and at two months, five months, and for the first cohort only nine months after CHESS implementation.

At the two-month postimplementation phase, Gustafson et al. (1999) found that CHESS participants (all three cohorts) rated their perceptions of quality-of-life (QOL) significantly higher on four of eight QOL measures (e.g., higher cognitive functioning, lower negative emotions, more active lifestyle, and greater social support) than the 97 controls who did not receive CHESS services. At the five-month postimplementation phase, CHESS users reported significantly higher QOL on three of eight measures (e.g., increased participation in their own health care and more active life) than that of control participants.

In addition, Gustafson et al. (1999) assessed differences in maintenance of gains in QOL between the two cohorts that received CHESS for three months and the one cohort that had CHESS for six months. They found that duration of treatment conferred a substantial advantage in maintenance of gains. Participants who received CHESS for six months showed maintenance of gains on three of eight QOL measures (i.e., active participation in their own health care, less negative emotion, and more social support) at follow-up. In contrast, the three-month cohorts showed lasting improvement only on one of the QOL measures (i.e., cognitive functioning) at follow-up.

Gustafson et al. (1999) also compared efficiencies in the use of medical services between the two conditions. During the active treatment phase, experimental participants (all three cohorts) reported fewer and shorter hospitalizations than those of routine care controls. The authors attributed this positive effect to CHESS users' increased knowledge and vigilance in recognizing and treating opportunistic infections. Note, however, that after the removal of CHESS, no differences in hospitalization rates and length of stays were found between the experimental and control groups.

The investigators also examined the impact of CHESS on the use of ambulatory care services. Although the total number of ambulatory care visits was similar for both experimental and control groups during the active treatment phase, CHESS participants reported significantly less time in medical visits and higher rates of phone consultations than control participants. The authors attributed CHESS users' shorter visits to better preparation with questions, clearer expectations for treatment, and increased empowerment to raise questions. No group differences in duration of medical visits were evidenced following the removal of CHESS. However, rates of phone consultation with providers continued to differentiate between experimental and control participants at the follow-up phase.

Thus, the overall pattern of findings suggested that CHESS led to substantial health benefits for HIV-positive individuals, including higher perceptions of quality of life, fewer hospitalizations, and less time in medical visits. However, maintenance of gains on the QOL measures was found mainly for participants who received CHESS services for six months. The authors argued that these positive effects were attributable to the increased duration of treatment.

In a related investigation, Flatley-Brennan (1998) assessed the effects of an Intranet-based, decision-making skills program (i.e., ComputerLink) on the social, psychological, and physical functioning of persons with HIV. Fifty-seven community-dwelling, HIV-positive individuals were randomly assigned to either the ComputerLink program ($n = 26$) or standard medical care ($n = 31$). Ninety-three percent of the participants were male and 61% were Caucasian. Their average age and mean years of education was 33 and 13.5, respectively. Thirty-five percent of the sample were employed at the time of the study, and mean years of education was 13.5 years. The Computer-Link equipment consisted of a Wyse 30 terminal with a 1200-baud modem that was linked to a public access computer network. ComputerLink services consisted of an encyclopedia of information about AIDS, self-care, medications, and local services, e-mail, and a public message board. In addition, participants received instruction in the use of a decision support system that helped to clarify their values and preferences in selecting self-care strategies. The control condition received routine medical care at an outpatient immunology clinic as well as printed information and a monthly telephone call.

The primary objectives of the study were to assess the differential effects of the ComputerLink program versus routine medical care on participants' (a) self-confidence in decision-making skills, (b) functional status, and (c) extent of social participation. In addition, the investigator examined the relationship between changes in health status and network use, as well as the extent of use of the ComputerLink system.

The dependent measures consisted of (a) a modified version of the Saunders and Courtney (1985) scale of decision-making success; (b) a count of unique alternative solutions for participant-identified problems; (c) a seven-item Activities of Daily Living subscale of the Multidimensional Functional Assessment device (Duke University Center for the Study of Aging and Human Development, 1978), and a 26-item self-report questionnaire that measured the participants' perceptions of the adequacy of social support (Ensel & Woelfel, 1986). Both ComputerLink and control participants received two administrations of the dependent measures: the first at pretreatment and the second six months later.

Only the level of social support significantly differentiated between the ComputerLink and routine care control condition from pre- to the six-month posttesting. No substantial posttreatment differences between ComputerLink and control participants were found among the measures of decision-making confidence and skill, as well as activities of daily living. Flatley-Brennan attributed the null findings across three of the four dependent measures to both the difficulty level of HIV-related information and decision-making materials as well as the use of weak measurement tools. The investigator also examined the extent of use of the major components of the ComputerLink network. Of the five different user options, participants used the communication function (i.e., message board and e-mail) most often, with e-mail exceeding the rate of message board submissions (6,086 hits for e-mail versus 4,886 hits for the message board). Similar to Gustafson et al. (1999), electronic mail and message boards, both of which involve social contact with peers, were used significantly more than the other user options.

Next, Gray and colleagues (2000) conducted a randomized clinical trial of the effects of an innovative Internet-based telehealth program, Baby CareLink, on the quality of care of high-risk infants at Beth Israel Deaconess Medical Center. Within 10 days of birth, families of very low birth weight (VLBW) babies were randomly assigned to either Baby CareLink (n = 26) or routine neonatal intensive care (n = 30). The Baby CareLink program was carried out in two phases: hospitalization and postdischarge. During hospitalization Baby CareLink provided virtual baby visits (i.e., "see your infant" in the neonatal intensive care unit (NICU), daily clinical reports, a confidential message center between parents and hospital staff, and distance learning for family members. Following discharge from the NICU, the Baby CareLink program offered virtual house calls from hospital and community-based providers, remote monitoring of the infant's health, a family room option that provided answers to common questions, information about services available to family members, links to Web-based resources, and an on-line library for browsing available print and video resources. Control group families received standard treatment at the neonatal intensive care unit, including specialized medical and nursing services, didactic information about the infant's medical condition and care, and emotional support from hospital staff.

The primary dependent measures of the study included family ratings of quality of care, the infant's length of hospital stay, frequency of family visitations, time spent interacting with infants in person, time spent interacting with staff, and disposition of discharge (e.g., home, transfer to a community hospital, or death). Standardized quality-of-care questionnaires (Picker

Institute NICU Family Satisfaction Survey; Picker Institute, 2000) were administered to all families after discharge from the hospital.

Gray et al. found that the average rating of quality of care was significantly higher for the Baby CareLink families than that for standard treatment controls. CareLink families also endorsed significantly fewer problems with hospital care, the neonatal care physical environment, and visitation policies than did control group participants. In contrast, no substantial differences were found between the two conditions on frequency of family visits, telephone calls to the neonatal care unit, and holding of the infant. Duration of hospital stay was also similar across Baby CareLink and standard treatment (M = 68.5 days, SD = 28.3 versus M = 70.6 days, SD = 35.6, respectively). Most noteworthy, all infants in the CareLink program were discharged directly to home, whereas 6 of 30 control group infants were transferred to their referring level II hospital facilities before they were finally discharged to their homes. This led to reduced costs in the Baby CareLink group.

Gray et al. concluded that the Baby CareLink program significantly improved family satisfaction, with VLBW patient care and reduced costs associated with hospital-to-hospital transfers. The investigators ascribed the differential effects of the Internet-based program on family satisfaction with quality of care to heightened perceptions of skill, knowledge, confidence, and comfort in assuming the primary caregiver role. They also suggested that lower rates of transfer to level II facilities in the CareLink condition might have resulted from increased parental confidence and comfort in managing their infant's care. Transfer to level II hospitals before discharge was standard practice at Beth Israel Deaconess unless families actively declined this option.

Next, in a conceptually driven investigation, McKay, Glasgow, Feil, Boles, and Barrera (2002) reported the initial outcomes of their randomized controlled trial of the impact of Internet-based education and support for individuals with diabetes. One hundred sixty adults with type 2 diabetes (ages ranging from 40 to 75) who had no previous Internet experience were randomly assigned to one of four conditions: (a) Internet-based information (IO) only, (b) IO and personalized self-management coaching (I + PC), (c) IO and peer support (I + PS), and (d) a combination of all three conditions (I + PC + PS). The IO condition consisted of Web-based readings on diabetes-related medical information, nutrition, and lifestyle management; the I + PC condition included information provided to the IO group, with the addition of an Internet-based professional who acted as a coach, helping participants work on their specific dietary goals; the I + PS included IO-group information, with the addition of peer interaction via Internet discussion groups, chat, and message boards; the I + PC + PS condition was an amalgamation of all three treatments (i.e., IO + PC + PS).

All participants received a computer that remained in their home over the 10-month duration of the study. The dependent measures consisted of reported eating behavior (Block Fat Screener; Block, Clifford, Naughton, Henderson, & McAdams, 1989; Kristal Food and Fiber Behavior Questionnaire; Kristal, Shattuck, & Henry, 1990), mental health status [Symptom Frequency–12 (SF–12); Stewart, Hays, & Ware, 1989; Center for Epidemiological Studies-Depression scale (CES–D), Radloff, 1977], and physiological changes measured by blood level of HbA_{1c} and total cholesterol. All measures were administered at baseline and at three months after installation of the computer equipment.

McKay et al. (2002) found significant and equivalent reductions in reported fat intake and ineffective eating habits across all four treatment groups. In contrast, no significant improvements in HBA_{1c} and cholesterol levels were evidenced from pretreatment to the three-month postimplementation phase. The investigators had predicted that improvements in dietary habits would enhance physiological functioning of patients with diabetes over time, particularly HbA_{1c} and cholesterol levels. Such positive changes in eating habits, however, may require more than three months to have a measurable effect on physiological indicators such as HbA_{1c}. McKay et al. also expected improvements in mental health indicators, such as depressive affect and psychological well-being. Note that only a trend for an interaction between condition and time (p = .10) was obtained. The personalized coaching and the combined condition showed substantial increases in psychological well-being from pretreatment to the three-month assessment phase, whereas the peer support and information-only conditions showed little or no change over time.

Turning to Web site utilization patterns, user activity varied considerably both between groups and within participants across time. Overall usage of the Web site, however, was modest. The investigators reported that the two support conditions (i.e., PS and PS + PC + IO) generated significantly more log-ons than the IO and the PC + IO conditions. This finding was consistent with those of Gustafson et al. (1999) and Flatley-Brennan (1998), who showed substantially increased use of services that provide social interaction. Thus, consumers with disabilities may tend to make greater use of Web-based health care resources that involve substantial peer interaction than stand-alone information or professional instruction.

In summary, McKay et al.'s initial findings suggested that Internet-based information and support interventions exert a positive impact on health-promoting behaviors of patients with Type 2 diabetes. Improvements in health behaviors, however, were circumscribed to eating behavior, specifically reported reduction of fat intake and poor dietary practices. It is notable that the gains in reported dietary intake were found for participants who had no previous Internet experience, suggesting that this intervention could be helpful to a wide segment of the population and not simply those who are already comfortable with computers. Although the current study permitted comparisons of different types of Internet-based diabetes-related services, it also would have been beneficial to compare all four groups against a routine medical care group. Such a design would have tested whether the Web-based interventions yielded gains beyond those typically obtained from standard care.

Overall, Internet-based technologies appear to be a promising vehicle for providing health care education and support to individuals coping with effects of chronic medical problems (e.g., HIV/AIDS, IDDM) and life-threatening medical conditions at birth (e.g., very low birth weight). Preliminary support for the efficacy of Internet-based interventions was found across three different populations using a combination of group chat, electronic mail, message board, and stand-alone information modules. The studies showed self-reported improvements in health-related quality-of-life and a reduction in the need for health care services. In addition, preliminary evidence from Gustafson and colleagues (1999) and Flatley-Brennan (1998) illustrates the potential value of offering both public and private modes of communication in Internet-based interventions as a means of enhancing communication among peers (e.g., patients), families, community, and health care professionals. These investigators also reported intriguing data suggesting that participants used the communication aspects (e.g., e-mail, message board, and group chat) of the intervention programs most often, particularly e-mail. Finally, caution should be exercised in interpreting the findings of these early Internet studies. Both Gustafson et al. (1999) and McKay et al.'s (2002) investigations are seminal efforts and require replication to ensure that the obtained effects are reliable.

Telephone Studies

Telephone-based telehealth research can be classified into two major categories: (a) first-generation evaluations of telephone counseling and assessment procedures using standard POTS equipment and (b) second-generation studies of automated telephone systems that offer a variety of services, including access to health education modules, consultation with health care experts, and telephone support groups for peers with similar medical conditions or their caregivers.

Evans and colleagues have conducted the majority of first-generation telephone counseling studies (e.g., Evans, Fox, Pritzl, & Halar, 1984; Evans & Jaureguy, 1982; Evans, Smith, Werkhoven, Fox, & Pritzl, 1986). In one of the first controlled telephone studies, Evans and Jaureguy (1982) assigned veterans with visual disabilities to one of two groups: telephone group counseling ($n = 12$) or standard office-based treatment ($n = 12$). They found significantly lower levels of depression and loneliness and higher participation in social activities for counseling participants than for no-treatment controls who showed no change over time. The veterans' positive response to telephone-mediated counseling was consistent with findings from similar studies that relied on uncontrolled, single group designs (Evans et al., 1984, 1986; Stein, Rothman, & Nakanishi, 1993).

Turning to second-generation studies, Follick, Gorkin, Smith, and Capone (1988) assessed the impact of transtelephonic electrocardiography (ECG) on the quality of life of adults with a recent myocardial infarction (MI). Participants were randomly assigned to a transtelephonic monitoring system (TMS) plus standard medical care or to standard care only. TMS participants were encouraged to make regularly scheduled calls to a hospital hub site to transmit ECG readings. In the case of symptomatic chest pain or other heart-related symptoms (e.g., numbness or pain in the left arm), patients were instructed to contact the on-call nurse who subsequently downloaded and interpreted their EEG recordings. If necessary, the on-call nurse sent out a rescue team, instructed the participant to self-administer Lidocaine, or both.

The primary dependent variables of the study included psychological distress and functional status [Symptom Checklist–90 (SCL–90); Derogatis, Lipman, & Covi, 1973; Sickness Impact Profile; Bergner, Bobbitt, Carter, & Gilson, 1981] as well as self-confidence in coping with symptoms (a Likert-type rating scale of an undisclosed number of items, designed for this study and based on a similar scale used by Taylor, Bandura, Ewart, Miller, & DeBusk, 1985). These measures were administered at baseline and one, three, and nine months following randomization to condition.

Although both groups showed initial improvement with treatment, TMS participants were significantly less preoccupied with their condition and showed significantly fewer depressive symptoms than controls at the nine-month postimplementation phase. Furthermore, subsequent nonparametric statistical analysis revealed a substantial discrepancy between the two groups in the proportion of participants falling within the clinically depressed range on the SCL–90. Although rates were similar in the two groups at baseline, clinical levels of depression were twice as likely to occur in the control group as in the TMS condition at the nine-month follow-up. No significant posttreatment group differences in reported functional status were found based on the Sickness Impact Profile. However, TMS users returned to work at a significantly higher rate (92%) than controls (76%).

In a second innovative cardiology intervention, Robert Friedman and colleagues (1996) randomly assigned 267 individuals with hypertension to a telephone-linked computer (TLC) system or to standard treatment over a period of six months. TLC interacted with home-based participants over the telephone via computer-controlled speech. The participants, in turn, communicated using a touch-tone keypad on their telephones. The primary functions of the TLC system were to inquire about the health status of users and to promote adherence to the treatment regimen. During TLC conversations, patients reported self-measured blood pressures, data on adherence to antihypertensive medications, and—if pertinent—medication side effects. This information was stored in a database and subsequently was transmitted to each patient's physician in printed form. Standard-treatment patients received usual care from their health care providers.

Friedman et al. found that TLC patients reported significantly greater average adherence to treatment and lower diastolic blood pressure compared to controls who showed little change over time on these measures. Note, however, that these effects were largely attributable to gains made by nonadherent patients in the TLC condition. TLC participants who were nonadherent before treatment (i.e., those who took less than 80% of their antihypertensive medications) showed significant improvements in mean adherence at the six-month posttest, whereas nonadherent standard treatment controls showed no change over time. Furthermore, adherent TLC and adherent control participants showed no significant between- or within-groups differences on both blood pressure and behavioral (i.e., adherence) outcomes. Cost-effectiveness ratios also were calculated for the TLC users. The cost per 1 mm Hg improvement in diastolic blood pressure across all TLC participants was approximately $5.00, and it was $1.00 in the nonadherent TLC group.

In a diabetes application of automated telephone technology, Piette, Weinberger, and McPhee (2000) recently conducted a randomized, controlled trial of Automated Telephone Disease Management (ATDM) plus nurse follow-up for adults with diabetes (diabetes subtypes were not specified). The authors randomly assigned 248 primarily low-income, underinsured individuals from a multilingual population (approximately half of the population was Hispanic; approximately 75% of the total participants were primarily English-speaking, and 25% were Spanish-speaking) with diabetes to either ATDM plus nurse follow-up or usual care. ATDM participants received biweekly automated calls for a period of 12 months reminding them of the importance of diabetes care behaviors, providing them with diabetes care tips, and asking participants to enter blood glucose levels. Participants interacted with the ATDM system using their telephone keypads to enter blood glucose levels and other information, and to access the diabetes care tips. Individuals who had additional questions were encouraged to call the study nurse. Controls received typical care (i.e., standard office-based care) and did not have access to the ATDM system. The investigators collected data on patient glycemic control (i.e., HbA_{1c} and fasting serum glucose) and psychosocial variables, including depression (CES–D; Radloff, 1977), anxiety (Rand Mental Health Inventory Anxiety subscale; Veit &

Ware, 1993), diabetes-related self-efficacy (an 11-item rating scale developed by the authors of this study to measure patients' confidence about their ability to conduct diabetes self-care—i.e., medication taking, blood glucose monitoring, etc.), days of reduced activity or confinement to bed, diabetes-specific QOL [Diabetes Quality of Life scale; Diabetes Control and Complications Trial (DCCT) Research Group, 1988] from all participants at baseline and 12-month follow-up. Data were also collected at baseline and follow-up on satisfaction with care and general health-related QOL [Symptom Frequency–36 (SF–36); Ware & Sherbourne, 1992] for primarily English-speaking participants (no Spanish translations of these measures were available).

The overall pattern of findings suggested that the ATDM system had a positive impact on both diabetes management and psychosocial functioning. In regard to diabetes management, the ATDM group reported significantly lower mean blood glucose levels and were twice as likely to be within the normal range on this measure as compared with the control group. Piette et al. (2000) also examined the impact of ATDM on several areas of psychosocial functioning, including depressive symptoms, anxiety, health-related QOL, satisfaction with care, and self-efficacy in performing diabetes care behaviors. ATDM participants reported significantly fewer depressive symptoms, greater satisfaction with care (for the subgroup of participants whose primary language was English), greater self-efficacy, and fewer days of reduced activity than controls. No significant differences were observed between the treatment and control groups for anxiety or overall health-related quality of life. No treatment effects were noted based on language spoken (English vs. Spanish), and no analyses were reported on ethnic differences. A major weakness of this study was that the ATDM intervention contained two disparate components: telephone and nurse visitation in the home. It is unclear which aspect of the intervention had the largest impact on results because all participants in the experimental condition received both components. Disaggregation studies need to be performed to assess the specific contributions of telephone and home visitation to the success of the intervention.

In summary, there is mounting evidence that automated telephone systems may be effective in enhancing adherence to intervention and reducing depressive symptoms in persons with chronic disabling conditions. Automated telephone systems that combine medication or health care regimen reminders with access to condition-specific educational modules may be particularly powerful methods for enhancing adherence to treatment and emotional well-being. However, there continues to be a lack of basic information about the social–psychological mechanisms that link telephone-based communications (e.g., reminders) to changes in health behaviors and emotional functioning. Future studies need to elucidate the specific health-promoting processes that automated telephone care appears to trigger in consumers with disabilities and, in turn, the relationship between these health promoting processes and positive health outcomes. In addition, disaggregation studies are needed to determine which elements (i.e., reminders vs. educational modules) of automated telephone systems account for improvements in health functioning.

Videoconferencing Studies

Two major types of controlled videoconferencing studies have been performed: (a) comparisons between videoconferencing technology (VCT)-based and face-to-face interviews, and (b) evaluations of the reliability (e.g., interrater agreement) of VCT-based mental status exams (e.g., Ball, Scott, McLaren, & Watson, 1993; Elford et al., 2000; Hubble, Pahwa, Michalek, Thomas, & Koller, 1993). Although the latter represent an important domain of research (see Ball & McLaren, 1997), we will not review these studies because they are not consonant with the telehealth intervention focus of this chapter. Furthermore, these studies generally make no explicit linkages between assessment and rehabilitation treatment.

Using the well-established University of Missouri hub-and-spoke teleconferencing network, Schopp, Johnstone, and Merrell (2000) assessed the impact of performing initial neuropsychological assessment interviews across two delivery modes: remote interactive videoconferencing versus standard face-to-face interaction. The participants of the study were adults with a wide range of neuropsychological problems (e.g., learning disabilities, traumatic brain injuries, and vascular dementia) referred by the Missouri Division of Vocational Rehabilitation for evaluation to assist in developing comprehensive vocational plans. Forty-nine participants were randomly assigned to each condition for a total of 98 participants. The videoteleconferencing group included 27 men and 22 women; the control group had 30 men and 19 women. Ninety-two percent of participants ($n = 90$) were White; 6% of the sample were African American ($n = 6$). The two groups were matched based on age and diagnosis. The mean age of participants and years of education was 33.8 and 12.8, respectively. The nine interviewers in the study included University of Missouri (UM) neuropsychologists ($n = 4$), neuropsychology postdoctoral fellows ($n = 3$), and neuropsychology interns ($n = 2$), each of whom performed both in-person and video interviews. The telehealth network used in the study included the UM medical center hub and 18 rural hospital and clinic spoke sites. Dedicated T1 connections were used to conduct the videoconferencing interviews, thus ensuring good quality video and audio transmission. A psychometrist, who later administered neuropsychological tests, also attended the videoconference at the rural locale. In-person interviews were carried out at the first two authors' neuropsychology laboratory located in the UM medical center. After each interview, both clients and interviewers completed closed-ended questionnaires. Clients rated their global satisfaction with the interview, how relaxed or tense they felt during the interview, ease of communication, perceived caring by the examiner, and whether or not they would repeat the experience under the same condition (i.e., videoconference or in-person). The neuropsychology staff rated their level of satisfaction with the interview after each videoconference or in-person control session. No significant differences were found between the two conditions on client global satisfaction, ease of communication, level of relaxation during the interview, and psychologist caring. Also, a significantly larger proportion of clients in the video condition reported that they would repeat their experience than that of the control group. In contrast, the neuropsychology staff expressed significantly less satisfaction with the videoconferencing-based than the in-person interview approach. The authors attributed this discrepancy to interviewers' unrealistically high expectations for transmission speed and reliability. Apparently, they were frustrated by even small delays in establishing digital connections between UM and the rural spoke sites. Finally, the authors compared the cost of videoconferencing against two alternative scenarios: (a) a client traveling to and from the hospital and (b) a psychologist traveling to and from the rural site. In both cases, the composite cost of the videoconferencing-based interview was significantly lower than that of the two travel scenarios.

Next, Johnston and colleagues (2000) have conducted the first multi-population clinical trial of videoconferencing technology-based home care. The overarching goal of the Tele-Home Health program was to assess the feasibility and desirability of replacing a portion of patient home care visits for adults with chronic illnesses with video-conferencing technology (VCT)-mediated intervention. The specific objectives of this quasi-experimental evaluation were to assess the differential effects of VCT-based home care plus routine care vs. stand-alone traditional in-person home care on patients' perceptions of quality of care, program satisfaction, and on cost-effectiveness. Johnston et al. assigned newly referred Kaiser-Permanente outpatients with chronic illnesses (e.g., congestive heart failure, pulmonary disease, stroke, and cancer) to one of two conditions: (a) ISDN-based Tele-Home Health ($n = 102$) plus routine home care or (b) routine home health care only ($n = 110$). The Tele-Home Health intervention included on-demand, 24 hours per day, VCT interaction between patients and nursing staff, as well as remote monitoring of vital signs and medication compliance. In addition, Tele-Home Health participants received routine home health care. Controls received only routine home health care, consisting of regularly scheduled home visits plus telephone contact. The mean duration of the Tele-Home Health and the standard home care interventions was 53 days ($SD = 38.4$) and 40 days ($SD = 51.1$), respectively.

Primary outcomes included three quality of care indicators (i.e., medication compliance, knowledge of disease, and ability or self-care); 12-item Short-Form Health Survey (SF–12; Ware, Kosinski, & Keller, 1996), a measure of health quality of life; patient satisfaction; rates and duration of service use rates; and costs of VCT-based and routine home health care services. The average costs for both the Tele-Home Health and routine home care programs were based on the following calculations: (a) outpatient costs for physician and emergency room visits as well as for laboratory and pharmacy tests, (b) inpatient hospital costs, and (c) home health care costs, including payroll, benefits, travel, and cellular phone expenses. In addition, the costs of the VCT equipment and telecommunication charges (e.g., ISDN fees) were included in estimating the mean cost for the Tele-Home Health condition.

The overall pattern of findings of the study were mixed. Tele-Home Health posttest ratings of quality of care and of program satisfaction were high and equivalent to those of standard home health care treatment. In addition, no significant differences in health quality of life (i.e., SF–12 mean scores) were found between the two treatment programs. Surprisingly, however, the frequency of in-person home health visits for Tele-Home Health (n = 1,003) was similar to that of standard home care (n = 1,197).

Johnston et al. conducted two separate cost analyses: (a) a cross-program comparison of outpatient and inpatient hospital costs and (b) a cross-program comparison of total costs of health services. First, the mean cost of outpatient and inpatient hospital services was significantly lower for Tele-Home Care patients ($1,948) than that for controls ($2,674). The reduced cost of hospital-based services in the Tele-Home Care group was attributable primarily to lower rates of hospitalization. Note, however, that this pattern of findings was not replicated in the analysis of overall costs. The total cost of health services, including equipment and telecommunications expenses, was $1,830 for the Tele-Home Health group versus $1,167 for standard home health care group.

In explaining the findings of the cost analysis, Johnston and colleagues contended that the overall expense of Tele-Home Care would have been significantly lower (approximately $900 rather than $1,830) had the telecommunications equipment been leased or amortized over several years rather than purchased at the outset of the study. Although this argument may be valid, one of the primary reasons for the lack of cost savings may be found in the study's design. Johnston et al. bundled telehealth and traditional home services in the Tele-Home Care condition rather than creating a stand-alone telehealth intervention. The effect of bundling these services into one treatment package may have been to decrease substantially the likelihood of detecting differences in overall costs between Tele-Home Care and routine home health services.

In summary, the overall results of the two studies suggested that consumer perceptions of the desirability and utility of VCT-based health services were high. Health professionals, on the other hand, may not share the same high levels of satisfaction. Schopp et al. (2000) noted that neuropsychology staff tended to express less satisfaction with VCT-based interviews compared with those performed in the clinic. This finding was consistent with the results of closed-circuit television interview studies with mental health populations that showed substantial discrepancies in perceptions of satisfaction with VCT between professionals and psychiatric patients (e.g., Ball, McLaren, Summerfield, Lipsedge, & Watson, 1995; Dongier, Tempier, Lalinec-Michaud, & Meuneir, 1986).

Only partial support was obtained for cost reductions in the use of videoconferencing-based clinical interventions. On the positive side, Schopp et al. (2000) provided preliminary evidence that remote neuropsychological assessment interviews led to significant cost savings compared with traditional professional outreach methods. Johnston, Wheeler, Denser, and Sousa (2000), however, reported equivocal results on cost savings in their home-based VCT evaluation. Additional research is needed to determine the specific settings (e.g., home versus outpatient clinic) and types of health services (clinic consultations versus home care services) that result in substantial cost savings.

Comparative Studies of Telecommunication Technologies

Glueckauf and colleagues (e.g., Glueckauf, Whitton, Baxter, et al., 1998; Glueckauf, Whitton, Kain, et al., 1998; Glueckauf, Fritz, et al., 2002) have performed, to our knowledge, the only randomized controlled trial of the differential effects of video versus speakerphone versus face-to-face counseling for individuals with chronic medical conditions. This multisite investigation is ongoing and ultimately will involve more than 75 families of rural teenagers with seizure disorders across five Midwestern and three Southeastern U.S. states.

Glueckauf et al.'s most recent paper highlighted the findings of phase 1 (i.e., the Midwest phase) of the study. Thirty-nine teenagers with uncontrolled epileptic seizures and their parents from the rural Midwest were randomly assigned to one of three conditions following initial assessment: (a) home-based (HB), family videocounseling (or HB speakerphone counseling when digital services were not available in the community); (b) traditional, office-based family counseling; or (c) a waiting list control group (after three months these participants were reassessed and randomly assigned to one of the first two conditions). The intervention consisted of six sessions of issue-specific family counseling, an integrative family therapy approach, which matches the specific concerns of teenagers and their parents to specific intervention strategies (Glueckauf et al., 1992). The differential effects of the issue-specific counseling intervention on outcome were assessed one week posttreatment and six months later. Twenty-two families completed the six-session counseling program; 12 families dropped out before the first assessment session; and five families dropped out after the initial assessment session. Dropout was differentially associated with office counseling, which required long-distance travel.

The investigators used a multimethod approach in assessing key intervention and process variables. Their outcome measures were (a) problem-specific rating scales derived from the Family and Disability Assessment System (FDAS; Glueckauf, 2001; Glueckauf et al., 1992) and (b) the Social Skills Rating System (SSRS; Gresham & Elliott, 1990). Process measures included the family version of the Working Alliance Inventory (Glueckauf, McQuillen, et al., 2002) and Homework Completion Ratings and Missed Appointments (Glueckauf, Fritz, et al., 2002).

On the FDAS measures, teenagers and parents reported significant reductions in both severity and frequency of identified family problems across all three modalities, from pretreatment to one-week posttreatment and from pretreatment to the six-month follow-up. On the SSRS scales, parents reported significant improvement in prosocial behaviors (e.g., agreeing to perform chores and avoiding arguments with siblings) from pretreatment to one-week posttreatment, whereas teachers reported no substantial changes in classroom behavior over time. Consistent with previous telehealth research, mode of transmission did not differentially influence the outcomes of treatment. Significant and equivalent treatment gains were found across HB desktop-video, HB speakerphone, and face-to-face office counseling for all measures except for teachers' ratings of prosocial and problem behavior.

Next, Glueckauf, Fritz, et al. (2002) found that the overall level of therapeutic alliance was moderately high across treatment conditions and family members. However, teenagers' perceptions of the therapeutic alliance varied with the mode of transmission. Teenagers reported significantly higher levels of alliance with therapists in the office and speakerphone conditions compared with the video condition. Parents, on the other hand, reported similar levels of therapeutic alliance across the three therapy modes.

Turning to treatment adherence, the researchers had anticipated that video and speakerphone families would show higher levels of homework completion and fewer missed appointments as a result of the placement of the intervention in the home environment. Contrary to prediction, no substantial differences were found across conditions on completion of therapy homework assignments and number of missed appointments. The investigators hypothesized that the convenience of the home-based video and speakerphone sessions needed to be weighed against the ease with which appointments could be rescheduled. Parents and teenagers may have concluded that their therapists could reschedule sessions with only limited difficulties, similar to the experience of calling someone back on the telephone at a later hour of the day.

In summary, consistent with telehealth research on clinical interviews (e.g., Schopp et al., 2000), Glueckauf, Fritz, et al. (2002) found that mode of transmission of telehealth services did not substantially influence treatment outcomes. In addition, therapeutic alliance was shown to be moderately high across all modalities. Although a preliminary finding, alliance was found to vary significantly with type of modality and family member. Glueckauf and colleagues noted that additional research is needed to evaluate the potential interactions among modality attributes, client characteristics, and situational factors on user perception of the quality of the therapeutic relationship. There currently exists only limited information about the factors that both enhance and reduce the quality of therapeutic alliance across modalities and disability groups and, in turn, their relationship with treatment outcome. Last, Glueckauf and colleagues suggested caution should be exercised in interpreting the findings of their study primarily as a result of small sample size and the need for replication in their southeastern sample.

FUTURE DIRECTIONS FOR TELEHEALTH IN HEALTH CARE PSYCHOLOGY SETTINGS

As discussed previously, telehealth holds considerable promise for resolving the access barriers of persons in rural areas and to homebound populations who require psychological services. However, we continue to lack basic information about how and under what conditions telecommunication-mediated services lead to positive psychological and health care outcomes. We also have limited information about the cost-effectiveness of telehealth services. This is especially true for cost-effectiveness of telehealth applications in rehabilitation and health psychology. In a health care marketplace increasingly focused on both the cost and quality of care, this research will be important to payers and policy makers and will ensure that rehabilitation and health psychology have a place in future technology-laden iterations of our health care system.

Outcome and Cost-Effectiveness Studies

It is imperative that large-scale evaluations of the differential effects of telecommunications-mediated interventions become a funding priority for federal health care agencies, such as the National Institutes of Health, Health Resources and Services Administration's Office for the Advancement of Telehealth, and the Department of Education's National Institute on Disability and Rehabilitation Research. Although a substantial number of demonstration grants have been awarded over the past 10 years, funding for randomized, clinical trials of the benefits of telehealth with chronic medical populations (e.g., persons with traumatic brain injuries and progressive dementia) has been slow to emerge. We can no longer tout the benefits of telehealth services for persons with chronic medical conditions without solid empirical evidence for their effectiveness. If we are to advance as a responsible scientific enterprise, we must begin to subject our basic assumptions about "what works" in telecommunications with our clients to scientific scrutiny.

Cost-effectiveness studies are also an integral component of the acceptance of large-scale telehealth interventions. To become a viable health service option, telehealth networks must show that the costs of treatment are at least equal to or less than those of alternative approaches that produce similar outcomes. Although several studies have documented the cost-effectiveness of psychotherapeutic interventions for psychiatric, substance abuse, and geriatric populations (see Glen, Lazar, Hornberger, & Spiegel, 1997; Krupnick & Pincus, 1992), there has been little published research on the cost-effectiveness of telecommunication-mediated psychological interventions for persons with chronic disabilities (e.g., Cheung et al., 1998; Trott & Blignault, 1998).

Process Studies

Although randomized, controlled field studies are the litmus test of the effectiveness of telehealth, it is essential to understand the social–psychological mechanisms that link intervention and outcome. We currently lack basic information about the factors that both enhance and reduce the quality (clarity, ease of use, distractibility, and comfort) of telehealth communications across modalities, age groups, minorities, and ethnic groups, and in turn, their relationship with treatment outcome. We also have only limited knowledge about the impact of different telecommunication modalities (e.g., home-based videoconferencing vs. e-mail) on intervention adherence, attendance, and attrition.

Practice Guidelines and Client Training Material

Practice guidelines are potentially powerful tools to enhance quality control. Guidelines provide a method of determining the most effective treatment of a disorder and establish accepted treatment approaches and duration of treatment modalities. They are likely to be critical to the broad-based acceptance of telehealth interventions and may help to establish the appropriate level of expertise of telehealth providers (cf., DeLeon, Frank, & Wedding, 1995). The Joint Working Group on Telemedicine has outlined the critical questions that the health professions need to work together to answer in the development of practice guidelines for the delivery of telehealth services (NTIA, 1997; Office for the Advancement of Telehealth, 2001). The time is ripe for developing and evaluating the use of practice guidelines in the delivery of telecommunication-mediated psychological services to persons with chronic disabilities and their families. Furthermore, we also need to create training materials for consumers of telehealth services. At the present time, the lay public has little guidance about how to purchase, install, and effectively use home-based telecommunications services.

CONCLUSION

As computer technologies, telecommunication networks, and health care systems continue to evolve, specific developments are difficult to predict. However, the convergence of these evolutions—coupled with increasing consumer demand and investor interests—have increased substantially the likelihood that telehealth practice and evaluation will become integral elements of our health care system. To take full advantage of these opportunities, psychologists need to become knowledgeable about the legislative, legal, marketplace, and consumer education forces that are driving the telehealth revolution and our changing health care system.

REFERENCES

American Telemedicine Service Providers. (1999). *ATSP report of telemedicine activity*. Portland, OR: Author.

Association of State and Provincial Psychology Boards. (1998). *Model act for the practice of psychology*. Mobile, AL: Author.

Balanced Budget Act of 1997. (1997). Pub. L. No. 105-33.

Ball, C., & McLaren, P. (1997). The tele-assessment of cognitive state: A review. *Journal of Telemedicine and Telecare, 3*, 126–131.

Ball, C. J., McLaren, P. M., Summerfield, A. B., Lipsedge, M. S., & Watson, J. P. (1995). A comparison of communication modes in adult psychiatry. *Journal of Telemedicine and Telecare, 1*, 22–26.

Ball, C. J., Scott, N., McLaren, P. M., & Watson, J. P. (1993). Preliminary evaluation of a low-cost videoconferencing (LCVC) system for remote cognitive testing of adult psychiatric patients. *British Journal of Clinical Psychology, 32*, 303–307.

Bergner, M., Bobbitt, R. A., Carter, W. B., & Gilson, B. S. (1981, Aug.). The Sickness Impact Profile: Development and final revision of a health status measure. *Medical Care, 19,* 787–805.

Block, G., Clifford, C., Naughton, M. D., Henderson, M. & McAdams, M. (1989). A brief dietary screen for high fat intake. *Journal of Nutrition Education, 21,* 199–207.

Cheung, S., Davies, R. F., Smith, K., Marsh, R., Sherrard, H., & Keon, W. J. (1998). The Ottawa telehealth project. *Telemedicine Journal, 4,* 259–266.

Council on Competitiveness. (1994). *Breaking barriers to the national information infrastructure.* Washington, DC: Author.

Council on Competitiveness. (1996). *Highway to health: Transforming U.S. health care in the information age.* Washington, DC: Author.

DeLeon, P. H., Frank, R. G., & Wedding, D. (1995). Health psychology and public policy: The political press. *Health Psychology, 14,* 493–499.

Derogatis L. R., Lipman R. S., & Covi L. (1973). SCL–90: An outpatient psychiatric rating scale—Preliminary report. *Psychopharmacology Bulletin, 9*(1),13–28.

Diabetes Control and Complications Trial (DCCT) Research Group. (1988). Reliability and validity of a diabetes quality-of-life measure for the diabetes control and complications trial (DCCT). *Diabetes Care, 11,* 725–732.

Dongier, M., Tempier, R., Lalinec-Michaud, M., & Meuneir, D. (1986). Telepsychiatry: Psychiatric consultation through two-way television: A controlled study. *Canadian Journal of Psychiatry, 31,* 32–34.

Duke University Center for the Study of Aging and Human Development. (1978). *Multidimensional functional assessment: The OARS methodology.* Durham, NC: Duke University.

Elford, R., White, H., Bowering, R., Ghandi, A., Maddiggan, B., St. John, K., et al. (2000). A randomized, controlled trial of child psychiatric assessments conducted using videoconferencing. *Journal of Telemedicine and Telecare, 6,* 73–82.

Ensel, W., & Woelfel, M. (1986). Measuring the instrumental and expressive functions of social support. In N. Lin & A. Dean (Eds.), *Social support, life events, and depression* (pp. 129–152). Orlando, FL: Academic Press.

Evans, R. L., Fox, H. R., Pritzl, D. O., & Halar, E. M. (1984). Group treatment of physically disabled adults by telephone. *Social Work in Health Care, 9*(3), 77–84.

Evans, R. L., & Jaureguy, B. M. (1982). Group therapy by phone: A cognitive behavioral program for visually impaired elderly. *Social Work in Health Care, 7*(2), 79–90.

Evans, R. L., Smith, K. M., Werkhoven, W. S., Fox, H. R., & Pritzl, D. O. (1986). Cognitive telephone group therapy with physically disabled elderly persons. *Gerontologist, 26*(1), 8–10.

Flatley-Brennan, P (1998). Computer network home care demonstration: A randomized trial in persons living with AIDS. *Computers in Biology and Medicine, 28*(5), 489–508.

Follick M. J., Gorkin, L., Smith, T. W., & Capone, R. J. (1988). Quality of life post-myocardial infarction: Effects of a transtelephonic coronary intervention system. *Health Psychology, 7,* 169–182.

Friedman, R. H., Kazis, L. E., Jette, A., Smith, M. B., Stollerman, J., Torgerson, J., et al. (1996). A telecommunications system for monitoring and counseling patients with hypertension: Impact on medication adherence and blood pressure control. *American Journal of Hypertension, 9,* 285–292.

Glen, G. O., Lazar, S. G., Hornberger, J., & Spiegel, D. (1997). The economic impact of psychotherapy: A review. *American Journal of Psychiatry, 154,* 147–155.

Glueckauf, R. L. (1990). Program evaluation guidelines for the rehabilitation professional. In M. G. Eisenberg & R. C. Grzesiak (Eds.), *Advances in clinical rehabilitation* (Vol. 3, pp. 250–266). New York: Springer.

Glueckauf, R. L. (2000). Doctoral education in rehabilitation and health care psychology: Principles and strategies for unifying subspecialty training. In R. G. Frank & T. R. Elliott (Eds.), *Handbook of rehabilitation psychology* (pp. 621–624). Washington, DC: American Psychological Association.

Glueckauf, R. L. (2001). The Family and Disability Assessment System. In J. Touliatos, B. F. Perlmutter, & G. W. Holden (Eds.), *Handbook of family measurement techniques: Vol. 2.* Newbury Park, CA: Sage.

Glueckauf, R. L. (2002). Telehealth and chronic disabilities: New frontier for research and development. *Rehabilitation Psychology, 47,* 3–7.

Glueckauf, R. L., Fritz, S. P., Ecklund-Johnson, E. P., Liss, H. J., Dages, P., et al. (2002). Videoconferencing-based family counseling for rural teenagers with epilepsy: Phase 1 findings. *Rehabilitation Psychology, 47,* 8–30.

Glueckauf, R. L., Hufford, B., Whitton, J., Baxter, J., Schneider, P., Kain, J., et al. (1999). Telehealth: Emerging technology in rehabilitation and health care. In M. G. Eisenberg, R. L. Glueckauf, & H. H. Zaretsky (Eds.), *Medical aspects of disability: A handbook for the rehabilitation professional* (2nd ed., pp. 625–639). New York: Springer.

Glueckauf, R. L., Ketterson, T. U., Loomis, J. S., & Dages, P. (in press). Online support and education for dementia caregivers: Overview, strategic marketing, and initial program evaluation. *Telemedicine Journal and e-Health.*

Glueckauf, R. L., & Loomis, J. S. (2003). Alzheimer's Caregiver Support Online: Overview, lessons learned, and future directions. *NeuroRehabilitation, 18,* 135–146.

Glueckauf, R. L., McQuillen, D. E., Liss, H. J., Webb, P. M., Dairaghi, J., & Carter, C. B. (2002). Therapeutic alliance in family therapy for adolescents with epilepsy: An exploratory study. *American Journal of Family Therapy, 30*(2), 125–140.

Glueckauf, R. L., Webb, P., Papandria-Long, M., Rasmussen, J. L., Markand, O., & Farlow, M. (1992). The Family and Disability Assessment System: Consistency and accuracy of judgments across coders and measures. *Rehabilitation Psychology, 37,* 291–304.

Glueckauf, R. L., Whitton, J., Baxter, J., Kain, J., Vogelgesang, S., Hudson, M., et al. (1998, July). Videocounseling for families of rural teens with epilepsy: Project update. *TeleHealth News, 2*(2). Retrieved November 3, 2003, from http://cybertowers.com/ct/telehealth

Glueckauf, R., Whitton, J., Kain, J., Vogelgesang, S., Hudson, M., Hufford, B., et al. (1998). Home-based, videocounseling for families of rural teens with epilepsy: Program rationale and objectives. *Telehealth News, 2*(1). Retrieved November 3, 2003, from http://cybertowers.com/ct/telehealth

Glueckauf, R. L., Whitton, J. D., & Nickelson, D. W. (2002). Telehealth: The new frontier in rehabilitation and health care. In M. J. Scherer (Ed.), *Assistive technology: Matching device and consumer for successful rehabilitation* (pp. 197–213). Washington, DC: American Psychological Association.

Gray, J. E., Safran, C., Davis, R. B., Pompilio-Weitzner, G., Stewart, J. E., Zaccagnini, L., et al. (2000). Baby CareLink: Using the internet and telemedicine to improve care for high-risk infants. *Pediatrics, 106*, 1318–1324.

Gresham, F. M., & Elliott, S. N. (1990). *Social skills rating system manual.* Circle Pines, MN: American Guidance Service.

Grigsby, B., & Brown, N. (2000). *The 1999 ATSP report on U.S. telemedicine activity.* Portland, OR: Association of Telehealth Service Providers.

Gustafson D. H., Hawkins R., Boberg, E., Pingree, S., Serlin, R. E., Graziano F., et al. (1999). Impact of a patient-centered, computer-based health information/support system. *American Journal of Preventive Medicine, 16*(1), 1–9.

Gustafson, D. H., Wise, M., McTavish, F., Taylor, J. O., Wolberg, W., Stewart, J., et al. (1993). Development and pilot evaluation of a computer–based support system for women with breast cancer. *Journal of Psychosocial Oncology, 11*(4), 69–93.

Haas, L. J., Benedict, J. G., & Kobos, J. C. (1996). Psychotherapy by telephone: Risks and benefits for psychologists and consumers. *Professional Psychology: Research and Practice, 27*, 154–160.

Harris Interactive. (2002). *Cyberchondriacs updates.* Retrieved May 1, 2002, from http://www.harrisinteractive.com/harris—poll/index.asp?PID=299

H.B. 2953. (1999). Washington State assembly, 57th Leg.

H.B. 4073. (1999). West Virginia assembly.

H.R. 5661. (2000). Medicare, Medicaid, and SCHIP Improvement Act of 2000. 106th Cong., 2nd Sess.

Hubble, J. P., Pahwa, R., Michalek, D. K., Thomas, C., & Koller, W. C. (1993). Interactive video conferencing: A means of providing interim care to Parkinson's Disease patients. *Movement Disorders, 8*, 380–382.

Jerome, L. W., DeLeon, P. H., James, L. C., Folen, R., Earles, J., & Gedney, J. J. (2000). The coming of age of telecommunications in psychological research and practice. *Professional Psychology: Research and Practice, 55*, 407–421.

Johnston, B., Wheeler, L., Deuser, J., & Sousa, K. H. (2000). Outcomes of the Kaiser Permanente Tele-Home Health Research Project. *Archives of Family Medicine, 9*(1), 40–45.

Kristal, A. R., Shattuck, A. L., & Henry, H. J. (1990). Patterns of dietary behavior associated with selecting diets low in fat: Reliability and validity of a behavioral approach to dietary assessment. *Journal of the American Dietetic Association, 90*, 214–220.

Krupnick, J. L., & Pincus, H. A. (1992). The cost-effectiveness of psychotherapy: A plan for research. *American Journal of Psychiatry, 149*, 1295–1305.

Magaletta, P. R., Fagan, T. J., & Ax, R. K. (1998). Advancing psychology services through telehealth in the Federal Bureau of Prisons. *Professional Psychology: Research and Practice, 29*, 543–548.

Mahone, D. F., Tarlow, B., & Sandaire, J. (1998). A computer-mediated intervention for Alzheimer's caregivers. *Computers in Nursing, 16*(4), 208–216.

McKay, H. G., Glasgow, R. E., Feil, E. G., Boles, S. M., & Barrera, M. M. (2002). Internet-based diabetes self-management and support: Initial outcomes from the Diabetes Network Project. *Rehabilitation Psychology, 47*, 31–48.

Mittman, R., & Cain, M. (1999). *The future of the Internet in health care: Five-year forecast.* Menlo Park: California Health Care Foundation.

National Telecommunications and Information Administration (NTIA). (1997). *Telemedicine report to Congress.* Retrieved November 2, 2003, from http://www.ntia.doc.gov/reports/telemed/

Newman, R. (1998, May). How are managed care and telehealth alike? [electronic version]. *APA Monitor, 29.* Retrieved November 3, 2003, from http://www.apa.org/monitor/may98/pp.html

Nickelson, D. W. (1997). Wired on capitol hill. In G. Levy & K. Coughlin (Eds.), *Telemedicine source book: 1999: A resource guide for the practical application of telemedicine in the health care marketplace* (pp. 99–104). New York: Faulkner & Gray.

Nickelson, D. W. (1998). Telehealth and the evolving health care system: Strategic opportunities for professional psychology. *Professional Psychology: Research and Practice, 29*, 527–535.

Nickelson, D. W. (2000). Telehealth, healthcare services & healthcare policy: A plan of action in the new millennium. *New Jersey Psychologist, 50*(1), 24–27.

Office for the Advancement of Telehealth. (2001). *2001 Report to Congress on Telemedicine.* Retrieved November 2, 2003, from http://telehealth.hrsa.gov/pubs/report2001/main.htm

Office of Technology Assessment. (1990). *Health care in rural America* (OTA-H-434). Washington, DC: Government Printing Office.

Picker Institute. (2000). *Improving the quality of health care through the eyes of patients: Surveys 2000.* Retrieved April 19, 2002, from http://www.pickereurope.ac.uk/research/default.htm

Piette, J. D., Weinberger, M., & McPhee, S. J. (2000). Impact of automated calls with nurse follow-up on patient-centered outcomes of diabetes care: A randomized controlled trial. *Medical Care, 38*, 218–230.

Radloff, L. S. (1977). The Center for Epidemiological Studies–Depression (CES–D) Scale: A self-report depression scale for research in the general population. *Applied Psychological Measurement, 1*(3), 385.

S. 770. (1999). 106th Cong., 1st Sess.

S. 980. (1999). 106th Cong., 1st Sess.

S. 2505. (2000). 106th Cong., 2nd Sess.

Saunders, G., & Courtney, J. (1985). A field study of the organizational factors influencing DDS success. *MIS Quarterly, 9*, 77.

Scherer, M. J. (Ed.). (2002). *Assistive technology: Matching device and consumer for successful rehabilitation.* Washington, DC: American Psychological Association.

Schopp, L., Johnstone, B., & Merrell, D. (2000). Telehealth and neuropsychological assessment: New opportunities for psychologists. *Professional Psychology: Research and Practice, 31*, 179–183.

Segal, D. (1999, Nov. 12). Tag team lawyers make businesses blink. *Washington Post*, pp. A1.

Stein, L., Rothman, B., & Nakanishi, M. (1993). The telephone group: Accessing group service to the homebound. *Social Work with Groups, 16*(1–2), 203–215.

Stewart, A. L., Hays, R. D., & Ware, J. E. (1989). The MOS short-form general health survey: Reliability and validity in a patient population. *Medicare Care, 26*(7), 724–735.

Taylor, C. B., Bandura, A., Ewart, C. K., Miller, N. H., & DeBusk, R. F. (1985). Exercise testing to enhance wives' confidence in their husbands' cardiac capability soon after clinically uncomplicated acute myocardial infarction. *American Journal of Cardiology, 55*, 635–638.

Trott, P., & Blignault, I. (1998). Cost evaluation of a telepsychiatry service in northern Queensland. *Journal of Telemedicine and Telecare, 4*(Suppl. 1), 66–68.

U.S. Department of Commerce. (1997). *Telemedicine Report to Congress.* Washington, DC: Author.

U.S. General Accounting Office. (1997). *Telemedicine: Federal strategy is needed to guide investments* (GAO Publication No. GAO/NCIAD/HEHS-97-67). Gaithersburg, MD: Author.

Veit, C. T., & Ware, J. E. (1993). The structure of psychological distress and well-being in general populations. *Journal of Consulting and Clinical Psychology, 51*, 730–742.

Ware, J., Kosinski, M., & Keller, S. D. (1996). A 12-item short-form health survey: Construction of scales and preliminary tests of reliability and validity. *Medical Care, 34*(3), 220–233.

Ware, J. E., & Sherbourne, C. D. (1992). The MOS 36-item short-form health survey (SF–36). *Medical Care, 30*, 473–483.

IV

PUBLIC HEALTH AND
POLICY PERSPECTIVES

12

HEALTH PSYCHOLOGY:
A PUBLIC POLICY PERSPECTIVE

PATRICK H. DeLEON, RUTH ULLMANN PAIGE, BRIAN D. SMEDLEY,
AND MORGAN T. SAMMONS

There have been a number of substantial changes within the discipline of psychology during the past quarter of a century that cumulatively have redefined the field. From a public policy perspective, perhaps the most significant has been the gradual realization by members of the profession (and ultimately, by society at large) that psychological services *are* fundamentally health care services. This change in orientation represents a transition from what was traditionally an intraprofessional and laboratory-focused academic–scientific perspective to one that by necessity involves active interdisciplinary collaboration; careful attention to health care delivery structural issues, as well as patient-specific systemic concerns; and proactive involvement in the public policy (e.g., political) process. Although this change in emphasis has been gradually evolving for some time, it is by no means complete, nor is its long-term significance truly appreciated by many in

Views expressed are personal in nature and do not reflect those of the U.S. Navy or the Department of Defense.

the field. Within the practitioner community, for example, the conceptual movement from being deemed a "mental health provider" to a "behavioral health specialist" has been particularly difficult for many. Within our professional training institutions, the necessary programmatic modifications have been particularly slow in coming. We suggest that herein is the essence of the often reported scientist–practitioner tensions that exist within the governance of the American Psychological Association (APA).

Although the discipline of psychology dates back to the founding of Wilhelm Wundt's laboratory in 1879, on September 21, 1970, classes began at the first independent professional school of psychology—the California School of Professional Psychology (now Alliant University; Street, 1994). This was to become the era of the Doctor of Psychology degree (PsyD), the first program being launched in the Department of Psychology at the University of Illinois at Champaign–Urbana in 1968. There can be little disagreement that the paradigm shift from the traditional research-oriented PhD degree to the professional-oriented PsyD degree represented a fundamental change in psychology's self-image and underlying mission. It also resulted in ever-increasing graduate school enrollments and, equally important, different kinds of graduates with different professional expectations and aspirations.

Within the health field we *are* a relatively young profession. When President Jimmy Carter signed Executive Order No. 11973 on February 19, 1977, thereby establishing his landmark President's Commission on Mental Health, there were approximately 59,900 members and affiliates of the APA. That same year, Missouri became the last state in the nation to license–certify practicing psychologists. A decade later (1988), responding to the extraordinary interest in psychology at the undergraduate and graduate level, the Committee for the American Psychological Association of Graduate Students (APAGS) was established by the APA Council of Representatives. The comparable APA membership numbers have grown today to 155,000, with APAGS presently enrolling 59,700 members. These are impressive figures and they speak well for the future of psychology. The advent of the professional school model has heralded a change that is not likely to be reversed (Wright & Cummings, 2001). At the beginning of the 21st century, there are 48 accredited PsyD programs in the United States, most of which are within professional schools that now graduate 58% of all clinical students (P. Nelson, personal communication, September 5, 2001). The APA also has begun formally accrediting postdoctoral training programs. This latter development is particularly relevant to the evolving environment of the U.S. health care delivery market. One of the fundamental policy lessons we have learned is that to be long-lasting, change within any profession must closely parallel overall developments within society at large.

LEGISLATIVE DEVELOPMENTS

At the national level, the mid-1970s was a time when professional psychologists legislatively succeeded in becoming recognized as autonomous providers under every health care initiative in which the federal government's role was that of the "payer of the bill" for federal beneficiaries. Some of the specific programs targeted by psychology included the Federal Employees' Health Benefit Program (FEHBP); the Department of Defense (DoD) Civilian Health and Medical Program of the Uniformed Services (CHAMPUS) and CHAMPVA for the Veterans Administration (VA); the Federal Workers' Compensation Act; the Social Security Disability Benefits program; and eventually Medicare and Medicaid (Dorken and Associates, 1986). During this process, organized psychology was successful in obtaining parity with medicine in the forensic arena, being formally recognized to make competency determinations throughout the federal criminal code, under the relevant provisions of the DoD code, and in various American Bar Association (ABA) policy documents. Other accomplishments included psychology's statutory inclusion in the U.S. Public Health Regular Corps, which allowed a psychologist to be appointed Surgeon General of the United States, if the president so desired. Efforts were successful in obtaining statutory authority to provide various federal psychologists with retention pay bonuses, similar to those received by other health professionals. Of considerable long-term policy significance, as the relevant federal agencies collected health professions data for developing the administration's programmatic recommendations to the Congress, psychology began to be specifically included in their calculations, pursuant to Congressional directives.

Similar legislative successes were increasingly obtained at the state level, principally with the enactment of "freedom of choice" legislation that required private insurance companies to treat psychology's practitioners in the same manner as they did other health care providers (i.e., physicians), when determining reimbursement policies (Thomas & Cummings, 2000). During this time period, increasing numbers of psychologists were also being selected by their governors to serve as chief state mental health officers, as well as being selected for high-level federal public health responsibilities by the White House and cabinet secretaries. These far-reaching legislative efforts and administrative accomplishments have served psychology's practitioners admirably. They have also nicely paralleled the development of a robust Practice Directorate capacity within the APA and, in particular, its concerted efforts to develop a cadre of seasoned state psychological associations. As one of the "learned professions," the 1970s was a time when professional psychology entered into a new era of public policy maturation (DeLeon & Zimbardo, in press).

INCREASING INTERNAL POLITICAL INVOLVEMENT

It has been our observation that the decade of the 1990s saw professional psychology gradually assert its dominance over the internal governance of the APA. If one reviews the composition of the Board of Directors or the Council of Representatives, the practitioners' voice was increasingly heard. The seemingly seamless transition from membership on the Board of Directors to or from the Committee for the Advancement of Professional Practice (CAPP), the major APA practice policy board, underscored this transformation. This was not always the case, however. Early in the 1990s, the practice community was just beginning to get itself organized—it was learning how to elect practitioner Board members. The APA Board of Directors was elected much as the president is elected currently. Individuals who were respected by virtue of their research or publications were chosen. Finally, during that period the practice community recognized and valued its unique needs and interests and realized that unless it began to vote those interests and become personally involved in the political process, these interests would not be addressed. During the 1990s increased numbers of practitioners were elected to the APA Board of Directors, as well as to the other association policy boards and committees. Also during this period, CAPP was undergoing its own transformation.

Although it had always been the voice of practice, how practice was defined by CAPP was shifting. Early in the decade CAPP still saw itself as representing a *mental health* profession and particularly those colleagues in private practice. Although CAPP never voted to make an official policy change, it made increasingly more decisions that reflected an underlying conceptual shift—namely, understanding psychology practice to be that of a broader health care discipline, including institutional practice. An early decision was to undertake the *CAPP v. Rank* (1990) case, which gave California psychologists independent hospital privileges. Under the changed leadership of the Practice Directorate at that time, still more initiatives were promoted that envisioned enlarged roles for psychologists in health care. A "tool box" for practitioners was developed that not only taught practice management skills but also supported expanded roles in a variety of settings. In addition, a document defining schools as health care settings was completed and distributed. In addition, CAPP established a task force on psychology as a primary care discipline. The task force outlined steps practitioners could take to move into new roles in primary care. In our judgment, however, nothing captured CAPP's broader conceptual shift in defining psychology practice so much as the evolution of its attitude toward psychologists' obtaining prescriptive authority (RxP-). Early in the decade CAPP was not on record as supporting RxP-. In fact, there was opposition to the notion. Each time the issue came up for a vote, following increasingly persuasive discussion about the need for practitioner autonomy as part of its shift into broader health care, the vote on CAPP was closer and closer. Additional discussions centered on practitioners' capacity to respond more broadly and independently to addressing societal behavioral health problems. Finally, the transformation on CAPP was complete. CAPP saw the need for psychologists to obtain independent prescriptive authority and it voted accordingly. With that vote, CAPP demonstrated it also had a changed image of psychological practice.

The steady movement within the governance over a period of years to ensure that all state, provincial, and territorial psychological associations, regardless of their membership size, would have at least one voting seat on Council is viewed by many within the scientific–academic community as increasing the practitioner's voice at the highest level of APA governance. State associations, which are predominately practice-oriented, inherently possess different policy agendas than the traditional APA divisions, especially those state associations that are supported primarily by academic psychologists. Not surprisingly, membership surveys have increasingly indicated that the top priorities of the governance and the membership at large are essentially practice oriented concerns, albeit broadly defined. Accordingly, there is probably considerable truth to the growing perception among those involved within the APA governance that the only elected position that is not readily within the control of the practice community is the APA presidency. We would note, however, that since full-time practitioner Ted Blau was elected as the Association's 85th president, an increasing number of practitioners have, in fact, been elected to that critical office.

The next step is to ensure increased practitioner awareness exists about the important role the office of the APA presidency plays in advancing the practice agenda. This gap in awareness has been demonstrated by the election to APA president in recent years of individuals (who have not always been familiar with professional psychology's concerns) primarily because they are well known authors and researchers. These individuals could not have been elected without practitioner votes. That practitioners vote for someone based on name recognition, rather than for the less known but more practice-friendly candidate, reflects a need for the profession's leaders to further educate its members about the significance of APA activities to professional psychology's survival and vitality.

THE NEED FOR FUTURISTIC VISION

In our judgment, the field of psychology should next expect (and genuinely hope for) a level of public policy conceptualization within the APA governance (and subsequently, within its legislative and administrative priorities) that demonstrates an appreciation for the inherent interdependence of practice aspirations and professional education (e.g., training) *and* the importance of public policy involvement by the leadership of both communities. Currently efforts are underway in the Education Directorate to establish an Educational Federal Advocacy Network, similar to the practice advocacy network. Practitioners, under the leadership of the APA Practice Directorate, have long had an organized network that can be rapidly mobilized to contact national legislative leaders to inform them about the behavioral health and public policy impact of proposed legislation. Forward-thinking academicians are beginning to recognize that those who train professional psychologists also have a responsibility to engage in advocacy efforts so they can obtain funds and support for innovative, socially responsive training programs. Until recently this was not something in which educators were inclined to participate. Instead, they saw advocacy as falling entirely within the purview of the practice community. Recent cross-constituency activities such as the meetings of the Commission on Education Leading to Credentialing and Licensure in Psychology and the APA Board of Directors' invited breakfast focused on the Wisdom of Prevention as Public Policy have gone a long way to raising educators' awareness. At one of the meetings, an educator specifically requested developing a summer institute to "train the trainers" in advocacy.

As practitioners increase their dominance within the APA governance, it is critical for the profession of psychology that its leaders determine how to effectively use the association's national stature and resources in furtherance of policy agendas that will benefit *all* elements of the discipline of psychology (e.g., practice, education, science, and public interest). If overly narrow or individual-based agendas ultimately supercede the development of a broader and truly inclusive vision, an unprecedented opportunity will be lost. Yet it is our impression that the crafting of this necessary futuristic vision and the resulting implementing strategies are, at best, only in their earliest stages. We were pleased, therefore. that recently two examples of such cross-constituency collaboration have surfaced. As a result of the September 11, 2001, terrorist attacks on the United States, the APA Board of Directors formed a task force comprising the leadership of the four Directorates, the Publications Office, and the Public Information Office. The task force, under the leadership of Recording Secretary Ron Levant and coordinated by the Science Directorate, is developing across constituency responses, psychology's responses, to this major crisis and public interest issue. Only with this kind of collaboration will a truly useful and meaningful response be formed. Also, under the leadership of President Norine Johnson, all the Directorates, under the coordination of the Practice Directorate, have begun to examine the resources and activities currently allocated to health policy activities in science, practice, education, and public interest.

The goal is to develop unified and strengthened attention to psychology's role in public well-being through increased attention to health maintenance, health promotion, and health care in the eyes of psychologists, as well as in the eyes of the public. This pioneering activity may well set the stage for similar future collaboration.

Our nation's elected officials have a long tradition of ensuring that those professions for whom they provide significant public financial training support are, in fact, recognized and appropriately reimbursed by all relevant payment mechanisms (DeLeon, Hagglund, Ragusea, & Sammons, 2003). In addition, over the years, the federal government has developed a number of health care initiatives targeted specifically toward addressing evolving federal priorities, almost always involving the active participation of health professional training institutions and their faculty. Increasing the overall numbers of health professionals, addressing ethnic and geographical disparities, targeting the unique needs of special populations, and capitalizing on the potential for ensuring quality health care by effectively using the incredible technological advances occurring (particularly within the communications arena) all reflect changing federal priorities, at different times in our history. Title VII of the U.S. Public Health Service Act, for example, currently authorizes a number of special project initiatives that should be of considerable interest to psychology—for example, increasing the availability of quality health care to children, elderly individuals, and those in rural America—as well as encouraging interdisciplinary training. The Graduate Medical Education (GME) account of Medicare, established in 1965 (and increasingly paralleled by other federal health care delivery programs), provides a significant economic incentive for hospitals to serve elderly individuals, in conjunction with academic health care institutions. The Medicare (and Medicaid) GME expenditure is estimated to approximate $11 billion annually. In 1999, a children's' hospital-based GME initiative was authorized under Title VII, which received more than $240 million in fiscal year 2002.

These federal programs represent exciting opportunities for the behavioral sciences. However, over the years we have observed only minimal interest within the discipline's training institutions in participating. Nevertheless, we were pleased to learn that after considerable legislative effort by the Practice and Education Directorates of the APA (in conjunction with two or three farsighted training programs), in fiscal year 2002 psychology's postdoctoral training fellows were deemed eligible for Medicare GME support, and $2 million of Title VII funding is expressly available for health psychology training initiatives. In many ways, the GME eligibility, in particular, possesses the potential for revolutionizing psychology's training programs and should result in opening up entirely new market places within the health care arena. The long-term effect may well parallel that of the VA's initial investment in psychology in the aftermath of World War II. To provide a financial perspective, within five years of comprehensive GME eligibility, psychology's training programs are projected to receive $50 million annually; in contrast, with the exception of support from the VA (which exceeded $9 million in fiscal year 2001), psychology's training programs annually receive approximately $2 million under all the other federal training initiatives. We further note that the VA stipends are oriented to individual students, rather than based on institutional programmatic efforts.

Notwithstanding these recent impressive GME and Title VII developments, it remains our considered impression that the leadership of psychology's professional training institutions have yet to fully appreciate the critical importance of public policy involvement to their underlying academic mission. Whereas many (perhaps even the majority) of our practitioners have a history of enthusiastically working closely with the APA Practice Directorate in furtherance of commonly developed legislative agendas (paying an individual-based "special assessment"), professional psychology's educators have yet to demonstrate a similar commitment to their national organization—either by institutionally making economic commitments to the APA Education Directorate or by becoming personally involved within the association's governance. Surprisingly, this has been true even for the leadership of psychology's professional schools.

It seems to us that the only plausible explanation for this lack of involvement is that psychology's academic leaders do not appreciate the extent to which their personal participation within the public policy (e.g., political) process will have a direct bearing on their institutional livelihood and their graduates' future. As a result, little systematic effort has been made by the APA during the past decade to establish new psychology-oriented health professional initiatives under Title VII or to have psychology effectively included in the various ongoing federal training initiatives, other than the traditional student loan programs (which are essentially undergraduate-based). This minimal interest extends even to effectively participating in those already established programmatic initiatives (i.e., the Burdick Rural Interdisciplinary training program) in which psychology is expressly authorized. Perhaps this is because the federal programs require considerable faculty involvement to address perceived federal priorities. There is a qualitative difference between being institutionally involved in programmatic activities and benefiting from the availability of traditional student oriented stipends. In this light, the recent Congressional movement to replace the designation of *psychology* with the more generic *mental health specialist* phrase throughout the various Title VII provisions should not be surprising. It should, however, definitely be considered a step backward, if not outright legislative failure.

In our judgment, it is absolutely essential for the future of the profession of psychology that the leadership of training institutions actively endorse interdisciplinary collaboration and training *and* for the leadership of the practice community to appreciate the consequences of this action (or inaction) on their future. Both groups should become actively involved with their counterparts within the leadership of U.S. schools of public health, health services administration, clinical pharmacy, business, law, medicine, nursing, and so forth, to develop proactive efforts to effectively expand the boundaries of psychological clinical practice beyond the traditional and status quo. These other disciplines have, over the years, played a significant role in shaping our health delivery system. And this would, of course, include the establishment of psychology-based comprehensive treatment centers— for example, for those patients requiring rehabilitative care or treatment for chronic illnesses.

PRESCRIPTIVE AUTHORITY

Perhaps the most important—and challenging—practice expansion initiative being currently undertaken by the profession is the effort to obtain RxP- for appropriately trained psychologists. From the standpoint of social responsibility, this initiative is fundamentally important, given evidence that psychotropic drugs are commonly inappropriately prescribed, at the same time their skilled administration is unavailable to populations that may benefit from them. From the standpoint of challenge to the profession, prescriptive authority presents several significant conceptual and political obstacles. Solving these problems will likely serve to advance not only the RxP- agenda but will also further accrete the profession's standing as the premier provider of behavioral health care services.

Social Responsibility

From the beginning of the prescriptive authority movement in psychology, it has been asserted that augmenting our clinical armamentarium with this additional tool is fundamentally an issue of social responsibility (DeLeon, Sammons, & Sexton, 1995). Lack of psychiatric resources, the existence of large numbers of underserved patients (primarily in rural and inner-city environments), and a widespread tendency by psychiatrists to use medication as the sole therapeutic modality were cited as fundamental inequities in mental health service provision that RxP- could ameliorate. All these factors remain potent arguments, but in the more recent past a new issue has arisen that must be factored into the social responsibility equation: In spite of the rapidly escalating prescription of psychotropics (Croghan, 2001), and the demonstrated efficacy of many psychotropics, they have not (as currently used), reduced the burden to society incurred by many forms of mental illness (Moncrieff, 2001). Psychologists advocating prescriptive authority believe that this is the result of essential flaws in the biomedical model of treating mental distress, and that it is incumbent on the profession to devise more rationale and effective pharmacotherapeutic interventions than currently exist.

Conceptual Obstacles

Psychologists have not been trained in the allopathic, medically based model that characterizes modern psychopharmacology. Therefore, the first conceptual hurdle to be overcome before integrating this skill into psychological practice is the absence of an academic–intellectual tradition of psychopharmacological service provision. There are two facets to this problem. One is based in science and encompasses the domain of knowledge required to *safely* use psychopharmaceutical agents. This domain covers what can be considered the mechanical aspects of prescribing psychotropics—pharmacology, pharmacokinetics, and pharmacodynamics. Acquisition of this knowledge base is not particularly intellectually challenging, and we can easily draw on extant medical models to acquire the basic knowledge requisite to safe provision of psychotropics. The second domain, however, is more ephemeral and intellectually difficult and deals more with the *effectiveness* of prescribing psychotropics. It is not, for highly transparent reasons, the intent of psychology to mimic the medical model in acquiring prescriptive skills, but rather to create a unique model that combines extensive training in assessment and psychotherapeutic intervention with the provision of medications. This uniquely psychological model of pharmacological service provision has been characterized by Newman (2000) as "a systems-oriented, holistic, integrative approach. It presumes a continuum of function and dysfunction, equates health with integrity of function and adaptability, and, to the extent that medication is appropriate, assumes it is but one aspect of treatment" (p. 45). But such an integrative heuristic has been elusive. Calls for a psychologically based, nonmedical approach to psychopharmacology service provision have existed since the dawn of the modern psychopharmacological era (Kubie, 1954). Although the lack of success in producing a guiding integrative theory are primarily a result of the medical–allopathic models' excessive reliance on biological causation, the fact remains that the interplay between psychology and biology in the production and amelioration of mental distress is poorly understood. Greater understanding of this highly complex area provides a challenge to be overcome, but also gives the promise of great advances in understanding and treating mental distress.

Pragmatic and Political Obstacles

Organized medicine is steadfastly opposed to the expansion of the scope of practice of most nonphysician health care providers (Greene, 2001). As would be expected, organized psychiatry is particularly opposed to the acquisition of prescriptive authority by psychologists. Groups representing organized medicine and psychiatry assert that nonphysician prescribing will endanger patients. But available evidence does not support this. In general, nonphysician health care providers achieve equivalent outcomes to physicians when their practices are compared, and are often preferred by patients (Sammons, Paige, & Levant, 2003). In addition, large-scale investigations such as the Institute of Medicine report *To Err Is Human* (IOM, 1999) find that physician medication errors are among the largest causes of patient morbidity, indicating that physicians' medication use provides an uncertain standard by which to gauge the performance of other professions. Decisions expanding a profession's scope of practice are, however, based in politics and not science. Psychology is a young profession that until recently has not seen the need to pursue political as well as academic agendas. The lengthy experience and numerous political successes of organized medicine represent a potent obstacle to successful passage of legislation enabling psychologists to prescribe.

We suggest, however, that the alternative is to become intellectually stagnant and ultimately to be replaced within the health care arena by ongoing developments occurring within the other health care professions. One cannot merely assume that the "best and brightest" of our nation's undergraduates will continue to be attracted to psychology—particularly if the discipline itself loses its fundamental relevance to society. To effectively expand our profession's scope of clinical influence, it is absolutely necessary that we collectively appreciate the magnitude of change that is evolving within the broader health care arena and society at large (DeLeon, Rossomando, & Smedley, 2004). The overwhelming membership vote in May, 2001 to expressly add "health" to the APA mission statement, pursuant to the recommendation of President Johnson, clearly suggests that the grassroots of psychology appreciates the magnitude of change occurring. The efforts referenced earlier by the Board of Directors under Johnson's leadership further suggests that the association's governance is not far behind. We are confident that psychology *will* respond affirmatively to the challenges of the 21st century.

Public Policy Developments

Historically, Americans (including the enlightened leadership of our nation's health and legal systems) have traditionally conceptualized the delivery of health care services as being predominantly, if not exclusively, what we today, as behavioral scientists, would consider "medical care." There was (and unfortunately still remains) a definite stigma associated with receiving mental health care or behavioral health services. Within the judicial system, for example, physical contact, no matter how slight, was an essential requirement for recognizing any trauma—merely witnessing a loved one being horribly injured would not suffice under this definition. The mind–body dualism was, at best, considered an interesting but totally abstract construct.

During President Carter's administration the Surgeon General of the United States released an extraordinarily farsighted document, *Healthy People: The Surgeon General's Report on Health Promotion and Disease Prevention* (U.S. HEW, 1979). To our knowledge, this was the first time within our nation's health policy deliberations that the importance of behavioral health had been raised to the level of presidential consideration. In his receiving statement, the President Carter stated, "I have long advocated a greater emphasis on preventing illness and injury by reducing environmental and occupational hazards and by urging people to choose to lead healthier lives. So I welcome this Surgeon General's Report on Health Promotion and Disease Prevention. It sets out a national program for improving the health of our people—a program that relies on prevention along with cure. This program is ambitious but achievable" (U.S. HEW, 1979, p. v).

Subsequent U.S. Surgeon Generals of both political parties have issued equally impressive follow-up policy documents, one of the most recent being *Healthy People 2010: Understanding and Improving Health* (U.S. DHHS, 2000), which was committed to the single, overarching purpose of promoting health and preventing illness, disability, and premature death. Over the past two decades-plus, the underlying health policy themes voiced at the highest levels by Democratic and Republican administrations have remained consistent: "Over the years, it has become clear that individual health is closely linked to community health—the health of the community and environment in which individuals live, work, and play. Likewise, community health is profoundly affected by the collective behaviors, attitudes, and beliefs of everyone who lives in the community. Indeed, the underlying premise of *Healthy People 2010* is that the health of the individual is almost inseparable from the health of the larger community and that the health of every community in every State and territory determines the overall health status of the Nation. That is why the vision for *Healthy People 2010* is "Healthy People in Healthy Communities" (U.S. DHHS, 2000, p. 3). All of psychology should be excited that the broad behavioral and psychosocial aspects of health care have been recognized at the highest levels of American public policy determination.

The Institute of Medicine

The Institute of Medicine (IOM) has long served as a health policy think tank for various administrations and for the Congress. The IOM was chartered in 1970 by the National Academy of Sciences, acting under the academy's 1863 Congressional charter responsibility to be an advisor to the federal government. In 1982, the IOM released its report *Health and Behavior: Frontiers of Research in the Biobehavioral Sciences* (Hamburg, Elliott, & Parron, 1982). In many ways, this IOM report laid out the foundation for our nation's health policy agenda for the remainder of the century and well into the 21st century.

The document's underlying policy theme, not surprisingly, stressed the importance of integrating the behavioral sciences throughout the nation's health delivery system clinically *and* when designing research protocols and programmatic strategies.

> The heaviest burdens of illness in the United States today are related to aspects of individual behavior, especially long-term patterns of behavior often referred to as "lifestyle." As much as 50 percent of mortality from the 10 leading causes of death in the United States can be traced to lifestyle. . . . One important advance of the twentieth century is recognition that it is possible to employ scientific methods to gain a better understanding of human behavior. The task is difficult and complex, but human behavior can be observed systematically, reliably, and reproducibly. As knowledge progresses, observations can become increasingly quantitative and have considerable predictive power. (Hamburg et al., 1982, pp. 3–4)

From a public policy perspective, there can be no question that this ongoing evolution has provided an extraordinary opportunity for all of psychology. The behavioral sciences *are* the key to the 21st century. However, critical policy questions still remain to be determined, one of which is, How do these evolving and admittedly quite broad and diffuse health policy objectives ultimately become transmitted into the budgetary priorities of our nation, and more specifically, how are they viewed by the National Institutes of Health (NIH)? The NIH has become the premier spokesperson for our nation's vision of world class health care.

A View From Within

Shortly after assuming the position of director of the NIH, Nobel laureate Harold Varmus was quoted as saying that he was trying to "learn more" about the behavioral and social sciences, but admitted that he "didn't find tremendous intellectual stimulation" from some of the research the field had produced (Greenberg, 1999). Advocates for a larger NIH investment in behavioral and social science research were hardly surprised by the statement, because it seemed to reflect the attitudes of many at the NIH that a greater return on research investments could be found in areas such as gene research.

But the tenor of the times at the NIH have changed rapidly since 1993, when Director Varmus made his statement. The NIH now supports a broad range of behavioral and social science research, stimulated in large part by the Congressionally mandated creation of the NIH Office of Behavioral and Social Science Research (OBSSR), which became functionally operational in July 1995. Although a full sea change of attitudes toward the various social and behavioral science disciplines has yet to be achieved in many of the NIH's Institutes and Centers, it is clear that the NIH's leadership has gained a better appreciation that some of the most cost-effective health research—measured in terms of extending and improving the quality of life—can be gained from a better understanding of the behavioral and social underpinnings of health and human behavior. Perhaps the best indication of the improved status of behavioral and social science research can be found in at least three areas of the NIH's research agenda.

First, several NIH Institutes and Centers are collaborating with OBSSR to help develop models of interdisciplinary research and training that are designed to integrate behavioral and social science research with biological levels of analysis. In 1997, OBSSR organized a trans-NIH request for applications that resulted in the development of 10 workshops aimed at stimulating collaboration among young researchers and at improving the quality of biobehavioral research applications. OBSSR has also organized an NIH working group to identify and document successful models of interdisciplinary research.

Second, all of the NIH's Institutes and Centers have developed "strategic plans"—or blueprints for future research—to address racial, ethnic, and socioeconomic health disparities. Each institute has developed plans based on the pressing health disparities in its respective fields or areas of disease research. Strikingly, many of these strategic plans recognize the central role of social and behavioral processes in contributing to health disparities. For example, the NIH is devoting increasing attention to the "socioeconomic gradient"—the fact that health status improves at each step of increasing socioeconomic status—and will likely increase its research efforts in this area.

Third, many of the individual Institutes and Centers at the NIH are developing extensive research programs in the behavioral and social sciences. The National Cancer Institute, for example, supports a large behavioral and social research portfolio via its Division of Cancer Control and Populations Sciences (DCCPS), among other divisions. DCCPS supports cancer surveillance, basic and applied biobehavioral research, prevention (including tobacco control and behavioral risk reduction research), health communication research, and research to better understand how behavioral and emotional states may influence immune response.

A number of factors have spurred this increase in behavioral and social science research at the NIH. OBSSR's first director, Norman Anderson, and his successor, Raynard Kington, skillfully championed a research agenda that has enhanced the NIH's capacity to respond to the nation's need for a greater investment in prevention research and social and behavioral interventions to manage and treat chronic diseases. In the process, they positioned OBSSR as a vital resource for other institutes and centers. External to the NIH, public advocates have played an important role in impressing on Congress the importance of behavioral research to improve the nation's overall health status. Perhaps most important, the quality of behavioral and social science health research and research methodologies have improved significantly over the past two decades, advancing the field and increasing its relevance as a vital tool in health research.

NIH support for behavioral and social science research has also benefited from several recent reports of the Institute of Medicine (IOM). The integration of biobehavioral research and training in the neurosciences, for example, was explored in the IOM report *Bridging Disciplines in the Brain, Behavioral and Clinical Sciences* (Pellmar & Eisenberg, 2000). The 1999 IOM report *The Unequal Burden of Cancer* (Haynes & Smedley, 1999) assessed the quality and scope of NIH cancer research pertaining to minorities and the medially underserved. The IOM concluded that the NIH had yet to take full advantage of the promise of behavioral and social science research to improve cancer prevention and control efforts. In addition, the report's finding that the NIH lacked a blueprint to guide research on the higher incidence of cancer among minorities contributed to the broad directive from the NIH director that all institutes and centers should develop a research agenda to improve minority health.

More recently, several IOM reports have specifically provided guidance on the most promising areas of behavioral and social science health research. The 2000 IOM report *New Horizons in Health: An Integrative Approach* (Singer & Ryff, 2000), which was commissioned by OBSSR to evaluate the potential contributions of behavioral and social science research to the NIH mission and to develop research priorities to complement the work of the Institutes, concluded that "behavioral and psychosocial processes have broad significance and are fundamental to a comprehensive understanding of disease etiology as well as to promotion of health and well-being" (p. 2). Among the 10 priority areas that the report identified for research investment were recommendations to better examine predisease pathways (including the identification of behavioral, biological, psychological, and social factors that affect disease early in the lifespan), social and behavioral factors that contribute to positive health (including factors that contribute to resilience, disease resistance, and wellness), social and environmental factors that shape gene expression; the mechanisms through which socioeconomic hierarchies, racism, discrimination, and stigmatization contribute to health disparities; and the properties of communities and physical environments that affect health and disease outcomes.

Similarly, the 2000 IOM report *Promoting Health: Intervention Strategies From Social and Behavioral Research* (Smedley & Syme, 2000) concluded that a research focus on the generic social and behavioral determinants of disease, injury, and disability is critical to the next wave of public health interventions. The report also urged that interventions use multiple approaches (e.g., behavioral change programs, education, social support, and public policies) applied at multiple levels (e.g., individual, families, communities) simultaneously to fully reap their benefits. These interventions should be targeted to population groups that face similar socioeconomic or social disadvantage, and should involve a variety of sectors that have not traditionally been involved in public health efforts, such as the business community, the media, social service organizations, and other stakeholders.

Challenges to greater federal support for health-related behavioral and social science research remain. *Promoting Health* urged greater support for behavioral and social research to address the fundamental causes of disease but noted that this support suffers from the disease-oriented funding structure at the NIH. The NIH's Institutes and Centers tend to focus on research that can be directly linked to improving prevention and treatment of cancer, diabetes, arthritis, heart disease, and a host of other disorders. Research on behavioral and social factors that may contribute to the development of many of these illnesses—such as stress, risky behavior, inadequate social support, and many other factors—may find little support within a research funding agency that compartmentalizes research by disease areas. What is needed, the *Promoting Health* committee argued, is an additional funding structure organized around behavioral and social risk factors to complement the existing disease orientation. The broad impacts of socioeconomic status and the socioeconomic gradient on health, for example, is an area where both basic and applied social science research is critically needed.

Promoting Health noted that "approximately half of all causes of mortality in the United States are linked to social and behavioral factors such as smoking, diet, alcohol use, sedentary life-style, and accidents. Yet less than 5% of the approximately $1 trillion spent annually on health care in the United States is devoted to reducing risks posed by these preventable conditions" (Smedley & Syme, 2000, p. 1). The NIH *is* increasing its investment in research to address these risks, but clearly the investment remains disproportionally low. Public advocates, behavioral and social scientists, and policy makers must increase their efforts to advance the field and make a most persuasive case that investments in social and behavioral research may reap greater benefits for the nation as a whole than even the dramatic breakthroughs in our understanding of the human genome.

CONCLUSION

We are confident that the profession and discipline of psychology will genuinely flourish as we move deeper into the 21st century. These are extraordinarily exciting times, and the behavioral sciences are the key to providing the highest possible quality of health care to our nation's citizenry (e.g., the psychosocial aspects of health care). Psychology is a relatively young profession. The conceptual movement from being a narrowly defined "mental health specialist" to the broader "behavioral health care provider" has been difficult for many psychologists, in practice and in education. However, there are increasing indications of our collective maturation. As one of the learned professions, psychology continues to attract the best and brightest of undergraduate and graduate students, and there is every reason to expect that this will continue for decades to come. For the field to fulfill its true potential, however, it is necessary that the leadership of the APA, the practice community, and our educational institutions enthusiastically embrace the changes evolving within our health care arena and, equally important, that they come to appreciate the inherent interconnectiveness of practice, education, science, and public interest. As one reflects on the changes occurring within organized psychology and society at large, it becomes evident that the foundation for effective cross-constituency collaboration and a true appreciation for psychology's potential contributions have gradually been evolving over the past several decades. In our judgment, as long as professional psychology continues to address society's pressing concerns, our nation's public officials will respond to our unique needs. Accordingly, we are ultimately in control of our own destiny, and the future remains bright.

REFERENCES

CAPP v. Rank. (1990). 51 Cal. 3d 1, 793.

Croghan, T. W. (2001). Increased spending for antidepressants. *Health Affairs, 20,* 129–135.

DeLeon, P. H., Hagglund, K. J., Ragusea, S. A., & Sammons, M. T. (2003). Expanding roles for psychologists: The 21st century. In G. Stricker & T. A. Widiger (Eds.), *Clinical psychology* (Vol. 8, pp. 551-568). New York: John Wiley & Sons.

DeLeon, P. H., Rossomando, N. P., & Smedley, B. D. (2004). The future is primary care. In R. G. Frank, S. H. McDainiel, J. H. Bray, & M. Heldring (Eds.), *Primary care psychology* (pp. 317–325). Washington, DC: American Psychological Association.

DeLeon, P. H., Sammons, M. T., & Sexton, J. L. (1995). Focusing on society's real needs: Prescription privileges for psychology? *American Psychologist, 50,* 1022–1031.

DeLeon, P. H., & Zimbardo, P. G. (in press). Presidential reflections—Past and future. *American Psychologist.*

Dorken, H., and Associates. (1986). *Professional psychology in transition: Meeting today's challenges.* San Francisco: Jossey-Bass.

Greenberg, D. S. (1999). Hardly an ounce for prevention. *Washington Post,* March 22, 1999, p. 19A.

Greene, J. (2001). AMA backs limits on scope on nonphysician practice. *American Medical News. Retrieved* January 1–8, 2001, from www.ama.-assn.org/sci-pubs/amnews/pic—01/prsb0101.htm

Hamburg, D. A., Elliott, G. R., & Parron, D. L. (1982). *Health and behavior: Frontiers of research in the biobehavioral sciences.* Washington, DC: National Academy Press.

Haynes, M. A., & Smedley, B. D. (Eds.). (1999). *The unequal burden of cancer: An assessment of NIH research and programs for ethnic minorities and the medically underserved.* Washington, DC: National Academy Press.

Institute of Medicine (IOM). (1999). Errors in healthcare. In L. T. Kohn, J. M. Corrigan, & M. S. Donaldson (Eds.), *To err is human: Building a safer health system* (pp. 26–48). Washington, DC: National Academy Press.

Kubie, L. S. (1954). The pros and cons of a new profession: A doctorate in medical psychology. *Texas Reports on Biology and Medicine, 12,* 692–737.

Moncrieff, J. (2001). Are antidepressants overrated? A review of methodological problems in antidepressant trials. *Journal of Nervous and Mental Disease, 189,* 285–295.

Newman, R. (2000). A psychological model for prescribing. *American Psychological Association Monitor on Psychology, 31*(3), 45.

Pellmar, T. C., & Eisenberg, L. (Eds.). (2000). *Bridging disciplines in the brain, behavioral, and clinical sciences.* Washington, DC: National Academy Press.

Sammons, M. T., Paige, R. U., & Levant, R. L. (2003). Prescribing psychologists: The future. In M. T. Sammons, R. U. Paige, & R. L. Levant, (Eds.), *Prescriptive authority: A history and guide* (pp. xi–xxiv). Washington, DC: American Psychological Association.

Singer, B. H., & Ryff, C. D. (Eds.). (2000). *New horizons in health: An integrative approach.* Washington, DC: National Academy Press.

Smedley, B. D., & Syme, S. L. (Eds.). (2000). *Promoting health: Intervention strategies from social and behavioral research.* Washington, DC: National Academy Press.

Street, W. R. (1994). *A chronology of noteworthy events in American psychology.* Washington, DC: American Psychological Association.

Thomas, J. L., & Cummings, J. L. (Eds.). (2000). *The value of psychological treatment: The collected papers of Nicholas A. Cummings.* Phoenix, AZ: Zeig, Tucker, & Theisen.

U.S. Department of Health, Education, and Welfare (U.S. HEW). (1979). *Healthy people: The surgeon general's report on health promotion and disease prevention* (DHEW Pub. No (PHS) 79-55071). Washington, DC: U.S. Government Printing Office.

U.S. Department of Health and Human Services (U.S. DHHS). (2000). *Healthy people 2010: Understanding and improving health.* Washington, DC: U.S. Government Printing Office.

Wright, R. H., & Cummings, N. A. (Eds.). (2001). *The practice of psychology: The battle for professionalism.* Phoenix, AZ: Zeig, Tucker, & Theisen.

13

BEHAVIORAL EPIDEMIOLOGY AND HEALTH PSYCHOLOGY

JALIE A. TUCKER, MARTHA M. PHILLIPS, JAMES G. MURPHY, AND
JAMES M. RACZYNSKI

Health psychologists have been leaders in expanding the settings and scope of practice for psychologists beyond the specialty mental health clinic into a growing range of health care, worksite, organizational, and community settings. Concurrent with this expansion, models and methods of service delivery have necessarily evolved beyond the dominant clinical model of care in the direction of public health approaches, thus forming a more optimal continuum of care that spans specialty mental health, nonspecialty health care, and other community settings. Clinical services for individuals such as psychotherapy have been augmented by an increasingly articulated continuum of interventions that range from individual clinical services to targeted, focused interventions for select risk groups to brief, low-intensity interventions for communities or populations.

In clinical care, individuals who have already developed a problem cross the threshold for specialty care through a variety of referral mechanisms and receive interventions from professional providers that are relatively

Manuscript preparation was supported in part by NIAAA grant no. K02 AA00209 to J. Tucker.

intensive and effective, but costly. Relative to the larger population with problems that could benefit from psychological interventions, the subgroup served by clinical interventions is quite small, largely self-selected, and typically encompasses only problems at the more serious end of the continuum of problem severity (Regier et al., 1993). The reach and impact of clinical services into populations that could benefit are not extensive.

In public health programs, populations or at-risk groups are actively targeted with brief interventions that usually are more preventive than therapeutic. The interventions typically are delivered in nonspecialty settings by trained nonprofessionals using methods that do not involve much personal contact (e.g., using written or videotaped materials; by phone or via the Internet; through media campaigns). At the individual level, public health interventions typically are lower in cost, although less effective than clinical interventions. Because they reach many more people, however, in the aggregate they may be more effective in promoting positive health and mental health changes in the affected population or risk group.

Continued development of a continuum of behavioral health services for the population in need requires that psychologists adopt more of a population sensibility about health, mental health, and other behavioral problems that could be prevented or ameliorated by psychological interventions. Vital to this endeavor is an understanding of the population distribution and dynamics of relevant health and behavioral health problems, as provided by the field of epidemiology and its subspecialty of behavioral epidemiology, which is the focus of this chapter. Key concepts and findings from the discipline of epidemiology are selectively summarized, with an eye toward informing the continued expansion of behavioral health services beyond specialty mental health care and supporting the integration of those services into mainstream health care. In addition to their research acumen, psychologists have unique, comprehensive knowledge and skills concerning mental health disorders, behavior change, theory and measurement of behavior, and the role of behavior in health and disease. By merging this disciplinary base with population-based concepts and methods to study relations among health, disease, and behavior, psychologists can allocate their professional resources across the continuum of need in ways that maximize the impact of their services on the health and behavioral health of the population.

The first section of the chapter is a primer on behavioral epidemiology, written for health psychologists who do not have much expertise on the topic. Similarities and differences in the orienting assumptions, scientific methods, and scope of application are drawn between psychology and behavioral epidemiology, and the reader is introduced to basic concepts, dependent variables, research designs and methods, and measures of association in behavioral epidemiology. The second section elaborates the concept of *risk factors* using coronary heart disease (CHD) and cigarette smoking as examples. CHD is a common medical problem with a substantial behavioral component, and smoking is a common behavioral health problem that is essential to target for disease prevention and management. The final section discusses priority areas to foster cross-disciplinary interactions between health psychology and behavioral epidemiology that span educational, conceptual, and research issues. Future research directions of mutual relevance include research on health and behavioral health services utilization and on behavioral health problems in primary care patient populations. Clinicians typically interact with only a minority of the population with problems, and developing a continuum of behavioral health services that spans clinical and nonclinical settings depends on adopting a population perspective on relations between need, access, and utilization.

BEHAVIORAL EPIDEMIOLOGY

The origins of public health and epidemiology go hand in hand. Regarded as the queen science of public health, epidemiology is the study of the determinants of disease in populations. Behavioral epidemiology is a recently developed subspecialty devoted to understanding the role of behavior and psychological constructs in health and disease at the population level. Health psychology and behavioral epidemiology thus share a common interest in understanding and modifying health/behavior relationships and other psychological factors in disease. They vary, however, in their adoption of a predominantly individual focus in the case of health psychology or a predominantly population perspective in the case of epidemiology, and the corresponding scope and methods of their research and practice vary accordingly.

The origins of epidemiology can be traced to the mid-1800s and classic early studies of infectious disease transmission, such as John Snow's analysis of how cholera was transmitted by contaminated well water in London (Turnock, 1997). Then, as now, epidemiology involves the use of scientific methods to investigate associations between patterns of disease in populations and their putative determinants. Nonexperimental, observational methods are commonly used to assess the strength of association between potential causes of diseases and patterns of disease onset, transmission, and death.

Until quite recently, epidemiology was predominately an observational science and did not routinely use random assignment and independent variable manipulations. Thus, much epidemiological research falls short of the standards for causal inference as typically defined in experimental psychology, and observed relations at the population level cannot be used to predict disease in individuals (Kaplan, 1984). This distinction is critical to understanding the utility and limitations of risk factors for disease, which is a central concept in epidemiology. As discussed later, some epidemiological designs provide stronger support for possible causal inferences than others, and the population level of analysis in epidemiology supports a degree of generalization that is absent in much applied research in psychology.

Until the widespread availability of antibiotics in the mid-20th century, epidemiology primarily involved the study of infectious diseases, then the main sources of morbidity and mortality. The re-emergence of infectious diseases in the late 20th century (e.g., HIV/AIDS, drug-resistant infections) renewed research on the topic, but for most of the second half of the century, much epidemiological research focused on chronic diseases, which have become a significant cause of morbidity and mortality in developed nations. Studying chronic diseases raised new scientific complexities related to (a) assessing associations between potential causes that occurred years before the onset of chronic, often irreversible health problems; and (b) the likelihood that multiple variables operating over different time frames contribute to chronic disease onset, instead of a single pathogen as is the case for most infectious diseases. As discussed later, these features led to innovations in research methods (e.g., case-control designs) and multivariate statistics that are useful for studying relations between health and behavior that are of interest to health psychologists.

The focus on chronic diseases also promoted interest in causes of disease other than pathogens, including environmental, behavioral, and psychological–emotional determinants. Although still not recognized by some traditional epidemiologists, this expanded study of determinants, which include those in which health psychologists have expertise, led to the emergence over the past two decades of a subspecialty dedicated to the study of behavioral determinants of disease known as behavioral epidemiology (e.g., Kaplan, 1984; Mason & Powell, 1985; Sallis, Owen, & Fotheringham, 2000; Sexton, 1979). Published studies of relations between behavior and psychological–emotional constructs and disease first appeared with some regularity in the 1960s, including landmark epidemiological investigations such as the Framingham Heart Study (Dawber, Meadors, & Moore, 1951), Western Collaborative Group Study (Rosenman, Brand, Sholtz, & Friedman, 1976), and the NHANES I Epidemiologic Follow-up Study (Cohen et al., 1987). These and numerous other studies assessed behavioral, lifestyle factors and helped to establish the now widely accepted premise that health status is the result of complex interactions between genetic, physiological, environmental, cognitive, social, behavioral, emotional, and psychosocial factors (Kaplan, 1984).

A second, related feature of behavioral epidemiology is the use of epidemiological research methods to understand behaviors that predict or modify health status, including their determinants and population distribution (Kaplan, 1984; Mason & Powell, 1985; Sallis et al., 2000). As noted by Sallis and colleagues (2000), this information is crucial to developing intervention programs aimed at health promotion and disease prevention and management. By using epidemiological methods to study behavior, information can be obtained about which populations or groups are more or less likely to engage in healthy or harmful behaviors, which factors are associated with expression of health-relevant behaviors, and how factors interact with one another, often in complex ways, to influence those behaviors.

Behavioral epidemiology and health psychology thus share key objectives concerning the identification of behaviors and psychological–emotional factors associated with disease occurrence and outcomes (both mortality and morbidity) and the development of strategies to promote healthy behaviors and to reduce high-risk or harmful behaviors. Like health psychology, behavioral epidemiology is a relative newcomer to the broader field of epidemiology, and recognition of the subspecialty is a recent and continuing development.

Population-Based Concepts in Epidemiology

To fulfill their disciplinary mission to study the occurrence and determinants of disease in populations, epidemiologists have developed concepts, measures, and research designs that may be unfamiliar to psychologists. This section summarizes measures of disease frequency in populations and the central concept of risk factors for disease. The next section describes research designs used to investigate associations between risk factors and disease in populations. The glossary at the end of the chapter summarizes key terms and definitions, which are discussed in the following sections.

Incidence and Prevalence

Incidence is a measure of the rate of disease onset and reflects the number of new cases in a population over a specified interval. Although incidence can be expressed as a simple count (e.g., number of new cases of influenza in January), it commonly is expressed as a rate that incorporates the dimension of time (number of new cases per unit time).

When the population under study is static (i.e., the duration of the period of risk is the same for all individuals in the sample), the incidence rate is calculated as the number of new cases of disease detected during the measurement interval divided by the number of persons in the sample. Many populations, however, are dynamic. Individuals move in and out of the group at risk of developing a disease at different points in time, which results in the interval of risk being different for different members of the population. Under these circumstances, the incidence rate is calculated by dividing the number of new cases of disease detected during the assessment interval by the sum of time at risk across all persons in the population; different individuals thus contribute different amounts of time to the computation of the total incidence rate. In this case, the rate is expressed as the number of new cases of disease per time unit, usually expressed as *person-years* (i.e., 200 cases of cancer per 10,000 person-years).

Prevalence reflects the total number of cases in a population at a single point in time (point prevalence) or over a specified time period (e.g., annual or lifetime prevalence). Prevalence can be expressed as a count of cases (e.g., 100 persons with low back pain in manufacturing plant A) or it can be computed as the number of cases of disease divided by the number of persons in the sample (e.g., 25% of the employees in plant A report low back pain).

Prevalence and incidence are intrinsically related, because prevalence is a function of both the rate of new occurrences (incidence) and the duration of disease. For both incidence and prevalence, only those persons at risk of developing a disease are included in the calculations. For example, calculations of the prevalence of pediatric asthma would include in the denominator only persons 17 years of age or younger. Similarly, in calculating the incidence of breast cancer, calculations would likely include only women in the denominator.

Different diseases have characteristic incidence and prevalence patterns that are meaningful to epidemiologists. For instance, an acute infectious disease with a high mortality rate typically has a high incidence for a short time and a low prevalence, and it may die out quickly because transmission opportunities are limited by its lethal nature (e.g., Ebola infections in Africa). A highly infectious acute infection with a high survival rate will have both a high incidence and prevalence for a longer time until the infection spreads through the population (e.g., influenza). An infectious disease with high mortality and a long survival period provides many transmission opportunities and will show a high prevalence, and incidence will vary with the success of prevention and supportive treatment programs (e.g., HIV/AIDS in the United States).

Risk and Risk Factors

Epidemiologists define risk as the likelihood that individuals who are exposed to a particular factor or have a particular characteristic will develop the disease of interest (Fletcher, Fletcher, & Wagner, 1996). *Risk factors* are those characteristics, behaviors, or circumstances that are associated with an increased risk of disease occurrence. Health psychologists may refer to risk factors as mediators of health status (Kaplan, 1984). *Exposure* to a risk factor indicates that an individual has, before developing a disease, come in contact with or exhibited the factor in question (Fletcher et al.,

1996). Exposure can be a single occurrence (e.g., radiation during one x-ray), involve repeated intermittent occurrences (e.g., sunburns), or entail more or less continuous exposure over variable periods of time (e.g., smoking).

Schemes for classifying risk factors vary, but most fall into one of the following six categories: (a) *genetic* (e.g., race/ethnicity, gender, presence of a specific gene in DNA profile); (b) *physiological/medical* (e.g., hypertension, diabetes, atherosclerosis); (c) *environmental* (e.g., tobacco smoke exposure, poor air quality, proximity to toxic waste); (d) *behavioral* (e.g., dietary fat or alcohol intake, smoking, lack of exercise, failure to use seatbelts); (e) *psychosocial* (e.g., coping skills, depression, lack of social support); or (f) *sociocultural* (e.g., education or income level, geographic region; Kaplan, 1984). Another consideration that affects health status is access to health care and barriers to utilization, which are determined by an array of economic, geographic, social, and behavioral variables. Finally, risk factors can be classified as *modifiable* or *nonmodifiable*. Modifiable behavioral risk factors, like smoking and diet, probably are of greatest interest to health psychologists and behavioral epidemiologists, although understanding the influence of nonmodifiable risk factors also is relevant to developing targeted interventions.

Epidemiological Research Designs and Statistical Considerations

Epidemiologists engage in both experimental and nonexperimental research, although experimental work is a recent development. Common experimental designs include (a) *clinical trials*, in which participants are individually randomized to intervention and control conditions; (b) *field trials*, in which community residents are individually randomized to intervention or control conditions; and (c) *community intervention trials*, in which whole communities or other naturally occurring units (e.g., schools, worksites) are randomized to intervention or control conditions (Rothman & Greenland, 1998). Because experimental designs are familiar to most psychologists, they are not discussed further.

During exploratory research or when interventions are not feasible or appropriate, epidemiologists use nonexperimental or observational study designs, in which groups of individuals are observed without intervention to assess the existence and extent of association between risk factors or exposure and the disease or health outcomes of interest. Three study designs are common in epidemiology: (a) cross-sectional, or prevalence, studies; (b) follow-up, or cohort, studies; and (c) case-control studies. As discussed next and as summarized in Table 13.1, the designs vary in their inclusion criteria and ability to address different research questions, and they have specific advantages and limitations. Measures of frequency and association that each design characteristically yields also are briefly described. Whereas psychologists often use continuous measures, epidemiologists are more likely to use categorical measures of disease and behavior (e.g., disease present–absent, smoker–nonsmoker) and thus must rely on statistics for categorical data, such as chi-square analysis or logistical regression.

Cross-Sectional Studies

These studies are designed to estimate the prevalence of disease in a population and, to a limited degree, to assess associations between disease and risk factors at a single point or interval in time. The sample is chosen without consideration of disease or exposure status and includes all persons in the population or a representative sample of such persons. Thus, it is expected (but not assured) that the sample will include a mix of persons who do and do not have the disease and who have and have not been exposed to the risk factors. Selection bias can be a problem for cross-sectional studies, particularly self-selection bias. For example, if patients can refer themselves for inclusion, persons with the disease may be overrepresented in the sample because of their interest in the topic, which can skew prevalence estimates and measures of association.

Data collection usually occurs once through surveys or record reviews. Information is collected on disease and exposure status and is used to estimate disease prevalence at one point in time. Relationships between risk factors and multiple diseases also can be assessed. Prevalence ratios are calculated by dividing the prevalence of disease in exposed persons by the prevalence of disease in unexposed persons (the reference group). Results typically are expressed as a percentage increase in the presence of disease among exposed persons compared to unexposed persons. Because data typically are collected at a single point in time, temporal relations between exposure and disease cannot be evaluated, which precludes inferences about potential causal relations. Nevertheless, prevalence estimates and measures of association can be compared over time as long as the same methods are used at all measurement points.

Follow-Up (Cohort) Studies

These studies identify a cohort of disease-free individuals and classify them into two groups based on the presence or absence of exposure to risk factors for the disease of interest. The cohort is then followed over time and new occurrences of the disease (incidence) or other health status changes are measured. Because risk factors are measured before outcome variables, temporal relationships between risk factors and outcomes can be evaluated, and these data can support limited inferences about potential causal relationships. Cohort studies can be very expensive, however, because many participants have to be followed over time. They also can be relatively inefficient,

TABLE 13.1

Characteristics of Common Observational Epidemiologic Research Designs

Design	Cross-sectional	Follow-up (cohort)	Case-control
Inclusion criteria for study group selection	Population or representative sample without regard to disease status	Exposed and nonexposed groups who are initially disease free	Groups with and without disease
Primary application	Prevalence estimates; assessment of associations between risk factors and disease	Determination of relative risk of disease due to exposure; more useful when a disease is prevalent or has a short latency to onset	Determination of how exposure to risk factors varies with disease status
Strengths	Can measure multiple diseases and risk factors simultaneously	Can measure multiple diseases; can assess temporal relationships between disease(s) and risk factor(s)	Appropriate for rare diseases; relatively quick results
Limitations	"Snapshot" view of a population; yields only general correlations between risk factors and disease status	Often requires a very large sample and lengthy follow-up to capture sufficient cases of disease for meaningful analysis; subject to attrition	Susceptible to sample bias or non-equivalence of cases and controls on dimensions other than disease status; retrospective data quality problematic
Cost	Variable depending on scope/type of sampling	Relatively expensive	Relatively inexpensive
Significance	Descriptive research useful for characterizing population distributions of disease and risk factors	Yields high quality data to evaluate strength of relations between risk factors and disease	Scientific validity will depend on extent of sample bias; if absent, this is a powerful design to assess risk factor-disease relations

particularly for rare diseases (e.g., birth defects) or when the latency between exposure and disease onset is lengthy (e.g., cancer).

Cohort studies generate incidence rates and estimates of relative risk. When the risk status of individuals in the cohort is static, the *risk ratio*, which compares the risk of developing a disease in the two groups, is calculated by dividing the rate of disease occurrence among the exposed group by the rate of disease among the unexposed group. When the risk status of individuals in the cohort changes over the observation period, the *incidence rate ratio* (incidence rate among the exposed divided by the rate among the unexposed) is used to compare incidence rates across groups. If the disease outcome under study is mortality, then *mortality rates* and *mortality rate ratios* are calculated in the same manner as incidence rates and ratios. All three ratios (risk, incidence rate, and mortality ratios) evaluate whether the group with the risk factor is more or less likely to develop the disease (or die) than the group without the risk factor.

Case-Control Studies

Two groups of individuals are recruited based on their current disease status ("cases" have the disease and "controls" do not), and the exposure status of participants is assessed retrospectively. The design is well-suited for rare diseases and for diseases with long latencies of onset. Case-control studies are relatively inexpensive and efficient and yield rapid results about associations between risk factors and disease.

Despite these advantages, case-control studies are susceptible to error and bias from several sources (Cole, 1980; Rothman & Greenland, 1998). First, risk factors are difficult to measure precisely and without bias after disease has occurred. For example, if exposure is measured by participant recall, then persons with the disease may be more apt to recall possible causes compared to persons who are disease-free. Similarly, if medical records are used to measure exposure, documentation may be more complete or simply different for cases compared to controls. Second, the control group must be carefully selected, so that cases and controls are as comparable as possible, particularly with respect to the possibility of exposure to the risk factors. This is often more difficult than it may seem, and the potential for confounding variables to affect measures of association is not trivial.

The *odds ratio* is the main measure of association in case-control studies and is calculated as the odds of exposure among cases (number of exposed cases/number of unexposed cases) over the odds of exposure among controls (number of exposed controls/number of unexposed controls). An odds ratio of 1.0 indicates that exposure did not differentiate the groups, and deviations from 1.0 must meet statistical criteria for significance for a risk factor to be implicated in disease status; for example, a ratio of 2.0 would indicate that children with leukemia were twice as likely to have been exposed to a toxin of interest compared to healthy children. Note that because participants are purposively recruited based on disease status, case-control studies do not assess prevalence.

Summary of Epidemiological Research Designs and Statistical Considerations

Epidemiological research designs vary in their ability to address certain research questions, have characteristic strengths and limitations, and must be chosen accordingly. Because relations between risk factors and disease are evaluated at the population level, the observed relations do not necessarily hold for particular individuals. Indeed, many individuals who experience an adverse health event have no known risk factors, even though a robust relationship between risk factors and disease exists at the population level. Moreover, support for such relationships from nonexperimental epidemiological designs does not provide unequivocal evidence of causal connections; for example, a positive association between dietary cholesterol and heart disease does not necessarily mean that an individual who eats less food with cholesterol and saturated fat will lower his or her personal risk of disease (Kaplan, 1984). As discussed in the next section, complex relations often exist among risk factors for disease, and other variables that have no direct relation to outcomes may influence or predict the risk factors that have a direct association with outcomes.

UNDERSTANDING HEALTH RISKS: EXAMPLES FROM BEHAVIORAL EPIDEMIOLOGY

This section presents examples of how behavioral risk factors influence disease occurrence and outcomes and interact with other risk factors in complex ways. CHD is presented as an example of a disease with a well-researched, multifactorial etiology including genetic, environmental, and behavioral contributions. CHD research shows (behavioral) epidemiology has helped to untangle these relationships and directs attention to areas that need additional work. Smoking is then discussed to illustrate the role that harmful health behaviors play in disease processes and outcomes and to show how behavioral epidemiology affords opportunities to study the problem behavior itself.

Coronary Heart Disease: Example of a Chronic Disease

CHD is the leading cause of mortality among men and women of all ethnic groups in the United States (AHA, 2000). U.S. rates of CHD are higher than in other industrialized countries (WHO, 1988). CHD develops as plaque builds up in coronary arteries, restricting blood flow to sections of the heart. Acute myocardial infarction (AMI) usually occurs when the blood supply to part of the heart muscle is severely restricted or stopped, because of a blockage in the coronary arteries of someone with CHD. About 1.1 million Americans have an AMI each year, and about a third die (AHA, 2000).

The multiple risk factors for CHD are commonly classified into categories of nonmodifiable (e.g., genetics, demographics), physiological–medical, lifestyle–behavioral, and psychosocial risk factors, although these categories overlap because of etiological interactions across factors. In general, risk factors remain similar as the disease progresses, although physiological factors begin to emerge as stronger predictors of morbidity and mortality as CHD worsens.

Nonmodifiable Risk Factors

Nonmodifiable risk factors include age, gender, ethnicity, and family history. CHD risk increases with age, and older age is associated with changes in behavioral risk factors, including increased weight and decreased activity. About 55% of all AMIs and 80% of fatal AMIs occur among people aged 65 and older (AHA, 2000). Younger men are at greater risk for CHD than younger women, although the risk for postmenopausal women approaches the risk for older men in the absence of hormone replacement therapy. Younger Black individuals also are at greater risk for CHD mortality than younger White individuals. A family history of CHD and certain other medical risk factors for CHD (e.g., hypertension, diabetes) are highly related to CHD risk, and the heritability of CHD is estimated to be about 65% (Emery & Mueller, 1992).

Medical and Physiological Risk Factors

Strong predictors of CHD include hypertension, which affects nearly 25% of U.S. adults (AHA, 2000), and several blood lipids, particularly elevated total cholesterol and elevated low density lipoprotein (LDL) (Bittner & Oparil, 1997; National Heart, Lung, and Blood Institute, NHLBI, 1994). Individuals with diabetes also have an increased AMI incidence, larger sized infarcts (Cohn, 1989), more silent ischemia (Muller et al., 1985), and higher rates of major cardiac complications, such as congestive heart failure (NHLBI, 1994). They are more likely to develop other medical problems that are risk factors for CHD, such as hypertension and dyslipidemia (NHLBI, 1994). Finally, obesity is likely an independent risk factor for CHD (Bild, 1994) and increases risk for other CHD risk factors, including diabetes, hypertension, and high-risk lipid levels (National Institutes of

Health NIH Consensus Development on the Health Implication of Obesity, 1985; Wood, Stefanick, & Williams, 1991).

Lifestyle and Behavioral Risk Factors

Diet, smoking, and inactivity are independent risk factors for CHD, and, as noted earlier, they also affect medical risk factors such as obesity, diabetes, dyslipidemia, and hypertension. CHD risk increases with diets high in cholesterol and certain other fats (NHLBI, 1994) and decreases with consumption of antioxidants (e.g., beta carotene, vitamins C and E), low to moderate amounts of alcohol (Fuchs et al., 1995; Kuller, 1991), and possibly fish oils (NHLBI, 1994). Heavy drinking, however, increases mortality from all causes (Fuchs et al., 1995), and even moderate drinking may increase the risk of hypertension (Klatsky, Friedman, Siegelaub, & Gerard, 1977).

Smoking increases risk of CHD and AMI two- to six-fold (LaCroix, Lang, & Scherr, 1991) and is especially involved in cases that develop before age 55. Women who smoke and use oral contraceptives at the same time increase their risk even more (AHA, 2000; NHLBI, 1994). Physical inactivity appears to be an independent risk factor for CHD (NHLBI, 1994) and for other factors associated with elevated CHD risk, including obesity (e.g., Owens, Matthews, Wing, & Kuller, 1990), hypertension (e.g., Blair, Goodyear, Gibbons, & Cooper, 1984), unfavorable lipid levels (e.g., Leon, 1989), and diabetes (e.g., Helmrich, Ragland, Leung, & Paffenbarger, 1991). Even modest increases in activity may lower CHD risk (Pate et al., 1995).

Psychosocial Risk Factors

Hostility, depression, and low social support are associated with increased CHD risk. The relationship with hostility appears to be stronger among women than men (Helmers et al., 1993). Hostility also may interact with other risk factors to affect CHD risk (Weidner, 1994), including lower education and less social support (Scherwitz, Perkins, Chesney, & Hughes, 1991), negative health behaviors (Houston & Vavak, 1991), and unfavorable lipid profiles (Dujovne & Houston, 1991; Siegler et al. 1990).

Depression at the time of an AMI is predictive of greater cardiac morbidity and mortality, even after adjustment for disease severity (Frasure-Smith, Lesperance, & Talajic, 1993), and low social support is associated with increased mortality (Berkman, Leo-Summers, & Horowitz, 1992). Physiological changes associated with stress have been suggested to contribute to the onset and development of CHD (Williams, 1989), but insufficient evidence exists to regard stress as an established risk factor. Nevertheless, hostility, depression, and stress are all associated with increased catecholamine levels (Barefoot, Haney, Hershkowitz, & Williams, 1991), which increase heart rate and blood pressure. Increased cardiovascular stimulation may, in turn, contribute to the development and worsening of CHD.

The Complexity of Risk Factors: CHD as an Exemplar

In addition to increasing the risk of developing a particular disease, in this case CHD risk factors often influence and interact with one another in ways that affect overall risk. Moreover, the likelihood of developing a given risk factor may be influenced by additional factors that have no direct effect on the disease of interest. These relationships are shown in Figure 13.1 for CHD. The middle panel summarizes known risk factors for CHD. The arrows to the left that interconnect the risk factor boxes represent complex interactions that may occur among independent risk factors. The box to the left represents other variables that predict and influence the independent risk factors for CHD. They have no direct relation to disease outcomes but exert indirect effects through their relation with the CHD risk factors. For example, a high-salt diet increases the risk of hypertension (a CHD risk factor) in some individuals, but it is not an independent risk factor for CHD.

The overall risk of CHD morbidity and morality is thus influenced by direct effects of risk factors, by interactions among the independent risk factors, and by the indirect effects of other variables that affect the risk factors, but have no direct relation with CHD. These pathways of association also apply to many other disease outcomes. They can become quite complex when all of the individual factors and their independent and mediated associations are considered. Although the risk factors and their interactions are probably more thoroughly examined for CHD than for other diseases, the associations and manner in which they influence one another are not completely known even for this disease.

CHD research illustrates how behavioral epidemiology and health psychology can mutually inform and advance one another. In this case, epidemiological research identified numerous behaviors that predict or modify CHD status, including their determinants and population distribution. This information is essential to developing intervention programs aimed at health promotion and disease prevention and management. Health psychology research in turn can inform effective behavior change strategies for health-relevant behaviors, help untangle the complex relations among modifiable and nonmodifiable risk factors, and bring an experimental analysis to bear on those factors that are amenable to manipulation.

Cigarette Smoking: Example of a Harmful Health Behavior

Harmful health behaviors contribute to an array of poor health outcomes. Knowledge of their distribution, risk factors, and determinants is basic

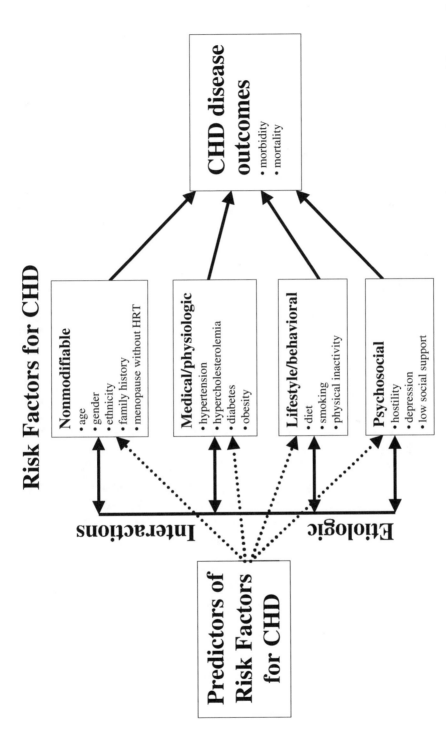

Figure 13.1. Schematic depiction of possible interactions among risk factors for cardiovascular heart disease (CHD) in determining overall risk and disease outcomes. Prediction variables have no independent relationship to CHD outcomes.

to targeting at-risk groups for interventions aimed at health maintenance and disease prevention. This section discusses smoking from a population–public health perspective. Discussion of health behavior change strategies, ranging from individual to community to media and marketplace interventions, is beyond the scope of this chapter.

In terms of morbidity, mortality, and cost, cigarette smoking is the most harmful form of substance misuse. About 48% of U.S. adults have smoked cigarettes at some time, and 23% currently smoke (CDC, 2000). Although overall smoking rates declined in the 1990s, the number of new smokers increased during the same period (Substance Abuse and Mental Health Services Administration [SAMHSA], 2000). Smoking is implicated in 20% of deaths in the United States, accounting for more than twice the number attributable, collectively, to alcohol, motor vehicle accidents, suicide, homicide, AIDS, and other drug-related causes (CDC, 2000).

Smoking has been implicated as a risk factor for many diseases, including cardiovascular disease (including atherosclerosis, AMI, hypertension, CHD, cerebrovascular and peripheral vascular disease), cancers (including cancers of the lung, trachea, bronchus, larynx, pharynx, oral cavity, esophagus, pancreas, kidney, bladder, and cervix), respiratory diseases (e.g., chronic obstructive lung disease, emphysema), and osteoporosis (U.S. Preventive Services Task Force, 1996). In addition, some 25% of residential fires, with resultant property loss, burns, other injuries, and deaths, are attributable to smoking (U.S. Preventive Services Task Force, 1996). Smoking poses special health risks for women as a result of its association with reduced fertility, early menopause, and poor pregnancy outcomes (U.S. DHHS, 1990). Smoking during pregnancy is associated with increased risk of premature birth, low birth weight, perinatal death, and asthma among offspring. Furthermore, smoking in combination with oral contraceptive use increases a woman's risk of vascular complications, such as blood clots (AHA, 2000).

Nonmodifiable Risk Factors

Smoking rates vary by age, gender, and ethnicity. Smoking is more common among men (36%) than women (21%; CDC, 2000), and women are more likely than men to have never smoked (U.S. DHHS, 1998). This pattern holds for all ethnic groups (U.S. DHHS, 1998). Smoking rates are twice as high among adults under age 65 compared to older adults (CDC, 2000). Among teenagers, the prevalence of smoking rose from 12.7% in 1991 to 16.8% in 1999 (CDC, 2000), and initiation is occurring at younger ages (CDC, 1991).

With respect to race and ethnicity, the highest rates of smoking are found among American Indians and Alaskan Natives (37%), and the lowest rates are found among Asian Americans (16%; U.S. DHHS, 1998). Black,

Asian American, and Hispanic smokers tend to smoke fewer cigarettes per day than do their White and Native American counterparts, but White individuals have higher quit rates (U.S. DHHS, 1998).

Medical and Physiological Risk Factors

Nicotine is an addictive substance that enhances the release of neurotransmitters such as acetylcholine, norephinephrine, dopamine, and serotonin (U.S. DHHS, 1998). The pleasurable effects reported by smokers, including arousal, improved vigilance and concentration, relaxation, reduction in stress and anxiety, and hunger reduction, are postulated to be related to the release of these neurotransmitters (Pomerleau & Pomerleau, 1984). Neurotransmitter release is thought to be associated with the initiation and maintenance of smoking before the establishment of physical dependence. Continued daily exposure leads to nicotine tolerance and dependence.

Compared to White smokers, Black smokers have higher cotinine levels, a nicotine metabolite, even after adjustment for number and type of cigarettes smoked per day and other exposure factors (U.S. DHHS, 1998). These findings suggest that differences in nicotine metabolism may influence the development of dependence and affect smoking cessation rates.

Lifestyle and Behavioral Risk Factors

Among adults, smoking is related to education, employment, geographic region, and use of other substances such as alcohol and illicit drugs (SAMHSA, 2000). In the 1999 National Household Survey on Drug Abuse (SAMHSA, 2000), persons with less than a high school education were nearly twice as likely to be smokers as were persons with a college degree. In the same survey, full-time employed persons were less likely to smoke than unemployed peers. Smoking rates varied by region of the country; the Northwest had the lowest rates, and the Southeast had the highest (SAMHSA, 2000).

Because most smokers begin smoking during their teenage years (U.S. DHHS, 1994, 1998), much research on modifiable risk factors for initiation has focused on young people. Youths who have lower school achievement and evidence behavior problems in school are more likely to smoke. Youth smoking also tends to co-occur with other risk-taking behaviors, such as not wearing helmets or seatbelts, using alcohol or other drugs, engaging in unprotected sex, and riding with drivers who may be drinking. Smoking thus appears to be part of a constellation of high-risk behaviors in adolescents.

Psychosocial Risk Factors

Both teenagers and adults report that smoking is used as a coping mechanism to combat boredom, stress, and anxiety. Additional risk factors for smoking among youths include low socioeconomic status, peer pressure to smoke, exposure to other smokers (e.g., family, friends), and poor self-esteem (U.S. DHHS, 1994). Youths who report a belief that smoking is a positive factor in their peer relationships or social image are more likely to smoke than youths who do not endorse such beliefs.

The Complexity of Risk Factors: Smoking as an Exemplar

As with CHD (Figure 13.1), cigarette smoking is likely influenced by direct effects of risk factors, by interactions among the independent risk factors, and by the indirect effects of other variables that affect the risk factors, but have no direct relation with smoking per se. As an example of risk factor interactions, the previously described hypothesized differences in nicotine metabolism between Black and White individuals may influence the development of nicotine dependence and contribute to the variable rates of cessation in these two groups (U.S. DHHS, 1998). More generally, risk factor profiles appear to vary somewhat across different phases of the smoking process, including initiation, maintenance, cessation, and relapse. Pleasurable effects related to neurotransmitter release are likely related to initiation and maintenance, whereas physical dependence becomes a more prominent factor in long-term maintenance of smoking and the outcomes of cessation efforts (Pomerleau & Pomerleau, 1984).

Additional understanding of the epidemiology of initiation, maintenance, cessation, and relapse may enhance the effectiveness of intervention programs. It is interesting to note that about 1.3 million U.S. smokers quit each year, typically without interventions, at a rate of remission higher than for alcohol or other drug misuse (Finney, Moos, & Timko, 1999). Understanding factors that predict success during both programmatic and self-initiated cessation attempts should help guide the development of more effective smoking cessation interventions that span the continua of cost and effectiveness and population impact (cf. Abrams, Clark, & King, 1999).

FUTURE DIRECTIONS IN BEHAVIORAL EPIDEMIOLOGY AND HEALTH PSYCHOLOGY: FOSTERING CROSS-DISCIPLINARY INTERACTIONS

Researchers with a background in health psychology and epidemiology have made substantial contributions to understanding factors that influence disease risk and wellness, and greater fertilization across disciplines holds promise for advancing knowledge and for broadening the scope of research and applications. However, behavioral scientists with expertise in both disciplines are fairly uncommon, and creating opportunities for cross-training should be a priority (National Institute of Mental Health, 2000).

Although both disciplines make the study of behavior in health and disease an explicit and central goal, they have variable, and often complementary, strengths and limitations. For example, behavioral epidemiologists bring breadth, generalizability, and real world relevance to an analysis of health-related issues, whereas health psychologists bring depth, conceptual elegance, experimental methods, and measurement skills. The behavioral epidemiological view thus can help to expand and, on occasion to correct, the limited clinical view of conventional mental health practice and its applied research base. Behavioral epidemiologists, however, may lack the conceptual model-building and measurement skills of psychologists, a limitation apparent in several well-known, longitudinal epidemiological studies of health risk factors. Incorporating psychological theories, such as the transtheoretical model (e.g., Prochaska & DiClemente, 1983) or behavioral economics (e.g., Bickel & Vuchinich, 2000) into health risk models will support greater precision in targeting groups with variable risk profiles with appropriately tailored interventions. In the CHD exemplar discussed previously, epidemiological research helped identify the multitude and nature of modifiable and nonmodifiable risk factors, whereas health psychology research helped provide more in-depth understanding of how relevant environment–behavior relationships can be modified in targeted intervention programs for high risk groups.

In the remainder of the chapter, we discuss two priority areas for future research and practice that have relevance for both disciplines: (a) patterns and determinants of health services utilization, using care-seeking for AMI symptoms as an example; and (b) behavioral health problems in medical patient populations, using depressive symptoms in primary care patients as an example. The topics illustrate how adopting a population perspective on behavioral and psychological phenomena relevant to health status can enhance the provision of services across the population in need.

Influences on Service Utilization: Acute Myocardial Infarction Symptoms as an Example

Understanding the complex set of variables that influence the use of health services is basic to improving proper utilization and, in turn, the quality of care and health outcomes. Some people in need do not use services, others delay utilization, and others present in settings that are not well-suited for their problem. Furthermore, the subset seen by clinicians is rarely representative of the larger population with problems and tends to include an excess proportion of more serious cases.

Lack of health insurance, which covaries with socioeconomic status and race, is a serious impediment to care-seeking. However, the influential variables extend far beyond economic considerations to include social and behavioral variables (Tucker & Davison, 2000; U.S. DHHS, 1999). For example, seeking care is positively related to impairment in daily functioning, often more so than to objective measures of disease severity or health status. In addition, social network responses about the need for help and where to obtain it heavily influence patterns of care-seeking, often more so than financial and geographic barriers to care.

To illustrate these complex relations, we consider research on care-seeking following the onset of symptoms of AMI. Rapid help-seeking, even when symptoms are ambiguous, promotes better health outcomes and averts monetary costs because of the increased morbidity and mortality that results from delayed care. Specifically, reperfusion therapies based on thrombolytic medications, or mechanically through methods such as angioplasty, can substantially reduce morbidity and mortality when treatment is initiated within the first few hours of symptom onset. The same is true for strokes caused by blood clots. However, delays in seeking treatment are often unacceptably long, resulting in most patients being ineligible for reperfusion therapies.

Several factors that influence the rapidity of care-seeking after the onset of AMI symptoms have been identified (Dracup et al., 1995; Raczynski et al., 1999), of which some are amenable to psychological and behavioral interventions. Older adults, females, Black individuals, and—although not consistently—persons of lower socioeconomic status and those without insurance tend to have longer delays. Acute chest pain prompts more rapid help-seeking compared to slowly developing, diffuse symptoms, and symptoms tend to differ by age, gender, and ethnicity; for example, women are less likely to have classic symptoms or to consider themselves at risk. Attributing symptoms to noncardiac sources is associated with longer delays, whereas believing that CHD is preventable is associated with shorter delays. Longer delays also are associated with being at home during symptom onset or traveling home afterward; having family members as opposed to nonfamily members present; and attempting to cope with symptoms or to contact a physician.

Although some symptoms provide clear cues for action, seeking care for AMI symptoms is interesting from a behavioral perspective in that it occurs with little or no learning history or behavioral rehearsal. Research on predictors of AMI delay suggests the importance of educating people to attribute appropriate symptoms to possible AMI and to seek medical care immediately. To address this issue, in 1991 the NHLBI initiated the National Heart Attack Alert Program (NHAAP), which focused on promoting prompt assessment and treatment of AMI symptoms in emergency departments (Dracup et al., 1997). Thereafter, the Rapid Early Action for Coronary Treatment (REACT) trial was initiated to help develop effective public education programs to reduce delays in hospital care-seeking for AMI symptoms. This four-year randomized trial evaluated a multicomponent intervention to reduce patient delays (e.g., Raczynski et al., 1999) and differs from other CHD risk reduction programs in focusing on care-seeking for an acute event rather than on changing risk factors related to repetitive lifestyle behaviors.

The core intervention message in the REACT trial focused on symptom identification and plans for action. Because bystanders and family members influence care-seeking, both were targeted in the message. Results suggested that patients and families would benefit from interventions to promote realistic expectations about AMI symptoms, including correcting misperceptions that severe and crippling pain is typical of AMIs; planning for AMI symptoms; building confidence in symptom attribution; and the benefits of calling 911 to obtain medical assistance rather than providing transport themselves. Intervention and control communities both showed reductions in delays, but only the intervention communities showed a significant increase in the use of emergency medical services (Luepker, Raczynski, Osganian, et al., 2000).

The REACT project speaks to the complexities involved in patterns and determinants of care-seeking. This area is in need of greater involvement by behavioral epidemiologists and health psychologists because many of the influential variables are behavioral. For example, behavioral epidemiologists can continue to facilitate knowledge about patterns of care-seeking and potentially modifiable variables in the health care system involved in rapid cardiac care. Health psychologists can address the complex psychological and behavioral process that are involved in the care-seeking decisions of symptomatic persons and their social network members.

Behavioral Health Problems in Medical Patient Populations

Comorbid relations between medical and psychological problems have long been a focus of health psychology, and recent constraints imposed by managed care organizations on access to specialty behavioral health care continue to move patients with such problems into primary care settings. Thus, understanding the distribution of and risk factors for psychological and behavioral problems in primary care populations has grown in significance.

Such problems are common but can be difficult to diagnosis and treat because many primary care patients do not self-identify. Nevertheless, most people (60–75%) who seek help for psychological symptoms turn first to primary care (Ustun, 2000). The chief complaint of about 60% of primary care patients has a psychological or behavioral basis (Kroenke & Mangelsdorff, 1989), although only a subset meet all diagnostic criteria for a mental disorder. For example, Pini, Perkonnig, Tansella, and Wittchen (1999) found that 12.4% of primary care patients met all criteria for a mental disorder, and an additional 14.2% reported subthreshold symptoms. Depressive (6.7%), anxiety (5.8%), and alcohol-related (3.1%) problems were most common.

Primary care physicians are less than optimal diagnosticians for behavioral health disorders (Borowsky et al., 2000; Pini et al., 1999). For example, in the Medical Outcomes Study, primary care physicians correctly identified 59% of major depressive cases, 56.5% of dysthymic cases, and 46.5% of cases of subthreshold depression (Borowsky et al., 2000). Detection rates were lower for patients who were Black, Hispanic, or under age 35, and were higher for females, older patients, and patients with diabetes or hypertension. Accuracy was better among younger physicians and those with a proclivity for providing mental health counseling. When behavioral health problems are detected, many primary care physicians are poorly equipped to manage them; for example, they have little relevant education, are pressed for time, or patients' access to specialty mental health services is limited in their insurance plans.

Assessment and management of harmful health behaviors are similarly limited in primary care settings. For example, among patients who had a physical last year, only 77% were asked about smoking, 56% about exercise, and 50% about diet (Nawaz, Adams, & Katz, 2000). Diet or exercise queries were relatively independent of risk status but had a positive effect on behavior. Asking about smoking, however, had no effect on cessation, which suggests the need for additional research on physician-facilitated behavior change.

Depressive symptoms are especially instructive about the complex relations between psychological and medical disorders, including relations with care-seeking. Nearly half (48%) of people who receive an intervention for depression are treated by primary care physicians (Narrow, Regier, Rae, Manderschied, & Locke, 1993), who write most of the prescriptions for antidepressant medications. In the general population, 20% to 30% of adults experience subthreshold depressive symptoms (Wells, Stewart, & Hayes, 1989; Zerbe, 1999), which may remit without interventions. Major depression, the most severe form of the disorder, is less common (4–10%; Kessler et al., 1994) but tends to recur—50% of persons who have had one major depressive episode will have another, and 70% who have had two episodes will have a third (Arean, McQuaid, & Munoz, 1997). Thus, monitoring medical patients who have a history of major depression is a priority (Whooley & Simon, 2000). However, only 33% of depressed individuals seek treatment, and even fewer (16–23%) present for specialty mental health care (Regier et al., 1993). Patients who use specialty mental health care for depression tend to be White, female, single, and well-educated (Wells et al., 1989).

Risk factors for depression include a positive family history, female gender, younger age, substance abuse, other medical problems, stressful life events, and low social support. For example, the lifetime prevalence of major depression in women is 21%, almost twice that of men (13%; Kessler et al., 1994). Depression is more prevalent among younger adults (ages 25–34), lower socioeconomic groups, and among Black compared to White individuals. Black individuals also tend to report relatively more somatic and fewer affective symptoms.

Depression is comorbid with many medical disorders and often leads to poor medical outcomes (Stevens, Merikangas, & Merikangas, 1995). Differential diagnosis can be complicated because many depressive symptoms involve changes that can be caused by physical diseases (e.g., hypothyroidism, CHD, dementia). From 12% to 36% of medical outpatients and 33% of inpatients meet criteria for a depressive disorder. Depression is particularly likely to co-occur with cancer, CHD, migraine, epilepsy, Parkinson's disease, multiple sclerosis, and Huntington's disease (Stevens et al., 1995). When depression and medical problems co-occur, the negative effects on functioning tend to be additive (Wells et al., 1989). Furthermore, depressed patients experience functional impairment and decreased subjective well-being comparable to or greater than patients with chronic medical conditions (e.g., CHD, diabetes, hypertension, angina, arthritis, peptic ulcer, and lung disease). Only patients with advanced coronary artery disease are relatively more impaired. Depression also is associated with heightened risk of suicide attempts and completions (Arean et al., 1997).

Finally, depressed patients are a substantial economic burden in primary care settings (Zerbe, 1999). The average annual primary care cost associated with depressed patients ($4,246) is almost double that of nondepressed patients ($2,371). The majority (80%) of the cost for depressed patients is for medical rather than for psychiatric care. Including behavioral health services in primary care and covering them in comprehensive health plans tends to reduce the utilization and cost of medical services (Campbell et al., 2000; Glabbard, Lazar, Hornberger, & Spiegel, 1997).

These findings collectively point to challenges and opportunities in today's health care environment with respect to detecting and managing behavioral health problems. The boundaries between medical and behavioral health care populations continue to blur. Behavioral epidemiologists can monitor the shifting distributions of treatment-seeking and general populations and the risk factors for the different disorders. This information is basic to intervention development and delivery at multiple levels, ranging from individual treatment to modification of relevant features of the health care system to changes in health plan reimbursement policies.

CONCLUSION

The complex relations between health, disease, behavior, and psychological disorders provide compelling arguments for greater inclusion of behavioral scientists with expertise in behavioral epidemiology and health psychology. Historically, the practice of psychology was grounded in the specialty mental health clinic, and this reality has shaped professional and research priorities in directions that are not well synchronized with population base rates of psychological and behavioral disorders, including in health care populations. An overarching theme of the chapter is that the professional resource allocation, reach, and effectiveness of health psychology can be enhanced by adopting a population sensibility on these relations.

When intervention and applied research opportunities are viewed from a population perspective, many new directions are suggested that make use of psychologists' unique knowledge and skills in assessment, behavior change, theoretical model-building, and research, in combination with epidemiological methods and concerns. Central among these are (a) incorporating psychosocial and behavioral factors into models of and research on health and disease; (b) continuing to develop and apply theory-based interventions to facilitate behavior patterns that promote and maintain health across a broader segment of the population than presents in clinical settings; and (c) aligning professional resources and attention to a greater extent with population base rates of disease, risk factors, health-relevant behaviors, and care-seeking patterns. The potential salutary effects on population health status of expanding health psychology in these ways are considerable, and doing so will require moving beyond a clinical model of care and adopting a population perspective on health, disease, behavior, systems of care, and relations among them.

GLOSSARY

Incidence: Number of new cases of disease in a population that occurs within a specified period of time; commonly expressed as a rate (# new cases per unit time).

Prevalence: Total number of cases of disease in a population at a single point in time (point prevalence) or over a specified time period (e.g., annual or lifetime prevalence); usually expressed as a proportion (percentage).

Person years: Unit of measurement used in expressing incidence rates that takes into account the differing periods of time that individuals may be at risk for disease occurrence within an observation period.

Risk: Likelihood that individuals who are exposed to a given factor (e.g., infectious agent) or have a given characteristic (e.g., genetic marker) will develop a given disease.

Risk factor: Characteristics, behavior, or circumstances associated with increased risk of disease occurrence; risk factors may be modifiable (e.g., behavior patterns, exposure to harmful environmental agents) or nonmodifiable (e.g., age, gender, genetic characteristics, country of origin).

Exposure: When an individual has had contact with or exhibited a given risk factor before disease onset; exposure may be a single occurrence, intermittent, or continuous.

Risk ratio: Measure of association in cohort studies when the risk status of persons in the cohort is static during the observation period; calculated by dividing the rate of disease occurrence among the exposed group by the rate among the unexposed group.

Incidence rate ratio: Measure of association in cohort studies when the risk status of persons in the cohort varies during the observation period; calculated by dividing the incidence rate among the exposed by the incidence rate among the unexposed.

Odds-ratio: Measure of association in case-control studies; calculated as the odds of exposure among cases (number of exposed cases/number of unexposed cases) divided by the odds of exposure among the controls (number of exposed controls/number of unexposed controls).

Note. These terms are used in text and are set in italic type at first mention.

REFERENCES

Abrams, D. B., Clark, M. M., & King, T. (1999). Increasing the impact of nicotine dependence treatment: Conceptual and practical considerations in a stepped-care plus treatment-matching approach. In J. A. Tucker, D. M. Donovan, & G. A. Marlatt (Eds.), *Changing addictive behavior: Bridging clinical and public health strategies* (pp. 307–330). New York: Guilford Press.

American Heart Association (AHA). (2000). *2001 heart and stroke statistical update.* Dallas, TX: American Heart Association.

Arean, P. A., McQuaid, J., & Munoz, R. F. (1997). Mood disorders: Depressive disorders. In S. M. Turner & M. Herson (Eds.), *Adult psychopathology and diagnosis* (3rd ed., pp. 230–255). New York: Wiley.

Barefoot, J. C., Haney, T. L., Hershkowitz, B. D., & Williams, R. B. (1991, March). *Hostility and coronary artery disease in women and men.* Paper presented at the annual meeting of the Society of Behavioral Medicine, Washington, DC.

Berkman, L. F., Leo-Summers, L., & Horowitz, R. I. (1992). Emotional support and survival after myocardial infarction: A prospective, population-based study of the elderly. *Annals of Internal Medicine, 117,* 1003–1009.

Bickel, W. K., & Vuchinich, R. E. (Eds.). (2000). *Reframing health behavior change with behavioral economics* (pp. 219–264). Mahwah, NJ: Erlbaum.

Bild, D. E. (1994). Overview of cardiovascular disease risk factors in women. In S. M. Czajkowski, D. R. Hill, & T. B. Clarkson (Eds.), *Women, behavior, and cardiovascular disease* (NIH Publication No. 94–3309). Washington, DC: U.S. Department of Health and Human Services.

Bittner, V., & Oparil, S. (1997). Hypertension. In D. G. Julian & N. K. Wenger (Eds.), *Women and heart disease* (pp. 299–327). London: Martin Dunitz.

Blair, S. N., Goodyear, N. N., Gibbons, L. W., & Cooper, K. H. (1984). Physical fitness and incidence of hypertension in healthy normotensive men and women. *Journal of American Medical Association, 252,* 487–490.

Borowsky, S. J., Rubenstein, L. V., Meredith, L. S., Camp, P., Jackson-Triche, M., & Wells, K. B. (2000). Who is at risk for nondetection of mental health problems in primary care? *Journal of General Internal Medicine, 15,* 381–388.

Campbell, T. L., Franks, P., Fiscella, K., McDaniel, S. H., Zwanziger, J., Mooney, C., et al. (2000). Do physicians who diagnose more mental health disorders generate lower health care costs? *Journal of Family Practice, 49,* 305–310.

Centers for Disease Control and Prevention (CDC). (1991). Difference in age of smoking initiation between Blacks and Whites—United States. *Morbidity and Mortality Weekly Report, 40,* 754–775.

Centers for Disease Control and Prevention (CDC). (2000). Comparative causes of annual deaths in the United States. *Tobacco Information and Prevention Service (TIPS)*. Atlanta, GA: Author.

Cohen, B. B., Barbano, H. E., & Cox, C. S., Feldman, J. J., Finucane, F. F., Kleinman, J. C., et al. (1987). Plan and operation of the NHANES I epidemiologic followup study: 1982–84. *Vital and Health Statistics—Series 1: Programs and Collection Procedures, 22,* 1–142.

Cohn, J. N. (1989). Sympathetic nervous system activity and the heart. *American Journal of Hypertension, 2,* 353S–356S.

Cole, P. (1980). The analysis of case-control studies (Introduction). In N. E. Breslow & N. E. Day (Eds.), *Statistical methods in cancer research* (Vol. 1, pp. 14–40). Lyon, France: World Health Organization.

Dawber, T. R., Meadors, G. F., & Moore, Jr., F. E. (1951). Epidemiological approaches to heart disease: the Framingham study. *American Journal of Public Health, 41,* 279–286.

Dracup, K., Alonzo, A. A., Atkins, J. M., Bennett, N. M., Braslow, A., Clark, L. T., et al. (1997). The physician's role in minimizing prehospital delay in patients at high risk for acute myocardial infarction: Recommendations from the National Heart Attack Alert Program. *Annals of Internal Medicine, 126,* 645–651.

Dracup, K., Moser, D. K., Eisnberg, R. J., Fore, J. M., Meischke, H., Alonzo, A. A., et al. (1995). Causes of delay in seeking treatment for heart attack symptoms. *Social Science Medicine, 40,* 379–392.

Dujovene, V. F., & Houston, B. K. (1991). Hostility-related variables and plasma lipid levels. *Journal of Behavioral Medicine, 14,* 555–565.

Emery, A. E. H., & Mueller, R. F. (1992). *Elements of medical genetics* (8th ed.). Edinburgh: Churchill Livingstone.

Finney, J. W., Moos, R. H., & Timko, C. (1999). The course of treated and untreated substance use disorders: Remission and resolution, relapse and mortality. In

B. S. McCrady, & E. E. Epstein (Eds.), *Addictions: A comprehensive guidebook* (pp. 30–49). New York: Oxford University Press.

Fletcher, R. H., Fletcher, S. W., & Wagner, E. H. (1996). *Clinical epidemiology: The essentials.* Baltimore: Williams & Wilkins.

Frasure-Smith, N., Lesperance, F., & Talajic, M. (1993). Depression following myocardial infarction: Impact on 6-month survival. *Journal of the American Medical Association, 270,* 1819–1825.

Fuchs, F. C., Stampfer, M. J., Colditz, G. A., Giozannucci, E. L., Manson, J. E., Kawachi, I., et al. (1995). A prospective study of alcohol consumption and mortality among women. *New England Journal of Medicine, 332,* 1245–1250.

Glabbard, G. O., Lazar, S. G., Hornberger, J., & Spiegel, D. (1997). The economic impact of psychotherapy: A review. *American Journal of Psychiatry, 154,* 147–155.

Helmers, K. F., Krantz, D. S., Howell, R. H., Klein, J., Bairey, C. N., & Rozanski, A. (1993). Hostility and myocardial ischemia in coronary artery disease patients: Evaluation by gender and ischemic index. *Psychosomatic Medicine, 55,* 29–36.

Helmrich, S. P., Ragland, D. R., Leung, R. W., & Paffenbarger, R. S. (1991). Physical activity and reduced occurrence of non-insulin-dependent diabetes mellitus. *New England Journal of Medicine, 325,* 147–152.

Houston, B. K., & Vavak, C. R. (1991). Cynical hostility: Developmental factors, psychological correlates, and health behaviors. *Health Psychology, 10,* 9–17.

Kaplan, R. M. (1984). The connection between clinical health promotion and health status: A critical overview. *American Psychologist, 39,* 755–765.

Kessler, R. C., McGonagle, K. A., Zhao, S. A., Nelson, C. B., Hughes, M., Eshleman, S., et al. (1994). Lifetime and 12-month prevalence of *DSM–III–R* psychiatric disorders in the U.S.: Results from the National Comorbidity Study. *Archives of General Psychiatry, 51,* 8–19.

Klatsky, A. L., Friedman, G. D., Siegelaub, A. B., & Gerard, M. J. (1977). Alcohol consumption and blood pressure: Kaiser-Permanente multiphasic health examination data. *New England Journal of Medicine, 296,* 1194–2000.

Kroenke, K., & Mangelsdorff, D. (1989). Common symptoms in ambulatory care: Incidence, evaluation, therapy and outcome. *American Journal of Medicine, 86,* 262–266.

Kuller, L. H. (1991). Epidemiologic data. Proceedings of interdepartmental dean's conference. Alcohol and atherosclerosis. *Annals of Internal Medicine, 114,* 967–976.

LaCroix, A. Z., Lang, J., & Scherr, P. (1991). Smoking and mortality among older men and women in three communities. *New England Journal of Medicine, 324,* 1619–1625.

Leon, A. S. (1989). Effects of physical activity and fitness on health. In *National Center for Health Statistics, Assessing physical fitness and physical activities in population-based surveys* (DHHS Publication No. PHS 89-1253). Hyattsville, MD: U.S. Department of Health and Human Services.

Luepker, R. V., Raczynski, J. M., Osganian, S., Goldberg, R. J., Finnegan, J. R., Jr., Hedges, J. R., et al. (2000). Effect of a community intervention on patient delay and emergency medical service use in acute coronary heart disease: The Rapid Early Action for Coronary Treatment (REACT) Trial. *Journal of the American Medical Association, 284*, 60–67.

Mason, J. O., & Powell, K. E. (1985). Physical activity, behavioral epidemiology, and public health. *Public Health Reports, 100*, 113–115.

Muller, J. E., Stone, P. H., Turi, Z. G., Rutherford, J. D., Czeisler, C. A., Parker, C., et al. (1985). Circadian variation in the frequency of onset of acute myocardial infarction. *New England Journal of Medicine, 313*, 1315–1322.

Narrow, W. E., Regier, D. A., Rae, D. S., Manderscheid, R. W., & Locke, B. A. (1993). Use of services by persons with mental and addictive disorders. *Archives of General Psychiatry, 50*, 95–107.

National Heart, Lung, and Blood Institute (NHLBI). (1994). *Report of the task force on research in epidemiology and prevention of cardiovascular diseases.* Washington, DC: U.S. Department of Health and Human Services.

National Institute of Mental Health. (2000, November). *Research on mental disorders: Overcoming barriers to collaborations between basic behavioral scientists and public health scientists.* Bethesda, MD: Author.

National Institutes of Health Consensus Development Panel on the Health Implications of Obesity. (1985). Health implications of obesity: National Institutes of Health Consensus Development Conference statement. *Annals of Internal Medicine, 103*, 1073–1077.

Nawaz, H., Adams, M. L., & Katz, D. L. (2000). Physician–patient interactions regarding diet, exercise, and smoking. *Preventive Medicine, 31*, 652–657.

Owens, J. F., Matthews, K. A., Wing, A. L., & Kuller, L. H. (1990). Physical activity and cardiovascular risk: A cross-sectional study of middle-aged premenopausal women. *Preventive Medicine, 19*, 147–157.

Pate, R. R., Pratt, M., Blair, S. N., Haskell, W. L., Macera, C. A., Bouchard, C., et al. (1995). Physical activity and public health: A recommendation from the Centers for Disease Control and Prevention and the American College of Sports Medicine. *Journal of the American Medical Association, 273*, 402–407.

Pini, S., Perkonnig, A., Tansella, M., & Wittchen, H. U. (1999). Prevalence and 12-month outcome of threshold and subthreshold mental disorders in primary care. *Journal of Affective Disorders, 56*, 37–48.

Pomerleau, O. F., & Pomerleau, C. S. (1984). Neuroregulators and the reinforcement of smoking: Towards a biobehavioral explanation. *Neuroscience and Biobehavioral Reviews, 8*, 503–513.

Prochaska, J. O., & DiClemente, C. C. (1983). Stages and processes of self-change in smoking cessation: Toward an integrated model of change. *Journal of Consulting and Clinical Psychology, 51*, 390–395.

Raczynski J. M., Finnegan J. R., Zapka J. G., Meischke H., Meshack A., Stone E. J., et al. (1999). REACT theory-based intervention to reduce treatment-seeking delay for acute MI. *American Journal of Preventive Medicine, 16*, 325–224.

Regier, D. A., Narrow, W. E., Rae, D. S., Manderscheid, R. W., Locke, B. Z., & Goodwin, R. K. (1993). The de facto U.S. mental and addictive disorders service system. *Archives of General Psychiatry, 50*, 85–94.

Rosenman, R. H., Brand, R. J., Sholtz, R. I., & Friedman, M. (1976). Multivariate prediction of coronary heart disease during 8.5-year follow-up in the Western Collaborative Group Study. *American Journal of Cardiology, 37*, 903–910.

Rothman, K. J., & Greenland, S. (1998). *Modern epidemiology*. Philadelphia: Lippincott-Raven.

Sallis, J. F., Owen, N., & Fotheringham, M. J. (2000). Behavioral epidemiology: A systematic framework to classify phases of research on health promotion and disease prevention. *Annals of Behavioral Medicine, 22*, 294–298.

Scherwitz, L., Perkins, L., Chesney, M., & Hughes, G. (1991). Cook-Medley Hostility Scale and subscales: Relationship to demographic and psychosocial characteristics in CARDIA. *Psychosomatic Medicine, 53*, 36–49.

Sexton, M. M. (1979). Behavioral epidemiology. In O. F. Pomerleau & J. P. Brady (Eds.), *Behavioral medicine: Theory and practice* (pp. 3–21). Baltimore: Williams & Wilkens.

Siegler, I. C., Peterson, B. L., Barefoot, J. C., Dahlstrom, W. G., Suarez, E. C., & Williams, R. B. (1990). Hostility levels at age 19 predict lipid risk profiles at age 42. *Circulation, 82*(Suppl. III), III228.

Stevens, D. E., Merikangas, K. R., & Merikangas, J. R. (1995). Comorbidity of depression and other medical conditions. In E. E. Beckham & W. R. Leber (Eds.), *Handbook of depression* (2nd ed., pp. 147–199). New York: Guilford Press.

Substance Abuse and Mental Health Services Administration (SAMHSA). (2000). *National household survey on drug abuse main findings, 1999*. Rockville, MD: Author.

Tucker, J. A., & Davison, J. W. (2000). Waiting to see the doctor: The role of time constraints in the utilization of health and behavioral health services. In W. K. Bickel & R. E. Vuchinich (Eds.), *Reframing health behavior change with behavioral economics* (pp. 219–264). Mahwah, NJ: Erlbaum.

Turnock, B. J. (1997). *Public health: What it is and how it works*. Gaithersburg, MD: Aspen.

U.S. Department of Health and Human Services. (1990). *The health benefits of smoking cessation* (DHHS publication no. (CDC) 90–8416). Rockville, MD: Author.

U.S. Department of Health and Human Services. (1994). *Preventing tobacco use among young people: A report of the Surgeon General*. Atlanta, GA: U.S. Department of Health and Human Services, Centers for Disease Control and Prevention, National Center for Chronic Disease Prevention and Health Promotion, and Office on Smoking and Health.

U.S. Department of Health and Human Services. (1998). *Tobacco use among U.S. racial/ethnic minority groups: a report of the Surgeon General.* Atlanta, GA: U.S. Department of Health and Human Services, Centers for Disease Control and Prevention, National Center for Chronic Disease Prevention and Health Promotion, and Office on Smoking and Health.

U.S. Department of Health and Human Services. (1999). *Mental health: A report of the Surgeon General.* Rockville, MD: Department of Health & Human Services, Substance Abuse & Mental Health Services Administration, Center for Mental Health Services, National Institutes of Health, and National Institute of Mental Health.

U.S. Preventive Services Task Force. (1996). *Guide to clinical preventive services* (2nd ed.). Baltimore: Williams & Wilkins.

Ustun, T. B. (2000). Mainstreaming mental health. *Bulletin of the World Health Organization, 78*(4), 412.

Weidner, G. (1994). The role of hostility and coronary-prone behaviors in the etiology of cardiovascular disease in women. In S. M. Czajkowski, D. R. Hill, & T. B. Clarkson (Eds.), *Women, behavior, and cardiovascular disease* (NIH Publication No. 94–3309, pp. 103–116). Washington, DC: U.S. Department of Health and Human Services.

Wells, K. B., Stewart, A., & Hayes, R. D. (1989). The functioning and well-being of depressed patients: Results of the Medical Outcomes Study. *Journal of the American Medical Association, 262,* 914–919.

Whooley, M. A., & Simon, G. E. (2000). Managing depression in medical outpatients. *New England Journal of Medicine, 343,* 1942–1950.

Williams, R. B., Jr. (1989). Biological mechanisms mediating the relationship between behavior and coronary heart disease. In A. W. Siegman & T. M. Dembroski (Eds.), *In search of coronary-prone behavior* (pp. 195–205). New York: Erlbaum.

Wood, P. D., Stefanick, M. I., Williams, P. T., & Haskell, W. L. (1991). The effects of plasma lipoproteins of a prudent weight-reducing diet, with or without exercise, in overweight men and women. *New England Journal of Medicine, 325,* 461–466.

World Health Organization (WHO). (1988). Geographical variation in the major risk factors of coronary heart disease in men and women aged 35–64 years. The WHO MONICA Project. *World Health Statistics Quarterly, 41,* 115–140.

Zerbe, K. J. (1999). *Women's mental health in primary care.* Philadelphia: Sounders.

14

THE ROLE OF BEHAVIORAL FACTORS IN ACHIEVING NATIONAL HEALTH OUTCOMES

C. TRACY ORLEANS, CHERYL C. ULMER, AND JESSIE C. GRUMAN

There is growing recognition of health-related behaviors and lifestyle factors in fostering individual and national health. In a landmark study, McGinnis and Foege (1993) reported that approximately 50% of all mortality from the 10 leading causes of death is linked to tobacco use, unhealthy diet, sedentary lifestyle, alcohol and drug abuse, and risky sexual practices related to transmission of HIV/AIDS. *Healthy People 2010*, an articulation of national health objectives, recognized the public health burden these behaviors impose (U.S. Department of Health and Human Services [DHHS], 2000a).

Unfortunately, psychologists are rarely involved in the assessment and implementation of health goals. This chapter illuminates opportunities for psychologists as we review the impact of health-related behaviors on morbidity and mortality in the United States and examine trends for selected *Healthy People 2010* measures, lay out why this is an opportune time for pressing behavioral and lifestyle issues, present theoretical and scientific advances that allow us to make real progress in shaping healthy behaviors and preventing or changing health-damaging ones, and outline next steps in the research and practice of health behavior change.

465

SCOPE OF THE PROBLEM AND NATIONAL GOALS

Through lifestyle health risks and nonadherence with medical recommendations, health behavior plays a role in the onset, progression, and management of many diseases. Given the overarching goals of *Healthy People 2010* to promote longer, healthier lives and to eliminate health disparities, it is not surprising that half of the leading health indicators tracked in the initiative relate to tobacco use, diet, physical exercise, alcohol and drug abuse, and risky sexual practices. Trend data for these health objectives show that much work remains to be done and that these health behaviors present some of the major research, practice, and public health policy opportunities for psychologists in the 21st century.[1]

Tobacco Use

Each year, tobacco is responsible for more than 430,000 premature deaths from cancer, cardiovascular disease, lung disease, and low birthweight (McGinnis & Foege, 1999; U.S. DHHS, 2000a). To put this figure in context, that is more than the combined deaths from AIDS, alcohol, homicide, motor vehicle crashes, cocaine, heroin, suicide, and fires. Clearly, tobacco use is the single most important preventable cause of death and disease.

Turning a smoker into a nonsmoker not only improves health but can decrease health care use (Wagner, Curry, Grothaus, Saunders, & McBride, 1995). One study showed employee health claims for smokers were 31% higher than for nonsmokers (Milliman & Robertson, 1995).

Not surprisingly, *Healthy People 2010* set objectives to stop smoking initiation and increase successful smoking cessation efforts (Table 14.1). Smoking prevalence has dropped 40% since the first Surgeon General's report on smoking in 1964. Yet one in four adults still smoke, and the highest prevalence today (33%) and greatest burden of disease is borne among Americans with the least income and education.

Youth and pregnant women are important targets for primary and secondary prevention. Each day more than 3,000 children and teenagers become new smokers, with 30% acquiring a daily and addictive smoking habit. Cigarette smoking is responsible for 17 to 26% of low birthweight babies, yet smoking cessation during pregnancy has decreased (National Center for Health Statistics, 1999).

---

[1]Other important indicators for improving the health of the country (e.g., mental health, injury and violence, environmental quality, access to health care and specific chronic diseases) are beyond the scope of this chapter but can be examined in more detail in the *Healthy People 2010* materials (U.S. DHHS, 2000a).

TABLE 14.1
Illustrative *Healthy People 2010* Objectives

	1997 baseline	2010 goals
Tobacco use		
Cigarette smoking adults	24%	12%
Current tobacco use by youth (past 30 days)	43%	21%
Smoking cessation attempts		
Adults	43%	75%
Pregnant women	12%	30%
Adolescents (grades 9–12)	73%	84%
Nutrition and physical activity		
Obesity[a] in adults (20 years and older)	23%	15%
Obesity in children and teens (6–19 years)	11%	5%
No leisure-time physical activity (18 years and older)	40%	20%
Moderate physical activity[b]		
Adults (18 years and older)	15%	30%
Adolescents (grades 9–12)	20%	30%
Alcohol misuse		
Alcohol-related auto deaths	6.1/100,000	4/100,000
American Indian or Alaska Native	19.2/100,000	(Data not collected)
High school seniors never using alcohol	19%	29%
Binge drinking		
Adolescents (12–17 years)	8.3%	6%
High school seniors	32%	11%
College students	39%	20%
Adults	16%	6%
Illicit drug use		
High school seniors never using illicit drugs	46%	56%
Adults using any illicit drug in past 30 days	5.8%	3.0%
Risky sexual practices		
Unmarried females (18–44 years) whose partners used condoms	23%	50%
HIV infected persons receiving Highly Active Antiretroviral Therapy (HAART)	54%	95%
Teenagers abstain from sex or use condoms	85%	95%

Note. Adapted from "Healthy People 2010—Conference Edition," by U.S Department of Health and Human Services. CD-ROM, January 2000. In the public domain.
[a]BMI (body mass index) of 30 or more.
[b]Moderate activity of 30 minutes a day five or more days a week.

Nutrition and Physical Activity

For those who do not smoke or drink to excess, diet and activity level are the most significant risk factors that one can modify (Frazao, 1996). Together inappropriate diet and inactivity are associated with 22 to 30% of cardiovascular deaths, 30 to 35% of cancer deaths, and 50 to 80% of

Type 2 diabetes (American Cancer Society, 1995; McGinnis & Foege, 1993) and are at the heart of the nation's twin obesity and diabetes epidemics (CDC, 2003; Mokdad, Ford, Bowman, & Dietz, 2003).

Lifestyle modifications have been shown to

- prevent and control high blood pressure and diabetes (Cleroux, Feldman, & Petrella, 1999; Eriksson et al., 1999; Harsha et al., 1999);
- affect the incidence and prognosis of cancers of the breast, colon, lung, and prostate (Glanz, 1997);
- be cost-effective in reducing population-wide coronary heart disease unlike cholesterol-lowering medications that are not, except for individuals at highest risk (Tosteson et al., 1997);
- reduce by about 30% the risk of coronary heart disease through leisure-time activities such as walking (averaging about 30 minutes a day), a magnitude of risk reduction comparable to smoking cessation (Leon, Myers & Connett, 1997; Manson et al., 1999).

Currently, an estimated 44.3 million adults in the United States are obese, an increase of 74% since 1991 (Mokdad et al., 2003). Overweight and obesity are also increasing among children. About 15% of children and adolescents aged 6 to 19 are overweight, a three-fold increase since 1980 (CDC, 2003). Accordingly, obesity-related physician visits are on the rise, jumping between 1988 and 1994 (Wolf & Colditz, 1998). More than 60% of the U.S. adult population is inactive or underactive. Obesity prevalence and rates of no leisure time physical activity are greater for women, minority groups, and low-income groups (U.S. DHHS, 2000a; see Table 14.1 for objectives).

Scientific consensus has emerged on the need to cut fat and cholesterol and maintain an optimal weight. Food-based recommendations include eating more fruits and vegetables and less red meat, increasing complex carbohydrates and fiber, and reducing the amount of full-fat dairy products (Glanz, 1999; USDA & U.S. DHHS, 1995). The Centers for Disease Control and Prevention, the American College of Sports Medicine, and the Surgeon General's report on physical activity and health endorse the health benefits of moderate-intensity activity accumulated throughout the day (CDC/ACSM, 1995; U.S. DHHS, 1996). They underscore the need for environmental supports (worksite programs, community walking and bicycling, safe play areas, daily school physical education) to provide for so-called lifestyle activities.

Alcohol Misuse

About 5% of the adult population are alcoholics, and another 20% are considered "risky drinkers" because they misuse alcohol, placing themselves at increased risk for accidental injury and physical and psychological problems (Higgins-Biddle, Babor, Mullahy, Daniels, & McRee, 1997). Alcohol is associated with 60 to 90% of cirrhosis deaths, 40 to 50% of traffic fatalities, and 16 to 67% of home and work injuries (McGinnis & Foege, 1993; National Institute on Alcohol Abuse and Alcoholism, 1996). Health care costs for untreated alcoholics are 100 to 300% higher than those of nonalcoholics, but alcoholism treatment would more than offset those increased medical care costs (Holder, 1998).

Alcohol abstinence rates increase with age and are inversely related to family income and education (U.S. DHHS, 1994b). Abuse is most prevalent during young adulthood, particularly among White and Native American males. Alcohol-related cirrhosis and auto death rates are two to three times higher for Native Americans and Alaska Natives (U.S. DHHS, 2000a).

Alcohol-related auto deaths have decreased by about 40% over the past decade, in part because the public has become less tolerant of heavy drinking and of driving after drinking (Babor, Aguirre-Molina, Marlatt, & Clayton, 1999). Although there has been some decline in youth use of alcohol, much less progress has been made among college-aged young people, with heavy drinking being the norm for about 40% of college students (see Table 14.1 for objectives).

Illicit Drug Use

Each year illicit drug use is responsible for about 20,000 deaths, and this figure is likely very low, because drug use is significantly underreported as a cause of death (McGinnis & Foege, 1993). Drug abuse is a major vector for transmission of HIV/AIDS, hepatitis, tuberculosis, and violence. In addition, employees with substance abuse diagnoses often have average health care charges higher than those for persons with asthma and diabetes (Garnick, Hendricks, Comstock, & Horgan, 1997). Unfortunately, fewer than one in four users actually received substance abuse treatment, which has been proven vastly more cost-effective than supply-side and criminal justice interventions (Leshner, 1996; Luborsky, Barber, Siqueland, McLellan, & Woody, 1997).

About 6% of those over age 12 years are current users of illicit drugs (Table 14.1). Most at risk for drug-induced deaths are male, economically disadvantaged, undereducated, under- or unemployed, and minority populations. However, many drug abusers do not fit this profile (e.g., Whites are more likely to abuse marijuana or inhalants; U.S. DHHS, 2000a).

Adolescent drug use had been declining since the late 1970s. However, a dramatic doubling of use by youth occurred during the 1990s (for example, from 11 to 22% among eighth graders; Johnston, O'Malley, & Bachman,

1997). At the same time, social disapproval and perception of harm among teenagers declined (National Center for Health Statistics, 1999).

Risky Sexual Practices

Persons with HIV/AIDS (human immunodeficiency virus/acquired immunodeficiency syndrome) are now living longer, although there is still no cure. Advances in treatment and declines in new infections among men having sex with men resulted in an almost 42% decline in death rate from 1996 to 1997 (U.S. DHHS, 2000a; see objectives in Table 14.1). Substantial progress has also been made in reducing perinatal transmission, but heterosexual transmission is accounting for an increasing proportion.

Prevention through behavior change has substantial economic benefits compared with the lifetime cost of HIV treatment (estimated as $155,000 per person; Holtgrave & Pinkerton, 1997). Safer behaviors not only prevent HIV/AIDS but also other sexually transmitted infections. Each year, more than 13 million persons become infected with STDs other than HIV. Among those becoming infected is a core group with recurrent but curable STDs. Standard medical care without attention to behavior change has not proven sufficient to protect against reinfection (J. Howland, personal communication, July 5, 2000).

An alarming number of young people are still being infected with HIV, and incidence rates are increasing for Black, female, and Hispanic individuals (U.S. DHHS, 2000a). Yet condom use among sexually active teenagers and injecting drug users remains low. In addition, recent therapeutic advances have led to alarming laxity in condom use even among men having sex with men (Kalichman, Nachimson, Cherry, & Williams, 1998).

Noncompliance With Medical Regimens and Behavioral Self-Management

Noncompliance with a wide range of preventive and curative actions also constitute a critical determinant of health care outcomes. *Healthy People 2010* sets objectives for improvement of preventive services and behavioral self-management of chronic diseases as well:

- Childhood immunization, mammography, and colorectal cancer screening and other preventive services remain a public health challenge, especially in low-income and disadvantaged populations;
- Typically, one third of patients are fully compliant with their medical regimen, one third comply at least some of the time, and the remainder are noncompliant. These patterns persist

across all economic classes and educational status (DiMatteo 1994a, 1994b); and

- Chronic disease by its very nature requires continuous, multistep treatment over a long period of time. The length and complexity of such regimens can negatively influence compliance.

Sobel (1995) noted that there is often a "critical mismatch" between patients' psychosocial needs and the medical systems response. Changes are recommended in provider–patient interaction, such as giving patients a greater role in medical decision making and teaching them better ways to manage their own daily care. Providing patients with tools for better self-management can reduce medical services use by 20% (Fries, Koop, Sokolov, Beadle, & Wright, 1998), yet fewer than 40% of people with diabetes and about 10% of people with asthma receive formal self-management education.

WHY FOCUS NOW ON THE BEHAVIORAL DETERMINANTS OF HEALTH?

Efforts to achieve *Healthy People 2010* objectives must respond to demographic trends and health system changes that make this a critical time for initiatives to shape healthy behaviors and prevent or modify health-damaging ones. These efforts can capitalize on growing scientific knowledge of basic mechanisms linking behavior and health and on advances in methods of health behavior change at individual and population levels.

Demographics and Health System Changes

A number of demographic changes, especially those related to the graying of America and to the increasing diversity of the population, underscore the importance of behavioral approaches to the prevention and management of chronic disease and for effective outreach to low-income and racial-ethnic minority populations to eliminate disparities in the prevalence of behavioral risks and resultant disease. The emergence of managed care and the informatics revolution brought on the one hand more population-based (versus individually oriented) models of health promotion and disease management and prevention, and on the other hand, unprecedented capacity and tools for tailoring health behavior change interventions within these broader population-based approaches.

Aging Population and Growth in Chronic Illness

Aging post-World War II baby boomers will push the number of people 65 years and older to 13% of the population in 2010 and to 20% by 2030

(U.S. Census Bureau, 1999). Advances in public health and acute care medicine mean that Americans are living longer, but the quality of those longer years is not necessarily better:

- Chronic disease prevalence is rising steadily, from 105 million Americans having chronic disease today to 120 million predicted in 2010; and
- Chronic disease accounts for more than 70% of all health care dollars spent and will cost an estimated $582 billion in 2010 (Hoffman & Rice, 1996).

The 1992 Institute of Medicine report, *The Second Fifty Years*, argued that standard health promotion–disease prevention activities are seldom applied in older populations. Yet these activities could substantially enhance physical, mental, and social well-being while reducing functional disability, shortening exposure to expensive medical services, and postponing long-term care. More recently, emphasis has been placed on addressing lifestyle behaviors and chronic disease management strategies for successful aging (Rowe & Kahn, 1998; Wagner, Austin, & Von Korff, 1996). Clearly, effective and efficient behavior change strategies have great potential to improve health and functioning and control health care costs in an aging society.

Growth in Low-Income and Minority Populations

The gulf between the richest and the poorest is widening. In 1997, 10% of the nation's families lived in poverty, including one out of every five children (Dalaker & Naifeh, 1998). More than 20% of adults are functionally illiterate. Low socioeconomic status and low literacy are strongly associated with poorer health and poorer health behaviors and present a barrier to health behavior change programs.

By the year 2050, today's ethnic and racial minorities will make up almost 50% of the U.S. population (Day, 1996). Risky health behaviors and their consequences are more prevalent in disadvantaged racial–ethnic populations: HIV/AIDS in Black and Latino populations; tobacco use in Native Americans and Black men; improper diet–obesity among Hispanics, Native Hawaiians, Native Americans, and Black women. Accordingly, *Healthy People 2010* recognizes that improving the nation's health will increasingly depend on reducing these disparities. Research is continuing to clarify the mechanisms underlying the complex relationships between sociocultural factors (low income, low socioeconomic status, limited education, racism) and behavioral health risks and to explain their interdependent effects on health.

Managed Care

Most Americans covered by private insurance and by Medicaid are now enrolled in managed care plans. Managed health care systems have an unprecedented ability to identify defined populations of patients and providers; new incentives for keeping people healthy; and new information systems and databases that can be harnessed for proactive health behavior change interventions on a population basis. These plans also bring access to new tools for practice improvement (clinical practice guidelines, prevention report cards, performance feedback, computer-based reminder systems) to motivate and standardize behavioral interventions and better integrate these interventions into routine primary care.

Health Plan Employee Data and Information Set (HEDIS) health plan "report cards" cover clinical preventive services, but not health behavior change programs or outcomes, except for measures of provider smoking cessation advice and treatment (National Committee for Quality Assurance [NCQA], 2003). These report cards have induced some improvements in use of some clinical preventive services (e.g., mammography and cervical PAP screening, tobacco use treatment), but aside from tobacco, programs that target health behavior change remain poorly integrated (Orleans & Alper, 2002; Partnership for Prevention, 1998; Wagner, Davis, Schaefer, Von Korff, & Austin 1999). In light of growing evidence that physical activity and diet are significant contributors to health care costs, not just long-term but within a short time of enrolling in managed care plans, and that effective counseling interventions can significantly improve health and reduce health care costs (Pronk, Goodman, O'Connor, & Martinson, 1999), the NCQA is likely to expand HEDIS measures to cover a wider range of behavioral risk factors and medical interventions.

The Informatics Revolution

Computer-based, interactive communication technologies are rapidly evolving into new media forms for delivering behavior change interventions. Computer-tailored print materials, interactive television, video, phone, and other two-way interactive communications bring unprecedented potential to target and personalize health information and behavior change strategies (Eng & Gustafson, 1999; Skinner, Campbell, Rimer, Curry, & Prochaska, 1999).

Individually tailored health behavior change advice and feedback can improve outcomes of self-help, primary care, and worksite programs, such as for dietary behavior change, physical activity, and smoking cessation (Brug, Glanz, van Assema, Kok, & van Breukelen, 1998; Bull, Kreuter, & Scharff, 1999; Campbell et al., 1994; Prochaska, DiClemente, Velicer, & Rossi, 1993; Strecher et al., 1994). Computer-based systems provide capabilities to coordinate interventions for multiple health risks. For instance, systems can determine optimal timing and sequencing of related behavior-change programs, integrate multiple strategies into chronic disease care, and map key behavioral "cost drivers" for cost-effective disease management (Fries, 1992; Pronk, O'Connor, Isham, & Hawkins, 1997).

When used to supplement brief provider advice, interactive computer-based technologies remove the burden of time-consuming counseling from providers (Glasgow, McKay, Boles, & Vogt, 1999; Strecher et al., 1994). Moreover, computer-based reminder systems can improve provider adherence to guidelines, thus easing use of increasingly complex screening, treatment, and triage algorithms (Palmer, Wright, Orav, Hargraves, & Louis, 1996; Yarnall et al., 1998).

Advances in Biobehavioral Research

Important advances in basic biobehavioral research, especially interdisciplinary or "transdisciplinary" research, have pointed the way to the development of more effective applied health behavior change interventions—those involving both behavioral and pharmacological interventions—and have propelled important policy changes as well. The sequencing of the human genome represents new challenges and opportunities for focusing behavioral strategies on the reduction and management of genetic disease susceptibilities.

New Models of Health and Health Behavior

Advances in interdisciplinary behavioral and biomedical research have shed new light on pathophysiological mechanisms linking health and behavior. For instance, it is now clear that smoking, diet, physical exercise, substance abuse, chronic stress, and socioeconomic status have profound effects on the central nervous, endocrine, and immune systems. Some fruits of collaborative research include the following:

- Twenty-five years ago, smoking was treated as a "bad habit." Today nicotine addiction is recognized as no less complex an addiction than that to alcohol or cocaine. Pharmacological approaches (i.e., nicotine replacement, Zyban), although ineffective on their own, are now standard in combination with cognitive–behavioral approaches—boosting quit rates as much as 200% over cognitive–behavioral approaches alone (AHCPR, 1996; U.S. PHS, 2000).
- A picture of drug addiction as a brain disease, expressed in behavioral ways and occurring in a social context, has emerged.

Findings that psychoactive drugs of abuse may enhance dopamine transmission suggest new treatment strategies. And evidence that drug-related cues trigger both subjective cravings and changes in brain chemistry suggests a new biobehavioral paradigm for preventing relapse (Leshner, 1999).

- The psychobiology of fat appetite and metabolic factors as promoters of fat and protein intake offer intriguing possibilities for biobehavioral models (Stunkard, 1996). Discovery of the "obese gene" may lead to new drugs that regulate appetite and energy expenditure, radically transforming behavioral–pharmacological weight loss and lipid-lowering treatments.

Improved knowledge of basic mechanisms also shapes public policy. Irrefutable evidence for the addicting effects of nicotine was the essential premise for proposing Food and Drug Administration jurisdiction to curb the sale and promotion of tobacco products to youth. Furthermore, the efficacy and cost-effectiveness of smoking cessation interventions undergirds recommendations for health plan and insurance coverage (U.S. PHS, 2000).

Beyond the Genome

The ability to identify genes that predispose to illness and the individuals who carry them will intensify, rather than obviate, the need for effective health behavior change strategies. Given the complex, subtle, and pervasive interactions among behavioral, environmental, and genetic factors over the life span, estimates of their relative separate influence are difficult to obtain. One population estimate suggests that 5 to 10% of cancer etiology is hereditary, with carcinogens, tobacco use, and diet-related free-radicals accounting for the rest at about 30% each (American Cancer Society, 1995; Li, 1995).

Although progress is stunning in developing genetically tailored pharmacotherapies, it is still the case, as geneticists Baird (1994) and Li (1995) argued almost a decade ago, that few inherited diseases are likely to be candidates for gene therapy in the near future and that identification of risk genotypes carries an obligation to develop effective prevention strategies. Prevention strategies can be behavioral (such as dietary fat reduction in the case of familial hypercholesterolemia). Likewise with new gene-based drug treatments, behavioral interventions will be needed to promote adherence to lifelong medication regimens. Exciting psychological research is underway examining the effects of genetic screening on well-being, health behaviors, future medical decision making, and social and family relationships (Lerman & Croyle, 1996). These will provide a foundation for improving outcomes of the testing process—enhancing psychological adjustment and adoption of preventive health practices (Audrain et al., 1999; Lerman et al., 1997; Smith, West, Croyle, & Botkin, 1999).

Advances in the Science and Practice of Health Behavior Change

A great deal more is known today about the requirements of programs that help people adopt and maintain healthy lifestyles. Bandura's social learning theory and the related health belief model are the basis for the most effective individually oriented approaches (Bandura, 1986). Changing health-related behaviors requires (a) perceiving the benefits of change will outweigh the costs; (b) feeling personally "at-risk" or susceptible to poor health outcomes; (c) having or acquiring skills to substitute ingrained unhealthy habits with healthy alternatives, to cope effectively with withdrawal from addictive substances, and to resist unavoidable relapse temptations; and (d) having adequate social support. Hence, traditional programs seek to supply the motivations, skills, and supports people need. These approaches can be improved on by adding an understanding of the stages and processes involved in individual and population-based health behavior change.

Stages of Change Model

This model, first proposed in 1983 by Prochaska, DiClemente and their colleagues, has had a profound impact on the design and delivery of health behavior change programs not only for individuals but also for populations. Based on naturalistic studies of how people went about quitting smoking on their own, these researchers identified six sequential stages and discovered that different skills and knowledge (and different types of treatment) were needed to help people in each stage:

- *Precontemplation:* Behavior is not seen as a problem; there is no intention to change behavior, a result part to limited self-efficacy/support;
- *Contemplation:* Person is seriously planning to change behavior within six months, weighing the pros and cons, building supports and confidence;
- *Preparation:* Plans to change are imminent, small initial steps are taken, psychological preparation has begun;
- *Action:* Active attempts are made—to quit smoking, exercise more, drink less, reduce fat/calories in diet—and sustained for up to six months;
- *Maintenance:* Change is sustained beyond six months; and
- *Relapse:* Individual returns to any earlier stage from action and can begin to recycle again through the stages of change.

Treatment interventions have moved away from a one-size-fits-all approach to targeting a person's readiness to change. This model has been successfully applied to multiple health-related behaviors, including all of the risk factors considered in this chapter (Prochaska & Velicer, 1997).

Most individually oriented health behavior change programs were designed for people who already were motivated to change. Yet population surveys repeatedly found that only a minority (20%) with any given health risk are in the preparation and action stages, with most (80%) in earlier contemplation and precontemplation stages (Nigg et al., 1999; Prochaska & Velicer, 1997). This disparity in population readiness helps to explain why so few people enroll in weight loss or quit smoking clinics, even when free and accessible. Accordingly, stage theory spurred development of innovative *motivational* treatments to move those in early stages toward greater treatment readiness (e.g., Miller & Rollnick, 1991) and provided new tools for detecting shifts in stage in entire populations. When applied in communities, worksites, and health care settings, programs with components in all stages have vastly improved the reach and efficacy of traditional approaches. Work to refine and expand the stage model continues, including applying it to how health behaviors are shaped and changed in childhood.

In another important development, social marketing approaches have been systemically applied to designing more appealing, better targeted, and more effective media and behavior change programs (Lefebvre & Rochlin, 1997). Basic marketing principles and methods (e.g., market analysis and segmentation, qualitative–descriptive research, consumer focus groups, "academic" detailing) are now routinely used when promoting healthy lifestyles. The greatest dividends have been the development of more widely applicable and user-friendly interventions and communications and use of better targeted, culturally appropriate, and more cost-effective strategies for reaching high-risk groups (Glanz & Rimer, 1997).

Evolution of Population-Based Models of Prevention

An important paradigm shift has occurred away from a strictly clinical treatment model toward broader public health and public policy models of prevention. In the early 1980s, there was a shift in focus from individuals to communities (Table 14.2).

This shift continued in the 1990s away from "downstream" individually oriented treatments for those with a specific risk factor like tobacco use. Too many early downstream efforts served to "(a) *divert limited resources* away from upstream healthy public policies; (b) *blame the victim;* (c) *produce a lifestyle approach to health policy*, rather than a social policy approach to healthy lifestyles; (d) *decontextualize risk behaviors* and overlook the ways in which such behaviors are culturally generated and structurally maintained" (McKinlay, 1995, p. 93). As a result, outcomes were disappointing.

TABLE 14.2
Clinical Versus Public Health Perspective on Health Behavior Change

Characteristic	Clinical perspective	Public health perspective
Problem definition	Individual, lifestyle	Community, environment
Target	Self-referred or recruited samples	Populations or high-risk groups
Setting	Medical/psychological	Natural environments (worksites, primary care)
Provider	Trained professionals	Lay, automated
Intervention	Intensive, multi-session	Brief, low- cost, self-help
Reach and Cost-effectiveness	Lower	Higher

Note. From "Smoking Cessation: What Have We Learned Over the Past Decade?" by E. Lichtenstein and R. E. Glasgow, 1992, *Journal of Consulting Clinical Psychology 60(4)*, p. 518. Copyright 1992 by the American Psychological Association. Adapted with permission of the author.

J. B. McKinlay argued that effective population-level behavior change requires applications *across the full spectrum of downstream to upstream activities*. "Midstream" approaches focus on primary and secondary prevention activities of providers, schools, worksites, and communities, and advances in "upstream" approaches involve macro-level state and national healthy public policies and environmental interventions powerful enough to redirect strong societal and industry counterforces. Successful upstream approaches require new health advocacy roles and partnerships.

Like other social–ecological models of health promotion and disease prevention (e.g., McLeroy, Bibeau, Steckler, & Glanz, 1988; Sallis & Owen, 1997), McKinlay's population model of prevention brings the importance of societal norms and macro-level societal influences and policies into sharper focus and has major implications for efforts to promote the challenge of long-term *maintenance* of behavior change (Orleans, 2000).

PROGRESS IN ADDRESSING THE BEHAVIORAL DETERMINANTS OF HEALTH

Using McKinlay's model, the following section highlights progress in individually oriented downstream treatments, organizationally mediated midstream interventions, and upstream macro-level programs–campaigns and healthy public policies for each of the primary behavioral risk factors featured in this chapter (Orleans, Gruman, Ulmer, Emont & Hollendonner, 1999). Table 14.3 outlines interventions under J. B. McKinlay's population-based intervention model.

TABLE 14.3
Overview of McKinlay's Population-Based Intervention Model

Downstream interventions

Individual-level interventions for those who possess the risk factor (e.g., tobacco use, sedentary lifestyle) or suffer from risk-related diseases/conditions (e.g., diabetes, obesity) with an emphasis on changing rather than preventing health damaging behaviors, including:

- Group and individual counseling
- Patient health education/cognitive behavioral interventions
- Self-help programs and tailored health communications
- Pharmacologic treatments

Midstream interventions

Population-level interventions that target defined populations for the purpose of changing and/or preventing health-damaging behaviors and involve mediation through important organizational channels or natural environments, including:

- Worksite and community-based health promotion/disease prevention programs
- Primary care screening/intervention programs that reach entire populations
- School-based youth prevention activities
- Community-based interventions focused on defined at-risk populations (e.g., gay men in HIV epicenters)

Upstream interventions

Macro-level state and national public policy/environmental interventions to strengthen social norms and supports for healthy behaviors and to redirect unhealthy societal and industry counterforces including:

- Nationwide public education/media campaigns
- Economic incentives (e.g., excise taxes on high fat and tobacco products, reimbursement for health behavior change treatments)
- Policies reducing access to unhealthy products (e.g., pricing, access, labeling)
- Policies reducing the advertising and promotion of unhealthy products and behaviors

Note. From "Rating Our Progress in Population Health Promotion: Report Card on Six Behaviors," by C. T. Orleans, J. Gruman, C. Ulmer, S. L. Emont, and J. K. Hollendonner, 1999, *American Journal of Health Promotion 14*, p. 76. Copyright 1999 by the *American Journal of Health Promotion*. Reprinted with permission.

Downstream Individually Oriented Treatments

The downstream emphasis is on changing rather than preventing the risk behaviors or the associated conditions. Many interventions, generally based on social learning theory, work reasonably well. Addictive behaviors often require combined behavioral and pharmacological approaches (Gutman & Clayton, 1999; Warner, Slade, & Sweanor, 1997) and sometimes harm-reduction interventions (Normand, Vlahov, & Moses, 1995). Some examples follow.

- *Smoking cessation:* Cognitive–behavioral individual and group strategies can produce 25 to 30% long-term quit rates among motivated volunteers. Nicotine replacement therapy can almost double quit rates (Orleans & Cummings, 1999).

- *Drug treatment:* State-of-the-art treatments can result in 30 to 50% of drug-abusing clients remaining abstinent one year after formal treatment. Major reductions have been sustained at least three years (Gutman & Clayton, 1999).

- *Alcohol treatment:* A variety of theory-based interventions have proven effective, including a 12-step facilitation approach that encourages participation in Alcoholics Anonymous. Naltrexone (the first new pharmacological treatment in 50 years) has doubled successful outcomes when treating alcoholics (Babor et al., 1999).

- *Changing risky sexual behaviors:* Changes in risky sexual behavior are most dramatic among persons who test HIV-positive; thus, counseling interventions are most successful as secondary prevention (Carey, 1999). Cutting down instances of unprotected sex reduces risks for other sexually transmitted diseases as well (National Institute of Mental Health, 1998).

- *Improving dietary practices:* Reductions in dietary fat intake and other dietary changes can be sustained among motivated individuals (having or at risk for diet-related disease such as breast cancer or heart disease) with intensive educational and behavioral interventions (Glanz, 1999).

- *Fostering physical activity:* Individual cognitive–behavioral interventions can lead to a 10 to 25% increase in physical activity compared with no-treatment controls (Marcus & Forsyth, 1999).

Findings from tobacco, diet, and alcohol research has contributed to the design and application of effective interventions for broader dissemination. One such result is the first-ever formal Agency for Health Care Policy and Research (AHCPR) smoking cessation guideline recommending combining medical provider advice to quit, ongoing provider and social support, skills-based cessation training, and adjunctive pharmacotherapy (i.e., nicotine gum and patches). The recently updated guideline (U.S. PHS, 2000) added telephone quitline counseling and several additional effective nicotine and non-nicotine medications. Minimal contact interventions and self-help strategies (e.g., print guides, tailored messages, supportive telephone counseling) have been found to provide effective and cost-effective treatment formats, with diet and tobacco interventions able to produce clinically meaningful changes at the population level (Abrams et al., 1996; Beresford et al., 1997; Campbell et al., 1994; Skinner et al., 1999; U.S. PHS, 2000).

Of course, room for improvement remains—to increase both the efficacy and dissemination of state-of-the-art protocols. Only a small fraction receive the best interventions because of inadequate treatment infrastructure or lack of policies supportive of dissemination such as reimbursement for behavioral interventions. For instance, only 20 to 30% of U.S. smokers and former smokers have ever used a formal treatment program—and those who have are likely to be better educated, White smokers (Orleans & Alper, 2002). Fewer than one quarter of illicit drug users receive treatment (Luborsky et al., 1997). Typically, poorest access is among low-income subgroups with the greatest prevalence of unhealthy behaviors and among those suffering with both addiction and psychiatric disorders. Even with growing consensus on effective treatments for smoking cessation and an increasing number of health plans providing coverage (McPhillips-Tangum, 1998), only 22 of the 50 states cover these treatments for low-income Medicaid beneficiaries (McMenamin, Halpin, Ibrahim, & Orleans, in press).

Midstream Organizationally Mediated and Community-Based Interventions

Effective health behavior change programs have been launched in worksites, clinics, hospitals, and schools. Tailored messages and stage-based treatments have increased the reach and impact of many traditional behavioral programs (Velicer, Prochaska, Fava, Laforge, & Rossi, 1999). However, the success and dissemination of midstream programs has been uneven. Consider the following examples.

- *Primary care:* Surveys of physicians indicate widespread acceptance of clinical prevention services, but low rates of behavior change interventions or even inquiry about risk behaviors. This occurs despite increasing evidence that even brief interventions can be effective at doubling smoking quit rates, reducing alcohol consumption, and increasing exercise levels (AHCPR, 1996; Marcus et al., 1995; Orleans et al., 1999; Wilk, Jensen, & Havinghurst, 1997). Although a majority of physicians advise improving one's diet—especially lowering fat and cholesterol intake—few evaluate a patient's overall diet, citing lack of time, insurance coverage, and training in intervention techniques (Glanz, Tziraki, Albright & Fernandes, 1995). Similarly citing lack of time during primary care visits, physicians often fail to provide adequate self-management counseling to persons with diabetes (Glasgow & Strycker, 2000). Screening for illegal drug use or safe-sex behaviors is even more rare, and this is of increasing concern as HIV infection spreads to a wider community (Gutman & Clayton, 1999; Taira, Safran, Seto, Rogers, & Tarlov, 1997).

- *School-based programs:* Primary prevention programs have had limited success. Commonly available programs addressing tobacco, drug, alcohol, and sexual activity tend to delay experimentation but do not always have lasting power (Babor et al., 1999; Glynn, 1989; Kirby, 1997). For example, the widespread Drug Abuse Resistance Education (DARE) informational program has shown little sustained effect (Clayton, Cattarello, & Johnstone, 1996), but others incorporating resistance-skills training, parent interventions, media, and community organization are promising (Botvin, Baker, Dusenbury, Botvin, & Diaz, 1995; Dishion, Kavanaugh, & Kiesner, 2003). The most effective sex education programs tend to be controversial and not widely implemented because they are not just abstinence-oriented but teach negotiation skills and reinforce values against unprotected sex (Carey, 1999). Similarly among college students, abstinence-based alcohol interventions have been less successful than skill-training programs (e.g., drink-refusal skills, alternative coping styles, setting drinking limits, estimating blood-alcohol levels; Marlatt et al., 1998). Although school-based interventions have altered dietary practices and physical activity, less is known about their lasting effectiveness outside the school environment (Marcus & Forsyth, 1999).
- *Worksite programs:* Worksites offer a venue in which individual treatment can be combined with supportive changes in policy and environment (e.g., smoking restrictions, space for exercise, nutritious food choices at modest prices). The impact of worksite health promotion has been limited in that it tends to attract only the most motivated and economically advantaged workers and is generally offered only by larger employers (Lewis, Huebner, & Yarborough, 1996). The most effective institute reinforcements and target people in all stages of change (Strycker et al., 1997).
- *Community-based initiatives:* Evidence from smoking and alcohol interventions has shown that combining community- and school-based prevention programs with upstream interventions (e.g., higher excise taxes, enforcement of youth access laws) has the most potential, but these more comprehensive programs are not widely available (Babor et al., 1999; Orleans & Cummings, 1999; Pierce et al., 1998). Community interventions for HIV/AIDS prevention, particularly in epicenters of the disease,

have achieved success, but these have not always stemmed from evidence-based protocols that would facilitate replication (Carey, 1999). Disappointing outcomes from a number of community-based initiatives (e.g., COMMIT smoking cessation trial; Center for Substance Abuse Prevention Community Partnerships Program) may in part reflect the choice of inappropriate statistical methods and outcome measures. J. B. McKinlay and others argue that poor results reflect measurement of the wrong outcomes, with too much focus on individual-level measures of health and behavior and too little effort to measure important intervention and policy-related changes in the organizations, worksites, communities, neighborhoods, and families (McKinlay, 1986, 1996; Murray, 1995). Better results emerge with greater local community involvement in program design, longer follow-up, and stronger research designs (e.g., higher response rates, intervention-control treatment matching; Sellers, Crawford, Bullock, & McKinlay, 1996).

Upstream Policy and Environmental Strategies

Recent evidence has made it clear that downstream and midstream initiatives depend on macro-level policies and programs for their success, and that full-spectrum interventions (downstream to upstream) will be the most effective. Upstream policy advocacy strategies may involve

- statewide or nationwide public education campaigns (e.g., changing norms about driving after drinking, media campaign of Partnership for a Drug-Free America);
- economic incentives (e.g., increasing excise taxes on high-fat, alcohol, and tobacco products; providing insurance coverage for health behavior change counseling);
- environmental change (e.g., reducing access to dangerous products by raising alcohol purchasing age or restricting hours of sale; increasing children's and adults' access to safe and convenient play/exercise facilities, requiring no smoking areas); and
- countering exposure to advertising or promotion of unhealthy behaviors (e.g., food labeling, counteradvertising to youth about tobacco use).

Public education and advertising, although they can help change public norms of thinking and deglamorize unhealthy behaviors, are often insufficient. More directive strategies—such as changing environmental access, providing for economic sanctions on harmful products, and removing financial barriers to seeking care—will further enhance behavior change (Orleans et al., 1999).

PROMISING TRENDS AND NEXT STEPS

To increase their population impact, the next generation of health behavior change programs need to improve their reach and power. This final section highlights the most promising areas for development and remaining challenges.

Promising Directions

Several trends hold potential to increase the overall population impact of health behavior change programs. They include the development of more proactive population-based approaches to health promotion—including the emergence of computer-tailored interventions and wider use of motivational interventions appropriate for people not yet read for action-oriented interventions—along with the integration of pharmacological and health behavior change strategies and the wider use of effective harm reduction and behavioral chronic disease management strategies. Perhaps the greatest benefits have come from important advances in public policy.

Proactive Models of Population-Based Health Promotion

Several trends hold potential to increase the overall population impact of health behavior change programs. The new application of theories (stages of change) and tools (user-friendly self-help guides and videos, brief telephone counseling) for population-based health promotion are beginning to emerge as market-ready. These include motivational strategies designed for people at low stages of readiness and are suitable for use in a variety of midstream organizationally mediated and community-based interventions. Now low-cost, self-help versions of effective clinic treatments are being more widely disseminated, and social marketing has impelled more sophisticated use of media. Minimal intervention strategies for smoking cessation, dietary change, and mammography screening already have demonstrated clinically meaningful changes at the population level in managed care settings (Beresford et al., 1997; Curry et al., 1993, 1995).

Computer-Tailored Health Behavior Change Advice

Computerized tailoring for individuals and for specific populations (including demographically vulnerable and medically high-risk groups) holds promise for better patient–treatment matching to improve treatment receptivity and outcome. Computer-based print, telephone, and video communications have boosted treatment outcomes over standard one-size-fits-all interventions (e.g., medication compliance, smoking cessation, cancer screening, diet modification), with greatest benefits sometimes seen in low-income populations (e.g., Skinner et al., 1999). These reduce provider burden and can be readily launched using the administrative and clinical databases of managed care organizations.

The Internet presents a far-reaching delivery channel for tailored information and interventions (Winkler et al., 2000). Yet how to best ensure access to new forms of communication technology for socially disadvantaged groups and to preserve patient confidentiality and confidence in the source of tailored health messages must be addressed (Orleans, 1999).

Motivational Interventions to Concretize Personal Health Risks

The stages of change model has stimulated new approaches for raising motivation. Motivational interviewing, originally developed to enhance motivation and self-efficacy in substance abuse treatment, are being creatively applied to a wide range of interventions. Scientific research continues to identify biomarkers of harm or risk, useful in boosting motivation or as reinforcement. Smokers, for instance, given feedback on biomarkers of health damage or health risk (e.g., precancerous lesions, impaired lung function) can have double the quit rates (Audrain et al., 1997). In others, as with feedback of genetic lung cancer susceptibility, no benefits (and some harms) have been observed (Lerman et al., 1997). Newer theories are guiding development of interventions to undermine pervasive "optimistic" biases about personal health risks and to maximize benefits and minimize harm of genetic risk feedback. These can also improve our understanding of how to facilitate patient (and provider) decision making under circumstances of uncertainty (Rimer, 1997).

Emergence of Combined Behavioral and Pharmacological Medical Treatments

Systematic behavioral medicine research has identified powerful new combinations of behavioral interventions and drug treatments (e.g., methadone for illegal drugs, naltrexone for alcohol dependence, nicotine replacement for tobacco addiction, new pharmacological treatments for obesity). These combinations have proven more powerful than either component alone (Babor et al., 1999; Campfield, Smith, & Burn 1998; Gutman & Clayton, 1999; Orleans & Cummings, 1999).

Harm Reduction Strategies

Broader applications are being explored for treatment of addictive behaviors (e.g., methadone maintenance, needle exchange, controlled drinking for risky drinkers, maintenance nicotine replacement therapy). These strategies include abstinence as an ideal endstate but offer an alternative to zero tolerance and may reach those not helped by abstinence-only approaches (Marlatt, 1996).

A New Focus on Behavioral "Chronic Disease Management"

Disease management involves identifying and changing patient behaviors to prevent progression of illness, avert costly flare-ups and complications, and prevent unnecessary resource use. Mounting evidence reveals that behavior change and self-management training can improve patient outcomes and reduce health care costs in diabetes, asthma, arthritis, hypertension, coronary heart disease, and other chronic diseases (Von Korff, Gruman, Schaefer, Curry, & Wagner, 1997). Growing chronic illness costs can motivate health plan re-engineering toward behaviorally oriented chronic care and development of system infrastructure that can be harnessed to improve preventive behavioral treatment as well (e.g., Solberg et al., 1998).

Public Support for Healthy Public Policy

Upstream interventions have gained attention in most behavioral risk areas. Educational approaches, whether warning labels or nutritional labels, provide information for transforming cultural norms. Environmental changes such as limiting youth access to alcohol or increasing recreational spaces further induce healthier lifestyle behaviors. Directive policy approaches, including economic sanctions (e.g., raising excise taxes on cigarettes) and incentives (e.g., reimbursement for smoking cessation treatment) have emerged as critical for expanding the impact of downstream, midstream, and even upstream educational approaches (e.g., Orleans & Alper, 2002). As Schroeder (2000) has argued, successful citizen action campaigns by antismoking activists and organizations such as Mothers Against Drunk Driving have done more to reduce the nation's death rates in the past 20 years than biomedical research conducted during the same period.

Taking the Next Steps

The efficacy of health behavior change interventions at all levels, although respectable, can and should be improved. Additional research and better dissemination of existing effective strategies will improve prospects for population-based health promotion. Major improvements will come only from the development and application of new theories and from greater support and incentives for interdisciplinary biobehavioral research collaboration (Center for the Advancement of Health, 2000; Rimer, 1997).

Understanding Determinants of Healthy Behavior Among Children and Adolescents

Health psychologists have focused much more on psychosocial vulnerabilities to *unhealthy behaviors* in childhood and adolescence than on protective factors (individual characteristics, family–socialization influences, and external neighborhood–school–community–societal influences). Both the 1994 Surgeon General's report (U.S. DHHS, 1994a) and the similar 1994 Institute of Medicine report on tobacco use prevention, for instance, underscored the need to identify positive skills that children and teenagers need to resist damaging influences and cope with problems of self-esteem–depression. Genetic and biological mechanisms, on the one hand, and policy influences (e.g., tobacco access, exposure to tobacco advertising), on the other, are required. Risk behaviors in adolescence are inversely related to socioeconomic status, so community and school prevention programs must be strengthened (Lowry, Kann, Collins, & Kolbe, 1996). School-based prevention curricula with demonstrated long-term impacts are lacking.

Improving Maintenance of Health Behavior Change

Downstream (individual-level) interventions now work reasonably well to produce short-term change, but there is much less progress in promoting maintenance. Recent reviews underscore the need for more research attention to this challenge (Wing, 2000) and highlight the need for new models that integrate individual-level with broader environmental and macro-level policy influences (Orleans, 2000).

Improving Health Behavior Change Programs for Vulnerable Populations

Healthy People 2010 focuses on reducing health disparities that are unexplained by information about biological and genetic characteristics of ethnic and racial minority populations. Empowering people to make informed decisions about their health and health care is one of the best opportunities for reducing disparities. Despite the greater vulnerability of low-income, blue-collar and ethnic–racial minority groups, these populations remain least likely to be reached by effective behavior change interventions. Quantitative and qualitative studies should systematically examine determinants of unhealthy behavior in these populations; identify unique health behavior change motives, resources, and barriers; and develop innovative, culturally sensitive models for health professional training and service delivery.

Moving Away From Single-Risk (One-Risk-at-a-Time) Approaches

The need continues to grow for systems of care that integrate and prioritize co-occurring risk behaviors in individuals (Pronk et al., 1997).

Clearly, risks cluster. For instance, individuals who smoke are more likely to have unhealthy eating and exercise patterns, more risky drinking, and poorer adherence to medical regimens. In addition, many behaviorally linked health problems involve more than one risk factor (e.g., diet and exercise in obesity and diabetes; tobacco and alcohol in bronchogenic cancers). Yet most programs have focused on a single risk factor at a time. Current applications of the stage model to multiple risks suggest that smoking cessation may serve as a gateway to other positive behavior changes in much the same way as smoking initiation serves as a gateway to addiction. More effort must be devoted to developing programs that help prioritize and sequence multiple health behavior change strategies, using more efficient delivery systems and more appealing, realistic, and holistic approaches to change.

CONCLUSION

In clinical settings, from managed care plans to public health clinics, interventions to modify behavioral risk factors are underused, even in the presence of clear evidence of clinical and cost effectiveness (e.g., Partnership for Prevention, 1998; Tobacco Use and Dependence Clinical Practice Guideline Panel, 2000). For example, the Surgeon General recently noted, "Our lack of greater progress in tobacco control is more the result of failure to implement proven strategies than it is the lack of knowledge about what to do" (U.S. DHHS, 2000b). Wider use of health behavior interventions will depend on better technology transfer and greater dissemination efforts (Kelly et al., 2000; Oldenburg, Ffrench, & Sallis, 2000). Unfortunately, health psychology and behavioral medicine have lacked an effective "science of applications."

Evidence-based medicine and growing recognition of the gap between best practice and usual practice in today's health care system (e.g., Schuster, McGlynn, & Brook, 1998) has generated new interest in clinical quality improvement strategies. Increasing the adoption, reach, and impact of evidence-based health behavior change interventions ultimately will require simultaneous efforts on three fronts, as outlined in Figure 14.1.

Increasing the *science/technology push* for behavioral interventions generally involves proving the intervention for wide population use and includes the development and promulgation of authoritative evidence-based clinical practice guidelines. *Building delivery capacity* includes training and technical assistance for intervention delivery, as well as system-level changes that come about through quality improvement strategies. New systems for delivering and monitoring health behavior change treatments as part of routine medical care are needed (Solberg et al., 1998), along

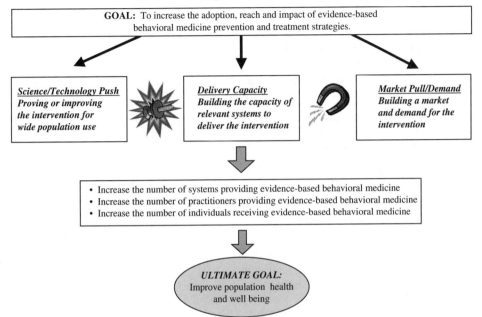

Figure 14.1. Getting evidence-based health behavior change into practice. From *Roadmaps for the Next Frontier: Getting Evidence-Based Behavioral Medicine Into Practice,* by C. T. Orleans, J. Gruman, and N. Anderson, paper presented at the annual scientific meeting of the Society of Behavioral Medicine, San Diego, CA, March 1999. Reprinted with permission of authors.

with changes in the culture and practice of medicine and medical education, not just for physicians but also for the widening range of providers (nurses, physician assistants, health educators, case managers) on the frontlines of primary care and serving schools, worksites, and communities. Finally, *building a market demand* for interventions includes social marketing and communications efforts to build consumer demand, better cost-effectiveness data, and policy changes that drive implementation and reimbursement for effective treatments. Most needed are policies that mandate or reimburse health behavior change programs as part of standard benefit packages and the addition of health behavior change programs to health plan report cards. Only synergistic efforts in each area will ensure the greatest population benefit.

Without efforts like these to address the behavioral aspects of health, the major health problems and causes of death in the United States cannot be solved, and we will not reach the *Healthy People 2010* goals.

REFERENCES

Abrams D., Orleans, C. T., Niaura, R. S., Goldstein, M. G., Velicer, W., Prochaska, J. O., et al. (1996). Integrating individual and public health perspectives for treatment of tobacco dependence under managed health care: A combined stepped-care and matching model. *Annals of Behavioral Medicine, 18,* 290–304.

Agency for Health Care Policy and Research (AHCPR). (1996). *Smoking cessation clinical practice guideline* (Publication No. 96-0692). Rockville, MD: U.S. Department of Health and Human Services, Public Health Service.

American Cancer Society. (1995). *Cancer in the 21st century futures symposium: Graphic summary of proceedings.* Atlanta, GA: Author.

Audrain, J., Boyd, N. R., Roth, J., Main, D., Caporaso, N. F., & Lerman, C. (1997). Genetic susceptibility testing in smoking-cessation treatment: One-year outcomes of a randomized trial. *Addictive Behaviors, 22*(6), 741–751.

Audrain, J., Rimer, B., Cella, D., Stefanek, M., Garber, J., Pennanen, M., et al. (1999). The impact of a brief coping skills intervention on adherence to breast self-examination among first degree relatives of newly diagnosed breast cancer patients. *Psychooncology, 8*(3), 220–229.

Babor, T. F., Aguirre-Molina, M., Marlatt, G. A., & Clayton, R. (1999). Managing alcohol problems and risky drinking. *American Journal of Health Promotion, 14*(2), 98–103.

Baird, P. A. (1994). The role of genetics in population health. In R. G. Evans, M. L. Barer, & T. R. Marmor (Eds.), *Why are some people healthy and others are not? The determinants of health of populations* (pp. 133–161). New York: Aldine de Gruyter.

Bandura, A. (1986). *Social foundations of thought and action. A social cognitive theory.* Englewood Cliffs, NJ: Prentice-Hall.

Beresford, S. A., Curry, S. J., Kristal, A. R., Lazovich, D., Feng, Z., & Wagner, E. H. (1997). A dietary intervention in primary care practice: The Eating Patterns Study. *American Journal of Public Health, 87*(4), 610–616.

Botvin, G. J., Baker, E., Dusenbury, L., Botvin, E. M., & Diaz, T. (1995). Long-term follow-up results of a randomized drug abuse prevention trial in a White middle-class population. *Journal of the American Medical Association, 273*(14), 1106–1112.

Brug, J., Glanz, K., van Assema, P., Kok, G., & van Breukelen, G. J. (1998). The impact of a computer-tailored feedback and iterative feedback on fat, fruit and vegetable intake. *Health Education and Behavior 25*(4), 517–531.

Bull, F. C., Kreuter, M. W., & Scharff, D. P. (1999). Effects of tailored, personalized and general health messages on physical activity. *Patient Education and Counseling, 36*(2), 181–192.

Campbell, M. K., DeVellis, B. M., Strecher, V. J., Ammerman, A. S., DeVellis, R. F., & Sandler, R. S. (1994). Improving dietary behavior: The effectiveness of tailored messages in primary care settings. *American Journal of Public Health, 84*(5), 783–787.

Campfield, L. A., Smith, F. J., & Burn, P. (1998). Strategies and potential molecular targets for obesity treatment. *Science, 280*(5368), 1383–1387.

Carey, M. P. (1999). Prevention of HIV Infection through changes in sexual behavior. *American Journal of Health Promotion, 14*(2), 104–111.

Centers for Disease Control and Prevention (CDC). (2003). *Physical activity and good nutrition: Essential elements to prevent chronic diseases and obesity.* Atlanta, GA: U.S. Department of Health and Human Services.

Centers for Disease Control and Prevention and the American College of Sports Medicine (CDC/ACSM). (1995). Physical activity and public health—A recommendation from the Centers for Disease Control and Prevention and the American College of Sports Medicine. *Journal of the American Medical Association, 273,* 402–407.

Center for the Advancement of Health. (2000). *The challenge of interdisciplinary research.* Washington, DC: Author.

Clayton, R. R., Cattarello, A. M., & Johnstone, B. M. (1996). The effectiveness of Drug Abuse Resistance Education (Project DARE): 5-year follow-up results. *Preventive Medicine, 25*(3), 307–318.

Cleroux, J., Feldman, R. D., & Petrella, R. J. (1999). Lifestyle modifications to prevent and control hypertension. 4. Recommendations on physical exercise training. Canadian Hypertension Society, Canadian Coalition for High Blood Pressure Prevention and Control, Laboratory Centre for Disease Control at Health Canada, Heart and Stroke Foundation of Canada. *Canadian Medical Association Journal, 160*(9 Suppl.), S21–S28.

Curry, S. J., McBride, C., Grothaus, L.C., Louie, D., & Wagner, E. (1995). A randomized trial of self-help materials, personalized feedback and telephone counseling with nonvolunteer smokers. *Journal of Consulting and Clinical Psychology, 63*(6), 1005–1014.

Curry, S., Taplin, S., Barlow, W., Anderman, C., & McBride, C. (1993). A randomized trial of the impact of risk assessment and feedback on participation in mammography screening. *Preventive Medicine, 22*(3), 350–360.

Dalaker, J., & Naifeh, M. (1998). *Poverty in the United States: 1997* (U.S. Bureau of the Census, *Current Populations Reports,* Series P60-201). Washington, DC: U.S. Government Printing Office.

Day, J. C. (1996). Population projections of the United States by age, sex, race, and Hispanic origin: 1995 to 2050 (U.S. Bureau of the Census, *Current Populations Reports,* Series P25-1130). Washington, DC: U.S. Government Printing Office.

DiMatteo, M. R. (1994a). Enhancing patient adherence to medical recommendations. *Journal of the American Medical Association, 271*(1), 79, 83.

DiMatteo, M. R. (1994b). The physician–patient relationship: Effects on the quality of health care. *Clinical Obstetrics and Gynecology, 37*(1), 149–161.

Dishion, T. J., Kavanaugh, K., & Kiesner, J. (2003). Prevention of early adolescent substance abuse among high risk youth: A multiple gating approach to parent intervention. *NIDA Monograph 177,* 208–228.

Eng, T. R., & Gustafson, D. H. (1999). Wired for health and well-being: *The emergence of interactive health communication*. Washington, DC: Office of Disease Prevention and Health Promotion, DHHS.

Eriksson, J., Lindstrom, J., Valle, T., Aunola, S., Hamalainen, H., Ilanne-Parikka, P., et al. (1999). Prevention of type II diabetes in subjects with impaired glucose tolerance: The Diabetes Prevention Study (DPS) in Finland. Study design and 1-year interim report on the feasibility of the lifestyle intervention programme. *Diabetologia, 42*(7), 793–801.

Feldman, H. A., & McKinlay, S. M. (1994). Cohort versus cross-sectional design in large field trials: Precision, sample size, and a unifying model. *Statistics in Medicine, 13,* 61–78.

Frazao, E. (1996). The American diet: A costly problem. *Food Review, 19,* 2–6.

Fries, J. F. (1992). The chronic disease data bank model: A conceptual framework for the computer-based medical record. *Computers and Biomedical Research, 25*(6), 586–601.

Fries, J. F., Koop, C. E., Sokolov, J., Beadle, C. E., & Wright, D. (1998). Beyond health promotion: Reducing need and demand for medical care. *Health Affairs (Millwood), 17*(2), 70–84.

Garnick, D. W., Hendricks, A. M., Comstock C., & Horgan C. (1997). Do individuals with substance abuse diagnoses incur higher charges than individuals with other chronic conditions? *Journal of Substance Abuse Treatment, 14*(5), 457–465.

Glanz, K. (1997). Behavioral research contributions and needs in cancer prevention and control: Dietary change. *Preventive Medicine, 26*(5), S43–S55.

Glanz, K. (1999). Progress in dietary behavior change. *American Journal of Health Promotion, 14*(2), 112–117.

Glanz, K., & Rimer, B. K. (1997). *Theory at a glance: A guide for health promotion practice*. Washington, DC: U.S. Department of Health and Human Services, Public Health Service, National Institutes of Health, National Cancer Institute.

Glanz, K., Tziraki, C., Albright, C. L., & Fernandes, J. (1995). Nutrition assessment and counseling practices: Attitudes and interests of primary care physicians. *Journal of General Internal Medicine, 10*(2), 89–92.

Glasgow, R. E., McKay, H. G., Boles, S. M., & Vogt, T. M. (1999). Interactive computer technology, behavioral science, and family practice. *Journal of Family Practice, 48*(6), 464–470.

Glasgow, R. E., & Strycker, L. A. (2000). Preventive care practices for diabetes management in two primary care samples. *American Journal of Preventive Medicine, 19*(1), 9–14.

Glynn, T. J. (1989). Essential elements of school-based smoking prevention programs. *Journal of School Health, 59*(5), 181–188.

Gutman, M., & Clayton, R. (1999). Treatment and prevention of use and abuse of illegal drugs: Progress on interventions and future directions. *American Journal of Health Promotion, 14*(2), 92–97.

Harsha, D. W., Lin, P. H., Obarzanek, E., Karanja, N. M., Moore, T. J., & Caballero, B. (1999). Dietary approaches to stop hypertension: A summary of study results. *Journal of the American Dietetic Association*, 99(Suppl. 8), S35–S39.

Higgins-Biddle, J. C., Babor, T. F., Mullahy, J., Daniels, J., & McRee, B. (1997). Alcohol screening and brief interventions: Where research meets practice. *Connecticut Medicine*, 61(9), 565–575.

Hoffman, C., & Rice, D. (1996). *Chronic care in America: A 21st century challenge.* Princeton, NJ: Robert Wood Johnson Foundation.

Holder, H. D. (1998). The cost offsets of alcoholism treatment. *Recent Developments in Alcoholism*, *14*, 361–374.

Holtgrave, D. R., & Pinkerton, S. D. (1997). Updates of cost of illness and quality of life estimates for use in economic evaluations of HIV prevention programs. *Journal of Acquired Immune Deficiency Syndrome and Human Retrovirology*, 16(1), 54–62.

Institute of Medicine (IOM). (1992). *The second fifty years: Promoting health and preventing disability.* In R. L. Berg & J. S. Cassells (Eds.), *Committee on health promotion and disability prevention for the second fifty* (pp. 1–332). Washington, DC: Author.

Institute of Medicine. (1994). *Growing up tobacco free: Preventing nicotine addiction in children and youths* (B. S. Lynch & R. J. Bonner, Eds.). Washington, DC: National Academy Press.

Johnston, L. D., O'Malley, P. M., & Bachman, J. G. (1997, Dec. 18). *Drug use among American teens shows some signs of leveling off after a long rise* (press release). Ann Arbor: University of Michigan.

Kalichman, S. C., Nachimson, D., Cherry, C., & Williams, E. (1998). AIDS treatment advances and behavioral prevention setbacks: Preliminary assessment of reduced perceived threat of HIV–AIDS. *Health Psychology*, *17*, 546–550.

Kelly, J. A., Somlai, A. M., DiFranceisco, W. J., Otto-Salaj, L. L., Mcauliffe, T.L., Hackl, K. L., et al. (2000). Bridging the gap between the science and service of HIV prevention: Transferring effective research-based HIV prevention interventions to community AIDS service providers. *American Journal of Public Health* 90(7), 1082–1088.

Kirby, D. (1997). *No easy answers: Research findings on programs to reduce teen pregnancy.* Washington, DC: National Campaign to Prevent Teen Pregnancy.

Lefebvre, R. C., & Rochlin, L. (1997). Social marketing. In K. Glanz, F. M. Lewis, & B. K. Rimer (Eds.), *Health behavior and health education: Theory, research, and practice* (pp. 384–402). San Francisco: Jossey-Bass.

Leon, A. S., Myers, M. J., & Connett, J. (1997). Leisure time physical activity and the 16-year risks of mortality from coronary heart disease and all-causes in the Multiple Risk Factor Intervention Trial (MRFIT). *International Journal of Sports Medicine*, *18* (Suppl. 3), S208–S215.

Lerman, C., & Croyle, R. T. (1996). Emotional and behavioral responses to genetic testing for susceptibility to cancer. *Oncology*, *10*(2), 191–195, 199, 200–202.

Lerman, C., Gold, K., Audrain, J., Lin, T. H., Boyd, N. R., Orleans, C. T., et al. (1997). Incorporating biomarkers of exposure and genetic susceptibility into smoking cessation treatment: Effects on smoking-related cognitions, emotions, and behavior change. *Health Psychology, 16*(1), 87–99.

Leshner, A. (1996, March). *Drug abuse is a health issue.* Paper presented ·at the annual meeting of the Society of Behavioral Medicine, Washington, DC.

Leshner, A. I. (1999). Science-based views of drug addiction and its treatment. *Journal of the American Medical Association, 282*(14), 1314–1316.

Lewis, R. J., Huebner, W. W., & Yarborough, C. M., III. (1996). Characteristics of participants and nonparticipants in worksite health promotion. *American Journal of Health Promotion, 11*, 99–106.

Li, F. P. (1995). Phenotypes, genotypes, interventions for hereditary cancers. *Cancer Epidemiology, Biomarkers, and Prevention, 4*, 579–582.

Lowry, R., Kann, L., Collins, J. L., & Kolbe, L. J. (1996). The effect of socioeconomic status on chronic disease risk behaviors among US adolescents. *Journal of the American Medical Association, 276*(10), 792–797.

Luborsky, L., Barber, J. P., Siqueland, L., McLellan, A. T., & Woody, G. (1997). Establishing a therapeutic alliance with substance abusers. In L. S. Onken, J. D. Blaine, & J. J. Boren (Eds.), *Beyond the therapeutic alliance: Keeping the drug dependent individual in treatment* (pp. 233–244). Rockville, MD: National Institute of Drug Abuse.

Manson, J. E., Hu, F. B., Rich-Edwards, J. W., Colditz, G. A., Stampfer, M. J., Willett, W. C., Speizer, F. E., & Hennekens, C. H. (1999). A prospective study of walking as compared with vigorous exercise in the prevention of coronary heart disease in women. *New England Journal of Medicine, 341*(9), 650–658.

Marcus, B. H., & Forsyth, L. H. (1999). How are we doing with physical activity? *American Journal of Health Promotion, 14*(2), 118–124.

Marcus, B. H., Pinto, B. M., Clark, M. C., DePue, J. D., Goldstein, M. G., & Simkin-Silverman, L. (1995). Physician delivered physical activity and nutrition interventions. *Medical Exercise, Nutrition, and Health, 4*, 324–334.

Marlatt, G. A. (1996). Harm reduction: Come as you are. *Addictive Behaviors, 21*(6), 779–788.

Marlatt, G. A., Baer, J. S., Kivlahan, D. R., Dimeff, L. A., Larimer, M. E., Quigley, L. A., et al. (1998). Screening and brief intervention for high-risk college student drinkers: Results from a 2-year follow-up assessment. *Journal of Consulting and Clinical Psychology, 66*(4), 604–615.

McGinnis, J. M., & Foege, W. H. (1993). Actual causes of death in the United States. *Journal of the American Medical Association, 270*(18), 2207–2211.

McGinnis, J. M., & Foege, W. H. (1999). Mortality and morbidity attributable to use of addictive substances in the United States. *Proceedings of the Association of American Physicians, 111*(2), 109–118.

McKinlay, J. B. (1995). The new public health approach to improving physical activity and autonomy in older populations. In E. Heikkinen, J. Kuusinen, & I. Ruoppila (Eds.), *Preparation for aging* (pp. 87–103). New York: Plenum Press.

McKinlay, J. B. (1996). More appropriate evaluation methods for community-level health interventions. Introduction to the special issue. *Evaluation Review, 20*(3), 237–243.

McLeroy, K. R., Bibeau, D., Steckler, A., & Glanz, K. (1988). An ecological perspective on health promotion programs. *Health Education Quarterly, 15,* 351–378.

McMenamin, S. B., Halpin, H., Ibrahim, J., & Orleans, C. T. (in press). Physician and enrollee knowledge of Medicaid coverage for tobacco dependence treatments. *American Journal of Preventive Medicine.*

McPhillips-Tangum, C. (1998). Results from the first annual survey of addressing tobacco in managed care. *Tobacco Control, 7*(Suppl.), S11–S13.

Miller, W. R., & Rollnick, S. M. (1991). *Motivational interviewing: Preparing people to change addictive behavior.* New York: Guilford Press.

Milliman & Robertson, Inc. (1995). *Health risks and their impact on medical costs.* Minneapolis, MN: Author.

Mokdad, A. H., Ford, E. S., Bowman, B. A., & Dietz, W. H. (2003). Prevalence of obesity, diabetes, and obesity-related health risk factors. *Journal of the American Medical Association, 289,* 76–79.

Murray, D. M. (1995). Design and analysis of community trials: Lessons from the Minnesota heart health program. *American Journal of Epidemiology, 142,* 569–575.

National Center for Health Statistics. (1999). *Healthy People 2000 Review, 1998–1999.* Hyattsville, MD: Public Health Service.

National Committee for Quality Assurance. (2003). The state of health care quality: 2003. Retrieved November 6, 2003, from http://www.ncqa.org/Communications/State%20Of%20Managed%20Care/SOHCREPORT2003.pdf

National Institute on Alcohol Abuse and Alcoholism. (1996). *Alcohol alert no. 31: Drinking and driving.* Bethesda, MD: Author.

National Institute of Mental Health Multisite HIV Prevention Trial Group. (1998). The NIMH Multisite HIV Prevention Trial: Reducing HIV sexual risk behavior. *Science, 280,* 1889–1894.

Nigg, C. R., Burbank, P. M., Padula, C., Dufresne, R., Rossi, J. S., Velicer, W. F., et al. (1999). Stages of change across ten health risk behaviors for older adults. *Gerontologist, 39*(4), 473–482.

Normand, J., Vlahov, D., & Moses, L. E. (Eds.). (1995). *Preventing HIV transmission: The role of sterile needles and bleach.* Washington, DC: Institute of Medicine and National Research Council, Panel on Needle Exchange and Bleach Distribution Programs.

Oldenburg, B. F., Ffrench, M. L., & Sallis, J. F. (2000). Health behavior research: The quality of the evidence base. *American Journal of Health Promotion, 14*(4), 253–257.

Orleans, C. T. (1995). Review of the current status of smoking cessation in the USA: Progress and opportunities. *Tobacco Control, 4*(Suppl. 2), S3–S9.

Orleans, C. T. (1999). Context, confidentiality, and consent in tailored health communications: A cautionary note. *Annals of Behavioral Medicine, 21,* 307–310.

Orleans, C. T. (2000). Promoting the maintenance of health behavior change: Recommendations for the next generation of research and practice. *Health Psychology, 19,* 76–83.

Orleans, C. T., & Alper, J. (2002). Helping addicted smokers quit. In S. Isaacs & J. Knickman (Eds.), *To improve health and health care: The Robert Wood Johnson Foundation Anthology* (Vol. 7, pp. 125–149). San Francisco: Jossey-Bass.

Orleans, C. T., & Cummings, K. M. (1999). Population-based tobacco control: Progress and prospects. *American Journal of Health Promotion, 14*(2), 83–91.

Orleans, C. T., Gruman, J., Ulmer, C., Emont, S. L., & Hollendonner, J. K. (1999). Rating our progress in population health promotion: Report card on six behaviors. *American Journal of Health Promotion, 14*(2), 75–82.

Palmer, R. H., Wright, E. A., Orav, E. J., Hargraves, J. L., & Louis, T. A. (1996). Consistency in performance among primary care practitioners. *Medical Care 34*(9), SS52–SS66.

Partnership for Prevention. (1998). *Why invest in disease prevention?* Washington DC: Author.

Pierce, J. P., Gilpin, E. A., Emery, S. L., White, M. M., Rosbrook, B., & Berry, C. C. (1998). Has the California tobacco control program reduced smoking? *Journal of the American Medical Association, 280,* 893–899.

Prochaska, J. O., & DiClemente, C. C. (1983). Stages and processes of self-change in smoking: Towards an integrative model of change. *Journal of Consulting and Clinical Psychology, 51,* 390–395.

Prochaska, J. O., DiClemente, C. C., Velicer, W. F., & Rossi, J. S. (1993). Standardized, individualized, interactive, and personalized self-help programs for smoking cessation. *Health Psychology, 12*(5), 399–405.

Prochaska, J. O., & Velicer, W. F. (1997). The transtheoretical model of health behavior change. *American Journal of Health Promotion, 12*(1), 38–48.

Pronk, N. P., Goodman, M. J., O'Connor, P. J., & Martinson, B. C. (1999). Relationship between modifiable health risks and short-term health care charges. *Journal of the American Medical Association, 282*(23), 2235–2239.

Pronk, N. P., O'Connor, P., Isham, G., & Hawkins, C. (1997). Building a patient registry for implementation of health promotion initiatives: Targeting high-risk individuals. *HMO Practice, 11*(1), 43–46.

Rimer, B. (1997). Toward an improved behavioral medicine. *Annals of Behavioral Medicine, 19*(1), 6–10.

Rowe, J. W., & Kahn, R. L. (1998). *Successful aging*. New York: Pantheon Books.

Sallis, J. F., & Owen, N. (1997). Ecological models. In K. Glanz, F. M. Lewis, & B. K. Rimer (Eds.), *Health behavior and health education: Theory, research, and practice* (pp. 403–424). San Francisco: Jossey-Bass.

Schroeder, S. A. (2000). Understanding human behavior is central to improving health. *Proceedings of the Society for Experimental Biology and Medicine, 223*(4), 329–330.

Schuster, M. A., McGlynn, E. A., & Brook, R. H. (1998). How good is the quality of health care in the United States? *Milbank Quarterly, 76,* 517–563.

Sellars, D. E., Crawford, S., Bullock, K., & McKinlay, J. B. (1996). *A meta-analysis of community heart health programs.* Unpublished manuscript.

Skinner, C. S., Campbell, M. K., Rimer, B. K., Curry, S. J., & Prochaska, J. O. (1999). How effective is tailored print communication? *Annals of Behavioral Medicine, 21,* 290–298.

Smith, K. R., West, J. A., Croyle, R. T., & Botkin, J. R. (1999). Familial context of genetic testing for cancer susceptibility: Moderating effect of siblings' test results on psychological distress one to two weeks after BRCA1 mutation testing. *Cancer Epidemiology, Biomarkers, and Prevention, 8*(4), 385–392.

Sobel, D. S. (1995). Rethinking medicine: Improving health outcomes with cost-effective psychosocial interventions. *Psychosomatic Medicine, 57*(3), 234–244.

Solberg, L. I., Kottke, T. E., Brekke, M. L., Conn, S. A., Magnan, S., & Amundson, G. (1998). The case of the missing clinical preventive services systems. *Effective Clinical Practice, 1,* 33–38.

Strecher, V. J., Kreuter, M., Den Boer, D. J., Kobrin, S., Hospers, H. J., & Skinner, C. S. (1994). The effects of computer-tailored smoking cessation messages in family practice settings. *Journal of Family Practice, 39*(3), 262–270.

Strycker, L. A., Foster, L. S., Pettigrew, L., Donnelly-Perry, J., Jordan, S., & Glasgow, R. E. (1997). Steering Committee enhancements on health promotion program delivery. *American Journal of Health Promotion, 11*(6), 437–440.

Stunkard, A. J. (1996). Current views on obesity. *American Journal of Medicine, 100*(2), 230–236.

Taira, D. A., Safran, D. G., Seto, T. B., Rogers, W. H., & Tarlov, A. R. (1997). The relationship between patient income and physician discussion of health risk behaviors. *Journal of the American Medical Association, 278*(17), 1412–1417.

Tobacco Use and Dependence Clinical Practice Guideline Panel. (2000). A clinical practice guideline for treating tobacco use and dependence: A US Public Health Service report. *Journal of the American Medical Association, 283,* 3244–3254.

Tosteson, A. N., Weinstein, M. C., Hunink, M. G., Mittleman, M. A., Williams, L. W., Goldman, P. A., et al. (1997). Cost-effectiveness of population wide educational approaches to reduce serum cholesterol levels. *Circulation, 95*(1), 24–30.

U.S. Census Bureau. (1999). *Projections of total resident population by 5-year age groups, and sex with special age categories: Middle series, 2006-2010 (NP-T3-C) and 2025 to 2045 (NP-T3-F)*. Washington, DC: Population Projections Program, Population Division.

U.S. Department of Agriculture (USDA) and U.S. Department of Health and Human Services (U.S. DHHS). (1995). *Nutrition and your health: Dietary guidelines for Americans* (4th ed.). Washington, DC: U.S. Government Printing Office.

U.S. Department of Health and Human Services. (1994a). *Preventing tobacco use among young people: A report of the Surgeon General*. Atlanta, GA: Public Health Service, Centers for Disease Control and Prevention, National Center for Chronic Disease Prevention and Health Promotion, Office of Smoking and Health.

U.S. Department of Health and Human Services. (1994b). *Signs of effectiveness II: Preventing alcohol, tobacco and other drug use: A risk factor/resiliency based approach*. Washington, DC: U.S. Government Printing Office.

U.S. Department of Health and Human Services. (1996). *Physical activity and health: A report of the Surgeon General*. Atlanta, GA: Centers for Disease Control and Prevention, National Center for Chronic Disease Prevention and Health Promotion.

U.S. Department of Health and Human Services. (2000a). *Healthy People 2010. Conference Edition*. [CD-ROM]. Washington, DC: Author. (Also available online at *http://www.health.gov/healthypeople*)

U.S. Department of Health and Human Services. (2000b). *Reducing tobacco use. A report of the Surgeon General—2000*. Atlanta, GA: Centers for Disease Control and Prevention, National Center for Chronic Disease Prevention and Health Promotion, Office on Smoking and Health. (Also available online at *http://www.cdc.gov/tobacco/sgr—tobacco—use.htm*)

U.S. Public Health Service (U.S. PHS). (2000). *Treating tobacco use and dependence: A clinical practice guideline* (AHRQ Publication No. 00-0032). Washington, DC: U.S. Department of Health and Human Services.

Velicer, W. F., Prochaska, J. O., Fava, J. L., Laforge, R. G., & Rossi, J. S. (1999). Interactive versus noninteractive interventions and dose-response relationships for stage-matched smoking cessation programs in a managed care setting. *Health Psychology, 18*(1), 21–28.

Von Korff, M., Gruman, J., Schaefer, J., Curry, S. J., & Wagner, E. H. (1997). Collaborative management of chronic illness. *Annals of Internal Medicine, 127*(12), 1097–1102.

Wagner, E. H., Austin, B. T., & Von Korff, M. (1996). Organizing care for patients with chronic illness. *Milbank Quarterly, 74*, 511–544.

Wagner, E. H., Curry, S. J., Grothaus, L., Saunders, K. W., & McBride, C. M. (1995). The impact of smoking and quitting on health care use. *Archives of Internal Medicine, 155*(16), 1789–1795.

Wagner, E. H., Davis, C., Schaefer, J., Von Korff, M., & Austin, B. (1999). A survey of leading chronic disease management programs: Are they consistent with the literature? *Managed Care Quarterly, 7*(3), 56–66.

Warner, K. E., Slade, J., & Sweanor, D. T. (1997). The emerging market for long-term nicotine maintenance. *Journal of the American Medical Association, 278*(13), 1087–1092.

Wilk, A. I., Jensen, N. M., & Havinghurst, T. C. (1997). Meta-analysis of randomized control trials addressing brief interventions in heavy alcohol drinkers. *Journal of General Internal Medicine, 12*(5), 274–283.

Wing, R. R. (2000). Cross-cutting themes in maintenance of behavior change. *Health Psychology, 19*(Suppl. 1), 84–88.

Winkler, M. A., Flanagin, A., Chilum, B., White, J., Andrews, K., Kennett, R. L., et al. (2000). Guidelines for medical and health information sites on the Internet. *Journal of the American Medical Association, 283*, 1600–1606.

Wolf, A. M., & Colditz, G. A. (1998). Current estimates of the economic cost of obesity in the United States. *Obesity Research, 6*(2), 97–106.

Yarnall, K. S., Rimer, B. K., Hynes, D., Watson, G., Lyna, P. R., Woods-Powell, C. T., et al. (1998). Computerized prompts for cancer screening in a community health center. *Journal of the American Board of Family Practice, 11*(2), 96–104.

15

INTERVENTIONS IN
COMMUNITY SETTINGS

LAURA C. LEVITON AND JAMES M. RACZYNSKI

This chapter addresses effective planning and research to introduce health behavior interventions into community settings. These settings may be entire communities or subgroups of individuals within a particular geopolitically defined group, consisting of individuals defined by the church or school they attend, their place of work, their ethnic or cultural group, or other means of segmentation of a broader community. The focus is thus on changing the behavior of numbers of individuals within the defined community rather than creating change within a collection of unassociated individuals. Community-based interventions are designed with the recognition that most people are embedded within a variety of communities and networks of social ties (Berkman & Glass, 1999). This is thus a population-based perspective rather than a focus on the individual client as is typically the case in most clinical and health care psychology. This distinction between a clinical focus and a population-based focus is critical to understanding issues related to community interventions.

Preparation of this chapter was supported through funding from the Centers for Disease Control and Prevention, Grant #U48/CCU409679, which provides core funding for the UAB Center for Health Promotion and funding for "Peer Support Intervention for CVD Risk Among African-American Women" through a cooperative agreement with the National Institutes of Health's Women's Health Initiative.

Many writers in psychology (both social and community), evaluation research, health promotion, and public health have spoken to the issues that follow (e.g., Cook, 1993; Cronbach, 1982; Green & Kreuter, 1999; Leviton, 1996, 2001; Windsor, Baranowski, & Clark, 1994). Most recently, Glasgow, Vogt, and Boles (1999) have articulated some of them in the RE-AIM framework, in a form that is most clearly addressed to the health psychology audience.

At the simplest level, communities are composed of individuals, and the approaches adopted to promote behavior changes when working exclusively with individuals are applicable within the planning and implementation of community changes. Theoretical approaches for individual behavior change, including those developed within clinical and social psychology, thus commonly serve as the theories on which community programs are structured. Nonetheless, community interventions are also different from those directed at individuals. Individually directed interventions typically are focused on those individuals who have sought treatment and are ready to change. Community interventions, on the other hand, typically focus on changing the behavior(s), not only of those who are ready to change, but also those who may not be at the stage of readiness to change. By making a distinction about who is being targeted for the intervention, community trials often incorporate theoretical models to affect individuals who are not yet at an action stage of readiness to change, as well as those who are seeking a change.

We first describe the advantages and special nature of this setting for behavior change initiatives as well as challenges of community-level interventions for research purposes and service programs. We then review approaches to planning. Complete planning is an important strategy to increase the likelihood of an effective intervention. Interventions that ignore such planning are often less imaginative, less tailored to local circumstances, and can be wasteful, because they are less likely to obtain community attention, trust, and cooperation and more likely to ignore a community's existing resources. Planning and community participation will generally lead to more effective, sustainable interventions. We discuss the need to select appropriate behavioral theories to guide the planning, development, implementation, and evaluation of interventions and the process of tailoring theories to interventions in communities. Finally, we speak to some special research issues that arise in community settings. Throughout, we use the following three examples to illustrate the points being made.

1. *The Heart Attack–REACT Project.* In 1994 the National Heart, Lung, and Blood Institute (NHLBI) initiated the REACT study (Rapid Early Action for Coronary Treatment), a theory-based community intervention to reduce patient delay time,

defined as the period from onset of heart attack symptoms until a patient's contact with the medical care system. REACT was a four-year, randomized, multicenter collaborative community trial, with five academic study field centers, each affiliated with four communities (Raczynski et al., 1999; Simons-Morton et al., 1998). REACT used community organization, community and media education methods, provider education, and patient education to convey the message about the importance of seeking help quickly when heart attack symptoms begin. A Web site outlining intervention components can be found at http://www.epi.umn.edu/react/welcome.html. Although greater reduction in delay in seeking treatment was not found in the intervention versus comparison communities, beneficial increases in the use of emergency medical services (EMS) was found in the intervention versus comparison communities (Luepker et al., 2000).

2. *The AIDS Community Demonstration Projects.* One of the earliest multisite evaluations of HIV prevention conducted by the federal Centers for Disease Control and Prevention (CDC), this initiative used a quasi-experimental design in which 10 communities were matched on relevant characteristics (AIDS Community Demonstration Projects Research Group, 1999; Higgins et al., 1996). The program's aim was to promote consistent condom and bleach use among injection drug users, female sex partners of injection drug users, female commercial sex workers, at-risk youth, and non–gay-identified men who have sex with men. Compared to control communities, intervention in the target communities achieved a 54% exposure rate to messages, significantly greater progress toward more consistent condom use, and a significant increase in carrying of condoms by those at risk. A bibliography and complete program description can be found at http://www.cdc.gov/nchstp/hiv—aids/projects/acdp/acdp.htm.

3. *The Uniontown Community Health Project.* This demonstration intervention program is being implemented in Uniontown, Alabama, as one of the Women's Health Initiative (WHI) programs. Funded by cooperative agreement, this program includes activities that specifically target knowledge, attitudes, and behaviors relevant to cardiovascular disease (CVD) risk-reduction in women, with a focus on increasing physical activity, dietary changes, and tobacco cessation (Raczynski et al., 2001). The program was developed in collaboration with the Uniontown Community Health Council (CHC) and

community health advisors (CHAs). Following initial CHA training, action teams are formed consisting of individuals who are interested in receiving advanced training in physical activity, tobacco cessation, or nutrition. One action team focuses on each of the three content areas. CHAs are free to belong to more than one action team but are asked to designate a primary content area of interest. The advanced training prepares CHAs to conduct risk-reduction classes in their chosen content area(s), as well as to conduct interpersonal counseling and community-based social marketing and other activities focused on reduction of risk for cancer and CVD. The findings of this project suggest significant decreases in smoking prevalence and improved food preparation behaviors to reduce risks for CHD [coronary heart disease] relative to a comparison community and maintained physical activity levels relative to reductions in physical activity in the comparison community (Cornell et al., 2000).

WHY INTERVENE IN COMMUNITY SETTINGS?

The fields of health promotion and public health have outlined some compelling reasons to intervene in community settings, in addition to the more narrowly focused patient care settings, workplace settings, and school settings (Green & Kreuter, 1999).

Many People Can Be Reached in the Community Who Are Not Seen in Other Settings

A variety of authors maintain that health psychology programs, like other health programs, should be evaluated on the basis of their public health impact—in other words, their impact on entire populations at risk of a disease (Glasgow et al., 1999; Leviton, 1996). Achieving public health impact requires "reach" into the target population. The RE-AIM Web site defines *reach* as "the absolute number, proportion, and representativeness of individuals who are willing to participate in a given initiative." From this perspective, community-located programs are highly desirable because of their ability under certain conditions to penetrate to a higher percentage of the target population than individually oriented programs.

Community-located and community-based programs are particularly important for low-income and minority community segments who are less likely than the middle-class to use health care services on a routine basis, as well as those who are unemployed and therefore not accessible through worksites (Center for the Study of Health Systems Change, 1997). For example, the AIDS Community Demonstration Projects identified specific community venues where hard-to-reach populations at risk of HIV would congregate. The Uniontown Project was focused on older, rural African American women who were largely not employed out of the home and had few avenues to receive care or to access primary prevention programs.

Health Messages and Strategies Can Be Delivered Through More Channels

This principle originally derived from communications research via the social psychology of attitude change (McGuire, 1969) and was adopted by the emerging field of health promotion (Green & Kreuter, 1999). Messages delivered through multiple channels, defined as avenues of disseminating a message, are often more effective than single-channel messages. This is because not everyone relies on the same channel and because people may not be reached on any single occasion by a single message. Most important, through word of mouth the community can amplify messages aired through mass and small media, health fairs, community associations, and other venues. Awareness of a health issue increases as the number of such venues increases. For example, in the Heart Attack–REACT project, many sites held programs that used channels available through senior residential facilities and senior centers. These programs aimed to assist elderly individuals in developing a plan for seeking help in the event of a heart attack. Word-of-mouth was key to developing such a plan, because it would naturally rely on friends, relatives, and others within the elderly person's network of social ties.

Trust in the Message and in the Provider Can Increase

Recently, social science has begun to focus on trust as a key variable that promotes the common good within nations, regions, and communities (Putnam, 2000). Although empirical data are sparse in this frontier area, the expectation is that health-promotion activities are more likely to be effective when such trust exists (Kreuter, Young, & Lezin, 1998). Although health promotion research has rarely investigated trust systematically, related areas of research have done so. Trust has been found to be a key variable for using medical care (Mechanic, 1998), and the field of communications has long understood the importance of credibility of the message (McGuire, 1969). It is likely that trust is a necessary, but not a sufficient, condition for many health behavior changes. However, not everyone trusts a health provider's message. The level of trust in medical care providers has declined in recent years (Mechanic, 1998), especially in marginalized groups and those who do not share a common culture with the health care provider.

Trust can often be increased when key influentials and community leaders endorse a project or message (Leviton, Needleman, & Shapiro, 1997). Because these leaders are trusted sources, trust in the health education message will increase (McGuire, 1969). Trust can also increase when community leaders are engaged in an effort, because their engagement can countervail against the forces that produce distrust. The social psychology of intergroup relations offers some reasons both for the lack of trust and the positive influence that trust can exert in affected communities. For example, disadvantaged communities often hold negative stereotypes of the more privileged groups that may approach communities "to help them," just as the more privileged groups may hold their own stereotypes about disadvantaged communities. Exposure to the "outsiders" under positive circumstances can help to overcome these negative stereotypes. As long as progress is seen, groups that work together for a common goal tend to increase positive feelings toward outsiders (e.g., Brown, 1988). Also, community leaders and service providers can often feel that they are in competition with outsiders, conditions that promote hostility (Brown, 1988). On entering communities, to gain trust it is essential to demonstrate why and how the newcomers are not in competition for resources or power.

Access to the Population in Need Can Increase

Community interventions to change health behaviors often need to work through community "gatekeepers," those individuals who can identify members of the population in need or at risk and who can facilitate contact with the population (Higgins et al., 1996). For example, the directors of senior centers in several Heart Attack–REACT communities were at first doubtful about permitting educational activities to go forward in these settings. They were concerned that the message might frighten seniors. However, greater overall familiarity with the goals of Heart Attack–REACT convinced these gatekeepers that the program was beneficial. In the Uniontown Project, CHAs were identified among the community's natural helpers, providing access to many more residents in need than might be possible through alternative mechanisms. A key mistake is to ignore community leaders and gatekeepers in community interventions, a tendency that is all too common in hierarchical., professionalized health care organizations (Leviton et al., 1997). In some projects, such as the Uniontown Project, involving community residents directly is central to achieving project goals. Even when community involvement is not centrally important to the plan, however, the support of community gatekeepers can be important to avoid their active opposition to a health intervention. For instance, the Minnesota Heart Project (Mittelmark et al., 1986) encountered active resistance from local dairy farmers until steps could be taken to enlist support from farming community members to promote low-fat milk options (John Finnegan, personal communication, August 15, 2001).

To this point, we have been speaking of pragmatics rather than ethics— but on ethical grounds, ignoring community leaders is inconsistent with democratic process and not even consistent with the protection of individuals' research rights. Community groups have long complained that a failure to consult them in research treats them like guinea pigs instead of thinking, feeling participants in problem-solving. We would find such treatment unacceptable in our own communities or in other forms of research.

When entire communities experience risks and benefits from research participation, an increasing number of bioethicists advocate that researchers should obtain consent at two levels, both from the community leaders and from individuals (CDC/ATSDR Committee on Community Engagement, 1997; Nuffield Council on Bioethics, 2002). The risks to entire communities can be very real: for example, minority communities and public health professionals are concerned about reporting sexually transmitted disease rates by census tract and race. Too often, media descriptions turn such information into a weapon to further denigrate those communities (Leviton, 2003). Principles for identifying and engaging community leaders can be found at the Web site of the Association for the Study and Development of Community (2000) or in Leviton, Needleman, and Shapiro (1997).

Treating community members as the passive recipients of services does not build community capacity and is not likely to result in sustained improvements once the researchers leave the scene. John McKnight (1996) has made the strongest case that professionals can actually undermine community capacity when they supplant natural helpers with professionalization of services. Indirect evidence that community engagement helps to sustain health promotion efforts comes from the long-term community–university partnerships in Michigan (Israel, Schulz, Parker, & Becker, 1998), North Carolina (Parker, Eng, et al., 1998), and East Baltimore (Bruce & McKane, 2000). Other examples of sustained efforts that engaged community participants can be found in Berkowitz and Wolff (2000). The literature on collaboration indicates that such efforts are often more sustainable than are stand-alone projects (Gray, 1989). Of course, one can make the case for sustained health promotion efforts that did not use a specific community partnership, as for example efforts that might be carried out by a medical care organization that views prevention as part of its mission. Moreover, coalitions can themselves take time, are not always successful, and can actually sap community and professional capacity for a time before they become sustained (Gray, 1989).

Community Interventions Can Use Community Resources and Capacities

Health promotion interventions commonly have limited resources, but enlisting those already available within communities can increase the chances for a successful and sustained program. To produce widespread effects in populations, therefore, those seeking to undertake health promotion interventions need to collaborate with communities and access their resources (Leviton, 1996). Along with acceptance and endorsement by community leaders, these resources can be key to two of the RE-AIM framework's criteria for effective programs: sustainment of the intervention and appropriate implementation (Glasgow et al., 1999). Several writers on community development and health promotion have coined the term "community capacities" as those resources that a given community has that can be brought to bear on a health or social problem (Bracht, 1999; Clark & McLeroy, 1995; Kretzman & McKnight, 1993; McKnight, 1996). For example, such capacities include volunteers who can be trained in aspects of an intervention. In the AIDS Community Demonstration Projects, for example, investigators recruited volunteers from among the affected at-risk groups to hand out role model stories designed to encourage HIV risk reduction. The volunteers were more effective than outsiders would have been in identifying those at risk. They were also effective spokespeople in conversations about HIV risk behaviors and the beliefs and attitudes that may promote those behaviors (AIDS Community Demonstration Projects Research Group, 1999). By recruiting the volunteers, the project tapped existing community capacity, but training them created new capacity. Similar interventions have been conducted by investigators in gay men's bars (Kelly et al., 1992) and among women in public housing communities (Sikkema et al., 2000). In general, both paid and unpaid community members are effective in many venues for their ability to engage community members in preventive activities and services (Centers for Disease Control and Prevention, 1998). Some evidence is also available that with proper backup and support in the form of needed knowledge and skill training and available professional consultative support, paraprofessionals can deliver theory-based preventive health interventions with fidelity (Cabral et al., 1996).

Although building on existing community capacities is critical to the success of community interventions, we have yet to understand the full potential of planned community interventions to build capacity. For example, the Uniontown Project, in which we participate, is being implemented in Uniontown, Alabama, a very poor community with high risk of heart disease among Black residents. Recently, volunteer residents underwent training as leaders of aerobic exercise, tobacco cessation and prevention, and heart-healthy dietary programs as part of their CHA training. Although this training assisted them to become more effective role models and active interventionists within their communities, training of the aerobic group leaders also gave them marketable skills and national certification as aerobic exercise instructors, contributing to increased capacity overall within the community.

Community capacities include not only human resources but other resources as well, such as libraries or other locations for meetings in community buildings and even vacant lots when converted to vegetable gardens (Kretzman & McKnight, 1993). In the Uniontown Project, residents converted an underused building into an exercise facility. The new capacity increases the likelihood that residents will continue to exercise in inclement weather. Some health facilities in the Heart Attack–REACT communities donated public relations and media assistance, which greatly extended the reach of the program's media budget.

Finally, it should be noted that some intervention programs and even the theoretical models on which they are based rely extensively on methods to build community capacities. Some intervention theories and methods simply require a focus on the community. For example, the focus of the CHA training in the Uniontown Project and the peer volunteers recruited for the AIDS Community Demonstration Projects both necessitated the active participation of identifiable lay leaders within these communities, and could only be implemented with the active participation of key community segments. Diffusion of innovation theory (Rogers, 1983) defines what happens as innovations are introduced and adopted throughout communities. Social marketing also describes the process of change within communities, as tools of marketing are incorporated into approaches to promote social changes (Andreasen, 1995; Maibach & Parrott, 1995).

Interventions Can Be Tailored to Community Conditions

Just as tailoring of individual lifestyle changes increases the likelihood of behavior change (Prochaska, DiClemente, & Norcross, 1992), so does tailoring of interventions at the community level. For example, the AIDS Community Demonstration Projects used role model stories that were aimed at changing community norms, beliefs, and skills for reducing HIV risk. The role model stories all used basic principles known to encourage behavior change; however, they were all developed locally from true-life stories, for the specific populations at risk (AIDS Community Demonstration Projects Research Group, 1999). Local development increased the immediate relevance of the stories and held people's interest to a greater degree than would materials developed for national distribution. The Heart Attack–REACT trial offers numerous examples of tailoring to community circumstances. In Brownsville, Texas, the Hispanic community did not respond to volunteers' door-to-door educational efforts. However, the volunteers formed a well-publicized "parade," complete with ambulances, sirens sounding, and lights flashing. Community members came to the door to see what was going on and felt safe talking with volunteers during such a public event (National Heart, Lung, and Blood Institute, 1994).

Community-Level Interventions Can Affect Forces Operating Beyond the Individual Level

By enlisting gatekeepers and community leaders, accessing community capacity, and improving the credibility of the message, health behavior interventions can affect factors in the *environment* that may facilitate or impede positive behavior changes, as well as the *perceived norms* of behavior within a community or at-risk group. These two sources of influence are important to the application of behavioral theories. For example, social cognitive theory (Bandura, 1986) posits that individual decisions to take action occur within a community and social environment that shape our perceptions and outcome expectations in the first place. Behavior change occurs in individuals largely through expectancies that behavior will result in personal benefit, that one can successfully perform the behavior in question (self-efficacy), and that interpersonal and environmental forces make the behavior possible in the first place.

Environmental changes that support behavior change efforts and the maintenance of healthful behaviors include structural changes, changes in social norms, and policy changes. The Healthy Cities movement (World Health Organization, 1995) offers a good example of the progress that can be made in lifestyle change when structural environmental factors are addressed; for example, advocacy for bicycle and walking trails has increased the ease with which people can exercise. Advocacy is more effective in producing changes when it martials the interest and efforts of community groups. The Community Health Advisory Network model anticipates that natural helpers will develop a variety of skills to advocate for structural and policy improvements in their communities (Eng & Parker, 1994). In the Uniontown Community Health Project, community CHAs advocated both for the installation of lights at a local track and renovation and air conditioning for an in-door exercise area. Examples also exist of policy approaches for creating environmental changes such as with advocacy to create policies to prohibit smoking from public areas that may reduce the temptation some people feel to relapse into smoking (e.g., Patten, Gilpin, Calvin, & Pierce, 1995). Zero drug tolerance throughout communities also appears to be a key policy feature of effective substance abuse prevention programs (Chou et al., 1998; Pentz et al., 1989).

The theory of reasoned action (Ajzen & Fishbein, 1980) posits that in any given situation, our intention to act is, in part, a function of our beliefs concerning relevant norms and the importance we give to those norms. For example, a powerful factor that facilitates HIV risk reduction in men who have sex with men (MSM) has been the perception that their peers (and potential lovers) support safer sex. This factor has been a key component in both small group and community-based interventions for MSM (Kelly et al., 1992; Leviton et al., 1990; Leviton & Valdiserri, 1990; Valdiserri et al., 1989). In the AIDS Community Demonstration Projects Research Group (1999), this effort was taken one step farther through attempts to influence relevant community norms and perceptions of those norms directly. The techniques of social marketing used in this study were also used in the North Karelia Project and Stanford Five Communities project, which saw reductions of smoking and other heart attack risks (Puska et al., 1989; Schooler, Farquhar, Fortmann, & Flora, 1997).

The Special Challenges of Community-Level Interventions

Many benefits accrue to promoting health and preventing disease at the community level, including allowing the intervention to reach people who cannot be reached through other avenues; enabling access to people who are in the most need; allowing community resources and capacities to be used to tailor the intervention for the community; and affecting forces beyond the individual level. Nonetheless, despite these benefits of community-level intervention programs, clear challenges also exist, both for service programs (those delivered strictly for their clinical benefit) as well as those that are being undertaken for research purposes. Even for service programs that are not being undertaken with a research purpose, the very nature of attempting to mobilize idiosyncratic community resources and capacities, although ultimately of great potential benefit in tailoring the program, is a major service challenge. Even for service programs, which often originate within community-based organizations, issues of sustainability also emerge as long-term challenges. For research programs involving community-level interventions that typically originate from academicians located outside of the community, these challenges are even greater.

The Challenges of Community-Level Service Programs

Community-level service programs, even in the absence of additional issues encountered with community research programs, face considerable challenges. Funding levels for service programs are often low, and problems with sustaining funding are often encountered. Categorical (single-purpose) funding streams are the norm, making it difficult to coordinate services and to address within the same program the array of problems that may stand in the way of health promotion. For example, women who use crack cocaine often have many other problems besides the need for abstinence, ranging from legal problems, to child care, to housing and transportation. Encouraging physical activity in urban areas may be discouraged by the lack of sidewalks and playgrounds, fear of crime, and isolation from neighbors, even if the most engaging and enthusiastic health promotion campaign were to encourage people to exercise.

In addition, service programs, such as research-based interventions, must sustain community support and enlist community capacities and resources if they are to realize the real benefits of working at the community level. Yet sustaining community interest and commitment in the face of competing needs can be difficult. Volunteers, for example, have many demands on their time, and resources may dwindle if the health promotion issue loses a sense of urgency or priority. For example, Detroit has mounted a highly effective community-based arson control program around Halloween. It relied on a city-wide effort and an active neighborhood watch approach. Yet in 1994, people thought the problem was solved; the program saw a substantial loss in volunteer effort and a corresponding rise in fires around the Halloween period (Maciak, Moore, Leviton, & Guinan, 1998).

Community decision-making processes can be slow and cumbersome, and from the perspective of an outsider, they may never get anywhere. When a program is community-driven, it takes both patience and appropriate facilitation to make sure that community groups stay on course to develop an action plan related to a program's goals. An excellent resource to provide context on these issues and suggestions for overcoming roadblocks in community decision-making processes is the Community Tool Box (2003), an Internet resource for health promotion that has been applied widely by community groups around the world.

The Challenges of Community-Level Research Programs

Beyond the challenges of service programs, four basic challenges are encountered in community-level research programs:

1. Like the service programs, researchers must deal with the challenges of funding that is most often categorical in nature. Unlike the service programs, they face another challenge, because funding is relatively short-term—as short as a year, for example. This creates three problems for researchers. First, it presents an ethical problem for the researcher who wants to benefit communities, because the funded project may very

well divert community energies from other projects, only to disappear within a relatively short time. In essence, short funding periods can actually *diminish* the capacity of small, community-based agencies unless substantial care is taken to anticipate this problem. Second, short periods of research funding create a public relations problem for researchers, in that communities rightly question the commitment and motivations of researchers who want to study their problems then move on to other research once funding ends. Third, short funding periods create a scientific problem for the research. It takes time for community-based projects to get through the start-up phase and into operation; the project may end just when it is starting to have an effect, such as occurred in the Heart Attack–REACT project.

2. Researchers must address the methodological and quantitative analytical challenges of nested or hierarchical designs in which communities (churches, schools, or some other unit) are randomized and in which other subunits (such as classrooms within schools) and ultimately individuals are aggregated. Furthermore, some designs must be used with care in community settings. Randomized experiments are feasible to conduct in community settings, but there are an array of dangers, both ethical and logistical, that require careful planning and implementation (Dennis, 1994). In some cases, group randomized studies may be feasible (Murray, 1998); in other cases resources or logistics may require a fall-back design, such as a recurring institutional design or a matched community or venue design in which intervention is staggered across time with multiple baselines (Cook & Campbell, 1979; Miller, 1995; Miller, Klotz, & Eckholdt, 1998).

3. Researchers often study an intervention that to be effective must be responsive to varying community resources and capacities. Therefore, the researchers need to balance flexibility of tailored implementation, while at the same time avoiding creation of disparate and noncomparable interventions in those communities receiving the intervention.

4. The evaluation is a challenge to researchers as well, because for each community they must determine what outcomes occurred, characterize the process by which the intervention in each community was implemented, and assess the impact of the intervention on intermediary variables that are hypothesized to affect the final outcome(s).

SIMILARITIES AND DIFFERENCES BETWEEN COMMUNITY AND INDIVIDUAL-LEVEL INTERVENTIONS

Although there are many dissimilar characteristics between interventions directed at individuals and those directed at a community or subset of the population, many similarities exist also.

Similar Features

Individually and community-directed interventions have some commonalities. The theories's approaches adopted to promote behavior changes when working exclusively with individuals are thus applicable within the planning and implementation of community changes. For example, the Heart Attack–REACT program was developed primarily based on social cognitive theory (Bandura, 1986) as the most commonly used theoretical model for community-based interventions, providing the best evidence of effective methods (Raczynski et al., 1999). However, aspects of self-regulatory theory (Cameron, Leventhal, & Leventhal, 1993, 1995; Leventhal & Nerenz, 1985) were useful in framing the intervention, because this theory specifically addresses illness behavior and help-seeking (Raczynski et al., 1999). The final theoretical approach, combining these two theories, incorporating relevant theoretical elements as appropriate, is represented in Figure 15.1.

Dissimilar Features

Nonetheless, community interventions also differ from those directed at individuals. Individually directed interventions commonly address the needs of individuals who have sought treatment and are ready to change. Community interventions, on the other hand, typically attempt to change the behavior of everyone possible within the community, both those who are ready to change as well as those who are not ready to attempt or even contemplating making any kind of risk-reduction change. This distinction has been termed a difference in efficacy versus effectiveness (Flay, 1986)— that is, a difference in a trial with a select sample of participants versus a trial with all individuals whether ready to make a change or not. Of course, effectiveness trials can also be conducted with individually directed interventions, but community trials are almost always conducted as effectiveness trials, whereas individually directed trials are most commonly conducted as efficacy trials. The outcome measures of community trials are thus typically derived from respondents randomly sampled throughout the entire community. This difference in focus thus often necessitates community trials incorporating theoretical models that conceptualize how to affect individuals

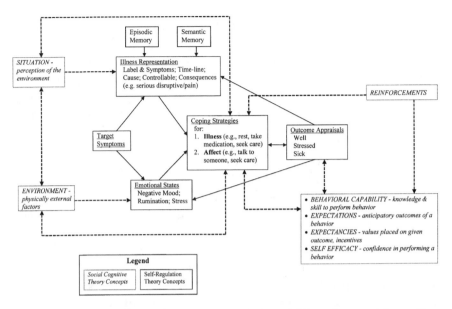

Figure 15.1. The REACT intervention theoretical model based on social cognitive theory and the self-regulatory model of health and illness behavior. From "REACT Theory-Based Intervention to Reduce Treatment-Seeking Delay for Acute MI," by J. M. Raczynski, et al. 2001, *American Journal of Preventive Medicine, 16,* p. 325. Copyright 2001 by *American Journal of Preventive Medicine.* Reprinted with permission of Elsevier Science.

who are not yet at an action stage of readiness to change. The use of theoretical models such as diffusion of innovations (Rogers, 1983) and the transtheoretical model of change (Prochaska et al., 1992) thus become important in community trials.

Diffusion theory (Rogers, 1983) describes how "innovations" are adopted through (a) knowledge (awareness), (b) persuasion, (c) decision, (d) implementation, and (e) confirmation. Diffusion research suggests that mass media has the greatest impact on awareness, whereas interpersonal channels are more effective in persuading individuals to adopt an innovation (Rogers, 1983). Rogers (1983) identifies different adoption groups. Innovators can most readily be persuaded to adopt an innovation. Other groups (in order of their likelihood of adopting an innovation: early adopters, early majority, late adopters, and laggards) are also important to identify so that the intervention may initially focus on those most likely to change. Guided by these principles, community intervention trials, such as REACT, the Uniontown Community Health Project, and the HIV Community Demonstrations, often incorporate some form of early community analysis to identify potential early adopters who are opinion leaders and to solicit their involvement.

The transtheoretical model of change (TCM) also outlines why community members and populations of people, as a whole, may not be prepared to change features of their behavior during any given time period. This is true for a variety of lifestyle issues, including smoking and substance use, sexual behavior, nutrition, and exercise (Prochaska et al., 1992). Considered as a group, some individuals will have changed their behavior already and are maintaining the change over time (maintenance stage); others will have initiated changes but are struggling to maintain the change (action); others will be prepared to make a change (preparation); still others will be at the stage of serious consideration (contemplation); and finally, a substantial portion are likely to have given no serious consideration to making a change (preparation). These stages are often defined by time periods—for example, someone who intends to change a feature of lifestyle within the next six months is often placed in the contemplation stage; any longer than that and the seriousness of the intention is questionable. Interventions appropriate for those in the preparation and action stages (the kind that would be applied to individual health promotion) are simply not well-tailored to those in precontemplation or contemplation. We should either save our resources or seek methods to move people to the preparation and action stages. This can be accomplished through various mechanisms of change, and these are often suggested spontaneously by other community members (e.g., support for a change, consciousness raising). Community-wide interventions attempt to alter the distribution of the population at each stage, moving a higher proportion to the later stages.

Ecological Variables

In the context of a community-level intervention, it is possible to address ecological variables as part of the overall intervention. These potential mediators can influence individual behavior but often cannot be addressed within individual interventions. These ecological variables can include group norms or rules of what constitutes good and bad conduct. For example, in the AIDS Community Demonstrations, a specific goal of intervention was the development of group norms conducive to risk reduction in each of the five groups at risk. These group norms were assessed over time by a street intercept survey that also assessed risk behaviors. Although measured at the individual level, changes in norms only made sense in aggregate. Other ecological variables can be termed environmental; in urban health promotion for example, we might measure the barriers and facilitators to physical exercise in various cities; in violence prevention, we might measure citizens' perceptions of neighborhood safety or the degree to which children remain unsupervised during after-school hours. The neighborhood in which children reside appears to be a potent predictor of their future risk for crime and violence (Leviton, Snell, & McGinnis, 2000; Wandersman & Nation, 1998).

Ecological variables such as neighborhoods and networks are often ignored in analyses of behaviors' contribution to health. Both science and practice are forcing a change. In her critique of the misuse of the ecological fallacy in epidemiology, Schwartz (1994) asserted that it "fosters a dismissal of social variables as causal factors in disease . . . it denies that ecological variables can affect individual processes" (p. 819). Syme (1997) makes a persuasive case for specific ways to change structures and ecologies to facilitate health promotion.

Frameworks for Community Interventions

The assumptions that interventionists make about communities also provide a major difference between community interventions and those aimed at individuals. Many different frameworks for understanding communities are available: typological perspectives classify different kinds of territorial groupings that share values, cohesion, and continuity; ecological perspectives map spatial, economic, and health indicators; conflict perspectives analyze struggles over resources; and in functional perspectives, networks and linkages among people are analyzed as social systems (e.g., Warren, 1978). Some of these perspectives are more obviously relevant than others—for example, the networks and linkages can be used to communicate health education messages or to improve social supports for a behavior change. However, planners ignore the other perspectives at their peril. Assuming a community exists on the basis of geographic definition ignores people who share values and interests, as in "the Chinese American community."

The conflict perspectives are especially familiar to behavioral scientists who have become involved in addressing environmental health issues, because these help us understand why conflict over health risks can escalate beyond all reference to the actual physical health problems that are likely to ensue (Edelstein & Wandersman, 1987; Kasperson et al., 1988; Renn, Burns, Kasperson, Kasperson, & Slovic, 1992; Wandersman & Hallman, 1993, 1994). The AIDS epidemic also illustrates the importance of the conflict frameworks, both for the attitudes of the general public and those of AIDS activists. So does the issue of teenage pregnancy (Clark, Rhodes, Rogers, & Liddon, 2004), in terms of what the community will find acceptable as intervention.

Social networks and the functions they serve, in particular social support, have been a central feature of social epidemiology and promise some powerful ways to intervene at the community level in the future. In the modern day, social networks are often impaired by use (Leviton et al., 2000). However, they are often merely dormant and can be accessed, for example, to provide social supports (Berkman & Glass, 1999), to communicate information or appraise a situation (Cohen, Underwood, & Gottlieb, 2000), or through family and school, to protect children and teenagers from various health risks (Resnick et al., 1997).

The complexity of community interventions raises a final point about the differences between interventions directed at individuals compared to those focused on communities. Multiple theoretical perspectives are often needed to incorporate the frameworks to understand the communities and to meet the broad scope of community interventions. Although their objectives are not necessarily easier, the scope of individually directed interventions are often more limited by contrast, allowing the use of more focused approaches and theoretical perspectives. Thus, the combination of theoretical approaches represented in Figure 15.1 for the Heart Attack–REACT trial is not unusual for community trials. However, this figure does not represent all of the theoretical perspectives incorporated into this trial. Although social cognitive theory and self-regulatory theory provided the overall theoretical framework, the REACT trial combined perspectives from other theories, as appropriate, to create *implementation theories* (Raczynski et al., 1999). A framework for these theories is seen in Figure 15.2. Implementation focused on community organization is one of the four intervention components; therefore community organization theories and principles were incorporated into the overall intervention (e.g., Bracht, 1999). Because other intervention components focused on providers, diffusion of innovation theory (Rogers, 1983) contributed appropriate methods to promote awareness of program goals among providers. In addition, this theory led the implementers to identify and involve early adopters in planning the intervention. Finally, social marketing principles were used to formulate community and patient education components (Novelli, 1991). Another example is provided by the Uniontown Project, in which the focus is to implement community-level changes under the guidance of CHAs. The framework in the Uniontown Project involves theoretical methods developed to follow Freire's model of working with community residents as "subjects" (capable of taking charge of their own destiny) rather than "objects" (acceptance of being acted on by outside forces; Freire, 1970). This model has been adapted to address global health outcomes (Wallerstein & Berstein, 1988) as well as in particular categorically based foci (Raczynski et al., 2001). Thus, the complexity of the intervention led to more complexity, or at least diversity, in theoretical development than is commonly found in individually directed interventions.

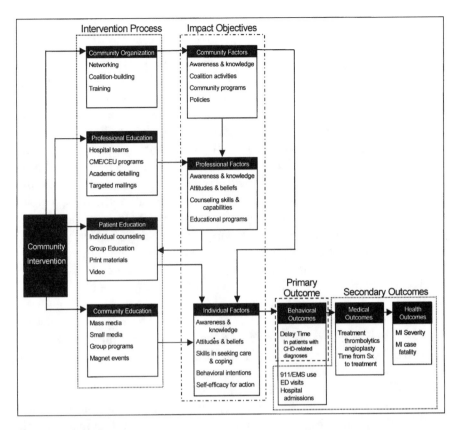

Figure 15.2. REACT framework of intervention components, and outcomes, processes, and impact variables. From "REACT Theory-Based Intervention to Reduce Treatment-Seeking Delay for Acute MI," by J. M. Raczynski, et al. 1999, *American Journal of Preventive Medicine, 16,* p. 325. Copyright 1999 by *American Journal of Preventive Medicine.* Reprinted with permission of Elsevier Science.

PLANNING FOR BEHAVIORAL INTERVENTIONS
IN THE COMMUNITY

A planning framework is decidedly different from a theoretical framework, describing process steps in the development and implementation of the intervention without specifying the theories that serve as the basis for guiding particular elements of the intervention. First we briefly describe some recommended frameworks, then describe a set of questions that can guide the reader's choice. In point of fact, all are valuable. Indeed, their real value may lie in the abundant illustrations and practice-based examples that reveal the art behind the acknowledged science.

Recommended Planning Frameworks

The PRECEDE/PROCEED framework is probably the best known planning framework for community interventions (Green & Kreuter, 1999). The framework was developed to counteract a lack of planning and hence effectiveness in health education and health promotion programs. Several stages are identified; however, the interventionist or researcher is often able to abbreviate the early stages based on the considerations listed earlier. The framework begins by considering the variety of health and social problems a society may have; some of these will be independent of health issues and relate to quality of life, justice, traditions, and other values that people hold. Among those problems that relate to health, the next stage determines which health conditions are the most important and also considers which are most modifiable—either through direct behavior change or environmental influence. Note that both are relevant to community health promotion efforts—for example, reducing disability and death because of car crashes depends both on behaviors (safe driving, seat belt use) and on the environment (improved car engineering, air bags, improved roads, emergency response). Improvements in the environment can sometimes be achieved through political advocacy by communities, as when residents of a developing world slum advocate for a sewage system.

The next phases of PRECEDE/PROCEED apply to most behavioral intervention programs: the inventory of predisposing, enabling, and reinforcing factors that produce a risky behavior. The most important and modifiable of those factors are then selected to design an intervention. For example, the Uniontown Community Health Project identified smoking, fat consumption, salt use, and physical inactivity as the most important behavioral risk factors in the Black community (hypertension control was considered separately). Some of the important and modifiable factors maintaining those behaviors included lack of information and skill to cook foods that tasted good without animal fats and salt; perceived preference for foods cooked with those fats and salt; lack of venues to try new, healthier recipes and taste them; lack of venues for exercise; lack of proper instruction in exercise; and lack of effective methods to quit smoking. To address these factors, CHAs in the community were recruited and trained in heart-healthy cooking, in aerobics instruction, and in smoking cessation methods. People meet in groups to model heart-healthy cooking skills and to try new and adapted recipes and taste them, and they continue to exercise together in a variety of ways, including group aerobics and indoor and outdoor walking. CHAs function both as peer role models and as program leaders, reinforcing and supporting community residents to maintain these lifestyle changes.

The final phase of planning before implementation is the administrative diagnosis: an assessment of the implementing organization, including an estimate of the resources needed, assessment of resources available, and barriers to implementation. For example, although the AIDS Community Demonstrations did not explicitly use PRECEDE, it is clear that program planners did a careful administrative diagnosis. Federal resources were limited to implement the intervention. Paying staff to distribute the educational materials would have been prohibitively expensive and it would probably not have been cost-effective by comparison to volunteers. Concurrent with the administrative diagnosis of the organizations delivering the intervention, a policy diagnosis is undertaken of the organizational policies and the local politics, which may help or hinder an effort. For example, an obvious barrier to HIV-related media materials is that frank, targeted messages about HIV risk reduction would never be shown on television in most American cities. Instead, the AIDS Community Demonstrations used small media materials, delivered one-on-one.

The PATCH model (Centers for Disease Control, 1985) derives from PRECEDE/PROCEED in most ways; however, it represents a manual for implementers concerning how to gain participation of community representatives in planning groups, how to define needs and select targets for action, how to assemble relevant data, how to mobilize communities, and other topics. PATCH has been evaluated and, in general, the results are favorable. However, the evaluation also revealed a common problem that extends beyond PATCH to many forms of community planning: Community-based initiatives sometimes falter once the assessment process is complete and the project must move to implementation (Wandersman & Hallman, 1994). Indeed, the most important need for professional technical assistance may be in the start-up phase of implementation, because project implementation is a skill like others and must be modeled.

Getting to Outcomes

With the implementation problem in mind, and to engage community leaders in a more active way, Wandersman and his colleagues developed the Getting to Outcomes (GTO) framework (Chinman et al., 2001). Developed primarily in the field of substance abuse prevention, GTO was designed to ensure that practitioners implement the most appropriate programs for the needs of the communities in which they work. Derived from participatory planning and evaluation, GTO looks relatively straightforward, but obtaining legitimate, participatory answers is part of the art of engaging communities in a meaningful way. The framework addresses, in order, 10 questions concerning the underlying needs and conditions that must be addressed; the goals, priority populations, and objectives; the choice of science-based and best-practice models to address the problems; how to fit the program to the community context; organizational capacities needed to implement the program; implementation plan for the program; assessment of program quality and implementation; how well did the program work; incorporation of continuous quality improvement methods; and methods to sustain the program. Case studies are offered to illustrate how a participatory approach can work to implement this framework.

The RE-AIM Framework

From the health psychology standpoint, RE-AIM (Glasgow, et al., 1999) offers the advantage that it melds criteria for efficacy and effectiveness of individual prevention programs with those of population health. Glasgow and his colleagues maintain that health psychology programs need to be judged by the degree to which they have the potential to reach large portions of the target community in an effective way. They would construct, test, and adapt health programs on five dimensions: reach, efficacy, or effectiveness, adoption by target settings or institutions, consistent implementation in the delivery of an intervention, and maintenance of intervention effects in both individuals and institutions over time. At the RE-AIM Web site, abundant examples are given illustrating how these dimensions can be maximized in practice.

Issues Involved in Planning Frameworks

Frameworks for planning are readily available from the health promotion and public health literature. In making a choice, interventionists and researchers want to pose several questions, considered next.

Is it necessary to choose a health problem, or has the choice been made already? Health departments often face this issue as they grapple with allocating scarce local resources. Grant applicants responding to a request for applications (RFA) are more likely to plan to address a particular health risk that interests them or that is already viewed as a priority by the federal government or other funding agencies.

Is a community partnership envisioned? If so, to what extent is there a partnership? In the rhetoric of community-based health programs, a wide variety of arrangements are termed "partnerships with a community." However, some partnerships are more equal than others. Bracht (1999) discusses some ways to organize partnerships, depending on the degree of shared power with communities and the individuals and community agencies that are engaged as representatives of the community in the partnership. At one extreme, the goal may be simply to obtain community consent or "buy-in" to an intervention. There is nothing wrong with a limited partnership of this type, as long as expectations about the partnership are clearly understood. At the other extreme, professionals may be committed to addressing the priorities that community members identify, then building community capacity to address their current and future priorities through training, political advocacy, or infrastructure development (Altpeter, Earp, Bishop, & Eng, 1999; Goodman, 1998; Goodman et al., 1998; Israel et al., 1998; Parker, Eng, et al., 1998; Parker, Schulz, Israel, & Hollis 1998; Raczynski et al., 2001). The Uniontown Project is an example of this latter extreme in which CHAs are being trained in leadership skills and methods of effecting community change. Many models fall somewhere in between. For example, the AIDS Community Demonstration Projects is aimed at stimulating community discussion of HIV risk reduction by enlisting volunteers and by linking HIV risk, where possible, to the perceived needs of community residents. The REACT Project similarly had a community organization component for the 18-month intervention, designed primarily to obtain community support but also to enlist volunteers where possible (Raczynski et al., 1999). A related issue is to come to agreement about the length of the partnership. Communities are becoming wary of professionals who work with them for the duration of a single grant and leave no sustained program when the grant ends (Telfair, Leviton, & Merchant, 1999). If a commitment cannot be long-term, then it is important to show community members what the sustained benefit is likely to be.

Whose priorities will be addressed, professional priorities or community priorities? Professional interventionists and researchers may have a clear sense of the problems they want to address. These may be based on their own interests and capabilities, as when professionals trained in diabetes self-care move into an impoverished community setting. The priorities may also be based on the most important causes of disability and death, as identified by epidemiological information or from the goals of *Healthy People 2000*. Although community interests may be compatible with professional priorities, particularly once the basis for the professionals' priorities has been explained, communities are often likely to have a somewhat different set of priorities. Often, crime, drugs, violence, employment opportunities, job training, and the physical condition of the neighborhood will take precedence over less immediate issues, such as heart disease and cancer (Leviton et al., 1997). Sometimes, partnerships can reach a balance between these priorities. For example, the CHA approach adopted in the Uniontown Project was funded in response to an RFA that was originally titled "Peer Support Intervention for CVD Risk Reduction in African American Women Aged 40 and Older." The approach (i.e., a peer support intervention), the focus of the intervention (i.e., risk reduction for cardiovascular disease), and the population (i.e., African American women 40 years old and older) were all defined by the RFA. Nonetheless, the intervention that was implemented, a community health advisor (CHA) model, was developed in collaboration with the Uniontown Community Health Council (CHC), and

CHAs who volunteered to participate were initially identified by the CHC and other community leaders. Participation in the programs was determined in collaboration with the CHC to be open to all who wanted to participate, rather than to just those who had been identified by the RFA. Initial training of these CHAs was based on Community Health Advisor Network (CHAN) concepts, with modifications to enable a particular focus on cardiovascular disease, involving training these natural helpers to enhance their knowledge, skills, and understanding of community issues and methods of promoting change. The modified CHAN program developed out of efforts to follow the Freire model of working with community residents (Freire, 1970; Wallerstein, & Berstein, 1988). Based on this initial CHAN training, CHAs identified their own community priorities to begin to address their identified issues, which were not CVD in nature. After the initial CHAN training, action teams were formed of individuals who were interested in receiving advanced training in physical activity, tobacco cessation, or nutrition. Thus, a balance was sought in establishing priorities. Although cardiovascular disease was an issue for the community, it was not as high a priority as community development was; thus, action teams addressed the research goals of the project, and CHAs and investigators worked together to address community development needs as well.

As we have discussed elsewhere (Raczynski et al., 2001), this partnership with Uniontown has also resulted in other funded research projects, each with its own evaluation to determine the impact of the individual projects. Through this approach, we believe that the community capacity continues to develop. Examples, albeit anecdotal in nature, exist of new initiatives, which are being developed by community members and organizations directly, rather than arising from our research group, providing evidence of enhanced community capacity (Raczynski et al., 2001).

If implemented as a research project, what design and evaluation plan will be incorporated that is acceptable to involved community partners? It has been our experience that all individuals volunteering to participate in a research program, whether in a traditional clinical trial or as a member of a community for a community-based research project, are becoming increasingly concerned about what they will receive when randomized to a no-treatment or usual-care comparison group. Because participants in a traditional clinical trial must individually consent to participate, relegating the study in most cases to an efficacy trial, these concerns are generally less of an issue than they are in community studies because individuals who have excessive concerns are not likely to consent to participate in the traditional clinical trial but may be involved in the community study simply if they reside in the community. Although all researchers should probably be concerned about addressing these issues, community researchers, in particular, must be sensitive to issues about community members' concerns of being randomized to comparison groups. These issues may lead to consideration of delayed treatment control designs so that all communities will ultimately receive the intervention or attention placebo controlled interventions so that all communities receive some form of intervention even if the intervention they receive is an attention control intervention for the main outcome of interest.

Understanding the Forces at Work

Whenever interventionists begin work in a new community, they bring a variety of assumptions to the task. Some of these assumptions are important, because they frame the feasible interventions. For example, basic behavioral theories, theories of social marketing, and theories of implementation are all important tools to help understand forces at work. Earlier research concerning effective interventions is important, based on literature reviews. Also, earlier research on the forces-at-work for any given population are essential tools.

However, the interventionist may also bring a variety of assumptions about the community to bear that need to be challenged. Many of our own assumptions are automatic and based in our own culture. Indeed, recent definitions from the literature on cross-cultural communication define culture as shared expectations (Singer, 1998). Our assumptions may simply not be shared with those we are trying to assist. It is easier to double-check our own assumptions when we know that we do not share a common culture with the community. Newly arrived immigrants or impoverished rural Black Americans clearly may look different and seem different for many interventionists, and so the interventionists must be sensitive to the need to gather more information. However, even people who look and sound like the majority of professionals may not share the same culture. For example, blue-collar workers in rural central Pennsylvania had a substantially different culture than interventionists trying to screen them for bladder cancer (Leviton, Marsh, Talbott, Pavlock, & Callahan, 1991). It became essential to understand the special sensitivities of the community before substantial progress could be made in cancer control.

Beyond the forces within particular communities, additional data collection is often required to develop effective interventions. These data can be quantitative or qualitative in nature. Both types of data are valuable in a given context; both help us to reduce the uncertainty about important features of implementation of health behavior interventions (Leviton et al., 1999; Leviton, 2003). For example, as we discuss later, in REACT although substantial data were available within the literature to enumerate symptoms associated with an acute myocardial infarction, data were limited on the key features that needed to be incorporated into the message to try to encourage people to seek treatment.

RESEARCH AT THE COMMUNITY LEVEL: SPECIAL CONSIDERATIONS IN DESIGN

So far, we have described the advantages and challenges of the community setting, how community settings affect the way that behavioral researchers use theory, and the way that interventions derived from theory can be tailored to various community problems. In these final sections, we will describe how the community setting introduces special considerations in research. These special considerations fall into the categories of protocols and implementation, research design, data collection, and data analysis.

In clinical trials, efficacy studies precede effectiveness studies—that is, theory-based interventions are tested under ideal conditions before being used in less than perfect ones (Flay, 1986). In community research studies, however, the efficacy step is often skipped. Indeed, it must be skipped to the extent that communities always represent open systems with less than perfect implementation. Under these circumstances, in addition to outcomes, a well-conceived evaluation will measure and analyze implementation (also known as process measures) and intermediate outcomes (such as variables that can be predicted to mediate the effects of outcomes). By carefully measuring process and mediating variables, evaluations avoid the problems of testing "black box" interventions. Black box interventions are those that do not address the processes at work when health behavior does, or does not, change. Should a study conclude that there is no effect, it is not possible in black box evaluations to determine why that is the case. Nor is it possible to gain additional insights about what caused the outcomes. Health behavior research is increasingly driven by well-articulated theories, such as those outlined earlier. Such research can maximize explanatory power by measuring and analyzing process, intermediate outcomes and mediators, and ultimate outcomes.

A word on terminology is important. The evaluation literature refers to implementation measurement, and the health education literature's cognate concept is process measurement. The mediating variables such as attitudes and beliefs are intermediate outcomes in evaluation but termed impact by health education, which also refers to the behavioral end-points that are desired as impact variables. The health end-points are referred to as outcomes or ultimate outcomes in both terminologies. The use of terminology is less important than is consistency in conveying the underlying concepts, but we present the issue here to avoid the misconception that one or the other field possesses a special expertise.

Implementation and the Role of the Protocol

When community studies are conducted, there is clearly a need for standardized study protocols as for all trials. The common reasons cited for standardized protocols include (Raczynski et al., 1999) (a) to ensure clear guidance for intervention staff; (b) to establish specific intervention goals and subsequent process evaluation to document progress toward achieving these goals; (c) to enable the intervention to be conceptualized overall as one intervention across communities rather than as an independent intervention in each community so that the impact and outcome data could be pooled across sites; and (d) to provide a clear description of the intervention for others to replicate or extend. Nonetheless, as already discussed, flexibility is also needed to address differences between study communities based on factors such as (a) cultural, socioeconomic, and ethnic diversity as they influence the particular behavior change being promoted and affect factors to be considered in the intervention (Raczynski et al., 1999); (b) cultural and ethnic diversity as they affect access to population segments (Schooler et al., 1997); (c) variations in community capacities and variations in ability to mobilize these capacities (Raczynski et al., 1999); (d) variations in organizations, such as health care system variations and the mix of insurance and managed care plans as they affect intervention plans for gaining the assistance of providers (Raczynski et al., 1999); (e) existing media outlets available for media-based interventions (Raczynski et al., 1999); and (f) variations in existing community structures as they influence approaches to organizing communities to support the intervention (Schooler et al., 1997).

Hence, there is a need to balance standardization with flexibility. This need for balance was addressed in the Heart Attack–REACT trial by developing a minimum core of exposure standards for each intervention component that delineated interpersonal and impersonal strategies (Glanz, Lewis, & Rimer, 1997; Windsor et al., 1994), which could be used to meet specific exposure standards. For instance, taking provider education as an example, the exposure standards specified the minimum number and type of interpersonal and impersonal strategies that had to incorporate at each site for different types of provider groups. Site Action Plans were then developed for each intervention community to detail and to document specific methods to meet the standards. This approach standardized the intervention while allowing necessary flexibility in methods. These exposure standards for each component of the REACT intervention are available on the study's Web site (http://epihub.epi.umn.edu/~react/welcome.html).

Although other approaches can certainly be adopted to address the need to balance standardization with flexibility, the REACT trial represents a good model for how this balance can be achieved.

Quantitative Data Collection in Community Settings

The published, quantitative literature is obviously an important source to consider in developing community intervention programs. Obviously, intervention programs should be driven by the research literature in determining what behaviors should be changed and what theories and methods will be most appropriate for changing them. Consideration should also be given during intervention planning to the collection of new quantitative data. In addition to research "gaps" in the literature that may need filling to plan adequately for an intervention, survey data to characterize community attitudes and beliefs concerning risk factors and behavior changes are often considered.

Special Community Applications of Quantitative Data: Culturally Appropriate Measurement

Too often, researchers use existing scales and instruments without assessing whether they are valid for the group to which they are being applied. This is particularly important in community settings where low income and minority group members are assessed. Instruments that are available should be revalidated with members of the new target population. Additional measures should be developed through qualitative means, to ensure that the investigators understand the cultural significance of the responses. Although not aimed at community level research, the methods developed by Fischhoff, Bostrom, and Quadrel (1993) to assess knowledge of health risks illustrate the advantages of developing relevant measures systematically whenever there is reason to believe that the investigators do not share the same worldview as the target audience. Although their approach has been used primarily in the area of environmental health, it can be valuable in other contexts as well. The process begins by eliciting from experts the causes of a problem, likely routes of exposure or infection, effects on the body, and ways to avoid the risk. For example, an expert might outline radon in the home as a health risk: Where does it come from, what are the mechanisms whereby it is released into the home environment, how does it act on the body, what are the likely results alone and in combination with other respiratory health risks such as smoking, how it can be avoided or household conditions remediated, and so forth. Next, lay people's understanding of radon is elicited through open-ended interviews that probe for additional detail until the person's store of information about the health risk is exhausted ("Tell me more about radon in basements"). A similar process can be applied to any health problem, even prevalent health problems such as diabetes and heart disease, where members of the target audience may not have adequate health knowledge or in which their health knowledge is confounded with folk beliefs. This process thus begins to pinpoint those portions of the overall health risk situation that the layperson readily understands as well as areas of misconception or lack of information. Then more structured survey instruments collect information about the prevalence of such misconceptions and lack of knowledge. These become the focus of tailored risk communication and also provide tailored instruments to assess change in the prevalence of knowledge, misconceptions, and relevant attitudes.

Special Community Applications of Quantitative Data: Use of Paraprofessional Interviewers

In some community settings, residents may have better luck than outsiders in asking others to take part in surveys and other forms of data collection. Moreover, in some community settings there are the special issues of community employment and resident participation. How can we answer low-income minority communities who report being "researched to death," even when our projects would be beneficial for them? One very important way to respond is to show where and how community residents participate in the research enterprise.

It is feasible for community residents in low-income neighborhoods to gather quantitative data. The keys to the data quality are the same as they would be for any data collection enterprise: selection of motivated people, training, supervision, and quality control. The first author has hired community residents to conduct extensive interviews of injection drug users in the context of an inner-city AIDS outreach and intervention project and has done the same for street intercept interviews of poor women at risk of HIV in public housing communities. In both cases the keys to the resulting high quality data were the same. Interviewers were selected with care. They were trained in the use of the instruments until they met a fairly high standard. They underwent regular supervision and monitoring—very heavily at first, and lighter as time went on. They met regularly with the data entry team to discuss such problems as missing data, errors resulting from incorrectly skipping around questions that should have been asked, and data out of range for various reasons. As long as these discussions were conducted in an atmosphere of mutual respect, they worked well.

Community residents should not be expected to make decisions about the research under conditions in which any other lay individuals would also make mistakes. In particular, it is our observation that lay individuals seldom understand the need to adhere to sampling frames—a key issue in many community research settings—particularly when they are expected to meet a quota of interviews each day. In general, paying interviewers of any kind on a per-interview basis is an invitation to low quality and even fraud. Community residents should never be expected to collect systematic data in the absence of supervision. For example, in the Uniontown Project we have asked CHAs to keep rosters of attendees at various cooking classes that aim to cut fat out of the diet. Research staff reviewed with CHAs the need for these rosters and the importance of a complete count of participants on a regular basis.

Qualitative Data Collection

In the field of behavioral health, qualitative data collection is often relegated to low priority and viewed with suspicion as somewhat less-than-scientific. The field of health behavior has been relatively untouched by the debates over the priorities given to qualitative and quantitative data and analysis, which are reaching resolution or at least accommodation in other fields of social intervention and evaluation (Reichardt & Rallis, 1994). We would argue that a qualitative data collection and analysis capacity are often particularly important in community interventions. We will offer examples of the value of qualitative data in program planning to assist interpretation of outcomes. At the planning stage, qualitative data are essential to community analysis before project implementation. They also allow better tailoring of intervention to the particular communities. For instance, in the Heart Attack–REACT project, data were available to describe symptoms that accompany heart attacks. However, qualitative data collected through focus groups and interviews from health care providers (primary care physicians and nursing staff, cardiologists, emergency department physicians and nurses), patients (those who had suffered from a heart attack as well as those at high risk for a heart attack), and family members of patients, were critical in supplementing quantitative data and defining the nature and scope of the intervention program (Raczynski et al., 1999). Among other findings, these qualitative data were essential in determining that, although quantitative data suggest that chest pain is the most common heart attack symptom (e.g., Raczynski et al., 1994), chest pain is very often accompanied by other symptoms that may be more prominent (Finnegan et al., 2000). Other data revealed through this qualitative assessment concerning the beliefs and attitudes of providers, patients, and families provide compelling evidence of the importance of qualitative data in intervention planning (Finnegan et al., 2000; Leviton et al., 1999; Zapka et al., 1999).

The AIDS Community Demonstration Projects offer another illustration of the value of qualitative approaches in planning (Higgins et al., 1996). Systematic, rapid ethnographic studies were conducted in each of the target communities, first with gatekeepers and key informants who were in a position to know the forces at work for the populations at risk, then with members of the populations themselves. The information assisted the intervention in developing culturally appropriate, specifically tailored small media materials for the very elusive and understudied populations at risk (e.g., men who have sex with men but do not self-identify as being gay). In addition, ethnographic study identified those locations in the communities where the populations at risk were most likely to congregate at various hours of the day. This permitted the demonstration projects to efficiently distribute small media materials and also to conduct random intercept interviews with the populations at risk (AIDS Community Demonstration Projects Research Group, 1999; Higgins et al., 1996).

Behavioral health professionals are generally more familiar with the value of qualitative data in program planning than with their explanatory power once implementation is under way. Yet the importance of qualitative data to offer a discovery capacity to accompany evaluation of outcomes cannot be overstated (Shadish, Cook, & Leviton, 1991). The reason for this is that in open systems such as communities, it is often not possible to anticipate new developments. These can include important features of implementation, as well as the unintended consequences or side effects of interventions. This reality of health promotion argues for the importance of a qualitative discovery capacity in evaluation, because qualitative data are frequently more flexible than quantitative data that must be planned in advance. In study after study, qualitative data offer important insights for learning about implementation and program improvement, in ways that could not be accomplished by planned data collection. For examples of this learning, the reader should visit the Heart Attack–REACT Web site and attend to the many examples described in this chapter. Unanticipated side effects of interventions are illustrated in the Uniontown Project:

- Some CHAs became certified exercise instructors.
- CHAs shared their expertise with leadership in another poor community nearby—which then initiated a heart-healthy program of their own.

Sometimes qualitative data offer solutions to data-based puzzles. For example, the AIDS Community Demonstration Projects discovered an apparent anomaly: Injection drug users were lowering their risk from sexual behavior but not their risks from needle sharing—the reverse of the pattern seen in other HIV outreach and education programs with this population

(Leviton & Schuh, 1999). Some limited qualitative data indicated that this may have been a result of a change in the CDC's message concerning needle-cleaning during the implementation period.

Special Applications of Qualitative Data:
Focus Groups and Key Informant Interviews

These methods are a familiar feature of health promotion studies at the planning phase. Key informants are individuals who are in a position to know certain facts about the target community or who have perceptions of the community. Key informants are often identified through a nomination process, often through "snowball" sampling in which certain key informants name additional informants for the investigators. Focus groups (Krueger & Casey, 2000) are small group discussions in which the group process stimulates group members to generate discussion themes and information that might not emerge in the context of individual interviews. A complete discussion of these methods can be found in Miles and Huberman (1994).

One issue does deserve attention, because planning and community analysis can frequently seem very complex. Particularly in community intervention, people become puzzled concerning how many focus groups or key informant interviews are enough. When can we be certain that all the relevant information has been obtained? The key principles are redundancy and replication. When the investigators begin hearing the same themes over and over, with little new information, data collection is complete (redundancy). However, it is useful to replicate findings so that a critic could not attribute them to the mode of data collection or the investigator or analyst: For this purpose, planned replication of data collection that varies these extraneous features will add confidence to the conclusions (Leviton et al., 1999). For example, the Heart Attack–REACT study conducted at least two focus groups with each major age group and each target group for communication (e.g., women, bystanders, those with chronic heart conditions).

Other sources can provide important qualitative information as well. Archival sources are especially important whenever a community intervention uses, or interacts with, the media. For example, a special effort was made in the early 1980s to notify former chemical workers that they were exposed to a potent bladder carcinogen (Leviton et al., 1997). Because of significant community tensions over the notification effort, media commentary and coverage were tracked and content was analyzed. An important finding was that the local newspaper focused almost exclusively on the danger and misfortune of workers, and very little if at all on the benefits of early detection and treatment. This finding was essential in planning for later community-based worker notification projects (Leviton et al., 1991).

Special Issues in Analysis

In open systems, the most commonly used methods of analysis may not be appropriate or sensitive enough to detect changes when they exist. In this section, we address three general approaches to deal with the issue of sensitivity.

Sensitivity of the Analysis in Light of Underlying Secular Trends

Sometimes, behavioral changes are moving in a desired direction at the same time that an intervention to promote similar changes is being initiated. It is perhaps not surprising in this age of rapid information diffusion that funding agencies, investigators, and the public at large all become aware of the benefits of certain changes at about the same time. Instances in which this has occurred include

- in the COMMIT program, which saw disappointing reductions in the number of cigarette smokers in states that implemented the intensive intervention (The COMMIT Study Group, 1995a, 1995b)—most people who were able to quit had already done so;
- in the AIDS Prevention Project for gay and bisexual men (Valdiserri et al., 1989), the average number of sexual partners was on the decline at the same time that intervention aimed at producing a reduction in the number of partners; and
- in the Heart Attack–REACT project (Luepker et al., 2000), a number of changes were occurring that resulted in clear reductions in delay in seeking treatment for heart attacks in line with the intervention program goals, such as chest pain clinics were being developed and were trying to attract patients by educating them about the symptoms of heart attack; pharmaceutical companies were promoting thrombolytic agents and encouraging people to seek treatment quickly to be eligible to receive these treatments; and national media had begun drawing attention to the problem of delaying in seeking treatment for heart attacks as well.

Under these circumstances, it is wise to project the underlying trends in the society, also called *secular trends* (Bauman, Suchindran, & Murray, 1999). Often, the trends look like what is illustrated in Figure 15.3, which plots the percentage of people adopting an innovation over time (Rogers, 1983). Given the state of affairs at any given time, intervention may or may not be warranted to establish clinical significance. If a health behavior is in the process of being adopted widely, perhaps intervention is not needed.

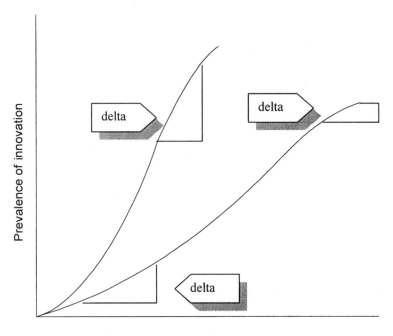

Figure 15.3. Adoption of a health behavior over time in three different situations.

On the other hand, intervention might speed its adoption and might promote its adoption in specific communities or social networks who have yet to begin adopting the innovation. Timing may be everything: Intervention may produce a steeper adoption curve, or by intervening at the point of most rapid adoption, ensure a more robust effect of intervention. Finally, if the stage of diffusion for any given behavior indicates that only small changes are likely (but still clinically significant changes), then adequate power to detect those changes is a must.

Because diffusion patterns are such important considerations, the choice of measures becomes an important matter of judgment. In the AIDS Prevention Projects, for example, the focus was not solely on the reduction of sexual partners but also on consistent condom use with all partners. An effect of intervention was seen on percentage of partners with whom condoms were used, regardless of the secular trend for reducing total number of partners (Valdiserri et al., 1989). Similarly, in the Heart Attack–REACT project, although delay in seeking treatment for heart attacks declined in both intervention and comparison communities and did not statistically differ between the two groups of communities, use of emergency medical services (EMS), a secondary outcome for the project, significantly increased in the intervention relative to the comparison communities (Luepker et al., 2000). These outcomes were detected because the studies adhered to an important principle of evaluation: the use of multiple measures on multiple outcomes.

Level of Analysis and Hierarchical Modeling

Because the diffusion of health information offers great potential for contamination in community-based trials, investigators frequently use the community or neighborhood as the unit of assignment. Under such conditions, it is accepted practice to analyze the data at both individual and aggregate levels (Bryk & Raudenbush, 1993; Goldstein, 1995). However, it is also the case that an adequately powered study is likely to be very expensive, because a rule of thumb is that between 7 and 15 aggregate units (such as communities) are needed for each arm of a randomized experiment, depending on the intraclass correlation, a measure of association among individual members within the unit (Murray, 1998).

Under these conditions, many researchers seek alternatives. For example, a central reason to use hierarchical models under these conditions is that the intraclass correlation within communities is likely to be substantial, and this will inflate the obtained differences at the individual level of analysis. When the intraclass correlation is low, investigators feel justified in proceeding with individual-level analyses.

The constraints because of budget are all too real. Yet it is important to note that there are costs associated with doing analysis at the individual level only. Specifically, some important information can be lost in the process. For example, it may not be feasible to study the ecological variables affecting entire communities directly. Instead, the fallback option may be to assess the degree to which an ecological variable (such as neighborhood crime) has affected individual cases. Also, it is increasingly the case that patterns of data aggregated to the community level are seen to behave differently than do pooled individual-level data. Without studying the community level, important patterns may be missed. A third problem with the focus on individuals exclusively is that a large degree of variation is often seen between the aggregated units of study (Weiss, 1998). For example, one community might reduce its AIDS risk substantially from a fairly high level of risk; another might reduce it very little from a similarly high level. Why should this be? This variation may be extraordinarily important to explore to understand the behavior of communities more completely.

Theory-Driven Research and Causal Modeling

In any case, it is sometimes not feasible or politically desirable to develop randomized experiments in communities. Although randomized experiments are not as difficult or expensive as often believed, and although they can be conducted in ways that are both ethical and perceived to be fair, these perceptions do persist (Dennis, 1994). Yet randomized experiments continue to be the standard of evidence for testing effectiveness of interventions (Cook & Campbell, 1979). When randomized experiments are not feasible, how then can community interventions be rigorously assessed?

The answer may lie in causal modeling, and adequate causal modeling depends critically on the quality of a study's theoretical framework. Both Weiss (1998) and Lipsey (1993) make the argument that the more well-articulated the theory is that lies behind an intervention, the more specific its predictions are likely to be, and the more difficult it will be for alternative explanations to rival the statement that interventions caused outcomes. This is especially likely when interventions possess a well-articulated implementation theory, as seen in the framework of the Heart Attack–REACT study. However, specific predictions will be required about the relationships between intervention and mediating variables and between mediating variables and outcomes. The study in question will need to invest heavily in measurement of high quality to permit the kind of causal modeling that can rule out specific alternative explanations.

WHY DO SOME COMMUNITY INTERVENTIONS "FAIL"?

As mentioned at the beginning of this chapter, there are many benefits of community-level interventions, including allowing the intervention to reach people who cannot be reached through other avenues, people who are often in the most need; community resources and capacities to be enlisted in tailoring the intervention for the community; and forces beyond the individual level to be incorporated into the intervention to produce potentially more powerful and mutually reinforcing program elements. Sustainment and institutionalization of interventions are more likely in well-implemented community programs and are key criteria in both the GTO and RE-AIM frameworks. Yet despite these potential benefits, results of community-based research programs have been mixed. Examples exist of positive outcomes from community-based intervention efforts (e.g., Kotchen et al., 1987; Puska et al., 1985; Lando, Koken, Howard-Pitney, & Pechacek, 1990); yet examples of disappointing outcomes also exist (e.g., Hancock et al., 1992; COMMIT Research Group, 1995a, 1995b). Even within the same project delivering the same intervention in different communities, great variability in outcomes can emerge between communities (e.g., REACT; COMMIT Research Group, 1995a, 1995b).

As we noted earlier in this chapter, there can be a number of factors that account for negative outcomes. Aside, of course, from possibly confirming the null hypothesis in studies with negative outcomes associated with the intervention theories and methods used, implementation drift, uneven implementation, and secular trends that overshadow intervention effects can be reasons for negative outcomes. "Social capital" is also a factor that is starting to be viewed as a major determinant of the likelihood of the effectiveness of programs (Coleman, 1988; Putnam, 1993). Social capital is defined as the willingness of individuals and organizations within a community to work cooperatively and is presumably built on trust (Putnam, 1993). Participation of individuals and organizations within a community is now recognized as an essential component for adequate implementation of interventions (Schooler et al., 1997). Social capital within a community at the time of intervention implementation will thus influence the extent to which community individuals and organizations are likely to work together and contribute to the implementation of an intervention, presumably increasing the effectiveness of the intervention. On the other end of the social capital continuum, presumably there are communities who are so deficient in social capital that major barriers will be encountered in adequately implementing the intervention, compromising severely the effectiveness of the intervention. Thus, knowing more about methods of identifying communities who have sufficient social capital to benefit from a particular intervention and knowing how to increase social capital so that communities might benefit more from the interventions is important for maximizing the outcomes of such programs.

Social Capital: Means of Developing Capital and Effecting Greater Community Change

The means to develop social capital and associated community capacity is based on spending social capital itself (Cox, 1995). By creating opportunities for individuals and organizations within a community to work cooperatively, social capital increases and the community is more likely to be able to address other issues. It is thus likely, as predicted by social cognitive theory (Bandura, 1986), that behavioral performance—in other words, providing opportunities for and actual acts of cooperation within a community—leads to enhanced social capital. The more that individuals, organizations, and systems (i.e., different social, political, religious, educational, private sector, and other systems) within a community work cooperatively, the stronger the network of social capital. Enhancing maximally the extent, breadth, and strength of a community's social capital and capacity to work cooperatively for the betterment of the community requires maximizing the involvement of community segments within the community.

Despite beliefs concerning the importance of social capital in determining the effectiveness of community-based interventions, methods of building social capital to improve health benefits in health promotion and disease prevention programs have rarely been examined. In part at least, such efforts have not been systematically examined because funding for community-based projects typically limit their focus to a particular disease outcome or risk factor for a relatively short funding period. In addition, the methodology for evaluation of social capital is not well-developed. These limitations make it difficult to examine issues involving social capacity that, by their very nature, do not directly address particular health outcomes and require long durations to examine changes. Approaches are clearly needed for determining systematic methods to develop community capacity to address multiple community needs that remain important over sustained periods of time if we are to examine the influence of these sustained efforts to build social capital and capacity.

SHORT-TERM VERSUS LONG-TERM QUESTIONS IN COMMUNITY-BASED RESEARCH AND SERVICE PROGRAMS

Most community-based research and many service programs have been relatively short-term in duration, largely as a result of categorical-funding restraints of most funding agencies; major challenges for community-based research programs, discussed earlier, which often only continue throughout the partnership between academicians and their community partners; and changes in the participants and their priorities on both the university and community side of the partnership. Service programs also frequently encounter similar challenges even when there is not a research component to the programs. The short-term nature of these programs affects the types of questions that can be posed. The questions being addressed by short-term studies attempt to address statistically significant changes but often preclude questions addressing truly clinically significant changes at the community level as well as questions about the sustainability of what changes occur.

There are two other ways in which short-term as opposed to long-term funding affects the types of questions that can be posed in community-based research. First, as discussed earlier, emerging thinking suggests that social capital may have powerful influences on the effectiveness of community-based programs. Social capital is built on creating opportunities for individuals and organizations within a community to work cooperatively (Cox, 1995). Thus, questions involving efforts to increase social capital within communities require sufficiently long periods to allow these changes to emerge. If we are truly interested in issues of clinical importance and methods of increasing widespread community capacity to address these issues, then methods need to be identified to generate the continuity in funding to allow sufficient time to pose and to attempt to answer these questions.

The second influence of categorical funding is that the funding, in essence, becomes narrowly focused on a particular disease outcome or risk factor with two results: (a) this narrow focus may not address the identified needs of community members, resulting in challenges in adequately engaging individuals and organizations; and (b) this narrow focus is somewhat anti-thetical to broad-based health disparity issues faced by ethnic minority and other underserved population subgroups. As we mentioned earlier, commu-nity members will often enumerate needs that often include health issues but also include, at least in underserved communities, a variety of more immediate, nonhealth issues, such as for job training, employment opportu-nities, recreational programs, and the like. Within just the realm of health needs, focusing on those in minority communities, particularly those that are impoverished or have poor access to health programs, excess morbidity and mortality is associated with a variety of health outcomes, not a single outcome. If we are to realize the objective of eliminating health disparities, then our research programs need to expand to address methods of producing broad-scale changes rather than the narrow, isolated ones supported by most categorical funding.

Addressing Long-Term and Multiple-Outcome Questions With Short-Term, Categorical Funding

The short-term and focused nature of categorical funding is not ideal for questions of building and sustaining social capital and addressing multiple health outcomes and risk factors. Nonetheless, categorical and relatively short-term funding is the basis on which most research projects in the United States are funded. Within the constraints imposed by categorical funding, we believe that the longer term and broader questions of methods to build social capital and affect multiple risk factors for disparate health outcomes can be achieved by conducting multiple categorical projects, each with its own separate evaluation plan, within a defined community (Raczynski et al., 2001). Staggering and even "layering" projects within communities has the potential to extend the duration of intervention activi-ties sufficiently to examine issues of increasing social capital; allow outcomes associated with increased community capacity to emerge; and enable a blend of projects each with different narrow focus of a categorically funded project but collectively addressing an array of risk factors. This approach thus provides one means of researchers beginning to address what we believe are extremely important issues of community-based intervention methods (Raczynski et al., 2001).

CONCLUSION

Community-based intervention programs offer unique challenges over individually directed programs. These are now starting to be addressed in health psychology, thanks in part to the attention that both the RE-AIM and GTO frameworks have received (Chinman et al., 2001; Glasgow et al., 1999). Community-located and community-based interventions offer unique advantages, including reaching people who cannot be reached through other means, who may be those in most need and be at the greatest risk or have the poorest access to other sources of care; enabling community resources and capacities to be enlisted to tailor the intervention for individuals with the community; and allowing elements to be incorporated into the intervention, such as environmental, cultural, and social support elements, to produce potentially more powerful and mutually reinforcing programs. Despite these benefits, community-based research and even clinical programs present many challenges, which we addressed in this chapter. For research programs and even many clinical programs, prominent among these challenges is the short-term and categorical nature of most funding in the United States. Categorical funding often limits programs to examining periods in which statistically significant changes may be detected but true clinical benefit is not realized. The narrow focus of programs that can be mounted with categorical funding also limits what can be learned about methods of addressing multiple risk factors and health outcomes and limits what can be examined to build social capital and community capacity to potentially increase the effectiveness and sustainability of community-based programs. There is thus a critical need for future community-based research programs to develop methods of examining these issues.

One method of beginning to address these issues and the limitations of categorical funding is to develop multiple and overlapping projects, each with its own categorical funding, within the same communities as we are attempting to do in Uniontown (Raczynski et al., 2001). Multiple, overlapping projects potentially allow contact to be sustained with a community for a sufficiently long enough time to have clinically meaning outcomes emerge and be reinforced; sufficient segments of the community to be involved in working together collaboratively, building trust and increasing capacity to work together on other projects; and sufficient activities to build knowledge and skill levels within the community both related to specific outcomes as well as more generally in terms of leadership and general problem-solving skills. These changes that might be possible with multiple and overlapping projects within particular communities may result, through the enhanced capacity that may result, in outcomes that develop beyond the foci of the individual projects.

REFERENCES

AIDS Community Demonstration Projects Research Group. (1999). Community-level HIV intervention in 5 cities: Final outcome data from the CDC AIDS Community Demonstration Projects. *American Journal of Public Health, 3*, 336–345.

Ajzen, I., & Fishbein, M. (1980). *Understanding attitudes and predicting social behavior.* New York: Prentice-Hall.

Altpeter, M., Earp, J. A., Bishop, C., & Eng, E. (1999). Lay health advisor activity levels: Definitions from the field. *Health Education and Behavior, 26*(4), 495–512.

Andreasen, A. R. (1995). *Marketing social change: Changing behavior to promote health, social development, and the environment.* San Francisco: Jossey-Bass.

Association for the Study and Development of Community. (2000). *Principles for evaluating comprehensive community initiatives.* Retrieved October 18, 2002, from http://www.capablecommunity.com/pubs/NFCVP062001.pdf

Bandura, A. (1986). *Social foundation of thought and action: A social cognitive theory.* Englewood Cliffs, NJ: Prentice-Hall.

Bauman, K. E., Suchindran, C. M., & Murray, D. M. (1999). The paucity of effects in community trials: Is secular trend the culprit? *Preventive Medicine, 28*(4), 426–429.

Berkman, L. F., & Glass, T. (1999). Social integration, social networks, social support, and health. In L. F. Berkman & I. Kawachi (Eds.), *Social epidemiology* (pp. 137–173). New York: Oxford University Press.

Berkowitz, W., & Wolff, T. (2000). *The spirit of the coalition.* Washington, DC: American Public Health Association.

Bracht, N. (1999). *Health promotion at the community level: New advances.* Thousand Oaks, CA: Sage.

Brown, R. J. (1988). *Group processes: Dynamics within and between groups.* Oxford: Blackwell.

Bruce, T. A., & McKane, S. U. (Eds.). (2000). *Community-based public health: A partnership model.* Washington, DC: American Public Health Association.

Bryk, A. S., & Raudenbusch. S. W. (1993). *Hierarchical linear models: Applications and data analysis methods.* Newbury Park, CA: Sage.

Cabral, R. J., Galavotti, C., Gargiullo, P. M., Armstrong, K., Cohen, A., Gielen, A. C., et al. (1996). Paraprofessional delivery of a theory based HIV prevention counseling intervention for women. *Public Health Reports, 111*, 75–82.

Cameron, L., Leventhal, E. A., & Leventhal, H. (1993). Emotional and behavioral processes. In J. Johnston & L. Wallace (Eds.), *Stress and medical procedures* (pp. 7–30). New York: Pergamon Press.

Cameron, L., Leventhal, E. A., & Leventhal, H. (1995). Seeking medical care in response to symptoms and life stress. *Psychosomatic Medicine, 5,* 737–47.

Centers for Disease Control. (1985). *PATCH: Planned approach to community health.* Atlanta, GA: Author.

Centers for Disease Control and Prevention. (1998). *Community health advisors/ workers: Selected annotations and programs in the United States* (Volume III). Atlanta, GA: CDC, National Center for Chronic Disease Prevention and Health Promotion.

Center for the Study of Health Systems Change. (1997, April). Access to health care: Bridging the gap between policy and research. *Issue Brief Center for the Study of Health Systems Change, 8,* 1–6.

CDC/ATSDR Committee on Community Engagement. (1997). *Principles of community engagement.* Atlanta GA: Author.

Chinman, M., Imm, P., Wandersman, A., Kaftarian, S., Neal, J., Pendleton, K. T., et al. (2001). Using the getting-to-outcomes (GTO) model in a statewide prevention initiative. *Health Promotion Practice, 2,* 302–309.

Chou, C. P., Montgomery, S., Pentz, M. A., Rohrbach, L. A., Johnson, C. A., Flay, B. R., et al. (1998). Effects of a community-based prevention program on decreasing drug use in high-risk adolescents. *American Journal of Public Health, 88*(6), 944–948.

Clark, L. F., Rhodes, S. D., Rogers, W., & Liddon, N. (2004). The context of sexual risk behavior. In J. Raczynski, L. Bradley, & L. Leviton (Eds.), *Handbook of clinical health psychology: Volume 2. Disorders of behavior and health* (pp. 121–146). Washington, DC: American Psychological Association.

Clark, N. M., & McLeroy, K. R. (1995). Creating capacity through health education: What we know and what we don't. *Health Education Quarterly, 22*(3), 273–289.

Cohen, S., Underwood, L., & Gottlieb, B. H. (2000). *Social support measurement and intervention: A guide for health and social scientists.* New York: Oxford University Press.

Coleman, J. S. (1988). Social capital in the creation of human capital. *American Journal of Sociology, 94*(Suppl.), 95–120.

COMMIT Study Group. (1995a). Community Intervention Trial for Smoking Cessation (COMMIT): I. Cohort results from a four-year community intervention. *American Journal of Public Health, 85*(2), 183–192.

COMMIT Study Group. (1995b). Community Intervention Trial for Smoking Cessation (COMMIT): II. Changes in adult cigarette smoking prevalence. *American Journal of Public Health, 85*(2), 193–200.

Community Tool Box. (2003). Retrieved December 11, 2003, from http:// ukans.edu/

Cook, T. D. (1993). A quasi-sampling theory of the generalization of causal relationships. In L. B. Sechrest & A. G. Scott (Eds.), *Understanding causes and generalizing about them. New directions for program evaluation 57* (pp. 39–82). San Francisco: Jossey-Bass.

Cook, T. D., & Campbell, D. T. (1979). *Quasi-experimentation*. Boston: Houghton-Mifflin.

Cornell, C. E., Raczynski, J. M., Stalker, V. G., Greene, P. G., Sanderson, B. K., Kirk, K., et al. (2000, October). Paper presented at the Community Prevention Research in Women's Health Conference, National Institutes of Health, Bethesda, MD.

Cox, E. (1995). *A truly civil society, 1995 Boyer lectures*. Sydney: Australian Broadcasting Company Books.

Cronbach, L. J. (1982). *Designing evaluations of educational and social programs*. San Francisco: Jossey-Bass.

Dennis, M. L. (1994). Ethical and practical randomized field experiments. In J. S. Wholey, H. P. Hatry, & K. E. Newcomer (Eds.), *Handbook of practical program evaluation* (pp. 155–197). San Francisco: Jossey-Bass.

Edelstein, M. R., & Wandersman, A. (1987). Community dynamics in coping with toxic contaminants. In I. Altman, & A. Wandersman (Eds.), *Neighborhood and community environments*. New York: Plenum Press.

Eng, E., & Parker, E. (1994). Measuring community competence in the Mississippi Delta: Interface between program evaluation and empowerment. *Health Education Quarterly, 21*(2), 199–220.

Finnegan, J. R., Meischke, H., Zapka, J. G., Leviton, L., Meshack, A., Benjamin-Garner, R., et al. (2000). Patient delay in seeking care for heart attack symptoms: Findings from focus conducted in five U.S. regions. *Preventive Medicine, 31*, 205–213.

Fischhoff, B., Bostrom, A., & Quadrel, M. J. (1993). Risk perception and communication. *Annual Review of Public Health, 14*, 183–203.

Flay, B. R. (1986). Efficacy and effectiveness trials (and other phases of research) in the development of health promotion programs. *Preventive Medicine, 15*(5), 451–474.

Freire, P. (1970). *Pedagogy of the oppressed*. New York: Seabury.

Glanz, K., Lewis, F. M., & Rimer, B. K. (1997). *Health behavior and health education: Theory, research, and practice*. San Francisco: Jossey-Bass.

Glasgow, R. E., Vogt, T. M., & Boles, S. M. (1999). Evaluating the public health impact of health promotion interventions: The RE-AIM framework. *American Journal of Public Health, 89*, 1323–1327.

Goldstein, H. (1995). *Multilevel statistical models* (2nd ed.). London: Edward Arnold.

Goodman, R. M. (1998). Principles and tools for evaluating community-based prevention and health promotion programs. *Journal of Public Health Management and Practice, 4*(2), 37–47.

Goodman, R. M., Speers, M. A., McLeroy, K., Fawcett, S., Kegler, M., Parker, E., et al. (1998). Identifying and defining the dimensions of community capacity to provide a basis for measurement. *Health Education and Behavior, 25*(3), 258–278.

Gray, B. (1989). *Collaborating: Finding common ground for multiparty problems*. San Francisco: Jossey-Bass.

Green, L. W., & Kreuter, M. W. (1999). *Health promotion planning: An educational and ecological approach* (3rd ed.). Mountainview, CA: Mayfield.

Hancock, L., Sanson-Fisher, R. W., Redman, S., Burton, R., Burton, L., Butler, J., et al. (1992). Community action for health promotion: A review of methods and outcomes 1990–1995. *American Journal of Preventive Medicine, 13*, 229–239.

Higgins, D. L., O'Reilly, K., Tashima, N., Crain, C., Beeker, C., Goldbaum, G., et al. (1996). Using formative research to lay the foundation for community level HIV prevention efforts: An example from the AIDS Community Demonstration Projects. *Public Health Reports, 111*(Suppl.), 28–35.

Israel, B. A., Schulz, A. J., Parker, E. A., & Becker, A. B. (1998). Review of community-based research: Assessing partnership approaches to improve public health. *Annual Review of Public Health, 19*, 173–202.

Kasperson, R. E., Renn, O., Brown, H. S., Emel, J., Govle, R., Kasperson, J. X., et al. (1988). The social amplification of risk: A conceptual framework. *Risk Analysis, 8*, 177–204.

Kelly, J. A., St. Lawrence, J. S., Stevenson, L. Y., Hauth, A. C., Kalichman, S. C., Diaz, Y. E., et al. (1992). Community AIDS/HIV risk reduction: The effects of endorsements by popular people in three cities. *American Journal of Public Health, 82*, 1483–1489.

Kotchen, J. M., McKean, H. E., Jackson-Thayer, S., Moore, R. W., Straus, R., & Kotchen, T. A. (1987). The impact of a high blood pressure control program on hypertension control and CVD mortality. *Journal of the American Medical Association, 257*, 3382–3386.

Kretzman, J., & McKnight, J. (1993). *Building communities from the inside out: A pathway toward finding and mobilizing a community's assets*. Evanston, IL: Center for Urban Affairs and Policy Research.

Kreuter, M. W., Young, L. A., & Lezin, N. A. (1998). *Measuring social capital in small communities*. Atlanta, GA: Health 2000.

Krueger, R. A., & Casey, M. A. (2000). *Focus groups: A practical guide for applied research* (3rd ed.). Thousand Oaks, CA: Sage.

Lando, H. A., Koken, B., Howard-Pitney, B., & Pechacek, T. (1990). Community impact of localized smoking cessation contest. *American Journal of Public Health, 80*, 601–603.

Leventhal, H., & Nerenz, D. (1985). The assessment of illness cognition. In P. Karoly (Ed.), *Measurement strategies in health* (pp. 517–554). New York: John Wiley & Sons.

Leviton, L. C. (2001). External validity. In N. J. Smelser & P. B. Baltes (Eds.), *The International Encyclopedia of the Social & Behavioral Sciences* (pp. 5195–5200). Oxford: Elsevier Sciences.

Leviton, L. C. (2003). Ethical challenges commentary: Encouraging the community in evaluation. *American Journal of Evaluation, 24(1)*, 86–90.

Leviton, L. C. (1996). Integrating psychology and public health: Challenges and opportunities. *American Psychologist, 51*(1), 42–51.

Leviton, L. C., Finnegan, J. R., Zapka, J. G., Meischke, H., Estabrook, B., Gilliland, J., et al. (1999). Formative research methods to understand patient and provider responses to heart attack symptoms. *Evaluation and Program Planning, 22*(4), 385–397.

Leviton, L. C., Marsh, G. M., Talbott, E., Pavlock, D., & Callahan, C. (1991). Drake Chemical Workers' Health Registry: Coping with community tension in health protection. *American Journal of Public Health, 81*(6), 689–693.

Leviton, L. C., Needleman, C. E., & Shapiro, M. (1997). *Confronting public health risks: A decision maker's guide.* Thousand Oaks, CA: Sage.

Leviton, L. C., & Schuh, R. G. (1999). The importance of a discovery capacity in community-based health program evaluation. *New Directions in Program Evaluation, 44*, 17–36.

Leviton, L. C., Snell, E., & McGinnis, J. M. (2000). Penalties and problems in urban health promotion. *American Journal of Public Health, 90*(6), 863–866.

Leviton, L. C., & Valdiserri, R. O. (1990). Evaluating AIDS prevention: Outcome, implementation and mediating variables. *Evaluation and Program Planning, 13*(2), 55–65.

Leviton, L. C., Valdiserri, R., Lyter, D., Callahan, K., Kingsley, L., & Rinaldo, C. (1990). Preventing HIV infection in gay and bisexual men: Experimental evaluation of attitude change from two risk reduction interventions. *AIDS Education and Prevention, 2*(2), 95–109.

Lipsey, M. W. (1993). Theory as method: Small theories of treatments. *New Directions for Program Evaluation, 57*, 5–38.

Luepker, R. V., Raczynski, J. M., Osganian, S., Goldberg, R. J., Finnegan, J. R., Jr., Hedges, J. R., et al. (2000). Effect of a community intervention on patient delay and emergency medical service use in acute coronary heart disease: The Rapid Early Action for Coronary Treatment (REACT) Trial. *Journal of the American Medical Association, 284*(1), 60–67.

Maciak, B., Moore, M., Leviton, L. C., & Guinan, M. (1998, April). Preventing Halloween arson in an urban setting. *Health Education and Behavior, 25*(2), 194–211.

Maibach, E., & Parrott, R. L. (1995). *Designing health messages: Approaches from communication theory and public health practice.* Thousand Oaks, CA: Sage.

McGuire, W. J. (1969). The nature of attitudes and attitude change. In G. Lindsey & E. Aronson (Eds.). *The handbook of social psychology* (2nd ed., pp. 136–314). Reading, MA: Addison-Wesley.

McKnight, J. (1996). *The careless society: Community and its counterfeits.* New York: Basic Books.

Mechanic, D. (1998). Public trust and initiatives for new health care partnerships. *Millbank Quarterly, 76,* 281–302.

Miles, M. B, & Huberman, A. M. (1994). *Qualitative data analysis* (2nd ed.). Thousand Oaks, CA: Sage.

Miller, R. L. (1995). Assisting gay men to maintain safer sex: An evaluation of an AIDS service organization's safer sex maintenance program. *AIDS Education and Prevention, 7*(Suppl. 5), 48–63.

Miller, R. L., Klotz, D., & Eckholdt, H. M. (1998). HIV prevention with male prostitutes and patrons of hustler bars: Replication of an HIV prevention intervention. *American Journal of Community Psychology, 26*(1), 97–131.

Mittelmark, M. B., Leupker, R. V., Murray, D. M., Jacobs, D. R., Bracht, N., Carlaw, R., et al. (1986). Community education for cardiovascular disease prevention: Risk factor changes in the Minnesota Heart Health Program. *American Journal of Public Health, 84,* 1383–1393.

Murray, D. M (1998). *Design and analysis of group-randomized trials.* Oxford: Oxford University Press.

National Heart, Lung, and Blood Institute. (1994). *REACT study.* Retrieved January 22, 2004, from http://epihab.epi.umn.edu/react/welcome/html

Novelli, W. D. (1991). Applying social marketing to health promotion and disease prevention. In K. Glanz, F. M. Lewis, & B. K. Rimer (Eds.), *Health behavior and health education: Theory, research, and practice.* San Francisco: Jossey-Bass.

Nuffield Council on Bioethics. (2002). *The ethics of research related to healthcare in developing countries: The assent/involvement of the community.* Retrieved October 18, 2002, from http://www.nuffieldbioethics.org/publications/developingcoun tries/rep0000000889.asp

Parker, E. A., Eng, E., Laraia, B., Ammerman, A., Dodds, J., Margolis, L., et al. (1998). Coalition building for prevention: Lessons learned from the North Carolina Community-Based Public Health Initiative. *Journal of Public Health Management and Practice, 4*(2), 25–36.

Parker, E. A., Schulz, A. J., Israel, B. A., & Hollis, R. (1998). Detroit's East Side Village Health Worker Partnership: Community-based lay health advisor intervention in an urban area. *Health Education and Behavior, 25*(1), 24–45.

Patten, C. A., Gilpin, E., Calvin, S. W., & Pierce, J. P. (1995). Workplace smoking policy and changes in smoking behavior in California: A suggested association. *Tobacco Control, 4,* 36–41.

Pentz, M. A., Dwyer, J. H., MacKinnon, D. P., Flay, B. R., Hansen, W. B., Wang, E. Y., et al. (1989). A multicommunity trial for primary prevention of adolescent drug abuse. Effects on drug use prevalence. *Journal of the American Medical Association, 261*(22), 3259–3266.

Prochaska, J. O., DiClemente, C. C., & Norcross, J. C. (1992). In search of how people change. Applications to addictive behaviors. *American Psychologist, 47*(9), 1102–1114.

Puska, P., Nissinen, A., Tuomilehto, J., Koskela, K., McAlister, A., Kottke, T. E., et al. (1985). The community-based strategy to prevent coronary heart disease: Conclusions from the ten years of the North Karelia project. *Annual Review of Public Health, 6*, 147.

Puska, P., Tuomilehto, J., Nissinen, A., Salonen, J. T., Vartiainen, E., Pietinen, P., et al. (1989). The North Karelia project: 15 years of community-based prevention of coronary heart disease. *Annals of Medicine, 21*(3), 169–173.

Putnam, R. D. (1993). *Making democracy work: Civic traditions in modern Italy.* Princeton, NJ: Princeton University Press.

Putnam, R. D. (2000). *Bowling alone: The collapse and revival of American community.* New York: Simon & Schuster.

Raczynski, J. M., Cornell, C. E., Stalker, V., Dignan, M., Pulley, L., Phillips, M., et al. (2001). Developing community capacity and improving health in African-American communities. *American Journal of Medical Sciences, 322*, 269–275.

Raczynski, J. M., Cornell, C. E., Stalker, V., Phillips, M., Dignan, M., Pulley, L., et al. (2001). A multi-project, systems approach to developing community trust and building capacity. *Journal of Public Health Management Practice, 7*, 10–20.

Raczynski, J. M., Finnegan, J. R., Zapka, J. G., Meischke, H., Meshack, A., Stone, E. J., et al. (1999). REACT theory-based intervention to reduce treatment-seeking delay for acute MI. *American Journal of Preventive Medicine, 16*, 325–324.

Raczynski, J. M., Taylor, H., Rappaport, N., Cutter, G., Hardin, M., & Oberman, A. (1994). Diagnoses, acute symptoms and attributions for symptoms among Black and White inpatients admitted for coronary heart disease: Findings of the Birmingham-BHS Project. *American Journal of Public Health, 84*, 951–956.

Reichardt, C. S., & Rallis, S. F. (Eds.). (1994). *The qualitative–quantitative debate: New perspectives. New directions for program evaluation* (Number 61). San Francisco: Jossey-Bass.

Renn, O., Burns, W. J., Kasperson, J. X., Kasperson, R. E., & Slovic, P. (1992). The social amplification of risk: Theoretical foundations and empirical applications. *Journal of Social Issues, 48*, 137–160.

Resnick, M. D., Bearman, P. S., Blum, R. W., Bauman, K. E., Harris, K. M., Jones, J., et al. (1997). Protecting adolescents from harm. Findings from the National Longitudinal Study on Adolescent Health. *Journal of the American Medical Association, 278*(10), 823–832.

Rogers, E. M. (1983). *Diffusion of innovations* (3rd ed.). New York: Free Press.

Schooler, C., Farquhar, J. W., Fortmann, S. P., & Flora, J. A. (1997). Synthesis of findings and issues from community prevention trials. *Annals of Epidemiology, 7*, S54–S68.

Schwartz, S. (1994). The fallacy of the ecological fallacy: The potential misuse of a concept and the consequences. *American Journal of Public Health, 84*, 819–824.

Shadish, W. R., Cook, T. D., & Leviton, L. C. (1991). *Foundations of program evaluation: Theorists and their theories.* Newbury Park, CA: Sage.

Sikkema, K. J., Kelly, J. A., Winett, R. A., Solomon, L. J., Cargill, V. A., Roffman, R. A., et al. (2000). Outcomes of a randomized community-level HIV prevention intervention for women living in 18 low-income housing developments. *American Journal of Public Health, 90*(1), 57–63.

Simons-Morton, D. G., Goff, D. C., Osganian, S., Goldberg, R. J., Raczynski, J. M., Finnegan, J. R., et al. (1998). Rapid early action for coronary treatment: Rationale, design, and baseline characteristics. *Academic Emergency Medicine, 5*, 726–738.

Singer, M. R. (1998). Culture: A perceptual approach. In M. J. Bennett (Ed.), *Basic concepts of intercultural communication* (pp. 97–110). Yarmouth, ME: Intercultural Press.

Syme, S. L. (1997). *Community participation, empowerment, and health: Development of a wellness guide for California.* Berkeley: University of California, Berkeley, School of Public Health.

Telfair, J., Leviton, L. C., & Merchant, J. S. (1999). *Evaluating health and human service programs in community settings.* New directions in evaluation (Number 83). San Francisco: Jossey-Bass.

Valdiserri, R. O., Lyter, D. W., Leviton, L. C., Callahan, C. M., Kingsley, L. A., & Rinaldo, C. R. (1989). AIDS prevention in gay and bisexual men: Results of a randomized trial evaluating two risk reduction interventions. *AIDS, 3*(1), 21–26.

Wallerstein, N., & Berstein, E. (1988). Empowerment education: Freire's ideas adapted to health education. *Health Education Quarterly, 15,* (4), 379–394.

Wandersman, A. H., & Hallman, W. K. (1993). Are people acting irrationally? Understanding public concerns about environmental threats. *American Psychologist, 48*, 681–686.

Wandersman, A., & Hallman, W. (1994, April). *Environmental threats: Perception of risk, stress, and coping.* Paper presented at the Spanish Congress of Environmental Psychology, Tenerife, Spain.

Wandersman, A., & Nation, M. (1998). Urban neighborhoods and mental health: Psychological contributions to understanding toxicity, resilience, and interventions. *American Psychologist, 53*, 647–656.

Warren, R. L. (1978). *The community in America* (3rd ed.). Chicago: Rand McNally.

Weiss, C. H. (1998). *Evaluation* (2nd ed.). Upper Saddle River, NJ: Prentice-Hall.

Windsor, R., Baranowski, T., & Clark, N. (1994). *Evaluation of health promotion, health education and disease prevention programs* (2nd ed.). Palo Alto, CA: Mayfield.

World Health Organization. (1995). *WHO Healthy Cities: A Programme framework. A review of the operation and future development of the WHO Healthy Cities Programme.* Geneva, Switzerland: Author.

Zapka, J., Estabrook, B., Gilliland, J., Leviton, L., Meischke, H., Melville, S., et al. (1999). Health care providers' perspectives on patient delay for seeking care for symptoms of acute myocardial infarction. *Health Education and Behavior, 26*, 714–733.

16

MEASURING HEALTH OUTCOMES: APPLICATIONS FOR HEALTH PSYCHOLOGY

JOSHUA C. KLAPOW, ROBERT M. KAPLAN, AND JASON N. DOCTOR

The measurement of health and health outcomes presents a formidable challenge for researchers and clinicians alike. Defining health outcomes, quantifying them, and evaluating them offers an important opportunity for health psychology. The intention of this chapter is to outline the basic concepts in the evaluation of health, discuss challenges in transitioning health psychology into health outcomes measurement, and highlight areas of immediate and future focus.

A single definition of health outcome has eluded both researchers and clinicians. Outcome measurement has typically referred to the endpoint of a health service that accounts for patient experiences, preferences, and values (Clancy & Eisenberg, 1998). Donabedian (1966) referred to outcome as "A change in patients' current and future health status that can be attributed to antecedent health care." Although it is conventional to consider an outcome as the endpoint of a particular intervention or service, outcome may also refer to an endpoint of any number of factors, including disease progression, environmental changes, or psychological processes (Klapow et al., 1993). In the end, outcomes measurement within a health care context functions to provide empirical evidence for decisions made by all those involved in the health care setting (Clancy & Eisenberg, 1998). Because the term *outcome* is so broad, and generally speaking within the health care setting outcome typically refers to an evaluation of health, the definition and measurement of *health* must be considered.

This chapter covers a variety of topics important to understanding health psychology's role in outcomes measurement. First, operational definitions of health are examined from epidemiological, historical, medical, and outcomes perspectives. Second, key dimensions of health are identified and targeted for measurement. Third, health psychology's current role in the measurement of health outcomes is examined and recommendations are offered for increasing the presence of health psychology in the field. Fourth, specific areas of measurement research that are immediately applicable for health psychology are identified and reviewed. Fifth, applications of health outcomes research are characterized that should be targeted by health psychology as areas for future research.

DEFINING HEALTH: VARYING PERSPECTIVES

For centuries, scholars have debated about the definition of health. Different definitions emphasize related, but divergent, concepts. Some terms used to describe health are positive concepts, such as *wellness* or *normality*. Other terms emphasize negative concepts, such as *disability* and *illness*. Much of the debate has centered on whether health is a continuum. Are disability and illness distinct from health, or are they opposite ends of the same continuum (Patrick & Erickson, 1993)?

Because the concept of health lacked conceptual clarity, the World Health Organization (WHO) proposed a comprehensive definition of health in their charter document. Health was defined as "a state of complete physical, mental, and social well-being and not merely the absence of infirmity" (World Health Organization, 1948). In the 50 years since the introduction of this definition, there has been some convergence of thought. It is now widely recognized that health has multiple dimensions. Also, it is now accepted that measures of mortality alone cannot summarize the health status of populations (Field & Gold, 1998). However, there is still considerable debate about what constitutes health and health status.

Historical Perspective

Some of the debate about the definition of health originates from sociologists. From the sociological perspective, illness represents deviation from society's standards for physical and mental well-being. Often, this deviation is recognized when a person cannot perform activities usual for his or her social role. In addition to observable functioning, illness may cause reports of symptoms or pain, and these deviate from societies norms of wellness. Parsons (1951) defined illness as "a state of disturbance in normal functioning of the total human individual including both the state of the organism as a biological system, and/or his personal and social adjustments" (Parsons, 1951, p. 431). For Parsons, health represented the capacity to perform valued tasks.

Epidemiological Perspective

Epidemiologists have addressed the issue of health status by tabulating the frequency of various outcomes. Their methodologies emphasize rates of morbidity and mortality. Healthy populations, for example, are those where life expectancy is longer and infant mortality rates are lower. The limitations of mortality rates as measures of health are well-recognized. A 1998 Institute of Medicine report summarizing methods for measuring population health concluded that mortality measures are incomplete, insensitive, and cannot be used to summarize population health (Field & Gold, 1998). Just as mortality measures exclude morbidity, morbidity measures often exclude information on mortality. The comprehensive definition of health requires some integration of morbidity and mortality. The major shortcoming of defining health only by mortality is that death is only one dimension of health outcome. Diseases and disabilities affect multiple aspects of wellness. Within the past few decades, attention has turned toward the definition of health-related quality of life.

Traditional Biomedical Perspective

From a biomedical perspective, people are healthy if they are free of disease. A disease is recognized in a human organism through the manifestation of clinical signs and symptoms. These signs and symptoms are associated with underlying lesions or pathology. Diagnostic tests are used to identify pathology, and interventions are designed to repair the lesion or stop the pathological process. Thus underlying pathology is the ultimate target of assessment and treatment. The traditional biomedical model is predicated on finding a specific biological problem and repairing the problem.

Outcomes Perspective

Kaplan (1990) posed the question, "If a disease or condition had an impact upon a tissue or organ system and had no effect on life expectancy, no effect on function, no effect on appearance or symptoms, would it be of concern?" This question is the foundation of an outcomes model of health. An outcomes model of health is defined from the patient's perspective. Measurement of health outcome is focused on those endpoints that have direct meaning to the patient. Typically these outcomes include two broad categories: length of life and quality of life. Defining health in terms of quality of life will be addressed in detail in the next section. For now, health-related quality of life may be understood as the value assigned to those dimensions of health that are most important to the patient. In an outcomes model of health, biochemical measures do not have meaning as endpoints in and of themselves. Rather, they are important to the extent that they are associated with length and quality of life.

Limitations of a Traditional Biomedical Perspective in Evaluating Health Outcomes

Diagnostic Testing

The biomedical model is appealing and useful in numerous applications of medicine and surgery. However, there is evidence that the biomedical perspective may fall short across indicators of health other than pathophysiology. For example, there is little evidence that life expectancy, infant mortality, or functioning has changed dramatically in the past 20 years. At the same time, however, there have been remarkable increases in the number of people with diagnosed disease. In part, the apparent epidemics in disease are the result of improved diagnostic technologies. New spiral CT scans can now detect hepatic lesions that are less than 2 millimeters. Twenty years ago, only lesions 20 millimeters or greater could be diagnosed. It is apparent there are large reservoirs of undiagnosed disease. As technology has improved, more disease is revealed. For example, about 3% of women eventually die of breast cancer, and about 3% of men die of prostate cancer. However, autopsy studies suggest that nearly 40% of women over 70 have some form of breast cancer (including ductile tumors). Nearly half of men age 70 and above have prostate cancer. The great majority of tumors found at autopsy were not known before and had little consequence for the affected individuals (Black & Welsch, 1993). Because disease is very common, the more we look for disease the more we find. Either greater screening or improved diagnostic technology will reveal more problems (Black & Welsch, 1997).

There are numerous examples of disease reservoirs being unmasked as more diagnostic tests are applied. For example, orthopedic surgeons have used radiographic evidence to confirm that reports of back pain represent disease. However, studies of volunteers without back pain reveal bulging disks in nearly half of all adults. Figure 16.1 shows the percentage of adults without back pain who had bulging disks as revealed by MRI images broken

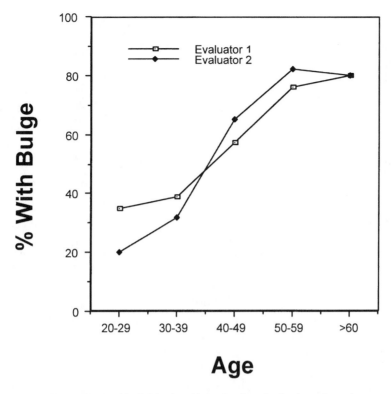

Figure 16.1. Percentage of individuals without back pain, broken down by age, with bulges identified by MRI of the lumbar spine (data from Jensen et al., 1994, tab. 2, pg. 70).

down by age. The two lines represent readings of the MRI images by different radiologists. For adults older than age 60, 80% of those without pain or disability had "disease" (Jensen, Kelly, & Brant-Zawadzki, 1994).

Similarly, there are substantial discrepancies between studies of X-ray evidence of osteoarthritis and performance of usual activities. Studies on back pain help illustrate some of these issues. Radiographic studies show that an estimated 57% of Americans age 60 years or older have ruptured discs or spinal stenosis. However, these patients often report little or no pain. Surgery to correct spinal stenosis may be of little value on patients who are not impaired. Conversely, pain is often reported by patients who have no abnormalities on X-ray. According to traditional measures, these patients have no problems.

Diagnostic Approaches

Although disease is usually regarded as a binary variable (present or absent) most health problems are on a continuum. By changing the thresholds for the disease label, many more people are regarded as sick. Overweight, for example, used to be defined as a body weight index greater than 28. This threshold was recently reset at 25 (National Heart, Lung and Blood Institute, 1998), making most of the adult population overweight. Likewise, new methods for assessing subthreshold depression greatly increased the number of people with a mental health "problem" (Judd, Paulus, Wells, & Rapaport, 1996). Just over 5% of patients in general medical practice qualify for a *DSM–IV* (American Psychiatric Association, 1994) diagnosis of depression. However, more than a quarter of all general medical patients might be labeled as having subsyndromal depression (Wells, 1996).

Reliability and Validity of Biological Measures

Advocates of the biomedical model argue that only biological measures of disease pathology taken with precise instruments have clinical meaning. Unfortunately, not all biological markers are measures of health status or health outcome. As Kaplan (1990) noted, elevated blood pressure is important as a predictor of premature mortality or disability resulting from coronary heart disease and stroke. If blood pressure had no bearing on these outcomes, then it would have little relevance as an endpoint. Elevated blood cholesterol can be predictive of heart disease and early mortality; however, other blood lipids, including low density lipoproteins or chylomicrons, may have very little relationship to health outcomes in the majority of cases. Serological abnormalities in patients with rheumatoid arthritis are poorly correlated with joint inflammation (McCarty, 1986), and erythrocyte sedimentation rate is not consistently associated with pain or dysfunction levels. Thus biological markers may serve as useful predictors of health outcomes but may be less useful as primary outcome measures.

Advocates of the biomedical model also argue that biological markers of health are more reliable than measures of patient perceptions. Measures of patient perspective are often devalued as meaningless and unreliable. Unfortunately, the reliability of many biological markers is often not well studied and the validity of such markers is often justified by their close link with physical or biological theory. Moreover, relatively poor reliability has been demonstrated in several commonly used biological markers. Blood pressure is an important example because it is commonly used as an outcome measure in clinical practice as well as in health psychology research. Conventional sphygomomangometric measurements have demonstrated poor test–retest reliability. This may be accounted for by the variety of sources of error in the process of blood pressure measurement, including environmental conditions (e.g., white coat hypertension), misreading biases, and sampling biases (e.g., changes in blood pressure minute to minute). All of these factors function to reduce the reliability of blood pressure as an outcome variable.

Similar to blood pressure, Fries (1983) noted the questionable reliability and validity of several biological outcome indexes ranging from measures of erythrocyte sedimentation rate (ESR) to latex fixation titer to hemoglobin.

A growing number of studies demonstrate that simple subjective measures of wellness are significant predictors of longevity for patients with chronic illnesses (Coates, Porzsott, & Osoba, 1997; Idler & Benyamini, 1997; Kaplan, Ries, Prewitt, & Eakin, 1994). Typically, simple self-report measures perform as well as, or better than, key physiological indicators in predicting mortality (Squier et al., 1995). Many studies show that a simple one-item rating of wellness predicts survival even after adjustment for other risk factors (Idler & Kasl, 1995). Thus, measurement from a patient's perspective may be as precise as physiological markers *and* have greater relevance to the patient.

The emerging evidence-based medicine paradigm raises questions about the biomedical perspective. Evidence-based medicine advocates argue that a test must have "therapeutic" benefit. This benefit occurs only if the test provides meaningful information that will result in benefit to a patient. In addition, it must be determined whether the test leads to treatment that will result in reduced life expectancy or quality of life (Sackett, 1996). In summary, defining health solely on the criterion of the absence of disease is problematic. In summary, traditional measures of clinical status, including X-rays or clinical tests, do not tell the whole story with regard to health benefit. Measures of health outcome are required to demonstrate the benefits of treatment from the patient's perspective (Kaplan, Anderson, & Ganiats, 1993). There is no "right" answer to the question of how to best conceptualize health. The examination of epidemiological, medical, and outcomes perspectives highlight strengths and weaknesses in each. However, it is important to build an approach to health outcomes assessment on a conceptual foundation. Given the patient-centered focus in the outcomes perspective, it is ideally suited as a conceptual foundation for the field of health psychology.

DIMENSIONS OF HEALTH

To better understand the measurement of health from an outcomes perspective, it is necessary to build a comprehensive theoretical model of health status—that is, a conceptualization of health from the patient's perspective. The major aspects of such a model include mortality (death) and morbidity, where morbidity refers to dimensions of health associated with quality of life (e.g. health-related quality of life). Diseases and disabilities are important for two reasons. First, illness may cause life expectancy to be shortened. Second, illness may make life less desirable at times before death (diminished health-related quality of life; Kaplan & Anderson, 1996; Kaplan et al., 1997). Environmental exposures or risky health behaviors might reduce life expectancy or quality of life, even if we do not understand their effects on disease process. Treatments might make life better or longer, even though we do not understand the mechanisms through which they influence a biological process. However, to understand health outcomes, it is necessary to quantify health using measures that do not necessarily depend on medical diagnosis.

Nearly all definitions of health recognize that health is multidimensional. Spilker (1996) argued that there are five major domains of life quality: (a) physical status and functional abilities, (b) psychological status and well-being, (c) social interactions, (d) economic or vocational status and factors, and (e) religious or spiritual status. Various approaches to the measurement of health outcome typically attempt to assess different dimensions, although the exact dimensions vary considerably.

An emerging consensus suggests that the concept of health must integrate the concept of mortality with multiple dimensions of life quality. More than 30 years ago, Sullivan (1966) offered a comprehensive review of concepts relevant to health. He noted that three types of evidence supported most definitions of morbidity: clinical, subjective, and behavioral. Sullivan's review concluded that clinical and objective evidence could not be used solely as valid and reliable indicators of health status. Instead, he focused on behavioral evidence including absenteeism, bed–disability days, and institutional confinement. The concept of disability was attractive to Sullivan because it represented deviation from societal standards and was consistent with Parson's (1951) conceptualization of health. Although people may be sick from many different diseases, they all represent deviation from society's ideal of well-being.

By themselves, measures of both mortality and morbidity are incomplete indicators of health. Combined indexes of morbidity and mortality may more accurately represent the level of wellness. In most attempts to define health, the measurable components include behavioral functioning and both physical and mental symptoms. Symptoms might be pain, cough, anxiety, or depressed mood. Physical functioning is usually measured in terms of limitations in ambulating or disruptions in functioning because of restrictions of mobility, confinement to home, or bed. Social functioning might be represented by limitations in performance of usual social roles; this would include attendance at school, ability to work, or participation in recreational activities. The concept of health-related quality of life usually attaches value to combinations of these attributes (Erickson, Wilson, & Shannon, 1995; Patrick & Erickson, 1993).

The models introduced by Sullivan require combining morbidity and mortality into a single index. Within morbidity, there is also the need to combine or integrate the information. Tabulating the frequencies of different dimensions of wellness results in an incomplete description of health. For example, consider two people with different health problems. Person 1 has pain from arthritis of the knee and walks with difficulty. However, she is able to work and perform a wide variety of social activities. Person 2 has persistent depressed mood. Although able to ambulate with no difficulty, he is limited in the amount or kind of work he is able to do. Which person is healthier? If we are able to make a judgment, it is only because we are using some system of weighting the circumstances of the two people. If we say person 1 is worse off, more weight is given to mobility. A judgment that person 2 is worse off implies that social functioning is given more weight. Value judgments about the relative importance of dimensions are common. However, weighting is typically done implicitly, arbitrarily, and in an idiosyncratic way. Formal models of health measurement attempt to make the value or preference dimension of health status clear (Kaplan & Anderson, 1996; Torrence & Feeny, 1989).

Time

The concept of health implies a time dimension. In addition to current wellness, future outlook must be considered. A person infected with the HIV virus may appear very well today. However, this person might not be described as healthy because he or she is at increased risk for poor health outcomes in the future. The term *prognosis* is used to describe transitions in health status over the course of time.

Acute care medicine, like preventive medicine, attempts to prevent or limit future problems. For example, cancer surgery or treatments of myocardial infarction are performed not only to treat current symptoms but also to prevent disease progression and death. Conceptual models of health separate levels of function at one point in time (such as today) from the probability of transition to other levels of function in the future. The failure to separate current health from prognosis is one of the major conceptual obstacles to defining heath. Health and severity of illness must be examined in relation to the two independent constructs of current functioning and prognosis.

In sum, measures of health must incorporate several components if they are to be maximally effective in evaluating outcomes. Measures that focus solely on one or more of the dimensions of morbidity (e.g., functional status, psychological and social status, and symptoms) are useful for specific research questions (e.g., documentation of functional abilities after a surgical procedure, improvement in psychological well-being as a function of psychotherapy) but are not as useful for evaluating the overall construct of health. To accomplish this, mortality, morbidity, preferences for health outcomes, and time must all be accounted for in a single metric.

Quality-Adjusted Life Years

Quality-adjusted life years (QALYs) are a metric of health that incorporates mortality, morbidity, preferences, and time. Specifically, QALYs are measures of life expectancy with adjustments for quality of life (Gold et al., 1996; Kaplan, Alcaraz, Anderson, & Weisman, 1996). QALYs integrate mortality and morbidity to express health status in terms of equivalents of well years of life. For example, if a woman dies of breast cancer at age 50 and one would have expected her to live to age 75, the disease was associated with 25 lost life years. If 100 women died at age 50 (and also had life expectancies of 75 years) 2,500 (100 x 25 years) life years would be lost.

Death is not the only outcome of concern in cancer. Many adults continue to suffer from the disease, leaving them somewhat disabled over long periods of time. Although still alive, the quality of their lives has diminished. Quality-adjusted life years take into consideration the quality of life consequences of these illnesses. For example, a disease that reduces quality of life by one half will take away 0.5 QALYs over the course of one year. If it affects two people, it will take away one QALY (equal 2 X 0.5) over a one-year period. A pharmaceutical treatment that improves quality of life by 0.2 for each of five individuals will result in the equivalent of 1 QALY if the benefit is maintained over a one-year period. The basic assumption is that two years scored as 0.5 add up to the equivalent of one year of complete wellness. Similarly, four years scored as 0.25 are equivalent to one completely well-year of life. A treatment that boosts a patient's health from 0.50 to 0.75 adds the equivalent of 0.25 QALYs. If applied to four individuals, and the duration of the treatment effect is one year, the effect of the treatment would be equivalent to one complete well-year of life. This system has the advantage of considering both benefits and side effects of treatment programs in terms of the common QALY units. Although QALYs are typically used to assess patients, they can also be measured for others, including caregivers that are placed at risk because they experience stressful life events. In their report, *Summarizing Population Health*, the Institute of Medicine (IOM) recommended that population health metrics be used to evaluate public programs and to assist the decision making process (Field & Gold, 1998). Methods for eliciting these QALY units will be discussed later.

In summary, the concept of the quality-adjusted life year attends to issues historically raised by Parsons (1951), Sullivan (1966), and Patrick and Erickson (1993). QALYs combine measures of morbidity and mortality. Specific medical diagnoses (e.g., hypertension, cancer, and depression) are not incorporated into QALYs but rather are accounted for by the morbidity and mortality outcomes they produce. QALYs also include time or prognosis and incorporate preferences for health outcomes. A consensus conference with the Department of Health and Human Services recommended the use of QALYs to evaluate health programs (Gold et al., 1996). A recent IOM report on the measurement of population health came to similar conclusions (Field & Gold, 1998).

Can an Outcomes Model of Health Be Applied to Evaluate Traditional Medical Interventions?

Because the medical model has dominated the evaluation of health for so long, the assessment of medical interventions in terms of mortality and biological markers is commonplace. Thus, it is important to consider an outcomes model of health in relationship to traditional medical interventions—specifically, to examine whether or not an outcomes model is relevant in evaluating traditional medical interventions. For example, most surgical interventions are justified on the basis of saving lives. However, the great majority of surgical procedures has no effect on life expectancy but may affect quality of life. This issue was recently reviewed by Fowler, Cleary, Magaziner, Patrick, and Benjamin (1994). Four of the most common indications for surgery in the United States are transurethral resection prostatectomy (TURP) for benign hyperplasia of the prostate (BPH), extractions of cataracts, joint replacement for severe osteoarthritis of the knee or hip, and hysterectomy for diseases of the uterus. Although it is often argued that these procedures prevent deaths, reviews of the evidence suggest that these procedures are rarely performed to extend life expectancy. In each case, however, the surgery may lead to improvements in functioning or the reporting of symptoms. For example, TURP may reduce the symptom of urinary frequency in men. Similarly, cataract extraction may help older patients function better with reading, night driving, and other activities of daily living. Joint arthroplasty may increase mobility for older patients. For most of these cases, traditional physiological markers of outcome provide little information. Patients seek these procedures because they want relief of symptoms or improvement in functioning. As such, it appears that for a variety of surgical interventions, an outcomes model of health is both applicable and relevant.

In summary, disease and disability reduce health-related quality of life. The outcomes research movement argues that quality of life outcomes (along with mortality), rather than physiological outcomes, are the most important objective of health care. During the last two decades there has been a remarkable growth in the number of studies on health–related quality of life (Figure 16.2). Quality of life measures are now common in clinical trials, epidemiological studies, and other clinical investigations (Spilker, 1996). Many different compendia of quality of life measures are now available (Schumaker & Berzon, 1995; Spilker, 1996). The challenges associated with evaluating such concepts as health status and health-related quality of life

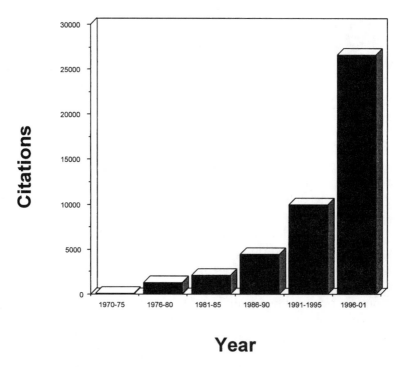

Figure 16.2. Medline citations to quality of life by five-year interval. Last interval represents three years.

lend themselves to the skills and training of health psychologists. Unfortunately, health psychology has played a relatively limited role in this area of inquiry. Next, we examine why this has been the case.

HEALTH PSYCHOLOGY'S CURRENT ROLE IN THE MEASUREMENT OF HEALTH OUTCOMES

Measurement is a cornerstone of psychology. The field of health psychology has made significant progress transitioning the principles of psychometric theory into a variety of assessment applications within the medical community. However, measurement within the field of health psychology for the most part has focused on (a) identifying psychological processes associated with health and illness, (b) evaluating psychological and social context variables and their relationship to biological markers of health, and (c) assessing psychological distress as a primary outcome. Although these are important contributions, the focus is somewhat narrow and limits health psychology's role in health outcome measurement.

Measures of Process

The role of psychological factors in the mediation and moderation of biological markers of health has improved the understanding of medical outcomes by accounting for systematic factors that are typically regarded as error variance in predictive models. Moreover, these factors have helped to define behavioral and psychological treatment modalities that complement biomedical interventions. Although these are clearly important contributions, there has been very little work in the field directed specifically toward the measurement of the construct of health as a whole (i.e., symptoms, physical function, and social and psychological function).

From an outcomes model perspective, the dimensions of quality of life (symptoms, physical functioning, and psychosocial functioning) serve as primary endpoints. Thus constructs such as stress, coping, social support, and health beliefs are best conceptualized as process indicators. Their contribution to health outcome evaluation lays predominately in their ability to explain changes in symptoms, function, and well-being. Much of health psychology research has focused on the interrelationships between these variables and has used these variables as primary endpoints. The evaluation of health outcomes has received relatively less attention. The distinction between process variables and outcome variables is always arbitrary and often draws debate among researchers. However, given the general consensus that health outcomes refer to an evaluation of patient symptoms, physical functioning, and psychosocial functioning (Kaplan, 1989; Patrick & Erickson, 1994; Spilker, 1996), we must distinguish between health outcomes and their psychosocial predictors (e.g., stress, coping, and social support). Health psychology can play a vital role in improving the evaluation of health outcomes. Increased attention to the development and validation of instruments designed to evaluate health status, symptoms, and quality of life as well as increased use of these variables as primary endpoints for the evaluation of psychological and behavioral interventions is greatly needed. Health psychology is in a position to expand its scope of research so that measurement of psychological process variables can be seen as complementary to the measurement of health outcomes rather than as a primary domain.

Biological Markers of Outcome

A great deal of measurement models in health psychology examine the relationship between behavioral and psychological process factors and biological outcomes. This focus has occurred in part as an attempt to justify the importance of behavioral and psychological factors within the medical community. Unfortunately, biological outcomes are often limited in their direct relevance to the patient and fail to encompass a complete characterization of health status. Therefore, reliance on them as primary endpoints may be quite limiting. Over the past 15 years, however, the emphasis on biological outcomes has continued to grow. In 1985, Grunberg and Baum emphasized new technologies for evaluating physiological outcomes, including portable blood withdrawal pumps, blood pressure monitors, and biochemical assessment tools. Rodin and Salovey in 1989 underscored the importance of disease endpoints and encouraged the field of health psychology to focus within specific disease categories (e.g., cancer and heart disease). There has been significant focus on the study of stress and measurable aspects of immune function (e.g., Pennebaker, Kiecolt-Glaser, & Glaser, 1988). As Kaplan (1990) noted, several reviews of the field of health psychology have emphasized the role of behavior and psychological factors in the development, maintenance, and treatment of disease, emphasizing the role of stress and distress in physiological processes.

With a shift away from the medical model of health and toward an outcome model, the emphasis on biological markers as primary endpoints is not as valuable or useful in health outcome assessment. The major limitation with disease measures is that biological measures of disease process may only be modestly associated with health outcome. The poor correlation between measures of disease process and patient outcome has been documented for many different areas of medicine (Feinstein, 1994). For example, rheumatologists often measure disease activity by sedimentation rates or numbers of swollen joints. However, these measures are poorly correlated with patient disability and capacity to function. Thus, the biological measure serves only a limited role in explaining the patient outcome. From an outcomes perspective, the functional disability and capacity to function (i.e., ability to carry out activities of daily living) are more relevant to the patient than sedimentation rates or numbers of swollen joints. Biological measures such as psychosocial process measures (stress, coping, health behaviors, etc.) serve an important role in contributing to the prediction of health outcomes. Reliance solely on biological measures as correlates of health outcomes may not be the most powerful line of research for health psychologists to pursue.

Psychological Distress: Necessary But Not Sufficient

Although process variables have been an area of concentration in health psychology research, the field has also contributed to the evaluation of distress-related outcomes. The contribution of health psychology in the conceptualization and systematic evaluation of psychological distress has been a cornerstone in the evaluation of health. Measures focused on evaluating psychopathology; symptoms of distress, including depression, anxiety, and hostility; and measures of cognitive status and function are an important component of health outcome assessment. However, the tendency to develop measurements focused solely on "psychological" symptoms and "mental" health perpetuates a dualistic model and serves once again to narrow health psychology's role in the measurement of health. This issue of separating mental health from physical health in the evaluation of outcome is not just a barrier to health psychology in the evaluation of outcome; it is also a topic of debate in the field of quality of life measurement. Two of the most frequently used quality of life measures, the Medical Outcomes Story Short Form 36 (MOS–SF36; Ware, Phillips, Yody, & Adamczyk, 1996) and the Quality of Well-Being Scale (QWB; Kaplan, Bush, & Berry, 1976) take very different perspectives on this issue. Illustration of these differences in the conceptualization and quantification of quality of life may be useful for appreciating the complexities in health outcome measurement.

The MOS–SF36 consists of 36 items assessing eight dimensions of health (general health perceptions, physical functioning, social functioning, role functioning, emotional well-being, and pain and vitality). Using factor analytic weights, these eight scales are combined into two summary scales representing mental health status and physical health status. The authors of the instrument have conducted validation studies that support the presence of two factors in the structure of health status (Ware et al., 1996) and suggest that health outcomes are best described in two dimensions (physical and mental). Thus, scores on the MOS–SF36 are always presented in physical and mental domains; a single index combining the two domains is not used to characterize quality of life.

The QWB is a measure of health-related quality of life comprising four subscales (symptoms, mobility, physical activity, and social activity) that are combined into a single score. This score incorporates societal preferences or weightings for each of the states described within the subscales. In contrast to the MOS–SF36, symptoms associated with psychological problems (e.g., depressed mood, anxiety, and loss of control) are combined with a list of "physical" symptoms (i.e., fatigue, dizziness, pain, etc.) in a single symptom subscale.

Kaplan, Ganiats, Sieber, and Anderson (1998) have argued that both mental and physical health problems produce symptoms and that those symptoms are associated with decrements in function. In this argument, the characterization of the symptoms are not as important as the severity when it comes to quantifying health status. Thus, an individual may suffer from a cough. The cough may be mild and have virtually no impact on the individual's ability to function in normal activities. In this situation the individual's health status remains essentially in tact. If, however, the individual has a cough that makes performance of daily activities nearly impossible, the impact on health status is significant. The cough itself is less important than the severity and impact on health status. This same scenario can be envisioned with a substitution of cough with the symptom of depressed mood. An individual with a mildly depressed mood may not be limited in normal activities. However, if that individual's mood is severely depressed, normal activities may be next to impossible and health status is likely diminished.

Like the definition of health itself, there is no one "right" way to conceptualize symptoms of psychological distress. However, the QWB provides one illustration of how psychological symptoms can be conceptualized as components of a larger group of general symptoms associated with health status rather than as a distinct entity. Although health psychologists may be particularly adept at evaluating psychological symptoms, they need not be limited to this class of symptoms. Focusing on the evaluation of symptoms in general and their relationship to levels of function enables health psychologists to evaluate the larger constructs of health status and health-related quality of life.

TRANSITIONING HEALTH PSYCHOLOGY INTO THE FIELD OF OUTCOMES MEASUREMENT

Why should health psychology play a major role in the evaluation of health outcomes? As discussed earlier, health is a complex, multidimensional construct. Viewed from the outcomes model it encompasses symptoms, behaviors, and both psychological and social functioning. Operationalizing such a construct and systematically evaluating it is well within the expertise of health psychology. Skills in psychometrics, behavioral assessment, instrument development, and validation are a cornerstone of training for most health psychologists. Because the *definitions* of health are increasingly shifting from a biomedical process model (i.e., physiological markers of health) to a patient-focused outcomes model (i.e., symptoms and function distress) so too must the *measurement* of health shift from biomedical process to outcome. This poses an incredible challenge for the medical community, because it requires a new paradigm in evaluation. This paradigm falls within familiar territory for health psychology. The process of defining and operationalizing a construct (e.g., health, anger, pain, and hostility), quantifying it through instrument development, validating the instrument to ensure both reliability and accuracy in measurement, and interpreting data obtained from such an instrument is common practice within health psychology. In fact, existing measures of health beliefs, coping strategies, adjustment to illness, health behaviors, and psychological distress are clear evidence of health psychology's skills in measurement and evaluation. This foundation of behavioral science, which is needed for the evaluation of health-related quality of life, is basic to healthy psychology and is new to medicine.

Health psychology is poised to be a leader in the evaluation of health outcomes. As medicine is increasingly faced with evaluating the impact of interventions on chronic conditions, the rationing of services based on improvement in general health status and quality of life, and the role of the patient as a consumer of health care services, a patient-focused model of outcome will prosper. Health psychology has the opportunity to apply its expertise in measurement across the health care field. Limiting measurement to distress and psychological factors associated with health and illness simply limits the field. Broadening the scope of health psychology to include all patient-based measures of health outcome opens the door to several areas of measurement.

MEASURING HEALTH: TARGET AREAS FOR HEALTH PSYCHOLOGY

Health psychology can contribute to the evaluation of health in numerous ways. In the following section, we highlight several key areas that are particularly well-suited for the field.

Decision Making in Health

As discussed previously, definitions of health are often ambiguous and are laden with implicit or idiosyncratic assumptions about the value of being free from specific impairments, limitations in daily activity, and restrictions from fully participating in society. Patrick and Erickson (1994) have argued that even the notion of disability or illness as distinct from health is a value judgment; what distinguishes health concepts are subjective interpretations of what is and is not desirable. Health services researchers are beginning to realize that to establish coherence within health and health policy research, they must study how best to value health outcomes. Human judgment, decision making, and valuation of health are growing areas of research well suited for health psychology.

Research on valuing health outcomes is of central importance to health policy decision making. Health policy decision makers have a simple objective: Optimize health of the population given budget constraints. This requires decisions about which health programs to fund and which not to fund. Because health programs can both improve health and use resources (i.e., cost money) to varying degrees, a goal in the decision-making process is to rank-order programs according to their cost per unit health effect (i.e., cost-effectiveness). Such a rank-ordered list could be used to fund the most cost-effective programs that fall within a particular health care budget

(Weinstein, 1995). Essential to this method is an interval scale measure of unit health effect.

Unit health effect can be thought of as a measure of health productivity. The goal of the health policy decision maker is to decrease the cost per unit of health productivity achieved. The question then becomes, "What is health productivity?"

What most people want in exchange for payment for health services is a combination of two things: (a) longer life, and (b) better health status (i.e., reduced symptoms and problems). Therefore, health as a commodity can be thought of as a combination of these two things. In this chapter, we will call any sequence of health states over a given time horizon a *health profile*.

Just thinking of health in this way does not solve the problem of measurement of a unit health effect. For instance, is greater health productivity achieved when someone lives for five years in perfect health or 10 years in poor health? Such a question requires the measurement of the value people place on health profiles. In the next section, we discuss how the value of different health profiles can be placed on a scale of preference, where a year of life in perfect health serves as the unit of measure. We present different models of preference-based health measurement and health psychology's role in the measurement development. The first set of models we discuss are the health utility models.

HEALTH UTILITY MODELS

Health utility models are mathematical models of considerable technical complexity that describe preference for health profiles for medical choices made under risk or uncertainty that are used in medical decision analysis and cost-effectiveness analysis. The mathematical nature of health utility models should not discourage psychologists from participating in health utility research. In fact, several psychologists have made a number of important contributions to health utility research (Chapman, 1996; Kaplan & Ernst, 1983; Miyamoto & Eraker, 1988, 1989; Treadwell & Lenert, 1999). In this section, we discuss health utility models and the role of psychology in their development and application.

Most medical decisions are made in the context of risk or uncertainty (i.e., death or shortened survival is a possible outcome). Utility measurement is the quantification of preferences under either risk or uncertainty. This type of measurement is necessary to place values on health profiles. Utility for health profiles is often discussed in terms of QALYs, defined earlier in this chapter. In traditional survival analysis, a person receives 1 unit of credit for each year he or she survives. Statistically, those who survive are coded 1.0 and those who die are coded as 0. Traditional survival analysis does not make the distinction between those who are perfectly well and those who are alive with severe disability. Each is given 1 unit of credit for surviving the year. The QALY concept holds that years of survival should be valued somewhere along the continuum between 0 (death) and 1.0 for (full health). How those numbers are assigned is a matter of major importance and of considerable debate. There are both theoretical and methodological arguments that assignment of these numbers must be based on an individual's willingness to risk death. The other extreme involves simple state valuations using rating scales, or trade-offs between health quality and length of life when no risk of death is involved. All of the different approaches make the assumptions that preferences along the 0 to 1.0 continuum are measured on a linear or interval response scale. Verification of these assumptions is essential to the application of the models.

Mathematical models begin with premises, or axioms. From a set of axioms, other conclusions can be deduced from the theory. These conclusions are often called theorems. If a mathematical model represents a phenomenon well, the axioms and theorems will provide a researcher with information about how individuals will behave in various situations. If not, then the theory is likely false, and axioms need to be revised to better account for behavior. The mathematical model as a whole should also tell us something about how numbers can be used to represent the objects of empirical study.

Clearly, mathematical models of preference are of great import to health policy research. Consider the health policy analyst: She is interested in health productivity (i.e., a unit health effect) and has empirical knowledge about the changes in health status and survival duration different medical treatments produce. Each person in the population she represents will have their own health profiles (i.e., each person in the populations will experience a sequence of health states over varying survival duration). Moreover, members of the populations will have preferences for these health profiles (e.g., they may prefer full health for 7 years to back pain for 10 years, and back pain for 10 years to coma for 12 years). If numbers can represent these preferences, then the analyst can recommend funding for health services that *maximize* preference, and thus health productivity is maximized. Knowing how individuals make choices with respect to their health under a multitude of circumstances is paramount for maximizing health productivity in a population. Thus, the inherent usefulness of mathematical models in health policy is clear.

Another key point is that health utility models are measurement models. Most psychologists are trained in a psychometric tradition. This tradition emphasizes the use of scaling procedures that assume the validity of a mathematical measurement model and produce a numerical representation that best fits the data (Krantz, Luce, Suppes, & Tversky, 1971). Examples of these approaches include Thurstonian scaling (Torgerson, 1958), factor analysis (Harman, 1976), and test theory (Lord & Novick, 1968). In sharp contrast, health utility models are concerned with the validity of the underlying axioms of a mathematical model that explain a person's decision-making behavior in the health context. A psychometric approach to measurement of health would, in a sense, assume it knows what the people in a given population want. This is an approach to be aware of if *actual* preference for health profiles in a given population are to be maximized. Let us now discuss specific health utility models.

Health utility models originate from a theory of decision under risk, developed by von Neumann and Morgenstern (1944), and called von Neumann and Morgenstern (vNM) utility theory. The theory is notable for being the first to prove that preferences for choices made under risk could be quantified under specific assumptions about decision-making behavior. The theory is about *individual* decision making under risk but has been extended to health policy situations by adopting specific assumptions about aggregation of individual utilities (see Bleichrodt, 1997).

In the case of vNM theory, a set of axioms (which amount to rules for rational decision making behavior under risk) are outlined. From this set of axioms, it can be deduced that there must exist a utility function unique up to positive linear transformations (i.e., an interval scale of preference). Interval and ratio scales of preference are the only two scale types that are appropriate for measuring health productivity. The theory was further extended to cover decisions with multiple objectives (i.e., a multiattribute theory of vNM utility by Keeney & Raiffa, 1976).

Health utility, or preferences for health states, was first conceived by Fanshel and Bush (1970). Later, the theory was summarized in the context of vNM utility theory by Pliskin, Shepard, and Weinstein (1980). Pliskin et al. (1980) realized the multiple objectives one faces over any health decision: improving health quality and increasing longevity (i.e., the health profile). This group developed a multiattribute theory of health utility that consisted of two attributes: survival duration and health quality. The crux of the theory is that vNM utility, within the health domain, is a function of these two attributes. The theory has some reasonable implications. For instance, the theory implies that the longer one lives in a constant health state, better than death, the greater one's utility. Similarly, at constant survival duration, utility increases as health quality improves.

QALYs represent utility for various levels of health quality over survival duration. Pliskin et al. (1980) developed the theory under a somewhat complex set of axioms. Only recently has it been shown that by introducing a self-evident assumption, that for duration of zero life years (i.e., immediate death), all quality of life levels are equivalent, (called "the zero condition"), the theory of health utility can be greatly simplified, resulting in simple tests with direct empirical meaning (Bliechrodt, Wakker, & Johannesson, 1997).

Health utility theory has largely been developed by economists. They have approached the problem of health preference measurement axiomatically, or deductively, by postulating a small parsimonious set of organizing principles. Economists place great importance on formal mathematical models. Such methods provide a concise language for communicating scientific ideas and offer specific predictions about the behavior of individuals. Often these predictions go untested because economists place a greater importance on theory development than on empirical tests of theory. In contrast, most psychologists emphasize inductive tests of theory (Anderson, 1981). Inductively driven theories within health psychology are often nonmathematical. These theories are not conceived from a few fundamental postulates and, hence, lack a clear axiomatic basis. Yet, health psychologists are trained within a strong empiricist tradition. This tradition values research design and statistical hypothesis testing as important tools in theory testing.

Psychology's contribution to the study of health utility theory has been the conduct of systematic experiments that test the axioms of health utility models. For instance, Miyamoto and Eraker (1988) tested the independence axiom, a necessary axiom in QALY theory. This axiom asserts that utility (i.e., preference) for survival duration and health quality do not depend on each other. The parsimony of any health utility model is threatened if preference for particular health states depends idiosyncratically on the order in which the states are experienced or the particular time they are experienced. A policy analyst would have difficulty making policy recommendations if he or she had to evaluate a multitude of unique health profiles in determining the value placed on any point in time health state. The independence axiom in effect says that the independence axiom can be conceived of visually. Visually, independence implies that utility curves for various health states over survival duration do *not* intersect, except at zero duration. Figure 16.3 provides hypothetical illustrations of the satisfaction (see Figure 16.3a) and violation (see Figure 16.3b) of the independence axiom for three health states: full health, back pain, and below-knee amputation. In Figure 16.3a, we see that preference for survival duration increases in a manner that is *independent* of health state. In contrast, Figure 16.3b illustrates a situation where utility for survival duration is *dependent* on which health quality state is achieved. For below-knee amputation and full health, utility increases constantly over survival duration, whereas for back pain it increases, reaches a peak, and then decreases, crossing below the utility curve for below-knee amputation. Miyamoto and Eraker (1988) found that a majority of individuals satisfied the independence axiom when asked to make risky choices for various health states over different survival durations. This is an important finding because all current QALY health policy

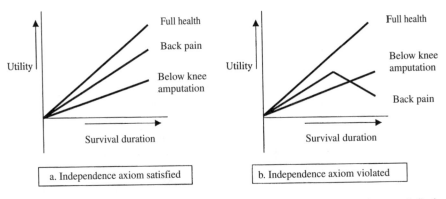

Figure 16.3. **(a)** Hypothetical illustration of the independence axiom satisfied. **(b)** Hypothetical illustration of the independence axiom violated.

models assume independence. For instance, with the general health policy model (GHPM) proposed by Kaplan and Anderson (1988), health preferences for various health states are determined by peer judges. Specific states are assigned weights, then patients are observed over time to empirically determine their transitions to other states of wellness. With this model, QALYs are accrued over an observation period, where point in time wellness is based on the weights assigned to specific health states. Point in time wellness is treated as *independent* of time. Hence, the GHPM imposes the independence axiom on outcomes data.

Independence greatly limits the general form a utility function can take, but it is still satisfied by several different parametric families of functions. Until one has a unique parametric utility function, it is impossible to compute a person's utility for health states. In a separate study, Miyamoto and Eraker (1989) examined the empirical plausibility of different parametric models for health utility. They tested the validity of different parametric equations for representing health utility functions. Specifically, they tested the class of the so-called log/power models against another class of models known as linear/exponential. The distinction between these models is beyond the scope of this chapter, but it is important to note that these different models have different implications for the allocation of health resources. In their work, Miyamoto and Eraker (1989) found that fewer individuals violated the qualitative tests of a linear/exponential QALY model than a log/power QALY model. This work has implications for which parametric form should be used for computing health state utilities in cost-effectiveness analysis. Currently, most health policy applications with QALYs assume a linear QALY model. This is a special case of the linear/exponential family of utility functions. Allowing QALYs to be computed using either linear or exponential utility functions may move health policy decision making closer to actual individual preferences under risk (Gold et al., 1996).

Health Utility Models and Time Preference

Most people would prefer to receive $1,000 today than in one year. This is one reason banks pay clients interest on their accounts. In addition, most people would prefer to pay $1,000 in one year than today. This is why credit card companies charge interest to customers carrying a balance. Time preference for money and other goods is an important factor in understanding utility. Health utility is no exception.

Health utility models all make assumptions about people's preferences for outcomes as a function of time. The simplest model, the linear QALY model, assumes that persons are indifferent to when they receive health benefits or decrements. For instance, the GHPM is a linear QALY model. Because utility is linear with respect to time, under the GHPM, a person confined to a wheelchair would accrue the same number of QALYs between the ages of 20 and 21 years as they would if they were confined to a wheelchair between the ages of 60 and 61 years. Other models relax this assumption and suggest that utility for health (much like utility for money) tends to decrease as consumption is delayed (Torrance & Feeny, 1989).

Of course, there are a number of psychological factors that may influence time preference. For instance, the bank account versus credit card example suggests an impatience–procrastination effect (Fishburn, 1982). People prefer to receive a good outcome sooner rather than later (impatience) but prefer to delay the receipt of a bad outcome (procrastination). Preliminary evidence suggests this principle tends to hold empirically in the domain of health as well (Chapman, 1996). However, other psychological theories of time preference and health are plausible. For instance, the notions of savoring and dread may, for some individuals, influence time preference for health (Fishburn, 1982). A person may actually experience anticipatory anxiety associated with a delayed health outcome that is negative (e.g., a surgery or painful procedure), causing dread. Or he or she may savor a delay in a positive health outcome (i.e., derive pleasure from knowing that they will achieve better health in the future). A savoring–dread effect is in opposition to the notion of impatience–procrastination. More empirical research is needed to determine people's time preference for positive and negative outcomes so that axiomatic theories of utilities can be developed to explain these effects.

In sum, health psychology's role in contributing health utility theory is one of applying improved research design and statistics to tests of health utility theory predictions. In this way, health psychologists compliment the elegant mathematical formulations of economists in modeling health decision making. Many advances in health utility theory have occurred through the multidisciplinary work between psychologists and economists.

Behavioral Economics

Despite advances in vNM utility formulations in the health domain, there has amassed considerable evidence that vNM utility theory is not valid as a descriptive theory of choice under risk. People tend to violate theory predictions in systematic ways (Kahneman & Tversky, 1979, 1984; Slovic, Lichtenstein, & Fischoff, 1988). Most of this research has been conducted by psychologists, and only recently has this research received significant notice from the economic profession (Laibson & Zeckhauser, 1998). This research has spawned the development of a field known as behavioral economics, which places its focus on behavioral tests of econometric models.

Behavioral economics has led to advances in mathematical formalizations of descriptive theories of choice under risk (Kahneman & Tversky, 1979; Quiggin, 1982; Tversky & Kahneman, 1992; Wakker & Tversky, 1993). Descriptive theories of choice represent concise revisions of the vNM utility theory. These theories are designed to account for violations of vNM utility theory that are caused by psychological factors that influence attitudes toward making decisions under risk. These new descriptive theories of choice are important for health policy decision making because they have implications for the unit health effects, or utilities, associated with particular health states (Bleichrodt & Quiggin, 1997; Miyamoto, 2000). This in turn influences the results of cost-effectiveness analyses.

Several anomalies of risky choice are emerging as important within descriptive theories of risky choice behavior. For instance, framing effects play a role in risk attitude (Kahneman & Tversky, 1979). For making decisions under risk, when outcomes are framed as gains, individuals tend to be risk-averse and when framed as losses they tend to be risk-seeking. In addition, persons appear to distort probabilities in specific ways. For instance, moving from an uncertain outcome (e.g., $p = 0.99$) to a certain outcome (i.e., $p = 1.0$) has a disproportionate impact on choice compared with moving between two uncertain outcomes over the same increment of probability (e.g., moving from $p = 0.98$ to $p = 0.99$). Finally, related to the framing example is the finding that losses appear to loom much larger than gains. This finding is called loss aversion, where the value curve for outcomes that are perceived as losses is steeper than it is for gains. An intuitive way to think about loss aversion is in the context of preference for money. As stated by Kahneman and Tversky (1979), "the aggravation that one experiences in losing a sum of money appears to be greater than the pleasure associated with gaining the same amount" (p. 279). For health utility, loss aversion may be tied to one's aspiration level for survival. People may have an aspiration level, or break-even point, with respect to longevity. If people do not make it to their break-even point, they may feel that they have been shortchanged. However, if they live beyond their break-even point for longevity, they may view those extra years as a gift. For instance, imagine a person who aspires to live 80 years. For this person, living any number of years beyond 80 is considered a gain, and living any number of years below 80 years is considered a loss. It is possible that decisions relating to risky prospects above and below such a reference level may prove to be different. This is an area of health outcomes measurement where psychological theory plays an important role and where validation of psychological theories has important health policy implications. A greater volume of quality research on judgment and decision making within health psychology will help address these important research questions.

Alternative Ways to Value Outcomes

Rating scales offer a highly efficient way of assigning numbers to health states such that the numbers represent preferences for those health states. However, the use of rating scales as a response mode has been the subject of controversy both within and outside the field of psychology (Luce & Galanter, 1963; Nord, 1992; Richardson, 1991; Stevens, 1966). Within the health state preference literature, economists have criticized rating scales for not having the axiomatic basis associated with vNM expected utility theory. Also, the rating response has been perceived as not being able to provide an interval scale of measurement for cost-effectiveness analysis (Nord, 1992; Richardson, 1991). However, the programmatic research of Norman H. Anderson on functional measurement (see Anderson, 1990, for review) has shown that, although rating scales are susceptible to biases, these biases can be controlled. Of equal importance, Anderson (1981, 1990) has shown that there are specific tests of the rating scale property that can be conducted to ensure that the numeric values associated with rating responses represent an interval scale of measurement. In addition, Luce (1981) has developed an axiomatic formalization of Anderson's methods.

Considerable research in the area of health outcomes measurement for health policy decision making has employed rating scales using Anderson's bias minimizing methods (Kaplan et al., 1979; Kaplan & Ernst, 1983; Patrick, Bush, & Chen, 1973). Other research has examined the relationship between physical and mental health constructs via Anderson's psychological measurement model (Cadman & Goldsmith, 1986; Viet, Rose, & Ware, 1982).

How best to use rating scales within the health outcomes measurement domain is an important area of research for health psychologists to address.

For instance, some health-related quality of life measures use a decomposed rating strategy, where each item on the measure receives a weight and these weights are summed and subtracted from full health to produce a health-related quality of life score. Other health-related quality of life measures, such as the European Quality of Life Scale (EQ–5D; EuroQol Group, 1990), use a holistic strategy. With a holistic strategy, a person's health problems are summarized and then the person is asked to give a rating response that represents how they value their current health (as described by the summary of endorsed items) in relation to full health and to death. Future research needs to determine the biases associated with these different approaches to health outcomes measurement. Finally, there is considerable evidence that psychological factors influence rating responses (Anderson, 1981, 1990; Birnbaum & Veit, 1974; Parducci, 1968). For instance, work by Bliechrodt and Johanneson (1998) has shown that for health preference elicitation, rating scale responses depend on the number of preferred alternatives in the rating task. However, a reanalysis of this data by Schwartz (1998) revealed that a psychological theory of judgment, known as range-frequency theory (Parducci, 1968), could be used to account for this effect. Findings such as these suggest that there is the need for the development and application of quantitative psychological theories of judgment within the area of rating-based health state preference elicitation.

In summary, health policy and decision-making research requires health outcomes measurement. Researchers largely agree that value or preference-based outcomes are necessary to accomplish health policy decision-making goals (e.g., funding health programs contingent on satisfactory cost-effectiveness ratios). However, psychological factors play a significant role in influencing judgments, choices, and trade-offs associated with health state valuation (Bliechrodt & Johanneson, 1998; Kahneman & Tversky, 1979; Miyamoto, 2000). Additional research is needed to identify biases and to establish valid methodologies for valuing health states. Such work will ensure that ratings accurately reflect preferences for health states.

Incorporating Costs Into Health

As mentioned, cost of care is an important factor in health outcomes research, particularly for cost-effectiveness analysis. Methodologies for estimating costs have now become standardized (Gold et al., 1996). From an administrative perspective, cost estimates include all costs of treatment and costs associated with caring for any side effects of treatment. Typically, economic discounting is applied to adjust for using current assets to achieve future benefits. From a societal perspective, costs are broader and may include the cost of family members staying off work to provide care.

When comparing programs for a given population with a given medical condition, cost-effectiveness is measured as the change in costs of care for the new program compared to the existing therapy or program, relative to the change in health measured in a standardized unit such as the QALY. The difference in costs over the difference in effectiveness is the incremental cost-effectiveness and is usually expressed as the cost per QALY. Because the objective of all programs is to produce QALYs, the cost–QALY ratio can be used to show the relative efficiency of different programs (Gold et al., 1996; Kaplan & Anderson, 1996).

More and more, health policy researchers, as well as health administrators, are interested in how much new interventions cost. Health psychologists need to be mindful of both costs and outcomes in their research. This is because, increasingly, the value of health research is being considered with respect to how the research affects costs. There are a few basic research questions that speak to this cost and outcomes issue: (a) "Does this research have an effect on cost of medical care, or other outside costs? And, if so, does it increase these costs or decrease them?" (b) "Are there ways to implement this health psychology intervention that are less costly, but equally effective?" (c) "If this intervention helps to reduce costs, does it do so at the expense of poorer health outcome?" Because health and medical researchers are becoming more vigilant about containing costs, these questions are important to consider in any health psychology research program or project.

FUTURE AREAS OF FOCUS: APPLYING AN OUTCOMES MODEL IN HEALTH POLICY

To refer to health policy as a "future" area of focus is a bit of a misnomer. The application of an outcomes model in the development and evaluation of health policy is a highly relevant endeavor that should be a primary target for health psychology researchers. The aforementioned areas of study will serve to facilitate health psychology's transition into broader applications such as health policy evaluation.

Using an outcomes model to evaluate health policy means reconceptualizing what health care systems and their providers' offer. There are important contrasts between the outcomes model and the existing traditional biomedical model when it comes to characterizing the provision of health care. The traditional model assumes that the role of a health care provider is to diagnose problems and to treat them. In other words, health care systems and their providers treat diseases. In contrast, the outcomes model argues that the role of health care is to treat patients, not just their diseases.

Sometimes treating the diseases of patients will make them live longer and feel better. However, there are other occasions in which treating diseases has no effect on life expectancy or quality of life and there are other occasions in which medical treatment causes harm (Kaplan, 1997). The outcomes model recognizes that health care is really about making decisions. Under most circumstances, a provider has alternative pathways, and the patient and provider together need to select the pathway that maximizes patient benefit. By using the tools of psychometrics and cognitive science, an outcomes model may improve the conceptualization and measurement of benefit and the decision process itself. The development of rigorous and empirical models of measurement and decision making will ultimately improve the process of health policy evaluation. Health psychologists can, and should, play a role in this process.

CONCLUSION

The field of health psychology was founded with a broad definition. As proposed by Mattarazzo (1980),

> Health psychology is the aggregate of the specific educational, scientific, and professional contributions of the discipline of psychology to the promotion and maintenance of health, the prevention and treatment of illness, and the identification of etiologic and diagnostic correlates of health, illness and related dysfunctions. (p. 8)

Although health psychology has made significant contributions to the health care field, most research in health psychology has focused on the study of illness correlates and psychological processes among those with chronic illnesses. Many health psychologists have focused attention on measures of biological process, believing these are more acceptable to mainstream biomedical researchers. Thus, research in health psychology has not been as broad-based as the definition that characterizes the field.

Within the past decade there has been a major paradigm shift in health care. New medical and surgical interventions are typically measured using evaluations of health-related quality of life. In addition, regulatory agencies, the National Institutes of Health, and pharmaceutical companies have accepted health outcome measurement as a central feature in clinical medical research. Although methods for health outcome assessment borrow from psychometric traditions, psychologists have been relatively uninvolved in this field.

The challenges ahead for health outcomes assessment and in medical decision making are enormous. There are significant opportunities for the study and application of health outcome measurement strategies and models for medical decision making. The field of health psychology is well suited to take on these challenges by applying its unique combination of expertise in psychometric theory and behavioral science to improve the evaluation of health outcomes and facilitate the process of medical decision making.

REFERENCES

American Psychiatric Association. (1994). *Diagnostic and statistical manual of mental disorders* (4th ed.). Washington, DC: Author.

Anderson, N. H. (1981). *Foundations of information integration theory*. New York: Academic Press.

Anderson, N. H. (1990) *Contributions to information integration theory* (3 vols.). Hillsdale, NJ: Erlbaum.

Birnbaum, M. H., & Veit, C. T. (1974). Scale convergence as a criterion for rescaling: Information integration with difference, ratio, and averaging tasks. *Perception and Psychophysics, 15,* 7–15.

Black, W. C., & Welch, H. G. (1993). Advances in diagnostic imaging and overestimations of disease prevalence and the benefits of therapy. *New England Journal of Medicine, 328,* 1237–1243.

Black, W. C., & Welch, H. G. (1997). Screening for disease. *American Journal of Roentgenology, 168,* 3–11.

Bleichrodt, H. (1997). Health utility indices and equity considerations. *Journal of Health Economics, 16*(1), 65–91.

Bleichrodt, H., & Johannesson, M. (1998). An experimental test of a theoretical foundation for rating-scale valuations. *Medical Decision Making, 17,* 208–216.

Bleichrodt, H., & Quiggin, J. (1997). Characterizing QALYs under a general rank dependent utility model. *Journal of Risk and Uncertainty, 15*(2), 151–165.

Bleichrodt, H., Wakker, P., & Johannesson, M. (1997). Characterizing QALYs by risk neutrality. *Journal of Risk and Uncertainty, 15,* 107–114.

Cadman, D., & Goldsmith, C. (1986). Construction of social value or utility-based health indices: The usefulness of factorial experimental design plans. *Journal of Chronic Disease, 39,* 643–651.

Chapman, B. (1996). When screening for wellness is right. *CAP Today, 10*(12), 1, 26–29.

Clancy, C. M., & Eisenberg, J. M. (1998). Outcomes research: Measuring the end results of health care. *Science, 282,* 245–246.

Coates, A., Porzsolt, F., & Osoba, D. (1997). Quality of life in oncology practice: Prognostic value of EORTC QLQ–C30 scores in patients with advanced malignancy. *European Cancer Journal, 33,* 1025–1030.

Donabedian, A. (1966). Evaluating the quality of medical care. *Milbank Memorial Fund Quarterly, 44*(3), 166–206.

Erickson, P., Wilson, R., & Shannon, I. (1995). *Years of healthy life. Healthy People 2000 statistical notes Number 7*. Washington, DC: U.S. DHHS, Public Health Service, Centers for Disease Control and Prevention, and NCHS.

European Quality of Life Measurement (EuroQol). (1990). A new facility for the measurement of health related quality of life. *Health Policy, 16*, 199–208.

Fanshel, S., & Bush, J. W. (1970). A health-status index and its applications to health-services outcomes. *Operations Research, 18*, 1021–1066.

Feinstein, A. R. (1994). Art, science, and the doctor–patient relationship. *Annals of the New York Academy of Sciences, 729*, 19–21.

Field, M. J., & Gold, M. R. (1998). *Summarizing population health*. Washington, DC: Institute of Medicine.

Fishburn, P. C. (1982). *The foundations of expected utility*. Boston: Kluwer Boston.

Fowler, F. J., Jr., Cleary, P. D., Magaziner, J., Patrick, D. L., & Benjamin, K. L. (1994). Methodological issues in measuring patient-reported outcomes: The agenda of the Work Group on Outcomes Assessment. *Medical Care, 32*, JS65–JS76.

Fries, J. F. (1983). The compression of morbidity. *Annals of Academic Medicine Singapore, 12*(3), 358–367.

Gold, M. R., Siegel, J. E., Russell, L. B., & Weinstein, M. C. (1996). *Cost-effectiveness in health and medicine*. New York: Oxford University Press.

Grunberg, N., & Baum, A. (1985). Biological commonalities of stress and substance abuse. In S. Schiffman & T. A. Wills (Eds.), *Coping and substance abuse*. New York: Academic Press.

Harman, H. H. (1976). *Modern factor analysis* (3rd ed.). Chicago: University of Chicago Press.

Idler, E. L., & Benyamini, Y. (1997). Self-rated health and mortality: A review of twenty-seven community studies. *Journal of Health and Social Behavior, 38*, 21–37.

Idler, E. L., & Kasl, S. V. (1995). Self-ratings of health: Do they also predict change in functional ability? *Journals of Gerontology Series B—Psychological Sciences and Social Sciences, 50*(6), S344–S353.

Jensen, M. C., Kelly, A. P., & Brant-Zawadzki, M. N. (1994). MRI of degenerative disease of the lumbar spine. *Magnetic Resonance Quarterly, 10*(3), 173–190.

Judd, L. L., Paulus, M. P., Wells, K. B., & Rapaport, M. H. (1996). Socioeconomic burden of subsyndromal depressive symptoms and major depression in a sample of the general population. *American Journal of Psychiatry, 153*(11), 1411–1417.

Kahneman, D., & Tversky, A. (1979). Prospect theory: An analysis of decision under risk. *Econometrica, 47*, 276–287.

Kahneman, D., & Tversky, A. (1984). Choices, values, and frames. *American Psychologist, 39*, 341–350.

Kaplan, R. M. (1989). Health outcome models for policy analysis. *Health Psychology, 8*, 723–735.

Kaplan, R. M. (1990). Behavior as the central outcome in health care. *American Psychologist, 45*(11), 1211–1220.

Kaplan, R. M. (1994). Value judgment in the Oregon Medicaid experiment. *Medical Care, 32*(10), 975–988.

Kaplan, R. M. (1997). Decisions about prostate cancer screening in managed care. *Current Opinion in Oncology, 9,* 480–486.

Kaplan, R. M., Alcaraz, J. E., Anderson, J. P., & Weisman, M. (1996). Quality-adjusted life years lost to arthritis: Effects of gender, race and social class. *Arthritis Care and Research 9*(6), 473–482.

Kaplan, R. M., & Anderson, J. P. (1996). The general health policy model: An integrated approach. In B. Spilker (Ed.), *Quality of life and pharmacoeconomics in clinical trials* (pp. 309–322). Philadelphia: Lippencott-Raven.

Kaplan, R. M., & Anderson, J. P. (1988). A general health policy model: Update and applications. *Health Services Research, 23*(2), 203–235.

Kaplan, R. M., Anderson, J. P., & Ganiats, T. G. (1993). The Quality of Well-being Scale: Rationale for a single quality of life index. In S. R. Walker & R. M. Rosser (Eds.), *Quality of life assessment: Key issues in the 1990s* (pp. 65–94). London: Kluwer Academic.

Kaplan, R. M., Bush, J. W., & Berry, C. C. (1976). Health status: Types of validity and the index of well-being. *Health Services Research 11*(4), 478–507.

Kaplan, R. M., Bush, J. W., & Berry, C. C. (1979). Health status index: Category rating versus magnitude estimation for measuring levels of well-being. *Medical Care, 17*(5), 501–525.

Kaplan, R. M., & Ernst, J. A. (1983). Do category rating scales produce biased preference weights for a health index? *Medical Care, 21*(2), 193–207.

Kaplan, R. M., Ganiats, T. G., Sieber, W. J., & Anderson, J. P. (1998). The Quality of Well-Being Scale: Critical similarities and differences with SF–36. *International Journal for Quality in Health Care, 10*(6), 509–520.

Kaplan, R. M., Patterson, T. L., Kerner, D. N., Atkinson, J. H., Heaton, R. K., & Grant, I. (1997). The quality of well-being scale in asympomatic HIV-infected patients. HNRC group. HIV neural behavioral research center. *Quality of Life Research, 6*(6), 507–514.

Kaplan, R. M., Ries, A. L., Prewitt, L. M., & Eakin, E. (1994). Self-efficacy expectations predict survival for patients with chronic obstructive pulmonary disease. *Health Psychology, 13,* 366–368.

Keeney, R. L., & Raiffa, H. (1976). *Decisions with multiple objectives.* New York: Wiley.

Klapow, J. C., Slater, M. A., Patterson, T., Atkinson, J. H., Doctor, J. N., & Garfin, S. (1993). An empirical evaluation of multidimensional clinical outcome in chronic low back pain patients. *Pain, 55,* 107–118.

Krantz, D., Luce, R. D., Suppes, P., & Tversky, A. (1971). *Foundations of measurement.* New York: Academic Press.

Laibson, D., & Zeckhauser, R. (1998). Amos Tversky and the ascent of behavioral economics. *Journal of Risk and Uncertainty, 16*, 7–47.

Lord, F. M., & Novick, M. R. (1968). *Statistical theories of mental test scores*. Reading, MA: Addison-Wesley.

Luce, R. D. (1981). Axioms for the averaging and addition representations of functional measurement. *Mathematical Social Sciences, 1*, 139–144.

Luce, R. D., & Galanter, E. (1963). Psychophysical scaling. In R. D. Luce, R. R. Bush, & E. Galanter (Eds.), *Handbook of mathematical psychology* (Vol. 1). New York: Wiley.

Matarazzo, J. D. (1980). Behavioral health and behavioral medicine. *American Psychologist, 35*, 807–817.

McCarty, D. J. (1986). Arthritis associated with crystals containing calcium. *Medical Clinics of North America, 70*(2), 437–454.

Miyamoto, J. M. (2000). Utility assessment under expected utility and rank dependent utility assumptions. In H. Chapman & F. Sonnenberg (Eds.), *Decision making in health care: Theory, psychology, and applications* (pp. 65–109). New York: Cambridge University Press.

Miyamoto, J. M., & Eraker, S. A. (1988). A multiplicative model of the utility of survival duration and health quality. *Journal of Experimental Psychology: General, 117*, 3–20.

Miyamoto, J. M., & Eraker, S. A. (1989). Parametric models of the utility of survival duration: Tests of axioms in a generic utility framework. *Organizational Behavior and Human Decision Processes, 44*, 166–202.

National Heart, Lung and Blood Institute. (1998). *Clinical guidelines on the identification, evaluation, and treatment of overweight and obesity in adults: The evidence report*. Washington, DC: U.S. Department of Health and Human Services.

Nord, E. (1992). Methods for quality adjustment of life years. *Social Science and Medicine, 34*(5), 559–569.

Parducci, A. (1968). The relativism of absolute judgments. *Scientific American, 219*(6), 84–90.

Parsons, T. (1951). *The social system*. Glencoe, IL: Free Press.

Patrick, D. L., Bush, J. W., & Chen, M. M. (1973). Methods for measuring levels of well-being for a health status index. *Health Services Research, 8*(3), 228–245.

Patrick, D. L., & Erickson, P. (1993). *Health status and health policy: Quality of life in health care evaluation and resource allocation*. Boston: Oxford University Press.

Patrick, D. L., & Erickson, P. (1994). *Health status and health policy: Allocating resources to health care*. New York: Oxford University Press.

Pennebaker, J. W., Kiecolt-Glaser, J., & Glaser, R. (1988). Disclosure of traumas and immune function: Health implications for psychotherapy. *Journal of Consulting and Clinical Psychology, 56*, 239–245.

Pliskin, J. S., Shepard, D. S., & Weinstein, M. C. (1980). Utility functions for life years and health status. *Operations Research, 28*, 206–224.

Quiggin, J. (1982). A theory of anticipated utility. *Journal of Economic Behavior and Organization, 3,* 323–343.

Richardson, J. (1991). Economic assessment of health care: Theory and practice. *Australian Economic Review, 81*(93), 4–21.

Rodin, J., & Salovey, P. (1989). Health psychology. *Annual Review of Psychology, 40,* 533–579.

Sackett, D. L. (1996). Evidence-based medicine: What it is and what it isn't. *British Medical Journal, 312*(7023), 71–72.

Schwartz, A. (1998). Rating scales in context. *Medical Decision Making, 18*(2), 236.

Schumaker, S. A., & Berzon, R. (1995). *The international assessment of health-related quality of life.* Oxford: Rapid Scientific Communications.

Schumaker, S. A., Schron, E. B., Ockene, J. K., & McBee, W. L. (Eds.). (1998). *The handbook of behavior change* (2nd ed.). New York: Springer.

Schwartz, A. (1998). Rating scales in context. *Medical Decision Making, 18*(2), 236.

Slovic, P., Lichtenstein, S., & Fischhoff, B. (1988). Decision making. In R. C. Atkinson, R. J. Herrnstein, G. Lindzey, & R. D. Luce (Eds.), *Steven's handbook of experimental psychology* (Vol. 2, pp. 673–738). New York: Wiley.

Spilker, B. (1996). *Quality of life and pharmacoeconomics in clinical trials* (2nd ed.). In B. Spilker (Ed.), Philadelphia: Lippincott-Raven.

Squier, H., Ries, A. L., Kaplan, R. M., Prewitt, L. M., Smith, C. M., Kriett, J. M., et al. (1995). Quality of well-being predicts survival in lung transplantation candidates. *American Journal of Respiratory and Critical Care Medicine, 152,* 2032–2036.

Stevens, S. S. (1966). A metric for the social consensus. *Science, 151,* 530–541.

Sullivan, D. F. (1966). *Conceptual problems in developing an index of health* (DHEW Publication No. (HRA) 76-1017, Series 2, No. 17). Rockville, MD: U.S. Department of Health and Welfare.

Torgerson, W. S. (1958). *Theory and methods of scaling.* New York: Wiley.

Torrance, G. W., & Feeny, D. (1989). Utilities and quality-adjusted life years. *International Journal of Technology Assessment in Health Care, 5,* 559–575.

Treadwell, J. R., & Lenert, L. A. (1999). Health values and prospect theory. *Medical Decision Making, 19*(3), 344–352.

Tversky, A., & Kahneman, D. (1992). Advances in prospect theory: Cumulative representation of uncertainty. *Journal of Risk and Uncertainty, 5,* 297–323.

Veit, T., Rose, B. J., & Ware, J.E., Jr. (1982). Effects of physical and mental health on health state preferences. *Medical Care, 20,* 368–301.

von Neumen, J., & Morgenstern, O. (1947). *Theory of games and economic behavior,* Princeton, NJ: Princeton University Press.

Wakker, P., & Tversky, A. (1993). An axiomatization of cumulative prospect theory. *Journal of Risk and Uncertainty, 7,* 147–176.

Ware, J. E., Jr., Phillips, J., Yody, B. B., & Adamczyk, J. (1996). Assessment tools: Functional health status and patient satisfaction. *American Journal of Medical Quality, 11,* S50–S53.

Weinstein, M. C. (1995). From cost-effectiveness ratios to resource allocation. In F. A. Sloan (Ed.), *Valuing health care* (pp. 77–97). New York: Cambridge University Press.

Wells, K. (1996). *Caring for depression.* Cambridge, MA: Harvard University Press.

World Health Organization. (1948). Constitution of the World Health Organization. In *Basic documents.* Geneva: Author.

AUTHOR INDEX

Numbers in italics refer to listings in reference sections.

Abbott, R., 171, *194*
Abdallah, R. M., 357, *374*
Abdul-Kabir, S., 205, *247*
Abdul-Karim, K. W., 172, *188*
Abeles, M., 176, *180*
Abraham, C., 231, *246*
Abraham, S., 38, *63*
Abrams, D. B., 227, 228, 230, *240*, 279, 286, 452, *459*
Abrams, D., 208, *232*, 480, *490*
Abrams, J. R., 350, *375*
Abramson, C., 206, 208, *232*
Abramson, J. L., 169, *199*
Acevedo, M. C., 156, *190*
Adamczyk, J., 573, *582*
Adams, A. H., 358, 360, *372*, *374*
Adams, D. O., 85, 88, *106*
Adams, M. L., 456, *462*
Adams, M. R., 35, *76*
Ader, R., 13, 14, 26, 82, 93, 94, 96, 100, *106*, *109*, *112*
Adih, W. K., 208, 209, 210, *232*
Adler, N. E., 143, 176, *192*, *197*, 205, 207, *232*
Affleck, G., 176, *179*, *180*, *185*
Agarwal, S. K., 100, *112*
Agras, W. S., 269, *285*
Aguirre-Molina, M., 469, 480, 482, 485, *490*
Ahern, D. K., 169, *180*, *185*
Ahijevych, K., 227–228, *232*
Ahmed, H. E., 346, 364, *371*
Ahmed, R., 88, *106*
Aiuta, F., 51, *77*
Ajzen, I., 202, 203, 205, 224, *232*, *237*, *245*, 257, 275, 283, 510, *541*
Akerstedt, T., 94, *112*
Albarracin, D., 206, 208, *232*
Albright, C. L., 481, *492*
Alcaraz, J. E., 558, *579*
Aldana, S. G., 217, *244*
Alderfer, M. A., 170, *198*
Aldwin, C. M., 168, *197*

Alemagno, S. A., 219, *240*
Alexander, C. S., 208, 209, 210, *232*
Alexander, F., 167, *180*
Alikoski, T., 37, *73*
Allan, S., 16, *27*
Allen, A., 149, *181*
Allport, G. W., 144, 148, *180*
Allred, K. D., 166, 167, *195*, *196*
Almog, S., 39, *73*
Alonzo, A. A., 454, *460*
Alper, J., 473, 481, 486, *496*
Altpeter, M., 523, *541*
Alvarez de Cienfuegos, G. A., 88, *108*
Ambler, S. K., 119, *135*
Ammerman, A. S., 473, 480, *490*
Ammerman, A., 523, *546*
Amos, C. L., 129, *141*
Amundson, G., 486, 488, *497*
Anda, R., 41, 60, 62, 169, 171, *180*
Anderman, C., 484, *491*
Andersen, B., 57, 58, 59, 60, 61, *62*
Anderson, E. A., 34, *62*
Anderson, J. E., 211, *232*
Anderson, J. L., 169, *180*
Anderson, J. P., 555, 557, 558, 563, 570, 575, *579*
Anderson, N., 429, *489*
Anderson, N. B., 158, 163, *195*
Anderson, N. H., 569, 573, 574, *577*
Andersson, S. A., 348, *374*
Ando, J., 166, *188*
Andreasen, A. R., 509, *541*
Andrews, K., 465, *499*
Angleitner, A., 166, *188*
Anglin, M. D., 206, *241*
Antoni, M. H., 4, 46, 47, 48, 50, 51, 52, 57, 62, 63, 65, 66, 74, 76, 79, 104, *106*, *109*, *111*, 208, 209, 210, *241*
Antoni, M., 4, 31, 46, 51, 55, 56, 59, 64, 65, 69, 72, 74
Appalsamy, M., 37, *75*

583

Fosher, K., 37, *75*
Foster, C., 102, *110*, 342, *371*
Foster, L. S., 482, *497*
Fotheringham, M. J., 438–439, *463*
Fournier, A. M., 39, *67*
Fournier, R. D., 34, *67*
Fowkes, F. G. R., 167, *198*
Fowler, F. J., Jr., 559, *578*
Fox, B., 57, 61, *75*, 143, *198*
Fox, H. R., 395, 396, *407*
Fox, J. D., 88, 89, 91, *113*
Franceschi, C., 84, *112*
Frank, J. B., 364, *371*
Frank, J. D., 364, *371*
Frank, J. S., 85, *107*
Frank, R. G., 3, 4, 321, 333, 334, *339*,
    406, *407*
Frankowski, J. J., 172, *188*, 194
Franks, P., 60, 70, 168. *188*, 457, *460*
Frasure-Smith, N., 40, 42, *67*, 169, *185*,
    186, 190, 447, *461*
Frautchi, N., 164, *187*
Fray, P. J., 35, *75*
Frazao, 468, *492*
Fredrikson, M., 156, *181*
Freedland, K., 16, *27*, 40, 42, 64, 169,
    170, 173, *181*
Freedman, A. M., 355, *373*
Freidenbergs, I., 55, *68*
Freidman, S. B., 100, *109*
Freire, P., 518, *543*
Freitas, A. L., 150, *184*
French, S. A., 280, *286*
Friedenrich, C. M., 214, 215, 216, *236*
Friedman, A., 51, *69*
Friedman, A. L., 123, 124, 131, *135*
Friedman, G. D., 37, *67*, 71, 447, *461*
Friedman, H. S., 169, 171, 172, *186*, *191*
Friedman, H., 171, *193*
Friedman, M., 162, *186*, 438, *463*
Friedman, R., 336, *339*, 381, 396, 397,
    408
Friedman, S. R., 281, 282, *285*
Fries, J. F., 471, 474, *492*, 555, *578*
Fritz, H. L., 147, 171, 177, *186*, *187*
Fritz, S. P., 402, 403, 404, *408*
Froberg, J., 44, *74*
Frobert, J., 94, *112*
Frohlich, E. D., 36, *75*
Frohm, K. D., 166, *196*
Fryer, J., 361, *370*

Frymore, J. W., 358, *371*
Fuchs, F. C., 447, *461*
Fulilove, M. T., 205, *235*
Fuller, R. W., 41, *67*
Fullilove, R. E., 281, *285*
Funch, D., 56, *67*
Funder, D. C., 149, *186*
Funk, S., 154, 172, *186*
Furukawa, H., 96, *107*

Gaard, M., 214, *247*
Gabay, C., 87, *109*
Gabel, J., 328, *339*
Gaby, A. R., 358, *371*
Gadia, M. T., 39, *67*
Gafni, A., 126, *139*
Gaines, J. G., 176, *182*
Galanter, E., 573, *580*
Galavotti, C., 211, 212, *238*, 508, *541*
Gale, M., 60, 76, 163, *195*
Gallacher, J., 169, *191*
Gallinger, S., 251, *288*
Gallo, L. C., 144, 146, 147, 151, 152,
    154, 155, 164, 166, 172, *186*,
    196, 270, *285*
Gallo, R., 53, 54, *73*
Gallois, C., 205, 207, *240*
Ganiats, T. G., 555, 563, *579*
Garancini, P., 38, *73*
Garber, J., 121, 123, 128, *135*, *136*, 476,
    490
Garcia, S., 150, 165, *188*
Gardea, M. A., 5, *341*
Gardiner, H., 42, *66*
Garfin, S., 549, *579*
Garfinkel, P. E., 94, 99, *108*
Gargiullo, P. M., 508, *541*
Garmezy, N., 258, *285*
Garnick, D. W., 469, *492*
Garrett, J., 361, *370*
Gartan, E., 94, *108*
Garvey, W. T., 38, *67*
Gassileth, B. R., 171, *182*
Gatchel, R. J., 5, 176, *186*, 341, 342,
    366, *371*
Gavin, J. R., III, 36, *69*
Gawin, F. H., 41, *67*
Gaynes, B. N., 50, *72*
Gedney, J. J., 378, *409*
Geller, G., 129, *137*

Goodwin, F. K., 41, 63
Goodwin, R. K., 436, 456, 463
Goodyear, N. N., 447, 460
Gordon, J. J., 174, 190
Gordon, J. S., 353, 372
Gordon, T., 37, 64
Gordon, W. A., 55, 68
Gorelik, E., 57, 68
Gorkin, L., 169, 180, 185, 396, 408
Gorlin, R., 40, 76
Gotay, C., 120, 123, 129, 137
Gottlieb, B. H., 518, 542
Gottlieb, N. H., 223, 239
Gould, J., 209, 246
Govle, R., 517, 544
Gracey, M. P., 204, 216, 217, 235
Graffin, N. F., 350, 372
Graham, I., 36, 69
Graham, S., 205, 226, 236, 248
Grandits, G. A., 164, 184
Grant, I., 44, 70, 100, 110, 579
Grant, P., 207, 241
Gray, B., 507, 544
Gray, J. E., 392, 393, 409
Gray, N., 88, 106
Gray, W., 219, 243
Graziano, F., 380, 389, 390, 392, 394,
    409
Graziano, W. G., 148, 186
Graziosi, C., 48, 54, 74
Green, C. J., 294, 316
Green, J., 128, 130, 137
Green, J. A., 351, 372
Green, J. M., 128, 140
Green, L. W., 502, 504, 505, 520,
    544
Greenberg, D. S., 428, 432
Greene, J., 425, 432
Greene, K., 205, 246
Greene, P. G., 504, 543
Greenland, S., 441, 444, 463
Greeno, C. G., 57, 68
Greenwald, P., 218, 239
Greenwood, A., 295, 304, 315
Greenwood, D., 44, 45, 70
Greer, S., 56, 57, 60, 68, 74, 78
Gresham, F. M., 402, 409
Griffith, P., 168, 187
Griffith, P. D., 49, 69
Grigsby, B., 378, 409
Grimley, D. M., 211, 212, 238, 239

Gritz, E. R., 129, 141
Gritzapis, A., 58, 63
Grogan, S., 219, 236
Grossman, A. H., 215, 216, 241
Grossman, P., 169, 198
Grothaus, L. C., 466, 484, 491, 498
Grove, J., 120, 123, 129, 137
Grube, J. W., 222, 223, 224, 229, 239
Gruman, J., 5, 465, 478, 479n, 481, 484,
    486, 489, 496, 498
Grunberg, N., 222, 239, 562, 578
Grundy, J. E., 49, 69
Gu, H., 50, 72
Guccione, M., 102, 111
Guijarro, M. L., 146, 165, 192
Guinan, M., 512, 545
Gumbs, A. A., 122, 141
Gump, B., 172, 193
Gunthert, K. C., 170, 186
Gunzerath, L., 118, 140
Gustafson, D. H., 380, 389, 390, 392,
    394, 409
Gustafson, K. E., 128, 141
Guthrie, D., 57, 61, 66
Guthrie, I. K., 273, 284
Gutman, M., 479, 480, 482, 485, 492
Guyer, P. M., 96, 112
Guyll, M., 166, 186
Gwaitney, J. M., 169, 183

Haas, L. J., 303, 316, 381, 409
Habicht, J. P., 38, 63
Hackl, K. L., 488, 493
Haddow, J. E., 37, 65
Hadicke, A., 99, 113
Haefner, D. P., 219, 233
Haettich, B., 49, 65
Hagdrup, N. A., 219, 239
Haggerty, R., 47, 75
Hagglund, K. J., 421, 431
Hain, J., 94, 108
Hair, E. C., 148, 186
Halar, E. M., 395, 396, 407
Halbert, S. C., 357, 372
Halderman, S., 363, 372
Halkin, H., 39, 73
Hall, C., 176, 180, 208, 209, 210,
    245
Hall, J. A., 350, 370
Hall, M., 88, 89, 98, 107, 110, 114

Herd, J. A., 143, *198*
Herlinger, H., 49, *72*
Hermann, C., 169, *187*
Hermayer, K. L., 38, *67*
Herrmann, W. M., 355, *372*
Hersch, L. E., *315*
Hersey, J. C., 225, *243*
Hershkowitz, B. D., 447, *459*
Hervig, L. K., 145, 153, 154, 171, *190,*
191
Herzog, T. A., 227, 228, 230, 240, 279,
286
Hewitt, J. K., 158, *197*
Hewitt, N., 206, *240*
Hibbard, M., 55, *68*
Hickey, N., 36, *69*
Hicklin, D., 45, 59, *63*
Higgins, D. L., 503, 506, 531, *544*
Higgins, P., 176, *180*
Higgins-Biddle, J. C., 469, *493*
Hilers, V. N., 219, *237*
Hilton, S., 220, *247*
Hinderliter, J. M., 36, *69*
Hirabayashi, H., 58, *78*
Hirschfeld, R., 168, *187*
Hjortland, M., 37, *64*
Ho, H., 34, *69*
Hoffman, B. B., 34, *69*
Hoffman, C., 472, *493*
Hoffman, P., 347, 348, *372*
Hoffman, R. P., 34, *62*
Hoffman, R. R., 174, *180*
Hogg, M. A., 203, 207, *248*
Holahan, C. J., 170, *193*
Holden, G., 258, *288*
Holder, H. D., 469, *493*
Hole, D. J., 38, *69*
Holland, D. R., 41, *67*
Holland, J. C., 123, *138, 141*
Hollenbeck, C., 36, *69*
Hollendonner, J. K., 478, 479n, 481, 484,
496
Holliday, J. E., 50, 68, 100, *109, 111*
Hollis, R., 523, *546*
Holm, N. V., 121, *139*
Holmes, K. K., 49, *68*
Holtgrave, D. R., 470, *493*
Holve, E., 328, *339*
Honig, A., 169, *193*
Hoover, D. R., 102, *111*
Hoover, R. N., 121, *137*

Hoppe, M. J., 222, 223, 224, *242*
Horgan, C., 469, *492*
Hornberger, J., 405, 408, 457, *461*
Hornyak, L., 309, *315*
Horowitz, R. I., 447, *459*
Horr, R., 355, *372*
Horsten, M., 169, *187*
Horwath, C., 220, *241*
Hospers, H. J., 220, 221, *234,* H. J., 473,
474, *497*
Hotz, S. B., 215, *236*
House, A., 169, *187*
Houston, B. K., 156, 163, 166–167, *187,*
188, 447, 460, *461*
Howard-Pinney, B., 536, *544*
Howell, R. H., 447, *461*
Howland, J., 470
Hsieh, C. C., 214, *244*
Hu, F. B., 468, *494*
Hu, S., 118, *140,* 166, *188,* 223, 224,
225, *240*
Hubble, J. P., 399, *409*
Huber, P., 346, *364*
Huberman, A. M., 532, *546*
Hubner, W. D., 355, *375*
Hudson, M., 402, *409*
Hufford, B., 377, 383, 395, 402, 408, *409*
Hufford, D. J., 363, 364, *372*
Hughes, C., 123, 127, 128, 129, 131,
133, 136, 137, 138, 139, 141
Hughes, G., 447, *463*
Hughes, J., 54, 74, 100, *109*
Hughes, M., 456–457, *461*
Huizinga, D., 256, *284*
Hulbert, J. R., 360, *370*
Hull, J. G., 153, *188*
Hulley, S., 163, *195*
Hulley, S. B., 37, *64*
Humphries, S. E., 43, *78*
Hunink, M. G., 468, *497*
Hunt, S. C., 158, *196*
Hupprich, W. R., 304, *315*
Hurley, K., 155, 166, 174, 175, *191*
Hurwitz, E. L., 358, 360, *372, 374*
Huskamp, H. A., 333, 335, *339*
Huston, D. P., 86, 87, 88, *110*
Huston, T. L., 256, *286*
Hwang, I. S., 34, *69*
Hyde, R. T., 36, 74, 214, *244*
Hynes, D., 474, *499*
Hyun, C. S., 55, 57, 61, *66*

Markland, D., 216, 217, *240*, *242*
Markland, O., 403, *408*
Markovitz, J. H., 165, 168, *184*, *188*, *190*
Markus, H. R., 263, *287*
Marlatt, G. A., 174, *183*, *190*, 469, 480, 482, 485, 486, 490, *494*
Marmot, M., 35, 63, 218, *234*
Marnane, D., 121, *140*
Marquart, L., 218, *240*
Marsh, G. M., 525, *545*
Marsh, R., 387, 405, *407*
Marshall, G. D., 100, *112*
Marshall, G. N., 145, 153, 154, 171, *190*, *191*
Marshall, J., 56, *67*
Marshall, P., 226, *242*
Marsland, A. L., 98, *107*, *110*
Martin, E., 219, *236*
Martin, L. R., 169, 171, *191*, *193*
Martin, N., 117, 118, *137*, *139*
Martin, R., 164, *191*
Martinson, B. C., 473, *496*
Marttila, J., 216, 217, *242*
Maruta, T., 171, *191*
Maseri, A., 35, 39, *72*, *79*
Mason, J. O., 438, *462*
Massie, M. J., 126, *138*
Masten, A. S., 258, *285*
Matarazzo, J. D., 13, *27*, 37, 64, 201, *242*, 576, *580*
Mathiesen, E. R., 39, *66*
Matloff, E., 122, *141*
Matthews, K. A., 156, 164, 165, 168, 171, 172, 176, *182*, *184*, *190*, *191*, *193*, *194*, 270, *284*, *285*, 447, *462*
Maurer, G., 41, *64*
MaxCornack, F. A., 361, *370*
May, M., 169, *191*
Maydeu-Olivares, A., 171, *182*
Mayer, K. H., 208, *242*
Mayne, T. J., 50, 60, *73*, 296, *316*
McAdams, D. P., 145, 148, *191*
McAdams, M., 121, 122, *141*, 394, *407*
McAlister, A., 536, *547*
McAllister, C. G., 98, *114*
McAllister-Sistilli, C. G., 88, *112*
Mcauliffe, T. L., 488, *493*
McBee, W. L., *581*
McBride, C. M., 218, *245*, 466, 484, 491, *498*

McBride, D. C., 208, *242*
McCabe, P., 53, *76*
McCaffery, J. M., 158, *193*
McCallum, R., 58, 59, 60, 61, *62*
McCamish, M., 205, 207, *240*
McCann, B. S., 35, 42, 64, *73*, 269, *284*
McCarron, P., 169, *191*
McCarty, D. J., 554, *580*
McCaul, K. D., 123, *139*, 228, 245, 280, *287*
McCormick, W. C., 38, *77*
McCrae, D. P., 145, 147, 148, *191*
McCrae, R. R., 146, 168, 169, *184*, *199*
McCulloch, J., 334, *339*
McCusker, J., 208, *242*
McDaniel, S. H., 457, *460*
McDermott, M., 102, *113*
McElrath, M. J., 54, *74*
McEwen, B. S., 45, 53, *73*
McGee, S. T., 222, 223, 224, 229, *239*
McGinnis, J. M., 14, *27*, 33, *7*, 465, 466, 468, 469, 494, 517, 518, *545*
McGlave, P., 57, 61, *73*
McGlynn, E. A., 488, *497*
McGonagle, K. A., 456–457, *461*
McGongile, M., 166, *196*
McGregor, M., 360, 362, *375*
McGrew, J., 222, *235*
McGuffin, P., 117, *139*, *140*
McGuire, L., 169, *191*
McGuire, T. G., 334, *339*
McGuire, W. J., 505, 506, *545*
McKane, S. U., 507, *541*
McKay, H. G., 393, 394, 395, *410*, 474, *492*
McKay, N., 4, *321*
McKean, H. E., 536, *544*
McKelvey, L., 166, *181*
McKinlay, J. B., 477, 478, 483, *495*, *497*
McKinlay, S. M., 483, *492*
McKinley, R., 214, 219, *243*
McKinnon, W., 44, 46, *73*
McKnight, J., 507, 508, 509, *544*, *545*
McKusick, D., 324, 326, 332, *339*
McKusick, V. A., 116, *136*
McLaren, P., 399, 402, *406*
McLaughlin, C., 361, *370*
McLaws, M. L., 205, 207, 208, 229, *246*
McLean, D. E., 208, *241*
McLellan, A. T., 469, 481, *494*
McLeod, R. S., 251, *288*

Nezu, A. M., 267. 287
Nguyet, N. M., 223, 224, 225, 243
Niaura, R., 35, 42, 64, 480, 490
Nickelson, D. W., 5, 377, 378, 379, 384,
 387, 388, 409, 410
Niederman, J. C., 94, 110
Nielsen, C. H., 86, 112
Nieman, D. C., 88, 114
Nieto, F. J., 41, 78, 165, 198
Nigg, C. R., 215, 217, 220, 221, 233,
 243, 477, 495
Nissinen, A., 511, 536, 547
Nixon, R., 344
Nogues, C., 128, 138
Norcross, J. C., 204, 205, 228, 244, 254,
 278, 279, 287, 509, 515, 516,
 546
Nord, E., 573, 580
Nordstrom, L., 258, 285
Norem, J. K., 170, 192
Noriega, V., 55, 64, 74, 176, 182
Norlock, F. E., 342, 371
Norman, G. J., 227, 248
Norman, P., 215, 219, 223, 243
Normand, J., 479, 495
Norris, A. E., 208, 210, 213, 238
North, W., 56, 75
Norusis, M., 163, 195
Noth, R. H., 37, 71
Nott, K. H., 91, 102, 113
Novelli, W. D., 518, 546
Novick, M. R., 568, 580
Nupponen, R., 216, 217, 242
Nusbaum, C., 115, 138
Nyamathi, A., 210, 243

Obarzanek, E., 468, 493
Öberg, B. E., 361, 374
Oberman, A., 530, 547
O'Brien, A. T., 100, 113
Obrist, P. A., 169, 197
O'Callaghan, F. V., 223, 224, 243
Ockene, J. K., 581
O'Connell, J. K., 214, 219, 243
O'Connor, A. M., 126–127, 139
O'Connor, P. J., 473, 474, 487, 496
Offord, K. P., 171, 191
O'Grady, N., 86, 113
Ogrocki, B. S., 100, 111
Ogrocki, P., 45, 71

O'Keefe, J. L., 166, 196
Oldenburg, B. F., 479, 496
O'Leary, A., 46, 78, 144, 153, 154, 172,
 183
O'Leary, J. E., 203, 247
Olfson, M., 336, 339
Olshavsky, R. W., 222, 223, 224, 235
Olsson, H., 125, 139
Olund, E., 214, 247
O'Malley, P. G., 165, 192
O'Malley, P. M., 469, 493
Omenn, G. S., 357, 374
Onaivi, E. S., 118, 135
O'Neill, B., 44, 74
Ong, E. L., 91, 102, 113
Oparil, S., 446, 460
Oppenheim, J., 86, 113
Orav, E. J., 474, 496
Orbell, S., 206, 231, 232, 246
Orci, L., 35, 69
O'Reilly, K., 503, 506, 531, 544
Orleans, C. T., 226, 241, 473, 475, 476,
 478, 479n, 480, 481, 482, 484,
 485, 486, 487, 489, 490, 494,
 495, 496
Orndorff, S., 53, 54, 73
O'Rourke, S. J., 171, 190
Orth-Gomer, K., 169, 187
Ortiz, L., 90, 107
Osborne, M. P., 123, 141
Osganian, S., 455, 462, 503, 533, 534–
 535, 545, 548
Oskamp, S., 208, 209, 210, 247
Osler, W., 143, 176, 192
Osmond, C., 56, 63
Osoba, D., 555, 577
Oss, M., 333, 340
Ostfeld, A. M., 60, 76, 169, 195
Ostroff, J. L., 14, 21, 27
Ostrow, D., 102, 110, 208, 242
Otero-Sabogal, R., 223, 224, 242
Otis, J., 223, 224, 225, 243
Ottaviani, E., 84, 112
Otto-Salaj, L. L., 488, 493
Owen, M. J., 117, 140
Owen, N., 438–439, 463, 478, 497
Owens, J. F., 165, 171, 172, 176, 191,
 193, 194, 447, 462
Owens, N. W., 226, 234
Ozer, D. J., 149, 152, 153, 154, 186,
 192

Zhu, S. H., 227, 229, 230, *237*
Ziegler, M., 44, *70*, 100, *110*
Zieler, K. L., 35, *79*
Zigler, E., 258, *287*
Zimbardo, P. G., 417, *432*
Zimmerman, E. A., 166, *197*
Zimmermans, N., 219, *247*
Zody, M. C., 115, *138*
Zollman, C., 345, *375*

Zonderman, A. B., 168, 169, *199*
Zubek, J., 176, *190*
Zuckerman, A., 150, 170, *181*
Zuckerman, M., 51, 52, *72*, *79*
Zuvekas, S. H., 326, 330, *340*
Zwanziger, J., 457, *460*
Zweifel, P., 332, *340*
Zweifler, A., 42, *66*
Zyzanski, S. J., 162, *188*, 219, *240*

SUBJECT INDEX

Clinical service payment systems, *continued*
   source of payment, 322–324
   third-party, 322–324, 330–331, 333
Clinical trials, 441
Cognitive–behavioral stress management, 24, 104
Cognitive mediation, 257
Cognitive–social perspective, 146–148, 172, 173, 174–175, 176
Cohort studies, 441, 442–444
Colon cancer, 122, 214
Commission on Education Leading to Credentialing and Licensure in Psychology, 420
Committee for the American Psychological Association of Graduate Students, 416
COMMIT program, 483, 533
Communications research, 505
Community health advisors (CHAs), 504, 506, 523–524, 531
Community Health Advisory Network, 510, 524
Community interventions, 481–483, 501–522
   analysis, 533–536
   described, 502
   frameworks, 517–518, 520–525
   individual-level versus, 514–518
   negative outcomes, 536–538
   planning, 519–526
   reasons for, 504–513
   research design, 526–536
   short-term versus long-term, 538–540
Community intervention trials, 441
Community partnership, 522–523
Community resources, 508–509
Community Tool Box, 512
Complementary health care, 341–369
   described, 341–344
   medicine technologies, 344–366
   physician guidelines, 368
   research needs, 366–368
Comprehensive Health Enhancement Support System (CHESS), 389–391
Computerized tailoring, 484–485
ComputerLink programs, 391–392
Condom use prediction, 205–214

Confidentiality, 302, 305
Conflict frameworks, 517
Conflict resolution, 268, 269
Congestive heart failure, 446
Conscientiousness, 146, 176
Consent, 507
Constitutional predisposition models, 158–159, 163
Constitutional vulnerability model, 158
Consulting staff, 312
Contextual influences, 272
Contextual model, 277
Control processes, 269
Coping
   maladaptive, 50, 51–52
   strategies, 56, 133
   symptom development and, 51–52
   transactional model, 131–133
Coping Effectiveness Training, 133
Coronary artery disease (CAD), 119, 165–167, 169
Coronary heart disease (CHD)
   biobehavioral risk factors, 33–38
   depressive symptoms, 39–41, 457
   dominance and 166–167
   hostility and, 164–166
   inflammation, 39–41
   insulin metabolic syndrome, 38–39
   neuroticism and, 168, 169
   optimism and, 171
   potential stress mechanisms, 41–43
   risk factors, 445–448, 449
   stress and, 33–43
   Type A personality, 163
Corticotropin-releasing hormone, 43
Cortisol, 96
Cost-effectiveness studies, 404–405, 574–575
Courtesy staff, 311
Credentialing, 309–312
Cronbach's alpha, 153
Cross-disciplinary interactions, 452–457
Cross-sectional studies, 441, 442, 443
Cues, 203–204, 226
Cultural issues, 363–366
Culturally appropriate measurement, 528–529
Curanderismo, 364–365
Curiosity, 172
Current procedural terminology, 297
Cytokines, 89–93

Introversion, 146
Irritability, 258

Jenkins Activity Survey, 162
Job loss, 35
Joint arthroplasty, 559
Joint Commission on Accreditation of
    Healthcare Organizations, 311
Joint Working Group on Telehealth, 384
Joint Working Group on Telemedicine,
    406

Karposi's sarcoma, 54
Key informant interviews, 532
Kristal Food and Fiber Behavior Question-
    naire, 394

Laboratory stress, 97–100
Law of similars, 351–352
Leisure Score Index, 216
Leukoplakia, 49
Life change stress, 94
Life quality domains, 556
Life stress, 35, 50–51
Lifestyle risk factor, 447, 449, 451
Linear/exponential models, 570
Log/power models, 570
Longevity, 171
Loss aversion, 572–573
Low-density lipoprotein (LDL), 34, 35,
    357, 466
Low-income population, 472, 481
Lumbar rehabilitation, 360
Lung cancer, 222, 357
Lung disease, 457
Lymphocytes, 87–88, 91
Lymphokine-activated killer (LAK) cells,
    58

Macrophages, 84, 85
Magnetic healing, 358
Ma huang, 353, 354
Major histocompatibility complex
    (MHC), 87
Maladaptive coping, 50, 51–52
Malpractice risks, 304–306
Mammography, 122
Managed care, 303, 328, 473

Managed care organization (MCO), 302,
    303
Marital conflict, 44, 268, 269
Massage, 348
Mast cells, 84, 86
Mastectomy, 121–122, 125, 126
Medicaid, 324
    capitated payment, 332
    carve-outs, 333, 334
    graduate medical education (GME)
        expenditure, 421
    smoking cessation coverage, 481
    telehealth reimbursement, 385, 387
Medical Expenditure Panel Survey, 326
Medical Outcomes Short Form 36 Health
    Survey, 347, 563
Medical Outcomes Survey, 390, 456
Medical risk factors, 441, 446–447, 449,
    451
Medical settings, 16–17, 23–24
Medicare, 324, 421–422
Medicare, Medicaid and State Children's
    Health Insurance Program
    (SCHIP) Benefits Improvement
    and Protection Act, 385
Megadosing, 356
Mental health services expenditures,
    324–326
Metaphysical causality, 363
Midstream interventions,, 478, 479,
    481–483
Migraine headaches, 360, 457
Mind–body dualism, 295–298
Minnesota Heart project, 507
Minority populations, 472, 507
Mitogen, 91
Mitogenic proliferation, 91–92
Modifiable risk factors, 441
Monoamine oxidase inhibitors, 355
Monocausal theory of disease, 359
Monocytes, 84, 85
Morbidity, 10–11, 14, 555–557
Mortality, 444, 555–557
Mothers Against Drunk Driving, 486
Motivation, 350
Motivational appraisal, 264–266
Motivational interventions, 485
Multidimensional Functional Assessment,
    391
Multidimensional Impact of Cancer Risk
    Assessment (MICRA), 127–128

University of Illinois Department of Psychology, 416
Unreliability, 146
Upper respiratory infection, 47
Upstream interventions, 478, 479, 483–484

Very low birth weight (VLBW) babies, 392–393
Very low-density lipoprotein (VLDL), 34, 35, 37, 42
Veterans Administration, 417
Videoconferencing studies, 399–402
Video teleconferencing, 381–382, 386
Vietnam Era Twin Registry, 118
Violated independence axiom, 569–570
Viral-challenge studies, 101
Vitamin supplements, 356–358
Von Neumann and Morgenstern (vNM) utility theory, 568, 572, 573

Weight gain, 37
Weight loss, 36
Wellness, defined, 251–252
Western Collaborative Group Study, 438
Wisdom of Prevention as Public Policy, 420
Women's Health Initiative, 503
Working Alliance Inventory, 403
Working Conference in Education and Training in Health Psychology, 307, 319
Worksite programs, 482
World Health Organization (WHO), 363
World Wide Web, 381, 386
Wu xing, 365

Xanthine, 353

Zero condition, 568
Zero drug tolerance, 510

ABOUT THE EDITORS

Editor-in-Chief

Thomas J. Boll, PhD, is director of the Neuropsychology Institute in Birmingham, Alabama. For 32 years, he was a professor at several universities and medical centers, including the University of Washington; the University of Virginia; Chicago Medical School; and, for the past 20 years, the University of Alabama at Birmingham (UAB). He was a professor in the Departments of Psychology, Pediatrics, and Neurological Surgery. He is board certified in clinical psychology, clinical neuropsychology, and clinical health psychology. His research investigations in the areas of health and human behavior include issues related to heart and lung transplantation and chronic pediatric illnesses, including congenital cytomegalovirus, low birthweight, seizure disorders, and learning disabilities. He has written on various aspects of educational and curriculum design for health psychology and was the founding chairman of the Department of Medical Psychology at Chicago Medical Center and the first director of clinical training for the Medical Psychology Program at UAB. He was the chair of the Doctoral Curriculum Committee at the Arden House Conference, which set the curriculum for health psychology doctoral training programs.

Volume Editors
Robert G. Frank, PhD, is dean of the College of Health and Health Professions at the University of Florida, where he is also a professor in the Department of Clinical and Health Psychology. His first appointment was at the University of Missouri–Columbia School of Medicine, Department of Physical Medicine and Rehabilitation, where he established the Division of Clinical Health Psychology and Neuropsychology. He was a Robert Wood

Johnson Health Policy Fellow from 1991 to 1992 and he worked with Senator Jeff Bingaman (D-NM). After completing the fellowship, Dr. Frank returned to the University of Missouri where, as assistant to the dean for health policy, he continued to work on federal and state health policy. He continued to work with Senator Bingaman and managed Missouri's state health reform effort, the ShowMe Health Reform Initiative. He has a doctorate in clinical psychology from the University of New Mexico. He is a diplomate in clinical psychology from the American Board of Professional Psychology; is past president of the Division of Rehabilitation Psychology of the American Psychological Association (APA) and a fellow in the Divisions of Rehabilitation Psychology and Health Psychology; and currently chairs the Health Care Task Force for the Florida Developmental Disabilities Council and has chaired the APA's Committee on Professional Continuing Education (1997) and its Board of Educational Affairs (2000).

Andrew Baum, PhD, is deputy director for Cancer Control and Population Sciences at the University of Pittsburgh Cancer Institute and is responsible for oversight and coordination of cancer control and prevention research activities. In this capacity he has fostered projects to better understand the basis of individual susceptibility to cancer; the conditions that promote cancer development; and the social and behavioral barriers to effective prevention, early detection, and treatment of cancer. His current research interests include the biobehavioral aspects of cancer and chronic illness, chronic stress and illness, and psychoneuroimmunology. He received his BS in psychology in 1970 from the University of Pittsburgh. He was awarded his PhD in psychology from the State University of New York at Stony Brook in 1974. Before joining the University of Pittsburgh in 1993, he was professor of psychology, psychiatry, and neuroscience, and assistant to the president for Research and Sponsored Programs at the Uniformed Services University of the Health Sciences, where he received the Achievement, Outstanding Service, and Distinguished Service Medals. He has also received awards from the American Psychological Association and its Health Psychology Division. He has authored or coauthored more than 150 scientific articles, chapters, and books and is editor of the *Journal of Applied Social Psychology* and the *Journal of Applied Biobehavioral Research*.

Jan L. Wallander, PhD, is principle research scientist at Sociometrics Corporation in Los Altos, California, as well as research professor of psychology at the University of Alabama at Birmingham (UAB). Previously, he was director of developmental psychology in the Department of Psychology, associate director for Human Development Research at the Civitan International Research Center, and director of research at the Alabama University Center for Developmental Disabilities at UAB. His research focuses on risk, resilience, and psychosocial development of children and adolescents who experience chronic health and developmental conditions and the impact they may have on their families. Dr. Wallander has held numerous leadership roles in national and international scientific and professional activities, including president of the Society of Pediatric Psychology, associate editor of the *Journal of Pediatric Psychology* and the *International Review of Research in Mental Retardation*, pediatric program chair for the 1996, 1998, 2000, and 2002 International Congress of Behavioral Medicine, and past member of the executive committees of the International Society of Behavioral Medicine and Alabama Psychological Association. His most recent book (co-edited with Hans Koot) is *Quality of Life in Children and Adolescents*. He has also chaired more than 30 theses or dissertations. Dr. Wallander has produced more than 200 scientific publications, and he has been invited to make presentations at meetings and institutions nationally and internationally. He is a recipient of the Lee Salk Distinguished Service Award from the Society of Pediatric Psychology.